Virginia Bible Records

Collected by
Jeannette Holland Austin

HERITAGE BOOKS
2008

HERITAGE BOOKS
AN IMPRINT OF HERITAGE BOOKS, INC.

Books, CDs, and more—Worldwide

For our listing of thousands of titles see our website
at
www.HeritageBooks.com

Published 2008 by
HERITAGE BOOKS, INC.
Publishing Division
100 Railroad Ave. #104
Westminster, Maryland 21157

Copyright © 1987, 1996 Jeannette Holland Austin

All rights reserved. No part of this book may be reproduced or transmitted in any form or by any means, electronic or mechanical, including photocopying, recording or by any information storage and retrieval system without written permission from the author, except for the inclusion of brief quotations in a review.

International Standard Book Number: 978-1-58549-619-8

Note to the Reader -

This collection of Virginia Bible records contains an itemized list of the births, marriages, and deaths found in approximately 478 family Bibles.

Many of the records were sent to me over the past twenty years or so by the actual owners, while others I copied from Bibles located in the Georgia State Archives, local libraries, or other genealogical publications. The collection spans a period of 1600's to 1900's and includes famous Statesmen, Burgesses, as well as pioneer settler. It is my express desire that many readers will be ass1sted by this effort, bearing in mind that many of the original owners are now deceased and/or otherwise difficult to locate.

Jeannette Holland Austin

TABLE OF CONTENTS

ADAMS, Littleton	84
ADAMS, Thomas	95
ALEXANDER, James and Jerusha, Rev. War Soldier	230
ALMANDER, John Regis	180-181
ALLEN, Daniel	223
ALLEN, Thomas of Fauquier County	95
ANDERSON, William and Elizabeth, Rev. War Soldier	236
APPLIN, Timothy Brown	192
ARCHER of City of Richmond	47
ARMISTEAD, James	50
ARMSTRONG, Ellis of Essex County	79
ARNOLD-GILL	91-92
ARTHUR, John of Bedford County	5
ASHBY, John of Fauquier County	214
ASHTON, Charles H. of Mt. Lebanon, King George County	215
BACON, Edmund	180
BACON, John	178
BACON, Mary, Mrs. of Lunenburg County	126-127
BAILEY, A., Sr.	120
BAKER, Peter	18
BALL, John Wesley	94
BANDY, Thomas, Rev. War Soldier	46
BANISTER, John	60-61
BARNES, Robert Leonard of Richmond	197-15
BARRET, William Overton	53-54
BARRETT, George	58
BASKERVILLE, George D.	64-65
BASS, John	172
BASS, Nathaniel of Norfolk Co.	34
BASS, William of Chesterfield	47-48
BASSETT, Burwell	61-62
BASSETT, George W.	63
BASSETT, William	60
BATES, Frederick	169
BAYLOR, George Daniel	65-66
BAYLOR, John of Caroline County	62
BAYLY, Thomas M.	67
BEADLES, James E.	63
BEALL, Thomas	50
BEAMAN, John	68
BEAR, John H. of Augusta County	46-47
BEARD, John, Captain	80
BEARD, Samuel	50
BELL of Long Glade, Augusta County	51
BELL, Seth of Accomack and Princess Anne Counties	75-76
BERKELEY	57-58
BIAS, Francis	242

BICKLEY, John of King and Queen County	84
BIGELOW, Joseph	85-86
BLAKER, John	168
BLANTON-ALLEN	55
BOLLING, Alexander of Prince George County	247-248
BONDURANT, Darby	25
BONDURANT, Jacob M.	26
BONDURANT, Robert M.	254
BONDURANT, Thomas M. and Marcia L.	22
BOYKIN, Nancy of Southampton County	207-208
BRAGG, Evens	17-18
BRANCH, Robert R.	55-56
BRANSCOME, Robert Lee of Roanoke	240-242
BRANSON, Jesse	11
BRASELTON, Joel, Sr.	141
BRENT, Charles of Upper Tidewater on Potomac River	168
BRICKER, John	51
BRIGHT, Samuel Francis	106
BRITT, Exum O. of Isle of Wight County	153
BROADDUS, Mordecai Redd of Cherry Grove, Caroline Co.	77
BROOKS, William, Rev. War Soldier	30
BROWN, Daniel	39
BROWN, Samuel, Captain	238
BROWNE, William	261
BRUCE, William N.	222
BRYANT	230
BURDINE, Wesley of Henry County	253
BURCH-BRUMFIELD	149
BURTON of Orange County	122
BURTON, Hutchins, Sr.	243
BURTON, May, Jr., Capt., of Orange Co.	213
BURTON-PRICE	26
BURWELL, Lewis	130
BURWELL-STEPTOE of Liberty, Bedford County	162
BUTTS, James	3-4
BUTTS, James, Sr.	225
BUTTS, Peter	3
CALLAWAY, Charles of Bedford County	201
CALLAWAY, John, Colonel, of Bedford and Campbell Co.'s	205
CALLAWAY, Thomas	204
CALLOWAY, Stephen	248-249
CAMDEN, Walker L. of Roanoke City	7-8
CAMM, John of King and Queen County	110
CAMPBELL, John, Rev. War Soldier	36
CARLETON, Thomas	208-209
CARR, Nathan of Isle of Wight County	154
CARR, Thomas, Colonel	4-5
CARSON, John R. of Isle of Wight County	245
CARTER, John Michel	283-284
CARTER, Landon of Loudoun County	157-159

CARTER, Raleigh	274
CARTER, Thomas of "Green Rock", Pittsylvania County	202
CARY, Miles of Southampton County	139
CASSELL, Deborah	11
CHANDLER, Oliver Mitchell	81-82
CHANDLER, Thomas B.	78-80
CHANNELL, Arthur of Isle of Wight County	154-155
CHAPMAN, John	156
CHAPMAN, Richard, Jr. of New Kent County	124-125
CHRISTIAN, Collier	112
CLARK, George of Williamsburg	98
CLARK, John	190-192
CLARK, Milley	14-15
CLAYBROOK-MALONE	89
COATES, John of Halifax County	172
COBBS, Robert, Captain of Bedford and Campbell Counties	205
COCKE, Samuel	227
CODY-LIGHTFOOT	101
COLLINS-GREEN	72
COLLINS-WORD	59
COMBS, James L. of Fauquier County	228
CONN-ELLIS	19-20
CONNER, John, Jr.	9-10
CONRAD, Jacob	237
CONWAY, Joseph, Sr.	160
CONWAY, Thomas of Westmoreland County	137
COOK, Reuben	209-210
COOK, Richard Pye of New Kent County	82-83
COOK, William Chamberlayne	73-74
COOPER, Joseph	210
CORN, Jesse, Rev. War Soldier	218-219
COX, Isaac	15
CRENSHAW, Nicholas and Mary	233
CROOM, C. Matthew of Isle of Wight County	153
CRUMP, Hammond Fletcher	74-75
CULVERIUS, Benjamin W. of Gloucester County	113
CURD, Joseph	97
CUSICK, Joseph	113
DADE, Robert Richards	2
DANCE, Lawson H. of Richmond	199
DANDRIDGE, Elizabeth	130-131
DANDRIDGE, Nathaniel West	135-136
DANZLER, William, Mrs. of Ft. Eustus	202
DAVEISS, Samuel of Rockbridge County	167-168
DAVENPORT, John, Town Clerk in Williamsburg	130
DAVIS, John C. of Fauquier County	87-88
DAVIS, John of Washington County	228-229
DAVIS, William of Dinwiddie County	131
DEARING, Albin Pasteur	196
DEARING, Thomas Hamilton	196-197

Name	Page
DEGGE, Joshua	132
DERIEUX, Justin L.	7
DEVEREAUX, Charles	219
DILLARD, Archibald Hall	138-139
DILLARD, John William of Lynchburg	23
DILLARD, Joseph of Amherst County	137
DODSON, Daniel of Dinwiddie County	173
DOUGLAS, Rev. William	281-283
DOUGLASS-RICHERSON	30
DRAPER, Martin	11
DUNBAR, Hamilton	229-230
DURRETT, John of Spotsylvania County	99-100
DYKE, James	108
EARLY, Jeremiah, Colonel, of Bedford County	201
EDMONDS, Colonel William of Fauquier County	280
EDMUNDS, Edwin Short of Williamsburg	99
EDWARDS, George McIntash	148-149
EDWARDS, Robert Andrew	135
EDWARDS, Robert of Northumberland County	133
EDWARDS, Thomas Andrew	132
EDWARDS-BARLOW	8
ELKIN, James, Rev. War Soldier	32
ESTES, Jackson of Orange County	162
FARMER, Henry and Jane Louisa	12
FAUNTLEROY, Thomas	200
FEILD, Charles Granview	186-187
FINKS, A. N.	69
FINKS, Lewis	39
FINKS, Wilmer P.	71
FITZGERALD, Edward	201
FITZHUGH, Philip of Caroline County	104-105
FOOTE, Richard	284
FORD, James, Rev. War Soldier	198
FOSTER, George	16
FOSTER, Isaac	220-221
FOSTER, William of Nansemond County	245
FRANCIS, John	86-86
FRASER, Alexander of Dinwiddie County	95
FREEMAN, William R.	89-90
FRIEND, Charles Washington	139-140
FULKERSON, James	12
FULTON, John	87
GEE, Henry	51
GIBBS, John of Isle of Wight County	154
GLADDING, George Washington of Accomack County	199
GLENN, George D.	234-235
GOODALL, John	70-71
GORDON, James of Lancaster County	270-272
GORDON, William	38
GORDON, William F., General, of Albemarle County	159

Name	Page
GRAHAM, John	4
GREEN, Albert Gallatin, Sr.	73
GREEN, Croxson and Sarah	122
GREEN, James	183
GREEN, John and Mildred	122
GRIFFIN, Samuel Stuart of Williamsburg	103
GRIGSBY, Redmond of "The Plains", Fanquier County	221
GUTHRIE, Philip William of Floyd County	255-256
HALL Thomas, Colonel	106
HAMLETT, James	71
HAMMOND, Peter	97
HANDY, Abram Ernest of Stuart	251
HANDY, Adam James of Stuart	250
HANKINS, George	98
HANKINS, William	93
HARDING, William of Northumberland County	218
HARRIS, Thomas, Sr.	195
HARRISON, Joseph	33
HARRISON-GOOSLEY-McCAW	119
HARWELL, Littleton Theodore Peterson	224-225
HATCHETT, Joseph of Nottoway County	170
HAY, William	138
HEALY, Thomas	203
HEALY, Thomas, Sr., of Middlesex County	165
HEALY, Waiter	167
HENDERSON, Robert	52-53
HENDERSON, William B.	257
HENDON, William of Greene County, Rev. War Soldier	193
HENDREN, William	261
HENKEL, Jonathan	251
HENRY, James Oliver	223
HENRY, Patrick	206
HENRY, William P.	218
HENRY, William S. B.	230-231
HERNDON, William of Greene Co., Rev. War Soldier	238
HICKS, Harris	6
HIGGINBOTHAM, Absalom	140-141
HIGHT, Alexander P.	176
HILL, Berryman J.	48-49
HILL, John	32
HITE, John of Rockingham County	88
HOAGLAND, James of Loudoun County, Rev. War Soldier	245
HODSDEN, Joseph Bridger	244
HOLLADAY-DAY-KELLY	163
HOLLAND, Jones M., Rev. War Soldier	142
HOLLEMAN, Moody	189
HOSICK, George F.	244
HOUGH, William of Loudoun County	195
HUBARD, William	136
HUDSON-GILMER	133

HUMBER, John, Jr. of "Air Hill", Goochland County	216
HUNT, Sion and Priscilla	217
HUNT-HARRIS	37
HUTCHESON, John of Caroline County	68
INGRAM, Benjamin of Brunswick County	221
IRBY, John, Rev. War Soldier	36
JACKSON, Green	120
JACKSON, William Lucas	96
JEFFERSON, Thomas of Henrico County	269-270
JENKINS, Henry J.	35
JENNINGS, William and Polly of Prince Edward County	237
JERDONE, Francis of Louisa County	144-145
JOBSON, John & Kesiah, Warden's Creek, Princess Anne Co.	214
JOHNS, Milton	18-19
JOHNSON, Philip	258
JOHNSON, Rev. William of Bedford County	257
JOHNSTON, James of Isle of Wight County	159
JONES, Isaac of Isle of Wight	156
JONES, Laines	106
JONES, Tallie V. Jolly of Loudoun County	212-213
JONES, William	33
JORDAN, John; Rev. War Soldier	145
JUSTIS, John	31
JUSTIS, Justinian	31
KELLY, George W.	78
KEMP, John	174
KENNEDY, James	5
KENNEDY, Sidney Manson	34
KENNON, Lewis	105
KERR, James	101
KIBRY, Bennett	111-112
LACY, John S.	83
LEAGUE, James	28
LEE, Hancock	84
LEE, Thomas, Captain	217
LEFTWICH, Alexander	203-204
LEFTWICH, James T. of Franklin County	40
LEVERETT, Thomas	100-101
LEWIS, Henry of Brunswick County	269
LEWIS, James L. of Fauquier County	260
LEWIS, John of Pittsylvania County	214
LEWIS, Thomas and Hannah, Rev. War Soldier	238-239
LEWIS, William	145
LIGHT, Stephen	13
LONDON, John and Tirzah	114
LOVVORN, Elijah	20
LOWRY, John	102
MABRY, Samuel	9
MACON, William	107
MADISON, Ambrose	108

MANSFIELD, Robert of Orange County	211
MANSFIELD, Thomas Martin of Franklin Co.	212
MARKHAM, George	164-165
MARTIN, Adam, Rev. War Soldier	147
MARTIN, Benjamin, Rev. War Soldier	147
MARTIN, George, Rev. War Soldier	146
MARTIN, James A.	148
MARTIN, Joseph, Rev. War Soldier	146
MASON, Thomas	252
MAURY, Matthew Fontaine	268-269
MELVIN, Samuel	67
MERIWETHER, Francis	216
MERRYMAN, John Thomas, Dr., of Lunenburg County	141-142
MILBY, Gilbert	129-130
MILLER, Daniel and Barbara, Rev. War Soldier	233
MILLER, John Willis	44
MILLS-SIMS of Hanover County	161
MINGE, John	114
MORRIS, Richard	2-3
MORT, Abraham	55
MOSBY, Woodson of Henrico County	253-254
MOSELEY, Alexander Trent, Greenbackville, Accomack Co.	24
MOSELEY, Bennett	190
MOSELEY, Hardaway, Rev. War Soldier	29
MOSELEY, William Henry of Bedford County	192
MOSELFI, William	29
MURDOCK, William	152-153
MURPHEY, William, Rev. War Soldier	229
MUSE-HEALY	115
McADAM, Joseph of Northumberland County	124-125
McCARTY, James	118
McCARTY, William	118
McCAULAY, Alexander	104
McKEE, John T.	170-171
McMULLEN, John	219-220
NALLE, Martin	256-266
NELSON, John, Rev. War Soldier	233
NISBET, Robert of Paisley, Scotland and Richmond, Va.	56-57
NOEL	39
NOLAN, George	193
NOLAND-HARRISON-POWELL-GILMER	109-111
NORTHCROSS, John Meglamre	24-25
NUNN, Josiah Wesley	19
NUNN, William R.	9
O'REAR, John of Prince William	87
OBENSHAIN, Samuel	10-11
OFFUTT, Ezra N.	128-129
OSBORN, Jeremiah of Augusta County	203
PACE, Alsa	260
PARIS, W. B.	122-123

PATMAN, William Henry	260
PAYNE, George B.	115
PAYNE, Lizzie K. of Campbell County	46
PAYNE-GLLLIAM of Goochland County	75
PENN, Clark, Major, of Patrick County	181-183
PENN, Robert Cowan of Bedford County	215
PENN, Thomas, Captain, of Patrick County	188-189
PETERS, Christian, Rev. War Soldier	193
PEYTON, Yelverton	161
PLEASANT, William	155-156
POAGE, John	27
POLLARD, Caleb D. of Nottoway County	40
POPE, William of Isle of Wight County	131
POPE-BAYNE of Westmoreland County	121-122
PORTER, William of Nansemond County	280
POSEY, Thomas and Mary	257
PRIDDY, Robert	93
PROVINCE, Mary Eugenia King	1
PRYOR, John C.	267-268
PURVIS, George W.	174
QUARLES, Solomon and Dorothy	231
RALLS-YATES	52
RAY, Leonard	90-91
READ, John T. W.	222
RICHARDS, William C.	177
RICHERSON, Holt	143-144
RICHIE, James and Martha of Lunenburg, Rev. War Soldier	239
RICKMAN, Philip R.	12-13
ROBERTSON, Hugh, Rev. War Soldier	42-43
RODGERS, Tabitha of Accomack County	149-150
RODGERS-BARTON	92
RODGERS-NEW	64
ROUNTREE, John	218
SAGE, James, Rev. War Soldier	215
SANDZFER, James	36
SANDRIDGE, Austin	44
SANFORD, Vincent of Loudoun County	219
SAVAGE, Southy Littleton	96
SCARBURGH, Edmund	134
SCOTT, Thomas W. of "Wildwood", Charlotte County	242
SCOTT, Thomas of Caroline County	265
SEATON, Hiram of Loudoun and Fauquier Counties	96
SEAY, James Gardam	115-116
SEAY, McElrath	145
SHELL, Herman of Brunswick County	147-148
SHORT, Dr. James Warren of Accomack County	23
SIMS, John of Hanover County	160-161
SIPPLE, Christopher	232
SLAUGHTER-BERREY	69
SMITH, Joshua	76-77

SMITH, Joshua, son of Dr. Charles Smith.	41-42
SMITH, Richard Graves	80-81
SMITH-DABNEY-CHAMBERLAYNE-BAGBY	70
SNIDER-GODWIN-AMMEN of Botetourt County	76
SOUTHALL, Daniel of Amelia County	171-172
SOUTHALL, Dasey	273-274
SPENCER-ARMISTEAD of Prince Edward County	69-70
SPRAGINS, Stith Belling of Halifax County	246-247
STANDEFER, Israel of Henry County	258-259
STARK, Jeremiah of Stafford County	202
STARK, William of York County	200
STITH, Drury	143
STITH, Richard	102
STOCKWELL, Joseph	45
STONE, Joshua of Pittsylvania County	200-201
STOVER, David of Shenandoah Valley	228
STREET, David of Lunenburg County	263-264
STREET, John of New Kent County	261-262
STRICKLER, Samuel and Maria of Shenandoah County	85
STUART, Henry	207
SYDNOR, Edward Garland of Hanover County	286
SYDNOR, William of Lunenburg County	285-286
TALIAFERRO, Nicholas (4/7/1756-2/3/1798)	179-180
TALIAFERRO, Nicholas of Culpepper County (b.12/29/1801)	40
TALLEY, Billey	34
TAYLOR, Edward of Accomack County	89
TAYLOR, James	43-44
TAYLOR, James, the Elder	287-288
TAYLOR, John	21-22
TAYLOR, John C.	43
TAYLOR, John of Orange County	175-176
TAYLOR, Peter	6
TAYLOR, William and Martha Waller of Lunenburg County	288
THARP, Timothy	265
THOMPSON, Frederick of Brunswick County	211
THOMPSON, Roger	249
THORNLEY, Jane Riding of Charlottesville	233-234
THORNLEY, John	235-236
THORNTON, George of Spotsylvania County	102
THORNTON, J. M.	199-200
THORNTON, Thomas of Richmond	250
THRUSTON, Edward, Jr. of Nansemond County	165-166
TIBBLE, Rev. Andrew	266-267
TUCKER, Joseph	88
TUCKER, Robert of Norfolk County	278-279
TURNBOLL, Rachel Robinson	134-135
TYREE, Cyrus of Richmond	146
UTTERBACK-COCKRILL of Fauquier County	42
VAN METTER, Garret of Hampshire County	246
VANDEVANTER, Cornelius M.	239

VANDIVER, William, Rev. War Soldier	33
VASSER, Hugh W., Mrs.	41
VICK, William of Southampton County	35
VIVION, Thacker of Spotsylvania and Orange Counties	173
WALKER, William	164
WALLER, Benjamin of Williamsburg	206-207
WALLER, Dabney Washington	184-186
WALTON, Robert Alfred	151-152
WARD, John, Rev. War Soldier	32
WARTENFIELD, Peter	151
WASHINGTON, Sarah Tayloe	274-278
WATSON, William and Mary, Rev. War Soldier	231
WEAVER, Jacob	243
WEST, Catherine	281
WEBB, Lewis	78
WEST, Joseph	190
WHITE, Samuel	104
WHITEHEAD, Jesse of Isle of Wight County	160
WILKERSON, William S. of King George County	229
WILKINS, John Limbrey of Brunswick County	31
WILLIAMS, E. A. of Charlotte and Mecklenburg Counties	117
WILLIAMS-CHILTON	53
WILLS, Mathew of Amelia County	216-217
WILLSON, Moses	27
WILSON, Thomas Poage	29
WINSTON, John, Sr., of Louisa County	194
WISEMAN, Joseph, Rev. War Soldier	28
WOOD, Abraham	224
WORD-SAUNDERS of Buckingham County	45
WOTEN, Bell of Rockingham County	91
YERBY, John	1

MARY EUGENIA KING PROVINCE BIBLE
Reconstruction of Bible previously burned
Owner: Mrs. Vernon Gomez, 4603 Cliffstone Cove, Austin, Tx. 78735

Children of Philip and Mary Broughton Johnson (he was b. 12/14/1766, d. 1849)

Phillip Johnson m. Mollie, lived N. C.
Marie Johnson married -- Arms, lived N. C. Judith Johnson m. Edwin Palmer, Halifax Co., Va.
Susan Johnson m. Elijah Hull, Halifax Co., Va.
Thomas Johnson m. Diana Roberta Chandler, Halifax Co., Va. 6/5/1833
Mary Johnson m. -- Taylor
Children of Willis and Rebecca Hill Chandler (Willis b. 1771 m. 6/20/1802 Halifax Co., Va. d. 9/10/1747; Rebecca d. 3/30/1834)

MARRIAGES

Diana Roberta Chandler to Dr. Thomas Johnson of Greenway, Halifax Co., Va.
Jane Chandler to Mr. Moseley Rowe Chandler to Miss Williams Kyle Chandler
Note: The three latter moved to Mississippi. Kyle Chandler moved
there in 1842. Thomas and Diana Roberta Chandler Johnson had only one child, Willis
Johnson. He m. Mary Blair Dennis 20/20/1861

JOHN YERBY BIBLE
Owner: Mrs. Wanda Karrant, Star Route, Box 18-A, Chester, Ark. 72934

BIRTHS

John Yearby b. Mecklenberg Co., Va.
John Yearby 1/13/1796-8/1/--
Tillie Y. Smith 9/9/1870
Sallie A. Smith 4/7/1872
George C. Smith 2/8/1882-2/13/1910
David C. Smith 5/16/1819-10/31/--
Hattie E. Smith 7/9/1875
S. A. Smith 7/15/1830-1/15/19--
Alfred Lee Smith 4/28/1878
Alfred Smith 12/8/1851-6/23/1921

Hattie O. Smith 4/27/-- - 5/5/1907.
Henry H. Smith 2/10/1880
Ida Smith 1/15/1887
David C. Smith 4/18/1873-6/6/--
Nellie Smith 11/11/1894
James Lesley Smith 4/9/1910
Maggie Mae Smith 5/19/1889-3/9/1929
Morata Smith 7/29/1885-7/27/---
Corbin Smith 7/13/1891-2/8/1892

H. H. Smith b. 2/10/1880, son of Alford and Hattie Ofelia Smith
Sallie Ann b. 1/30/1883, dau. of E. F. Rogers and Mary Rogers
A. G. Yearby 2/13/1806-1/1/--

BIRTHS

Earnest Dewitt Smith 11/3/1900
Opal Lee Smith 5/6/1911
Archie Columbus Smith 9/10/1905

Alla May Smith 2/17/1914
Rogers Morris Smith 10/8/1909

DEATHS

Alla May Smith 2/17/1914-10/19/1917
Rogers Smith 10/8/1951
H. H. Smith 12/1/1957

ROBERT RICHARDS DADE BIBLE
Owner: Mrs. Girard Dade, 304 White Ave., Fairhope, Ala.

Robert Richards Dade b. 8/1/1793 King George Court House, Va. Mary Dade, wife of Robert Dade, b. 7/29/1805

BIRTHS of THEIR CHILDREN:

Mary Elizabeth Dade 4/24/1822
Lucy Lane Dade 3/6/1835
Virginia Thompson Dade 5/25/1824
Susan Townsend Dade 2/6/1840
Benjamin Franklin Dade 2/2/1833
Kate Troup b. 10/11/1868
Wm Langhorn Dade 8/17/1857

Sarah Frances Dade 9/3/1826
Jane Parker Dade 6/23/1828
Robert Henry Dade 11/3/1842
Agnes Webster Dade 9/26/1830
Margaret Vail Dade 9/11/1845
Catherine Lewis Dade 1/10/1848

RICHARD MORRIS BIBLE
Owner: Mrs. Julian Miller, Athens, Ga.

MARRIAGES

Richard Morris, Jr., son of William and Elizabeth Dabney Morris, b. 3/19/1784 d. Hanover Co., Va. 8/13/1831 m. 11/27/1808 in Campbell Co., Va., by Abner Earley, a Methodist minister, to Mary Watts, dau. of William Watts and Mary Scott, b. 3/27/1784 in Prince Edward Co., Va., d. 11/7/1835, in Hanover Co., Va.

MARRIAGES of the Children of Richard and Mary Watts Morris

John D. Morris to Margaret Lewis, dau. of Dr. Charles Meriwether of Va. 5/6/1845 in Christen Co., Ky.
Sylvanus W. Morris to Laura Page, dau. of Dr. Robert Page Waller of Willtamsburg, Va. 10/15/1846. He d. 8/1773.
Charles Morris to Mary Minor, dau. of Dr. John Morris of Goochland Co., by Rev. William V. Bowers, an Episcopal minister, 10/12/1854
Mary Louisa Morris (d. 5/4/1852, age 42)to Thomas Belling, Jr., son of Col Wm Belling,2/7/1832
Richard Morris, Jr. to Mary Love, dau. of Col. James Love of Ky., 11/11/1841, at Galveston, Tx, Elizabeth W. Morris to Richard K. Cralle 5/10/1843 at Belling's Island
Edward Watts Morris to Matilda Elizabeth, dau. of Thomas and Mary O. Coleman 9/14/1848 at Chantilly, Hanover Co., Va., by Rev. Samuel Harris of the Baptist Church.

BIRTHS of Children of Richard and Mary W. Morris

Mary Louise Morris 8/11/1810 Campbell Co., Va.
John Dabney Morris 1/28/1813 Hanover Co., Va
Richard Morris 12/29/1815 Hanover Co., Va.
Elizabeth Morris 7/30/1818 Hanover Co., Va.
Edward W. Morris 2/1/1821 Hanover Co., Va.
Sylvanus William Morris 3/17/1823 Hanover Co., Va.
Charles Morris 4/27/1826 Hanover Co.,Va.

Children of Thomas and Mary Louisa Belling

Mary Elizabeth Belling 5/1/1833-6/18/1833
William Belling 5/1/1846-5/2/1847
Helen Wilmer Belling d.12/29/1848, age 7 mo, 29 das m. Wm Belling,1st, 10/17/1835-9/2/1839
William Morris, Sr. b. 2/6/1736 m. 5/13/1763 Elizabeth Dabney, dau. of William Dabney. He d. Hanover Co., Va. 4/26/1820, in his 85th yr.; she d. in Hanover Co., Va. 7/29/1818 aged 76 yrs.

(Richard Morris Bible, contd....)

BIRTHS of Children of William and Elizabeth Dabney Morris

Catherine Morris 5/23/1764
Charles Morris 12/25/1778
Ann Morris 4/14/1766
Mary Morris ---
Sylvanus Morris 6/16/1769

Richard Morris 3/19/1784
William Morris 12/25/1771
John Morris 5/8/1776
Susannah Dabney Morris 12/25/1773

DEATHS

Judge Richard Morris, son of Richard Morris of Hanover, in Galveston, Texas, of yellow fever. He left a wife, Mary Love, and one child to lament his untimely death.

PETER BUTTS BIBLE

Peter Butts, eldest son of Thomas Butts, b. 9/1/1715 Eliza Clements, his wife, b. 9/7/1724 Both were b. in South Hampton Co., Va.

BIRTHS of Children:

Francis Butts 11/7/1743
William Butts 8/12/1754
John Butts 2/3/1752

Thomas Butts 1/2/1745
James Butts 3/17/1757
Benjamin Butts 9/21/1747

Mollie Butts 4/14/1759
Lucy Butts 10/19/1749   Eliza Butts 4/22/1761
Daniel Butts 4/6/1765

DEATHS

Francis Butts 9/2/1747
Peter Butts 5/3/1780
John Butts 8/21/1781, d. a prisoner at Portsmouth, Va., aged 29 yrs. He was sent as courier to Hick's Ford on Meherrin River and on the way was captured by Tarleton's Cavalry, sent to Portsmouth where he died. He had been paroled on honor.
Eliza Butts 12/3/1781

JAMES BUTTS BIBLE

James Butts, 7th child of Peter Butts, b. 3/17/1757 South Hampton Co., Va.
Keziah Simmons, sister of Spratly Simmons, b. 3/27/1754
Simmons Butts, son of above, and only child of Reziah Simmons Butts, b. 2/5/1780
Fannie Lewis, 2nd wife of James Butts, m. 1783.

BIRTHS of Children of 2nd Marriage

Samuel Butts 11/18/1784
Parker Butts 5/22/1790
Richard Henry Butts 9/5/1786

Lewis Butts 10/12/1792
Rebecca Butts 6/30/1788
Elizabeth LeCay Butts 7/5/1796

BIRTHS of children by Sallie Simmons, his 3rd wife, was m. 1797

Matt Calvert Butts 4/29/1798
Washington Butts 1/26/1809
James Irwin Butts b. 4/13/1800
David Edward Butts 2/28/1812
Eliza Clements Butts 7/23/1802

John Floyd Butts 3/10/1814
Benjamin Kirby Butts 1/2/1805
Betsy Eleanor Butts 9/17/1806
Matt Calvert Butts d. 1887

Sarah Sophia Stebbens of Springfield, Mass. Georgia A. Hitchcock d. 12/25/1898
All are buried in Milledgeville Cemetery

(James Butts Bible, contd....)

DEATHS

Keziah Butts ca 1782
Richard Henry Butts 1/17/1805
Samuel Butts 1/27/1813

Fannie (Lewis) Butts, 2nd wife, 7/18/1796
Elizabeth LeGay Butts 7/24/1796 Rebecca Butts 11/2/1791

JOHN GRAHAM BIBLE
Owner: Mrs. Henry Carlton, Athens, Ga.

John Graham, b. 4/30/1711, son of John Graham, Esq. of Mackeston, in Pirthshire, North Britain, who was nearly related to Graham of Garter of Orchill.

My mother was named Margaret, oldest dau. of John Graham, Esq. of Killiarnin in the Shire of Sterling. He was heir-in-law to estate of Duke of Montrose in Scotland had the Duke left no Issue.

My father by my mother had 19 children and there is none living but myself, my sister, Catherine, who m. Mr. John Stuart of Balemuren, near Belfast, Ireland (a relative of hers), and my sister, Jean, if married, I know not to whom.

I was married to Christian, dau. of Dr. Gustavus Brown of Maryland 8/13/1742. She d. 9/17th following and lies interred under a marble st Dipple in Stafford Co. (Va.) 12/14/1746 I was 2nd time married to Elizabeth, dau. of Catesby Cocke, Esq., by whom we had the following issue:

John b. 9/14/1747 d. age of 3 mos, lies interred at Belmore in Fairfax Co., Va.
Duncan, b. 10/6/1748, christened the same day and died that night. He lies interred with his brother, John.
Margaret b. 10/13/1749
Robert b. 7/3/1751
Mary b. 5/2/1753 John b. 5/4/1755
William b. 4/1/1757 d. 9/28/1821

Walter b. 3/18/1759. William Bird, Esq., was his godfather Elizabeth b. 5/7/1761 d. 8/21/1764 of the same disorder Catherine had, which she got in the same way.

Catherine b. 8/22/1763 d. 8/6/1764 after being seized with violent flux, which she got from Allan, son of Allan McCrae. Catherine was the comeliest child we had. She died the fourth day after being taken sick. Catherine and Elizabeth lie interred at Belmont, near their brothers.

Jean, b. 3/23/1768 and privately baptised by Rev. Mr. James Scott. She had godfathers and godmothers afterwards, as had all the children except Duncan.

When Catesby Cocke, Esq., their grandfather, sold Belmont, he reserved a burying ground, which will appear by deeds made by the second Catesby Cocke to Benjamin Grayson, recorded in Fairfax Co.
Catesby b. 9/13/1765, privately baptised by Rev. Mr. James Scott. he had godfathers and godmothers afterward.

COLONEL THOMAS CARR BIBLE

MARRIAGES

Ignatius Few, attorney at law, to Selina Agnes Carr 8/29/1811 William A. Carr to Cynthia Walker, dau. of Elijah Walker (Brooke Co.) 7/31/1817
Thomas Carr to Fanny Law, his 2nd wife, 5/6/1813

William A. Carr to Jane Aiken, his 2nd wife, in Tallahassee, Fla. 2/18/1835

(Colonel Thomas Carr Bible, contd....)

BIRTHS

Thomas Carr, son of William and Susannah Carr, b. 10/4/1756 in Spotsylvania Co., Va.
Frances C., his wife, b. 11/16/1771

Thomas Walker Carr, son of William and Cynthia Cart, b. 9/17/1822
William Walker Carr, son of William and Cynthia Carr, b. 8/8/1824
Charles Nelson Carr, son of William and Cynthia Carr, b. 10/28/1826
Elijah Walker Carr, son of William and Cynthia Carr, b. 3/28/1829 Florida
Cynthia Carr, dau. of William and Cynthia Carr, b. 7/11/1831
Susan Agnes Carr, lst dau. of William and Jane Carr, his second wife, b. 12/16/1835
Frances Susan Carr, dau. of Thomas D. and Anne Watkins Carr, b. 3/29/1824
Mary Ann Selina Carr, dau. of Thomas D. and Anne Watkins Carr, b. 1/15/1826

DEATHS

William Bacon Carr 8/28/1793, aged 1 yr, 10 days
Alexander Waiter Carr 9/30/1803
Frances C. Carr, wife of Thomas Carr, 6/2/1812
Col. Thomas Carr 10/5/1820 Alexandria,Va., interred family burying ground beside Mrs. F. Carr.
Frances Selina Carr 12/16/1922, aged 4 yrs., 12 days
Charles Nelson Carr 10/25/1831, lacking 3 days of 5 yrs.
Mary Eliza Carr 11/6/1831, aged 11 yrs, 10 days
Cynthia, wife of William A. Carr, 7/12/1833.

JOHN ARTHUR BIBLE of Bedford County
From: Rev. War Pension #W5636

BIRTHS

Thomas Arthur 1/3/1787
Sally Arthur 4/27/1800
Dosia Arthur 11/23/1789
Caleb Arthur 7/2/1802
Willis Arthur 2/27/1791
Winnifred Arthur 1/8/1805
Larkin Arthur 2/5/1793

Nenah? Arthur 3/21/1807
Lilly Ann Arthur 3/12/1795
Melindah Arthur 1/17/1807
John Arthur 9/15/1797
Emley Jane Arthur 1/3/1816
Elizabeth Arthur 9/1816

Note: John Arthur's application dtd 5/17/1843, aged 85 yrs., Bedford Co. Va. States he m. 10/1784 Elizabeth Adams, b. 9/28/1769, dau. of John and Sarah Adams in Bedford Co., Va. States that his brother, Thomas, served in war and m. Sally Dixon.

JAMES KENNEDY BIBLE
From: His Revolutionary War Pension Application #R15594

BIRTHS of Children

Tully Kennedy 12/18/1787
Cyrus Kennedy 10/18/1799
Ann Kennedy 7/30/1790
Aralinta Kennedy 7/20/1802
Mary Kennedy 7/7/1792

Sophia Kennedy 10/29/1805
John Kennedy 10/11/1792
Josiah Kennedy 3/28/1808
William Kennedy 10/24/1796
Jefferson Kennedy 4/29/1811

Note: James Kennedy d. 3/10/1828. Claim for 1/2 pay pd to his admr, Granville Kennedy at Henrico Co., Va. He m. Mary McDonald b. 2/10/1768 Laurens Co., S. C. d. 10/6/1848 on 5/11/1786.

PETER TAYLOR BIBLE
From: Rev. War Pension f#6239

BIRTHS of Children of Peter and Elizabeth Taylor:

William Taylor 2/15/1787
Peggy Taylor 4/11/1790

James Taylor 2/15/1787
Peter Taylor 2/7/1791

BIRTHS of Children of William and Elizabeth Taylor Caroline Taylor 6/1/1832

William Henry Taylor 1/29/1827
Joseph Taylor 6/11/1825
Elizabeth Taylor 8/18/1835

Henry Taylor 1/29/1827
Babel Taylor, son, 12/24/1821
Thomas Taylor 7/29/1823-8/2/1825

Note: Reference is made in 1879 to grandchildren of soldier, Pete and wife, Elizabeth; Caroline Loomis; Mrs. William Ridgewell; Mrs. Ann Moore, all living in Portsmouth, Va., and Capt. Babel Taylor of the steamer "Lucy", Norfolk, Va., and Washington Taylor of Berkley, Va.

Peter Taylor states in his application that he m. 7/1783 in Accomack Co., Va., Elizabeth Kelly.

Peter Taylor d. 5/31/1824. Widow's application 8/21/1843 at Portsmouth, Va., aged 77 (she d. 9/1/1855 leaving three or four children).

HARRIS HICKS' BIBLE
From: Rev. War Pension #W4989

BIRTHS of Children of Harris and Temperance Hicks

Absalom Hicks 6/12/1786
William Hicks 8/29/1805
Jane Hicks 7/1/1788
Peyton Hicks 3/7/1808
John Hicks 5/20/1790
Elizabeth Hicks 9/1/1794
Willis Hicks 5/4/1797
Polly Hicks 1/20/1800
Robert Hicks 10/17/1802

Joseph John Hicks, son of Peyton and Eliza, 2/10/1832 Elethe Caroline Hicks, dau. of Peyton and Eliza, 1/9/1834

Eliza Hicks, wife of Peyton Hicks, 6/16/1817

Temperance Hicks, wife of Harris Hicks, 10/7/1765

Note: Willis Hicks, aged 47, 11/8/1844, Granville Co., N. C., made his declaration as one of children of Harris and Temperance Hicks, states father d. 4/6/1837, and mother d. 9/29/1841, leaving children: Willis, John, William, Peyton, Robert, Jane and Mary who intermarried with Ransom Smith.

Statement of William Hicks, Washington Co., Va. 7/26/1553, son of Harris Hicks, that –

Wife of Harris Hicks was Temperance Sears whom he m. 1789 in Granville Co., N. C., leaving issue: Absalom Hicks, Jane Hicks, Elizabeth Howell (decd), Willis Hicks, Mary Hicks, Robert Hicks (decd), William Hicks, Peyton Hicks, and John Hicks (decd). 9/4/1838 statement of John Sears, Granville Co., N. C. that his sister, Temperance Sears m. Harris Hicks at Ellis, Granville Co., N. C. in 1784. 6/1/1824 statement of Harris Hicks, Rev. War Soldier, Oglethorpe Co., Ga., aged 66.

JUSTIN L. DERIEUX BIBLE
Owner: Mrs. Willard Justin Derieux, Norfolk, Va.

(The Derieux family is descended from Justin Pierre Plumard de Rieux who immigrated to this country from France in 1784. He d. 12/23/1824 in Prince Edward County.)
Mary C. Derieux - presented by my husband, J. L. Derieux 1/1/1900

MARRIAGES

Justin L. Derieux of Essex Co., Va. to Mary C. Campbell of Essex Co., Va. 1/5/1882 at Edgehill by Rev. Joseph Hart
Robert L. Derieux 9/12/1922
James M. Derieux 4/4/1923
Willard J. Derieux 11/27/1922

BIRTHS

	James M. Derieux 12/23/1894	Campbell B. Derieux 4/10/1904
Alfred H. Derieux	Robert L. Derieux 8/28/1887	Willard J. Derieux 2/8/1890

DEATHS

Amanda M. Derieux 6/27/1899	Alfred Derieux 12/28/1906	Mary C. Campbell 10/8/1903
Justin L. Derieux 4/12/1922	Mary C. Derieux 8/16/1947	Alfred H. Derieux 6/25/1948

WALKER L. CAMDEN BIBLE of Roanoke City, Virginia

Presented to W. L. Camden by his sweet little wife, Lucy M. Camden 12/25/1891

W. L. Camden of Roanoke, Va. m. Lucy M. Campbell of Roanoke, Va. 12/23/1891 in presence of Miss Sallie C. Camden and   C. W. Francis. Signed Rev. Hamner and Rev. Greene.

BIRTHS

W. L.Camden 11/21/1861, Scottsville, Albemarle Co., Va.
Lucy M. Camden 9/29/1872, Mays Forge, Patrick Co., Va.
Ethel Claudine Camden 12/1/1892, Roanoke City
Lillie Bell Camden   4/25/1894,Roanoke City, Roanoke Co., Va
James Lewis Camden 11/2/1897, Roanoke City, Roanoke Co., Va.
Edward Norgrove Camden 7/14/1899, Roanoke City, Roanoke Co., Va.
Little Athy Camden 7/21/1902, Ogden, Roanoke Co., Va.
Margarett Ovedia Camden 3/17/1905, Roanoke City, Roanoke Co., Va.
William Wray Camden 3/26/1908, Gold Bills, Buckingham Co., Va. (Walker Lewis and 1st wife of W. T. Camden (Sally Davis) from Campbell Co. Child Luck d. 9 days after her)
Sue Maynard Wood 3/11/1926 Farmville, Va.
William Henry Wood 2/24/1926 Wealthia, Va.
Francis Eugene Wood 3/14/1928 Wealthia, Va.
Dorothea Ovedia Wood 2/6/1930 Wealthia, Va.
James Franklin Wood 5/21/1932 Wealthia, Va.
Stephen Lewis Wood 9/8/1934 Farmville, Va.
Walker Camden Wood 2/11/1937 Farmville, Va.
Margaret Rosalyn Wood 4/16/1939 Farmville, Va.
John Carter Wood 12/27/1940 Farmville, Va.
Lucy Estelle Wood 10/6/1843 Farmville, Va.

DEATHS

Ethel Claudine Camden 3/24/1893, Roanoke City, Va., 3 mos, 24 days
Little Athy Camden 1/18/1903, 5 mos., 25 days, Roanoke City, Va
Lucy Campbell Camden 12/24/1920 at John Hopkins Hospital, Baltimore, Md., aged 49 yrs., 2 mos., 27 days

(Walker L. Campbell Bible, DEATHS, contd....)

W. L. Camden 10/18/1947, Farmville, Va., aged 85 yrs., 10 mos, 28 days

DEATHS

Lilli.,aged 49 yrs., 2 mos., 27 days
W. L. Camden 10/18/1947, Farmville, Va., aged 85 yrs., 10 mos, 28 days

MARRIAGES

Lillian Belle Camden to Samuel G. Jolley at Dillwyn, Va. 8/26/1915
Margaret Ovedia Camden to William Henry Wood 6/9/1923 at Gold Hill, Va.
Edward Norgrove Camden to Florence Claiborne at Roanoke, Va.

In Memory of: Lucy M. Camden b. Henry Co., Va. d. John Hopkins Hospital 12/24/1920, aged 49 yrs., 2 mos., 25 days, interment: Evergreen Burial Park.

Golden Wedding Anniversary Card: 1876-1926, Mr. and Mrs. C. C. Camden, Tuesday, 11/23 six to twelve p.m. at home.

EDWARDS-BARLOW BIBLE

BIRTHS

Doctor Prince Alfred 5/1/1848 Mary Edwards 9/7/1881 Cora Perlina Edwards 7/20/1886
Sallie Edwards 2/22/1850 Etta Frances Edwards 8/22/1882 James M. Edwards 10/11/1867
Isaac Edwards 11/5/1884
Doctor Prince Edwards 5/9/1869
Joseph Edwards 2/22/1880

Caroline Edwards 1/25/1871
William Edwards 5/1888
Barbara Ann Barlow 12/9/1941
Boston Alexandra Edwards 1/23/1873 Mattie Keaton 9/22/1879
John Luke Edwards 8/9/1878
Rosa Lee Edwards 6/23/1874
Mary Elizabeth Barlow 4/13/1935

Sarah Edwards 10/22/1875
John Mathew Barlow 4/15/1918
George D. Barlow 9/5/1907
James Willie Barlow 5/12/1913
Fromis E. Barlow 11/20/1909

MARRIAGES

Carrie Edwards 1/15/1890
Arthur Taylor 3/3/1931
Rosa Lee Edwards 10/14/1894
Betsy Edwards --
Sallie Edwards 9/15/1897
Boston Edwards 9/27/1899
Joseph M. K. Edwards 12/1904
Mary C. Edwards ---
Frances E. Barlow 8/17/1935
James W. Barlow 2/15/1936

DEATHS

Mary Virginia Edwards 9/7/1881-9/14/1881 Doctor P. Edwards 4/1/1887
Isaac Edwards 4/5/1889

Carole Perlina Edwards 6/21/1892
James Edwards 3/26/1897
Boston Edwards 11/23/1899
Sallie Edwards 3/7/1899
Mary C. Edwarde 4/9/188- - 3/26/1922
John Matthew Barlow 4/1/1934-4/15/1918
James R. Barlow 7/13/1874-11/14/1942
Sally A. Barlow 9/22/1943

SAMUEL MABRY BIBLE

BIRTHS

Samuel Mabry, son of Charles Mabry, 3/10/1802 Tabitha Mabry, his wife, 12/23/1805

THEIR CHILDREN:

Absolom Mabry 6/26/1824
Samuel Mabry 1/5/1840
Sarah Mabry 6/2/1827
Tabitha Mabry 10/16/1842

Churchwell Mabry 8/6/1829
Greenberry Mabry 9/14/1845

Joseph Mabry 12/11/1831
Winfield S. Mabry 3/20/1848
Nancy Mabry 4/27/1834
Lucy Mabry 2/4/1837

America Mabry 12/28/1839 (Samuel Mabry, Jr.'s wife)   William Fielden Mabry 8/10/1860-10/26/1862

WILLIAM R. NUNN BIBLE
Owner: Col. William Preston, Roanoke, Va

BIRTHS

William R. Nunn 12/8/1850, Henry Co., Va.

Emma J. Draper 9/16/1858
Birdie Draper 2/12/1872
Virginia Nunn 12/22/1890
Frank Nunn 9/7/1878
Huldah Nunn 12/22/1890

Maggie Nunn 6/8/1880
William Oferall Nunn 3/2/1895
Ernest Nunn 12/8/1883
Wesley Irvin Nunn 4/6/1897

William R. Nunn of Henry Co., Va. m. Miss E. J. Draper of Rockingham Co., Va. 11/20/1877 at Inglewood, Va., by Rev. F. A. Strother of S. M. E. Church
William R. Nunn m. Birdie Draper 6/28/1894
Virginia Nunn m. Harold Williams 9/4/1912

DEATHS

Emma Jane Nunn 8/5/1893   Draper Nunn 12/6/1911   William Oferall Nunn 9/4/1893
William Riley Nunn 3/30/1918   Estelle Nunn Cross 11/30/1907   Birdie Draper Nunn 7/5/1897

JOHN J. CONNER BIBLE
Owner: Jean D. Powell, P. O. Box 207, Stuart, Va. 24171

John Conner, Jr. b. 8/9/1803
Milly Conner, dau. of William and Anna McAlexander, b. 3/5/1808 Our colored servant, Jennie, b. 5/7/1839
John Conner, Jr., son of John Conner, Sr. and Lucy, his wife, m. Milly McAlexander 11/16/1826

BIRTHS

Reed W. Conner 12/22/1847
George W. Conner 4/11/1873
Polly E. Conner 2/18/1852
Reed W. and Polly E. Conner m. 4/14/1870

R. W. Conner Jr. 5/31/1875
Thomas G. Conner 3/5/1871
Daniel W. Conner 4/13/1876

DEATHS

Polly E. Conner 9/6/1918   Reed W. Conner 2/28/1920

Wm McAlexander and Anna Booth, father and mother of these children, were m. 5/14/1807
John Helms m. Louvina McAlexander 10/7/1847
Jackson Dillon m. Elizabeth McAlexander 10/26/1841
William McAlexander m. Lucy Hubbard 11/26/1835

(John J., Conner Bible, contd...)

BIRTHS

William McAlexander 8/23/1779
Margaret McAlexander 7/31/1817
Isaac R. McAlexander 8/15/1819
Mille McAlexander 3/5/1808
Burke McAlexander 12/2/1809
Reuben R. McAlexander 11/3/1821
Nancy McAlexander 11/2/1810

Abner Booth 2/25/1781
Adah Booth 4/7/1797
Anna Booth 5/26/1791
Daniel Booth 4/5/1785
George Booth 4/20/1783
Jemimah Booth 5/6/1793
Zillah Booth 3/17/1795
Isaac Booth 4/17/1787
Freelove Booth 4/10/1789

Elizabeth McAlexander 9/15/1829
Anna McAlexander 10/31/1812
Anna Booth 5/26/1791
William McAlexander 9/29/1815
Adah McAlexander 3/2/1832
Isaac Booth 4/29/1758
Freelove Booth 4/17/1764
Elizabeth Booth 5/8/1799
Henry S. Booth 3/2/1846
Reubin McAlexander 10/29/1823
Burks McAlexander 12/26/1809
Anna McAlexander 8/30/1863
Adah McAlexander 6/7/1838
Nancy McAlexander 2/1811
Margaret McAlexander 7/27/1821
Millie McAlexander Conner 8/21/1859
Isaac R. McAlexander 12/7/1821
John Conner 2/8/1885

SAMUEL OBENSHAIN BIBLE
Owner: Mrs. J. P. Bovman, Roanoke, Va.

BIRTHS:

Zachary Obenshain 7/25/1846
Emma L. Obenshain 12/9/1864
Louisa Obershain 2/6/1855
Marcus D. Obenshain 7/28/1849
Samuel Theodore Bowman 12/22/1896
Lucy B. Obenshain 11/26/1866
James Thomas Obenshain 4/7/1852
Boyce Putney Obenshain 7/14/1871
Cora M. Obenshain 8/29/1847
Alonzo Waskey Obenshain 12/14/1873

Eleanor Blanche Bowman 10/1/1909
Annie Bell Obenshain 11/22/1861
Moffett Halley Bowman 3/15/1906
Albert Sidney Obenshain 1/25/1863
Halley Eidson Obenshain 2/25/1876
Julian Guy Hatcher 10/26/1882
George Price Bowmen 9/18/1900
Sidney Watson Hatcher 7/14/1903
Elise Ruth Bowman 10/4/1898
Richd Hatcher Bowman 1884

MARRIAGES

Samuel Obenshain to Ann Hardy 9/4/1845
Joyce P. Obenshain to Ida Shockley 10/14/1898
Samuel Obenshain to Lucy Halley 11/29/1860
Marcus O. Obershain to Lena B. Mason 1/16/1885
Z. Taylor Obenshain to Jennie Thrasher 1/1/1870
W. Taylor Thrasher to Louisa Obenshain 12/14/1871
Marcus 0. Obenshain to Mary M. C. Thrasher 5/1880
James T. Obenshain to Theodosia E. Graybill 1/25/1876
J. Watson Hatcher to Cora M. Obershain 12/15/1881
Joseph C. Bolton to Annie B. Obenshain 5/15/1883
James E. Stevens to Lucy Beale Obershain 3/23/1884
James William Bowie to Emma L. Obenshain 11/5/1884
J. Price Bowman to Blanche L. Obenshain 11/20/1894
Alonzo Waskey Obenshain to Mamie Carol Payne 9/20/1900

(Samuel Obenshain Bible, contd....)

DEATHS

Annie E. Obenshain 12/25/1858
Cora O. Hatcher 1/2/1909
Sidney J. Obenshain 5/7/1885
Joseph C. Bolton 8/10/1907
Ida Shockley Obenshain 10/7/1909
James W. Bowie 6/7/1915
J. Watson Hatcher 2/10/1885

Lucy Obenshain 7/12/1920
Samuel Obenshain 6/4/1890
Louisa Thrasher 5/17/1925
James T. Obenshain 9/30/1890
Annie Bolton 7/1933
Z. Taylor Obenshain 7/9/1900
Emma L. Bowie 12/6/1931

Marcus D. Obenshain 5/1903
Lucy Stevens 4/1936
William Taylor Thrasher 7/2/1906
Caswell L. Bolton 5/19/1908
Sidney Watson Hatcher 4/23/1897

JESSE BRANDON BIBLE

Jesse Brandon, His Book, 7/4/1824, m. Polly 3/5/1810

BIRTHS

Jesse Brandon 3/2/1793
Sary S. Brandon 9/9/1818

Polly Brandon 1/13/1794
Nancy Brandon 7/29/1820

John G. Brandon 1/13/1817

Negroes: Fanney 5/13/1804, Squire 7/3/1805, Leucy 1/25/--, Rachel 4/1824

MARTIN DRAPER BIBLE
Owner W. W. Phillips, Roanoke, Va.

BIRTHS

Martin Draper 3/4/1796
Letitia Amanda Draper 1832
Mary G. Draper 6/23/1799

John Harrison Draper -/27/1822
Emma Jane Draper 9/16/1856

Martin Draper m. Mary G. Williams 2/19/1818
John Harrison Draper m. Letitia Amanda Scott 1/27/1848
Emma Jane Draper m. William Riley Nunn 1/27/1877

DEATHS

Martin Draper 1/4/1878
Emma Jane Nunn 8/5/1893
Mary G. Draper 12/19/1824

Letitia Amanda Scott Draper 7/4/1900
John Harrison Draper 7/21/1891

DEBORAH CASSELL BIBLE
Owner: DAR Museum, Roanoke, Va

Bible printed in Edinburg, Scotland in 1752 by Adrian Watkins, His Majesty's Printer, imported by Cassell family to Philadelphia in 1686 on the "Jefries" Original owner: Deborah Cassell who was a war prisoner with her parents in Philadelphia when British occupied the city. Deborah Cassell m. John Banks of Gloucester, N. J., son of Capt. Richard Banks, who fought in Rev. War, age of 19, following the sample of his father. They had 12 children. Ruth Banks, dau. of John and Deborah Banks, b. New Jersey 8/23/1783. Mary Abigail Banks, dau. of John and Deborah, b. Montgomery Co., Va. 3/25/1798

HENRY AND LOUISA JANE FARMER BIBLE

MARRIAGES

Louisa Jane Osbourn, dau. of Thomas Osbourn, m. Henry Farmer 5/18/1837

BIRTHS

Henry Farmer 8/14/1814

Louisa J. Farmer 6/16/1817

THEIR CHILDREN:

Martha Ann Farmer 7/24/1839
James K. Polk Farmer 11/9/1851
Sally Henry Farmer 3/28/1842
Susan Emily Farmer 8/12/1854
David Thomas Farmer 5/3/1844
Eugenia Jackson Farmer 1/20/1847
Elizabeth Ellen Farmer 10/13/1849

(All children b. Halifax Co., Va. except Susan Emily)

DEATHS

Louisa J. Farmer 8/11/1876
Henry Farmer 1/14/1890
Eugenia J. McDaniel Crow 12/6/1900
James W. McDaniel 8/4/1871 (Husband of Eugenia J. Farmer)

Note: Family moved to Daviess Co., Ky. in 1852.

JAMES FULKERSON BIBLE
Owner: Mrs. Ryland Todhunter, Graystone Park, Lexington, Mo

BIRTHS of Children of James Fulkerson and Mary Van Hook

Jacob Van Hook Fulkerson 1773
John Fulkerson 1783
Hannah DeBough Fulkerson 1775
Peter Fulkerson
Frederick DeBough Fulkerson 1777

Dinah Fulkerson
Isaac Van Hook Fulkerson 1779
Abram Thomas Fulkerson
Caty Van Hook Fulkerson 1781

PHILIP R. RICKMAN BIBLE

MARRIAGES

Philip R. Rickman to Harriet A. Shepherd 11/29/1855
Robert L. Green to Narcissa E. Rickman 1/10/1882
M. Lee Rickman to Margaret Morrison 5/11/1892
John E. Rickman to Sarah C. Sanders 2/11/1887
Joseph W. Rickman to Jessie E. Mowatt 12/24/1895

John E. Rickman to Mary Jane Ports 3/3/1901
William R. Rickman to Martha Gladys Hall 8/6/1902
Thomas D. Lewis to Martha Jane Rickman 10/3/1907
C. C. Rickman to Mary ---

BIRTHS

Philip Riley Rickman 9/12/1835
Harriet Arzilla Rickman 5/20/1837
Sarah Emeline Rickman 10/4/1856
Miles Lee Rickman 5/2/1860
Harriet Naomi Rickman 1/21/1864
John Edwin Rickman 3/15/1866
William Riley Rickman 3/13/1869

Joseph Wiley Rickman 4/8/1871
Martha Jane Rickman 1/23/1874
Thomas Merit Fuller Rickman
Royal Graves Rickman 7/18/1876
Calvin Calaway Rickman 6/26/1877
3/2/1862 Narcissa Elizabeth Rickman 3/4/1858
Theodosia Arzilla Rickman 3/16/1880

(Philip R. Rickman Bible, BIRTHS, contd....)

William Riley Rickman 3/13/1869, Macon Co., N. C.
Martha Gladys Hall 9/28/1877, Caldwell Inst., N. C.
Grace Maddry Rickman 6/23/1903 Stevensville, Montana
Eunice Arzelia Rickman 6/18/1905 Hailey, Idaho
William Villfnes Rickman 5/7/1907 Covington, Va.
Willada Hall Rickman 9/8/1909 Pocahontas, Va.
Christine Briggs Rickman 10/30/1911 Pocahontas, Va.
Mary Nelson Rickman 6/5/1915 Pocohontas, Va.
Martha Lelia Brook Dent 8/18/1950 Medical College, Richmond, Va.

DEATHS

Sarah Emeline Rickman 8/3/1862, aged 5 yrs., 9 mos.; 30 days
Harriet Naomi Rickman 8/19/1866, aged 2 yrs, 16 mos., 28 das
Thomas Merritt Fuller Rickman 1/8/1872, age 9 yrs., 10 mos., 6 days
Theodosia Arzillia Rickman 7/28/1880, aged 4 mos., 12 days
Royal Grams Rickman 1/26/1906, aged 29 yrs., 5 mos., 8 days
Harriet Arzilla Rickman 8/3/1906, aged 69 yrs.
Narcissa Elizabeth Rickman 1/24/1929, aged 70 yr, 10 mos., 23 days
John Edwin Rickman 7/17/1942, aged 76 yrs., 4 mos., 2 days
Martha Jane Rickman Lewis ---
Miles Lee Rickman ---
William Riley Rickman 9/6/1947, aged 78 yrs., 5 mos., -- days
Joseph Wiley Rickman ---
John Edwin Rickman ---
Rev. C. C. ---- m. Col---- 6/1958

STEPHEN LIGHT BIBLE
Owner: Eunice W. Shorter, Star Rte, Box 225, Phenix, Va. 23959

BIRTHS

Stephen Light 7/30/1775
Joanne Light 12/24/1783
Tabitha Light 7/30/1777
Joel Light 11/1/1790
Agnes Light 2/28/1786

Temperance Light 11/9/1779
Mary Light 6/16/1788
Winifred Light 1/2/1782

DEATHS

John Light, Sr. 7/25/1824
Joanna Light 1/6/1806
Temperance Light 4/26/1848

BIRTHS of Children of James Carr and Agnes, his wife

Joel Carr 8/6/1807
Jemima Carr 5/18/1812
Joel Carr d. 9/28/1881

Joanna Carr 3/31/1810
Temperance Carr 12/8/1813

BIRTHS

John Light 7/29/1792
Sarah Light 9/18/1798
Elizabeth Light 10/18/1794
William Light 10/17/1800
Alexander Thomas Neal b. 8/--/-- d. 10/22/1841
Agnes Neal d. 4/31/1911
Temperance Neal d. 12/12/1845
Joel Carr 9/1861
James H. Neal m. M. D. Gilliland 12/3/1883

MILLEY CLARK BIBLE
Owner: Miss Rosa Alson

"Milley Clark is her name, a single life,-- obtain if any one would cherish it worth their while for."

Milley Clark, her hand and pen, and Burkit Field Clark, Polly Clark, Nancy Clark.
Thos. H. Gee
William Ellison Clark 5/1/1818-10/9/1907
Thos. Gee b. --/14/1814
Allison Clark, son of S. Clark, b. 11/20/1802
George Crymes b. 1766
Polly Clark.
Shadrick Clark and Rebecca his wife, dau. of Thomas Crymes were m. 9/7/1788
Thomas G. Clark b. 9/7/1790
Mela Clark b. 4/6/1793
Polly Clark b. 8/31/1795
Allison Clark, son of S. Clark, b. 3/20/1802
Peter Clark, son of Shadrick Clark, b. 8/14/1805
Dau. of Fanney, Estis, b. 9/11/1819
Dau. of Fanney, Craggy, b. 6/18/1821
Dau. of Fanney, Lucy,
Permelia, dau. of Fanney, b. 9/1/1825
Sarah Buck, dau. of Liza, b. 5/18/1826
Vilet b. 8/31/1828
Homer b. 8/11/1828 Robert b. 2/5/1829
Thomas C. Clark m. Susannah Jordan 7/22/1812

BIRTHS

Mary Rebecca Clark 8/29/1813
Henry Field Clark 3/9/1829
Andrew Jackson Clark 9/24/1837
Edward Thomas Clark 12/26/1815
Elizabeth Jane Clark 3/24/1821
Peter Francis Clark 9/5/1826

James Jefferson Clark 8/3/1831
William Ellison Clark 5/1/1818
Martha Jane Clark 3/1823
Joseph Washington Clark 2/24/1834
John Samuel Clark 4/12/1840

Alcy m. 4/17/1784 to Lewis Contales
Asolea and Bethey m. 5/26/1785

Molly, dau. of William and Mildred Killegrew, b. 4/3/1747
Lyse Tomson b. 10/8/1776
Elizabeth Tomson, dau. of Edward and Moley Tomson b. 9/19/1779
Archibald Lester m. Elizabeth Crymes 5/26/1785
William Crymes, their son, b. 10/13/1787
Mrs. Elizabeth B. Greene m. Thomas Smith
Pleasant Cox b. 4/22/1780

DEATHS

John Gardener 4/19/1796 at Shadrick Clark's, buried at the burying place at Mary Crymes, at side of the bro., Thomas Crymes.
Thomas C. Clark 7/5/1849
Peter F. Clark 7/14/1857
Edward F. Clark 11/9/1840
John S. Clark 3/26/1869 Mary R. Wood 7/17/1775
George Crymes, son of William and Christiana Crymes, b. 10/14/1710.
Christiana Crymes 11/2/1733
Ann Crymes //31/1737
Sarah Crymes 8/20/1744
Sarah Crymes, the mother of these children, d. 2/6/1745, aged 28 yrs., 2/1717.

(Milly Clark Bible, contd....)

By Ann, relict of Thomas Booker, Letty b. 11/23/1746 Thomas Booker b. 2/18/1748

BIRTHS By Mildred, dau. of William and Rebecca Bellamy, and relict of William Killegrew

Rebecca Killegrew 5/28/1757
George Killegrew 2/18/1766
Elizabeth Killegrew 6/25/1759

William Crymes, the father of George, d. 11/24/1712, aged 66 yrs. Christiana, his mother, d. 10/6/1758, aged 68 yrs.

Reuben Cox b. 4/22/1780. His name is Pleasant Mary Stevens Poindexter b. 9/26/1780
George Crymes d. 1743

Alscy was delivered of a child 4/18/1785.
Alcy, son, b. 4/18/1785.
Name is Lewis.
George Crymes came to Lunenburg 3/25/1755. Elizabeth Bowden b. 12/9/1757

Jane was the mother of Judy
Sarah b. 10/19/1778 Judy was b. 3/2/1760
Jane b. 3/6/1780 Martin, son of Judy, b. 1/12/1777
Artes b. 11/9/1783
Sarah b. 10/19/1778
Fereby b. 8/21/1785

Thomas C. Clark d. 7/5/1849 Susannah Clark d. 8/30/1853

Elizabeth Crymes, her hand, 6/28/1852:

John Davis d. 6/14/1771 Thomas Crymes, Jr. b. 2/8/1768
Thomas Crymes, 1717

ISAAC COX BIBLE

Bible printed 1748 Edinburgh, Scotland. Isaac Cox bought Bible in 1751. *"Sacred to the Memory of William Foster Nov 9,---"*

BIRTHS

Isaac Cox 2/21/1724-1813
Harmon Cox 1/2/1801-9/30/1839
Isaac Cox 11/17/1749
John Cox 1/2/1801
Thomas Cox -/20/1748
Jeane Cox 1/29/1811
William Cox 2/22/1750?-1817?
Edmund Cox d. 12/4/1813 (baby)
Amos Cox 3/12/1751
David Cox 2/1755-1832?
Solomon Mullins 5/5/1817
James Mullins 2/12/1821
Enoch Cox 4/19/1757
Isaac Cox 4/21/1858

Edmon Cox 6/16/1835-9/2/1880
Mary Cox 1/12/1837-1908
Thomas Triplet 1/12/1813
Olive Cox 1/1789-1877?
Harmon Cox -/30/1839
Hannah Cox 3/26/1792
Susy Ann Cox 1/16/1841
Mary Cox 3/1/1794
John Cox 2/1/1843-3/15/1883
Jeane Cox 12/9/1796
Olive Triplet 12/14/1808
David Cox 3/12/1799-6/25/1854
Mary Triplet 12/5/1810

GEORGE FOSTER BIBLE
Owner: Mrs. E. D. Myers, Roanoke, Va.

A. Foster, Turtle Rock, Floyd Co., Va. P. F. Huff, Turtle Rock, Va.

BIRTHS:

George Foster 1777   Jane Foster 1779

THEIR CHILDREN:

John Foster 7/1798   Agnes Foster 7/16/1816
Isaac Foster 7/27/1809   Eliza Foster 4/6/1806
Nancy Foster 3/12/1800   Elizabeth Foster 11/19/1807
George F. Foster 3/19/1812   William Foster 8/19/1818
Oney Foster 7/1/1802   Larkin Foster 4/8/1821
Hugh Foster 5/16/1814   Gabriel Foster 4/6/1807
Mary Foster 7/17/1804

William Foster's Family BIRTHS:

Orpha Foster, wife and consort of the above William Foster 8/5/1831

Mary Jane Foster 7/15/1849   Julianna Foster 12/30//1863
Ass Foster 12/29/1851   George William Foster 1/9/1867

Family BIRTHS of aforesaid Wm and Mary J. Mitchell, first grandchildren of Wm and Orpha Foster:

Dora Glen Mitchell 12/3/1868   Arthur Glenn Mitchell 2/3/1888
Minnie May Mitchell 12/24/1875   Carol Patra Mitchell 8/31/1882
George W. Mitchell 11/28/1870   James William Mitchell 1/9/1873
William Foster and Orpha Jones m. 4/6/1848
Mary J. Foster, dau. of above William and Orpha, m. William F. Mitchell 12/17/1867
Asa Foster, son of above William and Orpha, m. Bettie C. Ridinger 8/22/1872
Julia Ann Foster, dau. of above William and Orpha, m. 9/11/1889 Annie M. Blount
E. A. Foster, son of Asa and Bettie, m. Elizabeth Blake 11/11/1889
Lillie L. Foster, dau. of Asa and Bettie, m. Ell. Dobbins 11/3/1898
Pattie L. Foster m. E. D. Myers 8/25/1906
Hattie F. Foster m. Floyd Rieves 12/24/1906 Mattie W. Foster m. C. D. Koontz 10/23/1907

RECORDS OF E. A. FOSTER AND LIZZIE FOSTER (BIRTHS:)

Maida Ruth Foster m. 8/9/1898   Edwina Foster 4/1902
Earle Foster 12/1907

RECORD OF E. D. AND PATTIE L. MYERS (BIRTHS):

D. DeLos Myers 5/18/1907   Maids Foster Myers 2/27/1914

ASA FOSTER'S FAMILY BIRTHS:

Bettie Foster, wife and consort of Asa, 8/19/1855
Edgar A. Foster, son of Asa and Bettie, 8/21/1873

Lillian Alice Foster 1/13/1875   Hattie Funda Foster 5/25/1880
Mattie Martha Foster 11/19/1876   Pattie Lee Foster 1/12/1885

DEATHS

Edward L. Dobbins, husband of Lilian Alice Foster 6/6/1902
Lizzie Blake Foster, wife of Edgar Foster 5/1919
Bettie Ridinger Foster, wife of above Asa, 7/11/1926

TAZEWELL H. CANNADAY'S FAMILY RECORD:

Juliann Cannaday, wife and consort of T. H. Cannaday, 12/30/1863

THEIR CHILDREN:
E. C. Cannaday 3/19/1881
Annie Cannaday 8/30/1891
Frank W. Cannaday 9/26/1883
William Foster Cannaday 7/1894
Linnie Cannaday 8/10/1888
Iva Ella Cannaday 8/16/1901
Asa Howard Cannaday 11/1/1889
Kate Cannaday 12/1/1905

DEATHS
Edgar A. Foster 12/23/1924
George Foster 2/3/1830
Jane Foster, wife of above George Foster, 6/11/1857
William Foster, son of George and Jane, 11/28/1875
George P. Foster, son of George and Jane, 4/27/1876
Gabriel Foster, son of George and Jane, 7/18/1878
Larkin Foster, son of George and Jane, 11/17/1883
William T. Mitchell, son-in-law of William Foster, 3/19/1892
Annie Cannaday, dau. of Julia A. and T.Cannaday, 6/30/1893
Mary J. Mitchell, wife of W. F. Mitchell and dau. of William and Orpha Foster, 7/5/1897
Asa Foster, son of William and Orpha Foster, 4/15/1916 Lizzie Blake Foster, wife of E. A. Foster,son of Asa, 5/1919

FAMILY RECORDS OF GEORGE W. FOSTER

(BIRTHS):

Annie Foster,wife of G. W. Foster, 1/12/1873

THEIR CHILDREN:
Harry Holland Foster 8/13/1890
Margaret R. Foster 12/1/1905
Paul Harris Foster 1/16/1893

FAMILY RECORDS OF E. L. DOBBINS, SON-IN-LAW OF A. FOSTER:
Edward E. L. and Allie Dobbins, b. 4/26/1900

EVANS BRAGG BIBLE
Owner: Mrs. W. L. Schenk, Culpepper, Va.

BIRTHS

Evans Bragg 4/26/1777
William C. Bragg 11/1/1833
Gabriel James Bragg 5/20/1822
Lucy Rudersill 10/10/1793
Sarah Wade Bragg 6/12/1834
James F. Bragg 12/3/1812
Phillip T. Bragg 3/16/1836

Susan Frances Bragg 11/7/1825
Thomas Bragg 1/17/1791
Mary F. Bragg 12/18/1826
Elizabeth Janis Bragg 6/4/1801
Eliza Anne Bragg 2/18/1828
Lucy Ann Bragg 9/1/1817
Thomas E. G. Bragg 10/18/1819

Margaret Bragg 4/7/1831
Mary E. Bragg 4/13/1824
Amanda Melvira Fitzwallen Bragg 8/19/1829
Ann Elizabeth Bragg, great grandmother of Evans Bragg, dau. of Philip E. Bragg, 5/14/1874
Frances Roudesill, wife of James W. Bragg, 12/31/1807

Philip Evans Bragg, son of James W. Bragg, 1/16/1841
Emma Hudson Bragg 6/19/1845

DEATHS

Evans Bragg 4/22/1860, at "Rosewood", the home of his son, James W. Bragg
Lucy Rudisille Bragg 11/1/1858
Thomas Bragg 5/6/1833
Susan B. Robson 4/9/1883
Margaret B. Massie 8/10/1891
Elizer B. Hudson 11/15/1892
James W.Bragg 2/14/1894
Francis R. Bragg 7/27/1853

(Evans Bragg Bible, DEATHS, contd....)

Sarah B. Amiss 6/17/1909 Philip Evans Bragg 10/16/1919 Emma K. Bragg 8/31/1925

MARRIAGES

Evans Bragg to Lucy Rudisille 1/20/1825
James W. Bragg to Frances Rudisille 2/1/1830
Addison P. Hudson to Eliza Bragg 5/14/1844
Philip Evans Bragg to Emma K. Hudson 6/20/1866
Anna Elizabeth Bragg, great gtanddau. of Evans Bragg, dau. of Philip E. Bragg, b. 5/14/1874
Frances Rudisille, wife of James W. Bragg, b. 12/31/1837

PETER BAKER BIBLE
Owner: Tila Bland Mottley

Peter Baker and his four sons, George, Henry, Jacob and Peter, Jr.
George Peter Baker b. 1657 m. Christian Dillion
Peter Baker b. 1710 m. lst Leah Ferree?, 2nd Charlotte O. Lay
Joseph Baker 1747-1786 (now Wythe Co.) m.Nannie Smith
Joseph Baker, Jr. 1767-1870 Wythe Co. m. 1793 Elizabeth Alford
 Margaret Baker 4/5/1794 Wythe Co.-1/4/1887
Wythe Co. m. 10/29/1815 Berry Hurt 12/3/1786 Wythe Co.-2/16/1873 Wythe Co.
Cynthia Hurt 7/17/1842 Wythe Co.-3/L3/1920 Roanoke, Va. m. 2/3/1860 by Rev. James Fisher
Wytheville, Va. Isham Maness 1/19/1834 Greene Co., Tenn.-l0/l3/1917,
Laura Agnes Maness 11/24/1875-1/26/1948 m. 3/24/1897
William Preston Bland d. 10/19/1920
Tila Mae Bland b. 5/3/1899 Roanoke, Va. m. 9/5/1923
Robert Courtney Mottley b. 3/27/1899 Roanoke, Va.
Robert Courtney Mottley, Jr. b. 11/21/1942 Roanoke, Va.
Notes: Berry Hurt was son of Fannie Craig Mitchell (of Dutch descent) and Zachariah Hurt, b. 1763 who m. 6/8/1787 , had 9 children: Berry, Rhoda, James, Stephen, Washington, Meredith, Polly, Margaret and Calvin.

MILTON JOHNS BIBLE

MARRIAGES

Milton Johns to Clara Johns 12/18/18--, Halifax Co., Va.
Milton Johns to Pearlie W. Johns 6/25/1890
Pearl M. Johns to Stonewall Jackson Logan 1/25/1911
Verna M. France to Solomon Sutherlin 1/24/1907
Alma France to --- 12/--

BIRTHS

Milton Johns 6/18/-- ,Charlotte, Va.
Clara Johns 10/11/1862, Halifax Co., Va.
Lenora S. Johns 11/25/1891
Phoebe Smith 10/28/1842
Roscoe Morrell Johns 2/28/1893
Verna Mae France --

Stephen Smith 4/26/1846

Pearl M. Johns 1/31/1872
Alma Lovette France 11/7/1889
Alvin France Sutherlin 5/1/1908
Ed Dorsey Stewart 6/20/1888
Waldon Stephen France 9/17/1892

(Milton Johns Bible, contd....)

DEATHS

Preston Johns 12/14/1872, Charlotte Co., Va.
Milton B. Johns 8/18/1893
Phoebe Smith 6/30/1896
Sarah J. France 4/22/1909
L--ne Davis 12/30/1918
Ed Dorsey Stewart 11/16/1936
Rufus P. France 11/24/1912

Roscoe Morrell Jones 12/1/1935
Stephen Smith 3/11/1889
Waldon S. France 10/10/1918
Alma France Stewart 8/9/1937 Verna
M. Sutherlin 11/5/1918
Pearl Johns Logan 1/10/1942
Solomon Sutherlin 4/13/1919

JOSIAH WESLEY NUNN BIBLE
Owner: Herman Adkins, Roanoke, Va.

BIRTHS

Josiah Wesley Nunn 4/20/1827
Mary Virginia Nunn -27/1850
Lovina Ann Pedigo 7/22/1830
Martha Ann Nunn 10/25/1861
William R. Nunn 12/8/1850

Thomas Martin Nunn 1/9/1866
Joseph Henry Nunn 8/6/1853
John Wesley Nunn 8/29/1868
Sarah Jane Nunn 4/24/1856
Lillie Bell Nunn 5/1/1872

MARRIAGES

J. Wesley Nunn to Lovina Pedigo 10/17/1849 at residence of
Joseph Pedigo, by Arnold Walker, Oaklever, Henry Co., Va.
W. R. Nunn to Emma J. Draper 11/20/1877
J. H. Nunn to Lucy J. Stone 11/24/1881
Sarah J. Nunn to D. E. Marshall 12/18/1878
Martha A. Nunn to C. L. Holland 2/10/1886
Mary V. Nunn to B. L. Marshall 12/23/1898
T. M. Nunn to Bettie M. Carter 1895
John W. Nunn to Marie Womack---
Lillie H. Nunn to W. H. Adkins 1/30/1895
William R. Nunn to Roberta Susan Draper 6/27/1894
William Nunn to Lilian V. Shumate---

DEATHS

J. Wesley Nunn 3/14/1901
Emma J. Nunn 8/5/1893
Lovina A. Nunn Spring 1907

Robert S. Nunn 7/5/1897
Joseph H. Nunn 1908
W. R. Nunn 3/30/1818

CONN-ELLIS BIBLE
Presented to Isaac T. Conn by J. L. Ellis 5/11/1862

BIRTHS

J. L. Ellis 7/15/1839
Frances L. Conn 2/2/1857
Isaac T. Conn 10/15/1826
Hugh C. Conn 3/27/1860
E. C. Lamm 9/15/1827
Rhoda Jane Conn 4/1/1862
James L. Conn 7/30/1870
John N. Conn 3/23/1855
J. T. Conn m. E. C. Lamm 9/14/1847

Samuel 8. Conn 12/25/1863
Mary Elizabeth Conn 11/15/1848
William P. Conn 12/11/1865
Martha Ann Conn 8/25/1851
Manerva L. Conn 9/3/1867
Sarah P. Conn 7/18/1853

DEATHS

Mary Elizabeth Conn 10/15/1849   Martha Ann Conn 7/1857
Note: Paper in Bible states it was brought from Va. to Mo.

(Conn-Ellis Bible, contd....)

BIRTHS

Hugh Lee Conn 5/22/1814
Katharine Ann Boyd (1st wife of Hugh Lee Conn) 12/3/1813
Lydia Margaret Wilson (2nd wife of H. L. Conn) 7/6/1831

Children by 1st wife of Hugh Lee Conn

John W. Conn 3/14/1839
Singleton Norman Conn 12/17/1840
Thomas Middleton Conn 8/6/1843

Children by 2nd wife of Hugh Lee Conn

Trammel Conn 4/3/1850
Jesse James Conn 2/22/1860
Mary Crucilla Conn 2/15/1852
Josiah Francis Conn 5/11/1862
Hugh Edward Conn 1/9/1854
Nancy Jane Conn 4/8/1864

Mildred Ann Conn 9/10/1855
George Washington Conn 10/3/1865
Elizabeth Rebecca Conn 3/26/1857
Samuel Knotty Conn 10/2/1873
Margaret Katharine Conn 5/22/1858
Thomas Isaac Conn 9/1/1868

MARRIAGES

H. L. Conn to K. A. Boyd 4/11/1837 (Katharine Ann Boyd)
H. L. Conn to L. M. Wilson 12/28/1848 (Lydia Margaret Wilson)
J. W. (John W.) Conn to Mary Ann Hill 8/8/1881
M. A. (Mildred Ann) Conn to Isaac R. Moore 1/22/1874
M. K. (Margaret Katharine) Conn to John A. Pierce 12/31/1874 M. D.
(Mary Drucilla) Conn to Thomas W. Fogle 12/23/1875
H. E. (Hugh Edward) Conn to Alice E. Stroman 7/1877
J. J. (Jesse James) Conn to Ellen Pierce 12/31/1885
J. J. (Jesse James) Conn to Ellen Wycoff 1891
J. F. (Josiah Francis) Conn to Betty Campbell 11/1891
G. W. (George Washington) Conn to Ada Henkle 11/27/1889
T. I. (Thomas Isaac) Conn to Lou Quick 1895
S. K. (Samuel Knotty) Conn to Emma Turner 1897

DEATHS

K.A. Boyd Conn 5/1/1844 Ellen Pierce Conn (wife of J. J.) 1889
T. M. (Thomas Middleton) Conn 8/1845 J. W. (John W.) Conn 3/12/1909
Trammell Conn 4/6/1850 H. L. (Hugh Lee) Conn) 3/23/1884
E. R. (Elizabeth Rebecca) Conn 4/2/1860 N. J. (Nancy Jane) Conn 5/1864
S. N. (Singleton Norman) Conn slain at Ft. Donelson, La. 6/28/1863
L. Y. (Lydia Margaret Boyd) Conn 8/8/1902

ELIJAH LOVVORN BIBLE
Ref: 1812 Pension Application

Elijah Loving
Gincey Loving Matilda A. Loving

E. W. Loving J. C. Loving

BIRTHS

Elijah Lovvorn 3/5/1793
Thomas R. Lovvorn 1/16/1815

Thomas R. Lovvorn 8/16/--
William R. Lovvorn 10/22/1817

JOHN TAYLOR BIBLE of Orange Co., Va.
Owner: General Henry Lee Chapter NSDAR Library, Washington, D. C.

John Taylor, son of James Taylor and Mary, his wife, 11/18/1696-3/22/1780
Cathrine Pendleton, dau. of Phillip Pendleton and Isabella, his wife, 12/18/1699-7/26/1774, m. John Taylor 2/14/1716

BIRTHS of THEIR CHILDREN:

Mary Taylor 5/30/1718
Cathrine Taylor 12/30/1719-11/4/1774
Ann Taylor 5/10/1721-8/1761
Edmund Taylor 5/12/1723
Isabella Taylor 6/25/1725
William Taylor 12/19/1737, baptized 1/18, d. 11/5/1803
Joseph Taylor 2/19/1742, baptized 2/20/1742
William Taylor m. Elizabeth Anderson 7/28/1763.

John Taylor, Jr. 7/17/1727-10/26/1787
James Taylor 9/7/1729-9/26/1756
Phillip Taylor 2/17/1732-9/7/1765
Elizabeth Taylor 7/9/1735

BIRTHS of THEIR CHILDREN::

Sarah Taylor 3/5/1766
Anderson Taylor 12/9/1770-12/26/1854
John Taylor 2/22/1773-1847

7/4/1739 I gave my dau., Catherine Taylor in marriage to Moses Penn who d. 11/4/1759
John, son of Moses and Catherine Penn, 5/6/1740-9/14/1788
2/3/1735 I gave my dau., Mary Taylor, to Joseph Penn

BIRTHS of Children of Joseph and Mary Penn

George Penn 12/13/1736
Moses Penn 10/3/1744
Joseph Penn 9/27/1738
Elizabeth Penn 1740

Catherine Penn 3/11/1741
James Penn 8/12/174 –
Phillip Penn 2/6/1743
Thomas Penn 4/25/174-

1/25/1750 I gave my dau., Isabella Taylor in marriage to Samuel Hopkins.

BIRTHS of Children of Samuel and Isabella Hopkins

Samuel Hopkins 4/9/1753
John Hopkins 2/20/1762
Catherine Hopkins 3/3/1755
Mary Hopkins 3/13/1764

James Hopkins 7/27/1757-8/1758
Edmund Hopkins 2/27/1767
Elizabeth Hopkins 10/30/1759

BIRTHS of Children of Edmund and Ann Taylor

Lewis Taylor 8/17/1751
Edmund Taylor, Jr. 7/3/1763
Richard Taylor 10/16/1754
Ann Taylor 1765-1765

Capt. James Taylor 1729-5/21/1764
John Taylor 12/4/1758
Eliza Taylor 7/24/1771
Mary Taylor 12/3/1760

BIRTHS of Children of James and Ann Taylor

John Taylor 12/19/1753

Elizabeth Taylor 1/5/1756

BIRTHS of Children of Phillip and Mary Taylor:

Walker Taylor 11/3/1752-10/--
John Taylor 2/10/1763
Catherine Taylor 11/4/1754
Phillip Taylor 3/20/1761

Ann Taylor 3/20/1761
Mary Taylor 12/14/1756
James Taylor 1/8/1765

12/4/1752 I gave my dau., Elizabeth, in marriage to James Lewis

(John Taylor Bible, contd....)

BIRTHS of Children of James and Elizabeth Lewis:

Catherine Lewis 8/28/1755
Charles Lewis 8/2/1760

John Lewis 10/10/1757
Mary Lewis 11/22/1762

Joseph, son of John and Catherine Taylor, b. 2/19/1743
Frances Anderson, his wife, b. 3/30/1745, m 4/7/1763

BIRTHS of Children of Joseph and Frances Taylor

Elizabeth Taylor-10/11/1764
Mary Ann Taylor 9/24/1769
Thomas Taylor 8/14/1773
Lucy Penn Taylor 12/9/1782-8/22/1787
Frances Anderson Taylor 10/11/1786 m. John Somerville 12/18/1804
Frances Anderson Taylor b. 10/19/1801 m. William Shore 6/10/1819

BIRTHS of Children of William and Frances Shore

Ann Elizabeth Shore 12/2/1820-7/30/1821 Thomas William Shore 6/9/1825-1/15/1826
Sarah Ann Virginia Shore 9/7/1827-3/4/1847
Taylor Shore 5/17/1832-2/20/1882
Joseph T. Shore 9/18/1834
Robert Boiling Shore 1/19/1837
Sarah Ann Virginia Shore m. James Carter and had one son, James Drew Virginius Carter m. 2d 1/8/1873 Rosa A. Williams (nee Wright)

BIRTHS of Children of James and Rosa Carter

Sallie Ann Peable Carter 5/15 1876 m. William Trevathan 12/2/1896. He d. 1/2/1897. She then m. J. W. Eblen 12/15/1897 Grace Maudine Goodwin Eblen 10/17/1898-7/17/1899
Edward Phillpot Carter, son of James and Rosa Carter, b. 9/4/1878 m. Mollie E. Howe 9/4/1898
James Drew, son of Edward and Mollie Carter, 7/31/1899-9/1/1900
Mollie Magdeline, dau. of Edward and Mollie Carter, b. 3/10/1901

THOMAS M. AND MARCIA L. MOSELEY BONDURANT BIBLE
Virginia State Library

MARRIAGES

Thomas M. Bondurant to Marcia L. Moseley, dau. of Arthur Moseley,11/18/1823

BIRTHS

Thomas M. Bondurant 5/24/1797 Marcia L. Moseley 9/23/1799

THEIR CHILDREN:

Sarah Eliza 9/12/1826
Angelina Judith 8/12/1831
Amanda Harding 8/22/1827
Thomas Leigh (or Lee) 4/8/1834

William Arthur 7/13/1829
Joseph Alexander 3/19/1836
George Perkins 4/22/1838

DEATHS

William Arthur Bondurant 11/4/1832, aged 3 yrs, 3 mos, 22 days
Amanda Harding Bondurant 11/6/1832, aged 5 yrs, 2 mos, 15 days.

JOHN WILLIAM DILLARD BIBLE
Owner: Mrs. William B. Quilling Memphis, Tenn.

John William Dillard of Lynchburg, Va. m. Emma White of Appomattox, Va. 2/5/1880 at Bent Creek, Va. by Rev. T. M. Carson. Witnesses: Mrs. F. E. White, Dr. J. F. White.

DEATHS

Peter J. White 5/1879
Emma White Dillard 11/24/1943
Andrew L. Dillard 12/25/1880
William White Dillard 11/24/1943

Dr. John W. Dillard 5/17/1930
John Ruffner Dillard 3/10/1952
Dr. Oswald W. McCown 8/19/1952

BIRTHS

John W. Dillard 8/12/1852, Nelson Co., Va.
Emma White 8/18/1852, Putnam Co., W. Va.
William White Dillard 11/28/1881, Lynchburg, Va.
Fannie Elizabeth Dillard 9/24/1884, Lynchburg, Va.
John Ruffner Dillard 1/8/1890, Lynchburg, Va. (marked thru)
Oswald Stuart McCown, Jr. 8/23/1908, Memphis, Tenn. Frances Elizabeth McCovn 5/14/1912, Memphis, Tenn.

MARRIAGES

Fannie Elizabeth Dillard of Lynchburg, Va. to Dr. Oswald Stuart McCown of Memphis, Tenn. 2/5/1907
Nona Louise Blunt of Huntsville, Ala. to William White Dillard of Lynchburg, Va., 11/27/1919
Martha Ruth Henderson, Arrington, Va. to John R. Dillard of Lynchburg, Va., 6/2/1931, Washington, D. C.

JAMES WARREN SHORT BIBLE

John Jefferson, son of Richard and Polly W. Jefferson, b. 4/1761
Nancy T. Jefferson, dau. of Samuel and Agnes Tindal, b. 7/29/1762
John Jefferson m. Nancy Tindal 11/20/1782

BIRTHS of THEIR CHILDREN:

Hannah Jefferson 8/20/1783-11/21/1791
Warren Jefferson 5/14/1785
John Jefferson 9/24/1787

Samuel Jefferson 12/23/1792-10/22/1821
Unicy Jefferson 4/19/1795
Sabra Fooks 12/8/1783-1/28/1825
Warren Jefferson m. Sabra Fooks 12/27/1804.

THEIR CHILDREN:

Nancy T. Jefferson 11/20/1805
Sarah F. Jefferson 10/10/1810
James F. Jefferson 1/11/1808

John W. C. Jefferson 4/10/1813
Isaac P. Jefferson 9/26/1815
Samuel W. Jefferson 1/28/1825

John Hosea b. 9/11/1792 m. Nancy T. Jefferson 8/20/1823.

THEIR CHILDREN:

Sabra Jane Hosea 5/3/1827 at Georgetown, Delaware
John Jefferson 1/6/1825, 63 yrs. old
Nancy Jefferson was 70 yrs. old in 1833 when this was written.

ALEXANDER TRENT MOSELEY BIBLE of Greenbackville, Accomack County

BIRTHS

Alexander Trent Moseley 9/16/1811
Nicholas Bocock Moseley 8/25/1853
Maria Louisa Housewright 11/20/18-2
Florence Laselle Moseley 3/31/1855
Perkins Moseley 8/30/1857
Kate May Moseley 8/15/1859

Carrie Trent Moseley 4/11/1861
Lucy Page Moseley 9/10/1863
Elizabeth Montgomery Moseley 8/14/1866
Nannie Meredith Moseley 11/23/1868
Alexander and Arthur Moseley, twins, 1/10/1871
Hattie Heath Moseley 5/22/1872

Frank Trent Murrow 6/4/1884 at Buckingham C. H., Va.
Rachel Talbot Murrav 1/7/1887, at Columbia, Va.
John Eppea Hubard 7/21/1887 at Saratoga, Buckingham Co., Va.
Edmund Wilcox Hubard 11/4/1888 at Saratoga, Va.
Lorana Doone Hubard 8/4/1890 at Saratoga, Va.

MARRIAGES

Alexander Trent Moseley to Marie Louisa Housewright 12/23/1852 at Buckingham C. H., Va., by Rev. John Spencer
James Franklin Morrow to Carrie Trent Moseley 4/18/1883 at Buckingham C. H., Va.
John Eppes Hubard to Lucy Page Moseley 6/16/1886, Buckingham C. H., Va., by Rev. Mr. Ware
Whicome E. Pratt to Florence Lucille Moseley 4/6/1887, Buckingham C.H.,Va., Rev.Fitzgerald
Hattie Heath Moseley to Edward E. Hunter 12/5/1894, Buckingham C. H., Va., by Rev. Mr. Rice
Nicholas B. Moseley to Mrs. Pattie Moss 6/8/1893, Buckingham C.H., Va., by Rev. John Spencer

DEATHS

Kate May Moseley 4/27/1861
Alex and Arthur Moseley 11th and 12th of Jan. 1871
Newville Penn 2/26/1886
Frank Trent Murray, aged 20 mos, 22 days.
John Eppes Hubard 9/26/1889, Saratoga, Va., aged 2 yrs, 2 mos. Or. John E. Hubard 2/14/1892, Saratoga, Va,, aged 45 yrs.
Lorna Doone Hubard Forbes 3/12/1915 at Saratoga, Va.

JOHN MEGLAMRE NORTHCROSS BIBLE
Owner: Mrs. Margery Everett

John Meglamre Northcross 1799-1855 m. in Henry Co., Va., his wife, Sarah Larrison Cakes
Northcross 1809-1854

BIRTHS of Children of John and Sarah Northcross

Mary-Northcross 10/13/1829
Thomas Northcross 9/12/1834
James Northcross 12/14/1830

Elizabeth Northcross 1/20/1837
Hannah Northcross 2/10/1832
John Northcross 7/10/1839

Richard and Northern Nelms Northcross 10/4/1341
Northern Nelms Northcross 10/4/1841
Sarah Margery Northcross 10/26/1844

BIRTHS of African Children:

Nelms 10/20/1839
Alexander Campbell Northcross 1/19/1847
Sarah Margery Northcross 10/26/1844
Matt Northcross 9/23/1849
Walter Scott Northcross 6/10/1852
Thomas Northcross 9/12/1834
J. M. Northcross –

(John Meglamre Northcross Bible, contd....)

DEATHS

Hannah Northcross 4/17/1851
John M. Northcross 3/15/1855
Hannah L. Northcross 4/17/1851
Richard Northcross 1867
Sarah L. Northcross, wife of J. M., 2/18/1854
Elizabeth Northcross 8/8/1854, aged 17 yrs., 6 mos., 18 days

Mary McGee 8/1856
Nelms Northcross 1867
Martha O. Graham 6/10/1853
Thomas Northcross 10/1857

MARRIAGES

John M. Northcross to Sarah Cakes 3/8/1827

BIRTHS

John Meglamre Northcross 2/15/1799 Sarah L., his wife, 7/30/1809

BIRTHS of Children of Thomas and Hetty Northcross

J. M. Northcross 2/15/1799 -
Richard Northcross 2/5/1807
Sarah Northcross 9/8/1800

N.N. Northcross 7/18/1809
James Northcross 10/25/1802
Maria Northcross 2/15/1811

Ages of Black Children:

Bob 3/14/1801
Leathy 6/15/1824
Ned 2/6/1803
Fred 5/1/1824
Sly 7/14/1804
Martha 7/8/1825
Silas 6/14/1828

Charity 6/20/1811
Julia 3/20/1806
Dan D.
Stephen 11/19/1813
Scaly 3/9/1816
Delila 1/10/1808
Matilda 2/20/1827

Stith 9/10/1809
Thomas 1/8/1830
January 10/2/1832
Margery 2/27/1833
Anny 1818
Ann 9/27/1832

DARBY BONDURANT BIBLE

Rebecca Bondurant 1825
Darby Bondurant m. Ruth Igee 10/16/1777
Darby Bondurant m. Lucy Hall 7/12/1786
Darby Bondurant, son of Benjamin Bondurant, m. Salley C. Mosley 7/12/1797

Joseph Bondurant, son of Darby Bondurant, m. Rodney Tery 10/26/1797
David Bondurant m. Polley
Benjamin Bondurant 2/17/1773
Mary Bondurant 3/21/1778
Joseph Bondurant 4/22/1774
James Bondurant -/2/1789?

Salley E. Bondurant, wife of Benjamin Bondurant, 5/4/1781
Polly Garrett, wife of David Bondurant, 3/4/1787
Francis Walker 4/16/1790
William Bennett 9/8/1796
John Maxey, son of Sampson, 1/31/1788
James Agee Bondurant 12/2/1809
William M.? Bondurant 11/18/1827 son of Thomas and Mary Ann Rebecca Bondurant 5/20/1803, wife of Samuel Bondurant Mary Ann R. Moseley 12/1809, wife of Thomas Bondurant

Garrett 1/23/1803 Daniel Thomas m. Polley Bondurant 5/24/1797
James Bondurant, son of Darby Bondurant, m. 12/27/1802 to Cory Garrett, dau. of Isaac Garrett
Samuel Bondurant m. Rebecca M. Walker 7/30/1822
Thomas Bondurant m. Mary Ann R. Moseley 12/20/1826

BIRTHS
Lucy Hall 1/3/1748 Darby Bondurant 1/7/1747

BIRTHS of Children of Darby and Ruth Bondurant

David Bondurant 4/25/1775
---Bondurant 5/26/1792
Thomas Hall 5/6/1749

JACOB M. BONDURANT BIBLE
Owner: Mrs. Albert C. Scott Henderson, Tennessee

MARRIAGES

Jacob M. Bondurant to Elizabeth C. Read 11/17/1824 Elizabeth M., dau. of J. M. B. to Hubbard Sanders 6/22/1848 J. J. Bondurant to Susan Anthony (d. 1/18/1893) 4/22/1856
Edward P. Bondurant to Mary Franklin 4/14/1859
J. M. Bondurant to Mrs. Mary King Roney 4/13/1912
Jacob M. Bondurant Buckingham Co., Virginia 2/4/1795-12/25/1858
Elizabeth C. Reed 12/25/1803-6/25/1869
Martha Bondurant 10/4/1825-3/4/1836
John B. Bondurant 9/7/1827-10/1828
Samuel R. Bondurant 1/21/1832-2/3/1832
Elizabeth Bondurant 9/27/1829-10/2/1907
Jacob Jones Bondurant 7/19/1834-1/15/1898
Edward Poindexter Bondurant 11/10/1836-12/30/1902
Joseph R. Bondurant 7/1/1839-3/8/1922
Robert Leander Bondurant 1/21/1842-10/2/1845
James F. Bondurant, son of E. P., d. from gun shot 3/17/1893

BURTON-PRICE BIBLE
The ages of Hutchins Burton Cenr and his wife and children:

BIRTHS

Hutchins Burton Cenr. 4/9/1694
Susannah Burton 5/17/1700

Samuel Burton 12/25/1719
Ann Burton 12/7/1731
Drury Burton 11/23/1721
Charles Burton 5/4/1734
Hutchins Burton Jr. 9/25/1723
Robert Burton 12/4/1736
David Burton 6/25/1725
Richard Burton 2/5/1740
Susannah Burton 1/15/1738
William Allen Burton 7/25/1727
Nowell Burton 4/27/1729
Julius Burton 10/22/1742

William Price, Sr., now of Pittsylvania Co., b. Henrico Co., near City of Richmond, Va. 9/3/1730.
Susannah Burton b. near same place in same county 1/15/1738
The aforesaid William and Sarah were married in county aforesaid 3/29/1752. Their offspring:

BIRTHS

Sarah Price 1/8/1754
Daniel Price 8/27/1766
Susannah Price 3/26/1756
Robert Price 10/6/1768
Elizabeth Price 5/13/1758
Maraday Price 6/1/1770

John Price 3/25/1760
Molly Price 5/6/1772
William Price 3/2/1762
Nancy Price 3/15/1774
Cutburd Price 6/13/1764
Patsy Price 6/1/1776

Major Price 10/1779 (On one of leaves is written 3/10/1763---Julius Burton)
Mary Watson Hines b. 10/22/1744
David Allen is 15 yrs. old 5/8/---
Hanner Guinn did die 1/20/1755.

JOHN POAGE BIBLE
Owner: Mrs. Margaret Jordan Carroll

MARRIAGES

James Poage Moyers to Nancy S. Brown 9/1/1837

BIRTHS

James Poage 4/3/1805
Nancy S. Poage 6/16/1812

THEIR CHILDREN::

John Poage 4/15/1839
Mary Virginia Poage 7/26/1847
James B. Poage 10/9/1842
Annette Margaret Poage 6/26/1851
Rebecca Ann Poage 11/7/1844
John Poage 12/23/1757
Rebecca Poage 1/14/1765
John H. Poage 4/15/1793
Thomas C. Poage 7/30/1798

Polly Poage 4/15/1793
Betsy Poage 1/20/1801
Thomas Poage 1/18/1795
Ann Poage 12/1/1802
Jane Poage 4/22/1796
James Poage 4/3/1805
Robert G. Poage --
Cyrus Poage 3/13/1808

DEATHS

Rebecca Ann Poage 4/4/1846
Nancy S. Poage 1/8/1870
James B. Poage 4/7/1846

James Poage 11/15/1876
John Poage 3/26/1862

MOSES WILLSON BIBLE
Owner: J. F. McClure Fairfield, Va.

Moses Willson b. 1754 in Pennsylvania, d. 3/4/1826 in Virginia Thomas Willson m. Elizabeth Poage 10/24/1826
John Edward Willson b. 4/30/1833 m. Elvira Anna Brooks 2/11/1856
James William Willson m. Dottie Fruit 10/30/1901, Roswell, N. M.
John Edgar Willson m. Martha B. Dold 5/29/1879

BIRTHS of Children of Moses Willson

James Willson 3/13/1782 - William B. Willson 7/9/1790 Matthew Willson 3/17/1784
Thomas Willson 2/17/1794 John B. Willson 10/3/1787

BIRTHS of Children of Thomas Willson (b. 1794)

Amanda Jane Willson 5/7/1828-
Elvina Ann Willson 6/23/1837
Annette Louisa Willson 10/26/1829
Thos Mitchell Willson 2/6/1840
Mary Elizabeth Willson 9/29/1831

Matthew Willson 8/30/1844
Wm Norval Willson 12/13/1842
John Edgar Willson 4/30/1833-1887

BIRTHS of Children of John Edgar Willson (b. 1833)

Bette Hunter Willson 1/24/1859-1866
Mary Finley Willsod 1/19/1861
Annie Poage Willson 3/9/1863

Harriett Brooke Willson 5/31/1866
Lucy S. Willson 9/30/1868
James H. Willson 3/5/1872

DEATHS

J. E. Willson 4/23/1887, aged 54 yrs.
Elvira Lackey Willson 1/12/1884
Lucy Steel Willson 11/4/1898, aged 30 yrs.
Moses Wilson m. Elizabeth Finley 1761-9/6/1833

Harriett Brooks Willson 8/3/1908
James B. Willson 8/2/1922, aged 50 yrs.

JAMES LEAGUE BIBLE

James League 1725-3/4/1813
Mary, his wife, d. 11/5/1817

BIRTHS of Children of James and Mary League

Benjamin League 2/21/1755
Elijah League 12/28/1766
Joshua League 5/18/1756
Elisha League 5/17/1769
Oney League 1/8/1758
Ussilla League 10/3/1771
Joab League 5/5/1759

Candace League 7/24/1773
George League 10/6/1761
Rachel League 7/3/1776
Drusilla League 4/14/1763
Isham League 2/16/1780
Lucy League 3/8/1765
Anna League 5/10/1781

Joel League 7/11/1783-7/7/1857

Joel League m. Mary Holt 4/14/1791-1/18/1857.

BIRTHS of Children of Joel League and Mary Holt

Nathan League 6/10/1810
Jane P. League 4/22/1818
Archer League 4/22/1812
Joshua League 8/26/1819
Robert League 7/27/1813
William League 3/14/1825

Harriett League 8/22/1821
George B. League 11/29/1814
Edward League 9/4/1823
Elizabeth League 9/20/1816

Mary League 11/21/1826-5/1/1906 m. W. B. Jones 1813-93

Berry League b. 7/23/1828
Casander League b. 3/25/1832

Nancy League b. 7/21/1830
Sallie League b. 2/22/1834

JOSEPH WISEMAN BIBLE
From: Rev. War Pension #R11,741

Elizabeth Wiseman (8/26/1738-7/19/1807), soldier's mother, was dau. of Samuel Davis.

BIRTHS

Joseph Wiseman 3/29/1759
Elizabeth Wiseman, dau. of Henry and Elizabeth Bateman, 7/10/1762

James Wiseman 11/30/1783
Sarah Wiseman 1/13/1799
Isaac Wiseman 11/24/1785
Edith Wiseman 10/4/1800
Elizabeth Wiseman 7/10/1788
Samuel Wiseman 7/18/1792

Margret Wiseman 4/25/1803
Rachel Wiseman 4/23/1790
Joseph D. Wiseman 6/14/1805
Thomas B. Wiseman 12/23/1808
Owen Wiseman 7/21/1794

Joseph Ramsey Wiseman, son of Daniel and Elizabeth Ramsey, 12/27/1817
Isaac Wiseman, son of Isaac and Marey Wiseman, 8/18/1738-5/3/1818 James Wiseman, son of
Isaac and Marget Wiseman, 9/25/1818
Robert Wiseman, son of Owen and Jane Wiseman, 10/27/1818
Veldy Wiseman, dau. of Owen and Jane Wiseman, 3/14/1820
Keozah Wiseman, dau. of Owen and Jane Wiseman, 4/2-/1822
James Miller, son of Thomas and Sarah Miller, 10/10/1818
Christy T. Wiseman, dau. of Marget Wiseman, 9/22/1827
Elizabeth Lettey Wiseman, dau. of Thomas and Fanny Wiseman, 5/11/1833

THOMAS POAGE WILSON BIBLE
Owner: Claude Jordan, Ft. Defiance, Va.

MARRIAGES

Nannie M. Wilson to S. M. Wilkes 5/6/1874
Clara Winters Wilson to F. A. Jordan 4/30/1878
Katie McGuffin to W. A. Wilson 12/18/1889
W. M. Wilson of Augusta Co., Va., to C. J. Jordan 6/6/1849, by Rev. William Monroe.

BIRTHS

Nannie Miller Wilson 12/7/1854
Calvin Bird Wilkes 2/18/1875
Clara Winters Wilson 3/29/1857
Thomas P. Wilson 11/17/1803

Edna Wilson Jordan 3/13/1879
Lizzie Brown Wilson 9/8/1860
William Arthur Wilson 10/9/1865
William Miller Wilson 5/18/1828

Catherine F. Hanger 1/11/1829, wife of William M. Wilson   Katie McGuffin Wilson 3/4/1891

DEATHS

Edna Wilson Jordan 8/30/1879, aged 5 mos., 17 days.
Thomas P. Wilson 12/11/1879, aged 77 yrs.
William M. Wilson 11/16/1885
Katie F. Wilson 3/8/1890
Catherine June Wilson 12/16/1898
Theodore Miller Jordan 12/16/----
Bruce Jordan 3/10/1897

HARDAWAY MOSELEY BIBLE
From: War of 1812 Pension #W 30705, FWC 20689

BIRTHS

Hardaway Moseley 2/12/1787
Harriet, his wife, 8/16/1802
Emily Moseley 1/19/1822
Adeline Moseley 9/5/1831
Virginia Moseley 12/20/1823

Andrew J. Moseley 8/11/1834
Joseph Moseley 6/21/1826
John Moseley 6/2/1837
Benjamin Moseley 9/7/1828

From Pension: Soldier d. 9/19/1867. Brunswick Co., Va. 5/18/1878, Harriet Moseley, aged 75, wid.,states she was Harriet Richardson when she m. Hardaway Moseley on 4/6/1822 in Warren Co., N.C. (Mrs. Harriet Moseley d. 4/1889 Lawrenceville, Va.) Applications of Emily Conner (b. Emily Mosely in Brunswick Co., Va. 1/18/1822) and Adeline Edwards (b. Adeline Moseley 9/5/1831 Brunswick Co., Va.) stated that their father d. 9/19/1867.

WILLIAM MOSELEY BIBLE
From: War of 1812 Pension Certs. #27455, 20625, 38309, 28817.

William Moseley b. 2/5/1795
Mary Moseley, formerly Kirkland, b. 3/18/1804
Monroe Moseley 9/24/1826
George Moseley 2/20/1834
Evelina Moseley 9/16/1823
Maryan Moseley 11/6/1837
Mortimer Moseley 4/12/1830
Sargie Moseley 12/10/1842
Alford Moseley 2/17/1832
Martha Moseley 7/19/1847

Note: Application of William Moseley, aged 77, White Plains, Brunswick Co., Va. 6/6/1572, states he m. Mary A. Kirkland in Northampton Co., N. C. in 1829.

DOUGLASS-RICHESON BIBLE
Owner: William Evans Richeson Winding Branch Circle, Atlanta, Ga

On flyleaf: Scott's Bible. Mary Douglas (of Rockbridge Co., Va.), her Bible, 1852

BIRTHS

James S. Richeson 1/17/1817
Nancy M. Douglass 12/23/1820-11/2/1887 m. J. S. Richeson 9/22/1842

Children:

Ernest Richeson 9/25/1843
Andrew Jackson Richeson 1/17/1846
Mary Catherine Richeson 12/31/1847
Lucy Anna Richeson 1/16/1851
James Douglass Richeson 4/13/1859-5/24/1877

MARRIAGES

William and Mary Douglass 3/26/1818
Jane Douglass to Samuel McCorkle 12/30/1825
Elizabeth Douglass to Jefferson Crawford 5/22/1833
Nancy M. Douglass to William A. Richeson 11/2/1843
Sarah Douglass to John R. Maben 7/15/1847
M. Kate Richeson to S. B. Rucker 10/20/1869
Nannie L. Richeson to George E. Cunningham 11/28/1877
Andrew J. Richeson to Carrie Minor 11/6/1878

DEATHS

Ernest Richeson 1/27/1844
James Douglass Richeson 5/24/1877
Nancy M. Richeson 11/2/1887, wife of J. S. Richeson
Kathleen Temple Richeson, dau. of Carrie and Andrew Richeson,11/25/1894
Andrew Jackson Richeson, son of James and Nancy, 11/16/1896
Nancy M. Richeson, ne Nancy M. Douglass, wife of James S.Richeson, 11/2/1887
Jane McCorkle 4/15/1827
An infant of William and Mary Douglass 7/2/1827
William Douglass, Jr. 9/8/1838
William Douglass, Sr. 11/25/1843
Earnest Richeson 9/25/1843-1/1844
Mary Douglass, wife of William Douglass, 2/10/1855, age 60 yrs.

WILLIAM BROOKS BIBLE From: Rev. War Pension #W5908

BIRTHS of Children of William and Ann (or Nancy) Brooks

John Brooks 1/28/1790
William C. Brooks 7/28/1800
Frances Brooks 11/18/1792
James Brooks 1/21/1802 Elizabeth Brooks 6/29/1796
Catherine Brooks 12/6/1806

Note: Ann or Nancy Brooks d. 4/9/1849 and left above six children (alive). Catherine is called Catherine Roberts.William Brooks applied for pension 12/3/1833,Charlotte Co.,Va., stated that he was b. 1759 Essex Co., Va. Abt 40 yrs. ago he removed Charlotte Co., Va.Ann or Nancy Brooks applied 8/14/1838 saying she m. WmBrooks 5/1788 Essex Co.,Va.; that husband d. 10/14/183d

JUSTINIAN JUSTIS BIBLE

BIRTHS

Justinian Justis 12/25/1694
Prissilla, his wife, 2/5/1694 m. 5/28/1718.

THEIR CHILDREN:

John Justis 3/18/1719/20
David Justis 10/27/1729
Justinian Justis 12/14/1721
Phrame Justis 1/25/1732
Major Justis 5/16/1724
Prissilla Justis 5/16/1735
Judith Justis 12/7/1726

William Justis, grandson of Justinian Justis and Prissila, his wife, died in his childhood 7/8/1751.

JOHN JUSTIS BIBLE
From: Rev. War Pension #W7947

John Justis, son of Justinian Justice, b. 3/18/1720

BIRTHS of Children of John and Elizabeth Justis

Jemima Justis 1/29/1760
William Justis 2/27/1765
Pattey Justis 1/17/1762
Henry Justis 9/20/1768

David Justis 8/14/1763
Stephen Justis 7/24/1770
Kezie Justis 1/1/1774
Allen Justis 8/22/1775-10/11/1825

Samuel M. C. Addams, son of Joseph M. C. Addams, b. 10/9/1732

D. Justice m. Susan 12/27/1791

Patsey Justice 8/5/1792-4/5/1825
Polley Justice 10/1/1796
Elizabeth Justice 1/6/1799
John Justice 8/26/1802-
Nancy Justice 11/28/1803-

JOHN LIMBREY WILKINS BIBLE of Brunswick County

This fragment copied from the Bible before its destruction by fire at Belmont, the plantation of William Wyche Wilkins in Northampton Co., N. C.
John Limbrey Wilkins b. 3/4/1710
Susanna Wilkins b. 12/22/1724 m. J. L. Wilkins 2/26/1741.

BIRTHS of THEIR CHILDREN:

Douglass Wilkins 7/19/1743 -
William Wyche Wilkins 10/21/1768
Edmund Wilkins 8/30/1745
John Limbrey Wilkins 10/21/1768

Rebecca Wyche, wife of
Edmund Wilkins, 4/29/1749

DEATHS

Edmund Wilkins 2/1/1791, aged 45 yrs. Rebecca Wilkins 6/1810, aged 61 yrs.
William Wyche Wilkins m. Elizabeth Judkins Raines 9/26/1793, the said Elizabeth was b. 2/1776
Edmund Wilkins, son of William and Elizabeth, b. 10/2/1796 William Wilkins, son of William and Elizabeth, 1/1799-2/1802

JAMES ELKIN BIBLE From: Rev. War Pension #W8803

Katharine 6/2/1784-12/18/1824 m. 8/25/1801 ---- White. Mary Elkin b. 6/14/1786 m. 12/15/1808
Dorcas Elkin b. 6/20/1788 m. 9/13/1810
Martha Elkin b. 1791 m. 2/8/1810
Jean (or Jane) Elkin b. 1/15/1793 m. 9/10/1818
Rhoda Elkin b. 3/7/1796 m. 6/17/1819
Nancey Elkin b. 2/23/1799 m. 3/28/1824 James Elkin b. 5/19/1801 m. 12/12/1822
Zacheus (or Zachariah) Elkin b. 10/12/1803 m. 12/5/1822 William Elkin 12/30/1805-11/6/1807
Sibbo Elkin b. 8/11/1808
Elizabeth Elkin b. 4/17/1811
William Ferry Elkin b. 1/31/1824
James Mic Elkin b. 1/27/1826
Luvica Elkin b. 1/7/1828
Thomas B. Elkin b. 10/31/1831

DEATHS

William Elkin, son of James and Martha, 11/6/1807 Katharine White, dau. of James and Martha Elkin, 12/18/1824
Note: James Elkin, soldier, was b. 4/16/1755 in Henry Co., Va. m. 9/23/1782 on Virginia frontier, Martha Jackson, b. 2/6/1765. Widow's pension dtd 7/18/1839, Estill Co., Ky. Soldier's son-in-law, James Crow, was aged 38 in 1839.

JOHN HILL BIBLE
From: Rev. War Pension #W3814

BIRTHS of Children of John and Nancy Hill

Molly Hill 1/1781
Salley Hill 3/12/1792
Elizabeth Hill 5/26/1783
Martin Hill 7/1/1794
Nancy Hill 1/2/1790

Luce? Hill 12/15/1796
George Hill 3/24/1785
Dolley Hill 6/9/1787
Trisy Hill 3/17/1803
Henrietta Hill 10/20/1806

Chloe Kesterson, dau. of George and Mary Kesterson, b. 1/27/1763

Note: John Hill lived Northumberland Co., Va. when enlisted. After war, he removed to Md., then Hancock Co., Ga. His application 2/4/1833, Hancock Co., Ga., aged 82 or 83. He m. 1779 or 1780 Northumberland Co., Va.,Nancy, dau. of George and Mary Kosterson He d. 11/12/1842 Hancock Co., Ga. Nancy b. 5/29/1761 was m. in Church by Catholic Minister. She d. 12/10/1845,Hancock Co., Ga.

JOHN WARD BIBLE
From: Rev. War Pension #W8974

BIRTHS

Betsey Marshall Ward 1/13/17--
Frances Ward 4/2/1802
Anderson Ward 3/24/179-
Washington Ward 11/19/1804
Nancy Ward 12/10/--
Patsey Ward 5/4/1807

John Ward 3/23/1797
Rebeccah Ward 5/31/1809
Polly Ward 5/10/1799
Allen Donaphan Ward 5/19/1811

Note: John Ward's pension application dtd 9/25/1828, Mason Co., Ky., states he was b. 6/28/1765 in Nottoway Co., Va., son of Richard Ward and his wife, Anna Ford. His mother b. 12/28/1740 m.Richard Ward 10/20/1763. John Ward m. Nottoway Co., Va. 4/4/1789 Theodosia Anderson by baptist minister, Charles Anderson. Soldier d. 10/25/1846,Mason Co., Ky. Theodosia, widow,(1/17/17689/4/1854),was dau. of Henry Anderson. She applied for pension 7/12/1847. In 1829 brothers of John Ward - Albert B.and Robert Ward, made affidavits in Lunenburg Co., Va.

HENRY J. JENKINS BIBLE

Abraham Jenkins m. Martha Perkinson 2/7/1856 by Rev. Joseph Hay

BIRTHS of THEIR CHILDREN:

Louis Jenkins 2/10/1857
Clara Jenkins 3/2/1863
Nathaniel A. Jenkins 9/5/1858
Pattie Jenkins 1/21/1867
Betty Young Jenkins 2/19/1861
Asa D. Jenkins 1/15/1869
Henry Y. Jenkins b. 10/13/1792
Martha Brightwell, his wife, b. 6/10/1795, m. 1/15/1818 by Rev. Philip Mathews.

BIRTHS of Children of Henry Y. and Martha Jenkins

Mary E. Jenkins 10/26/--
Patsy Jenkins 6/17/182-
Sarah Ann Jenkins 8/29/182-
Henry Jenkins 6/22/18-

Abraham Jenkins 1/7/18
James Jenkins 1/6/18-
Jane W. Jenkins 1/15/1832
Benjamin Jenkins 12/10/1834

Thomas James Jenkins came to his death in Battle of the War at Malvern Hill, Richmond, 6/30/1862.------, the father of the above------- came to his death in ----- Hatacher's Run near Petersburg.

DEATHS of my white Family:

Sarah Ann Jenkins 1/15/1824, her funeral preached by Rev. William Johnson
Benjamin Jenkins 3/2/1837, funeral preached by Rev. J. H. C. Leach Mary E. Davis 6/7/1864, aged 48 yrs
Mrs. Martha Jenkins, wife of H. Y., 5/16/1868, aged 72 yrs., 11 mos, 6 days, his funeral preached by Rev. Askar Littleton
Jane W. Jenkins 4/10/1871, aged 39 yrs., 2 mos., 26 days, her funeral preached by Rev. F. M. Edwards

R. B. Jenkins m. Jane W. Jenkins 12/22/1852 by Elder Rev. James A. Riddick.

BIRTHS of THEIR CHILDREN:

Addie Nicolas Jenkins 9110/1855
Sally J. Jenkins 5/21/1863
Nannie E. Jenkins 11/16/1858

Mary Jenkins 9/18/1866
Charles W. Jenkins 8/29/1860

Thomas W. Porter m. Addie N. Jenkins 10/1/1872 by Rev. F. M. Edwards.
Magg B. Jenkins b. 12/6/1881

BIRTHS of Children of W. N. and M. E. Davis

Wille S. Davis 1/15/1858 - - -
HenryF,Davis 2/9/1861

WILLIAM VICK BIBLE
Loose Chancery Papers Southampton County (1830)

BIRTHS of Children of William and Polley Vick

Patsey Matilda Vick 5/1/1810 -
Cordall Vick 2/4/1816
Newt Vick 3/17/1812
Elizabeth Etna Vick 12/31/1820
Rebecah Vick 12/25/1813
William James Vick 10/28/1822

JOHN IRBY BIBLE
From: Rev. War Pension tW5003

John Irby b. 8/5/1761 Richmond Co., Va., applied for pension 1/22/1833, Lincoln Co., N. C. when 13-14 yrs. old, he lived in Dinwiddie Co.,Va., then Charlotte Co. with his father. His uncle Joseph Irby lived on Saluda River, S. C.Pension of widow, Anne, dtd 6/5/1845, age 78, Lincoln Co., N. C.,states husband d. 5/9/1843.
In 1845 Joseph K. Irby, son of soldier, lived in Cleveland Co., N. C.
In 1834, Richard Hanks, seed 73, cousin of soldier, testified in Lincoln Co., N. C.

BIRTHS

Joshua Mason Irby 11/9/1790
Betsey Irby 12/9/1800
Thomas Kendrick Irby 4/30/1793
William Irby 1/26/1804
Nansey Irby 5/7/1796
Joseph Irby 5/10/1808

JAMES SANDIFER BIBLE
From: Rev. War Pension #W8698

James and Martha m. 1/6/1781

BIRTHS of THEIR CHILDREN:

Martha Sandifer 11/13/1786-
Martha Ann Sandifer 9/25/1787
Robert Sandifer 5/10/1790

Note: Soldier applied for pension 1820, aged 70, Mercer Co., Ky. Affidavit of Martha Sandifer 9/24/1836, Perryville, Ky., widow, aged 72. Her maiden name was Martha Taylor. James Sandifer, bro. of soldier, states that the maiden name of wife of James Sandifer was Martha Coleman, abt 6 yrs. older than soldier, whom he m. 1/1781 in Mecklenberg Co., Va.

JOHN CAMPBELL BIBLE
From: Rev. War Pension #W1713

BIRTHS

Samuel Campbell 11/13/1797
Andrew Campbell 2/7/1810
Jane Campbell 12/19/1798
Robert Campbell 10/7/1812
Elizabeth Campbell 10/7/1800
William Campbell 10/-/1815
Archibald Campbell 1/9/1803
Alexander Campbell 6/11/1817
Mary Campbell 1/11/1805
Nancy Campbell 6/22/1820
James Campbell 8/11/1807

Note: Pension application dtd 9/21/1832, Preble Co., Ohio, of John Campbell, aged 71, states he enlisted Bedford Co., Va. where b. 2/6/1761, that he m. 12/1796 Sarah Vance, Jefferson Co., Tenn. Soldier d. 5/14/1846/1847. Widow, Sarah, applied for pension 4/11/1849, aged 75 yrs. James Vance,b. 1773, brother to Sarah, testified in 1850, states his sister was b. in 1770.

HUNT-HARRIS BIBLE
Owner: William L. Deyo
3203 Normandy Ave., Fredericksburg, Va. 22401

1/15/1796. This Bible is a gift of Daniel and Elener Hunt to -and S. Hunt

Daniel Hunt 4/17/1729-3/30/1806
Elener Hunt 7/4/1737-5/8/1817 Elizabeth Hunt 1762-1/18/1799
Ralph Hunt 1765-3/16/1838
Ishi Van Cleve Hunt 1767-8/25/1794

William Hunt 1769 8/25/1794
Benjamin V. Hunt 4/14/1773-12/31/1848
Jane S. Hunt 1/15/1776-10/24/1845
John Harris 1767-3/31/1845, aged 78 yrs.

Sarah A. Sneed b. 6/5/1807
William S. Harris m. Sarah Ann Martin 5/31/1836
John M. Harris 3/23/1837-10/31/1838
William Sneed Harris b. 12/5/1838
Sarah Sneed Harris b. 7/28/1840

Sarah Ann Harris d. 8/6/1840, aged 33 yrs.
Daniel Hunt Harris 2/14/1803-1/26/1871, aged 67 yrs., 11 mos., 12 days
Eleanor Eyre Hunt 7/22/1804-11/22/1849
Daniel Hunt Harris m. Eleanor Lyre Hunt 5/14/1839
They had three children. None lived more than one week.

John Harris m. Jane Smith Hunt 4/16/1798

Innes Todd Harris 2/18/1799-1/9/1837
William S. Harris 9/22/1800-5/15/1848
Daniel Hunt Harris 2/14/1803-1/16/1871, aged 67 yrs., 11 mos., 12 days
Hannah Stewart Harris 4/17/1805-9/26/1835

Elenor Vancleave Harris 12/23/1806-2/26/1807
Jon Fowler Harris b. 4/25/1808
Elener Vancleave Harris 12/6/1815-12/20/1811
Charles Henry Harris b. 1/15/1816

Lucy W. Buck 10/2/1815-1/22/1874 m. 12/13/1842 John F. Harris
John F. Harris 4/25/1808-10/6/1879

Innis T. Harris 9/12/1844-2/24/1882
Daniel H. Harris b. 10/7/185-

WILLIAM GORDON BIBLE

BIRTHS

William Gordon 3/13/1753
Hannah Ladd 4/11/1765

THEIR CHILDREN::

Simeon L. Gordon 11/28/1784
William Gordon 7/24/1795
Ruth A. Gordon 10/22/1786
James Gordon 6/11/1797
Clarissa Gordon 7/26/1788
Mary Ladd Gordon 7/9/1801
Elizabeth G. Gordon 6/27/1791
Clementina R. Gordon 8/30/1805
Caroline L. Gordon 8/2/1803
Rufus L. Gordon 4/24/1793

MARRIAGES

William Gordon Sr. to Hannah Ladd 3/25/1784
Simeon L. Gordon to Ruth Cheney 4/30/1812 Nathaniel Davis to Clarissa Gordon 4/12/1815
Stephen N. Morse to Elizabeth G. Gordon 12/28/1819
James Gordon to Susan Blaisdell 11/28/1821
Rufus L. Gordon to Sarah Floyd ---
William Gordon to Elizabeth Smith 10/28/1823
Mary Ladd Cordon to Charles Rogers 10/25/1827
Clementina R. Gordon to Jona P. Baker 6/4/1829

DEATHS

William Gordon Sr. 10/14/1818, aged 65 yrs., 7 mos., 1 day
Hannah Gordon 10/27/1843, aged 78 yrs., 6 mos, 16 days
Caroline L. Cordon 9/11/1834, aged 31 yrs., 1 mo., 9 days
Ruth A. Gordon, Mrs. Holt, 1/20/1844, aged 57 yrs., 3 mos., 28 days
Mary L. Gordon, Mrs. Rogers, 7/16/1844, aged 43 yrs., 8 days Elizabeth Gordon 10/22/1855, aged 64 yrs.
Sarah Floyd Gordon, wife of Rufus, 12/19/1856. She was b. in Danvers, Mass. 1800
Clemmentina R. Baker 3/1/1860, aged 54 yrs.
Ruth Cheney, wife of Simeon L. Gordon, 6/26/1861, aged 70 yrs., 6 mos.
James Cordon, Esq. 2/3/1868, aged 70 yrs, 7 mos., 22 days
Clarissa Davis d. Norfolk, a. 1868, aged 80 yrs. William Gordon 1/30/1871, aged 74 yrs, 6 mos, 6 days
Rufus L. Gordon d. 4/27/1872, aged 77 yrs., 3 days
Simeon Ladd Gordon 12/8/1879, aged 90 yrs., 1 wk., died Ashland,N. H.
Sally Cheney, wife of Thomas Blaisdell, 11/19/1877
Simeon Ladd Gordon 11/28/1784-12/8/1874 Ruth Cheney, his wife 1/1791-6/26/1861

THEIR CHILDREN:

Sallie S. Gordon 8/16/1814-6/4/1886
Elizabeth Ann Gordon 10/1816-10/9/1833
Marcia Lovejoy Gordon 1818-William Gordon 4/11/1821-
Henry Ladd Gordon 2/7/1823-11/15/1865
Mary Ladd Gordon 5/5/1825-1/22/1889
Clemmentina Amanda Gordon 5/1/1827
Hannah Maria Gordon 8/26/1829-6/10/1891 Emily Ann Gordon 3/27/1833-9/23/1912

DANIEL BROWN BIBLE
Owner: Mrs. Lucy Roberts Baltimore, Md.

BIRTHS

Daniel Brown 12/1/1748
Elizabeth Hill, wife of D. Brown, 11/30/1764
John H. Brown 7/22/1784
Frances H. Brown 2/12/1793
William Brown 7/26/1786
Daniel Brown Jr. 2/2/1795
Armistead Brown 10/14/1787
Lucy Brown 9/15/1791

Russel Brown 1/6/1798
Thomas C. Brown 11/19/1789
Richard Brown 5/10/1800
Mary Ann Brown 8/10/1801

BIRTHS of Children of John H. Brown:

John H. Brown Jr.
Sarah Jane Allen 8/22/1821
James C. Allen 4/24/1825

Elizabeth F. Allen 11/20/1833
John N. Allen 10/19/1827
Walter A. Brown 3/10/1821

MARRIAGES

Daniel Brown to Elizabeth Bill 12/25/1779
Newman Allen to Mary Ann Brown 9/21/1819

Edward Burgess to E. F. Allen 11/2/1841
Walter A. Brown to S. J. Allen 12/21/1843

DEATHS

Daniel Brown Sr. 7/1833
Newman Allen 1/20/1828
Elizabeth Brown 1/2/1838
John N. Allen 2/29/1828
Mary A. Allen 4/21/1875. Her home was burnt 4/16/1875.

Daniel Brown Jr. 2/24/1841
Walter A. Brown Sr. 8/27/1845
James C. Allen 6/29/1826
Elizabeth F. Burgess 10/12/1872

LEWIS FINKS' BIBLE
Owner: Robert Newton Finks Madison Co., Virginia

MARRIAGES

Lewis Finks to Juriah Berry 5/21/1812
Mark F. Finks to Sarah E. Carpenter 3/16/1873

BIRTHS

Lewis Finks 11/1788
Juriah Finks 6/23/1792
Lewis Fisher Finks 3/2/1814

Mary Eve Finks 6/5/1818
William Preston Finks 2/27/1822

NOEL BIBLE
Owner: Mrs. Ruth Powell
808 Veeden Street, Fredericksburg, Va.

BIRTHS

Berkley Muscoe Noel, son of Richard L. and Cathrine, 6/11/1847
Charles Muscoe Noel, son of James L. & Susannah S., 7/27/1850
Edwin Wellford Walker, son of John M. and Emily F., 10/28/185-
James L. Noel, son of Maria Noel, 4/15/1862

James R. Noel, son of Berkley and Alberta, 2/5/1877
William L. Noel, son of Berkley and Alberta, 10/2/1878
Elmer M. Noel 10/30/1880
Irene Noel 9/16/1881, dau. of Berkley M. and Alberta
Mary C. Noel, dau. of Berkley M. and Alberta, 2/26/1884
Grace D. Noel 2/12/1886
James R. Noel 6/12/--

NICHOLAS TALIAFERRO BIBLE of Culpepper Co.
Owner: Mrs. Rebecca W. Wroten
1517 Linden St., Pine Bluff, Ark.

MARRIAGES

Nicholas Taliaferro b. 12/29/1801 m. Ann Hill 2/24/1824 who was b. 12/18/1804

BIRTHS

Benjamin B. Taliaferro 2/1/1830
Malinda Margaret Taliaferro 5/30/1832
John Nicholas Taliaferro 5/10/1835
Miles Hill Taliaferro 1/23/1837
James Hampton Taliaferro 8/2/1842
Ann Amelia Taliaferro 8/13/1845
Martha Taliaferro 3/1/1847
Col. Ben Taliaferro 1/4/1756

James A. Hill 12/17/1797
Miles Hill 3/13/1774
Hampton W. Hill 3/9/1800
Tabitha Hill 1/11/1778
Ann Hill 12/18/1804
Blanton M. Hill 5/5/1802
Malinda Hill 7/3/1795

DEATHS

Benjamin Taliaferro 9/3/1821
James Hill 2/28/1831
Benjamin B. Taliaferro 11/18/1862

Miles Hill 11/4/1844
Miles Hill Taliaferro 10/12/1860
Martha Talfaferro 9/1812

CALEB D. POLLARD BIBLE of Nottoway County
Owner: Anna Elizabeth Vassar Pickett
Beechcroft, Rt. 3, Box 276, Farmville, Va. 23901

Caleb D. Pollard m. Olive K. Williams 11/9/1825.

BIRTHS

Caleb D. Pollard 2/24/1792

Olive K. Williams 11/11/1806

THEIR CHILDREN:

George James Pollard 9/16/1826
Elizar Jane Pollard 9/3/1829

Jemima Pollard 3/21/1828
Virginia Frances Pollard 10/--

DEATHS

Virginia Frances Pollard 9/20/1836
Caleb D. Pollard 7/3/1862

JAMES T. LEFTWICH BIBLE of Franklin County
Owner: Mrs. Catherine Schorn, 1331 E. 12th, Tulsa, Okla. 74104

MARRIAGES

James T. Leftwich to Frances A. Shaon 9/13/1854 by Rev. Benjamin Meaders
Harrison W. Holley to Susan A. Leftwich 2/5/1879 by Rev. Joel Peters

BIRTHS

James T. Leftwich 8/15/1834-7/20/1862
John O. Leftwich 7/6/1855 (m. Josephine Wilks)
William P. Leftwich 8/14/1857
Sarah E. Leftwich 2/17/1859 ("Sissie" m. Christopher C. Martin)
Susan A. Leftwich 3/12/1861

(Joshua Smith Bible, BIRTHS, contd....)

Martha E. Tarry, 2nd dau. of E. E. and G. W. Tarry, 1/14/1855

Frances Ann Bagby Smith 11/15/1856
Lelia Alice Smith 9/18/1858
Thomas W. Smith 9/14/1860
Emma Belle Smith 9/19/1867

Henry E. Tarry, 2nd son of G. W. and E. E. Tarry, 10/1856 William W. Tarry, 3rd son of G. W. and E. E. Tarry, 12/29/1858 Sidney Branch Betts , 1st son of Mollie Betts, 10/26/1863 Eliza Stokes Tarry, dau. of G. W. and Eliza E. Tarry, 12/15/1866

MARRIAGES

Joshua Smith to Susan Jones 4/7/1831
George W. Tarry to Eliza E. Smith 11/18/--
Joshua Smith to Bettie W. Pilkinton, his 2nd wife, 10/23/1855
Algenon Sidney Smith to Sarah M.Ingram 6/17/1857
Calvin Betts to Mary S. Smith 10/7/1863
Green W. Crowder to Susan C. Ellis 4/22/1868?

DEATHS

Susan Smith, consort of Joshua Smith, 5/1/---
William B. Tarry, Ist child of George W. and Eliza E. Terry, 9/20/1852, nearly one yr. Old Mrs. D. Jones 6/25/1855
George Lewis Smith 8/12/1862
Thomas Wise Smith, son of G. and E. E. Smith 1/3/1861, 15 mos. Eliza Stokes Tarry, dau. of George W. and Eliza E. Tarry, 7/10/1867

UTTERBACK-COCKRILL BIBLE of Fanquier County
Owner: Richard Lake, Falls Church, Va.

BIRTHS

Benjamin C. Leith 10/11/1813
Littleton J. Burgess 2/1/1862
Margaret C. Leith 8/16/186-
Susan C. Utterback 11/21/1828
Ida J. Utterback 3/15/1864
Redmonia J. Utterback 8/11/1851
Mary V. Utterback 8/29/1868
Fannie E. Utterback 8/2/1856
Mattie W. Utterback 9/23/1870
Annie L. Utterback 8/2/1862
Ernest M. Utterback 3/15/1864

DEATHS

Margaret L. Leith 9/16/1884
Edmonia J. Cockrill 11/19/1915
Annie L. Uutterback 5/20/1889
Clarence T. Lake 1/14/1926
Landon J. Cockrill 4/19/1926
John T. Cockrill 10/26/1930
Landon J. Cockrill, Jr. 4/29/1915
Hazel L. Pless 12/23/1944

HUGH ROBERTSON BIBLE
From: Rev. War Pension #W18836

BIRTHS

Cole Robertson, son of Hugh and Jemima, 12/29/1780
Elizabeth C. Robertson 1/16/1783
Camel Robertson 5/25/1784
Ede Robertson, dau. of Hugh and Susannah, 10/8/1787
William Robertson 3/18/1789
Anna Robertson 1/5/1791
William Albert Robertson, son of William and Polly, 11/28/1818. I was married the first time 8/17/1777. We were married 1/4/1787

Stuard? Robertson 7/21/1793
John Robertson 3/8/1800?
Richard Robertson 10/4/1795
Thomas Robertson 11/18/1802
Salley Robertson 9/24/1797
Hugh Robertson 6/16/1806
HughRobertson 10/9/1756 (son of Hugh and Susannah)
Susanah Robertson 6/24/1809
Mary Susanah Woody 2/26/1820
Richard Ligon, son of William, 9/10/1772
Thomas Robertson, son of Cole and Kesiah, 1/10/1809
William Woody, son of William and Edy,
10/6/1813 Richard W. Woody 12/13/1815
Nancey R. Woody 2/5/1818

JOHN C. TAYLOR BIBLE
Owner: Mrs. Ollie Platts Kidds Fork, Virginia

John C. Taylor m. 7/13/1842 Lucy Myra Dillard.

BIRTHS of THEIR CHILDREN:

Lucy M. Taylor 10/11/1828
John Lawrence Taylor 10/16/1858
Burton Lewis Taylor 10/19/1847
Letha R. Taylor 10/30/1861
Laura A. Taylor 1/23/1850
James L. Taylor 2/17/1852
Mary Elzie Taylor 2/17/1863
Virgin T. Taylor 1/13/1854
Francis L. Taylor 5/18/1866
Albert S. Taylor 1/22/1856

(John C. Taylor Bible continued...)

DEATHS

Thomas B. Taylor 1/24/1854

JAMES TAYLOR BIBLE

BIRTHS

James Taylor, son of William and Mary, 2/28/1731-4/4/1815 Ann, dau. of George and Elva Owen, 9/25/1738-4/12/1814

BIRTHS of Children of James and Ann Charity Taylor 6/16/1757 m. John May

George Taylor 4/8/1759
Daniel Taylor 8/13/1761

Patsy Taylor 5/4/1764 m. James Pittman Betty Taylor 11/1/1766 m. Edward Adams
Mary Taylor 9/4/1769 m. Joel Witt

Nancy Taylor 10/20/1772
Kisiah Taylor 3/3/1775-9/1/1781
Hughes Owen Taylor 10/19/1778-3/10/1837
E
lizabeth Taylor, dau. of Thomas Kennon and Rachel, 1/25/17831/24/1868

BIRTHS of Children of Hughes O. and Elizabeth Taylor Louisa Taylor 8/16/1801 - Amanda

Ann Taylor 12/7/1818
Hughes Woodson Taylor 9/22/1803
Thomas Daniel Taylor Amelia Taylor 8/12/1805

James Taylor 5/30/1809-8/6/1814
Jabin Snow Taylor 8/10/1823
Elika Adams Taylor 7/30/1811
Rachel Taylor 12/22/1813-7/17/1853

Elbert Elihu Taylor 4/7/1826
George Grant Taylor 3/16/1816-
Edna Elizabeth Taylor 11/12/1828-12/1/1847

MARRIAGES

James Taylor to Ann Owen 12/3/1755
Rachel Taylor to G. M. Witt
Hughes O. Taylor to Elizabeth 8/28/1800

(James Taylor Bible, contd....)

DEATHS

Kesiah Taylor 9/1/1781
Jabin Snow Taylor 2/22/1857
James Taylor 4/4/1815
Thomas Daniel Taylor 3/13/1867
Edna E. Jackson, formerly Edna E.Taylor, 12/1/1847, age 19 yrs
James Taylor, son of Hughes O. and Elizabeth, 8/6/1814

Ann Taylor 4/12/1814
Elizabeth Taylor 1/24/1868
Hughes O. Taylor 3/10/1837
George Grant Taylor 1/26/1869

AUSTIN SANDRIDGE BIBLE
Owner: Mrs. E. C. Hayden Sterling, Virginia

BIRTHS

Austin Sandridge ---
Anna Sandridge 5/26/1768
Sophfa Sandridge 12/12/1756
Zacharias Sandridge 9/9/1770

Larkin Sandridge 11/21/1758
Winifred Sandrfdge 6/10/1772
David Sandridge 1/8/1761-1/16/1806

Elizabeth Sandridge 7/6/1774-9/28/1802 Savannah, Ga.
William James Cason 11/17/1814
Anna Sophia Elizabeth Cason 8/16/1816, intermarried with James Rawlings
James Lewis Holladay b. 4/29/1802, baptized 11/16/1802

DEATHS

David Sandridge Sr. --/10/--
---Shackleford 7/23/1802
Winifred Pulliam 8/21/1831, aged 74 yrs., 11 mos.
Rebecca Holladay (nee Rawlings), wife of Captain William Holladay, 7/26/1838

MARRIAGES

Levis Holladay and Catherine, his wife, 7/3/1799
Polly Boxley Holladay, dau. of Lewis and Catherine, 2/23/1800; intermarried w/Rev. Frederick Frazer 11/8/1825, Louisa Co., Va.
Benjamin Cason to Anna Holladay 1/20/1814 by Rev. Hugh C. Boggs

DEATHS

Anna Holladay 8/16/1816, two hrs. after she had been delivered
Benjamin Cason 1/12/1821

JOHN WILLIS MILLER BIBLE
Owner: Mrs. Raymond Duquette 5316 Thayer Ave., Alexandria, Va. 22304

BIRTHS

John Willis Miller 9/2/1787

Peninnah Evans 4/11/1795

They were m. 3/5/1811. THEIR CHILDREN:
Henry Miller 5/6/1821

A son 3/17/1812
Mary Miller 2/17/1813
William Harrison Miller 7/17/1814
Evans Miller 4/1/1833
Thomas Evans Miller 3/17/1818
John Miller 11/21/1820

Philip Evans Miller 4/1/1826
Peninnah Miller 3/20/1829
William Miller 2/5/1832
George Miller 3/30/1836
Reuben Miller 10/4/1838
Matilda Miller 3/11/1841

WORD-SAUNDERS BIBLE
of Buckingham Co., Va.
Owner: Natalie Saunders Pease
3913 Kensington Ave., Richmond, Va. 23221

MARRIAGES

Benjamin F. Word to C. A. Housewright 9/14/1848 by Rev. James Gregory of the Method1st Church
Nathaniel M. Saunders to C. A. Word 5/13/1862 by Rev. J. R. Bowmen of the Presbyterian Church
Edward Claiborne Saunders to Pattie Venable Gaines 10/17/1889 by Dr. J. Y. Fair
Edward Claiborne Saunders to Sallie Garlick Gaines 11/28/1899 by Rev. Dr. D. K. Walthall

BIRTHS

Thomas Fletcher Word 6/19/1849
Franklin LaFayette Word 3/8/1859
John Robert Word 2/6/1851
Edward Claiborne Saunders Benjamin Heath Word 12/29/1852
Amelia Ann Word b & d 6/1/1855
Nathaniel Morris Saunders, Jr. 12/28/1863
James Henry Word 8/22/1856
Nathaniel Morris Saunders, Sr. 5/10/1804

DEATHS

Benny Heath Word 10/5/1856, aged 3 yrs., 9 mos., 7 days Thomas Fletcher Word 10/2/1857, aged 8 yrs., 3 mos., 14 days
Benjamin Franklin Word 7/25/1858, aged 40 yrs.
Franklin LaFayette Word 8/18/1859, aged 5 mos., 10 days
Nathaniel M. Saunders 5/26/1879, aged 75 yrs.
Katherine Anne Saunders 11/1893
Pattie Gaines Saunders 5/12/1896
N. M. Saunders, Jr. 5/20/1903, aged 36 yrs.

JOSEPH STOCKWELL BIBLE
Owner: Marion L. Stockwell Long Beach, New York

BIRTHS

Joseph Stockwell 5/5/1802
Anna M. Saxe Stockwell 2/10/1802
Joseph Stockwell m. Anna M. Saxe 7/8/1823 (or 1825).

BIRTHS of THEIR CHILDREN:

Mary A. Stockwell 5/18/1826
Mathew J. Stockwell 1835
Godfrey E. Stockwell 2/7/1827
Benajah L. Stockwell 8/14/1836
Abi R. Stockwell 12/23/1828
Hermit G. Stockwell 5/10/1838
David S. Stockwell 11/10/1830

Lucy Stockwell 8/13/1840
Harriet S. Stockwell 12/1532
Maloma Stockwell 6/20/1842
Joseph M. Stockwell 11/25/1834
Samuel S. Stockwell 5/28/1844

DEATHS

Joseph Stockwell 9/22/1870, aged 68 yrs., 4 mos., 17 days
Anna M. Stockwell 2/4/1890, aged 85 yrs., 11 mos., 22 days

LIZZIE K. PAYNE BIBLE
of Campbell County Owner: Mrs. John Y. Kerr, Alexandria, Va.

MARRIAGES

Welter Tazewell Payne of Campbell Co., Va. to Elizabeth (Lizzie) K. Ligon of Nelson Co., Va. 12/10/1851 by Rev. Robert Nowlin

BIRTHS

Walter T. Payne 12/1826
Lizzie Kimborough Ligon 1/6/1827
Rosa Kimbrough Payne 2/3/1853
Susan Scott Payne 10/4/1860

Walter Ligon Payne 4/7/1856
Nellie Payne 2/11/1864 Robert
Withers Payne 7/21/1858

MARRIAGES

Rosa Kimborough Payne to D. C. Jackson of Charlotte Co., Va. 5/3/1876
W. L. Payne to Jennie C. Treadway 1/7/1880
R. W. Payne to Lillie D. Jackson 3/30/1888
Nellie Payne to S. Franklin Heidelberg 8/28/1895

DEATHS

Mrs. Walter Tazewell Payne 3/14/1893
Walter L. Payne 8/14/1918
Mrs. D. C. Jackson 9/1/1900
D. C. Jackson 1/23/1928

Walter Tazewell Payne 6/1/1923
Susan Scott Payne 2/25/1928
Mrs. S. F. Heidelberg 2/5/1925
Walter L. Payne 8/14/1918

THOMAS BANDY BIBLE
From: Rev. War Pension S25497

BIRTHS of Children of Thomas and Polly Bandy

Phebe Chr1stian Bandy 10/1765
Elizabeth Bandy 8/7/1773
Cary Bandy 10/30/1769
Martha Bandy 8/8/1775 (twin)

Richard Bandy 7/10/1771
Thomas Bandy 8/8/1775 (twin)
Thomas Bandy 6/22/1744
Nancy Bandy 3/1757 (second wife)

James Bandy 12/27/1786
Robert Dobson Bandy 2/15/1792

Elihu Bandy 6/9/1788
Horsha? Bandy 8/13/1794

Note: Thomas Bandy (also so. Bany) applied for pension 11/12/1835, Franklin Co., Tenn., aged 85 yrs., stating that he was b. Cumberland Co., Va. in 1748, lived Botetourt Co until aged 18, then removed to Sumner Co., Tenn. His second wife, Nancy, stated she m. Thomas Bandy 10/12/1777 and that he d. 10/13/1835. (Notice variance of birthdates for Thomas Bandy)

JOHN K. BEAR BIBLE of Augusta Co., Virginia

BIRTHS

John K. Bear 5/3/1819
Nancy C. Bear 2/26/1820
John H. Campbell 8/1/1778
Elizabeth Campbell 2/13/1817
Darcus Campbell 2/6/1785

Nancy Campbell 2/26/1820
Lavinia Campbell 3/19/1810
Caroline Campbell 10/6/1824
Margaret Campbell 2/20/1912

DEATHS

Nancy Campbell Bear Thompson 11/26/1893, Radio Citty, aged 73 yrs., 9 mos.
Caroline McEffinger 7/29/1846

(John H. Bear Bible, BIRTHS, contd....)

Lavinia B. Hopkins 7/19/1549
John H. Campbell 6/2/1850, aged 71 yrs., 9 mos., 1 day Elizabeth A. Shumate 1/6/1851
Darcas Campbell 9/12/1865, aged 80 yrs.

BIRTHS

Darcus Ellen 4/22/1846
Sally Warren Bear 7/15/1850 Caroline Allice 1/1/1848

Mary Elizabeth Cooper, dau. of John and Elizabeth, 4/17/1842 Charles C. Thompson 10/10/1858
Addie Deen 3/30/1861

MARRIAGES

John K. Bear to Nancy C. Campbell 6/18/1844 Charles S. Thompson to Nancy C. Bear 5/5/1857
Charles B. Berry to Ella D. Bear 5/26/1869 John T. Calhoun to Sallie W. Bear 9/18/1872

ARCHER BIBLE
of City of Richmond

MARRIAGES

Alexander Archer to Mary B. Hatcher 11/12/1817 Alexander Archer to Eliza A. Mims 10/18/1834

BIRTHS of Children of Alexander and Mary B. Archer

Calvin Archer 8731/1818 Ann Bett Archer 11/9/--
Alexander Boisseau Archer 2/4/1830 Benjamin Hatcher Archer 3/27/1831
Virginia Susan Archer 6/11/-- Sallemaud Archer ---

BIRTHS of Children of Alexander and Eliza A. Archer

Susan Mims Archer 1-iT24/1835 Burke Archer 11/25/1837
Polly Eliza Archer 2/4/1840 Wilbur Archer 5/27/1842

DEATHS

The friends and acquaintances of Alexander Archer are requested to attend the funeral of his son, Wilbur, tomorrow morning at 11 o'clock Monday March 19, 1844.

WILLIAM BASS BIBLE Of Chesterfield County

Ester Bass b. 1682
---dau. of Christopher and ---- b. 2/27/1695 ---- b. 2/27/1695
William Bass m. CicLllia 10/9/1718

BIRTHS of Children of William and Cicillia Bass Chr1stopher Bass 3/5/1719/20-

Thomas Bass 3/23/1727/8 Peter Bass 12/23/1732
Mary Bass 1/9/1721 Archard Bass 1/31/1725/6
Edward Bass 7/31/1730 Joseph Bass ---
Thomas Bass 2/4/1723

DEATHS

Martha Bass, dau. of Henry and Mary Clay, wife of William Bass, Jr., 3/1/1745
Mary Bass, wife of William Bass, 11/5/1717, and at her death gave this Book to her son, William Bass

(William Bass Bible, contd....)

William Bass, son of William and Mary Bass m. 5/6/1731 Martha, dau. of Henry and Mary Clay
William Bass, son of William and Mary Bass, b. 12/5/1707

BIRTHS of Children of William and Martha Bass

William Bass 6/29/1732
John Bass 11/27/1738
Mary Bass 2/2/1733
Martha Bass 10/5/1740

Francis Bass 4/18/1735
Henry Bass 7/19/1744
William Bass 3/7/1736/7

William Bass, Jr., son of William and Mary Bass m. 10/31/1747
Mary Walthall, dau. of Henry and Mary Walthall

BIRTHS of Children of William and Mary Bass Elizabeth Bass 8/13/ 1748 -

Archard Bass 10/31/1752
Lucy Bass 4/29/1750

Edward Bass 8/15/1754

Edward Wesley Bass m. Mary Louisa Martin 8/28/1844

BIRTHS of Children of Edward Wesley and Mary Louisa Bass Richard Royall Bass 8/31/1845

Mary Louisa Bass 7/22/1852
Ann Keron Bass 10/7/1847
Colin Bass 4/25/1855

William Edward Bass 6/13/1849
Martha Evelin Bass 7/7/1856
Matoaca Bass 11/10/1850

DEATHS

Matoaca Bass, dau. of Edward Wesley and Mary Louisa Bass,5/31/1851
Martha Evelin Bass, dau. of Edward Wesley and Mary Louisa Bass,7/27/1856
Colin Bass, son of Edward Wesley and Mary Louisa Bass, 6/24/1856
Mrs. Mary Louise Bass, wife of Edward W. Bass of Powhatan Co.,Va., 7/19/1856
William Bass 1/21/1775
Mary Bass 6/11/1791, aged 72 yrs.
Edward Bass 4/26/1834
William Bass, son of William and Martha Bass, 11/10/1735
Martha Bass, dau. of William and Martha Bass, 2/7/1744

BERRYMAN J. HILL BIBLE

MARRIAGES

Berryman J. Hill to Margaret Greenway 9/25/1800
Martha D. Hill to Wright Robinson 2/22/1821
Braxton Robinson to Margaret Hill 6/12/1817
Green Hill to Ann M. Eldridge 2/10/1830
Green Hill to Louisa R. Y. Anderson 4/4/1850

Nathaniel Park Newbill to Martha Emma Hill 11/15/1860 by Rev. C.J. Gibson

BIRTHS

Berryman Jones Hill 8/5/1775
Margaret Greenway 4/15/1776
Martha D. Hill 10/21/1801

Mary Jones Hill 1/2/1809
Richard Hill 9/25/1803
Green Hill 2/28/1810

(Berryman J. Hill Bible continued...)

Robert G. Hill 9/12/1806
Ann M. Hill 1/6/1812

Martha Greenway...
Martha Dixon Hill Robinson 1/24/1822

Margaret Elizabeth Hill, dau. of Mary and Green Hill 4/10/1831, christened by Bishop Amory
Richard G. Hill 12/1/1835, christened by Rev. Lewis
James Robert Hill 7/22/1838, christened by Rev. J. M. Lewis
Martha Emma Hill 5/28/1840, christened 12/1/1841, by Rev. J. H. Bennett
Thomas Eldridge and Mary Jane Hill b. 9/5/1843, baptised

JAMES ARMISTEAD BIBLE

MARRIAGES

Elvira L. Arm1stead to John D. Kelly 11/2/1859

Robert D. Cosby to Lucie J. Arm1stead 7/3/1857, dau. of James Arm1stead, Esq. of Prince Edward Co., Va., by Rev. S. W. Watkins Mattie E. Parrish to D. B. Arm1stead 3/4/1868

BIRTHS

James A. Armistead, Jr. 10/11/1869
Alie M. Armistead 7/28/1876
Robert P. Armistead 5/5/1871
Mattie Sue Armistead 4/28/1881

Drury L. Armistead Jr. 6/22/1874
Corah J. Cosby 1/11/1858
Howard L. Armistead 6/22/1874

DEATHS

Thomas H. Howard 6/22/1858
Elizabeth D. Armistead 6/5/1860
Mary S. Arm1stead 2/11/1824

Elizabeth Ann Armistead 9/13/1846
Mary S. Arm1stead 7/19/1846
James A. Armistead 5/10/1876, aged 83 yrs

THOMAS BEALL BIBLE

Thomas Beall, son of Colonel George Beall, was b. 9/27/1748
Nancy Orme, eldest dau. of William John Orme, b. 7/29/1752 m. 9/26/1773 by Rev. Alex Williamson (at George Town)

BIRTHS of THEIR CHILDREN:

Elizabeth Ridgeley Beall 11/22/1786
Harriett Ann Beall 2/15/1791-8/20/1813 m. John Peter 7/5/1808
This 11/22/1807 Eliza R. Washington is 21 yrs. old. George C. Washington is 18 yrs. Old 8/20/1807
George C. Washington, 1st son of Thomas Beall Augustine Washington 6/7/1808-2/2/1809, 8 mos.old, wanting 5 days
John Peter and H. A. Beall's 1st child, a son, b. 6/30/1809, a son named John Thomas Peter who d. 1810.
Second son b. 9/20/1810 named Thomas Peter Beall Third son, Colon Peter, b. 8/10/1813
George Thomas Beall Washington, 2nd son, b. 2/26/1810
Third son, Augustine Bushrod Washington b. 6/10/1811 dead
Fourth son, Lewis William Washington b. 11/30/1812
Fifth son, Bushrod Washington b. 12/1814
First dau., Harriet Ann Bushrod Washington, b. 3/16/1816
Second dau., Cornelia Adelaide
Washington, b. 3/10/1818 Augustine Bushrod Washington d. 2/12/1812, aged 8 mos. Bushrod Washington d. 8/1815, aged --- mos.
H. A. B. Washington d. 12/4/1817, aged 21 mos.

SAMUEL BEARD BIBLE

BIRTHS

Samuel Beard 12/26/1820
Margaret Ann Beard 10/7/1323
Sarah Jane Beard 2/11/1844
Josiah O. Beard 4/29/1847

Lucretia Beard 6/1845
Samuel G. Beard 9/4/1850
Elizabeth A. Beard ---

DEATHS

Margaret A. Beard 9/29/1850

HENRY GEE BIBLE

BIRTHS of Children of Henry Gee and Rachel, his wife

Charles Gee 8/20/1731
James Gee 11/12/1741
John Gee 7/12/1736

Rebecah Gee 11/18/1745
Sarah Gee 5/24/1740

BELL BIBLE of Long Glade, Augusta County

BIRTHS

Nancy Bell 10/16/1814
David Bell 9/19/1828

John Hendren Bell 1/8/1826

DEATHS

John Hendren Bell d. 7/28/1830
Elizabeth Bell 7/23/1840

David Bell 8/1/1830
John Bell 10/17/1833

BIRTHS

John Young 5/21/1741
Margaret Young 2/10/1741
Elizabeth Bell 9/16/1791
John Bell 9/1/1755

Esther Gamble 1/27/1764
John Bell
Esther Gamble 7/29/1800

BIRTHS of THEIR CHILDREN:

Nancy Bell 10/16/1814
William Bell 6/10/1823
Able Bell 8/16/1816
John Hendren Bell 1/7/1826

James Bell 11/3/1818
David Sell 9/19/1828
Rebecca Bell 4/1/1820
Francis Bell 4/8/1831

John Young, his Book, God give him grave thereon to look. Bought in the year 1770.

JOHN BRICKER BIBLE
Owner: Mr. Meacham, Rising Sun, Iowa

John Bricker m. Naioma Craig 9/20/1824

BIRTHS

John Bricker 8/15/-- = 9/25/1858
Naoimi Craig 10/11/1809-9/19/1865
William Bricker 11/16/1828-1912
Margaret Bricker 9/13/1830
Christopher Bricker 12/6/1933
Truman Bricker 11/17/1834
Malissa Bricker 12/19/1836-10/14/1876 (twin)

Sarah Bricker 2/25/1839
Allen Bricker 6/7/1841-11/6/1926
Rebecca Bricker 2/28/1843
John Bricker 1/13/1845-6/24/1918
Eunice Bricker 1/11/1847
Mary Bricker 9/12/1849
Orpha Bricker 6/18/1852-9/25/1865

RALLS-YATES BIBLE
Owner: Bertie R. Yates Rt. 2, Box 180, Victoria, Va. 23974

BIRTHS

Charles Ralls 6/12/1787
Maria Williams 5/13/1792

BIRTHS of Children of Charles and Maria Rails

Sarah Emily Ralls 4/7/1814
Luther Nathl Ralls 3/29/1821
John Williams Ralls 4/1/1816
George Norton Ralls 10/10/1823

George Alexander Ralls 11/23/1817
Margaret Sophia Ralls 2/7/1832
Edward O. Ralls 8/1/1819

BIRTHS of Children of Benjamin L. and Sophia Yates

Sarah Louisa 6/18/1852
George Murray Yates 6/18/1870
John Leroy Yates 9/21/1854
Luther Edward Yates 7/12/1865
Charles Norton Yates 12/26/1857

Benjamin L. Yates 12/15/1858
Henry Tucker Ruffin Yates 6/14/1873
Anna Maria Yates 1/25/1860
Addie Maude Yates 4/15/1875
Joseph Marion Yates 4/25/1869

Thomas W. Smith, son of William and Sarah Smith, 11/11/1835
Anna Maria Smith 8/6/1857
Edward Oscar Smith ---
Jane Eliza Smith, dau. of William and Sarah Smith, 6/26/1839
George Edward Smith 5/16/1841
Mary Anderson Rails 11/9/1851, Henry Co., Va.
Charles Thomas Rails, son of Luther N. and Jane, 12/15/1851
Florence Yates Jeter 10/22/1881 Ethel Sue Yates 10/1/1886
Ruby Rivers Jeter 8/15/1883

MARRIAGES

Charles Ralls to Maria Williams 12/27/1812
William Smith to Sarah Ralls 9/1/1834
William Smith to Mary P. Wallace 5/6/1846
George A. Ralls to Martha J. Clarke 5/30/1851
George A. Ralls to Virginia M. Anderson 5/2/1849

Luther N. Ralls to Jane D. Davenport 1/15/1851
Annie M. Yates to W. E. Jeter 12/15/1886
Benjamin L. Yates to Sophia M. Ralls 5/21/1851
Luther E. Yates to Pattie H. Land 1/12/1892

DEATHS

Charles Rails 6/25/1832 John W. Ralls 10/12/1858
Sarah Emily Smith, wife of William, 7/24/1844, aged 30 yrs.

Maria Ralls 4/25/1866
Edward O. Ralls 8/30/1849, aged 30 yrs.
Joseph Marion Yates 8/31/1895

ROBERT HENDERSON BIBLE

Robert Henderson b. 4/3/1772 Augusta Co., Va. d. 7/31/1837, son of Joseph Henderson and Sarah Miller. Robert m. Hannah McClung 3/16/1803. Hannah was b. 6/24/1780 in Bath Co. d.3/23/1849 Staunton, Augusta Co., Va.

THEIR CHILDREN:

Joseph Henderson 4/9/1804-5/28/1875 m. 9/2/1830
Charity Litton Sally Henderson 12/24/1805-1812
John McClung Henderson 1/2/1808-6/1/1875 m. 10/25/1832
Sarah R. Hall, b. 10/20/1811
Shelton Jones Henderson 11/7/1809-2/16/1872
Adaline McCutchen Henderson b. 9/21/1811 m. William W. Peace
Nancy Cummins Henderson b.2/15/1814 m. John Paris

(Robert Henderson Bible, contd....)

William Harvey Henderson 10/23/1816-4/2/1891 m. 3/23/1843 Nancy Lavinia McCutchen
Robertus Henderson d. 2/6/1899 m. 10/18/1849 Catherine Ann Peck Rodney Boys Henderson b.
8/22/1821 m. Ruth Ann Wright
Nicholas Kinney Henderson 7/21/1824-6/15/1899 m. 7/15/1847 Jane Eliza Denison
        Children of John McClung Henderson and wife, Sarah R. Hall
Sarah Susan Henderson 9/21/1833-2/15/1913 m. 7/1/1852 John Deeds
Robertus Henderson b.3/16/1835 m. 3/14/1861 Nancy Mariah Looney 5/10/1842-7/25/1923
John A. Henderson b. 8/17/1840 m. 4/18/1867 Mary C. Moomaw
Harvey Henderson b. 6/19/1843 m 10/29/1873 Tabitha S. Henderson who d. 12/21/1877
Rosanna Rachel Henderson 5/17/1854-12/29/1887 m. 2/8/1878 James L. Henderson
Mary S. Henderson b. 5/2/1852 m. 3/7/1877 Henry E. Moomaw
Louvinia Ellen Henderson b. 1/11/1846 m. 9/4/1878 William L. Karr
Elizabeth A. Henderson b.1/10/1849

WILLIAMS-CHILTON BIBLE
Owner: Harriett A. Chilton, 3108 Annandale Rd., Falls Church, Va. 22042

BIRTHS

Littleton A. Williams 6/17/1836
John P. Chilton 7/15/1809
Addie E. Williams 8/14/1834
Adeline V. Hunter 3/29/1812

John W. Dillard 9/15/1863
Chapman A. Chilton 3/25/1832
W. Hunter Williams 1/1/1865

MARRIAGES

Addie E. Chilton to Littleton A. Williams 11/11/1857 Jemima S. Cheatham to William C. Chilton 5/1/1907

DEATHS

Thomas R. Williams 3/17/1858
John E. Williams 6/17/1864
Sarah W. Williams 10/24/1864
Sarah M. Hunter 2/23/1869
Thomas W. Williams 4/29/1871

John P. Chilton 7/15/1868
Adeline Virginia Chilton 9/29/1834
Littleton A. Williams 5/6/1907
Addie Elizabeth Williams 2/14/1911

WILLIAM OVERTON BARRET BIBLE
On Flyleaf: Nancy Barret d. 8/15/1825

BIRTHS

Elizabeth I. Barret 5/24/1805
Charles Nelson Barret 7/30/1816
Robert Bullock Barret 2/10/1807
David Bullock Barret 5/24/1819

Sary Jane Barret 9/19!1809
Nancy Bullock Barret 5/4/1822
Patsy H. Barret 5/17/1814

DEATHS

W. O. Barret, 3rd son of W. O. Barret and Mary, 2/12/1821 Robert Lewis Barret, 2d son, 8/4/1837
Ann C. Barrett 7/2/1832
Barbara Winston Barret, eldest dau. of William Overton Barret and Mary, 8/22/1855, aged 41 yrs., 8 mos., 11 days

BIRTHS

W. O. Barret 6/10/1783
Martha Yates 9/10/1798
Michael W. Yates 8/18/1785

Thomas C. Yates 8/18/1800
William Yates 6/16/1802
Reuben C. Yates 5/25/1789

(William Overton Barret Bible, BIRTHS, contd....)

Millicent Yates 5/15/1791
George Yates 11/17/1804
Mary Yates 6/9/1793
Ann C. Yates 2/7/1809
Abner Yates 3/4/1795
John M. Yates 8/29/1796

MARRIAGES

JohnY.Barret 9/8/1840 to Sarah A. Win
Barbara W. Barret to Daniel Pearee 4/14/1842
Joseph Roberson to Nancy C. May Field 8/7/1842
John P. Patton to Mary O. Barret 8/20/1844
Robert Barret to Barbara 8/15/1771, and he d. 6/9/1823

BIRTHS

Robert Barret, son of Robert and Barbara, 10/26/1772
Elizabeth Lewis Barret, dau. of Robert and Barbara, 5/2/1778

Lewis Barret 5/21/1785
Robert Barret, 2nd son, 12/24/1773
William Overton Barret 6/10/1783
John Winston Barret 12/10/1775-10/3/1821
James Winston Barret 2/16/1791
Nelson Berkley Barret 10/3/1793-4/8/1815
Elizabeth L. Barret 5/24/1805
Robert B. Barret 2/10/1807
John Yates Barret 3/28/1812
Barbara Winston Barret 12/3/1813
Nancy Coleman Barret 11/5/1815
Robert Lewis Barret 9/E/1818
William Overton Barret 2/3/1821
Mary Overton Barret 1/11/1825
Harriet Conner 11/13/1819
Catherine Hannah Tedder 9/9/1862
Louisa S. Emerson 5/20/1841
Harriet Adelia Tedder 2/19/1864
Resetter Tedder 1/28/1860

MARRIAGES

Robert Barret to Barbara Winston 8/15/1771
John Yates to Nancy Coleman 5/11/1785
William Overton Barret to Mary Yates 5/16/1811
Paul H. Burret to Ann C. Yates 11/17/1828
Dabney M. Anderson to Elizabeth L. Barret 7/25/1832
William T. Mayfield to Nancy C. Barret 5/15/1834

(William Overton Barret Bible, BIRTHS, contd....)

DEATHS

Robert Barret Sr. 6/9/1823
Barbara Barret, his wife, 11/6/1823
Nancy Yates, consort to John Yates, 12/1810
John Yates 12/1812
Barbara Overton 2/5/1690-10/12/1766

John Winston 1725-1/23/1772, aged 47 yrs.
Alice Winston 6/16/1773, aged 43 yrs.
William Overton Winston 11/16/1747
Mary Tod 3/16/1748-2/27/1752
Barbara Winston 11/30/1750-11/6/1823

BIRTHS

James Winston 3/12/1753
Joseph Winston 4/2/1763
Molly Winston 3/28/1755-11/13/1761

Martha Winston 6/21/1765
John Winston 10/14/1757
Bickerton Winston 1/28/1768
Elizabeth Winston 1/11/1760
Alice Ann Winston 8/8/1769

BLANTON-ALLEN BIBLE
Owner: Mrs. Dollie Allen Prohaska

DEATHS

Richard Blanton 7/5/1870, aged 74
Sallie H. Blanton, wife of George W., 5/22/1877, aged 44
Laura O. Blanton, wife of Julian A., 5/26/1878, 20 yrs, 27 days
George W. Blanton 8/13/1908, aged 80 yrs.
Aquilla J. Goodloe 3/29/1912, aged 85 yrs.
John T. Allen 10/4/1912, aged 58 yrs, 17 days

Bettie b. Allen 10/29/1937, aged 82 yrs.
John Shelby Allen 10/17/1949, aged 64, son of above couple
Emmett Lewis Allen 7/1/1950, aged 63, son of above couple
Lawrence Berkley Allen 3/27/1956, aged 62, son of above couple

MARRIAGES

George W. Blanton to Sarah H. Goodloe 11/17/1853
Laura O. Blanton, dau. of George W. and Sarah, to Julian A. Blanton 12/12/1876
George W. Blanton of Caroline Co., Va. to Mrs. C. H. Mountjoy of Washington, D. C. 9/16/1880
Bettie L. Blanton of Caroline Co., Va. to John T. Allen of same 12/16/1880

BIRTHS

Richard Blanton, Essex, Va., 10/30/1786 Mary Blanton, Prince William, 4,27/1790
Nettie S. Blanton, dau. of C. H. and George W., 9/3/1881
George W. Blanton, son of Richard and Mary, 9/15/1828
Sarah H. Blanton, dau. of Aquilla & Elizabeth Goodloe, 4/29/1834

Children of George W. and Sarah H. Blanton

Betty L. Blanton 9120/1855
SallieH. Blanton 5/28/1867
Laura O. Blanton 4/29/1858
Isla C.Blanton 4/6/1870

George Goodloe Blanton 6/28/1861
Mary J. Blanton 9/26/1872
James R..Blanton 2/15/1864

Children of Bettie L. and John T. Allen

George C. Allen 2/6/1883
Berkley Allen 7/26/1893
John Shelby Allen 3/24/1885
Sallie W.Allen 3/8/1895

Emmett L. Allen 3/13/1887
Mary G. Allen 11/29/1890
Earl Allen 7/14/190-

ROBERT R. BRANCH BIBLE
Owner: Mrs. Fisher Watkins Bruce, Chester, Virginia

BIRTHS:

Robert R. Branch 4/17/1811
Elvenia E. Flournoy, his wife, 10/11/1816
Sarah J. Porter, his wife, 4/10/1820
Sarah E. Branch 5/10/1339
Thermuthis Branch 3/9/1844
Aaron H. Branch 9/7/1840
Virginius R. Branch 3/30/1846
Lucian H. Branch 4/16/1842
Virginia Royster Branch 12/17/1847
Sarah E. Branch 12/11/1868
Robert Branch m. Elvenia E. Flournoy 12/10/1835
Robert Branch m. Sarah J. Porter 7/11/1838
Aaron H. Branch m. Martha E. Miller 12/17/1867

Aaron H. Branch 8/22/1875
Lilly L. Branch 2/23/1870
Lucian M. Branch 4/2/1878
Robert H. Branch 12/1/1872
Mary E. Branch 7/23/1880
Nesbit A. Bass 11/25/1861
Cabel B. Branch 10/23/1852
Montes Bass 1/18/1866
Stanley H. Branch 2/21/1885

(Robert R. Branch Bible, contd....)

Mary E. Branch d. 4/1/1887
Sarah J. Branch d. Chula, Va. at res. of R. H. Bruce, 10/8/1895, aged 76, bur. Grubb Hill Episcopal Church, Amelia Co., Va
Aaron H. Branch d. Lodore, Va., AmelLa Co., 1330/9/1896, bur. Grubb Hill, 10/10/1896, aged 57, Amelia Co., Va.
Mrs. Aaron H. Branch d. at W. H. Brazeal's Sunny Side, 7/19/1911, bur. Grove Church, Cumberland Co., Va., aged 63 (Aunt Monty) Robert R. Branch d. 5/11/1847
Elvenia E. Flournoy d. 11/12/1837
Virginius R. Branch d. 6/16/1847
Lucian W. Branch d. 7/24/1862, aged 20 yrs, 4 mos.
Thermuthis Branch d. 8/29/1862, aged 18 yrs., 5 mos., 10 days Sarah E.Bass, wife of Dr. Joseph Bass, d. 3/16/1868

Cabel B. Branch d. at W. H. Brazeal's 1/21/1911, bur. Grove Church, Cumberland, Va.,aged 25 yrs.

Mrs. Martha E. Branch d. at W. H. Brazeal's 7/19/1911, bur. Grove Church, Cumberland, Va., 7/20/1911, aged 64 yrs.

Stanley H. Branch d. at W. H. Brazeal's 1/1/1912, bur. Grove Church, Cumberland, Va. 1/2/1912, aged 26 yrs.

ABRAHAM MORT BIBLE

BIRTHS

Abraham Mort 9/16/1801 m. 1827
Catherine Dennison 2/25/1808
John Mort 9/26/1828
Mary Elin Mort 7/10/1841
Anna Maria Mort 9/20/1830
Soffia Mort 2/19/1843
Henry Mort 3/9/1832
Jeremiah Mort 1/4/1845

Catherine Mort 8/6/1834
Mehaly Jane Mort 3/22/1848
Elizabeth Mort 8/1/1836
Eliza Francis Mort -/22/1850
Mary Ann Mort 7/11/--
William David Mort 3/22/1854
Mehaly Jane Mort d. 3/15/1835, aged 6 yrs, 11 mos., 24 days

ROBERT NISBET BIBLE Of Paisley, Scotland and Richmond, Va.
"Paisley High Church Parish 15th March 15(03?)

That the bearer Mrs. Nisbet whose maiden name was Isabella Kemp resided in this Parish twenty five years immediately preceding this date during which time she lived soberly and honestly, free of public scandal.... John Findley,Minr., James Campbell, Session Clerk. Andrew Moody, Chief Maglstrate.

"Extracted from Town Reglster of Paisley on 3/15/1803 is attested by above officials.

BIRTHS of Children of Robert Nisbet and Isabella Kemp

Isabella Nisbet 4/2/1785, baptised, 472
David Nisbet 11/26/1787, baptised 11/29
Agnes Nisbet 3/26/1792, baptised 3/29

Janet Nisbet 5/1/1795. baptised 5/3
William Nisbet 11/26/1798, baptised 12/2

DEATHS

Robert Nisbet, native of Paisley Scotland, 8/181-, Richmond, Va.,aged 66 yrs, 6 mos. 14 days
Isabella Kemp Nisbet of Dumbartonshire, Scotland, 2/1/1846,Richmond, Va., 2/1/1846, 88 yrs.
Isabella Nisbet, dau. of Robert and Isabella K., 10/1836, Richmond, Va.
David Nisbet, son of Robert and Isabella K. Nisbet, d. Brooklyn, New York, aged 58 yrs.
Archibald Nisbet, son of Robert and Isabella K. Nisbet, 4/17/1849, Richmond, Va.

(Robert Nisbet Bible, DEATHS, contd....)

Agnes N. Btgelow, wid. of Joseph, 3/1863, Richmond, Va., aged 72 yrs., dau. of Robert and Isabella K. Nisbet.
William Nisbet, son of Robert and Isabella K. Nisbet, 2/24/--, in St. Louis, Missouri
Jane B. Maben, wid. of David, d. Amelia Co., Va. 4/5/1870, aged 75 yrs., dau of Robert and Isabella K. Nisbet.

Newspaper clippings pasted in Bible:"Died on Sunday night at 12 o'clock, Mrs. Isabella K. Nisbet, in the 88th year of her age. The friends and acquaintances of the family are requested to attend her funeral this morning at 11 o'clock from her residence on Grace Street, near the Grace Street Baptist Church, without further invitation."

"In Brooklyn, on the 20th last, after a long and severe illness, Mr. Davis Nisbet, aged 58 years."

BERKELEY BIBLE

MARRIAGES

Edmund and Lucy Burwell Berkeley 12/1/1703

BIRTHS of THEIR CHILDREN:

Edmund Berkeley 11/26/1704 - Mary Berkeley 5/24/1711 Lewis Berkeley 1/18/1706/7
Sarah Berkeley 2/9/1713/14 Lucy Berkeley 5/10/1709

MARRIAGES:

Edmund and Mary Nelson Berkeley 5/18/1728
Lucy Berkeley 6/15/1729
Mary Berkeley 1/15/1737/8
Edmund Berkeley 12/5/1730
Sarah Berkeley 1/27/1741/2
Nelson Berkeley 5/16/1733
Lucy Berkeley 6/9/1744

Edmund Berkeley 6/18/1804
William Henry Berkeley
--Betty Landon Berkeley ---
Sally Nelson Berkeley
--Catherine Robinson Berkeley ---
Carter Berkeley 11/27/1809

Carter Berkeley m. Catherine Spotswood Carter 5/7/1796
Elizabeth W. C. Berkeley 5/21/1797-8/21/1852
Charles Carter Berkeley 11/8/1798-7/3/1801, aged 2 yrs., 8 mos.
Edmund Berkeley 3/17/1801-4/7/1851
Anne Butler Berkley 12/26/1803-
Robert Carter Berkeley 6/2/1806-10/18/1851
Park Farley Berkeley 3/31/1808-3/24/1888
Catherine S. Berkeley, wife of C. Berkeley, d. 10/24/1809
Carter Berkeley m. Frances P. Nelson, his 2nd wife, 11/8/1810
Catherine Frances Berkeley 2/28/1813-6/29/185833
Carter Nelson Berkeley 6/12/1815-4/1842
Parke F. Berkeley m. Mary Eppes Thweatt 8/31/1837
Two sons b. the elder on the 7th and the younger on the 9th of May, 1832. Died the elder immediately after birth with the younger just before
William Berkeley m. Betty Randolph 1/5/1797

BIRTHS

Jacquelin A. Berkeley 11/20/1797
Landonia Carter Berkeley –
Lucy Ann Berkeley ---
Catherine Spotswood Berkeley –
Nelson Berkeley ---
William Randolph Berkeley

--Mary
Randolph Berkeley ---
Elizabeth W. C. Berkeley –
Peyton Randolph Berkeley ---
Kidder Randolph Berkeley ---

(Berkeley Bible, BIRTHS, contd....)

Mary E. Berkeley 10/25/1839
Parke Farley Berkeley 6/1/1841-11/10/1847
Lucy Thweatt Berkeley 3/24/1845
Cornelia LeLeigh Berkeley 8/30/1848
Carter Nelson Berkeley 11/14/1850
Lewis Berkeley m. Elizabeth Darracott 3/-Susan
Elizabeth Berkeley b.
Mary Nelson Berkeley b.
Nelson William Berkeley b.
Louisa Carter Berkeley d.
Landon Carter 10/14/1817

Parke Julian Berkeley b. 12/1853
Catherine Spotswood Berkeley b. 11/8/1856
Robert Berkeley m. M. Julia Carter
--Robert Carter Berkeley b. 4/14/1805
Landon Carter Berkeley b. 11/12/1806
Sophia Carter Berkeley b. 2/10/1808
Nelson Berkeley b. 7/12/1809
Julia Berkeley b. 6/28/1812
Benjamin Pasco Berkeley b. 2/26/1811
Elizabeth W. Berkeley b. 2/14/1814
Lucy Mary Berkeley b. 1/27/1816
Frances A. Tasker b. 1/1/1818

A Family in Heaven:

Landon Carter Berkeley m. 10/23/1811
Lucy Sheppard Landon C. Berkley d. 4/27/1813
Lucy S. Berkeley d. 6/13/1815

Their son, Landon C. Berkeley d. 4/17/1816

Another Landon Carter Berkeley has gone to Heaven. Died on Monday 4th of November L. C. Berkeley of Frederick Co. believing he had made his peace with God and was ready to receive glorious immortality. How blessed are those who died in the Lord. Year of our Lord 1833.

GEORGE BARRETT BIBLE

Mary Ann Foster b. 12/29/1781 m. George Barrett 1803

BIRTHS of THEIR CHILDREN:

George Barrett 2/15/1804
Milton Barrett 2/9/1819
Mary Anne Barrett 3/10/1808
Robert Foster Barrett 9/30/1820
Jane Smith Barrett 2/14/1809
Elizabeth Barrett 6/25/1803?
Henry and Bryan Barrett 11/28/1811, twins

DEATHS

John Smith Barrett 11/1/1810

William, David, Elizabeth, Josiah and John Smith, d. in infancy Bryan Barrett 7/17/1815. Henry survived.

The father, George Barrett, 1827
The mother, Mary Ann Foster Barrett, d. abt 1866 in Smithfield

COLLINS-WORD BIBLE

John H. Collins Sr. d. 6/17/1836, aged 89 yrs.
Judith Collins, formerly Judith Word, wife and relative of John H. Collins, Sr. and mother of William Collins, d. 1/7/1828, aged 81.

BIRTHS of Brothers and Slsters of William Collins, Children of John Collins and Judith, his wife

James Collins 11/11/1771
---- 11/30/1778
Nancy Collins 11/16/1772
William Collins 1/1/1781
Peter Collins 10/20/1774
Joseph Collins 11/7/1784
John Collins 1776
Elizabeth Collins 1785-decd
Elisha Collins 10/1788
William C. Collins 1/1/1781
Dolly C. Stone 5/6/1788
William C. Collins m. Dolly C. Stone 11/9/1810

DEATHS

William Collins Sr. 7/5/1847 Dolly C. Collins 1/16/1836

BIRTHS of Children of William and Dolly C. Collins

Dolly Haskins Collins 10/7/1815
Judith Word Collins 3/16/1817
Christopher Stone Collins 11/20/1818
Theophilus Jackson Collins
10/31/1820 Sally Ann Collins 5/29/1823
John H. Adams Collins 4/2/1824
Edwin Stone Collins 3/31/1826
William Collins 8/4/1832
Mary E. Collins 5/15/1835-4/6/1836

DEATHS

Virginia A. Word 2/23/1808
William Collins Jr. 1864
Sally A. Morton 12/26/1881
John A. Collins 9/2/1892

MARRIAGES

Dolly H. Collins to James T. Jordon 10/19/1836
Judith W. Collins to William P. Holland 11/8/1837
Theophilus Collins to Mary A. Dews 9/7/1840
John Collins to Mary E. Smith 5/17/1845
Virginia Collins to Thomas E. Word 9/2/1846
Sally Collins to Robert Alexander Morton 9/2/1846
Edwin Collins to Clara Reid of Charlotte, 1850
William Collins to Mollie Lou Green 10/1853

WILLIAM BASSETT BIBLE

Ages of the Children of William and Joanna Bassett who were married 11/28/1693

Martha Bassett 11/7/1694, baptised 7/16
Elizabeth Bassett 7/1697, baptised 7/13
Lucy Bassett 5/2/1699, baptised 5/31
Joanna Bassett 10/1701, baptised 10/30-d. 10/4/1708
William Bassett 3/27/1705, baptised 4/4
Lewis Bassett 8/10/1707, baptised 8/19-d. 9/30/1708
William Bassett 8/8/1709, baptised 8/10
Burwell Bassett 3/3/1702
Hannah Bassett 3/9/1713/14, baptised 3/19
Mary Bassett 8/7/1716
Nathaniell Bassett 1/16/1718/19

JOHN BANISTER BIBLE

DEATHS

Mrs. Anne Banlster, Relict of John Banlster, 12/23/1813, late of Battersea in co. of Dinwiddie

Thomas Yelverton Banister 10/10/1816
Augusta Banister 11/22/1844
Alonzo Banister 7/3/1885
James Conway Banister 10/7/1855
Henry Tudor Banister 11/1/1862
William S. P. Banister 7/31/1864
Thomas Yelverton Banister 2/26/1868
John Banlster, Esq. of Battersea 9/30/1788

Theodoric Blair Banister 11/8/1829, aged 49 yrs.
Ann Blair Banister 5/6/1835, aged 3 yrs
John Banlster 6/3/1835 aged 22 yrs.
Robert Jones Banister 1/11/1836, aged 20 yrs
John Blair Peachy 6/28/1838 at Tallahassee, Fla.
Anne Banister Peachy 9/21/1847
John Tabb of Clay Hill 8/27/1736-4/16/1798
Frances, his wife, 5/31/1752-4/12/1829.

THEIR CHILDREN:

Martana Tabb --
Martha Peyton 1777-8/1808 (wife of W. B. Lily)
Fanny Book 10/1780-11/6/1830 (wife of J. R. Archer)
Mary 5/1782-2/28/1832 (wife of Bathurst Randolph)
Thomas ---
John Yelverton ---
Virginia Peyton 7/27/1787-7/31/1864 (wife of J. B. Banister)
Harrtet Peyton 1791-1805
Marianna Elizabeth 3/17/1796-12/7/1856 (wife of W. T. Barksdale)
Fanny Peyton Barksdale
8/24/1824-2/23/1873 Richmond, Va. m. Monro Banister 9/12/1860

BIRTHS

Martha Peyton Tabb Banister 10/5/1808
Eliza Thompson Banister 5/21/1810
Augusta Banister 10/26/1811
John Banister 2/24/1813
Thomas Yelverton Banister 11/7/1814
Robert Jones Banister 3/20/1816
Monro Banister 1/8/1818
James Conway Banister 5/8/1819
Thomas Yelverton Banister (2d) 6/10/1822
Henry Tudor Banister 12/14/1823
Anne Blair Banister 10/10/1825

(John Banister Bible, contd....)

BIRTHS

Mary Blair, dau. of John Blair and Eliza T. Peachy, 9/1/1832 Augusta Banister Peachy, dau. of John Blair and Eliza Thompson Peachy, 3/20/1835
Ann Bannister Peachy, dau. of John Blair and Eliza T. Peachy, 6/23/1838

MARRIAGES

Theodoric Blair Banister to Susanna Peyton Tabb 12/22/1807 John Blair Peachy to Elite Thompson Banister 10/4/1832 Mary Blair Peachy to John Wilkinson, USN, 12/29/1857

BURWELL BASSETT BIBLE

----Chamberlayne m. Burwell Bassett 6/26/1755
Elizabeth Bassett b. 10/17/1756
Burwell Bassett m. Anna Maria Dandridge 1/7/1757
Elizabeth Bassett b. 1/26?/1758
Anna Maria Bassett b. 5/16/1760, d. 7/23rd following
William Bassett b. 9/19/1761

The Ages of the Children of William and Eliza. Bassett who were married 1/29/1729

Eliza. Bassett b. 12/13/1730

The Ages of the Children of Burwell and Anna Maria Bassett who were married 5/7/1757

Elizabeth Bassett 1/26/1759
Anna Maria Bassett 5/16/1760-7/23rd following Burwell Bassett 3/18/1764
John Bassett 8/30/1765
George Bassett 8/7/1766-d. abt 3 hrs. after his birth Frances Bassett 12/19/1767
----m. 5/31/1763 by Rev.-----following children
Mary Burnet b. 8/7/1765
Batty Carter b. 12/22/1768, Godparents? were Landon Carter, Sabine Hall, P. W. Claiborne, E. Chamberlayne, Carter Braselton, Esqr., Mrs. Claiborne,----Chamberlyane, Miss Polly (Braselton?),
Miss Claiborne.
Dau. b. d. 2/4/1771
Judith Walker b. 12/10/1773, Godfathers? were William Dandridge Claiborne, John Hill Carter, Mr. Thyring. Godmothers-Miss Betty Digges, Miss Carter, Miss Betty Carter.
A son b. d. 10/1/1778
Ph--- Harriss b. 9/3/1768 at Elsing Green
Wilber Harriss b. 8/17/1770 at Elsing Green
B.----s, on of Ben and Pheby b. at Elsing Green 8/1768
H. C. 2/1781
w. B. B. C. 12/1782
V. Herbert Claiborne b.
John Bassett m. Betty Carter Browne 9/12/1786

BIRTHS of THEIR CHILDREN:

Virginia Bassett 9/20/1787
Anna Maria Dandridge Bassett 3/15/1789
William Bassett 10/10/1790 st Elsing Green
Frances Carter Bassett 12/9/1792 at Wakefield-d. 1/4/1795

(Burwell Bassett Bible, BIRTHS, contd....)

John Burwell Bassett 12/27/1794 at Farmington-d. 4/12/1796 at Farmington.
John Churchill Bassett 5/1/1797 at Farmington-d. 9/12/1798 at Farmington.
Judith Carter Bassett 1/5/1799-d. 8/21/1800

George Washington Bassett 8/23/1800 at Farmington
Burwell Bassett 1/22/1802-d. 10/1/1802 at Elsing Green
Henry Alfred Bassett 11/17/1803 at Farmington-d. aged 15 mos.
Alfred Bassett 7/18/1805-d. 9/25/1805 at Farmington
Betty Carter Bassett 1/5/1807

Virginia Bassett m. Samuel William Sayre 9/20/1806 at Farmington
Philip Ludwell Sayre, Virginia's 1st child, b. 10/8/1807 in Middlesex Virginia lost a son 10/1808 at Highgate
Edward Sayre, her 3rd child, b. 9/22/1809 at Farmington
Burwell Bassett Sayre b. 12/20/1810 at Farmington
Stephen Sayre b. 6/10/1812 William Sayre b. 2/22/1814
John Bassett Sayre b. 3/24/1817
Josiah Lily Deans m. Anna Maria Dandridge Bassett 3/15/1808
Rosanna, their 1st child, b. at Middleway 3/5/1809-d. 5/16/1816
Josiah Lily Deans d. 8/28/1812 at Middleway, aged 34 yrs.
Josiah Lily Deans b. 5/26/1811 at Middleway
William Bassett d. 11/21/1812 at Middleway in Gloater Co., aged 22 yrs., 1 mo., 11 days.

John William Deans b. 12/31/1812 at Farmington, d.
Mrs. A. M. D. Deans m. Isaac Garretson 8/11/1815
B. Carter Garretson b. 5/1816

JOHN BAYLOR BIBLE of Caroline County

John and Frances Baylor m. at Parish Church of St. Olave, Hart Street, London, by Bev. Mr. Lett 11/18/177-

John Horace Upshaw, Esq. of Essex Co. m. 11/25/180-at New Market to Lucy Elizabeth Todd Baylor of Caroline Co.

Frances Courtenay Baylor, dau. of John and Frances, 10/10/1779 4/3/1780
Courtenay Orange Baylor, dau. of John and Frances, b. 5/31/1781. Sponsors: Mrs. Baylor, Sr., Miss F. Baylor
Susanna Frances Baylor, dau. of John and Frances, b. 3/2/1783. Sponsors: Miss Fanny Armistead, Mrs. Shield, Miss Pitt, Miss Betsey Baylor, Mr. Thomas, Mr. George Norton.

"I went to Alexander in April 1797 when C. O. B. and E. B. had the smallpox. Frances Baylor Mary ?, dau. of John and Lucy, b. at New Market 1811.

John and Courtenay Norton b. in York Town, Va. 12/10/1743. They went over to England in 11/1764, said John Norton of London, Merchant, d. 10/25/1777 , aged 58 yrs. and was bur. in St. Olaves, Heart Street, Crutched Fryers Parish Church, in the Doctr's Vault Middle Isle.

Doctor Owen, Rector of Parish buried him--his wife Courtenay Norton d. in Barbadoes 8/8/1780 -- also his son, Henry Norton, d. in Barbadoes 11/1780. Their loving dau., Frances Baylor, left could Square Crutched Frayers London where her Father and Mother had resided some years – on 11/21/1778 for America by way of Holland and St. Eustatia and arrived at New Market 6/1779.

John --- on 4/4/-----.

GEORGE W. BASSETT BIBLE

George W. Bassett, son of John and Betty Carter Bassett of Farmington, Hanover Co., Va. and Betty Burnet Lewis, dau. of Robert and Judith Lewis of Fredericksburg, Va. were m. 8/1/1826

Children of George W. Bassett and Betty Lewis

Betty Burwell Bassett m. 5124/1849 at Clover Lea to Ronald Mills of Richmond, Va.
Anna Virginia Bassett m. her cousin, John H. Claiborne of Richmond 5/13/1852 at Clover Lea
Ella More Bassett m. 11/6/1860 to Lewis W. Washington of Jefferson Co., Va.
Mary Burnett Bassett m. 12/22/1860 to Benjamin M. Bassett of Tx.
L. Frances Carter Bassett m. 12/1/1863 to Charles T. Mitchell of Charleston, S. C.
Annette L. Bassett m. Rev. Inhan E. Ingle of Maryland 1/23/1873
BIRTHS of Children of George W. Bassett and Betty Lewis
Betty Burwell 5/10/1827, baptised by Rev. John McGuire in Fredericksburg.
George Anna Maria 7/26/1929 at Lansdowne, baptised at St.George's Church, Fredericksburg, by Rev. E. C. McGuire. George Washington 3/25/1831 at Lansdowne, bapt. by E. C. McGuire

- Anna Virginia 1/17/1833 at Lansdowne, baptised in her 4th mo. by her Uncle the Rev. E. C. McGuire in St. George's Church,
- Fredericksburg.Ella More 9/7/1834 at Lansdowne,baptised in St. George's Church by Rev. E. C. McGuire,sponsors, Father and Mother, together with Mrs. Anna M. Thornburn Judith Frances Carter 12/19/1836 at Lansdowne, baptised St George's

Church, Fredericksburg,.by Rev. E. C. McGuire Mary Burnet 8/12/1839 in Fredericksburg, baptised the 3d month by her uncle E. C McGuire.
Annette Lewis 9/14/1842 at our summer house near Richmond,baptised there by Rev. Dr.Empie when 5 weeks old,sponsors her father and mother
Robert Lewis 9/28/1844 at Clover Lea, Hanover Co.,baptised Old Church in 6th mo by Rev E.A. Dairymple Rector.A dau.,3/9/1847-d. aged only 10 days. William Augustine 8/23/1854 (the same day of mo with his father), baptised Immanuel Church by Rev. David Caldwell, Rector 7/1/1855

DEATHS

Betty Burwell Mills 2/3/1875 in Bunham, Tx., aged 47 yrs .
George Washington Bassett of Clover Lea 8/27/1878, aged 79 yrs
Mary Burnet Bassett 11/10/1881
George Anna Maria 10/23/1831
Annette Lewis Ingle 11/19/1881
Anna Virginia Claiborne 8/25/1862, aged 29 yrs

JAMES E. BEADLES BIBLE

BIRTHS

James E. Beadles 11/16/1869 in Green Co., Va.
George W. R. Beadles 7/25/1871 in Green Co., Va.
Mareens Judson Beadles 5/20/1873 in Green Co., Va.
Lealila Francis Beadles 7/25/1875 in Orange Co., Va.
Hazletine Mary William Beadles 10/13/1877 in Charles City Co., Va.
Dianna Ann Beadles 5/20/1879 in Charles City Co., Va.
John Alonzo Beadles 4/20/1881 in Charles City Co., Va.
Cecilia Alice Beadles 8/23/1583 in Charles City Co., Va.
Thomas Newton Beadles 11/17/1885 in Hanover Co., Va.
Not named 2/9/1837? in New Kent Co. Va.
Tomasia C. Beadles, dau. of J. W. and Cecilia A., 4/1/1889 in New Kent Co., Va.
Allburn P. Beadles 9/26/1890 in New Kent Co., Va.

RODGERS-NEW BIBLE
Owner: Mrs. Kitty Joyner
On flyleaf: William T. Rodgers.

MARRIAGES

William T. Rodgers to Frances New, his wife, 1/25/1821
Theophilus R. New to Sarah Jane Rodgers 9//1841
Charles H. Wingfield to Annie M. New 12/21/1859
Charles A. Price to Jane Josephine New 12/23/1874
William T. New to Mary Taylor 6/1869

Samuel F. New to Lizzie L. Cox 12/12/1883
C. A. Pettft to Nannie P. Wingfield 6/5/1894
C. T. Smith to Edith Nelson Wingfield 10/29/1901
Marion Rodgers Wingfield to Mary E. New 10/16/1903
E. K. O'Brien to Ruby Evelyn Wingfield 7/7/1906

BIRTHS

William T. Rodgers 3/12/1799
Frances Rodgers 3/13/1799

Children of William T. and Frances Rodgers:

John H. Rodgers 11/29/1821
Sarah Jane Rodgers 8/12/1825
Edward Rodgers 4/3/1834
William B. Rodgers 10/23/1823

Isaac Newton Hyram Lafayette
Sarah Jane Rodgers 8/12/1825
Rodgers 12/4/1827

Children of William T. and Elvira Rodgers

Stephen Rodgers 8/29/1840
William T. Rodgers 1/6/1842

T. R. New b. 8/5/1804

Children of Theolphilus R. and Sarah Jane New

Francis Samuel New 5/3/1852
Wm Theophilus New 2/9/1848
Jane Josephine New 2/20/1845

Anne Marie New 1/27/1843
Samuel Frayser New 5/24/1855
James, slave of William T. Rodgers, b. 11/15/1832

Mary Ann, slave of William Rodgers, b. 1838
Marish Isabel, slave of William T. Rodgers, b. 11/11/1835

DEATHS

Isaac Newton H. L. Rodgers 5/30/1830
William Benjamin Rodgers 5/15/1830
Edward Rodgers 1/12/1835
Frances Rodgers 3/10/1850
Samuel F. New 3/5/1917

Frances L. New 5/8/1853
Theophilus R. New 8/21/1863
William T. New 6/8/1918
Sarah Jane New 11/8/1901
Annie M. C. New Wingfield 12/8/1904

GEORGE BASKERVILLE BIBLE

MARRIAGES

George D. Baskerville to Betsey E. Williams 11/23/18--
Robert Hall 10/6/1862
JohnW. Baskerville - Sally D. Young 11/8/1843
James L. Duke to Betsey P. Baskerville 7/23/1844
Albert C. Jones to Ann M. Baskerville 12/10/1844
George D. Baskerville Jr. to Emma V. Ferguson 1/26/1858
Charles H. Cuthbert to Isabella Baskerville 4/8/1855
Alexander Kennedy to Delha P. Baskerville 5/12/1858
Eugene Cole Dowell, M. D. to Mary Ranson Duke 11/20/1865
Albert C. Jones to Roberta P. Baskerville 8/7/1572 (2nd marr)

BIRTHS:

George D. Baskerville 11/12/1793
Betsey Eaten Willis 1/4/1800
Betsey P. Baskerville 9/22/1816
William J. Baskerville 4/23/1820
John U. Baskerville 7/23/1822
Sally T. Baskerville 7/25/1824
Anne M. Baskerville 11/28/1826
Delha P. Baskerville 4/1/1829
Mary Willis Baskerville 11/15/1833
Roberta P. Baskerville 11/15/1833
George D. Baskerville 1/26/1836
Lucy C. Baskerville 9/27/1838
Isabella H. Baskerville 3/28/1840
Albert C. Jones, husband of Ann M. Baskerville ---/20/1813
Charles H. Cuthbert, husband of Isabella H. Baskervtlle, b. in Petersburg 2/13/1828
Sally Dunn, wife of John Baskerville, 7/29/1824
James L. Duke, husband of Betsey P. Baskerville 1/7/1514

BIRTHS of Grandchildren

George D. Baskerville, son of John W. and Sally D., 9/7/1840
Mary Ransom Duke, dau. of Betsey Park C James Lawrence, 7/17/1845
Mary Ann Jones, dau. of Ann Minge and Robert C., 12/3/1846
Betsey E. Baskerville, dau. of Sally D. and John W.,
Mine Ruth Baskerville, dau. of Gee. D. Jr. & Emma Virginia, 8/1860
Lucy Cuthbert Hall, dau. of Robert R. and Lucy C., 7/7/1864
Annie Herbert Cuthbert, dau. of Isabella H. and C. H., 5/13/1865
Belle Kennedy Cuthbert, dau. of Isabella and C. M., 1/16/1867
Blanche Bragg Cuthbert, dau. of Isabella and C. M., 4/21/1871
James E. Cuthbert, son of H. and C. H.

DEATHS

Mary Eaten Baskerville 11/11/1820 William Wharton Baskerville 4/12/1821
Mary Williams Baskerville 11/24/1833 Sally Turner Baskerville 1/22/1836
Betsey Eaten Baskerville (wife of George D. Baskerville), 4/5/1847
Betsy P. Duke, wife of James L. Duke, 4/2/1850
Ann Minger Jones, wife of Albert C. Jones, 9/12/1850
Ro be rta Park Jones (2nd wife of Albert C. Jones), 10/24/1910 in home of her niece,
Mrs. Eugene Cole Powell. Mrs. Isabella H., wife of Charles H. Cuthbert, 2/6/1924
Annie Herbert Cuthbert, dau. of Isabella H. & Charles H., 9/5/1924
Elvira Cuthbert Scott, dau. of Charles H. Cuthbert (Ist wife's child), 4/20/--
Delha Park, wife of Alexander Kennedy, d.
Charles Cuthbert 7/12/1895 in Petersburg
Alexander Kennedy, husband of Delha P. Baskerville, 6/25/1870

GEORGE DANIEL BAYLOR BIBLE

MARRIAGES

George Daniel Baylor, son of John and Frances of New Market and Caroline Co., to Eliza Lewis Fox,dau. of John and Eleanor of Greenwich, Glouchester Co.,9/24/1814
John Baylor to Frances Norton at Parish Church of St. Olave, Hart Street, London by Rev. Mr. Pett 11/18/1778, recorded by their grandson, W. L. Baylor
W. L. Baylor, 3rd son of George D. and Eliza L. of Caroline Co.,Va. to Mary A. E. Chappell, dau. of R. W. Chappell of City of Petersburg, 1/27/1864,by Rev. C. J. Gibson, Pastor of Grace Church at res. of her mother on Halifax Street in same city.

(George Daniel Baylor Bible, contd....)

BIRTHS of Children of George Daniel and Eliza Lewis Baylor

John Norton Baylor 8/19/1816
Julia Ann Baylor 2/3/1828
Ellen Augusta Baylor 5/15/1818
Louisa Henrietta Baylor 10/13/1830?
George Robert Baylor 5/24/1820
Frances Courtenay Baylor 12/15/1822
Thomas Wiltshire Baylor 3/28/1833
Warner Lewis Baylor 6/22/1825
Alexander Galt Baylor 10/5/1835

BIRTHS of Children of John and Frances Baylor

George Daniel Baylor 1129/178- at New Market, Caroline Co.
Frances Courtenay Baylor 10/10/1779-4/3/1780, aged 5 mos.
Courtenay Orange Baylor 5/31/1781
Susanna Frances Baylor 3/2/1783-2/19/1837
Eliza Lewis Fox, dau. of John and Eleanor Fox, 12/8/1794 at Greenwich, Gloucester Co.
Warner Lewis Baylor, son of Dr. Warner Lewis and Mary A. E. Baylor, 10/27/1864 in City of Petersburg, Va.
George Marie Baylor, son of Dr. Warner Lewis and Mary A. E. Baylor, 3/8/1868 at Mrs. Chappell's in City of Petersburg, Va.

DEATHS

John Baylor 2/6/1808 of New Market, Caroline Co., Va., son of John and Frances Baylor of same place, aged 58 yrs. and upwards. He was b. 9/4/1750

Frances Baylor 2/18/1816, b. at York Town, Va., dau. of John and Courtenay Norton of Gould Square Crutched Friars London, aged 55 yrs and upwards. She was b. 12/5/1759

Mrs. Eliza Lewis Baylor 4/3/1837, dau. of John and Eleanor Fox of Greenwich, Gloucester Co., aged 41 yrs. and upwards. Recorded by her bereaved husband, George D. Baylor

Dr. George Daniel Baylor 4/17/1848, son of John and Frances Baylor of New Market, Caroline Co., aged 59 yrs. and upwards.

Ellen Augusta Garnett 4/25/1857, City of Petersburg, Va., aged 39 yrs., bur. in Blandford Churchyard

Mary A. E. Chappell 4/26/1868 at her mother's, Halifax Street, Petersburg, Va. wife of Dr. W. L. Baylor of Caroline Co., Va. and dau. of R. and Harriett Chappell of Petersburg b. at same house 4/22/1828.

Lewis Baylor 9/8/1869, son of Dr. W. I. Baylor and late Mary A. E. Baylor, aged 4 yrs., 10 mos., 8 days, buried in Blandford Churchyard 9/10/1869

George Marie Baylor 9/15/1869, son of W. L. Baylor and late Mary A. E. Baylor, aged 6 mos., 6 days, bur. Blandford Churchyard 9/15/1869

Mrs. Frances C. Pollard, wife of Charles W. Pollard, 7/23/1868 in City of Petersburg.

Marginal Notes by B. H. Baylor: "This record is from the Bible of his grandfather Dr. George Daniel Baylor of Lockleys (near Bowling Green) Caroline Co., Va. One of Dr. Baylor's daughters, Julia Ann Baylor, married Joseph Bray whose only surviving great grandchild (1939) was Miss Georella B.Jefferis.

Dr. Warner Lewis Baylor, Asst. Surgeon, C. S. A., married, first, Miss Chappell no living descendants; secondly, Miss Lizzie Hoskins Wright, Rappahannock, Essex Co., Va. By the marriage of Dr. Warner Lewis Bayhlor and Lizzie Hoskins Wright, there were the following living children (1939) Elizabeth Lewis, Bernard Hoskins, Thomas Booth, Frances Warner and George Daniel, all of whom were married with descendants."

THOMAS M. BAYLY BIBLE

On flyleaf: Elizabeth W. Melvin, a legacy from her father, Thomas M. Bayly; Fanny Melvin Watkins, a legacy from her mother, Elizabeth W. Melvin

Births of Children of Thomas M. and M. P. Bayly

Sally C. Bayly 12/22/1813
William P. Bayly 6/14/1820

Elizabeth Wharton Bayly 12/6/1815
Margaret Pettitt Baylor 1/15/1818

BIRTHS of Children of Thomas M. and Jane O. Bayly

Jane Bayly 10/31/1827
Rosy Bayly 8/67/1832

Samuel Bayly 4/23/1830

Thomas M. Baylor, son of Thomas and Ann Bayly, 3/26/1775
Margaret Pettitt Cropper, dau. of John and Margaret Cropper, 5/13/1784

MARRIAGES

Thomas M. Bayly to Margaret Pettitr Crooper at Bowman's Folly 3/24/1802
Samuel Melvin to Elizabeth Wharton Bayly 4/13/1835
Dec. P. F. Browne to Sally C. Bayly 11/14/1839 by Rev. H. M. Bartlett at Mr. Curtis.
James W. CustFs to Margaret P. Bayly 10/27/1840 at Mr. Custis, by Rev. W. G. Jackson.
Rev. Benjamin M. Miller to Ann D. Bayly 11/11/184- at St. James Church by Rev. William
Meade Robert Wharton Watklns to Fanny Mayo Melvin 12/23/1875 by Rev. O. A. Kinsolving at Halifax C. H., Va.

BIRTHS of Children of Thomas M. Bayly and Margaret Pettitt

Henry Custis Bayly 12/26/1802
Thomas H. Bayly 12/11/1809
Richard Drummond Bayly 3/15/1805

Ann Drummond Bayly 10/19/1811
John Cropper Bayly 1/28/1808

DEATHS

Richard Drummond Bayly 10/21/1807
John Cropper Bayly 9/1/1809

Thomas M. Bayly 1/7/1834
Henry C. Bayly 10/1/-

Margaret P. Bayly, wife of Thomas M. Bayly, 12/3/1824
Ann D. Miller, wife of Rev. B. M. Miller, Norfolk, Va., 11/28/184-, having first given birth to a child in Sept. previous which died in the birth.

SAMUEL MELVIN BIBLE
Owners: Thomas M. and Margaret Pettitt Bayly

BIRTHS of Children of Samuel and Elizabeth W. Melvin

Peggy Cropper Melvin 7/12/1836
Henry Bayly Melvin 5/7/1840

James Melvin 1/21/1839
Fanny Mayo Melvin 4/23/1842

BIRTHS of Children of Robert W. Melvin and Fanny M. Watkins

Mary Wharton Melvin 2/9/1877
Henry Bayly Melvin 11/10/1878
Margaret Cropper Melvin 7/26/1881

Katherine Custis Melvin 9/5/1884

DEATHS

Peggy Cropper Melvin 10/3/1837
James Melvin 6/8/1839
Margaret P. Custis, wife of James W. Custis, 3/18/1856
Sally C. Browne, wife of Dr. P. F. Browne, 1/1/1857
Elizabeth Wharton, wife of Samuel Melvin, 11/22/1885 in Halifax C. H., Va.

William P. Bayly 8/26/1948
Thomas H. Bayly 6/1856
Samuel Melvin 1/28/1862 in Richmond, Va.

JOHN BEAMAN BIBLE
Owner: Dr. Beaman Storey, Franklin, Virginia
John Beaman m. Mary 2/17/1825
BIRTHS

John Beaman, son of Cullen and Huldeth Beaman, 2/24/1798
Mary Beaman, dau. of Edmund Cotton and Milly, his wife, 12/24/1801
Nathaniel Williamson, son of Mathias Williamson and May, his wife, 10/10/1819
Edmund, son of Mathias Williamson and May, his wife, 10/10/1822

BIRTHS of Children of John Beaman and Mary, his wife

May Beaman 11/8/1825
John Cullen Beaman 9/26/1835
William Patrick Beaman 12/25/1827
John Wesley Beaman 5/4/1838

Joseph Thomas Beaman 2/26/1830
Martha M. Beaman 1/10/1841
George Munroe Beaman 2/10/1833
John Crowder Beaman 4/9/1847

DEATHS

John C. Beaman 6/15/1837 (son of John and Mary Beaman)
Mary Ann Beaman, dau. of John and Mary Beaman, 6/26/1837
John Wesley Beaman, son of John and Mary Beaman, 11/4/1839
John Beaman 3/20/1847, aged 49 yrs., 26 days
John Crowder Beaman, son of John and Mary Beaman, 4/28/1849, aged 2 yrs., 19 days
Martha Moore Beaman, dau. of John and Mary Beaman, 10/16/1854, aged 13 yrs., 9 mos., 7 days Mary Beaman 6/27/1875

JOHN HUTCHESON BIBLE of Caroline County
Owner: Smith Co. Historical Society, Tyler, Tx,
John Hutcheson m. Elizabeth Chiles of Caroline Co., Va. 8/30/1763

BIRTHS

Jemimah Hutcheson 8/4/1766
William Hutcheson 1/12/1776
Samuel Hutcheson 1/17/1774
Mary Hutcheson 4/18/1768
Susannah C. Hutcheson 7/27/1777

Chiles Hutcheson 4/30/1770
Elizabeth Hutcheson 8/13/1779
John Hutcheson 4/7/1772
Richard Hutcheson 8/30/1782

John Hutcheson m. Nancy Stone of Mecklenburg Co., Va. 12/24/1793

BIRTHS

Martha R. Hutcheson 10/9/1794
Elizabeth C. Hutcheson 7/12/1798
William Hutcheson 7/11/1796

BIRTHS

Rebecca I. Hutcheson 3/3/1803 Mary M. Hutcheson 8/12/1806 Ann J. Hutcheson b. 5/4/1841
Nancy Hutcheson, consort of John Hutcheson, d. 1/16/1801
Mary Hutcheson, consort of John Hutcheson, d. 6/25/1839
John Hutcheson m. Mary Clay of Mecklenburg Co. 2/25/1840

Frances A. Hutcheson 4/8/1800
John Hutcheson m. Mary
Sugget, widow (nee Jones) 9/10/1801
Mary Hutcheson, wife of John Hutcheson, d. 2/21/1863
Her husband d. 14 yrs. before in 12/1849
Thomas S. Legrand m. Annie Hutcheson 5/1/1861
BIRTHS:
John T. Legrand 5/7/1862
James A. Legrand 10/11/1867
Eveline G. Legrand 5/19/1866
John T. Legrand 1/18/1863

DEATHS

John T. Legrand 1/18/1863
Thomas S. Legrand 1/5/1869

Eveline G. Legrand 10/17/1868

SLAUGHTER-BERREY BIBLE
Owner: James Hay Berrey, Criglersville, Va.

Daniel F. Slaughter b. Rappahannock Co., Va. 7/8/1824 d.3/1901 Mary Elizabeth Berrey, consort of Daniel F. Slaughter, b. Madison Co.,Va 7/5/1835 d. 3/5/1876

BIRTHS

Bettie Florence Slaughter 5/28/1860
Lelia Stewart Slaughter 3/29/1863
David S. Berrey 12/8/1856
David Burnam Berrey 1896
Mary Slaughter Berrey 7/17/1890
Emma Deane Berrey 5/18/1897
Grace Woodward Berrey 3/1/1892

James Hay Berrey 11/3/1898
Winnie Davis Berrey 3/1893
Daniel Fischer Berrey 5/16/1900
Ray Berrey 10/9/1894
Berry Slaughter Berrey d. 3/9/1901
Lelia S. Berrey d. 11/13/1934

N. FINKS BIBLE

" Presented to my wife 11/18/1888, the 30th anniversary of our marriage" by A. N. Finks"

Alexander Newton Finks of Madison Co., Va. m. Judith Frances Story of Criglersville, Madison Co., Va. 11/18/1858 by William C. Lauck, witnesses: Dr. Thomas P. Carpenter and Miss M. F. Crisler

MARRIAGES

Wilmer P. Finks to Ola Smith 12/31/1884
John H. Finks to Mary E. Eggleston 10/22/1902 Emmet L. Finks to Mildred L. Lozano 5/25/1905
Fred W. Finks to Agnes Price 5/5/1908

BIRTHS:

Y. Finks 8/23/1835
Lula Clyde Finks 6/3/1872
J. F. Story 3/18/1838
Sallie Lewis Finks 11/29/1874
Wilmer P. Finks 10/26/1859
Emmett L. Finks 8/26/1877
Helen Elizabeth Finks 1/22/1943 (dau. of Louis Lozano)

John H. Finks 5/24/1862
Fred Neale Finks 5/9/1880
Henry L. Finks 2/8/1869
David Lee Finks 2/18/1885
Frances Story Finks 3/2/1906 (dau. of Emmett)
Louis Lozano Finks 11/11/1908 (dau. of Emmett)

DEATHS

Henry Linwood Finks 9/12/1870
John H. Finks 8/12/1936
Lula Clyde Finks 5/1/1876
Wilmer P. Finks 4/15/1944
Sallie Lewis Finks 9/28/1876
Fred Meal Finks 8/18/1945

Judith F. Finks 11/19/1900
Emmett Lester Finks 5/10/1957
N.Finks 12/8/1904
Louis Lozano Finks 2/13/1970
David Lee Finks 5/1918

Memo: "To Capt. Alexander Finks: Your son, Emmett Lester Finks died on the same day (May 10) as did Thomas Jonathan Jackson (Stonewall) whom I know to have been your ideal and Leader through your years of strife."

SPENCER-ARMISTEAD BIBLE of Prince Edward Co.

BIRTHS of Children of Sharp and Sarah Spencer

James A. Spencer 5/11/1760-
Frances Spencer 12/10/1769
Elizabeth Spencer 10/25/1761
John Spencer 3/20/1772
William Spencer 4/11/1764

Sharp Spencer 5/30/1776
George Spencer 1/21/1766
Sarah Spencer 1/8/1777
Savannah Spencer 1/19/1765
Thomas Spencer 9/16/1780

DEATHS

James A. Spencer 11/13/1777
John Armistead 10/25/1794
Sarah Walthall 11/2/1805
Thomas S. Armistead 2/26/1840
Sharp Spencer Sr. 4/19/1814
Sharp Spencer 2/3/1854

Sarah Spencer, his wife, 9/25/1819
John Armistead 4/18/1868
William Spencer 7/3/1819
Frances Holan 7/1832
Mary Armistead 7/30/1838
John Armistead m. Polley 4/15/1788

BIRTHS

Thomas S. Armistead 3/5/1791
John H. Armistead 12/5/1794

William S. Armistead 3/21/1789
James A. Armistead 8/12/1793

SMITH-DABNEY-CHAMBERLAYNE-BAGBY BIBLE
Owner: Montrose, The Chamberlayne House, Henrico Co., Va.

Augustus Smith m. Sarah Carber 11/9/1711.

THEIR CHILDREN:

Mary Smith 7/1713-6/8/1720
John Smith 11/13/1715-11/19/1771 m. Mary Jacquelin 1/17/1737.
Son, Augustus Smith, 1/3/1738-10/4/1764
Sarah Smith 9/8/1717-3/12/1720
Mildred Smith b. 9/22/1719 m. John Willis 1/23/1741
Elizabeth Smith b. 5/8/1722 m. Philip Aylett 3/16/1744
Ann Smith 2/18/1723-6/2/1724 Jane Smith 3/6/1730-3/29/1732
Rev. Thomas Smith b. Westmoreland Co., Va. 1739 d. 11/29/1801 m. Mary Smith 12/7/1765.

Their Children:

Lucy Cooke Smith 8/28/1766-2/18/1768
Mary Jacquelin Smith 6/23/1769-12/14/1791
Gregory Smith 4/1/1771-12/25/1775

Thomas Gregory Smith b. 1/17/1778
Benjamin Dabney b.10/11/1791
John Augustus Smith b. 8/29/1799

Ann Smith 1/31/1733-killed by lightening 7/12/1786
Benjamin Dabney 1750-5/25/1806 m. 1st Martha Burwell Armistead, 2nd, Sarah Smith
Sarah Smith 2/25/1775-12/21/1851 m. Benjamin Dabney 10/11/1791

BIRTHS of Children of Benjamin Dabney

Matt son 8/29/1794-d. age of 4 wks,without a name.Second son 5/11/1796, d. in Nov. following

Thomas Gregory Smith Dabney 1/4/1798
Philip Augustus Lee Dabney 3/4/1800
Martha Burwell Dabney 5/15/1802-3/19/1853 m. 4/11/1820

Dr. Lewis Webb Chamberlayne who d.1/27/1854.
William Alfred Baynham Dabney 1/5/1805-3/1809.
James Benjamin Dabney 11/12/1806

JOHN GOODALL BIBLE

BIRTHS

John Goodall, son of John and Mildred, 3/16/1768
Junior Turner Goodall, son of John and Mildred, 6/19/1770
Mary Goodall 10/22/1774
Lodowick Goodall 4/7/1788
Thomas Goodall 11/28/1780

Nancy Goodall 4/2/1791
Edward Goodall 2/29/1784
James Goodall 7/24/1792 Peter
Copeland Goodall 5/16/1786
Turner Goodall 8/14/1795

----, a negro boy, 5/7/1817
Salley, negro girl, 2/11/1788

Saline, a negro girl, 2/23/1815
Caroline, a negro girl, 11/27/1811

(John Goodall Bible, BIRTHS, contd....)

Lodowick Goodall 4/7/1788
Peter C. Goodall 5/19/1820
Mary Goodall 3/14/1789
Nancy G. Goodall 5/16/1822
William M. Goodall 8/23/1812

Rhoda G. Goodall -/17/1824
Lattitia Goodall -/14/1815
Turner L. Goodall 7/20/1826
James A. Goodall 12/2/1817

"My dear father, Junior Turner (Goodall),departed this life on Saturday evening two hours before sun it being the 11 of March 1769 he being in the 67 year of his age. Mildred Goodall."

WILMER P. FINKS BIBLE
Owner: Robert Newton Finks, Criglersville, Va.

Wilmer P. Finks 10/26/1859-4/15/1944
Ola E. Finks 2/20/1867 (nee Ola E. Smith)
Ruth L. Finks 7/7/1888-
Percy N. Finks 11/19/1890-5/18/1933
Robert Lynn Finks 10/4/1892-1/6/1950

Charles S. Finks 11/16/1895-
Frances Finks 10/9/1897-10/25/1925
Alice Ola Finks 11/7/1906-

MARRIAGES

John H. Finks of Criglersville, Va. to Mary E. Eggleston of Gordonsville, Va. 10/22/1902. /s/T. W. T.Wingfield
Virginia Frances Finks to Carmen Erselle Fields 1926 Robert N. Finks to Mary Virginia Brockett 11/23/1936
Genevieve Constance Finks to fames Williams Hicks 2/7/1953, Dartford, Kent Co. England
John Beverly Finks to Anna Elizabeth Edwards 4/25/1953

BIRTHS

Virginia Frances Finks 7/12/1903
Lewis Franklin Finks 1/21/1916
Edna Lee Hamilton Finks 4/23/1906
John Beverly Finks 3/16/1921

Sallie Eggleston Finks 1/25/1911
Robert Newton Finks 4/8/1908
Genevieve Constance Finks 4/22/1913

DEATHS

Sallie Eggleston Finks 10/14/1926
John H. Finks 8/12/1936

Virginia Frances Finks 8/18/1939
Edna Lee Finks 1/6/1945

JAMES HAMLETT BIBLE
Owner: Mrs. John E. Strain, Adams, Tennessee

James Hamlett 1751-1819, Cav. in Va. Line m. 1772 in Virginia,
Marv Bedford 1755-1772
James Hamlett 11/25/1795-5/2/1887, aged 92 yrs. m. Mary Atkins 6/27/1812-6/7/1875

BIRTHS of Children

John Elllott Hamlett 9/6/1817
Susan Elizabeth Hamlett 12/16/1819
Joseph James Hamlett 10/4/1524
Francis Marian Hamlett 11/16/1830
Andrew Jackson Hamlett 7/1/1832
Mary Jane Hamlett 11/16/1833
Wiley Norfleet Blunt Hamlett 12/30/1834
Josephine Hamlett 4/5/1838
Maria Louise Hamlett 9/1/1840
Margaret Ann Hamlett 5/4/1844

COLLINS-GREEN BIBLE

William Collins, Jr., son of William Collins, Sr. and Dolly C., b. 8/4/1856
Mary Lou Green, dau. of Albert G. & Sarah E. Green, b. 10/2/1834

BIRTHS of Children of William and Mary Lou Collins

Ida Coleman Collins 9/29/1854 at res. of A. G. Green
Millard Fillmore 6/26/1856 at res. of his Uncle C. S. Collins Sallie Willie' Collins 1/28/1859 at res. of Harvard Nunnilee Signora Alice Collins 6/30/1860 at Halifax Co.
William Collins 3/10/1863 at Halifax Co.

BIRTHS of Children of S. T. Rogers and Ida Coleman, his wife

Thomas Sidney Rogers 7/1875 in Nelson Co.
Coleman Whitehead Rogers 1/3/1878 in Nelson Co.
William Stuart Rogers 5/30/1880 in Albemarle Co.
Robert Sterling Rogers 11/28/1882 in Highland Co., Va.
Ethel June Rogers 6/6/1884 in Albemarle Co., Va.
Charlotte Embrer Rogers 10/12/188Louise Catherine Rogers 11/16 /188-
Ida Ruth Rogers 7/7/188- in Albemarle Co., Va.
Clifton Paul Rogers 8/22/1894 in Basic City, Augusta Co., Va. Stephen Virginius Rogers 8/25/1900 in Basic City, Augusta Co.

MARRIAGES

William Collins, Jr., son of William Collins, Sr. and Dolly C., to Mary Louise Green 10/31/1853 of Prince Edward Co., Va., dau. of Albert G. and Sarah E. Green
Stephen T. Rogers to Ida Coleman Collins 9/16/1874 by Dr. Preston of RLchmond, Va. at res. Of her Uncle J. A. Collins

DEATHS

Sallie Willie, dau. of William & Mary Lou Collins 9/12/1859, aged 7 mos., 15 days
Signora Alice, dau. of William and Mary Lou Collins, 8/31/1864, aged 4 yrs., 2 mos., 1 day
Capt. William Collins, Co. H, 3rd Va. Cavalry of Halifax Co., Va. d. 12/12/1864, house of John Roberts in Nelson Co., Va., 33 yrs.

Edward W. Rogers, son of S. T. Rogers, 3/21/1891, aged 22 yrs.
Ida Ruth, dau. of S. T. & Ida C. Rogers, 11/28/1893, 3 yrs., 5 mos
Coleman W. Rogers, son of S T.. Rogers and Ida C., his wife, was killed on 10/22/1896, aged 18 yrs.
Stephen T. Rogers 11/15/1915, aged 75 yrs.
Mary L. Collins 1/10/1917, aged 82 yrs., in Basic City, Va.
Ada Lee Rogers, dau. of S. T. Rogers 6/10/1918, aged 52 yrs. Millard F. Collins 1/22/1938, bur. San Antonio, Tx., aged 82 yrs.
Ids Collins Rogers 11/15/1938, aged 84 yrs., Richmond, Va., bur. in Waynesboro, Va.
Thomas Sidney Rogers 9/30/1944, bur. Waynesboro, Va. 10/2/1944, aged 69 yrs.
Robert Sterling Rogers 11/6/1946 in NYC, bur. Woodlawn Cemetery, NY, 11/8/1946, aged 64 yrs. Clifton Paul Rogers 6/27/1950 in NY, bur. Arlington Cemetery 7/3/1950, aged 55 yrs.
William Stuart Rogers 2/24/1956, bur. San Antonio, Tx. 2/25/1956, aged 76 yrs. on 5/20/1956

Louise Catherine Rogers Pratt, wid. of Dr. Frank C. Pratt, 5/9/1969 In Richmond, Va., bur. at Oak Hill Cemetery, Fredericksburg, Va., aged 79 yrs.

Charlotte Embrer Rogers Samis, wid. of Theodore A. Sammis, Sr., 5/10/1969, bur. at Forest Lawn Cemetery, Richmond, Va., 80 yrs.
Ethel Rogers Armitage, age 91, wid. of John H. 8/6/1976, Tampa, Florida.

ALBERT GALLATIN GREEN, SR. BIBLE

My great-grandfather, Thomas Embro Green d. 7/31/1827.
His wife, Elizabeth Julia Booker d. 5/3/30/1828.

THEIR CHILDREN:

Don Carlos Green 7/18/1786-12/6/1813
William Booker Green 12/30/1787-1870 (of Greenwood, Charlotte Co., Va., whom I remember).
Berryman Davis Green 7/14/1789-8/31/1815
His twin sister, Nancy Flournoy Green d. 4/8/1816
Thomas Hope Green 7/1/1791-9/7/1791
Gideon Flournoy Green 7/20/1793-3/21/1815 Elizabeth Julia Green 4/19/1795-5/30/1828
John Parish Green 3/6/1797-8/10/1825
Albert Gallatin Green (our grandfather, the 9th child) 6/15/1799-1872 or 1873

My Grandparents:

Albert Gallatin Green m. Sarah Elizabeth Scott 2/11/1830

BIRTHS of THEIR CHILDREN:

Pauline Elizabeth Green 1/17/1831
Thomas Embro Green 12/16/1832
Mary Louise Green, my mother, b. at "Marble Hill", Prince Edward
Co., Va. 10/2/1334 and d. at Basic, Augusta Co., Va. 1/10/1917
William Scott Green 11/4/1836, was killed at 2d Battle of Manassas.
Albert Gallatin Green, Jr. 1/2/1839
Sarah Catherine Green 11/13/1840
Infant son b. and d. 1842, lived 3 days Carlos Berryman Green 1/12/1845
Cornelia Stuart Green 1/16/1847
Ella Saline Green 6/2/1850
Frances Veola Green 5/10/1853
Nannie Read Green 5/11/1856-11/1/1861 in Tx., aged 5 yrs, 5 mos.

MARRIAGES of the Children of my Grandparents (Albert Green and Sarah Scott Green)

Pauline E. Green to Richard R. Puryear, M. D. in Va. 11/11/1851 Mary Louise Green (my
mother) to William (Button) Collins Jr. of Halifax Co., Va. 10/31/1853
Sarah Catherine Green (Salite Tip) to Nathan E. Bell in Va. 11/11/1857
Thomas Embro Green to Ella A. Faris, Tx., 4/27/1859 (Ella Athantha Green d. 3/4/1861 and Thomas E. Green was again married to Margie M. Patton 8/8/1865)
Cornelia S. Green to Dr. Sam B. Maney 1/16/1866
Albert G. Green, Jr. to Sophia Erskine Anderson of Sequin, Tx. 4/8/1866
Ella S. Green to John K. Pierce of Belmont, Tx.

WILLIAM CHAMBERLAYNE COOK BIBLE
Owner: Virginia Sister Sherman   New Kent Co., Virginia

MARRIAGES

William C. Cook to Minerva L. Chandler 5/18/1842
William C. Cook to Octavia R. Chandler 12/6/1848
William Henry Vaughan to Mary Eliza Cook at her father's res. in New Kent Co. 10/31/1860
Richard D. Cook to Leer M. Apperson 7/6/1870
James L. Ames to Mary E. Vaughan 7/28/1872
Gabriel S. Macknamara to Alice A. Cook 3/2/1881
Richard C. Boswell to Octavia W. Cook in Baltimore 9/3/1884

(William Chamberlayne Cook Bible, contd....)

BIRTHS

William Chamberlayne Cook 2/5/1815 Minerva Lipscomb Cook 11/5/1818
Mary Eliza Cook 3/9/1843, dau. of William C. and Minerva L. Cook
Richard Delaware Cook 1/31/1845
Minerva Frances Cook 1/17/1848, dau. of William C. and Minerva L. Cook
Octavia R. Cook 10/22/1829
Alice Ann Cook 4/2/1850, dau. of William C. and Octavia R. Cook
William Oliver Cook 11/24/1851, son of William C. and Octavia R. Cook
The son of William C. and O. R. Cook 7/18/1855
Marcus Lafayette Cook 11/16/1856 Octavia Willfnette Cook 5/22/1859
Silas Chandler Cook 7/13/1860 Robert Handsford Cook 6/16/1862
William H. Vaughan 1/30/1863, son of W. H. and Mary E. Vaughan
Elizabeth Conor Cora Cook 2/2/1865, dau. of William and O. R. Cook
Emmett Adolphus Cook 4/26/1868 Baby b. 11/14/1870

BIRTHS of Negroes

Susan Jefferson 7/17/1840
Jane 7/1837
Wilson Jefferson 11/9/1842
Martha Ann 5/6/1846 Jane 7/1837
John 11/5/1856
William Turner Jones b. 11/25/1859, son of Sinthey & Amsted Jones Martha Jane b. 1/27/1860
Becky b. 1/22/1862

DEATHS

Minerva L. Cook 1/25/1848, wife of William C. Cook
Minerva Frances Cook 1/28/1848, dau. of William C. and Minerva L. Cook
William Oliver Cook 5/18/1854, son of William C. and Octavia R. Cook
The son of William C. and O. 8. Cook 1/12/1856
Marcus Lafayette Cook 7/19/1857
William H. Vaughan 8/12/1862
Silas Chandler Cook 11/3/1866, son of O. R. and William C. Cook   James H. Cook 1/15/1870, aged 52 yrs, 26 days
Baby d. 9/11/1871
William A. Cook 3/30/1876, aged 31 yrs, 5 mos.
Allce A. McNamara 6/24/1882, aged 32 yrs, 1 mo., 22 days
Octavia R. Cook 9/10/1882, aged 53 yrs., 11 mos., 12 days
William C. Cook 12/6/1885
R. D. Cook 12/18/1910

HAMMOND FLETCHER CRUMP BIBLE
Owner: Mrs. Marius R. Barham, Norfolk, Va

MARRIAGES

R. G. Smith of Hanover Co., Va. to M. C. Cooke of New Kent Co., Va., 5/4/1858 at Chestnut Grove, res. of bride's father, by Rev. Simcoe
W. W. Jones-Annie E. Cooke 12/27/1871, New Kent Co., Va., Chestnut Grove, by Rev.T.P.Wise
H. F. Crump to Mollie A. Cook 1/24/1871 at New Rent Chapel by Rev. T. P. Wise
W. W. Jones to Maggie S. Patterson 9/29/1875 at Chestnut Grove by Rev. T. P. Wise
H. F. Crump to M. A. Smith 9/26/1888 at New Kent Chapel by Rev. S. H. Johnson

(Hammond Fletcher Crump Bible, contd....)

BIRTHS of Children of H. F. and Mollie A. Crump

Charles Prior Crump l/6/1872- -
Bessie Lee Crump 11/8/1877
Aurelius Byron Crump 6/29/1873
Rufus Stanley Crump 5/31/1879

Hamond Fletcher Crump 10/25/1874
Florence Aurelia Crump 12/28/1851
Annie Cordelia Crump 1/30/1876

BIRTHS of Children of H. F. and M. Aurelia Crump

Mary Cordelia Crump 7/6/1889
William Robert Crump 5/6/1896
Loveline Gladous Crump 4/16/1891
Floye Belle Crump 9/10/1897

Isaac Walker Crump 10/3/1892
Benjamin Franklin Crump 8/19/1899
Grosjean Graves Crump 12/16/1894

DEATHS

Annie Cordelia, dau. of H. F. and M. A, Crump, 7/11/1878, aged 5 mos., 11 days
?lary A., wife of H. F. Crump, 1/8/1886, aged 56 yrs., 5 mos., 15 days. She was b. 7/24/1840
Loveline Gladous Crump, dau. of H. F. and M. A. Crump, 1896
Aurelius Byron, son of H. F. Crump,1/21/1908
Hammond Fletcher Crump, Sr. 12/21/1840-2/28/1919
Margaret Aurelia Crump 10/15/1860-2/25/1940
Hammond Fletcher Crump, Jr. 5/8/1940
Rufus S. Crump 8/11/1948

PAYNE-GILLIAM BIBLE
Of Goochland Co., Virginia Owner: Va. State Archives

John W. Payne m. Polley G. Payne 12/24/1807
Emily C. Payne, their dau. m. Thomas Cornelius 12/3/1828
Elizabeth W. Randolph m. James Randolph 2/10/1831
John W. Payne b. 6/20/1784
Polley G. Payne, his wife, b. 3/6/1785

BIRTHS of Children of John W. and Polley G. Payne

Emily C. Payne 10/23/1808
John W. Payne 7/3/1817-8/3
Tarlton F. Payne 11/12/1809
Ann O. Payne 8/13/1818
Elizabeth W. Payne 6/30/1811

Mary T. Payne 8/13/1818
Susanna G. Payne 12/4/1813
Barbara W. Payne 10/24/1821
Jane C. Payne 9/20/1815
Caroline B. Payne 3/9/1827

Tarlton Payne, father of John W., d. 8/10/1817, aged 60 yrs. Elizabeth W. Payne, his wife and mother of John W. Payne, d. 4/12/1830, aged 71 yrs.
Barbara W. Cocke, dau. of above Tarlton and Elizabeth, d. 7/4/1832 Thomas Payne, son of above T.and Elizabeth, d. 11/26/1832
John Winston Cornelius, son of Thomas Cornelius, d. 2/20/1834, aged 4 yrs.

SETH BELL BIBLE Of Accomack and Princess Anne Counties
Owner: Museum of St. Paul's Episcopal Church
201 St. Paul's Blvd., Norfolk, Va.

MARRIAGES

Seth Bell of Accomac Co., Va. to Fanny B. Outten of Accomac Co., Va. 12/5/1525 at Accomac Co., Va.
James V. Hall to Johanna S. Bell 12/27/1855
Thomas P. Bell to Laura V. Stratton 9/3/1873
Henry F. Bell to Margie Hoggard 10/15/1873

BIRTHS

Seth Bell 1/27/1799
Fanny B. Bell 3/14/1805

BIRTHS of Children of Seth and Fanny Bell

Jane Bell 1/26/1827-
Thomas Pennell Bell 3/17/1838
Henrietta B. Bell 4/12/1829
Joseph W. Bell 12/27/1840
Henrietta Susan Bell 6/29/1831

Henry Franklin Bell 1/12/1846
Julianna Susan Bell 4/15/1835
Fanny Bell 8/16/1850

DEATHS

Seth Bell 8/5/1874
Henrietta Susan Bell 7/7/1835
Jane Bell 2/14/1827

Fanny Bell 8/23/1850
Henrietta B. Bell 7/11/1830

SNIDER-GODWIN-AMMEN BIBLE of Botetourt County

MARRIAGES

William T. Snyder to Harriet Godwin 7/25/1837 in Salem, Botetourt Co., Va. by Rev. John S. Martin of the Baltimore Conference
James Godwin to Blanche Redwood Booker In Houston, Tx. 6/29/1899
James Winchester Ridout to Ella Neville Godon at Ridgeley 10/8/1907, by Rev. F. A. Ridout

BIRTHS

William T. Snider, son of Henry and Catherine, 11/17/1816, Salem Baptist Godwin, dau. of James A. and Nancy, 3/31/1805, Salem The son of William and Harriet Snider b. & d. 8/12/1840
James A. Godwin, father of Harriet Snider, 6/2/1770 in Delaware Nancy Godwin, wife of James A., 9/1777 in Ireland
James Godwin, 4th son of Thomas G. and Martha M. Godwin, 2/21/1843 in Fincastle, Va.
Ann Eliza Amman, 2d dau. of Daniel and Hester Ammen, 5/2/1845, Willow Grove, Botetourt Co.
Frank, their 1st son, b. & d. 12/29/1871, bur. Godwin Cem., adj. Methodist Church,Fincastle, Va.
Constance, their 1st dau., 9/20/1873
Mary Sipkins Godwin 5/28/1875 at "Solitude" in Fincastle
Ella Neville, 3rd dau., Hayth House, Fincastle, Va. 10/20/1880

DEATHS

William T. Snider 12/21/1858 at Salem
Harriet Snider in Fincastle at res. of her bro. Thomas G. Godwin, 9/11/1874, bur.. beside her mother in the Methodist burying-ground
James A. Godwin 5/21/1842
Mrs. Nancy Godwin 5/31/1862
Constance Godwin 6/7/1874 in Fincastle, bur. Godwin Cemetery
Eliza Ammen Godwin, wife of James Godwin, 9/22/1881 in Staunton. her remains bur. in Godwin Cemetery at Fincastle, Va.
Emma Zulema Ammen 6/14/1882 Roanoke, Va., bur. beside her sister, Eliza, in Godwin Cemetery at Fincastle, Va.
Blanche Redwood Godon 10/15/1903 at "Ridgeley", Fincastle, Va., bur. in Godwin Cemetery at Fincastle, Va.

JOSHUA SMITH BIBLE
Owner: Col. John C. Bell, Nashville, Tenn.

On Flyleaf: Joshua Smith, his Book 11/12/1837 Upside down in pencil - Ida Ash

BIRTHS of His Children

Olive Francis Smith 3/4/1833-
Caroline Cageman Smith 10/29/1837

Martha Jane Smith 7/16/1835
Petronelo Susan Smith 8/7/1840

(different handwriting):-

Olive F. Smith 3/4/1833
Joshua Smith 12/24/1842
James Alexander Smith 6/27/1853
Martha Jane Smith 7/16/1835
Ann Smith 11/29/1845

Sarah Smith d. 6/27/1853
Caroline B. Smith 8/7/1840
Robert Chapel Smith 11/16/1848
Peteronelia Smith 8/7/1840

MORDECAI REDD BROADDUS BIBLE of Cherry Grove, Caroline County

BIRTHS of Children of Mordecai Redd and Sarah A. Broaddus (all b. Cherry Grove)

Alexander Woodford Broaddus 2/27/1834
Attaway Miller Broaddus 2/29/1836
John Prince Broaddus 3/23/1838.

Preston Broaddus 8/21/1840
Archibald Thomas Broaddus 2/16/1843
Susan S. Broaddus 2/17/1846

Roland Falconer Broaddus, son of Alexander Woodford and Fannie Ellen B and Elizabeth Haile Broaddus 2/5/1856 at Cherry Walk, Essex Co., Va.; Sallie Matilda Haile, dau. of Capt. Robert G., b. At Beaver's Hill, Essex Co., Va. 2/25/1839

BIRTHS of Children of A. W. and S. M. Broaddus (all b. Cherry Walk, Essex Co., Va.)

Junius M. Broaddus 2/26/1860.Nannie P. Broaddus 7/24/1861
Alexander Woodford Broaddus 8/21/1867 .Lena Madison Broaddus 12/21/1866
Matilda Haile Broaddus 3/7/1867 . Lucy Virginia Broaddus 2/17/1871
Attie Miller Broaddus 2/4/1873 at Cherry Walk, Essex Co., Va.
Alexander Preston Broaddus 2/4/1875 at Cherry Walk, Essex Co.
Sarah Elizabeth Broaddus 3/26/1879 at Cherry Walk, Essex Co.
John William Broaddus 9/22/1880 at Cherry Walk,Essex Co., Va.
Alexina Woodford Broaddus 9/12/1883 at Cherry Walk, Essex Co.

MARRIAGES

William B. Kidd to Miss Attaway Miller Broaddus 11/18/1858 at Salem Church, Caroline Co.
Alexander Woodford Broaddus to Sallie Matilda Haile, of Essex Co. 4/19/1859 at Beaver's Hill
Alexander Woodford Broaddus to Fanny Ellen Croxton 3/15/1855 at Laurel Grove, Essex Co.
Roland F. Broaddus, son of A. W. and F. E. Broaddus, b. 2/5/1856 at Cherry Walk, Essex Co.
Alexander Woodford Broaddus to Sallie M. Haile 4/19/1859 at Beaver's Hill, Essex Co., Va.,

DEATHS

Mordecai Broaddus 1/6/1837 John Prince Miller 1/21/1838
Mordecai Redd Broaddus 5/29/1859 in Caroline Co., aged 52 yrs.
 Mrs. Sarah Ann Miller Broaddus 9/24/1887, Caroline Co., aged 76
Miss Susie S. Broaddus 8/24/1886 in Caroline Co., aged 40 yrs.
Alexander Woodford Broaddus 10/7/1883 in Caroline Co., aged 49
William B. Kidd 12/27/1875 in Caroline Co
Alexander Woodford Broaddus, Jr., son of A. W. and S. M. Broaddus, 7/15/1869
Alexander W. Broaddus, son of M. R. and S. A. Broaddus, 10/7/1883
Mattie H. Broaddus, dau.of A.W. and S. M. Broaddus, 5/8/1890
S. M. Broaddus, dau. of Capt. R. G.&E. Haile, 12/29/1901.A. T. Broaddus 4/20/1915, aged 73
Roland F. Broaddus d. 12/4/1914 at Memorial Hospital, aged 59 Died at his home, 708
Wickham St., Barton Heights, Va., 1/25/1911, John P. Broaddus, aged 73 yrs.
Died at her home, 708 Wickham St., Barton Heights, Va., 8/6/1916, Mrs. Attie M. Kidd, aged 81

LEWIS WEBB BIBLE
Owner: Mrs. A. C. Duke
Jersey Ridge Rd., Maysville, Ky. 41056

BIRTHS:

Martha L. Webb 6/25/1788
Lewis Foster Webb 9/22/1801
Elizabeth Webb 9/12/1790
Martha Webb 3/8/1805
Ann Bickerton Webb 10/27/1790
George Bickerton Webb 12/9/1805
Theodocia Cocke Webb 9/17/1794

Pleasant Fleming Webb 6/26/1810
Catherine Power Webb 1/9/1808
Edward Cary Webb 12/22/1796
William Ross Webb 12/11/1798
Lucy A. Dandridge Webb 4/9/1815
Pleasant F. Webb had a dau. B. 11/1/1833

Susan Martha, dau. of Alfred H. & Lucy A. D. Tucker, b. 2/1/1840

MARRIAGES

Lewis Webb of New Kent Co., Va. to Lucy R. Cary of King William Co., Va. 9/29/1787
Foster L. Webb, son of Lewis Webb, to Martha Bilbo of Mercer Co. 1/27/1825
William R. Webb, son of Lewis Webb, to Jane More of Washington Co. 2/12/1824
Lucy R. Webb, wife of Lewis Webb, b. 4/5/1768
Bluford Mussen to my dau., Catherine P. Webb 4/19/1832 by Rev.Mr. Cane of Lebanon
Ragan Daviss of Green Co. to my dau., Ann B. Webb 7/5/1817 Pleasant F. Webb to Amanda C. Short of Lincoln Co. 6/7/1832

BIRTHS

Mary A. Fleming. dau. of F. L. Webb, 11/22/1825
William Levis 3/11/1829
William Levis Mussen, son of Bluford and Catherine Mussen, 12/26/1832 in Washington Co.
Martha Catherine Cary, dau. of Foster L. Webb, 12/14/1833
Frankling---- 2/10/1837

BIRTHS of William R. Webb's Children

Lucy A. Webb 10/13/1824
Jane Hawkins Webb 3/3/1834
Richard Webb 5/7/1829
Margaret More Webb 11/15/1826

Lewis Foster Webb 9/15/1836
Theodocia Webb 11/23/1831
William Alexander Webb 5/27/1839

DEATHS

A son b. 10/24/1800 and departed this life.
A dau. b. 12/9 and d. 12/1803
William Lewis Webb, son of Foster L. &Martha Webb, 1/20/1833,Washington Co., Ky., 10 ms.
Franklin Knot? 5/9/1839
Levis Webb 7/12/1841, aged abt 84 yrs.

GEORGE W. KELLY BIBLE
Found in log house near Bandy Cemetery, Roanoke Co., Va.

George W. Kelly 9/28/1837-2/25/1914
Matilda C. Kelly, wife of George W. Kelly, 8/14/1850-2/27/1914
Charles W. Kelly 6/11/1876-1/19/1904

Mary C. Kelly 9/22/1878-
Joe Rob. Kelly 3/17/1883-

John Thomas Kelly 6/11/1886-
George L. Kelly 7/10/1889-1/16/1912
Walter P. Kelly 2/11/1892-

ELLIS ARMSTRONG BIBLE of Essex Co., Va.

MARRIAGES

Polley Armstrong, dau. of Ellis and Phanney, to Richard Beazley, son of Ephraim, 1/14/1811
Elizabeth33 Garnett Armstrong, dau. of above, to Johnson Munday, son of Ben H. Munday 5/20/1813
--- Armstrong to Susan A. Haile, dau. of Richard, 5/14/1829

BIRTHS of Children of Ambrose and Mary Armstrong

Ambrose Armstrong 4/13/1760	William Armstrong 8/9/1768
Kills Armstrong 10/18/1766	Mary Armstrong 10/18/1764
John Armstrong 1/24/1762	

BIRTHS of Children of Ellis and Fanny Armstrong Polly Armstrong 3125/1792

Elizabeth Garnett Armstrong 6/14/1794
Joseph Noel Armstrong 5/17/1807
James Richards Armstrong 3/11/1812

BIRTHS of Children of Richard and Polly Beazley

Eliza Ann Beazley 10/23/1816	Richard Edward Beazley 9/29/1828
Ephraim Beazley 3/22/1819	Judith Armstrong 3/6/1834
Mary Elizabeth Beazley 12/28/1821	James Benjamin Beazley 1/24/1835
Ellis Armstrong Beazley 1/25/1826	

Robert Armstrong Munday, son of Johnson Munday and Elizabeth, his wife, 4/3/1821
---other entries, blurred---

DEATHS

Fanney Armstrong, wife of Ellis, 2/28/1836
Elliz Armstrong 8/11/1840 ---3/30/1868
---other entries

BIRTHS

Lucy Ann Key 5/3/1818	Polly Kay --/7/1833
Elizabeth Jane Kay 1/4/1829	Sarah Key 12/23/1822
Edward Key -/9/1820	Sally Kay 7/16/1836
William Kay 2/29/1831	Christopher Ray -/14/1824
James Key 9/11/1821	John Key 10/12/187
Richard H. Key 3/12/1827	

DEATHS

Richard Kay 11/11/1781-3/26/1868	Elizabeth Key 9/1852
Elizabeth Ray, his wife, b. 3/31/1794	John Key 2/9/1885
Richard H. Key 9/20/1863	

THOMAS B. CHANDLER BIBLE
Owner: Marius Barham, Norfolk, Va.
On flyleaf: Thomas Chandler

"The first steam boat seen in the Paaunkey River was on Saturday, the 4th day of June 1831 (named J. M.). H. C. Palmer."
Robert B. Chandler, son of James and Mary, b. 11/27/1791

BIRTHS of Children of James and Martha Chandler

John Chandler 11/2/1796	James Chandler 3/1/1809
Mary Ann Chandler 9/20/1805	William Chandler 8/26/1803
Harman Chandler 10/25/1798	

(Thomas B. Chandler Bible, contd....)

BIRTHS of Children of Thomas B. Chandler

James Chandler 7/18/1809
Augustine Chandler 1/2/1818
Parker B. Chandler 9/6/1811

Sara Chandler 3/15/1821
---Chandler 9/26/1814

BIRTHS of Children of Robert Bradenham Chandler Elizabeth

Roper Chandler 9/27/1816-3/26/1827
Robert Archer Chandler 6/6/1818-10/9/1855
Oliver Mitchell Chandler 3/25/1821

Fra-- Roper Chandler 6/22/1824
Mary Ann Eliza Chandler 4/5/1827
Octavia R. Chandler 10/22/1829

CAPT. JOHN BEARD BIBLE
Owner: Mrs. John Bell 1622 N. Augusta St., Staunton, Va.

Capt. John Beard b. 1733 Augusta Co., Va. d. 1819 near Lewisburg, W., Va., m. Jenet Wallace 1/16/1769. She was b. 1746 d. near Lewisburg, W. Va. 1819.

THEIR CHILDREN:

Margaret Beard was the 2nd wife of Thomas Price
Samuel Beard (Major, War of 1812) 9/24/1771-6/5/1850 m. Margaret walkup 5/12/1795
Jane Beard 8/6/1774-5/26/1848 m. John Armstrong 5/12/1812
Thomas Beard (Lt. Col., War of 1812) 1/1776-12/22/1853 m. 1st Katie Price, 2nd, Mary (Polly) Skiles
Agnes Beard b. 5/28/1779 m. John Walkup 11/24/1803
Jesse Beard 5/16/1782-9/13/1867 m. Sarah Lewis 11/8/1810
Sabina Beard b. 5/28/1729? m. Christopher Walkup
Mary Beard m. Rev. John Spotts 1/28/1819
William Ryneck Beard 1/8/1788-1/4/1878 m. Rachel Cameron Poage
Elizabeth (Betsy) Beard was 2nd wife of George W. Poage m. 5/1816
Katherine Beard d. 1803, aged 23.

RICHARD GRAVES SMITH BIBLE
Owner: Mrs. Richard G. Smith

MARRIAGES

Richard G. Smith to Margaret F. Cunningham 5/13/1822
Richard G. Smith to Margaret Cordelia Cook 5/4/1858
William Campbell Cook Smith to Clara Frances Ogg 4/30/1902

BIRTHS of Children of Richard Graves Smith and Margaret Farlie

Old Church Hanover Co., Va. Cunningham of "Eastern View",

William C. Smith 4/14/1823
Mary E. Smith 9/27/1834
John G. Smith 5/28/1825
Georgianna Smith 1/9/1836
Richard G. Smith 1/11/1829

Lewis Oliver Smith 6/14/1838
Larkin Smith 9/19/1831
Robert Harrison Smith 1/13/1841
Ann C. Smith 5/13/1833
Margaret Farlie Smith 10/19/1842

BIRTHS of Children of Margaret C. and Richard G. Smith Ann Farlie Smith 4/197183~

Margaret Aurelia Smith 10/15/1860
Eliza Georgiana Smith 3/15/1862
William Campbell Cook Smith 4/18/1566
Cordelia Cunningham Smith 12/26/1867
Richard Graves Smith 12/24/1869

(Richard Graves Smith Bible, BIRTHS, contd....)

Robert St. Patrick Smith 3/17/1871
John Grosjean Smith 7/30/1873 Delaware
John Smith 4/11/1875

Mary Fleming Smith 12/28/1976
Rose Wilnette Smith 3/11/1878
Ethel Virginia 3/20/1881

DEATHS

William Cunningham 6/15/1831, aged 54 yrs
John G. Smith 6/25/1832, aged 9 yrs.

Larkin Smith 7/21/1832, aged 10 mos., 2 days
Georgianna Smith 9/5/1843, aged 7 yrs.

Mrs. William (Mary) Cunningham, wid. of late William Cunningham, 11/21/1845, aged abt. 80
Margaret Farlie Smith, wife of Richard G. Smith, 11/11/1848, aged 42 yrs. She was the only child of the late William Cunningham. She was b. 12/2/1806
Robert H. Smith, youngest son of Richard G. Smith, 10/25/1853, aged 13 yrs.
Ann Cunningham Smith 9/3/1855, aged 23 yrs.
William Cunningham Smith was killed in battle near Ashland, Hanover Co., Va., 3/15/1865
Mrs. M. C. Smith 3/20/1913
William Campbell Smith 8/23/1922
Mrs. O. M. Chandler 6/5/1923
O. .M. Chandler 8/7/1926

OLIVER MITCHELL CHANDLER BIBLE
Owner: Cammie Chandler Barham

Oliver Mitchell Chandler, son of Robert Bradenham Chandler and Mary Meanly, his wife, b. at Cousaic, New Kent Co., Va., 3/25/1821

Sarah Elizabeth, wife of Oliver M. Chandler and dau. of Robert Liggan and Susan Coghill, b. 3/28/1831, City of Richmond

Oliver Mitchell Chandler m. Sarah E. Liggan 10/15/1851,City of Richmond by Rev.Thos Moore

BIRTHS of Children of Oliver M. and Sarah E. Chandler

Oliver Marious Chandler 9117/1854 at New Kent C. H.
Mary Susan Chandler 8/6/1857 at New Kent C. H.
Ann Elizabeth Chandler 11/29/1859-7/5/1862, New Kent C. H.
Stonewall Jackson Chandler 6/21/1862 New Kent C. H.
Eliza Ella Chandler 7/8/1864-9/20/1871 New Kent C. H.
Harman Cataline Chandler 12/25/1866-d. age 26 yrs., at Ellsworth, New Kent Co., Va.
James Cromwell Chandler 4/7/1869 New Kent C. H.
Minnie Blanche Chandler 10/24/1871 New Kent C. H.
Hester Chandler 1872, lived 8 days
Myrtle Mozelle Chandler 6/6/1878-4/26/1920

Sarah E. Chandler, wife of Oliver M. Chandler d. 3/24/1883 at Chestnut Grove, New Kent Co., Va.,aged 51 yrs., 361 days

Oliver M. Chandler d. Chestnut Grove 4/28/1889, 67 yrs, 27 days
Mary Susan Chandler Martin d. 5/29/1938, Richmond, Va.

Funeral services for Maude Allen Chandler, wife of J. C. Chandler of 2014 Princess Anne Ave. (Richmond) who died Sunday December 17, 1950, at a local hospital, were held at 3:30 p.m. today at Woody's Funeral Home with burial in Oakwood Cemetery. The pallbearers were Wiley Johnson, Oliver Johnson, Linwood Edwards, Merrill French, Preston Hicks and Dr. J. E. Meats,Sr Besides her husband, Mrs. Chandler is survived by a son, Oliver Allen Chandler, a granddaughter,Patricia 4. Chandler, and a grandson, Richard A. Chandler.

(Oliver Mitchell Chandler Bible, DEATHS, contd....)

Oliver Marious Chandler m. Ann Farlie Smith in Washington, D. C. 4/9/1878
Mary Susan Chandler m. William FranklLn Martin at Cornith Church in New Kent Co. 11/8/1882
Robert Archer Bradenham Chandler m. Ada Byron Apperson in 1875 New Kent Co. Children: Berkley and Wilmer.

Note: Oliver Mitchell Chandler was tavern keeper at New Kent Tavern in New Kent Co. for many yrs. All but one of his children were born at the tavern.

RICHARD PYE COOK BIBLE Of New Kent County
Owner: Thaddeus Chandler Cox, Silver Spring, Md.

MARRIAGES

William Cook to Rebecca Hays 1812
Richard Pye Cook to Sarah Ann Elizer Chandler 11/22/1836
Richard G. Smith to Margaret C. Cook 5/4/1858
William W. Jones to Annie Elizabeth Cook 12/27/1871
Hammond F. Crump to Mary A. Cook 1/24/1871
O. M. Chandler to Annie F. Smith in City of Washington, D. C., by Rev. B. Saunderlin 4/9/1878
Hammond F. Crump to Margaret Aurelia Smith 9/26/1888

BIRTHS

Richard Pye Cook 10/10/1813
Sarah Ann Elizer Chandler, wife of said R. P. Cook, 7/4/1814

Margaret Cordelia Cook 10/10/1837   Mary Aurella Cook 7/24/1840
Ann Elizabeth Cook 5/24/1838

Twin sons, William Giles and James Dandridge Chandler, both died in infancy

William Chamberlayne Cook 2/5/1819   James Battwell Cook 11/25/1820

The above named, W. C. and J. H. Cook, were bros. of R. P. Cook Oliver M. Chandler 9/17/1854 at New Kent C. H.
Annie Farlie Smith at Chestnut Grove 4/19/1859

BIRTHS of Children of O. M. and Annie F. Chandler

Richard-Oliver Stanley Chandler at Chestnut Grove 9/28/1879-3/1/1880
Marious Pye Chandler at Chestnut Grove 3/20/1881-3/27/1957, aged 76 years
Aurelia Blanche Chandler 12/4/1882 at Chestnut Grove
Annle Elizabeth Chandler 12/31/1884 at Chestnut Grove
Cordie Campbell Chandler at Chestnut Grove 3/19/1886
Addie Mozelle Chandler at Chestnut Grove 3/5/1889
Susie Valerie Chandler at Chestnut Grove 8/6/1892
Delaware T. Chandler at Chestnut Grove 12/22/1894-4/1/1919
Robert Harmon Chandler at Chestnut Grove 4/30/1897-6/25/1900

DEATHS

Rebecca Cook 1/12/1826
William Cook 7/4/1831
Ann Ridley Cook 10/16/1838

Ann Elizabeth Jones, formerly Cook 5/20/1872
James Hartwell Cook 1/15/1870

Sarah Ann Eliza Cook, formerly Miss Chandler, 10/30/1879
William Chamberlyane Cook 12/6/1885
O. S. Chandler 3/1/1880 at Chestnut Grove
Mary Aurelia Crump, formerly Miss Cook, 1/8/1887

Robert Harman Chandler 6/25/1900 at Chestnut Grove
Col. R. P. Cook 12/1889 R. G. Smith 12/6/1887
Susie Valerie Chandler 12/1/1911 at Memorial Hospital, Richmond, Va.

(Richard Pye Cook Bible, DEATHS, contd....)

Mrs. M. C. Smith 3/20/1913
Delaware Chandler 4/1/1919 at Burton Hospital, Newport News, Va.
Annie F. Chandler 6/5/1923 at Chestnut Grove

Newspaper Clippings: "Died, January 8th 1890 at the home of her brother-in-law,O. M. Chandler, in New Kent County, Va., Mrs. Cordie Williams, wife of Dr. R. M. Williams, aged twenty two years."

"Death of William Giles and James Dandridge Cook, twin infants of Capt. Richard P. Cook and Sarah A. E., his wife, at Chestnut Grove, their father's residence in the County of New Kent. William Giles departed this life on Tuesday the 4th June, aged 7 months and 20 days.... James Dandridge on Sunday evening, the 19th of June, aged 7 mos., 25 days...

Included in Bible on paper:

Marious Pye Chandler m. Sarah Jane Bagby 9/5/1906 First Baptist Church of West Point, Va., Rev. A. Bagby, D. D., grandfather of the bride, officiating, assisted by Dr. C. V. Waugh.
Ann Elizabeth Chandler m. Rev. Zesely B. T. Cox at First Baptist Church of West Point, Va. 10/17/1936, Rev. Herbert Carlton officiating
Thaddeus Chandler Cox b. 10/9/1937, Johnston-Willis Hospital, Richmond, Va.
Paul Hart Cox b. 8/19/1940, Jefferson Hospital, Roanoke, Va. Sarah Jane Cox b. in Woodard-Herring Hospital in Wilson, N. C., on 10/25/1947
Theodore Lipscomb Chandler d. 5/2/186, aged 70 yrs., 4 mos., 2 days
Delaware Chandler d. 3/4/1893

JOHN S. LACY BIBLE
Owner: Virginia Slater Sherman

MARRIAGES

John S. Lacy to Agnes J. Lacy 5/25/1831 by Rev. Gervas Keesee

BIRTHS

John S. Lacy, son of Edmund B. Lacy and Mary Harris, his wife, 10/12/1809
Agnes J. Lacy, dau. of Archibald and Juriah Lacy, 10/15/1810

BIRTHS of Children of John S. and Agnes J. Lacy Mary Jurian Elizabeth Lacy 8/21/1832

John Bacon Lacy 8/9/1836
Junietta Constance Lacy 11/1/1838
Salley Henry Lacy 12/17/1840
William Archibald Lacy 5/21/1846

DEATHS

Mary Juriah Elizabeth Lacy 10/13/1837, aged 5 yrs, 1 mo., 23 days
Junietta Constance Lacy 9/23/1839, aged 10 mos., 23 days
William Archibald Lacy, inf. son of John S. and Agnes J. Lacy, 6/26/1846, aged 1 mo. 5 days
Agnes J. Lacy, wife ; John S. Lacy, 6/2/1846
John S. Lacy 3/30/1872 at the home of his only child at Ward Town, Northampton Co., Va.

JOHN BICKLEY BIBLE
Of King and Queen County
Owner: Virginia State Library

John Bickley m. Mary 4/14/1736
Humphy Caleb Bickley b. 3/26/1737
James Hunt and Jane, his wife, and Charles Bickley, sureties for him
Sarah Bickley b. 10/26/1740. Ralph Shelton, Wm Pollard, Sarah Bickley and Elizabeth Shelton, sureties
Joseph Bickley b. 2/8/1742/3. James Hurt and Catherine Holliday, sureties
Hannah Bickley 1/8/1744/5. James Murray, Sephas Hart, Mary Johnson and Jane Nelson, sureties
Mary Bickley b. 2/3/1746/7, William Hurt, Mary Gosney, Elizabeth Johnson, sureties
John Bickley b. 3/25/1748, John Pemberton, James Rishe? and Elizabeth Pemberton, sureties
Elisabeth Bickley b. 1749/50
Jane Bickley b. 6/18/1751, John Shelton, Ann Johnson, Mary Oakes, sureties
Charles Bickley b. 7/27/1753, Charles Bickley, Thomas Tuck, Patience Bynes, Rachael Oakes, sureties.
Frances Bickley b. 2/19/1755, Hezekiah Pollard, Isabell----, Phebe Johnson, sureties
William Bickley b. 5/27/1757, Thomas Pollard, Humphrey Bickley, Elizabeth Pollard, sureties
Caroline Matilda Bickley b. ---, Henry Davis, Hannah Bickley, sureties

HANCOCK LEE BIBLE
Owner: Mrs. Melvin E. James, Charleston, W. Va.

Hancock Lee 3/4/1766-5/14/1811
Sinah Ellen Lee, his wife, 5/15/1769-7/24/1851

THEIR CHILDREN:

Richard Kendall Lee 11/27/1788-3/6/187
Betty Lee 1/21/1795-8/8/1881
Sarah McCarty Lee 2/22/1792-5/1/1867
Sinah Ellen Lee 3/6/1793-2/26/1807
Hancock Lee 4/9/1794-11/1/1794
John Hancock Lee 6/2/1795-8/9/1820
Hancock Lee 8/14/1796-1/18/1853
William Lancelot Lee 10/7/1797-4/20/1874
Mary K. Lee 11/17/1798-1/13/1865
Daniel Chichester Lee 4/14/1800-8/1/1849
Ann Catharine Lee 9/21/1801-
Doddridge Chicester Lee 9/7/1803-5/1/1863
Ann Me Lee 11/27/1804-2/8/1578
Sinah E. C. Lee 5/15/1806-6/18/1887

LITTLETON ADAMS BIBLE
Owner: Virginia State Library

MARRIAGES

Littleton Adams to Elizabeth Ash 9/23/1779
Littleton Adams to Harriet Smith 3/3/1793
Andrew Turner to Anna Adams, dau. of Littleton and Elizabeth Adams, 12/9/1801
Francis Adams to Chloe Parker 1/1805
Willis Adams to Sarah Chinn 1812

(Littleton Adams Bible, MARRIAGES, contd....)

George Adams to Ann Chinn --Thomas Adams to Frances Jett 1818
George Jackson to Mary Ann Adams 12/22/1835
Harriet V. Adams, dau. of George and Mary Jackson, to W. H. E. Morecock, 4/6/1865
John N. Fishback to Annie E, Jackson, dau. of George and Mary Jackson, 11/10/1870
Wilbur L. Jackson, son of George and Mary Jackson, to Sarah Winecoff 8/9/1882

BIRTHS

Littleton Adams 2/23/1752-2/9/1833 Elizabeth, his first wife, 1/24/--d. 8/10/1791
Harriet, his 2nd wife, 4/18/1764-6/16/1848
Anna, dau. of Littleton and Elizabeth, 7/25/1780-3/17/1805
Francis Adams 1/5/1783-1/20/1841
John Adams 2/26/1784-6/25/1813, in Battle of Hampton
George Adams 3/12/1786-10/5/1868
Willis Adams 7/2/1789-6/5/1847
Thomas Marshall Adams, son of Littleton and Harriet, 4/23/17949/8/1831
Elizabeth Marshall Adams 2/22 - d. 2/10/1873
Charles Brandt Adams 2/23/1798-8/11/1809
Mary Anne Adams 1/7/1804-1/20/1847
John A. Turner, son of Andrew and Anna, 9/16/1802-9/6/1840
Elizabeth Ann Turner b 1/17/1804.
Littleton Turner Adams, son of Francis and Chloe.
Elizabeth M. Adams and Harriet W. Adams, daus. of Thomas M. and Fannie Adams, 11/25/1821
Joanna M. Adams 5/31/1829
Mary Ann Adams 5/13/1830
Susan Thomas Adams 1/19/1832

SAMUEL AND MARIA STRICKLER BIBLE Of Shenandoah County
On flyleaf: David Strickler

BIRTHS

Samuel Strickler 11/20/1759
Daniel Strickler 10/28/1773
Annely Strickler 1/4/1762
David Strickler 2/28/1776
Note: Samuel Strickler m. Maria Bidler

JOSEPH BIGELOW BIBLE
Owner: Virginia State Library

MARRIAGES

Joseph Bigelow to Agnes Miller Nisbet 9/4/1813
Jane E. Bigelow, dau. of Joseph and Agnes, to Rev. John T. Hendrick of Goochland Co., Va. 9/30/1834
Isabella B. Bigelow, dau. of Joseph and Agnes, to John M. Royall of City of Richmond 10/27/1836
Archibald Nisbet Bigelow, son of Joseph and Agnes, to Frances Elizabeth Ballard of Albemarle Co., Va. 5/5/1846
Woodbury B. Bigelow, son of Joseph &Agnes, to Cornelia L. Rust, of Richmond, 10/3/1850

BIRTHS

Joseph Bigelow b. Harvard, Worcester, Mass. 3/27/1790
Agnes Miller Nisbet b. Paisley, Renfrew Co., Scotland 3/26/1792

(Joseph Bigelow Bible, BIRTHS, contd....)

Jane Elisabeth Bigelow b. Richmond, Henrico Co., Ga., 8/4/1814, dau. of Joseph and Agnes M. Bigelow
Archibald Nisbet Bigelow, b. Richmond, Henrico Co., Va. 10/22/1818, son of Joseph and Agnes M.
 Bigelow Robert William Bigelow 1/3/1825, Richmond, Henrico Co., Va., son of Joseph and Agnes M. Bigelow
Woodbury Bromfield Bigelow b. Richmond, Henrico Co., Va 10/5/1829, son of Joseph and Agnes M. Bigelow.

DEATHS

Woodbury B. Bigelow 10/3/1888
Joseph Bigelow 4/9/1846, Richmond, Va., husband of Agnes M.Bigelow
Jane Elizabeth Hendrick, wife of John T. Hendrick and eldest dau. of Joseph and Agnes Bigelow, in Clarksville, W. Tenn. 1/23/1852
Agnes M. Bigelow, wife of Joseph, Richmond, Va., 3/7/1863
Robt William Bigelow 1872 at Staunton, Va., bur. Richmond.

Archibald N. Bigelow 9/16/1892
Fannie Bigelow, his wife, 10/7/1892, Albemarle Co., at Mr. T. E.Paris. She was buried up there
My grandfather Richard Nisbet 8/14/1812 in Richmond, Va., 66 years, 6 months, 14 days
My grandmother Isabella Kemp Nisbet 2/1/1846 Richmond, Va., 88 years old
My Uncle David Nisbet d. in Brooklyn on 20th inst., aged 58 yrs.
My Uncle Archibald Nisbet d. in Richmond, Va. 4/16/1849, 66 yrs. Agnes M. Bigelow, dau. and sister of above, d. in Richmond, Va.,3/7/1863, aged 71 yrs

(She was my dear and beloved mother) My Aunt Isabella Nisbet d. in Richmond, Va.

William Nisbet d. St. Louis, Mo.

JOHN FRANCIS BIBLE
Owner: Mrs. Charles C. Bauthan Stuart, Virginia

BIRTHS

Elizabeth, dau. of Frank Scotts, 2/14/1770 Micajah Francis 1/9/1790
Hasten Francis 9/8/1793 Joseph Francis 11/10/1797
John Francis 6/11/1799 Melchezedick Francis 5/27/1802
Nancy Fisher Francis 3/4/1804
Polley Spence Francis 6/2/1806
Elizabeth Francis, dau. of Melchezedick Francis and Polley, his wife, 12/18/1825
Salley Cammel Francis 3/16/1808
Betsey Bennet Francis 10/30/1810
Rebecca Green Francis 12/21/1812
James Matterson Francis 5/2/1817
Haysten Loves, son of Richard and Nancy Loves, 12/15/1822
John Francis, his Bible, 1/12/1519. Wrote by John Collings

BIRTHS of Children of Melchezedick Francis and Nancy

Mary Francis 8/10/1827
William Francis 6/16/1835 John Francis 3/5/1829
Rebecca Francis 12/14/1836 Sarah Francis 5/17/1830
Mariah Francis 4/19/1840
Presley Francis 11/1/1831
Melchezedick Francis 3/13/1845
Elizabeth Francis 6/21/1833
Melchesedick Francis was cousin Tom Francis' daddy, they lived in Charleston, W. Va., but spelled their last name - France.33

(John Francis Bible, contd....)

John Francis 3/5/1829-3/20/1912
He m. Eliza Applin Hill. She was b. 3/17/1835, d. 9/27/1877

These are THEIR CHILDREN:

Nancy Ruth Ella Francis 8/8/1864-8/20/1954
William Madison Francis 12/12/1865-5/22/194(
Johnie Andrew Francis 7/4/1869-12/11/1956
Waiter Lee Francis 5/3/1873-4/21/1965
George-Leake Francis 12/7/1875-2/17/1956

JOHN O'REAR BIBLE
Of Prince William County
From: Rev. War Pension #S7376

BIRTHS

Jeremiah O'Rear 5/16/1744
Margaret O'Rear 2/13/1753
Mary O'Rear 8/21/1745
Jesse O'Rear 1/24/1756
Benjamin O'Rear 2/20/1747

Daniel O'Rear 12/23/1759
John O'Rear 3/21/1749
William O'Rear 12/1/1761
Elizabeth O'Rear 4/7/1751
Enoch O'Rear 2/18/1763

JOHN FULTON BIBLE

"This Book was purchased in 1804 by John Fulton"

MARRIAGES

John Fulton to Jane Reid 1/19/1804 John Fulton b. 5/20/1768
Jane Reid b. 11/18/1778

BIRTHS

Hugh Fulton 1/29/1805
John Fulton 10/29/1815
Nancy Ann Fulton 11/23/1806
Robert Campbell Fulton 11/24/1817

Sally Fulton 8/15/1809
George Henry Fulton 11/18/1819
Betsey Fulton 12/6/1811
Orlando Fulton 11/2/1822
James Reid Fulton 10/31/1813

DEATHS

HuldahFulton Sr. 5/16/1810, aged 84 yrs.
Ann Reid, 8/12/1818, aged 83 yrs.
Sally Fulton 9/22/1821, aged 13 yrs.

Orlando Fulton 9/19/1824, aged 1 yr., 10 mos., 13 days
John Fulton 1/20/1845, aged 76 yrs., 8 mos.
Jane Fulton 728/1851, aged 72 yrs., 8 mos.

JOHN C. DAVIS BIBLE of Fanquier County
Owner: John R. Gott, Arlington, Va.

John C. Davis b. 4/27/1783

Susan Davis b. 6/17/1783

BIRTHS of THEIR CHILDREN:

Francis B. Davis 12/18/1804
Susan J. Davis 3/1/1817
Caroline M. Davis 2/11/1806
Hamilton J. Davis 9/10/1818
Eliza Davis 6/23/1908
Lucy A. Davis 9/21/1820

William Davis 9/29/1810
James C. Davis 10/25/1822
Thomas T. Davis 4/28/1812
Juliet A. Davis 2/5/1827
John W. Davis 9/7/1814

(John C. Davis Bible, contd....)

DEATHS

James C. Davis 7/12/1890
John W. Davis 5/8/1891
Hamilton J. Davis 11/28/1892

Note: Marriage Bond of John C. Davis and Susanna Brown 2/27/1804 in Fanquier Co., Va.; Francis Brown as security. Marriage bonds of six of THEIR CHILDREN: are also of record in Fanquier Co., Va.

JOSEPH TUCKER BIBLE
DAR Collection, Atlanta Archives

Benjamin Tucker d. 7/29/1710, aged 79 yrs.
Joseph Tucker, son of Joseph, d. 10/28/1707
Littleberry Tucker 1768-11/1846 m. Priscilla Williamson b. Va.-d. 2/13/1841 Hancock Co., Ga.
Ann Collier Tucker b. Va. 10/13/1796 d. 12/12/1868 Warren Co., Ga.

JOHN HITE BIBLE of Rockingham County
Owner: Mrs. E. R. Chilcott, Pasadena, CA

John Hite 6/28/1751-6/12/1808 m. 3/24/1772
Susanna Hite, my wife, 12/25/1755-9/30/1792
Sally Hite 2/19/1775
Francis Asbury Hite 8/17/1790
John Hite 4/14/1776-4/7/1792
John Wesley Hite 9/26/1792
Jacob Hite 4/8/1778
Polly Hite 2/9/179-
William Hite 11/30/1779
Isaac Hite 11/9/1795
Peggy Hite 8/3/1782

Abraham Hite 8/6/1797
Samuel Hite 6/20/1784
Gabriel Hire 12/8/1799
Susanna Hite 3/20/1786
Gaberilla Hite 12/8/1799
Betsey Hite 7/12/1758
Melinda Hite 7/7/1802
Meliday Hite 7/7/1802
Strawther Hite 8/3/1804-6/27/18--
--- Hite 1/12/1807-
Ann Rawlings b. 6/1/1777

Ann Hite, consort of Samuel Hire d. 3/21/1870, aged 93 yrs.
Samuel Hite d. 7/20/1877, aged 93

Samuel Hite's Children

Charles Lewis Hite 3/17/1805-6/28J1806
Ann Hance Hite 2/1/1807-9/19/18--
Margaret Strawther Hite b. 4/15/1809 m. 3/3/18--
Benjamin Rawlings Hite b. 3/21/1811 m. 2/2/1830
Doctor Benjamin Bawling's son, ---- King Rawlings, b. 1/11/1811

BIRTHS of Children of Benjamin and Sarah Hite

Samuel Charles Lewis Hite 2/14/1831 Margaret Rebecca Hire b. & d. 3/5/1845
William Eberly Hite 3/5/1835-Elizabeth Ann Hite 7/23/1837
John Butler Hire 11/1/1839 Benjamin Gabriel Hite 8/21/1842
Henry Clay Hite 8/1844 Susan Harriett Hite 3/10/1847
Nancy Sarah Hite 3/19/1849 James? Hite 10/1851
William Seamen Wright b. 2/8/1805 Washington Co., Pa. m. 3/3/1825 Bloomingham, Ind.,
Margaret Strother Hite, b. 4/14/1809, both died in Mt. Pleasant, Iowa
John Hance Wright 2/11/1826
Samuel Asbury Wright 9/15/1827
Ann Isabel Wright 12/27/1829
Margaret Strother Wright 6/7/1834 (m. Ephraim Winans, minister and Pres. of Simpson College on 6/23/1858 at Mt. Pleasant, Iowa)

CLAYBROOK-MALONE BIBLE
Owner: James B. Cook, Jr. Chester, Virginia

MARRIAGES

Chastain Claybrook to Catharine Malone 10/31/1842
Marcus H. Walker to Lavinia A. Nash 2/27/1861
Henry C. Baylor to Lavinia A. Walker 12/14/1871

BIRTHS

William Kerr, half bro. of Chastain Claybrook, 12/28/1796, Amelia Co., Va.
Lucia Claybrook, aunt of Chastain, 1/4/1768
Herbert Lee Walker, son of Marcus H. and Lavinia A. Walker, 6/15/1863
Henry Vernon Baylor, son of H. C. and C. A. Baylor, 10/11/1872 Chastain Claybrook 4/1/1787, Amelia Co., Va.
Catharine Malone 5/17/1817 Brunswick Co., Va.
Mary C. Claybrook, inf. dau. of Chastain and Catharine, 5/24/1845-5/26/1845
Catharine Claybrook was sister of Amanda Malone Nash, grandmother of Iva Baylor Cook, Vernon Baylor and George David Baylor, also, Herbert Lee Walker, a son by a previous marriage. The above were children of Lavinia Nash Baylor.

EDWARD TAYLOR'S LEDGER Of Accomack Co., Virginia
Owner: Virginia State Library

BIRTHS

Edward Taylor 4/26/1741
Deidamia Taylor, wife of Edward Taylor and dau. of John Lilliston, 2/11/1750
Elizabeth Drummond, dau. of William Drummond, 2/25/1770

BIRTHS of Children of Edward and Deidamia Taylor

Thomas Teackle Taylor 10119/1775
William Taylor 9/18/1778-9/24/1778, aged 6 days
Sarah Taylor 12/26/1779

DEATHS

My honored father d. 4/21/1774, aged 67 yrs., 3 mos.
William Taylor 11/21/1767, aged 37 yrs., 7 mos., 25 days
Sarah Johnson 7/5/1760, aged 27 yrs., 11 mos, 17 days
Patience Baylor 3/7/1767, aged 24 yrs, 26 days
My honorable mother d. East Greenwich 11/20/1779 (Edward Baylor's mother, Patience Baylor)
Catharine Tillinghast 12/27/1780, aged 37 yrs. (dau. of Thomas Teackle Taylor of Newport)
Edvard Taylor m. 9/25/1774 to Deidamia, his wife.

WILLIAM R. FREEMAN BIBLE
Owner: Lucille Metzger 220 Mar Vista Dr., Aptos, Ca 95003

Howell Freeman 1760
Thomas Massie 12/26/1759
William R. Freeman 3/25/1786
Mary Massie 6/14/1789

BIRTHS of Children

Jordan L. Freeman 10/18/1808
Mary Ann Freeman 6/8/1822
Thomas M. Freeman 13/15/1810
Frances Freeman 6/6/1824

Elizabeth Freeman 11/20/1812
Pleasant M. Freeman 7/29/1826
John R. Freeman 7/10/1514
George W. Freeman 4/17/1828
Martha Ann Freeman 9/2/1816

Sylvanus Freeman 11/17/1829
William P. Freeman 4/7/1918
Cavil M. Freeman 4/12/1832
Howell Freeman 4/8/1820

DEATHS

Howell Freeman Sr. 5/4/1836
Francis Hazelrigg 6/30/1912
William R. Freeman 3/25/1872
George W. Freeman 10/3/1896
Mary Freeman 9/16/1868
Sylvanus Freeman 1/3/1900
Jordan L. Freeman 6/7/1882
Cavfl M. Freeman 10/4/1874

Elizabeth Rushing 5/4/1896
John R. Freeman 6/18/1833
Martha Ann Jones 1/19/1895
Thomas M. Freeman 8/20/1830
William P. Freeman 4/1/1907
Mary Ann Freeman 8/23/1832
Howell Freeman 8/22/1892
Pleasant M. Freeman 8/1850

MARRIAGES

William R. Freeman to Mary Massie 7/12/1807 Jordan L. Freeman to Sarah Shipman
Howell Freeman to Hanah Doty, 2nd wife, 3/4/1830
Elizabeth Freeman to Mark Rushing Martha Ann Freeman to Thomas Jones
Frances Freeman to John W. Hazelrigg Howell Freeman to Lucy J. Hazelrigg
William P. Freeman to Sarah Maston Sylvanus Freeman to Caroline Lippincott
George W. Freeman to Mary Black Cavil M. Freeman to Maggie Wilkerson

BIRTHS of Children

Jordan L. Freeman 5/31/1829
William P. Freeman 1/1/1843
Elizabeth Freeman 3/14/1830
Sylvanus Freeman 12/21/1851
Martha Ann Freeman 5/12/1833

George W. Freeman 3/19/1857
Frances Freeman 7/28/1842
Cavil M. Freeman 2/22/1858
Howell Freeman 7/28/1842

LEONARD RAY BIBLE

Leonard Ray b. 10/23/1780 m. 1/7/1803

BIRTHS of Children of Leonard Ray and Rebecca

John C. Ray 9/31/1804
George A. Ray 6/22/1814
Benjamin B. Ray 9/8/1806
Theney D. Ray 9/18/1824

Biddy Ray 2/25/1809
Washington N. Ray 4/29/1828
Nancy Ray 2/23/1811

BIRTHS of Children of John C. and Polly Ray

Amy Ray 4/17/1829 - -
Leonard Ray 12/12/1833

Magness L. Ray 7/2/1831
Martha Jane Ray 4/19/1836

Rebekah Stamps, dau. of Sanford and Nancy, 2/11/1834   John Winders, son of Elizabeth, 3/22/1829
Elizabeth Stamps 3/26/1836   Benjamin H. Ray 7/25/1839 Nancy Ray 2/4/1842
John H. Ray, son of B. B. Ray, 8/17/1837 James K. P. Ray 8/5/1844
Joseph L. Ray 12/4/18-Polly Ann Ray 6/27/184-
William Leonard Cooper, son of Nathan and Nancy, 2/1/1860

DEATHS

James P. K. Ray 4/15/1--George A. Ray 9/28/1838
Amy Ray, oldest dau. of John C. Ray and Polly, 8/11/1858
Leonard R. Ray, son of J. C. and Mary Ray, 2/1863

(Leonard Ray Bible, DEATHS, contd....)

James Polk Ray, son of -- X. Ray, 1/1861-1/9/1863
Sister Nancy Cox 3/29/1847
Leonard Ray ---
Mary A. Ray, dau. of -- R. Ray and S. J. Ray, b. 12/9/18-
Martha A. Ray, dau. of Leonard Ray and S. J. Ray b. 3/2/185-
Polly Ray, wife of J. C. Ray, 6/21/1873
Leonard Ray Sr. 9/10/1853
Polly Looper, wife of J. C. Ray, 4/21/1811-6/21/1873

BELL WOTEN BIBLE of Rockingham County

BIRTHS of Children of Bell and Jane Woten

Samuel Woten 12/21/1793
Anna Woten 11/17/1804
Elizabeth Woten 3/13/1795
Susannah Woten 10/14/1806
Sally Woten 8/22/1796
Ellender Woten 8/27/1809
Mary Woten 2/12/1799

John Woten 3/11/1811
Jane Woten 1/11/1801
Hugh Woten 11/23/1816
Senthe Woten 3/23/1813
Jonathan Woten 5/11/1815
Nathan Woten 1/8/1803

Note: Bell Woten purchased Bible in Gallipolis, Ohio. The last four children were born in Ohio. The first children born in Bath Co., Va.

ARNOLD-GILL BIBLE
Owner: Mrs. Nell Edmondson Baskerville, Virginia

MARRIAGES

Isaac Arnold to Ann H. Andrews 5/21/1795 (Mecklenburgh Co., Va.)

Joseph D.Arnold to Martha W. Harper 12/26/1820
Hartwell Arnold to Mary M. Harper 12/23/1830
Richard Harwell to Elvira A. Arnold 12/21/1831
Joseph D. Arnold to Mary Bennett (3rd wife) 11/9/1837
C. R. Edmondson to Ann E. drnold 12/18/1838
John Ellington to Catherine V. Arnold 3/3/1842

0. W. Thomas to Mary W. Arnold 9/4/1847
James L. Moss to V. F. Edmondson 12/31/1860
Sam F. Gill to E. W. Arnold 12/15/1853
C. A. Arnold to Mary Whitehead (Miss.) 5/8/1856
C. A. Arnold to Mrs. E. F. Pitchford (Ala.) 1/15/1873

BIRTHS of Children of Isaac (b. 1758 and Ann Arnold)

Joseph D. Arnold 3110/1798
Hartwell Arnold 5/19/1808
Isaac M. Arnold 5/18/1804
George A. Arnold 10/6/1799
Elvira A. Arnold 3/6/1810
Elisha Arnold 6/16/1801

Susan E Arnold 3/12/1812
John J. Arnold 1/31/1803
Silvanus J. Arnold 3/23/1815
Narcissus M. Arnold 1/29/1818
Charles G. Arnold 5/18/1806

BIRTHS of Children of Joseph and Martha W. Arnold

Ann E. E. Arnold 9/23/1821 -
Martha W. Arnold 475/1830
Catherine V. Arnold 10/3/1823
Charles A. Arnold 8/6/1832

Mary W. Arnold 3/1/1926
Emily W. Arnold 7/30/1834
Henry W. Arnold 3/27/1828
Richard H. Arnold 5/30/1837

BIRTHS of Children of C. R. and Ann E. E. Edmondson Angeline V. F. Edmondson 1/6/1840
Martha Edmondson 11/20/1841/2 Charles R. Edmondson 12/18/1845
Joseph H. Edmondson 10/27/1843 Martha V. E. Edmondson 8/18/1848

BIRTHS

Samuel F. Gill 11/2/1831
Emily W. Gill, nee Arnold, 7/30/1834, m. 12/15/1853

BIRTHS of Children of Samuel F. and Emily W. Gill

Rosella A. Gill 2/3/1855
Charles H.Gill 5/2/1865
Joseph P. Gill 8/18/1862
William F. Gill 4/1/1857
Samuel P. Gill 12/29/1867

Mary E. Gill 3/6/1873
Martha V. Bill 6/1859
Edwin Arnold Gill 6/22/1870
James R. Gill 1/24/1874

DEATHS

Isaac Arnold 7/7/1820
C. V. Nelson, nee Arnold, 1/27/1867
Silvanus J. Arnold 8/9/1828
Ann Arnold, his wife, 6/10/1822
Charles G. Arnold 4/26/1829
Elvira A. Harwell 9/7/1832

Martha W. Arnold 6/6/1837
Joseph D.Arnold 4/29/1835
Mary W. Thomas, nee Arnold, 12/1/1872
Martha W. Whitehead, nee Arnold, 9/18/1871
Ann E. E. Edmondson, nee Arnold, 12/22/1891

RODGERS-BARTON BIBLE
Owner: Frank E. Bradley, Jr.NewYork, New York

MARRIAGES

Samuel H. Rodgers to Nancy B. Davis 3/22/1831
Isaac C. Barton to Emma Rodgers 9/6/1855

Arthur L. Barton to America J. Rodgers 10/8/1850
Frank E. McClure to Addie Maud Barton 5/31/1900

BIRTHS

Samuel H. Rodgers 11/7/1809 Nancy B. Davis (now Rodgers) 11/8/1809

BIRTHS of Children of Samuel H. and Nancy B. Rodgers

America Jane Rodgers 7/25/1834
Martha Emily Rodgers 1/11/1839

Nancy Anjaline Rodgers 7/15/1836
Louisa Adalaide Rodgers 5/26/1841

BIRTHS of Children of Isaac C. and Emma Barton

Addie Maude Barton 5/13/1868 Earl Barton 1/9/1875
Byron Lemon Barton 2/25/1871 Pearl Barton 12/25/1878

DEATHS

Samuel H. Rodgers 9/3/1841
Byron Barton 1916
Isaac Barton 1903
Pearl Barton 1926

Ema Barton 1933
Maud Barton McClure 8/16/1950
Earl Barton 1888
Frank E. McClure, husband of Maud Barton, 1942

Letter in Bible "Circleville, Kan, 4/23/1888, To: I. C. Barton, Esq., Baldwin, KS My very dear sir. I have just read in the Ledger the Obituary of your little boy. Accept the honest sympathy of a true friend in the hour of your bereavement. May God sustain and bless you in the earnest prayer of your friend and brother . /s/ R. B. Taylor, M. D.,Circleville, Jackson Co.,Kan."
Newspaper Obituary in Bible: "Died on the 6th day of Aug. 1886, near Nevada, Mrs. Eliza Miller Mrs. Miller was born Jan. 24th, 1818 in Fayette Co., Penn. her maiden name was Eliza Barton...She was was the mother of four children, 2 boys and 2 girls, three of whom are now living. The first born died in infancy,...She raised 4 nephews of her brother, one of Allen Barton's who is now living in Dakota, near Rapids City, and three of Samuel C. Barton's children who lives in Osborne County, Kansas...She also raised two girls, the daughters of M. K. and Ella Ramsey...."

ROBERT PRIDDY BIBLE
Owner: Sydnor Y. Priddy Norfolk, Virginia

Robert Priddy 1/23/1789-10/5/1838
Nancy D. Frances, wife of Robert Priddy, 11/17/1800-2/17/1862
BIRTHS of Children of Robert and Nancy Priddy
John D. Priddy 11/6/1815-1/3/1887
Frances Ann Priddy 7/29/1817-3/1869 m. Richard Gray
Joseph S. Priddy 8/16/1819-2/9/1862
Elizabeth E. Priddy 10/9/1822-2/9/1862
Thomas G. Priddy 8/31/1823-8/12/1862
Robert W. Priddy 1/3/1828-12/6/1901
William K. Priddy 1/20/1831-
Martha R. B. Priddy 9/18/1833- , m. Henry Ellis 4/18/1864
John D. Priddy b. 11/6/1815 Mary K. Merryman b. 7/17/1823

BIRTHS of Children of John D. and Mary Priddy

Margaret Ann Priddy 12/27/1842
Cornelia F. Priddy 4/22/1851
Robert T. Priddy 10/21/1845
Lucy Alma Priddy 7/14/1856
Sarah Eliza Priddy 12/27/1849

Mary Helen Priddy 3/6/1858
John Gustevil Priddy 4/8/1854
Charles W. Priddy 10/6/1861

DEATHS

Sarah E. Priddy 1/1881
Mary W. Gilliam 12/3/1885
John D. Priddy 1/23/1887
Mary E. Priddy, wife of John D. Priddy, 2/6/1895
J. G. Priddy, son of John D. and Mary E. Priddy, 3/1892
M. A. Whitehead, dau. of John D. and Mary E. Priddy, 5/31/1903

MARRIAGES

John D. Priddy to Mary E. Merryman 10/31/1838
Margaret A. Priddy to John M. Whitehead 7/8/1863
Robert T. Priddy to Lavinia A. Watkins 10/27/1867
Lucy A. Priddy to Richard C. Bailey 11/13/1878
Mary M. Priddy to Richard M. Gilliam 11/13/1878
Charles W. Priddy to Myrtle G. Young 3/23/1887

WILLIAM HANKINS BIBLE
Owner: Mrs. L. S. Orrick, Ft. Worth, Tx.

BIRTHS

Elizabeth Hankins 5/10/1731
Sarah Hankins 9/11/1743
William Hankins Jr. 6/25/1733
Samuel Hankins 1/16/1745
Anne Hankins 8/3/1735
Robert Evilman Hankins 10/16/1747
Richard Hankins 12/18/1749
John Hankins -/9/1738
Sarah Hankins 1/9/1741
Mary Hankins 11/18/1752
William Hankins 6/3/1779

Margret Hankins 2/3/1794
Ann Hankins 1/16/1781
Sarah Hankins 11/15/1797
John Hankins 5/19/1784
Lorenda Hankins 10/26/1818
Mary Hankins 3/11/1786
William Hankins 1/14/1820
Elizabeth Hankins 5/19/1789
Clarinda Hankins 11/14/1823
Robert Hankins 1/20/1792

JOHN WESLEY BALL BIBLE
Owner: Mrs. Kenneth L. Moody Pittsburgh, Pa.

On flyleaf: Property of Wesley Ball, 1825.

Wesley Ball 10/4/1796-9/27/1875
Elizabeth Ball, wife of Wesley Ball, 1/28/1803-1/28/1872
Ann Liza Ball 11/30/1827-4/19/1893
Johnath Ball 8/25/1829-3/2/1874
Davis Henry Ball 10/24/1832
Abigail Ball 3/23/1835-
James Wesley Ball 9/22/1837-7/6/1863
Lucy Jane Ball 6/2/1840-5/27/1867
Jonathan Jones Ball 8/17/1843-

JOHN WESLEY BALL BIBLE
Owner: Mrs. Locie Hedges
Hurricane, West Virginia

Note: Another version.

Three Ball brothers.
John Wesley Ball m. Elizabeth Jones 12/2/1826.

Seven Children:

Anliza Henderson Ball 1827
James Wesley Ball 1837
John Maurice Ball 1829
Lucy Jane Ball 1840

Davis Henry Ball 1832
Jonathan Jones Ball 1843
Abigail Ball 1835

Isaac Munson Ball b. 10/3/1803 m. Sarah Hand in 1836.

Six Children:

William Pfinkney Ball 1833
John Henry Ball 1842
Naomi Ball 1836
Cad Welinder Ball 1845
Isaac Munson Ball m. 2nd Susan Frances Wallace

Francis Marion Ball 1839
Amanda Ball 1846

Nine Children:

Calvin Ball 1854
Isaac Ball 1865
Conwellsee Ball 1856
Sarah Isabel Ball 1868
George Wesley Ball 1858

Willie May Ball 1870
Emily Ball 1860
Mary Magdalene Ball 1872
Alice Ball 1863

Zachariah Ball m. Sarah Ball m. Mr. Gibson

Children:

John Ira Gibson
Dallas Gibson Calvin Gibson
Charles Gibson

Melvin Gibson
Walter Gibson James Gibson

THOMAS ALLEN BIBLE
Of Fauquier County
Owner: Mrs. Edith B. Keyser
Marshall, Virginia

MARRIAGES

Thomas Allen to Eliza Davis 3/19/1833

BIRTHS

Thomas Allen 11/25/1798
Mary Caroline Allen 1/1/1834
Eliza Davis 6/23/1808
Susan Frances Allen 12/8/1841
James Henderson Allen 8/13/1835
Lucy Davis Allen 12/1/1843
Thomas Catlett Allen 11/26/1836

Eliza Mildred Allen 6/26/1848
John Davis Allen 9/1/1838
Eleanor Henderson Allen 11/20/1850
George Tavvener Allen 6/8/1840
Edwin Forrest Allen 12/11/1845

DEATHS

James Henderson Allen 1/11/1836, aged 4 mos., 28 days
John Davis Allen 9/7/1842, aged 4 yrs., 7 days

ALEXANDER FRASER BIBLE
Of Dinwiddie County
Owner: Edwin Fraser
Brunswick, Virginia

Alexander Fraser m. Martha Reese 5/10/1803

Alexander Fraser 12/29/1777-1/6/1828
Martha Fraser, wife of Alexander Fraser, 11/4/1782-3/23/1861

BIRTHS of THEIR CHILDREN:

Betsy Fraser 5120/1804
Edwin Fraser 1/30/1806
Martha T. Fraser 1/30/1808
Frederick Fraser 1/10/1810-11/1/1846
Robert Fraser 11/6/1813-11/13/1841

Mary Ann Fraser 2/20/1817-6/6/1838
Caroline Fraser 3/20/1819-12/25/1868
John W. Fraser 11/13/1821
Harriet M. L. Fraser 8/24/1825-11/27/1828
George A. Whitmore 5/26/1838

MARRIAGES

Betsy Fraser to James Gresham 11/20/1820
Edwin Fraser to Polly Cheery 3/18/1831
Edwin Fraser to Mary Rieves 2/14/1844
Martha T. Fraser to Robert Rogers 3/13/1834

Frederick R. Fraser to Edna Rogers 6/18/1834
Robert B. Fraser to Martha Wainwright 12/12/1840
Mary A. Fraser to George Whitmore 2/18/1836
John W. Fraser to Lucy J. Tucker 6/14/1848
Caroline Fraser to William Thweatt 3/20/1847

HIRAM SEATON BIBLE
Of Loudoun and Fauquier Counties
Owner: Virginia Historical Society

On flyleaf: Margery Seaton, her Book 1807
Hiram Seaton m. Margery Hatcher 12/4/1806
William Seaton, son of Hiram and Margery, b. 3/20/1807
Margery Seaton, wife of Hiram Seaton, d. 2/21/1812
Hiram Seaton m. Nancy Powell 8/24/1815
James P. Seaton, son of Hiram and Nancy Seaton, b. 6/2/1815
George M. Seaton, son of Hiram and Nancy Seaton, b. 3/15/1818
John M. Seaton, son of Hiram and Nancy Seaton, b. 3/20/1820

WILLIAM LUCAS JACKSON BIBLE
Owner: Mrs. Arnold Staubach, Houston, Tx.

MARRIAGES

W. L. Jackson to Ann V. Bishop 9/28/1841
T. E. Jackson to C. W. Rankin 3/19/1874
O. P. Jackson to Jennie L. Moore 1880

BIRTHS

W. L. Jackson 9/28/1808
C. M. Jackson 4/2/1849
Ann V. Bishop 4/11/1820
W. L. Jackson Jr. 3/23/1851
Auguster M. Jackson 6/24/1842
P. O. Jackson 7/11/1854
T. L. Jackson 6/28/1844
Robert T. Jackson 11/3/1856
Green Jackson 11/30/1846
Zena Jackson 12/20/1874

DEATHS

W. L. Jackson 3/4/1858
Auguster M. Jackson 9/9/1844
Green Jackson 5/8/1858
Charles M. Jackson 3/9/1864
W. L. Jackson Jr. 3/9/1873
V. Jackson 3/26/1890
Robert T. Jackson 6/30/1890
O. P. Jackson 11/1934

SOUTHY LITTLETON SAVAGE BIBLE
Owner: Harriet Parker Hankins
Williamsburg, Virginia

Southy LIttleton Savage b. 3/24/1779
Harriet Reynolds b. 8/2/1784 m. at house of Thomas Lytt Savage in Northampton 4/25/1805 by Rev.Mr. Gardner
Nathaniel Littleton Savage 4/13/1806-1/8/1853 William Reynolds Savage b. 12/10/1808
Southy Littleton Savage d. New Kent Co. at place of his res. and birth 12/31/1811
Mary A. Susan Savage b. 1/6/1812 William Reynolds Savage d. 8/5/1853 Harriet Reynolds
Savage d. 8/27/1862

JOSEPH CURD BIBLE
Owner: Mrs. Andrew Brock Waddle
Somerset, Kentucky

Joseph Curd m. Mary 10/6/1772
Benjamin Curd, son of Joseph and Mary Curd, b. 12/24/1778
Pleasant Curd, son of Joseph and Mary Curd, b. 5/10/1781
Aaron Curd ----
Stephen Curd, son of Joseph and Mary Curd, b. 11/6/1786
Sarah Curd b. 3/6/1792
James Curd, son of Joseph and Mary Curd, b. 4/15/1795, being the 13tth Heir of my Little Land Estate.

PETER HAMMOND BIBLE
Owner: George A. Hammond
Smith Center, Kansas

BIRTHS

Peter Hammond 7/28/1791
Elizabeth Hammond 11/11/1802
Paul Hammond 7/12/1793
Samuel Hammond 5/18/1805
James Hammond 8/8/1795

Catherine Hammond 10/28/1807
Henry Hammond 3/28/1798
Jacob Hammond 1/10/1810
Mary Hammond 9/10/1800

DEATHS

Catherine Hammond 4/22/1828
Elizabeth Reasoner 2/22/1836
Henry Hammon d 11/20/1839

Daniel Hammond 4/28/1846
Henry Hammond 11/20/1839

BIRTHS

Peter Hammond, son of Daniel and Catherine Hammond, 7/28/1791
Christens Hammond, dau. of Henry and Rebecca S. Hammond, 7/15/1796

Elvira Hammond 1/13/1816
Daniel Louis Hammond 9/28/1823
Rebecca Hammond 10/13/1819
Samuel Sheplar Hammond 5/10/1827
Henry Oliver Hammond 10/30/1821
Wm Harrison Hammond 3/19/1833
Minerva Jane Hammond 9/1/1846
Eva Rose Ann Hammond 9/28/1862
Peter Horatio Hammond 10/16/1550

Lily May Hammond 6/22/1865
Hamilton Jefferson Hammond 8/11/1854
Mary E. Hammond 11/20/1867
Marie Angeline Hammond 10/19/1856
Samuel J. Hammond 5/7/1871
Elvira Adaline Hammond 3/30/1859
Sylvanus Hammond 8/19/1848
James Honnold 5/18/1785
Elizabeth Honnold 12/8/1785

BIRTHS of Children of James and Elizabeth Honnold

Samuel Honnold 12/t11808
Sarah Honnold 9712/1818
Martha Honnold 7/5/1810
Hamilton J. Honnold 3/1/1821
Richard Honnold 5/14/1812

Elizabeth C. Honnold 8/7/1823
Lucinda Honnold 5/4/1814
Rebecca M. Honnold 7/4/1826
James Honnold 9/18/1816
Julia Ann Honnold 3/6/1829

DEATHS

Christena Hammond 12/2/1851
Henry Oliver Hammond 9/16/1843
Peter Hammond 6/2/1851
Rebecca M. Hammond 2/3/1885

GEORGE HANKINS' BIBLE
Owner: Harriet Parker Hankins
Williamsburg, Virginia

MARRIAGES

George Hankins of James City Co. to Mary Ann Susan Savage of New Kent Co. 10/18/1836 at Windsor Forest by Rev. William H. Hart Robert B. Richardson to Harriet A. Hankins 3/11/1873 Southy S. Hankins to C. Texie Geddy 12/24/1873
Francis W. Hammond to Alice Browne Hankins 10/18/1876
George A. Hankins to Mary L. Savage 4/24/1877 William N. Hankins to Nannie James 12/26/1889

BIRTHS

George Hankins, only son of Archer and Alfce Hankins, 1/1/1800 Mary Ann Susan, only dau. of Southy and Harriet Savage, 1/6/1812

BIRTHS of Children of George and Mary Hankins

Alice Browne 9/21/1837 -
George Archer Hankins 1/7/1846
Harriet Ann Hankins 4/19/1839
Reynolds Hankins 7/3/1847
Southy Savage Hankins 2/27/1843
William Nathl Hankins 2/2/1854
William Edwin, son of William N. and Nannie V. Hankins, 11/9/1890

DEATHS

Reynolds Hankins 1/25/1872
George Hankins 4/10/1874
Alice Browne Hammond 12/2/1876
William N. Hankins 8/24/1892
Mary A. S. Hankins 8/11/1897, aged 86 yrs.
Catharine Texanna Hankins 5/4/1912, aged 67 yrs.
Southey Savage Hankins 8/27/1914, aged 71 yrs., 6 mos.
Robert B. Richardson, son of H. B. M. and Elizabeth T. Richardson, 11/17/1890
Harriet A. Richardson, wife of Dr. R. B., 2/19/1922, at house of her bro., Dr. G. A. Hankins in Williamsburg, Va., and bur. beside her husband at old home, Marlbrooke, James City Co., Va., aged 82 yrs., 10 mos.

GEORGE CLARK BIBLE
Of Williamsburg
Owner: William and Mary College
Williamsburg, Virginia

On flyleaf: "Presented to Barbara Wagner from her father, Philip Wagner...."

BIRTHS

Berbery Clark 10/25/1806
Archibald Clark 2/1830
George Clark 6/15/1793
Samuel Clark 1/1/1832

Sarah Clark 2/1/1825
Rebecca Clark 9/12/1835?
Mayry Clark 11/14/1828
Jane Clark 4/15/1836

EDWIN SHORT EDMUNDS' BIBLE
Owner: William and Mary College Williamsburg, Virginia

"Presented to William and Mary College by Sally Daingerfield 10/1936, granddaughter of Edwin Short Edmunds."

Thomas Edmunds d. 1791
Martha Short Edmunds 1/27/1763-4/1789
John Edmunds 1787-1830
Eliza Kennon Edmunds 1811-
Thomas W. R. Edmunds 8/20/1809-10/9/1833
Jack B. F. Edmunds 8/27/1814-6/27/1835
Martha E. M. Edmunds 3/27/1817-4/27/184-
Edwin S. Edmunds 4/30/1819-7/27/1891
Edward R. Edmunds 4/30/1819-10/22/1855
Georgia McAfee 11/7/1836-1911
Martha Eliza Nichol 2/23/1848-1857
Eliza H. Edmunds 1/4/1844-8/10/1932

MARRIAGES

Thomas Edmunds to Mary P. Green of Christian Co., Ky. 8/20/1811 by Rev. G. P. Giddings
Martha A. E. M. J. S. Edmunds to Rev. George G. McAfee 11/21/1835 by Rev. B. J. Wallace and to James Nichol 3/11/1847
Edward P. Edmunds to Eliza G. Henry 4/28/1841 by Rev. William D. Jones and to Anna Greathouse 1853
Edwin S. Edmunds to Sally McAfee 9/12/1843 by Rev. William D.Jones 9/12/1843
Children of E. S. E. and Sally McAfee:
America Edmunds 1/18/1845-12/21/1935
George M. Edmunds, no children, 5/7/1847-8/14/1929 Thomas M. Edmunds I.
1/23/1853-5/23/1911
Eliza Randolph Edmunds 8/16/1856-7/27/1857 Cornelia Edmunds 12/27/1859-10/6/1867
Grandchildren:
Marian Louise Daingerfield 2/16/1837-1/11/1875 Sally Daingerfield 9/21/1869-
Ealine Louise Edmunds 3/2/1882-
Marguerite Edmunds 12/11/1889- m. George Parker
Thomas McAfee Edmunds II 12/14/1891- m.Ethel Lauger Thomas McAfee Edmunds III 1926-

MARRIAGES

Christian Co., George McAfee to 9/8/1853 Dr. C. S. Ratcliffe of Ky. 11/7/1836-1911
Eliza H. Edmunds to 11/10/1867, W. E. Wallace of Crittenden Co.Ky. 1/4/1844-8/10/1932
America Edmunds to J. F. Daingerffeld, M. D. of Christian Co., Ky. 2/3/1869
Thomas M. Edmunds m. to Nettle Van Clear in Stockton, Ca. 4/14/1880
George M. Edmunds to Ida Craig in San Francisco, Ca. 11/22/1883
America Edmunds formerly m. to J. F. Daingerfield m. H. V. D. Nevius D.D. of Peoria, Ill. in San
Francisco by Dr. J. K. Smith 11/28/1888

JONATHAN DURRETT BIBLE of Spotsylvania County
Owner: Herman Baker, Woodford, Va.

BIRTHS

Jonathan Durrett 4/4/1771	Joseph Hart Baker 6/24/1879
Nancy Hedges 8/7/1797	Albert Durrett 7/19/1805
Polly H. Durrett, his wife, 6/28/1784	William Hines Durrett 2/27/1807

(Jonathan Durrett Bible, BIRTHS, contd....)

Oscar Fitzwallen Durrett 12/25/1808
Abigail Durrett 2/5/1816
Braxton Byrd Durrett 11/16/1819
Jonathan Jackson Durrett 6/24/1824
Mary Elizabeth Durrett 9/3/1829
Mary Ann Johnson Durrett 12/4/1828
Martha Ellen Durrett 10/6/1830
Judith Terrell Durrett 2/24/1833
Elliott Vermanet Durrett 9/24/1834
Mary Ann J. Carter 1/15/1836
William porter Carter 11/28/1837
Wallis Marion Carter 4/28/1838
Ellenorah Hassentine Carter 11/24/1840
Jonathan Melter Carter 3/13/1849
Kate Baker Durrett 10/16/1856
Cliveous Albert Baker 11/15/1856

Charles Lewis Durrett 4/14/1859
William Albert Durrett 3/20/1868
Judith T. Durrett 5/13/1870
Everett Vermanet Durrett 4/18/1872
Robert Henry Durrett 3/18/1874
Mary Virginia Durrett 11/10/1875
Ann Lewis Durrett 10/9/1877
Laurence Blanton Durrett 3/25/1880
Harvey John Thomas Durrett 10/18/1881
Ann Elizabeth Blanton 10/9/1878
Albert Riftin Baker 5/22/1881
Emmet Todd Blanton 6/11/1880
Richard Alfred Blanton 5/26/1882
Herman Cliveous Baker 3/28/1885
Andrew Ellis Baker 3/6/1888

MARRIAGES

Jonathan Durrett to Polly H. Lively 10/23/1804
Albert Durrett and Nancy Hedges 2/22/1827
William H. Durrert to Mary I. Dumkum 5/15/1832
Melter Carter to Abigail Durrett 10/16/1834
Braxton Byrd Durrett to Ann E. Williams 5/30/1844
Jonathan J. Durrett to Susan E. Jones 8/20/1848
Abner Hines to Mary Elizabeth Durrett 9/5/1855
Bushrod W. Baker to Judith T. Durrett 7/26/1855
Elliott V Durrett to Maria L. Hester 12/20/1855
Andrew Hart to Mary A. J. Durrett 1/16/1867
E. V. Durrett to Mary A. Blanton 5/16/1867
Jonathan J. Durrett to Margaret J. Tompkins 6/7/1866
Cliveous Albert Baker to Marie Lou Hart 12/19/1877

DEATHS

Oscar Fitzwallen Durrett 2/25/1816
Susan E. Durrett 9/16/1862
Abigail Carter 4/22/1851
Nancy Durrett -/17/1883
Polly H. Durrett 5/2/1851
Judith T. Baker 8/14/1857
Andrew Hart 10/21/1877
Maria L. Durrett 9/21/1861

Albert Durrett 9/26/1889
Jonathan Durrett 3/23/1855
Mary Ann Johnson Hart 8/12/1900
Mary E. Hines 4/26/1856
Martha E. Durrett 11/26/1916

THOMAS LEVERETT BIBLE
Owner: Benjamin Johnson

BIRTHS

Thomas Leverett 5/12/1755
Maria Leverett 5/-/1725
Marian Leverett 3/25/1772
Thomas Leverett 5/-/-
John Leverett 2/--
Gideon Leverett 7/1788
Ann Leverett 1/4/--

Myrtilla Leverett 3/
Jeremiah Leverett 12/22/1791
Alminda Leverett 1/-
Catharine Leverett 1792
Malitta Leverett
Abraham Leverett 3/18/1811

(Thomas Leverett Bible, contd....)

MARRIAGES

Ann Leverett 8/2/18-5
Mariah Leverett 3/15/1814
Jeremiah Leverett 7/--
Gideon Leverett 1/13/1819
Malitta Leverett 3/19/1817
Almmeda Leverett 1/1/1822
Jeremiah Carlis 12/7/1815
Mary E. Leverett 7/18/1832 8 miles southwest of LaGrange, Ga.
Abraham Leverett m. Emily H.Dozier 10/1834 8 miles west of LaGrange, Ga.

RICHARD STITH BIBLE
Owner: Jesse Stith, late of Breckenridge, Ky.

Richard Stith b. Brunswick Co., Va. 1727 m. Lucy Hall b. 1736

BIRTHS of THEIR CHILDREN:

Ann Stith 11/12/1757
Thomas Stith 10/8/1768
Joseph Stith 9/6/1759
John Stith 12/27/1770
Lucy Stith 3/12/1761
Katherine Stith 5/28/1773

Elizabeth Buckner Stith 10/25/1762
Martha Stith 5/8/1775
Mary Stith 11/12/1764
William Stith 10/8/1777
Benjamin Stith 8/25/1766
Richard Stith 12/9/1778

CODY-LIGHTFOOT BIBLE

John Cody of Maryland and his wife, Martha Womack
Edmun33d Cody of Virginia and his wife, Katherine Donaldson
Barnett Cody of Georgia and his wife Sinai, McCormick had McCormick, b. Warren Co., Ga. and m. Mr. Edwin Lightfoot in 1834. Children: James who m. Mrs. McAllister, Sarah m. Mr. Felix Reid, Thomas, killed in war for Southern Independence, William m. Miss Bertha Farmer, Caroline Donaldson m. Dr. R. L. Reeves at Auburn, Ala., 11/26/1868,---children Edwin Lightfoot, Frank Clyde, Margaret Caroline, John Richard.

BIRTHS

John A. Lightfoot 9/27/1780
Elizabeth Lightfoot, his wife, 2/26/1781
Elizabeth Liqhtfoot 11/6/1782
William Lightfoot 2/4/1805
Mary Lightfoot 3/20/1785
John W. Lightfoot 10/5/180
William C. Lightfoot 3/6/1790
Allen Lightfoot 11/13/1800
James T. Lightfoot 12/4/1792

Edwin Lightfoot 11/12/1810
Aseneth Lightfoot 11/12/1811
Catherine Lightfoot 7/30/1812
James Sharp 12/14/1792
Collin Lightfoot 9/11/1821
Thomas H. Lightfoot 9/26/1803
Anderson Lightfoot 8/31/1818
Peterson B. Lightfoot 10/23/1814

DEATHS

Catherine Jarrell 10/30/1847
Elizabeth Lightfoot 10/31/1844

John W. Lightfoot 7/10/1836
Thomas H. Lightfoot 10/8/1846
Peterson B. Lightfoot 6/20/1837

MARRIAGES

Thomas H. Lightfoot 1/1/1834
John W. Lightfoot 12/8/1835
W. T. Lightfoot 4/1/1834
Catherine Lightfoot 1/22/1829

Edwin B. Lightfoot 11/4/1833
Cullen A. Lightfoot 12/31/1850

JOHN LOWRY BIBLE
From: Williamsburg Chancery Court (lawsuit)

BIRTHS

William Lowry 9/25/1762
Robert Lowry 4/18/1772
Nancy Lowry 1/16/1765
Mary Hollier Lowry 2/13/1774
John Lowry 1/20/1767

Jane Lowry 1/27/1776
Thomas Lowry 2/8/1769
Edmond Lowry 8/21/1779
Francis Lowry 12/17/1770

"Elizabeth City September 16th 1794. Capt. Moses Robertson came before me, and maid Oath, that the above List was taken from the Family Register of John Lowry, deed, and that it was a true copy, given under my hand the above Year of date---William Moore."

GEORGE THORNTON BIBLE of Spotsylvania County
Owner: Historical Foundation of the
Presbyterian and Reformed Churches, Montreat, N. C.

George Thornton m. Mary Alexander 10/9/1773 in Stafford Co., St. Paul's Parish, by Rev.William Stewart

BIRTHS of Children of George and Mary Thornton

George Thornton 10/21/1774, baptised by Rev. James Marye in Fredericksburgh, Spotsylvania Co., St. George's Parish, d. 11/6/1776, 2 yrs., 16 days old
John Alexander Thornton 1/6/1776, baptised by Rev. James Marye in above church, d. 8/1st, aged 7 mos., 25 days
John Washington Thornton 3/28/1777, baptized by above Rev., d. 8/20th, aged 4 mos., 15 days old George Washington Thornton 12/31/1778, baptised by above Rev. Reuben Thornton
10/21/1780, baptized by Rev. Thomas Thornton. Lucy Frances Thornton 12/5/1781, baptised by Rev. Thomas Thornton; her godfathers were: Col. Ball, Col. Wallis, Francis Thornton, Jr., Abraham Maury,Phill.Thompson, Strawther Jones her godmothers:Mrs. Betsy Lewis, Mrs. Fanny Jones, Mrs. Fanny Ball.Melvina Thornton, Betsy Thornton and Mary Thornton, her mother.Mary Thornton remained a wid. 2 yrs, 8 mos., 22 days and then intermarried.
Thomas Posey and Mary Alexander Thornton m. 1/22/1784 in Spotsylvania Co., Parish of St. George by Rev. Mr. Stephens.

BIRTHS of THEIR CHILDREN:

Fayette Posey 10/24/1784
Thomas Posey 3/29/1791
Lloyd Posey 6/16/1786
Eliza Maria Posey 8/26/1792
Thornton Alexander Posey 2/21/1788

Alexander Posey 9/20/1794
William Churchill Posey 5/13/1789
Addison Posey 9/13/1796
Sarah Ann Thornton Taliaferro
Posey 8/20/1800

DEATHS

Addison Posey 8/1/1797
George Thornton 4/30/1781, aged 28 (38?) yrs.
Thornton Alexander Posey 9/17/1817, aged 29
Genl. Thomas Posey 3/18/1818, aged 68, at seat of his son-in-law, Genl. Joseph M. Street near Shawneetown, Illinois
Lloyd Posey 8/6/1820, aged 34
John Posey, son of Thomas Posey, by his first wife, b. 9/19/1774
Mrs. Mary Posey, the beloved consort of Genl. Thomas Posey, 5/18/1837, aged 81 yrs. at res. of her son-in-law, Capt. John Posey, Walnut Spring, Henderson Co., Ky. She survived her husband 19 yrs Sarah Ann T. T. Posey, mother of William P. Beverley.

SAMUEL STUART GRIFFIN BIBLE
Owner: William and Mary College
Williamsburg, Virginia

MARRIAGES

Samuel Stuart Griffin to Sarah Lewis of Gloucester Co., Va. 11/19/1808
Stephen D. Wright to Mary Louisa Griffin, dau. of Dr. S. S. and Mrs. S. S. Griffin, 11/23/1836 in Williamsburg, Va.
J. S. B. Griffin to Jane Hester Denning of St. Johns (Newfoundland), 6/30/1842
J. S. B. Griffin to Fannie Mary Denning of St. Johns, N. F., 3/15/1853
M. Dulaney Bell to Sallie Lewis, dau. of S. 0. and M. L. Wright, 10/17/1860

BIRTHS

S. S. Griffin 1/6/1782, Philadelphia, Pa.
Sarah Lewis, wife of S. S. G., 6/24/1787, Gloucester Town

Children of S. S. and S. Griffin Cyrus Anstruther Griffin 7/26/1810 at York Town

James Lewis Corbin Griffin, 3/.17/1814 at Lewisville, Gloucester Co., Va.
Mary Louisa Griffin 3/31/1817 at Lewisville, Va.
Thomas Stuart Griffin 5/16/1819-2/24/1822 at Lewisville, Va.
John Mercer Griffin 8/24/1822-9/3/1822 at Lewisville, Va.
Fayette Griffin 3/21/1824 at Williamsburg, Va.
Julia Amy Griffin 6/3/1828-6/20/1828 in Williamsburg, Va.
Mary Stuart Griffin 6/8/1830-6/20/1830 in Williamsburg, Va.
J. L. C. G., infant son, 6/20- 6/22, same year
Henry Stuart Griffin, infant son, 9/28/1856-9/2/1857 Sharon, Miss.

DEATHS

Samuel Stuart Griffin 12/19/1864 at Williamsburg, Va., 83 yrs. Sarah Lewis, consort of S. S. C. Griffin 11/12/1846 at Williamsburg, Va., aged 59 yrs.

Jane Hester Griffin, consort of J. L. C. G., 7/28/1848, Williamsburg, Va.
Cyrus Anstruther, son of S. S. and S. G. Griffin, 10/10/1834 in Williamsburg, Va.

Fayette, son of S. S. and S. G., 11/25/1850 near Williamsburg, bur. in Episcopal Churchyard of Williamsburg near his departed mother

Stephen Orren Wright, son of Stephen and Abby W. of Norfolk and husband of M. L. W., d. in that city 1/5/1853 and bur. in family cemetery of Norfolk near remains of his mother and mother. Lady Christina, mother of S. S. G., 10/8/1807, Williamsburg, Va. Cyrus Griffin, father of S. S. G., 12/10/1810 at York Town, Va. Sarah Tabb, mother of Sarah Griffin, 12/8/1821 at Gloucester Town, aged 68 yrs

John Griffin, bro. of S. S. G. and eldest child of Cyrus and C. S. G., 8/3/1849 in Philadelphia
Mrs. Louisa Mercer, relict of late Col. Hugh Mercer of Fredericksburg, Va., dau. of Cyrus and Lady Christina Griffin, 12/28/1859 at Savannah, Ga., at res. of her son, Hugh Mercer
Newspaper clipping from N. Y. Weekly Herald 10/4/-- : "Announcing death of Mrs. Mary Griffin, relict of the late Maj. Thomas Griffin of York Town, Virginia, and of the Revolutionary Army...."

SAMUEL WHITE BIBLE
Owner: George Smith Whitesburg, Tennessee

MARRIAGES

Sarah White, dau. of Samuel and Sarah, 5/28/1805
Joseph White, son of Samuel and Sarah, 1/9/1810
Martha White, dau. of Samuel and Sarah, 1/11/1810
Nancy White, dau. of Samuel, 4/1/1813
Richard White, son of Samuel

BIRTHS

Samuel White, father of said family, 4/1/1751 Sarah White, mother of said family, 3/15/1759

BIRTHS of Children of Samuel and Sarah White

Joseph White 10/7/1778
Richard White 5/17/1790
Samuel White 8/26/1780
Mary White 3/24/1792
Nancy White 4/6/1782
Elizabeth White 10/22/1795

Sarah White 1/28/1784
Hannah White 2/28/1797
Rebecca White 1/14/1787
George White 5/1/1799
Martha White 8/23/1788
Rebecca White 6/28/1801

DEATHS

Rebecca White, dau. of Samuel and Sarah, 10/11/1787
George White, son of Samuel and Sarah, 9/1800
Samuel White, father of said family, 9/23/1804
Samuel White, son o f Samuel and Sarah, 4/10/1854
Elizabeth Smith, dau. of Samuel and Sarah White, 2/8/1873
Mary Brown, dau. of Samuel and Sarah White, 1/5/1881, aged 88 yrs., 9 mos., 12 days
Martha Smith, 2nd Reynolds dau. to Samuel and Sarah White, 6/8/1848

ALEXANDER MACAULAY BIBLE
Owner: Elizabeth MaCaulay

Alexander MaCaulay m. Elizabeth Jerdone 12/5/1782

BIRTHS of THEIR CHILDREN: H

Helen Maxwell Macaulay 6/25/1784 Louisa Co., Va.
Alexander MaCaulay 2/20/1787 Yorktown, Va. d. South America in 1812/1813
Sarah MaCaulay 5/14/1789 Yorktown, Va.-d. 9/30th
John MaCaulay 10/11/1791 Yorktown, Va.-d. 1/20/1795
Francis MaCaulay 3/3/1793 Yorktown, Va.-d. 9/30/1811
Patrick MaCaulay 4/27/1795 Yorktown, Va.

PHILIP FITZHUGH BIBLE Of Caroline County

Died: Mrs. Mary Macon Fitzhugh 10/6/1836 Philip Fitzhugh 1790-12/28/1836

MARRIAGES

Philip Fitzhugh to Mary Macon Aylett 7/18/1813

BIRTHS of THEIR CHILDREN:

Elizabeth Henry Fitzhugh 5/12/1816
Patrick Henry Fitzhugh 12/2/1818 (killed 6/17/1864 at Petersburg, Va., in Civil War)
Lucy Redd Fitzhugh 10/8/1819

(Philip Fitzhugh Bible, BIRTHS, contd....)

John Fitzhugh 12/26/1821
philip Aylett Fitzhugh 6/14/1824 (d. 6/7/1908) Child unnamed 1/26/1826-2/18/1826
Lafayette Henry Fitzhugh 5/9/1829 (d. 8/1/1905) Edwin Fitzhugh 5/9/1830
Thadeus Fitzhugh 3/15/1855
Sons and daus. of John Fitzhugh of King Gee. Co., Va. and his wife, Lucy Fitzhugh (nee Reed) of Caroline Co., Va
Dennis, eldest son, m. a cousin, Miss Clark, moved to Louisville, Ky. Was afterwards Judge Samuel Temple, married his cousin, Miss Fitzhugh near Baltimore, Md., dau. of Col. Fitzhugh-- moved to Ky. Philip Fitzhugh remained in Va. and m. Mary Macon Aylett of King William Co., Va. Lucy m. Dr. Hall and lived in St. Louis, Mo.
Alexander - went to Pike Co., Mo., m. a Miss Carson.

(The above was written by my father, the late Dr. Philip Aylett Fitzhugh--6/14/1824-6/7/1908)

LEWIS KENNON BIBLE
Owner: Lewis Kennon

BIRTHS of Children of Lewis and Eliza Kennon

Charles Henry Kennon 3/8/1817
Lewis Willis Kennon 1/12/1829

BIRTHS of Children of Lewis and Rhoda Kennon

Elizabeth Rebecca Kennon 8/3/1830
Oswell Eve Kennon 9/30/1832
Robert Poe Kennon 1/19/1835
Mildred Susan Kennon 1/9/1839
Lewis Kennon, son of Charles Kennon and his wife, Mary, 6/14/1784 Halifax Co., Va.
Eliza Wyatt Winslow 5/6/1790 Orange Co., Va., m. Lewis Kennon 1/23/1816, d. 9/22/1824

MARRIAGES

Lewis Kennon to Eliza W. Jackson 1/23/1816 by Rev. J. McVean
Lewis Kennon to Rhoda Chadwick 1/10/1828 by Rev. Samuel Davis

DEATHS

Charles Henry, 1st son of Eliza W. and Lewis Kennon, 3/16/1817 Elizabeth Rebecca, dau. of Lewis and Rhoda Kennon, 7/17/1831 Oswald Eve, son of L. and R. Kennon, 7/17/1833
Mildred Susan Kennon 6/18/1869
Rhoda Kennon, wife of Lewis Kennon, 2/19/1847
Lewis Kennon 10/15/1847
Charles Kennon, in Wake Co., N. C., 4/21/1820
Howell Lewis in Granville Co., N. C., 11/20/1813
Nancy Millie in Wake Co., N. C., 10/24/1817
Lewis Wlllis Kennon in Grant Pass, Oregon 1/2/--

BIRTHS of my father's (Dr. Lewis Kennon) brothers and sisters

Elizabeth W. Kennon 9/20/1778	James Kennon 5/7/1806
Richard Kennon 3/28/1800	
Mildred L. Kennon 5/18/1781	Mary B. Kennon 4/3/1795
William Kennon 3/14/1802	Elisa Kennon 8/2/1808
Lewis Kennon 6/14/1784	Patsey Kennon 11/16/1796
Howell Kennon 3/14/1802	Erasmus Kennon 1/31/1810
Charles H. Kennon 8/3/1786	Lucy Kennon 5/26/1798
Rebecca Kennon 10/28/1804	Sally Kennon 11/20/1811
Nancy Kennon 12/16/1790	

LAINES JONES BIBLE

Memo taken of the ages (BIRTHS) of Mr. Laine Jones' children

Martha Jones 5/20/1728
Orlando Jones 4/19J1738

Anne Jones 9/24/1729
Frances Jones 1/26/1740 Laine Jones 9/15/1733
William Jones 11/7/1746

Lane, son of Orlando Jones and Martha, his wife, b. 6/15/1707 Francis, son of Orlando Jones and Martha, b. 8/6/1710
Martha, wife of Orlando Jones, Gent., d. 5/4/1716

SAMUEL FRANCIS BRIGHT BIBLE

Samuel Francis Bright m. Susan H. Bright 11/15/1827 in Gloucester Co., by Rev. Mr. Cairnes

BIRTHS of THEIR CHILDREN:

A son, 8/7/1828 in Elizabeth City Co., d. 11th of same mo. Susan Hannah Bright 3/8/1830 York Co.,Va. Susan H., wife of S. F. B., d. 3/20/1830, bur. at Porto Bello in York Co., Va.
Samuel F. Bright m. Elianna Maria Jerdone Southall, his 2nd wife, at res. of her uncle, Dr. Patrick Macaulay in Baltimore, Md. by Rev. Dr. Wyatt 11/19/1834.

BIRTHS of THEIR CHILDREN:

Francis Peyton Bright 11/25/1838Williamsburg, Va.-d. 9/28/1839
Robert Anderson Bright 3/23/1839 Williamsburg, Va
Elianna M. J., wife of S. F. B., d. Williamsburg 7/21/1839, bur. at Porto Bello, in York Co., and Francis Peyton, her son, d. 9/28/1839 in Williamsburg.
Samuel Francis Bright, son of Samuel and Jane Sinclair Jennings, b. on Back River in Elizabeth City Co., 1/5/1803

COLONEL THOMAS HALL BIBLE
Owner: Mrs. S. P. Ward
Bell Haven, Virginia

Printed in England 1725.

On flyleaf: "This Bible was imported from England by my greatgreat grandfather, Colonel Edmund Scarburgh. Signed, Anna Maria Smith."

BIRTHS of Children of Colonel Thomas Hall and his wife, Elizabeth Scarburgh

Margaret Hall 9/28/1735
Jane Hall 8/7/1743
Anna Maria Hall 11/30/1738
Elizabeth Hall 8/7/1743

WILLIAM MACON BIBLE

William Macon, a son of Gideon Macon and Martha, his wife, b. 11/11/1694 b. Mary Hartwell, dau. of William Hartwell and Ann, his wife, 6/18/1703 and m. William Macon 9/24/1719

BIRTHS of Children of William Macon and Mary Hartwell Macon

Ann Macon 10/21/1720-11/9/1736
Sarah Macon 2/21/1731
Martha Macon 8/12/1722-4/25/1863
Mary Macon 4/17/1735
William Macon 1/4/1725
Mary Macon 3/9/1723-1/29/1733
Mary Macon, mother of above, d. 11/19/1770
William Macon, father of above, d. 11/1/1773

Judy Macon 8/12/1737-2/1/1768
Hartwell Macon 6/30/1741
Henry Macon 9/1/1727-9/11/1785
Elizabeth Macon 2/15/1729
Anna Macon 7/31/1747

William Macon b. 1/4/1725 m. Lucy Scott 11/2/1753. She was b. 5/29/1737 and was dau. of John Scott and Elizabeth, his wife.

BIRTHS of THEIR CHILDREN:

William Hartwell Macon 3/2/1759
Thomas Macon 6/11/1765

Thomas Macon 9/11/1761-7/4/1762
Elizabeth Macon 5/21/1768 1/5/1802

William Hartwell Macon b. 3/2/1759 m. Hannah Seldon 12/22/1783. She was b. 2/7/1762-d. 9/19/1813 aged 51 years, 7 months, 11 days, she being the 2nd wife. His 1st wife was Sarah Ambler, to whom he was m. 3/25/1799.

BIRTHS of Children of William Hartwell Macon and Sarah

Mary Cary Macon 12/29/1779

Sarah Macon 6/30/1752-10/23/1782, called Sarah Ambler

BIRTHS of Children of William Hartwell Macon and Hannah Lucy

Scott Macon 11/2/1784
William Macon 12/5/1786
Miles Selden Macon 10/27/1788-5/5/1790
Rebecca Macon 8/26/1790-5/1/1809

Miles Macon 8/13/1791
Cary Selden Macon 5/23/1795
Thomas Macon 3/18/1797

Joseph Macon 12/22/1798-9/15/1807, called Joseph.
Ann Elizabeth Macon 1/15/1801
Sarah, 1st wife of William H. Macon, d. 10/23/1782
Lucy Macon, mother of William H. Macon, d. 12/1/1802

William Macon, father of William H. Macon, d. 11/24/1813
William H. Macon himself d. 8/24/1843, aged 85 yrs.

William H. Macon m. Sarah Dabney, wid. of Benjamin Dabney (who was Sarah Smith before Her marriage with Benjamin Dabney) 8/4/1814. She was b. 2/27/1775.

BIRTHS of THEIR CHILDREN:

Mary Smith Macon 7/18/185-
John Augustine Macon 6/22/1817-10/3/1817, aged 3 mos., 11 days
Elizabeth Macon, dau. of William and Lucy Macon, b. 5/21/1768 m. William Waller 11/30/1786.

BIRTHS of Children of Elizabeth Macon and William Waller

William Macon Waller 11/13/1789
Lucy Waller 12/10/1791

Dolly Ann Waller 7/1794-8/5/1797

William Waller d. 1/6/1799 and his wid., Elizabeth, m. George Nicholson 3/31/1800
Mary Cary Macon, dau. of William H. Macon and Sarah, his 1st wife, m. William Marshall, 12/10/1803. She d. 1/5/1812, aged 32 yrs, 7 days.
Lucy Scott Macon, dau. of William H. Macon, m. William Temple 8/28/1804

AMBROSE MADISON BIBLE

"The following Bible record of the Madisons was copied by Major Isaac Hite, of Belle Grove, Frederick County, Va., aid to General Muhlenburg at the siege of Yorktown, and was taken from his note book by Miss S. Jaquelin Davison for publication in this magazine:"

Ambrose Madison m. Frances Taylor 8/24/1721, d. 8/27/1732. His wife. d. 11/25/1761

James Madison Sr. b. 3/27/1723 m. Nelly Conway who was b. 1/9/1732 m. 9/11/1749

Elizabeth Madison 6/14/1725-1/6/1773
Frances Madison 3/6/1726, m. Tavener Beale and afterwards, Jacob Hire. Killed by the Indians 7/1776
James Madison, son of James and Nelly Madison, 3/5/1751-6/28/1836
Francis Madison, son of same, b. 6/18/1753
Ambrose Madison, son of same, 1/27/1755-10/1793
Catlett Madison 2/10/1758-3/18/1758

Nelly Conway Madison b. 2/14/1760 m. Isaac Hite, son of Isaac Hite, 2/2/1783
William Madison b. 5/5/1762 m. Fanny Throckmorton, d. 7/20/1843
Sarah Madison b. 8/17/1764 m.Thomas Macon
Elizabeth Madison 2/19/1768-6/1775
Reubin Madison 9/19/1771-5/17/1775
Frances Taylor Madison b. 10/4/1774 m. Dort Robert H. Rose, and she d. 10/1823

Col. James Madison Sr. d. 2/29/1801
His wife, Mrs. Nelly Madison, d. 2/11/1829, aged 78 yrs.

JAMES DYKE'S BIBLE

James Dyke d. 12/20/1853
Richard L. Dyke, son of James and Elizabeth Dyke, d. 6/21/1858 Elizabeth Dyke, wife of James Dyke, d. 10/14/1874
Peter Elliott Seward m. Dorothey E. Dyke 1/12/1854.

THEIR CHILDREN:

James Vernon Seward b. 11/7/1854 m. Alma P. Parrish 9/3/1894
Eldrid Benson Seward b. 9/7/1857 m. Brooke A. Broughton 2/10/1886
Henry Lewis Seward b. 9/1/1859
Elizabeth Eunice Seward b. 12/4/1861
Richard Hamilton Seward b. 4/13/1864
Clifton Elliott Seward b. 11/30/1866
Clara Brooke Seward b. 3/28/1869
Weston W. Seward b. 10/19/1871
Peter E. Seward d. 3/1/1893
Dorothey E. Seward d. 8/27/1915
Richard L. Dyke b. 4/19/1836

JAMES KERR BIBLE

Alexander Kerr Sr. b. 6/15/1726 in Scotland. His wife, Elizabeth Rice

BIRTHS

Elizabeth Kerr, 1st child, 9/1/1752
Mary Kerr 9/7/1761
Ann Kerr 10/16/1759
John Kerr 1/29/1754
Martha Kerr 8/30/1763
Sarah Kerr 10/12/1755
Frankey Kerr 10/14/1765
Susannah Kerr 8/12/1757
Lucy Kerr 5/2/1774
John Kerr, Sr., my father, 1/29/1754
Mary Kerr, my mother, 4/3/1756

Nancy Kerr, their 1st child, 12/18/1774
Alexander Kerr 8/9/1786
William Kerr, their 1st son, 12/1/1776
James Kerr 6/19/1788
Mary Kerr 10/12/1779
Isabella Kerr 6/12/1790
John Kerr Jr. 8/4/1782
Elizabeth Kerr 5/23/1793
Bazillac Kerr 8/21/1784
Solomon Kerr 3/20/1796

My Own Family:

James Kerr b. 8/19/1788
Frances Ann (McNeill) Kerr, my wife, b. 8/1/1803
Mary I. I. Kerr, our 1st dau., b. 10/1/1836
John and James, two twins, b. 11/12/1838, d. the same day Fanny L. Newell Kerr b. 8/16/1840
James Sadler? C. Kerr b. 5/2/1832
John H. McNeill Kerr b. 4/20/1844
Mary Isabella Mebane b. 6/16/1858 My Ist grandson b. 4/4/1861-8,

NOLAND-HARRISON-POWELL-GILMER BIBLE
Owner: Mrs. Rosalle M. Noland, Richmond, Va.

MARRIAGES

Burr Harrison to Ann Barnes 7/31/1722
Levin Powell to Sarah Harrison 2/6/1763
Burr Powell to Catherine Brooke 1/5/1792
Lloyd Noland to Ann Whiting Powell 1/5/1814
Lloyd Noland to Elizabeth W. Smith 1/22/1829
William B. Cochran to Catherine M. Powell Noland 11/5/1835
Burr P. Noland to Susan Chaplain Wilson 11/11/1845
R. W. N. Noland to Mary Louisa Minor 11/1/1843 by Rev. R. K. Mead R. W. N. Noland to Kate Y., dau. of John Spotswood Wellford 10/31/1861
Robert Gratton Noland to Ann Kerr

Preston Wellford Noland to Rosalie Sinclair Merrill 4/25/1905 by Rev. R. Grattan Noland and Rev.Jere Witherspoon

BIRTHS

Cloyd Noland, son of Thomas Noland (son of Philip) and Elinor Luckett, 12/4/1790
Bur Harrison 5/21/1690
Catherine Brooke 1737
Sarah Harrison 5/14/1768
Levin Powell 1739
Burr Powell 6/9/1770
Anne Whiting Powell 3/31/1793
Eliz. W. Smith 9/25/1801 Burr Powell, son of L. N. and A.W. P.,10/20/1818
Catherine Mary Powell, dau. of L. N. and A. W. P., 11/3/1814
R. W. N. 2/23/1822 Ann Whiting, dau. of L. N. and E. W. S., 3/12/1830
Sara Ella, dau. of L. N. and E. W. S., 4/6/1832
Anna Lloyd, dau. of L. N. and E. W. S., 4/25/1835

(Noland-Harrison-Powell-Gilmer Bible, BIRTHS, contd....)

Noble Barnedge, dau. of L. N. and E. W. S., 3/3/1838
Richard William Noland, son of Lloyd Noland and Ann Whiting Powell, 2/23/1822
Mary Louisa, dau. of Peter Minor and Lucy Gilmer, 7/8/1823
Lloyd, son of R. W. N. and M. L. Noland, 12/16/1844
Lucy 4/12/1846
Charles Minor 10/19/1847
Catherine 3/14/1850
Burr Powell 1/6/1853 Frank Minor 3/30/1855
Robert Grattan 1/8/1857
Preston Wellford, son of R. W. N. and Catherine Y. Noland, 2/16/1864, baptized by Rev.
Thomas
Walker Gilmer 10/27/1866
George Gilmer, son of George Gilmer and Mary Peachy Walker, 1/19/1743, m. Lucy Walker, dau. of Thomas Walker and Mildred Thornton (b. 5/16/1751) 8/27/1767.
Peter Minor 6/30/1783 m. Lucy Gilmer (b. 10/13/1785) 5/31/1806

BIRTHS of Children of Peter and Lucy Minor

Hugh Minor 7/31/1807
Peter Carr Minor 3/21/1816
Edward Minor 3/27/1809
Lucy Walker Minor 11/4/1818
Martha Divers Minor 11/30/1810

John Skinner Minor 10/3/1820
Franklin Minor 3/21/1812
May Louisa Minor 7/8/1823
George Gilmer Minor 12/4/1816

DEATHS

Ann Whiting Noland 1/21/1823
Thomas Lloyd Noland 7/4/1834
Ann Whiting Noland 3/31/1831
Anna Lloyd Noland 4/23/1838
Noble B. Noland 11/28/1858
Elizabeth W. L. Noland at Glenora, 10/28/1888
Lucy, dau. of R. W. N. Noland, 12/19/1846
Catherine 3/5/1851
Frank M. Noland 1/6/1873
Lloyd Noland 11/1875
Burr P. Noland 6/22/1902, New York City
Charles Minor Noland 9/28/1913 at Middleburg, Va. Robert Grattan Noland 4/7/1916 at Chillicothe, Ohio Mary Louisa Noland 9/20/1859, Middleburg, Va.
R. W. N. Noland 11/30/1886, Richmond, Va.
Kate Wellford Noland 2/17/1901, Richmond, Va.
A. M. Preston Wellford Noland 2/4/1919, Richmond, Va.

JOHN CAMM BIBLE Of King and Queen County

John Camm m. Mary Bullock 5/22/1722 by Rev. Mr. Lewis Lattany

BIRTHS of Children of John and Mary Camm

Ann Camm 1/5/1723, baptised by Rev. Mr. Goodwin; Humphrey Hill, Richard Bullock, Alice Bullock and Ann Arnold Gossips
Mary Camm 10/15/1725, baptised by Rev. Mr. Brunskill. John and Ann Madison, Christopher and Elizabeth Beverley Gossips.
Mary d. 8/22/1726
Mary Camm 10/16/1727, baptised by Rev. Mr. Hancock Dunbar. Richard Bagly, Thomas Hill, Sarah Powell, Catharine White Gossips Elizabeth Camm 2/12/1729, baptised by Rev. Mr. Dunbar.
Joseph and Ann Temple, Richard Gwathmey, Ann Aylett, Junior Gossips
John Camm 5/4/1731, baptised by Rev. Mr. Dunbar. Humphrey Hill, his wife, Joseph Temple
And Francis Orrill Gossips. John d. 30th of same mo.

(Noland-Harrison-Powell-Gilmer Bible, BIRTHS, contd....)

John Camm 5/30/1732, baptised by Rev. Mr. Dunbar. Joseph and Ann Temple, Benjamin Hubbard and Francis Hill Gossips. John d. 12/5th, aged 3 yrs., 6 mos., 6 days
Richard Camm 7/1/1736, baptised by Rev. Mr. Dunbar. John Gibson, John Walker, Alice Bullock and Mary Watkins Gossips. Richard d. aged 12 yrs., 1 mo., 21 days
Sarah Camm 2/28/1738, baptised by Rev. Mr. Dunbar. Holt Cluverius, James Taylor, Ann Camm and Sarah Gwathmey Gossips. Sarah m. Dr. John Walker and d. 10/13/1756, aged 18 yrs.
John Camm 1/17/1745, baptised by Rev. Mr. White. John Pendleton, William Temple, Philadelphia Gwathmey and Hannah Temple Gossips. John d. 7/30/1748, aged 2 yrs., 6 mos., 13 days
Mary Camm, wife of John Camm. d. 1/1/1753, aged 49 yrs., 1 mo., 17 days
Alice Bullock d. 8/22/1759, aged 76 yrs.
Robert Pollard d. 4/30/1819, aged 63 yrs.

BENNETT KIRBY BIBLE
Owner: Mrs. Samuel Tompkins Kirby, Dinwiddie Co., Va.

BIRTHS

Rebecca E. M. Vaughan 6/21/1807
Lucy M. Vaughan 6/2/1801
William Warwick 11/24/1816
Minerva W. Bonner 1802
Martha Bonner 3/31/1800
Samuel T. Kirby 6/3/1824
Mary Kirby 6/16/1826
William Kirby 2/4/1829

William R. Kirby 2/5/1832
John A. Kirby 2/9/1834
Martha E. F. Walker 10/29/1816
John Munford Walker Kirby 4/19/1836
Lucy W. Kirby 3/11/1838
Lula P. Kirby 1/9/1842
Eliza Ann Bonner 8/23/1813

Azuleka Rice, dau. of Robert Rice and Mary A. Shirley, 3/26/1837
Clay S. Rice 6/17/1819
Paul Rice
Lucy Kirby Rice 8/28/1842
Mary S. Rice
Robert R. Rice

Lucy McGruder Rice, dau. of S. T. Rice and Adelinoa Wyatt Rice

DEATHS

Bennett Kirby 11/17/1770
Wm Kirby, son of John, 9/20/1805
Martha Kirby 6/13/1779
Dorothy Kirby 11/7/1805
Thos Kirby 1/7/1794
Capt. John Kirby 9/9/1806
Bennett Kirby 1/17/1795

Mary D. Oliver 7/1809
William Kirby 4/28/1795
Charlotte Kirby 10/2/1798
Samuel T. Kirby 3/16/1803
Elizabeth C. Watts 4/1/1804
Bennett T. Kirby 9/3/1803
Minerva W. Bonner 7/21/1824

Frances Kirby, wife of Samuel T. Kirby, 9/23/1796
John B. Rice, 8/10/1822, aged 43 yrs., 7 mos., 27 days
James W. Rice 10/8/1814, aged 3 yrs., 8 mos., 7 days
William Rice 4/21/1827, aged 39 yrs., 2 mos., 14 days
Minerva W. Kirby 4/4/1827
Martha Kirby 4/6/1834
Mary Kirby 1826
William Kirby 1829
John Kirby 11/20/1837
John Kirby 6/1827
Eliza Ann Kirby 6/27/1837

(Bennett Kirby Bible, DEATHS, contd....)

John Munford Walker Kirby 6/13/1839, aged 3 yrs., 1 mo., 25 days Lucy Walker Kirby 6/21/1839, aged 15 mos., 10 days
Lucy T. Kirby Rice 7/9/1840, aged 67 yrs., 1 mo., 15 days Robert Richie Rice 12/23/1852
Mary J. Rice, wife of S. T. K. Rice, 6/12/1860
S. T. K. Rice 12/15/1870

COLLIER CHRISTIAN BIBLE
William & Mary Qtly, viii. p. 267

BIRTHS

New Kent Co., Va.
Collier Christian 12/25/1765
Nancy Bates, wife of Collier Christian, 2/14/1770

BIRTHS of Children of Collier and Nancy Christian

John Flemming Christian 2/4/17--
Caroline Matilda Christian 9/21/1793
Jordan Collier Christian 3/26/1795
Archibald Hunt Christian 12/19/1796
Sarah Ann Pleasants, wife of John Fleming Christian, 6/2/1798
Ann (Christian) Savage, 2nd wife of John Fleming Christian, 7/12/1792
Samuel Pleasants Christian, son of John Fleming and Sarah Ann Christian, 1/25/1821
Amelia Coleman Gordon, wife of Samuel P. Christian, 6/18/1829

BIRTHS of Children of S. P. and A. C. Christian

Sally. Ann Pleasants Christian 1/14/1851
John Fleming Christian 9/3/1858
Churchill Gordon Christian 3/12/1860
Julia Devereaux Christian 11/9/1861
Mary Blair Christian 12/14/1872

Alice Clifford Christian 11/18/1863
Arthur Christian 2/7/1865
Caroline Fitzhugh Christian 6/18/1869

MARRIAGES

Collier Christian to Nancy Bates 4/28/1790
John Fleming Christian to Sarah Ann Pleasants 10/21/1819
John Fleming Christian to Ann Savage 12/20/1827
Samuel Pleasants Christtan to Amelia Coleman Gordon 12/22/1847
Frank Rennie to Julia Devereaux Christian 6/18/1884
Samuel Pleasants Christian Jr. to Cornelia Lomax May 6/20/1901

DEATHS

Dr. Collier Christian 7/12/1814
Nancy, wife of Collier Christian, 3/9/1855
Sarah Ann, wife of John Fleming Christian, 11/6/1822
Alice Clifford Christian 11/1862
Arthur Newton Christian 6/26/1865
Mary Blair Christian 12/19/1873
Caroline Fitzhugh Christian 7/27/1890
Samuel Pleasants Christian 3/29/1909, aged 89 yrs.
Amelia Coleman Gordon, wife of Dr. S. P. Christian 6/14/1909, aged 80 yrs.
Sally A. P. Christian 11/7/1914
John Fleming Christian 3/2/1920 in Leith, Scotland

BENJAMIN W. CLUVERIUS BIBLE

MARRIAGES

Benjamin W. Cluverius to Dorothy Cluverius 11/16/1815
James Hill Lipscomb to Maria S. Cluverius, dau. of Joseph and Ann, 2/3/1820
Overton Seawell to Elizabeth Seawell 3/27/1815
Benjamin W. Cluverius to Mary E. Tyler, dau. of Dr. Watt H. Tyler of Hanover, 7/30/1835
William Vaughan to Ann F. Cluverius, dau. of Benjamin W. and Dorothy G. Cluverius, 2/25/1834
Harriet Elizabeth Cluverius, dau. of Benjamin and Dorothy Cluverius, 4/16/1835, to Francis Thornton
John T. Dobson to Sarah G. Cluverius, dau. of Benjamin and Dorothy Cluverius, 3/15/1849

BIRTHS of Children of Joseph and Ann Cluverius
Elizabeth Gibson Cluverius 12/13/1788, baptised by Rev. W. Elliott

Oranta Gibson Cluverius 3/2/1791, baptised by Rev. James Price Benjamin William Cluverius 6/23/1795, baptised by Rev. W. MacNorton
James Washington Adams Jefferson Cluverius 3/28/1801, baptised by Rev. W. Smith
Dorothy G. Cluverius 5/20/1797, dau. of Ann Cluverius

James W. Cluverius 4/5/1824, son of Benjamin W. and Dorothy Maria Sterling Cluverius, dau. of Joseph and Ann, 7/3/1803, baptised by Rev. H. Smith

Ann Frances Cluverius, dau. of Benjamin W. and Dorothy, 10/4/1815, baptised by Rev. Peter Billups

Harriet Elizabeth Cluverius, dau. of Benjamin and Dorothy G., 3/15/1819
Watt H. Cluverius, son of Benjamin W. and Mary Cluverius, 6/8/1836
Mary Jane Cluverius, dau. of Benjamin and Dorothy, 9/1/1820
Sarah Cluverius, dau. of Benjamin and Dorothy, 3/8/1827
Benjamin W. Cluverius, son of Benjamin and Dorothy, 2/1/1821
Joseph Cluverius, son of Benjamin and Dorothy, 10/10/1832

DEATHS

Cluverius, wife of Joseph, 9/22/1812
Joseph Cluverius 9/30/1820
Dorothy G. Cluverius, wife of Benjamin W. Cluverius, 9/23/1833 Benjamin W. Cluverius, son of Benjamin and Dorothy, 10/2/1849, aged 20 years, 7 months.
Joseph A. Cluverius, son of Dorothy and Benjamin W. Cluverius, 7/17/1851, aged 19 yrs.
James A. W. J. Cluverius, son of Ann Cluverius, 12/18/1804, aged 3 years.
Benjamin W. Cluverius, son of james and Ann Cluverius, 4/8/1836, aged 40 yrs.

JOSEPH CUSICK BIBLE
Owner: Macklin Bandy, Columbia, Mo.

Joseph Cusick 2/19/1772-10/15/1854
Jean Blackburn, his wife, 9/28/1771-9/1/1838

JOHN AND TIRZAH LONDON BIBLE

John London m. Tirzah Higginbotham 12/31/1809

BIRTHS

Frances Ann London 11/1/1810-11/3/1810
Frances Jane London 9/23/1811-4/26/1862
John James London 2/11/1813-10/10/1856
William Augustus London 5/15/1814-2/10/1815 Eliza
Ann London 10/31/1815-2/24/1887
Daniel Higginbotham London 2/17/1818-12/7/1875
Mary Banks London 2/18/1820-11/17/1892
William Augustus London 6/18/1821-8/2/1888

Thomas Higginbotham b. 6/10/1769 in Co. of Amherst near New Glasgow, d. 2/4/1835 at his res. in sd co. (son of Capt. John Higginbotham (1726-1814) and Rachel Banks)
Terzah Higginbotham b. Co. of Amherst near New Glasgow 2/17/1783 and m. John London 12/31/1809, and d. 8/1/1841 at her res. in sd co. (dau. of Capt. John Higginbotham (1726-1814) and Rachel Banks) John London b. Co. of Amherst 6/11/1774, m. Terzah Higginbotham 12/31/1809,d.3/21/1823, aged 48 yrs., 9 mos., 12 days

JOHN MINGE BIBLE

John Minge m. Sarah 6/6/1795, Richmond, Va.

BIRTHS of THEIR CHILDREN:

John Minge, M. D., 9/10/1796
James Minge 5/7/1807
William Henry Minge 12/3/1797
Anna Mercer Minge 1/19/1809
Collier Harrison Minge 11/17/1799
David Minge 12/16/1811
Benjamin Carter Minge 8/20/1801
Christians Minge 2/1/1803
Elizabeth Harrison Minge 4/7/1804
George Wm Hunt Minge, twin, 11/10/1805
Anna Mercer Minge, twin, 11/10/1805

Sarah Minge, wife of John, d. 2/27/1812, aged 42 yrs.
John Minge, M. D., son of John and Sarah, m. Mary Griffin Adams in Richmond, Va. 3/9/1820.

BIRTHS of Children of John Minge, M. D. and Mary

John Minge 2/11/1822
William Henry Minge 8/2/1827
Margaret Adams Minge 8/20/1824
Mary Griffin Minge 9/6/1832
Sally Harrison Steward Minge 8/9/1829
John. above, d. 3/10/1858, bur. St. Michaels near Faunsdale, Ala.
Margaret Adams Minge m. Richard A. Wilkins of Brunswick Co., Va. 1/8/1847
William Henry Minge d. Oct. following his birth
Sally Harrison Steward m. Capt. George E. Pickett of U. S. Army 1/28/1851 at res. of Col. R. A. Wilkins, Franklin, La. and d. at Ft. Gates, Tx. (US Army post)

GEORGE B. PAYNE BIBLE
Owner: George Booker Payne Micanopy, Florida

MARRIAGES

George B. Payne to Catherine G. Penn 10/9/1839 by Rev. Nelson Sale Marion L., son of same, to Jane Dupuis 12/--, Salts Spring, Fla. Sallie Penn, dau. of same, to J. C. Rembert in Savannah, Ca. 10/28/1870 by Rev. King
Rosalie, dau. of same, in Savannah, Ga. to D. Elwood McCuen 6/8/1881 by Rev. C. H. Strong
Newspaper Clippings:
"Married in this city, June 8, 1881, at the residence of J. B. G. O'Neill by the Rev. C. H. Strong, Mr D. E. McCuen, of Florida, to Miss Rosa L. Payne, daughter of the late Dr. George B. Payne of Florida"
"In Fernandina, November 16, 1881, at the residence of the bride's parents, by Rev. O. P. Thackara T. G. Pratt Thompson and Miss Jennetta M., daughter of Dr. A. C. Ford."

BIRTHS

George B. Payne, son of George M. and Susan M., 9/24/1816 Catherine G. Penn, dau. of Edmond and Jane, 6/19/1819
Ella Susan, dau. of G. B. and Catherine Payne, 10/13/1840
Ida, dau. of same, 9/6/1843
Rosalie Payne, dau. of same, 7/8/1850
Sallie Penn, dau. of same, 7/4/1852
Virginia Morton, dau. of same 9/17/1855
George Elwood McCuen, son of D. E. and Rosalie McCuen, 7/23/1882, in Savannah, Ga.
Edwin Burke G., son of D. E. and Rosalie McGuen, 11/22/1889 in Savannah, Ga.

DEATHS

Ella Susan Payne 11/9/1846, aged 6 yrs., 27 days
Catherine G. Payne, wife of George B. Payne, 7/6/1859 in Micanoph, Fla.
George B. Payne 11/22/1859 Micanopy, Fla.
Virginia Morton Payne 11/19/1800 Savannah, Ga.
D. E. McCuen 1/20/1893 at Savannah, Ga.
Newspaper Clipping: (Richmond Enquirer 4/24/1821) "Died in Buckingham, on the morning of the 14th inst. in the 24th year of her age, Mrs. Susan M. Payne, consort of George M. Payne, Esq..."

JAMES GARDAM SEAY BIBLE
Owner: James G. Seay, Atlanta, Georgia

BIRTHS

Samuel Seay 4/12/1760
Polly Seay, formerly Polly Grundy, 8/22/1778-11/21/1857, aged 79 yrs., 2 mos., 30 days
Elizabeth G. Seay 10/29/1797
Elizabeth M. Seay 7/14/1822
James G. Seay 3/22/1799
Charles T. Seay 12/18/1827
Moses A.Seay 12/5/1800
George W. Seay 10/24/1830
George G. H. Seay 5/14/1811
Malvina G. Seay 6/29/1832
John G. Seay 9/21/1815
Anna S. Parrott 4/21/1799
Amanda A. Seay 3/9/1835
John R.Seay 4/22/1837
Marion Wright 3/11/1808
Ann V. Seay 11/3/1845
Felix G. Seay 4/12/1848

(James Gardan Seay Bible, BIRTHS, contd....)

James T. Tittsworth 6/7/1842 Mary A. Tittsworth 2/12/1845
George F. Tittsworth 7/28/1849
Joseph I. Seay 2/14/1852
William Seay Alexander 2/5/1856
Richard Allin Lauderdale Alexander 7/14/1857
James Sardem Seay 1/26/1886
Salascha Annie Seay 3/19/1887
Emma Duke Seay, wife of James Gardem Seay, 12/29/1886
John Richard Seay, son of James Gardem Seay, 10/ 8/1921
Lou Ella Seay, wife of John R. Seay, 7/23/1920
Michael J. Seay 2/28/1947
Patrick Thomas Seay 1/5/1952
Carole Ann Seay 9/22/1954

MARRIAGES

Samuel Seay to Polly Seay, formerly Polly Grundy, 10/11/1796
James G. Seay to Anna S. Parrott 10/16/1821
James G. Seay to Marion Wright 3/19/1844
James G. Seay to Mrs. Melinda B. Bone 11/5/1862
John R. Seay to Selascha A. Kimball 2/24/1885
Ferrell Tittsworth to Elizabeth M. Seay 3/24/1841
Samuel R. Seay to Martha Hughes 12/10/1850
Dr. Charles Thomas Seay to Emily M. Lockridge 3/31/1852
R. B. Alexander to Elizabeth H. Seay Tittsworth 4/17/1855
S. B. Erwin to Annie V. Seay 1/31/1856
Felix Grundy Seay to Pattie R. May 1/8/1883
James Gardem Seay to Emma Duke 5/23/1913
Joseph A. Grubbs to Annie S. Seay 11/8/1922
John Richard Seay to Ella Thomas 1/26/1946

DEATHS

Melvina G. Seay 10/27/1834
Anna S. Seay 8/12/1843
Brother John G. Seay 9/19/1843
James T. Tittsworth 4/27/1847
Marion Seay 11/.1/1856
George Green H. Seay 7/8/1857
Mother Polly Seay 11/21/1857
Brother Morrison 8/30/1858
R. B. Alexander 6/8/1868
Charles Shelton Parrott 9/18/1874
George W. Seay 11/17/1878
Anna V. Erwin 3/6/1879
Elizabeth Parrott 2/20/1880, wife of C. S. Parrott
Melinda B. Seay 6/11/1880
Amanda A. Earle 7/29/1881
James Gardam Seay 11/30/1881, aged 82 yrs., 8 mos., 8 days
Elizabeth G. (Seay) Morrison 11/15/1884
Samuel R. Seay 6/25/1909, aged 81 yrs., 6 mos., 15 days
Dr. Charles T. Seay 11/7/1907, aged 82 yrs., 10 mos., 19 days
Dr. Felix Grundy Seay 6/26/1310
John R. Seay 1/19/1916

E. A. WILLIAMS BIBLE
Of Charlotte and Mecklenburg Counties

MARRIAGES

Edwin A. Williams to Elizabeth Ann Hamlet 5/10/1827
Edwin A. Williams to Lucy Page Kennon 3/4/1841
Charles E. Williams to Rosalie Overbey 9/30/1858
Robert C. Overbey to Anna Nelson Williams 8/20/1862
Henry S. Williams to Sue Dabney Withers 12/21/1865 Carter N. Williams to Rosa B. Hawkins 12/16/1874
Edwin A. Williams Jr. to Sallie J. Hamilton 3/5/1873
E. K. Willlams to Lela Ingram 4/27/1882
J. W. Cannon to L. Kennon Overbey 11/8/1888
William Spotswood Boyd to Alice Camille Overbey 6/22/1918

BIRTHS

Edwin A. Williams 4/14/1806 Elizabeth A. Hamlet --Lucy Page Kennon 10/3/1817

BIRTHS of Children of Edwin and Elizabeth Williams

Charles Edwin Williams 4/28/1828
William James Willtams 3/6/1830 Henry Sinclair Williams 6/2/1832
John Carter Williams 7/13/1834
Roger Andrew Williams 11/11/1837

BIRTHS of Edwin and Lucy Page Williams

Anna Roberta Williams 1/3/1842
Edwin Anderson Williams 5/6/1843
Roger Williams 10/14/1844
Carter Nelson Williams 12/14/1845
Erasmus Kennon Williams 12/31/1847
Thomas Williams 11/14/1849
Alice Rosely Kennon Williams 8/4/1852
Children or R. C. and Anna N. Overbey
Robert Camilrus Overbey 11/3/1863
Lucy Kennon Overbey 11/28/1864
Edwin Williams Overbey 11/1/1870
Mary Alice Overbey 10/23/1874
Anna Nelson Overbey 10/9/1881

DEATHS

William James Williams 3/6/1833
John Carter Williams 7/5/1837
Mrs. Elizabeth A. Williams 2/3/1838
Roger Andrew Williams 12/8/1838
Roger Williams 7/17/1845
Alice Kennon Williams 1/1/1874
Edwin A. Williams Jr. 10/10/1880
Edwin A. Williams 10/28/1879
Kennon Overbey Cannon 8/12/1957 Montgomery, Ala.

Newspaper Clipping: "Mrs. Kennon Page Overbey Cannon, widow of John W. Cannon, died at her residence on South Ferry Street this morning. Mrs. Cannon was born in Clarksville, Va., Nov. 28, 1864, the daughter of Robert C. and Anna Nelson Williams Overbey. She is survived by one son, John F. Cannon, of Montgomery; four grandchildren; and 11 great-grandchildren...."

JAMES McCARTY BIBLE
Owner: Mrs. Sharlie Cope Hill
Hawkins Co., Tennessee

BIRTHS of Children of Sarah and James McCarty

Anne McCarty 5l2311799
Mary McCar ty 1/8/1801

BIRTHS of Children of Elizabeth and Thomas Hamblen

Louisa Sidney Hamblen 9/25/1808
William Matterson Hamblen 9/23/1810
A. P. McCarty b. 7/16/1808
June 23, 1833, A. P. McCarty (signature)

BIRTHS of Children of James McCarty

William McCarty 4/1/1764
Hannah McCarty 10/5/1769
Isaac McCarty 3/2/1766
James McCarty Jr. 7/3/1773

----h McCarty 10/29/1767
John McCarty 9/27/1775
William McCarty, his Book, 1/7/1808

BIRTHS of Children of Robert and Polly Gamble

William Porter Gamble 9/3/1814
Written July 7th day 1829 ?

A. P. McCarty b. 7/16/1808

W. B. Kyle ----

L. J. Thomas McCarty b. 4/7/1853
Thomas Jefferson McCarty b. 4/7/1818
Thomas Hamblen m. dau. of William McCarty, Rachel, 12/10/1807
Thomas Hamblen b. 11/20/1788
Elizabeth Hamblen b. 10/3/1790

BIRTHS of Children of Darby and Hannah McCarty

James McCarty 7/4l1776
Hannah McCarty 12/9/1750
Mary McCarty 12/10/1738
Enoch McCarty 4/29/1753
Isaac McCarty 4/18/1741
Jonathan McCarty 4/29/1756

Sarah McCarty 7/3/1743
Lydia McCarty 4/30/1756?
Rachel McCarty 10/28/1745
Benjamin McCarty 12/22/1759
Elizabeth McCarty 6/18/1748

WILLIAM McCARTY BIBLE
Owner: Miss Daisy Poates Rogersville, Tennessee

BIRTHS of Children of William and Rachel McCarty

Elizabeth McCarty 10/3/1790-
Andrew R. McCarty 9/28/1804
Mary McCarty 6/18/1792
Sarah McCarty 8/10/1806
Leah McCarty 11/29/1793
Absalom P. McCarty 7/16/1808
Robert K. McCarty 10/23/1795

Rachel B. McCarty 4/15/1810
Martha McCarty 7/16/1797
John C. McCarty 12/25/1813
James P. McCarty 1/27/1799
Thomas J. McCarty 4/7/1818
William L. McCarty 2/20/1802

Rachel McCarty, wife of William McCarty, Sr., d. 6/24/1818
William McCarty Sr. d. 12/22/1818

HARRISON-GOOSLEY-McCAW BIBLE
Owner: James B. McCaw
Richmond, Virginia

A armory of the birth and marriage of Benjamin Harrison of Wakefield, in Surrey County

8/23/1739 he m. Susannah, dau. of Honorable Cole. Digges, Esg., by whom he had the following children

(BIRTHS):

Elizabeth Harrison 11/26/1740, baptised by Rev. Mr. Richard Heuit She d. 9/8/1748, aged 8 yrs.
Mary Harrison 10/22/1742, baptised by Rev. John Smith. She d. 9/2/1747, aged 5 yrs.
Nathaniel Harrison 8/24/1744, baptised by Rev. Mr. John Cemm
Susanna Harrison 11/23/1745, baptised by Rev. Mr. William Fife
Benjamin Harriaon 8/23/1747, beptised by Rev. Mr. Henry Eilbeck
Hannah Harrison 9/1/1749, baptised by Rev. Mr. Henry Eilbeck
Eliza Digges Harrison 8/24/1751, baptised by Rev. Mr. Eilbeck; She d. 11/8/1751, aged 2 mos., 15 days
Peter Cole Harriaon 2/11/1753, baptised by Rev. Mr. Richard Hopkins
Ludwell Harrison 12/31/1754, baptised by Rev. Mr. Alexander Finney
Benjamin Harrison d. 6/11/1757, aged 10 yrs. on 9/3rd ensuing

William Goosley m. Ludwell, dau. of Benjamin Harrison of Uakefield 1/16/1773 and had following children

(BIRTHS):

Martha Goolsley 11/11/1773, baptised by Rev. Mr. Andrews; d. 6/16/1774
Elizabeth Goolsley 5/14/1776, baptised by Rev. Mr. White of King William Co.
Anna Goolsley 8/23/1778-6/20/1779, baptised by Rev. Mr. Robert Andrews
George Goolsley 5/5/1780, baptised by Rev. Mr. Andrews

Lucy Goolsley 3/30/1782, baptised by Rev. Mr. Carter of King and Queen Co.
Frances Goolsley 12/29/1783, baptised by Rev. Mr. Andrews
William Goolsley 4/2/1786, baptised by Rev. Mr. Sam Shield
Benjamin Goolsby 1/23/1788, baptised by Rev. Mr. John Bracken; d. 2/25/1789

Sarah Carey Goolsley 2/5/1790, baptised by Rev. Mr. Shield.
Samuel Beall Coolsley 1/2/1792, baptised by Rev. Mr. Shield.
Anne Harrison Goolsley 9/15/1794, baptised by Rev. Mr. Henderson

Carey Goolsley 9/21/1797, baptised by Rev. Mr. Mendecson, d. March following.
Susan Goolsley 8/29/1799, baptised by Rev. Mr. Bracken
8/22nd, my Dr. son, George Goolsley. was lost on his way to Charleston, 1806.
12/31/1809, died, my beloved husband, William Goosley, of York Co.

"Richmond Va., 1/1/1870.

Presented to James Brown McCaw, M. D., oldest son of Anne Ludwell Brown. who married Dr. William R. HcCaw, oldest grandson of Francis Goolsley. wife of James Brown, Jr., great-grandson of Ludwell Harrison, wife of William Goolsley, Esq. of York, great-great-grandson of Benjamin Harrison, Esq. of Wakefield, by his great aunt, Susan Campbell, surviving child of Ludwell Harrison."

GREEN JACKSON BIBLE
Owner: Columbus Haile, Staunton, Va

MARRIAGES

Green Jackson to Rebecca R. Lucas 9/8/1807
Green Jackson to Temperance Jackson 1/12/1813, 2nd marriage
Ephraim Jackson to Mary C. Dyer 2/25/1835
Ira N. Green to Rebecca A. Jackson 10/13/1840
William b. Jackson to Ann V. Bishop 9/28/1841
Robert T. Jackson to Mary I. Bruce 7/30/1845
James M. Perry to Hannah E. Bruce, dau. of Green and Temperance Jackson 10/8/1851

BIRTHS

Green Jackson, son of Ephraim and Lucretia, 2/1/1780
William Lucas Jackson, son of Green and Rebecca, 9/28/1808
Temperance Jackson, 2nd wife of Green, 11/12/1791
Rebecca Ann Jackson, dau. of Green and Temperance, 6/8/1814
Ephraim Jackson, son of Green and Temperance, 10/17/1815
Lucretia Catherine Jackson, dau. of Green & Temperance, 6/23/1818
Martha Green Jackson, dau. of Green and Temperance, 1/26/1820
Emily Stith Jackson, dau. of Green and Temperance, 10/14/1821
Temperance, his wife, 10/14/1821
Robert Tucker Jackson, son of Green and Temperance, 6/9/1823
Mary Jones Jackson, dau. of Green and Temperance, 2/7/1825
Temperance Jackson b. 12/23/1826
Hannah E. M. Jackson, dau. of Green and Temperance, 7/7/1828

DEATHS

Rebecca R. Jackson 12/22/1808
Emily Stith, dau. of Green and Temperance Jackson, 11/19/1826
Frederick M. Jackson 8/25/1827
Ephraim W. Jackson, son of Green and Temperance, 3/4/1845
Mary Jones Jackson, dau. of Green and Temperance, 9/18/1845
Green Jackson, husband of Temperance, 5/18/1829
Rebecca Anne Green, dau. of Green and Temperance Jackson, 9/16/1852
Robert Tucker Jackson, son of Green and Temperance, 3/9/1835, aged 29 years, 9 months

A. BAILEY, SR. BIBLE
(Included with London Bible)

Andrew Bailey Sr. 8/1/1767-10/10/1852 Mary Anne Green 1/5/1784-4/29/1859

BIRTHS of THEIR CHILDREN:

Obedience Green Bailey 7/.28/1803-8/29/1844
Peter Renard Bailey 6/7/1807-4/29/1843
Andrew Bailey Jr. 4/4/1809-8/4/1872
Mildred Maranda Bailey 3/29/1811-8/5/1878
John Green Bailey 2/15/1813 m. Catherine
Joseph Richard Bailey 1/25/1815-8/28/1857
Daniel Edwin Bailey 2/17/1817-3/16/1884
Mary Ann Zorada Bailey 4/17/1819 m. Wyatt B. Paris
Seleuda Harriette Janette Bailey 8/1/1821-6/21/1887

Obedience Green Bailey, oldest child of Andrew and Mary Ann (Green) Bailey m. --- Williamson and d. 8/29/1844

CROXSON AND SARAH GREEN BIBLE
(Included with London Bible)

Croxson Green b. 10/4/1772 and intermarried with Sarah Crymes 2/19/1801
Sarah Crymes b. 3/2/1780

BIRTHS of THEIR CHILDREN:

John Thomas Green 11/23/1801
Jesse Davis and James Croxson Green, twins, 8/5/1811
William Davis Green 11/17/1803
Joseph Gressett Green 8/12/1806
John Randolph Green 1/13/1814
Thomas Crymes Green 1/5/1809
Abram Philmen Green 8/2/1816
Mary Ann Mildred Green 12/24/1822
Charles Richard, only son of A. P. and F. Green, 11/20/1864

DEATHS

John Thomas, 1st son of Croxson and Sarah Green, 8/28/1803
James C. Green (one of twins) 10/17/1814
John R. Green 6/13/1836 in Milton, N. C., 22 yrs., 5 mos., 5 days Joseph G. Green 8/28/1839, Augusta, Ga., 33 yrs., 16 days
Sarah Green, consort of Croxson Green, 2/6/1849
Croxson Green, husband of Sarah Green and 3rd child of John and Mildred Green, 4/3/1852
Thomas Crymes Green 10/17/1876 Halifax Co., Va., leaving a large family to mourn his loss.

JOHN AND MILDRED GREEN BIBLE
Included in London Bible)

John Green, son of William and Amy, b. 11/10/1744
John Green intermarried with Mildred Davis 11/25/1766
Mildred Davis b. 12/26/1742

BIRTHS of Children of John and Mildred Green

Jesse Davis Green 8/23/1767
Patsy Green 1/28/1779
Nancy Green 2/22/1777
Rebecca Green 1/15/1769
Amy Clay Green 2/3/1782
Coalman Green 9/13/1770

Polly Ann Green 7/5/1784
Croxson Green 10/4/1772
Letty Green 7/13/1786
Gressett Green 9/5/1774
Mildred Davis Green 7/17/1788

DEATHS

John Green, son of William and Amy, 8/20/1828
Mildred Green, his consort, 10/17/1829
Mrs. Mary A. Bailey, consort of Andrew Bailey, Sr. and dau. of John and Mildred Green 4/29/1859.
She d. at Staunton View at res.of her son-in-law, Wyatt B. Paris, Esq and her remains were carried.to Buck Mountain 5/1/1859 where they now repose in solitude by the dust of her much loved husband.

POPE-BAYNE BIBLE
Of Westmoreland County

BIRTHS of Children of Lawrence and Penelope Pope

Susan Pope 11/13/1794
Elliott Pope 3/18/1802
Patsey Pope 11/9/1797
Sallie Pope 4/19/1805

Lawrence Pope 2/18/1800
John Pope 5/31/1807
Kitty Pope 7/1/1809

Lawrence Pope d. 7/21/1810, aged 70 yrs. Penelope Pope, wife of Lawrence, d. 3/12/1826

(Pope-Payne Bible, contd....)

Richard Bayne, husband of Susan Bayne, dau. of above Lawrence and Penelope Pope b. 9/13/1789.

BIRTHS of Children of Lawrence B. and Rockey Pope Caty Pope 12/2/1821

John B. Pope 10/20/1829
Austin Pope 3/7/1825
Lawrence B. Pope 12/26/1831
Edwin Robertson Pope 10/23/1824
William Bayne Pope 2/7/1834
Cabrilla Pope 12/3/1826
Richard Bayne m. Susan 9/14/1813

BIRTHS of Children of Richard and Susan Bayne Lawrence

Pope Bayne 8/26/1814-
George H. Bayne 6/4/1820
William Bayne 10/12/1816
Washington Bayne 6/30/1822
Charles Bayne 11/5/1818
Patterson Bayne 10/9/1824
Richard Bayne, husband of Susan Bayne, d. 11/3/1829
Lawrence P. Bayne and his wife, Delia C. Bayne, dau. of Doctor Bushrod Rust, of Upperville, Fanquier Co., Va., m. 7/11/1837
George H. Bayne, 4th son of Susan and Richard Bayne, m. Marian E. Speiden, dau. of William Speiden of Washington City, D. C. 11/3/1853
George H. Bayne d. Culpepper C. H., Va., 3/28/1858, aged 38 yrs.

BURTON BIBLE
Owner: Mary Burton, Jr. Orange Co., Virginia

BIRTHS

Lucy Burton 4/28/1778 m. James Collins
Fanny Burton 2/6/1780 m. Baldwin M. Buckner Elizabeth Burton 6/17/1781
Benjamin Burton 6/22/1784
Hannah Burton 6/30/1786 m. Alexander Bradford
Jarth Burton 9/9/-- m. 1st Mr. Blakey, 2nd, John Webb Sarah Burton 5/9/1790 m. Melton 11/11/1811
Peggy Burton 2/13/1792 m. Mr. Douglas
Martha Burton 5/31/1794
Harriet Burton 2/27/1797
Mary Mariah Burton 10/8/1798

W. B. PARIS BIBLE
(Included in London Bible)

Wyatt B. Paris Sr. m. Mary A. Bailey 9/28/1836

BIRTHS

Julia Ellen Paris 8/8/1837 at Bruce's farm Andrew Bailey Paris 1/31/1839 at Rice's
William Richard Paris 5/23/1840 at Rice's Wyatt
Branch Paris 9/6/1842 Johnson's
Louisa Catharine Paris 3/7/1844, Chris Clark's Josiah Paris 12/1/1845, Chris Clark's
Mary Elizabeth Cardwell Paris 1/17/1848
John Clark Parts 2/7/1857
Charles Craddock Paris 4/21/1853
July 30th, 1884.

(W. B. Paris Bible, BIRTHS, contd....)

Andrew Isham Harvey 11/20/1835
Mary Green Buchanan 9/15/1846
Elizabeth Jordan Harvey 10/25/1837
Thomas C. Harvey 5/16/1848
John W. Harvey Jr. 2/20/1839
Mildred A. Vaughan 6/28/1850
Robert Hester Harvey 8/31/1841
Joseph Daniel Harvey 3/5/1854
Seluda Harriet Whitsitt 9/15/1844

These are the names of the living children of John William and Mildred M. Harvey who was married 12/18/1834:

John William Harvey 2/15/1811
Mildred M. Harvey 3/29/1811-8/6/1878
Peter R. Bailey d. 4/29/1843 at his res. in Pittsylvania Co., Va., aged 36 yrs.
Mrs. Obedience G. Williamson d. 8/29/1844, aged 41 yrs.

The funeral serman of Peter R. Bailey was preached at Midway by E. W. Roach on the last day of August 1843....

Preached at Midway on last day of October 1844 by E. W. Roach and Mr. Namonsly the funeral of O. G. Williamson. My beloved brother, Joseph R. Bailey, d. 8/28/1857 at Newcastle, Va., aged 42 yrs., 7 mos., and some days

Mrs. Julia A. Bailey d. in Bristol, Tenn. 12/31/1866, c onsort of Joseph R. Bailey, aged 55 yrs.

William A. London m. Harriette Bailey 4/13/1842 by Rev. E. W. Roach

Inf. dau. of W. A. and H. London, b. 3/1/1843, and being stillborn was bur. at Poplar Grove on the morning of the 2nd Second dau. of W. A. and H. London b. 1/13th and d. 3/20/1844

Daniel Higginbotham d. at Soldier's Joy, his res. in Nelson Co., 8/10/1845, aged 64 yrs. (son of Capt John Higginbotham (17261814) and Rachel Banks)

Mrs. Sarah Chappell d. at her res. in Charlotte Co. 4/22/1844, aged 79 yrs.

Sallie Marie Mourning, lOth child of Obedience G. Williamson, b. 8/29/1844-d. 2/16/1845

David Flournoy, 4th child of Joseph R. and Julia A. Bailey, b. 1/22/1845 at Buck Mountain, the res. of his grandfather Bailey

"Rough Creek, Va. Octo. 25th, 1872 Dear Sister London
Bro. Andrew and Sister Cats funeral will be preached at Salem on next Sabbath by old Bro. E. W. Roach. Sister Cat died Tuesday lid at Davids.....Judith with nannie and her two children is with us, but expecting to leave in a day or two. We expect to move Judith, Lucy and Walter down next Spring. I wish she could have gone to see you and Sister Paris, before she leaves....Your brother, Daniel E. Bailey"

Andrew Bailey d. 8/14/1872
Mrs. A. C. Bailey d. 10/22/1872 at Ridgeway, Charlotte Co., Va., relict of Andrew Bailey, decd, aged 62 yrs. (Member of New Salem Baptist Church)
Peter R. Bailey d. 4/29/1843 at his res. in Pittsylvania Co., Va., eldest son of Andrew Bailey Sr. of Charlotte Co., Va., aged 36 yrs.

A. Bailey m. A. C. Hamlet 9/27/1830
David H. White m. Bettie A. Bailey 5/21/1856

(W. B. Paris Bible, contd....)

"Fatal Accident.--On the evening of the 29th of August, a small company of young people, ladies and gentlemen, having met at a saw mill (circular saw) recently started in the neighborhood, Josiah Paris, son of Wyatt Paris, Esq., near Clarke's Ferry, Charlotte Co., Va., incautiously taking his seat on the log then under the saw, was, on the truck being reversed unobserved by him,
caught and terribly wounded in the back. He lived less than two hours. He was a young man of fine promise, and had served during the war in his brother's battery of light artillery."

Josiah Paris d. 8/29/1865

"Thursday, April 30th, 1874 Dear Aunt Pa died this morning about sunrise. Will be buried tomorrow at Buck Mountain at four or five o'clock.

We have great comfort in his death. Mr. Brown was with him to the last moment. Come and see us soon. Yours in great distress, Bettie C. Paris"

John William Bailey, son of John G. and Catharine Bailey, b. at Josiah Chappell's farm, Charlotte Co., Va., 11/24/1859

Newspaper clipping: "Died, March 16th, 1884, in the 68th year of his age,....Capt. Daniel E. Bailey. Capt. Bailey was raised in Charlotte County and was the last of a large and respectable family. He was a merchant and farmer and conducted business at Waugh's Ferry; where he married the amiable and accomplished Miss Judith Waugh; and thereby became proprietor of Waugh's ferry...He died at Big Island where he had been connected with his son-inlaw, Mr. S. B. Steger, in merchandising for the last several years...."

JOSEPH McADAM BIBLE of Northumberland Co.
Owner: William Broun, Washington City, Va.

Joseph McAdam m. Jane Muir 7/30/1712 by Rev. Mr. Charles Coates, Minister of Govan, in his own house

BIRTHS of Children of Joseph and Jane McAdam

James McAdam 4/21/1713
Hugh McAdam 7/5/1720
John McAdam 3/18/1715
Charles McAdam 11/8/1722

James McAdam 10/8/1717
Robert McAdam 9/18/1723
Joseph McAdam 5/28/1719

The sons of Joseph and Jane McAdam; their ages at present year, 1769:

James McAdam, 56
James McAdam, 52
Hugh McAdam, 49
John McAdam, 54

Joseph McAdam, 50
Charles McAdam, 47
Robert McAdam, 45

Children of my grandfather McAdam *(written on back of paper)*

William Broun, son of George and Margaret Broun, of North Britain, m. 10/22/1771 to Janetta McAdam, second dau. of Joseph and Sarah Ann McAdam of Virginia.

BIRTHS of Children of William and Janetta Broun

George McAdam Broun 1/8/1773-
Harriet Broun 10/4/1779
Ann Lee Broun 11/8/1775
Edwin Conway Broun 3/9/1781
Thomas Broun 6/11/1777

(Joseph McAdam Bible, contd....)

10/29/1807 Thomas Broun, son of William and Janetta Broun of Lancaster Co., Va., m. Elizabeth G. Lee, dau. of Charles and Sarah Lee of Northumberland Co., Va. by Rev. John Seward. Thomas Broun b. 6/11/1777, and Elizabeth, 11/12/1779
8/27/1808, they had issue, a son, who was christened by Rev. John Seward, and called William Waters.
9/20/1810 they had issue, two daus., who were christened by Rev. B. Burgess, the eldest called Sarah Elizabeth, and the youngest called Jane Ann. 2/1812 my dear little dau., Jane Ann d. at Cobbs Hall and was buried in family burying ground.

3/1/1813 they had issue, a son, christened by Rev. Samuel Low, and called Charles Lee
11/25/1814 they had issue, a dau., christened by Rev. B. Burgess, and called Jane Ann
1/26/1817 they had issue, a son, christened 2/11th following by Rev. Henry Padget, and called Thomas Kennerly, and d. 10/6/1826
9/30/1819 EdwLn, son of Thomas and Elizabeth Broun, b. and christened by Rev. B. Burgess, 1/2/1820
7/6/1822, my dear wife had issue, a dau., 2/15/1823, she was christened by Rev. Bishop Enoch George, and called Judith Lee.

9/10/1812 my dear bro., George McA.Broun, d. at Heathsville, alias Northumberland Courthouse.
4/11/1818 my sister Harriet d.

My dear son, Thomas Kennerly (Broun), d. 10/6/1826, aged 9 yrs., 8 mos., 11 days
Our aged mother, Mrs. Sarah Lee of Cobbs Hall, d. at my house 7/8/1829, aged 80 yrs.

RICHARD CHAPMAN JR. BIBLE Of New Kent County
William & Mary Qtly

Richard Chapman, son of Richard Chapman and his wife, Jane Johnson, b. at "Chericoke", King William Co., Va., 9/1741
Elizabeth Reynolds b. at "The Island" in New Kent 2/18/1757
Elizabeth Reynolds m. Richard Chapman 4/16/1775 by Rev. Mr. Ford.

BIRTHS of THEIR CHILDREN:

Jane Chapman 2/29/1776 at "Prior Park"
Reynolds Chapman 7/22/1778 at "Prior Park"
Johnson Chapman 12/26/1780 at "Prior Park", d. aged 4 yrs.

DEATHS

Richard Chapman 12/10/1789, aged 48 yrs.

Susannah Mosson Chapman 5/23/1789, aged 4 yrs.

Jane Price, dau. of Richard Chapman, 3/26/1796, after being delivered of twin daus., still living- one named Jane Chapman Price and the other, Susannah Smith Price

Susannah Smith Price 6/8/1797, youngest twin dau. of Nathaniel W. Price and his deed wife, Jane Chapman, aged 1 yr., 2 mos., 22 days; also d. 7/2/1797 Jane Chapman Price, the eldest twin of above, aged 1 yr., 3 mos. 18 days
George Green, husband ; Elizabeth (wid. or Richard Chapman),3/27/1798

Richard Chapman, Jr. Bible, contd....)

Richard Meriwether Chapman b. 12/4/1789, just 6 days before death of his father, Richard Chapman

Nathaniel W. Price m. Elizabeth Garland Smith 6/22/1797
David Mossom and Mary, wid. of Henry Claiborne (maiden name Major) m. 7/20/1740

BIRTHS of Children of David and Mary Mossom

Mary Mossom 9/6/1741, baptised 10/1st
Robert Mossom 5/13/1744, baptised 6/15th, d. 12/17/1744
Mary Mossom d. 11/23/1745
David Mossom and Elizabeth (wid. of Benskin Marston, dau. of Henry Sloane) m. 7/6/1755. She d. 4/2/1759
Rev. David Mossom, my dear father, d. 6/4/1767, aged 78 yrs. James Curtis, my dear husband, d. 3/13/1767, aged 28 yrs.
Jane Chapman, dau. of Richard and Elizabeth, m. 10/30/1794 Nathaniel W. Price of Hanover Co.

MRS. MARY BACON BIBLE of Lunenburg County

On flyleaf: "This blessed Holy Bible was the property of Mrs. Mary Bacon of Lunenburg County, who lived the widow of Col. Lyddall Bacon, and died in Lunenburg Co, Oct. 11, 1816. At her death it came into the possession of her son, Capt. Drury A. Bacon, and at his death, in the year 1845, it came into the possession of his son, Lyddall Bacon. It has been in the family of the Bacons from my earliest recollection. Lyddall Bacon, Aug. 24, 1872."

BIRTHS of Children of Lyddall Bacon (son of John and Sarah Law, b. 1719 m. 1740 Mary Allen

Elizabeth Bacon 12174/1741
Sarah Bacon 8/19/1753
Lucy Bacon 4/11/1744
Lyddall Bacon 11/17/1755
Mary Bacon 3/14/1758
Susannah Bacon 1/6/1750

Anne Bacon 10/11/1748
Richard Bacon 11/24/1760
Edmund Parks Bacon 11/17/1763
Langston Bacon 5/25/1746
Drury Allen Bacon 12/4/1765

BIRTHS of Children of Drury Allen Bacon and Polly Stokes Allen

Stokes Bacon 5122/1787
Langston Bacon 2/17/1789

BIRTHS of Children of Drury Allen Bacon and Nancy, 2nd wife

Lyddall Bacon 12/26/1793
Drury Allen Bacon 10/19/1795
Mary Ann Bacon, wife of Lyddall Bacon, son of Drury and Nancy, 2/23/1798-7/10/1862

BIRTHS of Children of Lyddall and Mary Ann Bacon

Nancy Aris Bacon 10/29/1818-6/1856
William Allen Bacon 3/25/1820-6/25/1901
Drury Allen Bacon 7/14/1821-11/8/1876
Mildred Hainey Carter Bacon 11/20/1822
James Lawrence Bacon 2/6/1824-2/12/1826
Robert Carter Bacon 7/20/1825-2/8/1835
Edmunds Cummins Bacon 2/16/1827-4/25/1860
Virginia Bacon 3/20/1828-5/15/1904
Lyddall Bacon Jr. 12/27/1830
Bacon Bacon 5/12/1832
Nathaniel Bacon 4/16/1833
Richard Parkes Bacon 12/25/1834

Thomas Alexander Bacon 7/7/1836
Mary Jane Bacon 5/20/1838-9/4/1889 Josephus Carter Bacon 4/1/1840-2/18/1902
Drury Allen Bacon m. lst Polly Stokes, and m. 2nd 12/16/1792 Mrs. Nancy Aris Jackson, dau. of
Frederick Nance. Their oldest son was Lyddall Bacon, who m. in 1817 Mary Ann Carter.

DEATHS

Mary Bacon, mother of Drury Allen Bacon, d. 10/11/1816 Lunenburg Co., Va.
Langston Bacon, son of Lyddall and Mary, 8/26/1831 Charlotte Co.
Mildred Hainey Carter Bacon, dau. of Lyddall and Mary Ann, 8/7/1823
Bacon Bacon, son of Lyddall and Mary Ann, 5/13/1832
Langston Bacon, son of Drury, 10/4/1838
Lyddall Bacon, son of Lyddall and Mary Ann, 8/15/1843
Richard Parkes Bacon, son of Lyddall and Mary Ann, 8/18/1843
Nathaniel Bacon, son of Lyddall and Mary Ann, 8/29/1843
Drury A. Bacon, son of Lyddall and Mary An, 9/3/1845, aged 80.
Allen Stokes Bacon of Roane Co., Tenn., 10/1/1848
James Lawrence Bacon, son of Lyddall and Mary Ann, 2/12/1853
Mary Ann Bacon, wife of Lyddall, 7/10/1862
Lyddall Bacon, son of Drury Allen and Nancy Aris Bacon, 6/23/1875, aged 81 yrs.
Thomas Alex. Bacon, son of Lyddall and Mary Ann, 10/10/1878, aged 39 yrs.
Nancy A. H. Spencer, dau., of Lyddall and Mary Bacon, 6/1856
Edmund C. Bacon, son of Lyddall and Mary 4/25/1860
Drury A. Bacon, son of Lyddall and Mary, 11/8/1876, aged 55 yrs.

MARRIAGES

Drury A. Bacon to Polly Stokes 5/22/1786
Drury Allen Bacon to Nancy Aris Jackson, dau. of Frederick Nance, 12/26/1792
Drury A. Bacon to Elizabeth Jones 8/1807
Lyddall Bacon, son of Drury A., to Mary Ann Carter 12/18/1817
Nancy A. M. Bacon, dau. of Lyddall and Mary Ann, to Capt. John R. Spencer 1846
William A. Bacon to Lucy Mangum of Mississippi, 6/7/1854
Edmund C. Bacon to Tabitha Tate of Arkansas, 1854
Robert C. Bacon to Nannie Fluke ot Monroe Co., now Summers Co., West Virginia.
Thomas A. Bacon-Pattie Farrar res of E. T. Kenne, Christianville, Mecklenburg,Va.1/1860
Mary J. Bacon to James Cunningham 12/1860
Mary J. Bacon Cunningham to Tyree G. Finch 2/1871
Virginia Bacon to William S. Harris of Powhatan Co., Va. 12/19/1866
Josephus Carter Bacon to Lottie H. Lewis of Granville Co., N. C., 10/17/1881
Anne Marion Harris, dau. of William S. and Virginia (Bacon) Harris to Henry Bedford Moseley
of Charlotte Co., Va., 10/17/1894
Robert H. Harris to Mary B. Harris 12/19/1811.
Robert Harris b. 6/2/1784.
Mary B. Harris b.7/9/1792

BIRTHS of Children of Robert H. and Mary B. Harris:

Stephen P. Harris 10/12/1812 –
James LaFayette Harris 1824
Charlotte Corde Harris 7/29/1818
Caroline R. W. Harris 7/5/1815
Adolphus Washington Harris 9/29/1828
Robert Edward Harris 3/4/1816
William Samuel Harris 12/15/1819
Martha Jane Eloise Harris 1/10/1826
Mary Magdeline Chastaine Harris 2/19/1822

"Mrs. Moseley's Bacon family Bible."

EZRA N. OFFUTT BIBLE
Owner: Ezra Offutt Witherspoon, Louisville, Kentucky

MARRIAGES

William Offutt to Elizabeth Macgruder 12/21/1750
Alexander Offutt to Ann Clagett 1/13/1791
Alexander Logan to Verlinda Offutt 12/12/1816
William Offutt to Malissa Pitts 4/13/1820
Henry C. Offutt to Mary Bell 9/22/1821

William M. Offutt to Elizabeth M. Offutt 2/22/1825
Bartlett Hall to Ann Offutt 12/18/1827
Ezra N. Offutt to Elizabeth A. Lemon 7/4/1836
Z. C. Offutt to Mary E. Ford 5/27/1837
H. C. Offutt to Mrs. Mary S. Glass 7/1/1840 (2nd wife)
Alexander Offutt to Emfline Smith 10/21/1840

Children of Ezra and Elizabeth Offutt:

Mere Mundy to Margaret Offutt 1/28/1858 by Rev. J. J. Bullock
W. H. Mundy to Laura V. Offutt 10/25/1865 by Rev. Daniel P. Young Dr. O. H. Witherspoon to
Mary Edmonia Offutt 9/22/1869 by Daniel P. Young
Ezra Offutt Witherspoon to Nell Eliot-Newman 10/14/1908 Louisville, Ky.
Joseph I. Lemon of Lexington, Ky. to Margaret Ann Leathers of Scott Co., Ky. 6/30/1817

BIRTHS

Mary Offutt 10/6/1721
Sara Offutt 8/9/1731
James Offutt 2/14/1725
Priscilla Offutt 8/17/1730

Jane Offutt 1/6/1727
Keziah Offutt 2/24/1734
William Ofutt 2/14/1729
Alexander Offutt 5/7/1736

BIRTHS of William Offutt's Children

Samuel Offutt 1b/2/1751
James D. Offutt 9/11/1765
William Macgr. Offutt 4/23/1753
Alex Offutt 2/18/1767
Sara Offutt 4/6/1755
Enoch Offutt 3/23/1768
James M. Offutt 8/3/1757
Jane Offutt 3/27/1770

Rezin Offutt 2/22/1759
James D. Offutt 5/29/1772
Margaret Offutt 7/22/1760
Elisha Offutt 4/12/1775
Nathaniel Offut 4/16/1762
Baruch Offutt 5/3/1777
Elizabeth Offutt 11/23/1763

BIRTHS of Alexander Offutt's Children

Henry C. Offutt 10/8/1791
Ann Offutt 10/27/1800
William C. Offutt 10/2/1793
Alex Offutt 10/10/1803

Verlinda Offutt 6/3/1794
Ezra Offutt 12/28/1806
Elizabeth M. Offutt 12/7/1799
Zachariah C. Offutt 11/4/1808

BIRTHS of Ezra and Elizabeth Offutt's Children

Margaret Offutt 5/20/1837
Joseph Ev-Alex. Offutt 2/14/1848
Jos F. Offutt 6/14/1841

Clarence L. Offutt 4/2/1851
Laura Verlinda Offutt 12/11/1842
Marion Ezra Offutt 12/28/1854

Birth of Mark and Margaret Mundy's Child

St. Marc Mundy 6/13/1865

BIRTHS of William H. and Laura Mundy's Children

Lizzie Mundy 7/25/1866
Clarence H. Mundy 3/1/1878
William Offutt Mundy 9/11/1873

Dr. Oran Haws Witherspoon 6/14/1842
Mary Edmonia Offutt 2/4/1845
Joseph Leathers 12/13/1839

Ezra Offutt Witherspoon 10/3/1878, son of O. H. & Edmonia
Elizabeth Ferguson Leathers, wife of Joseph Leathers, 10/27/1773 in Culpepper Co., Va.

(Ezra N. Offutt Bible, BIRTHS, contd....)

BIRTHS of Joseph and Elizabeth Leather's Children

Peter Ferguson Leathers 4/27/1793
Margaret Ann Leathers 3/23/1792

Joseph I. Lemon 6/15/1793, Georgetown, Scott Co., Ky.
Margaret Ann Leathers 3/23/1792, Madison Co., Va.

BIRTHS of Children of Joseph I. & Margaret Ann Lemon

Elizabeth Amelia Lemon 7/10/1818 Lexington, Ky
Mary Jane Lemon 11/15/1820
James Cavin Lemon 7/20/1824
Joshua Leathers Lemon 5/5/1823 at Bell Air Farm

Margaret Ann Lemon 10/20/1819
Mary Jane Lemon 2d, 12/4/1821

Joseph Innis Lemon 8/10/1827
Joseph Francis Marion Lemon 12/28/1828

William Thomas Lemon 11/9/1830
George Washington Lemon 2/20/1833

Josephine Isabella Francis Lemon 5/11/1826 in Scott Co., Ky.
Mary Elizabeth Carth, dau. of A. G. and M. A. Garth, 9/1/1837
Joseph Lemon Frost, son-in-law of J. M. and M. A. Frost, 1/1/1841

DEATHS

Alexander Offutt Sr. 10/31/1823
Ann Offutt 8/8/1833
Elizabeth M. Offutt 2/1831

William Offutt ---
Ann A. Hall 3/14/1861
William P. Offutt, son of William C. Offutt, 6/20/1833

DEATHS of Children of E. N. & E. A. Offutt

Clarence L. Offutt 7/24/1871, aged 20 yrs., 3 mos. 23 days
Dr. Oran Haws Witherspoon, son-in-law of E. N. & E. A. Offutt, 1/4/1900
Clarence H. Mundy 6/8/1878
Joseph Leathers 5/23/1825, aged 66 yrs.
Elizabeth Ferguson Leathers, wife of above, aged 52 yrs., 2/9/1525
Peter Ferguson Leathers, son of above, 9/27/1825, aged 23 yrs.
Joseph I. Lemon 6/17/1836, aged 51 yrs.
Margaret A. Lemon, wife of J. I. Lemon, aged 76 yrs., 8 mos., 7 days, 11/29/1868

Children of J. I. and M. A. Lemon

Mary Jane 6/28/1821 - - -
Joshua L. 2/14/1841
Mary Jane 2nd 9/11/1822

Joseph Francis Marion 9/25/1853
Joseph I. 8/22/1828
William T. 10/30/1869

Amelia, wife of James Lemon, Sr. 9/27/1806
Joseph Lemon, eldest son of James and Amelia Lemon, 5/22/1815

Thomas Lemon 10/4/1815
James Lemon Sr. 4/28/1832 (father of Joseph I. Lemon)
Albert G. Garth, son-in-law of Joseph T. and Margaret A. Lemon, 3/21/1838

James Lemon Jr. 1/22/1823

GILBERT MILBY BIBLE
Owner: Margaret Seymour Hall, 24 Monroe Place, Brooklyn, N. Y.

MARRIAGES

Gilbert Milby to Betsey 5/23/1799
George C. Ames to Hester Walter Milby 4/10/1828 on Hampton Creek

BIRTHS

Gilbert Milby, son of John and Rachel, 11/28/1767
Betsey Kellam, dau. of John and Margaret, 7/10/1773

John Kellam Milby, son of Gilbert and Betsey, 3/14/1800

(Gilbert Milby Bible, BIRTHS, contd....)

Katharine Milby, dau. of Gilbert and Betsey, 11/6/1801
Hester Waiter Milby, dau. of Gilbert and Betsey, 7/21/1805 George Christian Ames, son of Zerubabel and Margaret Ames, 12/16/1806

DEATHS

Gilbert Milby 9/30/1807, aged 39 yrs, 10 mos., 2 days John Kellam Milby 7/5/1801, aged 1 yrs., 3 mos., 21 days Katharine Milby 9/26/1805, aged 6 yrs., 10 mos., 26 days
Hester Milby Ames 12/5/1840, aged 35 yrs., 4 mos., 2 days

LEWIS BURWELL BIBLE
Owner Armlstead G. Gordon. Staunton, Virginia

Lewis Burwell m. Judith Kennon 5/30/1784

BIRTHS of THEIR CHILDREN:

Francis Page Burwell 9119/1790
William Kennon Burwell 9/26/1791
Elizabeth Ann Burwell 10/25/1793-10/15/1867
Alice Williams Burwell 3/12/1795
Lewis Burwell 8/19/1797
George Washington Burwell 4/1/1799

Ann Price Burwell 10/11/1801
John Perrin Burwell 4/5/--
Nathaniel Burwell 4/4/1806-7/5/1806
Peter B. Whiting Burwell 5/31/1809
Mary Blair Burwell 9/23/1811

JOSEPH DAVENPORT BIBLE
Town Clerk in Williamsburg, Va.

Printed in Glasgow 1745.
Hugo Grotius de Verilate Religionis Christianae.
On flyleaf: "Joseph Davenport, Jr. 7/23/1748
Joseph and Marg. uxoris liberi
Mat. 10/24/1734
Elizabeth Geminae, natoe 3/5/1729-30
Jud.
Mara
Jas
Joseph Jr. 2/21/173 1/2
Shank Davenport George 3/29/1733
Sarah
Peachy) Geminae
Johan)

ELIZABETH DANDRIDGE BIBLE
Owner: Mrs. Eliza Luce

On flyleaf: "Elizabeth Dandridge, 1749. Her Bible, given her by her affectionate mother, March 6, 1773"

John Dandridge m. Frances Jones 7/22/1730

BIRTHS of THEIR CHILDREN:

Martha Dandridge 6/2/1731
Anna Maria Dandridge 3/30/1739
John Dandridge 2/23/1732
Frances Dandridge 11/2/1744

William Dandridge 3/2/1734
Elizabeth Dandridge 5/25/1749
Bartholomew Dandridge 12/25/1737
Mary Dandridge 4/4/1756

(Elizabeth Dandridge Bible, contd....)

DEATHS

John Dandridge Jr. 7/23/1749
Mary Dandridge 9/25/1763
Frances Dandridge 2/10/1758
William Dandridge 1/22/1776 (suddenly drowned)
John Dandridge the elder 8/31/1756, aged 55 yrs.
Anna Maria Bassett 12/17/1777, aged 37 yrs.
My dear mother 4/9/1785, aged 75 yrs.
4/18/1785 my dear bro., Bartholomew Dandridge, aged 49 yrs.
John Aylett m. Elizabeth Dandridge 4/10/1773
William Aylett, their son, b. 6/15/1774
Mr. Aylett d. 2/7/1776, aged 29 yrs.
John Aylett 2/17/1776-8/24/1777
William Aylett d. 8/29/1777
Leonard Henley m. Elizabeth Aylett 1/31/1779

BIRTHS of THEIR CHILDREN:

Frances DandridgeHenley 11/17/1779
John Dandridge Henley 2/25/1781
Robert Henley 1/5/1782
William Henley 11/28/1784
Martha Henley 3/23/1786, d. 3 -1/2 yrs old.

Bartholomew Henley 3/14/1788
George Henley 2/7/1790-9/18/1790
Samuel Henley 2/25/1792
My dear Mr. Henley d. 11/19/1798

WILLIAM POPE of Isle of Wight County
Quaker Records published by Sou. HIstorical Assn.

William Pope and Maire, his wife, THEIR CHILDREN:'s nativities recorded as followeth:

William Pope 8/15/1662   Dau. 8/1667   Henry Pope 11/30/1663   John Pope 8/6/1670

WILLIAM DAVIS BIBLE of Dinwiddie County
Owner: Joseph Edmon Davis

Printed in Edinburg in 1760

William Davis m. Marion 3/14/1709
Jane Hardaway 3/12/1721-7/9/1795 m. 10/15/1737

DEATHS

Baxter Davis 1/30/1750
Elizabeth Davis 9/20/1785
Frances Davis 10/20/1759
Baxter Davis 11/19/1795
Mary Davis 10/20/1759
Mason Davis 11/14/1795
Elizabeth Davis 10/21/1759
Daniel Mason 11/26/1798
Baxter Davis Jr. 11/4/1759

James A. Watson 8/7/1797
Edith Davis 11/5/1759
Jane Morris 12/31/1799
Batty Smith 11/21/1790
William Davis 5/7/1810
Elizabeth Jane Roberson 7/8/1797
Lucy Davis 8/25/1770
Hardaway Davis 10/4/1795

Ann Morris, dau. of Hercules Morris and Jane, his wife, b. 8/1/1762

JOSHUA DEGGE BIBLE
Owner: W. W. Degge, Boulder, Col.

MARRIAGES

Joshua Degge to Elizabeth Degge 1762 Anthony Degge b. 1765 to --- Morris
John Lawson Degge b. 1802 to Mary Thomas 1826
William B. Degge b. 1829 to Eliza Burroughs 1853
William Winder Degge b. 1858 to Nellie Louise Avery 1887
Dudley Avery Degge b. 1890 to Allie Lee McKeehan 1910
William W. Degge Jr. b 1911.

DEATHS

Mary, dau. of Anthony and Avarilla Degge, 6/24/1759, aged 3 yrs., 5 mos.
Lawson, son of Anthony and Avarilla Degge, 8/1/1765
Allen Smith 5/5/1774
Avarilla, wire of Anthony Degge ---
An thony De gge, son ,of Anthony and Avarilla , also husband of Elizabeth Day, 4/30/1786
Johanna Degge, dau. of Anthony and Avarilla Degge, 9/11/1790
Anthony, son of John and Joanna Degge, b. 11/4/1714

THOMAS ANDREW EDWARDS BIBLE
Owner: Robert Wilmer Edwards, Ophelia, Virginia

Thomas Andrew Edwards m. Sallie A. Ball 11/6/1873 Thomas Andrew Edwards d. 4/22/1893

MARRIAGES

William Eskridge to Ann Edwards, dau. of Robert and Ann Edwards, 11/23/1797
James Wilkinson to Ann H. Eskridge 10/2/1817
Yarrett Hughlett to Elizabeth Baker Eskridge, dau. of William and Ann Eskridge, 5/29/1823
Royston B. Covington to Mary C. Eskridge, dau. of William and Ann Eskridge, 6/1/1826
Robert Edwards Eskridge to Ann Elizabeth Jett, dau. of Thomas and Elizabeth Jett, 12/23/1829
John H. Barney to Julia Ann Wilkinson 12/29/1836
Allucius J. Eskridge to Frances H. J. Harcum, dau. of William and Frances Harcum, 11/4/1856

BIRTHS

William Eskridge, son of William and Betty, 2/19/1774
Ann Edwards, dau. of Robert and Ann, 11/23/1777
Ann H. Eskridge, dau. of William and Ann, 3/5/1797
William Eskridge, son of William and Ann, 3/21/1801
Elizabeth Baker Eskridge, dau. of William and Ann, 9/3/1803
Mary Cedar Eskridge, dau. of William and Ann, 12/7/1805-3/4/1870
Robert Edwards Eskridge, son of William and Ann, 9/23/1810
Allucius Jett Eskridge, son of Robert and Ann, 3/12/1831
Ann Elizabeth, dau. of Robert E. and Ann E. Eskridge, 10/10/1844
William Eskridge Hughlett, son of Barrett and Elizabeth B. Hughlett, 4/15/1824

DEATHS

William Eskridge, Jr., son of William Edwards, Sr. and his wife, 6/30/1808
William Eskridge, Sr. 3/7/1823, aged 40 yrs.
Elizabeth Baker Hughlett, wife of Yarrett Hughlett and dau. of William Eskridge and Ann, 5/11/1824,aged 21 yrs
Ann Eskridge, wife of William Eskridge and dau. of Robert Ann Edwards, 3/28/1850, aged 72 yrs., 4 mos., 5 days
Robert Edwards Eskridge, son of William and Ann, 4/30/1850, aged 40 yrs.

HUDSON-GILMER BIBLE
Owner: Frank Gilmer, Charlottesville, Va.

MARRIAGES

Christopher Hudson to Sarah Anderson 3/19/1763
George Gilmer to Elizabeth A. Hudson 5/5/1801
Sarah Eliza Gilmer to Sam Tompkins 5/29/1825
Colin C. Spiller to Georgeanna Gilmer 4/5/1829
George C. Gilmer to Leeanna D. Lewis 8/24/1831
George C. Gilmer to Mildred Wirt Duke 8/19/1851
Thomas A. Cunningham to Maria Walker Gilmer 10/23/1878
Frank Gilmer to Decca S. Haskell 3/17/1886

BIRTHS

Christopher Hudson 3/30/1758
Sarah Hudson 7/20/1758
Elizabeth Anderson Hudson 4/30/1784
Ann Hudson 7/6/1787
George Anna Gilmer 5/27/1809
Sarah E. Gilmer 4/7/1835
George C. Gilmer 1/27/1811
Zachariah Lee Gilmer 6/18/1840

Leeanna D. Lewis 6/18/1811
George Walker Gilmer 7/10/1845
Maria Walker Gilmer 10/12/1854
Mildred Laura Cunningham 7/22/1879
James N. Gilmer 7/30/1833
Frank Gilmer 1/29/1857

DEATHS

Sarah Hudson 4/2/1807
George C. Gilmer 9/7/1887
Elizabeth Anderson Gilmer 8/8/1820
James N. Gilmer 8/27/1836
Chrlstopher Hudson 5/1/1825

Leeanna D. Gilmer 7/23/1845
Martha Jane Gilmer 1/12/1840
George Gilmer 10/6/1836
Maria Gilmer Cunningham 1/26/1880

ROBERT EDWARDS BIBLE
Of Northumberland County

Robert Edwards m. Ann Haynie 6/6/1775
Thomas Edwards, son of Robert and Ann, 4/24/1763-1/2/1818
Thomas Edwards m. 11/19/1768
Sarah, dau. of James and Mary Ball.
Sarah Ball Edwards d. 1842
Joseph Chinn Edwards, son of Thomas and Sarah, b. 11/21/1795
Joseph Chinn Edwards m. 12/26/1821 Elizabeth Ann, dau. of Thomas Harvey.

DEATHS

Joseph Chinn Edwards 1/1/183- Elizabeth Ann Edwards 1835
Americus Adams Edwards, son of Joseph C. and Elizabeth Ann Edwards, b. 2/4/1826
Americus Adams Edwards m. Sallie Carter 6/14/1860
Doctor Americus A. Edwards d. 7/28/1871
Thomas Andrew Edwards, son of Robert Andrew Edwards and Sarah Howorth Edwards (2nd wife) b.1/9/1846

EDMUND SCARBURGH BIBLE
DAR Records, Ga. State Archives

BIRTHS

Elizabeth Scarburgh 13/29/1720
Francis Wainhouse 4/4/1720
Margrate Wainhouse 1/15/1723

Sarah Potter, dau. of Edmund Scarburgh and Elizabeth, and wife of John Potter, d. 8/16/1727, aged 26 yrs.

Dorothy Wainhouse 8/4/1695
Mitchell Scarburgh 8/13/1695
Mitchell Scarburgh m. Dorothy Wainhouse 11/24/1715

BIRTHS of Children of Mitchell Scarburgh and Dorothy

Edmund Scarburgh 8/19/1716-
Mary Scarburgh 2/28/1725
Mitchell Scarburgh 11/18/1718
Matilda Scarburgh 2/29/1728

Margrate Scarbllrgh 4/26/1721
Dorothy Wainhouse Scarburgh 2/10/1730
Americus Scarburgh 9/17/1723
Mitchell Scarburgh d. 6/21/1763

3/28/1751 Edmund Scarburgh m. Mary Knot, in Nansemond Co., Va. Edmund Scarburgh d. 2/5/1764

"My dear son, Edmund Scarbrough set sail for Hampton in James River 3/20/1734 with John Sheppard, the wind at east, and at night there was a great storm at north east. God grant I may see him....for Jesus Chr1st his sake Rote the 21st by me. M. S.". 8/21/1742 Dorothy Scarburgh

Mitchell Scarburgh Jr. d. in March betwn 12th and 16th; he went from Pungoteague the 12th in a cainow and by misfortune was drowned, over to Wicocomco, and was found on the 16th.

Robert Thorowgood, son of John and Margaret Thorowgood, b. 1/1/1754

Thomas Scarburgh Thorowgood b. 6/29/1757

Mitchell Thorowgood, son of above parties, b. 4/13/1757/8
Mary Scarburgh b. 2/28/1725 m. Andrew Stewart 10/2/17--, d. 9/15/1759
Robert Thorowgood, son of John and Margaret, d. 10/175=
Pembrook Thorowgood, dau. of John and Margaret Thorowgood, b. 3/9/1760

RACHEL ROBINSON TURNBULL BIBLE

Printed in London 1753.

Major Anthony Robinson of Poquosan d. 3/17/1756
Diana, his wife, d. 11/13/1761
Mary Cole, dau. of Rosco and Rachel Colt, b. 11/10/1751
William Cole, son of Rosco and Rachel, b. 1/17/1753

Rachel Robinson, dau. of Major Anthony Robinson and Dianna Tabb, 10/4/1732-2/23/1767
George Turnbull, son of Alexander, d. 1/4/1763, bur. Br1stol Brick Churchyard

(Rachel Robinson Turnbull Bible, contd....)

in Scotland East Lothian m. Rachel Robinson (wid. of Roscoe Cole, Minlster of Gospel in Warwick Co.), dau. of Mr. Anthony Robinson of York Co., Parish of Charles, 9/29/1759, by Rev. Mr. Joseph Davenport, Minlster of Charles Parish, York Co., Va.

Robert Turnbull m. Mary Cole 9/16/1770 by Hon. James Horror, Commissary of Va. And President of William and Mary College and one of his Majesties Honorable Councellors of Virginia.

Mary, wife of Robert Turnbull, delivered of a boy named Charles, 12/8/1772
1/20/1775 delivered of a dau. named Anne
9/20/1776 delivered of a son named Thomas Crawford
12/21/1778 delivered of a son named Robert
10/31/1780 delivered of a son named William Cole. 11/9 he was chrlstioned and d. 11/11/1780
5/14/1782 delivered of a dau. named Mary Cole
Benjamin Harrison b. 12/19/1768
Anne Harrison b. 1/1775

Nathaniel Harrison, son of Benjamin and Anne Harrison, b. 10/12/1795

Mary Cole, dau. of Robert Turnbull, m. Armlstead Burwell, Esq. of Dinwiddie, only son of John Blair Burwell, Esq. 12/13/1800

ROBERT ANDREW EDWARDS BIBLE
Owner: Robert E. Lee Edwards
Fleets Point, Va.

Robert Andrew Edwards, son of Robert and Priscilla Edwards, b. 6/6/1806
Robert A. Edwards m. Mary Jane Adams 6/25/1859 (3rd wife)
Robert A. Edwards d. 10/22/1878

Robert E. Lee, son of Robert A. and Mary Jane Edwards, b. 3/26/1863
Robert E. Lee Edwards m. Mary L. Shipley 4/30/1885
Robert E. Lee Edwards d. 8/20/1930

NATHANIEL WEST DANDRIDGE BIBLE
Owner: Mrs. Mildred Spotswood Mathes Memphis, Tennessee

This Bible was printed by Thomas Baskett, printer to the King's most excellent majesty, 1751"

Nathaniel West Dandridge m. Dorothea Spotswood 6/18/1747

BIRTHS

Martha Dandridge 9/20/1748
Robert Dandridge 6/21/1760
William Dandridge 4/6/1750
N. W. Dandridge 10/26/1762
Alexander Spotswood Dandridge 8/1/1753
Eliza Dandridge 9/12/1764
Anna K. Dandridge 7/27/1767
John Dandridge 4/15/1756
Mary C. Dandridge 1/14/1772
Dorothea Dandridge 9/25/1757

(Nathaniel West Dandridge Bible, contd....)

N. W. Dandridge m. Jane Pollard 8/3/1779

Mrs. Dorothea Dandridge d. 9/25/1773

Nathaniel West Dandridge Sr. d. 1/16/1786, b. 9/7/1729 in King and Queen Co., Va.

Mrs. Martha Payne d. 9/28/1791

N. W. Dandridge m. Martha Fountaine 7/13/1797

N. W. Dandridge b. 1/14/1771

Martha Fountaine b. 7/4/1781

THEIR CHILDREN:

William Fountaine Dandridge
Martha Lightfoot Dandridge
Eliza Anne Dandridge
N. W. Dandridge, Jr.
Charles Fountaine Dandridge
Rosalie Spotswood Dandridge
Harry Belling Dandridge

Martha Dandridge d. 9/12/1845, bur. Ridgeway, Pontotoc, country seat of P. H. Fountaine, her bro. N. W. Dandridge d. 7/26/1847 in Pontotoc, bur. beside his wife at Ridgeway, the seat of P. H. Fountaine

Mrs. Martha Lightfoot Bolton d. 6/3/1850

WILLIAM HUBARD BIBLE
Owner: Col. James L. Bubard

BIRTHS

Matthew Hubard 3/11/1736
William Hubard 12/19/1744
Ann Hubard 3/26/1738
John Hubard 11/2/1747
Elizabeth Hubard 9/6/1739
Margaret Hubard 10/24/1749

Mary Hubard d. infant Elizabeth Hubard 9/13/1754

Mary Hubard 6/12/1752 James Hubard 2/6/1743

THOMAS CONWAY KELLY of Westmoreland County
Owner: J. Y. Kelly, Georgetown, Ky.

Thomas Conway Kelly b. 12/25/1799 in Virginia.
James Kelly, son of Alexander Kelly and Elizabeth, his wife, b. 3/12/1737.
Susan Wilson, his wife,b. 10/4/1741.
John Kelly, son of said James and Susan, b. 4/3/1761
Jane Payne, his 1st wife, b. 8/31/1760
Dinah Conway, his 2nd wife, b. 5/11/1773
James Y. Kelly, son of said James and Susan, b. 9/12/1765

Children of John Kelly (by Jane and Dinah)

Fanny Kelly
Jane P. Kelly
Spicer W. Kelly
John P. Kelly
Alexander D. Kelly
Mary Ann Kelly
George P. Kelly
William T. Kelly

Henry W. Kelly
Peter C. Kelly
Elizabeth Kelly
James W. Kelly
Susan W. Kelly
Richard P. Kelly
Thomas C. Kelly

Children of James Y. Kelly who m. Nancy Neale

Elizabeth Kelly
Susan Kelly
Sally Kelly
Penelope Kelly
James Kelly

Spicer Kelly

John Kelly (d. La. in 1837)
Nancy Kelly

Children of James and Susan Kelly

John Kelly b. 4/3/1761
Molly Kelly
Spicer Kelly

James Y. Kelly b. 9/12/1765
Jonathan Kelly
Alexander D. Kelly

JOSEPH DILLARD BIBLE of Amherst County
Owner: Peter H. Dillard

MARRIAGES

4/22/1781 Joseph Dillard b. 10/12/1776 to Judith Higginbotham b. on 1/26/1797

James H. Dillard to Mary Anne F. Lewis 10/30/1822
Thomas P. Dillard to Sophia F. Ferry 6/16/1824
George W. Dillard to Eliza Jane Hill 12/22/1828
Willis R. Plunket to Mahala R. Dillard 5/10/1832
Peter H. Joyner to Cassandra R. Dillard 2/23/1836
Gabriel H. Page to Susan Ann Dillard 12/26/1839

O. D. Dillard to Elizabeth C. J. Higginbotham 12/28/1840
Moses B. Hughes to Mary E. J .Dillard 3/2/1843
Chr1stopher C, Dillard to Edna Hill 8/31/1843
Barnett Cash to Elizabeth W. Dillard 9/17/1845
William S. Hughes to Paulina E. Dillard 12/22/1868

BIRTHS of Children of Joseph and Judith Dillard

James Higginbotham Dillard 12/1/1797
George Washington Dillard 1/13/1799
Betsey Watts Dillard 4/11/1800
Thomas Pettus Dillard 2/10/1802
Mahala Roberson Dillard 12/16/1803
Joseph Dillard 4/28/1805

Christopher Columbus Dillard 3/5/1813
Cassandra Rachel Dillard 6/12/1809
Paulina Smith Dillard 6/20/1811
Orgon Duvall Dillard 9/17/1815
Susan Ann Dillard 11/25/1818
Mary Ellen Judith Dillard 8/6/1822

WILLIAM HAY BIBLE

"William Hay, youngest son of James Hay and Helena (Rankin), his wife (by whom he had twelve children), was born in the town and Perish of Kilsyth and Shire of Sterling in North Birton on Thursday the l0th day of November O. S. being the 21st N. S. Anno Domini 1748. Having obtained an University Education in the City of Glasgow, he sailed from Greenoch for the Colony of Virginia on the 18th day of July An. Dom. 1768 and landed at Norfolk on Friday the 16th of September in the same year After visiting his brothers, .John and Peter who then, resided in the County of Southampton, he studied law under John Tazewell in the City of Williamsburg until the 7th day of May 1770 and on that day obtained a license to practice. He followed the Profession of the law until the Revolutionary War shut up the Courts and never resumed it again."

William Hay, aged 26 yrs, 27 days, m. 12/18/1774 Elizabeth, eldest dau. of Miles Cary Esq., Attorney at Law, decd, who was b. 12/18/1753 and by whom he had issue.

John Hay b. 1/5/1776, chrlstened 3/10th by Rev. William Harrison- his sponsors were Richard Taylor and Lady, Thomas Armlstead, his aunt Miss Hannah Cary and John Hay.

Willie Hay 6/12/1777-3/5/1778, aged 8 mos., 21 days

Mrs. Elizabeth Hay d. 3/9/1778, aged 24 yrs, 2 mos., 17 days.

William Hay m. again 5/22/1780 Elizabeth Tompkins, youngest dau.

Capt. Bennett Tompkins of Bennet's Creek in York Co. who was b. 1/2/1753 and was 1st cousin to his former wife, by whom he had issue –

Elizabeth Cary Hay b. 2/16/1783
William Hay b. 10/6/1784
James b. 2/26/1794
Mrs. Elizabeth Hay d. 12/9/1796

Miss Elizabeth Cary Hay d. 3/27/1807, aged 24 1 mo., 1 day

William Hay, Sr. d. 11/11/1825, wanting 11 days of being 77 yrs.

ARCHIBALD HALL DILLARD BIBLE

BIRTHS

Archibald Hall Dillard, son of Thomas P. and Sophia F. Dillard, 4/3/1835
Ann Eliza, dau. of Thomas P. and Sophia F. Dillard, 1/29/1836
Jesse Thomas, son of Thomas P. and Sophia F. Dillard, 5/17/1839
Paulous Marion, son of Susan Ann and Gabriel H. 10/20/1840
Oscar P. Dillard, son of O. D. and E. C. J. Dillard, 11/6/1841
Paulina E. Dillard 4/6/1544
Mary J. Dillard 10/8/1845
Cassandra W. Dillard 8/9/1847
Oscia Ella Joyner dau. of Peter H. and Cassandra R. Joyner, --/22/1837
Paulina Dillard Joyner 9/8/1839
William Warner Dillard, son of James H. and Mary Anne, 1/28/1824
Virginia Pettus, dau. of Thomas P. and Sophia Dillard, 6/22/1825
William Walker, son of above, 8/29/1826
James Edwin, son of above, 3/30/1828
Robert Franklin, son of above, 9/13/1829
Mary Elizabeth dau. of above, 7/8/1831

Cassandra Jane Plunket, dau. of Mahala and Willis R., 2/28/1833
Joseph Henry, son of Thomas P. and Sophia F. Dillard, 3/17/1833

(Archibald Hall Dillard Bible, contd....)

DEATHS

Joseph Dlllard, son of Joseph, 9/28/1805-8/21/1806
Joseph Dillard 2/24/1834, aged 57 yrs., 4 mos.
George W. Dillard, son of Joseph and Judith, in Mo., 8/26/1839
Eliza Jane Dillard, consort of George W., 8/24/1839 in Mo
Cassandra R. Joyner, consort of Peter H. Joyner and dau. of Joseph and Judith Dillard, 10/7/1842, Princess Ann Co., N. C. Judith Dillard, consort of Joseph Dillard, 1/6/1855, aged 74 yrs.

Relations of Joseph Dillard and wife

George Dillard, bro. to Joseph, 10/1911807, aged 39 yrs.
Sukey Dillard, mother to Joseph, 4/1813, aged 72 or 73 yrs. Rachel Higginbotham, mother to Judith Dillard and wife of James, 3/28/1809, aged 54 yrs.
Cole. James Higginbotham, consort to Rachel and father to Judith, 3/14/1813, aged 84 yrs.
Eliza Watts, wife of Henry H. Watts and dau. of George Dillard, bro. to Joseph, 7/22/1821
James Dillard, father to Joseph, 10/16/1823, aged 79 yrs.
James H. Dillard, son of Joseph and Judith, 10/13/1830, 33 yrs.

MILES CARY'S BIBLE
Of Southampton County

Miles Cary b. 5/28/1727 m. 5/23/1752 Elizabeth Taylor, b. 3/1/1733

BIRTHS of THEIR CHILDREN:

Elizabeth Cary 12/18/1753 -
Miles Cary 9/1/1757
Hannah Cary 11/10/1755
Mary Cary 8/29/1760

Nathaniel Cary 10/19/1763
Miles Cary d. 9/9/1766
Nathaniel Cary drowned in Nottoway 11/15/1767
Mrs. Elizabeth Cary d. 3/16/1774

CHARLES WASHINGTON FRIEND BIBLE
Owner: Mrs. Charles N. Friend Chester, Virginia

Thomas Friend 4/1700-4/14/1760
Frances Friend b. 3/1705

Thomas Friend, son of Thomas and Frances Cox, 7/7/1733-11/15/1768
Sarah Friend b. 9/8/1743 m. 10/25/1761 Sarah Friend, wife of Thomas Friend, 9/8/1743-10/1827

BIRTHS of Children of Thomas and Sarah Friend

Sarah Friend 8/14/1862 Charles Friend 12/6/1763-1/4/1799
Thomas Friend 10/23/1765-11/18/1767 William Friend 4/7/1767-2/7/1808
Ann Friend 2/4/1769 Ann Woodson Friend 2/4/1769-8/1827

BIRTHS of Children of William and Catherine Friend

Ann Stevenson Friend 12/28/1792-7/1793
Catherine Friend 7/4/1796-12/12/1797
Thomas Friend 7/3/1798
William Craig Friend 7/4/1800-summer 1802
Charles Washington Friend 6/28/1801 Chesterfield Co., "The Grove" Mother, Catherine Craig, d. when he was 11 days old, 7/9/1801
Martha Maria Friend, dau. of William and Nancy, 2/4/1803

(Charles Washington Friend Bible continued...)

Martha Cox, dau. of George and Mary Cox, 4/11/1804 Chesterfield Co., Va., m. Charles Washington Friend 4/16/1822

BIRTHS of Children of Charles W. and Martha Friend

Ann Catherine Friend 2/14/1824. Robert Whiting 4/5/1842
Sarah Frances Friend 10/18/1825 in Prince Edward Co., Va.-d. at Spring ,Hill, Chesterfield Co.,
Va.,4/26/1845, aged 19 yrs., 6 mos., 8 days
George William Friend 8/29/1827
Charles Woodson Friend 8/15/1829-9/11/1831, aged 2 yrs., 27 days
Robert Craig Friend 1/15/1832
Thomas Henry Friend 12/27/1834, baptised 5/17/1835
Mary Elizabeth Friend 3/3/1837, bapt1st Oct. 1st at Ware Bottom by Rev. George A. Bain
Charles Edward Friend 1/10/1842, baptised at Ware Bottom Church
by Rev. John W. Childs in August following-d. 9/28/1844
Charles Nathaniel Friend 9/25/1846 at Bollings in Chesterfield Co., Va., baptised by Rev. William B. Rowsie 1848
Sarah Woodson, wife of George, 8/14/1762-11/20/1798
Ann Woodson b. 6/2/1766
Sarah Woodson, dau. of George and Sarah, b. 11/19/1784
Caroline Matilda Woodson, dau. of same George, b. 7/28/1789
Robert Whiting, son of John
Whiting and Elizabeth, b. 5/17/1813 m. Ann Catherine Friend, dau. of Charles W. and Martha Friend,4/5/1842

ABSALOM HIGGINBOTHAM BIBLE
Mrs. B. D. Higginbotham, Buena VIsta, Va.

Absalom Higginbotham b. 5/2/1781
Mary C. (Sandidge, dau. of Benjamin Sandidge of Amherst Co.), b. 8/26/1789

BIRTHS of THEIR CHILDREN:

Betty Ann Higginbotham 10/5/1807
Nancy Croxton Higginbotham 12/4/1809
James Higginbotham 2/5/1812
Sallie Higginbotham 9/25/1783
Rufus A. Higginbotham 3/5/1814
Benjamin G. Higginbotham 8/21/1818
Absalom Higginbotham Jr. 7/3/1821
Thomas Higginbotham 3/1/1824
Aaron Higginbotham 12/31/1826
Paul Higginbotham 11/1/1831
Elizabeth Higginbotham 7/11/1778

John J. Higginbotham 1/16/1820
Nancy Higginbotham 10/7/1821
Nancy Higginbotham 6/12/1786
Anderson Sandidge 8/9/1793
Johannah Higginbotham 6/26/1794
Aaron Higginbotham 2/23/1789
Arthur White 8/1/1824
Clara G. Higginbotham 12/1/1791
William, son of Ann, 8/2/1855
Alexander B. Higginbotham 6/23/1818
John, son of Ann and Jack, 7/3/1856

MARRIAGES

Absalom-Hiigginbotham Sr. to Mary C. Sandidge 11/6/1806
Absalom Higginbotham Jr. to Elizabeth Tucker 12/14/1843
James Higginbotham to Ann Eliza London 12/17/1835
Aaron Higginbotham to Elizabeth Sandidge (dau. of Benjamin of Amherst Co.) 5/22/1817

DEATHS

Betty Ann Hill 5/26/1831, the oldest dau. of Absalom and Mary Higginbotham
Thomas Higginbotham 11/1/1841, aged 17 yrs., 8 mos.
Anderson Sandidge 8/9/1793-5/12/1859

(Absalom Higginbotham Bible, DEATHS, contd....)

Paul Higginbotham 8/26/1864
Nancy C. Royster 10/5/1865
Sarah A. Higginbotham, wife of A. L., 6/5/1860
Absalom Higginbotham Sr. 5/2/1781-7/7/1866
John W. Myers 9/23/1869
Mary C. Higginbotham 5/28/1871

James Higginbotham 9/11/1874
Rufus A. Higginbotham 12/28/1878
Elizabeth Higginbotham 9/23/1874
William Tucker 8/23/1884

JOEL BRASELTON SR. BIBLE
Owner: A. M. Evans, Gainesville, Ga.

Jacob Braselton b. 6/27/1749
(Hannah Braselton, Sr., dau. of Duff Green of Va. and niece of General Washington)

BIRTHS

John Braselton 2/27/1774
Green Braselton 12/5/1786
Elizabeth Braselton 11/5/1775
Reuben Braselton 12/30/1788
Henry Braselton 4/5/1777
Daniel Braselton 11/5/1790
William Braselton 3/26/1779
Job Braselton 12/30/1792

Hannah Braselton Jr. 6/24/1781
Rebecca Braselton 2/3/1795
Mary Braselton 2/21/1783
Amos Braselton 5/15/1797
Jacob Braselton, Jr. 9/17/1785
Sarah Braselton 10/29/1799

DEATHS

Elizabeth Brown 6/23/1805
Sarah Bell 2/27/1832

Hannah Braselton Jr. 10/11/1832

BIRTHS

Cynthia Brown 3/27/1798
John McClintick Brown 1/9/1803

Mary Brown 1/11/1801

Note--Braselton, Georgia (Jackson Co.) was named after one of these children who migrated there.

DR. JOHN THOMAS MERRYMAN
Of Lunenburg Co., Virginia

BIRTHS

Thomas F. Merryman 4/18/1782
Mary Scott 5/12/1791
Margaret Bauldin 9/28/1792
James Parke Street 6/10/1814
William James Merryman 4/17/1817
Waddy Street 3/7/1832

John Thomas Merryman 11/14/1819
Susan Frances Street 7/2/1828
Mary Elizabeth Merryman 7/17/1823
Mary Scott Merryman 12/5/1854
David Street 4/21/1770

Margaret Elizabeth Merryman b. 11/8/1857 m. William Alexander Neal, who was b. 2/3/1849.

Their Children

Frances Alma Neal
Elizabeth Merryman Meal
William Bernard Neal (d. infancy)

Virginia Montfort Neal Daisy Merryman Neal
Charles Alexander Neal Margaret Ann Neal

MARRIAGES

Thomas F. Merryman to Margaret Bauldin 2/21/1816 by Rev. Mathew Lyle
William Bauldin to Elizabeth Baker 3/25/1782 by Rev. Richard Sankey

(Dr. John Thomas Merryman Bible continued....)

David Street to Mary Scott (2nd wife) 9/7/1813 by Rev. Charles Price in Bedford Co., Va.
John D. Priddy to Mary E. Merryman 10/31/1838
John Thomas Merryman to Susan Frances Street 2/28/1854
Margaret Elizabeth Merryman to Wm Alexander Neal 4/12/1877, St. Paul's Church, Lunenburg Co., Va.
Frances Alma Neal to John Herbert Thompson 4/15/1896 by Rev. J. C. Hiden
Daisy Merryman Meal to John Nicholas Martin 6/16/1903 by Dr. William E. Evans
Margaret Ann Neal to Frost Hiram Herndon 8/17/1912 by Rev. Thomas C. Darst
Elizabeth Merryman Meal to (1) H. E. Boykin 2/1904; (2) Harry H. Warfield 11/24/1915
Virginia Montfort Meal to Dawson Edward Watkins 1/12/1905
Charles Alexander Meal to Mary Louise Cobb 3/15/1913

DEATHS

Thomas F. Merryman 8/16/1839
John Thomas Merryman 12/9/1862
William J. Merryman 1/19/1848
Mary Scott Street 1/18/1876
Margaret Bauldin Merryman 4/8/1853

Susan Frances Cheatham (nee David Street 5/3/1849) 2/8/1895
Mary Scott Merryman 9/4/1857
William Bernard Neal 3/1884
William Alexander Neal 7/18/1911
Elizabeth Merryman Neal 3/18/1914

Memorandum

Thomas F. Merryman was son of John and Mary Flippen Merryman of Cumberland Co., Va.
John Merryman was son of Thomas Merryman and Phebe James who were married 1/17/1752
John Merryman d. 6/16/1785
Thomas Merryman was son of John and Elizabeth Merryman of Goochland Co., Va.
Margaret (Peggy) Bauldin was dau. of William and Elizabeth Bauldin of Prince Edward Co., Va.
John Merryman m. Mary Flippen about 1781.

JONAS M. HOLLAND BIBLE
From: Rev. War Pension #W8944

BIRTHS

Jones M. Holland 12/20/1754
Theodosia 3/20/1761

THEIR CHILDREN:

Judy Holland 12/9/1784
John Holland 11/3/1796
Polly Holland 11/27/1786
Patsy Holland 2/8/1800
Nancy Holland 2/20/1791

Susanna Holland 12/20/1803
Anny Holland 12/9/1794
Elizabeth Holland 11/15/1806

MARRIAGES

Jonas Holland to Theodosia Belk
Judy Holland to J;ames Jones 4/4/1809
Polly Holland to Andrew Robins 10/1803

Anny Holland to David Graves 10/29/1815
Nancy Holland to R. Jones 3/13/1817

BIRTHS

James Jones 1/27/1818
John Holland Jones 11/7/1822
Polly Ann Jones 2/26/1820
Thomas J. U. Jones 4/1/1829
Zerelda Graves 8/29/1816

--an Graves 11/15/1824
John Washington Graves 12/25/1817
Elizabeth Holland Graves 9/10/--
Richard Evermont Graves 4/16/1819
Harrison Anderville Graves 10/24/1820

DRURY STITH BIBLE
Owner: Mrs. Thomas J. Stith
Ekron, Kentucky

Drury Stith and Elizabeth (nee Buckner), husband and wife

BIRTHS

Richard Stith 9/30/1727 m. 12/29/1756 Lucy Stith (nee Hall) b. 7/1736, dau. of John and Ann Hall
Richard Stith 12/9/1778 m. 12/27/1798
Elizabeth Stith (nee Jones) 1/1779, dau. of Thomas and Elizabeth Jones

BIRTHS of Children of Richard and Elizabeth Stith

Lucy Stith 3/2/1802-10/6/1876 m. Thomas Hawfield Stith
Elizabeth Stith 10/6/1803-6/7/1840.
Stith Saunders, husband Buckner Stith 5/31/1807-9/1/1856
Susan Stith 12/10/1808-8/4/1847 m. Griffin Stith 5/13/1825
John C. Stith 10/3/1810-3/1/1880
William Stith 4/21/1812-1/17/1880 m. Hannah Hayden
Edmund Stith 3/25/1814-4/2/1860 m. Marv Dowell
Martha Ann Stith 5/14/1816 m. 7/14/1832 Joseph E. Hardaway
Jesse J. Stith 3/14/1818-7/21/1895
Mary Ann Stith 1/23/1820-10/24/1873 m. Henry Stith
John Cain b. 10/2/1797 m. 11/30/1820
Olive Dismore b. 6/6/1800. issue: Lucinda b. 4/10/1824
Jesse J. Stith m. Lucinda Cain 10/6/1842

DEATHS

Husband, Richard Stith, 4/13/1843 Elizabeth Stith, wife, 8/24/1844
Richard Stith m. Lucy Hall 12/29/1756

BIRTHS of Children of Richard and Lucy Stith

Ann Stith 11/12/1757
Thomas Stith 10/8/1768
Joseph Stith 9/6/1759
John Stith 10/7/1770
Lucy Stith 3/12/1761

Catharine Stith 5/28/1773
Elizabeth Buckner Stith 10/25/1762
Martha Stith 5/8/1775
Mary Stith 11/12/1764 m. Saunders
Benjamin Stith 8/28/1766

William Stith 10/8/1777 m. Nancy, dau. of Thomas and Elizabeth Jones.
Richard Stith 12/9/1778 m. Elizabeth, dau. of Thomas and Elizabeth Jones.

DEATHS

Richard Stith Sr. 11/16/1802
John Stith 10/27/1840
Lucy Stith, Sr. 2/12/1815
Martha Saunders 7/1/1843
Ann Hightower 1/14/1831
Elizabeth Buckner

Joseph Stith 11/3/1837
Catharine Lucy Jordan 6/13/1802
William Stith, Sr.
Benjamin Stith 3/18/1837
Richard Stith 4/13/1843
Thomas Stith 7/27/1821

HOLT RICHERSON BIBLE
Owner: Mrs. George W. Bonte 330 W. 95th St., NYC

Holt Richerson (Col. Holt Richerson, officer in American Revolution), b. 9/30/1716
Susanna Richerson, wife of Col. Holt Richerson, dau. of Col. Francis West, b. 3/15/1744

(Holt Richerson Bible, contd....)

BIRTHS of THEIR CHILDREN:

Mary Evans Richerson 8/3/1765
Agnes Richerson 11/25/1774
James Richerson 8/7/1767
Holt C. Richerson 9/16/1776

Susanna W. Richerson 4/14/1770
Francis W. Richerson 12/20/1778
Francis W. Richerson -/13/1772
John A. Richerson 11/26/1780

BIRTHS of Children of Holt and Elizabeth Richerson

Jane P. Brete Richerson 3/8/1783
John B. Richerson 2/28/1787
Elizabeth H. Richerson 2/28/1785

Gracey B. Richerson 5/29/1789
Anderson Richerson 8/15/1793

BIRTHS of Children of Frances and Benjamin Quarles

Francis W. Quarles 1/5/1803
Thomas D. Quarles 7/20/1806

Susan Ann Quarles 1/27/1809

John Brete Richerson m. Mildred Anne Ragsdale 5/14/1812 by Rev. John Mills, all of King Wm Co., Va.

BIRTHS of Children of John Brete and Mildred Richerson William

West Richerson 3/13/1813
Ann Eliza Frances Richerson 2/14/1816
John Holt Richerson 1/21/1818
Ragsdale Anderson Richerson 10/5/1819
Maria Louisa Richerson 7/11/1821

Alfred Pleasants Richerson 12/30/1822
Edward Motier Richerson 10/29/1824
Charlotte Blatterman Richerson 2/24/1827
Mildred Dungleson Richerson 2/14/1829
Mary Jane Frances Richerson 12/28/1832

DEATHS

Susanna Richerson, wife of Holt Richerson, 12/5/1780
Francis W. Quarles, son of Benjamin and Frances Quarles, 6/8/1840
Frances Quarles, wife of Benjamin Quarles and dau. of Col. Holt Richerson, 1/1815
Francis W. Richerson 11/1816

FRANCIS JERDONE of Louisa County
Owner: "Stirling" Plantation, Charles City Co., Va.

"This Bible belongs to Francis Jerdone of Louisa County in Virginia, who was born in Jedburgh in the Shire of Tiviotdale in North Britain, the 30th of January 1720-21.Sarah Macon, his wife, was born in New Kent Co. in Virginia, the 21st of Feb 1732. They were married on the 10th of Feb 1753"

Children of Francis and Sarah Jerdone

Mary Jerdone 1/17/1751 New Kent Co. - 4/20/1837
Francis Jerdone 2/9/1756 Louisa Co. - 4/29/1841
Sarah Jerdone 9/12/1757 Louisa Co. - 4/1/1792 at Br1stol, N. B.
Elizabeth Jerdone 4/7/1759 Louisa Co. 2/3/1830 at York (she m. Alexander Macauley of Yorktown)
Isabella Jerdone 9/30/1761 Louisa Co. - 4/8/1825
Anne Jerdone 4/3/1763 Louisa Co. - 10/2/1794
John Jerdone 9/19/1764 Louisa Co. - 1/15/1786 at Jed'g, N. B.
Martha Jerdone 6/10/1767 Louisa Co. 9/12/1767
William Jerdone 3/26/1769 Louisa Co. - 12/2/1772

DEATHS

Francis Jerdone 8/5/1771 Sarah Jerdone, relict of Francis, 10/23/1818
Polly Byars 3/12/1821

(Francis Jerdone Bible, contd....)

Francis Jerdone m. Polly Byars 6/20/1799, who was b. 12/2/1781 Louisa Co., Va.

BIRTHS of Children of Francis and Polly Jerdone

John Jerdone 10/11/1800 Louisa Co.
Sarah Jerdone 2/10/1807 Louisa Co
Francis Jerdone 12/6/1802 Louisa Co.

William Jerdone 3/4/1805 Louisa Co.
James Jerdone 2/19/1812 Louisa Co. -- 2/15/1863

William Jerdone m. Maria A. G. Coleman 11/22/1832, who was b. in Spotsylvania Co., Va. 12/20/1812

BIRTHS of Children of William and Maria Jerdone

Maria C. Jerdone 11/27/1833 Louisa Co. -12/25/1833
William Jerdone m. Anne Burfitt (Burford) 12/1/1847

BIRTHS of Children of William and Anne Jerdone

William M. Jerdone 11/8/1848
Earnest Jerdone

Ellen Jerdone

WILLIAM LEWIS BIBLE

BIRTHS

William Lewis 7/11/1791
Joseph Martin Lewis
Elizabeth Lewis 11/13/1795-8/19/1819
Joseph Martin Lewis 8/17/1828
John Jefferson Lewis 6/5/1820
Elizabeth Didamia Lewis 10/1/1821

George Washington Lewis 1/31/1834
Dorcas Lewis 5/4/1823
Henry William Lewis 10/14/1824
Sara Ann Elizabeth Lewis 12/17/1835
William L. Lewis 10/28/1826

JOHN JORDAN BIBLE
From: Rev. War Pension #W29726

John Jordan, son of Burrell and Amy, b. 5/8/1756 Greenville Co., Va. m. Northampton Co., N. C., 2/19/1786 Winifred b. 9//1763, dau. of George Jordau.

BIRTHS of THEIR CHILDREN:

Brittain Jordan 6/18/1787
Burwell Jordan 9/30/--
Green H. Jordan 4/30/1789
John Jordan 4/16/1800

Priscilla Jordan 8/17/1791
Mary Jordan 7/3/1803-1/22/1893
Patience Jordan 9/30/1793
Mary Jordan m. John H. Newton

McELRATH-SEAY BIBLE
Owner: Dean Rathbone, Rt. 3, Box 178, Clyde, N. C. 27821

BIRTHS

Sarah Maria Seay 2/28/1827
John McElrath 3/21/1827

THEIR CHILDREN:

James Matthew McElrath 9/20/1852
Margaret Lula McElrath 11/4/1858
Wilmath C. McElrath 9/17/1853
William Joseph McElrath 4/18/1855

Nancy Jane McElrath 10/5/1859
Sarah Ann McElrath 6/9/1857
John Augustus McElrath 7/25/1863

GEORGE MARTIN BIBLE
From: Rev. War Pension #W4543

Joel Martin, son of George J. and Mary, b. 6/22/1787
Fatsy Jenkins d. --/16/1775?
Salley Martin, dau. of George, b. 5/24/1791

---tty, dau. of John -eanes and Paty, his wife, b. 1811
John Martin ---

Note: 8/12/1841 Martha Martin, Patrick Co., Va., testified she was s1ster of Mary Martin of Pittsylvania Co., Va. and saw Mary marry George Martin by Parson Lee Massie in Fairfax Co., Va. on 1/15/1775. Martha Martin stated that Mary Martin with her two children, William and George, stayed at her father's house (Joseph Bailey) while George was in service. George Martin d. when 33 yrs. old. 8/12/1841

Stephen Martin, aged 62, of Patrick Co., Va. stated George Martin was his uncle.
In 1841, Susan Hancock of Patrick Co., Va. stated George Martin was her uncle. Mary Martin,
widow, d. 10/22/1843 Pittsylvania Co., Va.
Thomas Bailey of Halifax Co., Va., bro. of Mary Martin, stated Mary was dau. of Joseph H. Bailey of Loudoun Co., Va. Patsy Martin made oath that she was s1ster of Mary Martin of Pitttsylvania Co., Va.from Stokes Co., N. C.

JOSEPH MARTIN BIBLE
From: Rev. War Pension #R6960

BIRTHS

John Martin 12/19/1787
Sarah Martin 6/1/1797
William Martin 4/6/1789
Abner Martin 11/9/1799
Elizabeth Martin 6/25/1791

Ephraim Martin 8/18/1803
Susannah Martin 7/26/1793
Joseph Martin 10/24/1806
Jane Martin 7/26/1795

Note: John Martin, father of Joseph, testified 10/5/1835. Athens Co., Va., that his son, Joseph, now decd, lived in Sussex Co., Va. when he enl1sted. Martha Martin, wid., applied for pension 7/9/1851, Tyler Co., Va., aged 84 or 85 yrs., stated she married soldier 1/1786 by Thaddeus Dodd, a Presbyterian minister, Washington Co., Pa., when she was about 19 yrs. old. Joseph Martin d. 4/23/1833.

CYRUS TYREE BIBLE of Richmond
Owner: Mrs. George Mahan, Jr.
590 S. Barksdale, Memphis, Tenn.

Cyrus Tyree of Richmond, Virginia m. Emily Pitts of Halifax, North Carolina 12/22/1825
Emily G. Pitts, b. Ringwood, North Carolina, dau. of John and Nancy Pitts, b. 9/16/1805

MARRIAGES

John P. Tyree to Eliza A. Farris 2/5/1852
F. D. Tyree to Lucy A. Jones 3/29/1853
Mary W. Tyree to William C. Burns 8/10/1854

BIRTHS

Francis D. Tyree 10/3/1826
Emily M. Tyree 2/12/1839
John P. Tyree 11/18/1828
Cyrus Hardy Tyree 10/18/1841
Thomas J. Tyree 6/10/1830
Sarah Elizabeth Tyree 1/8/1844
Mary W. Tyree 4/15/1832

Lemuel H. Tyree 6/18/1846
Martha Ann Virginia Tyree 4/22/1834
James L. Tyree 3/8/1848
Nancy C. Tyree 2/23/1837
Cora P. Tyree 9/17/1850
Cyrus Tyree d. 2/22/1854, aged 52 yrs., 6 mos., 26 days

ADAM MARTIN BIBLE
Revolutionary War Soldier

CHILDREN

Mary M. Martin
Adam Martin
Rebekah Martin
Jehoida Martin
John Martin
Jonathan P.
Letty
Lewis
Lucinda
Mary
Nancy A.

BENJAMIN MARTIN BIBLE
Revolutionary War Soldier

CHILDREN

Benjamin Martin
Benjamin H. Martin
Betsey Martin
David Martin
Elizabeth Martin
Henry Martin
Nathan Martin
Mary M.
Robert N. Martin

HERMAN SHELL BIBLE

CHILDREN:

Daniel Asbury Shell
Dorothea L. Shell
Elizabeth A. Shell
Herman Shell
James E. Shell
Jane E. Shell
Martha Shell
Mary A. Shell
Nancy L. Shell
Thomas H. Shell
William B. Shell

(Herman Shell Bible, contd....)

Children of Lemmon and Nancy, his wife

Charles W. Shell 5/8/1810   John Fletcher Shell 6/30/1813

DEATHS

Lemmon Shell 9/15/1814
Nancy Shell, wife of above, 10/13/1814
Dorothea, wife of Lemmon Shell, 12/10/1794
Dorothea L. Shell, dau. of Lemmon and Dorothea, 9/11/1795
John Fletcher Shell, son of Lemmon and Nancy, 8/9/1814
Thomas Shell, son of Lemmon and Dorothea, 5/4/1828
Precious Shell 9/1836
Clara T. Curtiss (wife of W. H. Perkins) 6/5/1859, Columbia, Mississippi
Mary F. Curtiss 6/25/1861, 14 yrs., 10 mos, 10 days, same place

BIRTHS

George Elliott Curtiss 11/4/1838-4/1839 Clara Thompson Curtiss 1/8/1839
Melissa Elizabeth Curtiss 8/15/184-Little Babe 12/18/1851-12/28/1851
Emm Curtiss 8/9/1845-1849 Mary F. Curtiss 8/15/1846
George Wesley Curtiss 10/29/1836-9/12/1837 John Dugan 12/6/1775
Nancy Dugan, wife to above, 10/30/1771

BIRTHS of THEIR CHILDREN:

Lucy L. Dugan 2/7/1802   Marthy E. Dugan 3/6/1809?
Elizabeth Ann Dugan 7/21/1807 Robert Dugan 6/10/1805
Mary J. Dugan 9/19/1803   Margaret C. Dugan 12/27/1811

JAMES H. MARTIN BIBLE
Owner: Mrs. Robert Ross Mangum

James H. Martin b. 1/22/1789 m. 4/6/1809 Charlotte De'Berry Kirby b. 4/5/1795

BIRTHS of THEIR CHILDREN:

Caroline K. Martin 2/20/1811   Benjamin K. Martin 8/12/1815
Julia E. Martin 1/25/1825   Lemuel K. Martin 10/5/1829
Ellenor F. Martin 4/23/1813   Emily A. Martin 11/22/1817
Melvina F. Martin 8/24/1827   Virginia Lafayette Martin 5/8/1832
James H. Martin, Jr. 10/1/1822 Edmund D. Martin 5/3/1820- 5/8/1832

DEATHS

James H. Martin 6/1/1836, aged 48
Charlotte De Martin 6/12/1858, aged 63 yrs., 3 mos., 7 days

GEORGE McINTOSH EDWARDS BIBLE
Owner: Mrs. G. S. Edwards, 519 Caroline St., Norfolk, Va.

MARRIAGES

George McIntosh Edwards to Mary Amanda Ball   Charles Edward Owens to Sarah Frances Edwards
Henry Shelton Edwards to Emma C. Daniel   James B. Groves to Alice Tellietha (Lillie) Edwards 4/1881
Benjamin Fuller Allen to Mary Cornelia Edwards 2/3/1876   George S. Edwards to May E Hope 3/20/1906

(George McIntosh Edwards Bible, contd....)

BIRTHS of Children of George S. and May E. Edwards

Henry Shelton Edwards 11/12l1909 Parksley, Va.
Mary Hope Edwards 10/23/1911 Norfolk, Va.
Louise Virginia Edwards 10/4/1914 Norfolk, Va.
Margaret Ball Edwards 9/14/1917 Norfolk, Va.-7/30/1918, aged 10 mos., 16 days
John Sumner Edwards d. 8/12/1942, aged 36 yrs.
George McIntosh, son of William Henry and Sally Sands Edwards, b. 1/31/1827
Mary Amanda Ball, wife of G. M. Edwards, b. 3/14/1831, Beaufort, S. C.
BIRTHS of Children of G. M. and Mary A. Edwards Henry Shelton Edwards 11/16/1850
Sarah Frances Edwards 8/14/1852
Elijah Ball Edwards 9/19/1854
Mary Cornelia Edwards 7/31/1856
Alice Tillietha (Lillie) Edwards
Ella Virginia Edwards 1/31/1863 Tattnall Co., Ga.

BIRTHS of Children of G. S. and Georgia Ware Edwards

George McIntosh Edwards 7/19/1888
Thomas Theodore Edwards 9/16/1894

DEATHS

Ella Virginia, dau. of G. M. and Mary A. Edwards, 8/31/1862, aged 1 yr, 1 mo., 15 days
Elijah Ball Edwards, son of G. M. and Mary A. Edwards, NYC, bur.Oakland Cemetery, Atlanta, Ga.
George McIntosh Edwards 11/28/1899, bur. Norfolk, Va.
Mary A., wife of George M. Edwards, 10/28/1903, aged 72 yrs. Georgia Ware, wife of George S. Edwards, 2/23/1898
Sarah Frances Edwards Owens, dau. of G. M. and Mary Edwards 1/5/1922 in Savannah, Va. (bur. Flemington Cem., Hinesville, Ga.

BURCH-BRUMFIELD BIBLE

BIRTHS

John R. Burch 1/9/1832
Oscar Monroe Burch 8/17/1871
Malissa S. Brumfield 10/11/1843
Arthur Wilmer Burch 7/17/1873
Lena Leota Burch 7/23/1864
Lewis B. Burch 12/30/1874
William V. Burch 7/22/1865

Rosa A. Burch 7/17/1876
Walter V. Burch 8/17/1866
Weston J. Burch 6/13/1878
Frances Cletena Burch 10/14/1868
Thomas E. Burch 8/17/1879
Mary Rebecca Burch 10/19/1869
Wilton E. Burch 10/18/1581

TABITHA RODGERS BIBLE
Of Accomack County
Owner: Mrs. George R. Miles, Atlantic, Va.

"Bible purchased November, 1818 by Tabitha Rodgers." Inside flyleaf: "John Read, his Book"
"Elizabeth Rodgers, her Book, 1828"
Richard Rodgers 1550-1730, aged 30 yrs.
John Rodgers, son of Richard, 9/8/1698-10/1756
Elizabeth Rodgers, wife of John Rodgers, 12/29/1696-5/18/1783
Abel Rodgers, son of John and Elizabeth, 4/20/1727-1768
Robert Rodgers, son of Abel and Rosey, his wife, b. 6/29/1753
Tabitha Rodgers, wife of Robert, 1/22/1755-11/28/1824

(Tabitha Rodgers Bible, contd....)
BIRTHS of Children of Robert and Tabitha Rodgers

Enoch Rodgers 1/21/1775-8111/1811
Emily Rodgers 11/27/1778
Elizabeth Rodgers 4/22/1781-6/25/1844
Abel R. Rodgers 3/25/1784-2/1/1820
Smith Rodgers 4/15/1787-11*18/1795
Asa J. Rodgers 1/18/1794
Peggy Smith Rodgers 5/8/1798-7/5/1800
Sarah Bundick, mother of Tabitha Rodgers, d. 2/14/1764, aged 56
Richard Rodgers emigrated to James Town from England in the year 1820, his son, John, b. 1626, and removed to Accomack Co. in 1650, his son, Richard, b. 1650, his son, John, b. 1698. The following is the order of the ancestral line of the oldest male branch. Richard from England in 1620, age not known.

His son, John, b. 1626 settled in this county 1650
His son, Richard 1650-1730, aged 80
His son, John 1698-1758, aged 58 His son, Abel 1727-1768, aged 40
His son, Robert 6/29/1753-12/14/1827, aged 75 yrs.
Richard Rodgers 1/21/1775-8/11/1811 m. 1/6/1808 Sarah C. B. Kendall 3/13/1789-2/16/1824, dau of William and Nancy Kendall
Margaret Annatha Parsons Rodgers, dau. of Richard Rodgers and Sarah, b. 3/9/1808
William Kendall b. 6/7/1735 m. Nancy Parsons 10/17/1771
My dear mother, Tabitha Rodgers, d. 11/28/1824 (/s/ Elizabeth Rodgers)
Robert Rodgers d. 12/14/1827
Sarah Elizabeth Read b. 3/23/1825, dau. of Richard and Annatha Read
John Read, son of Richard and Annatha, b. 3/19/1836
Margaret Annatha Parsons Rodgers d. 6/30/1831 Sarah Rodgers d. 1/30/1843
Samuel Griffin Savage, son of William A. Rosey, b. 1/8/1815
Elizabeth Rodgers d. 6/26/1844
Asa J. Rodgers d. 12/2/1846, aged 2 yrs.

BIRTHS of Children of John R. and Mary F. Read

Asa R. Read 1/26/1856
John R. Read 1/4/1861
William K. Read 3/21/1858
Ray Read 1/5/1864
Mary F. Read, wife of John R. Read and dau. of William Henderson and Sally, his wife, 5/8/1832-8/13/1869
John R. Read d. 11/9/1876, aged 46 yrs., 7 mos., 21 days
William K. Read m. Margie B. Ames 1/27/1880

BIRTHS of Children of William K. and Margie B. Read

George Rodgers Read 12/23/1891 –
Kathryn Ames Read 7/31/1901
Mary Irene Read 8/4/1843
Kendall Agnes Read 5/21/1905
Gladys E. Read 2/28/1897
Gladys E. Read m. Joseph E. Mayfield 9/17/1918
Margie B. Read, wife of W. K. Read, d. 6/2/1917
Kendall Agnes Read m. George Robert Miles 12/12/1923
William Kendall Read, husband of Margie B. Read, d. 3/22/1926, aged 87 yrs.
John R. Read d. 5/7/1942 Baltimore City Hospital, bur. 5/7/1942, London Park Cemetery, Route 6, Grave 105.

(William Murdock Bible, contd....)

DEATHS

Minerva E. C. Murdock 10/8/1863
John M. Austin 5/1/1868
C. E. Austin m. Ann E. Murdock 12/24/1870

BIRTHS of Children of C. E. and Ann E. Austin

William F. Austin 9/12/1871 -- 9/28/1905
Mary E. Austin 11/12/1885
John R. Austin 3/12/1874
John M. Austin 6/14/1820
Thaddeus W. Gilliam m. Mary P. Murdock 12/27/1866
John William Russell Gilliam b. 3/10/1868
Richard T. Adams m. Elizabeth J. Murdock 12/25/1865
Oscar Judson Adams b. 10/16/1866

Mary Austin 5/29/1877
C. Y. Austin 5/18/1880-1/14/1893
Cornelius E. Austin 6/14/1844

C. MATTHEW CROOM BIBLE
of Isle of Wight Co.
Owner: Mrs. F. C. Berryman

BIRTHS of Children of Edward and Sarah Croom

C. Matthew Croom 10/6/1734
Edward Croom 12/24/1741
Mary Croom -/13/1736

Joseph Croom 11/23/1744
Robert Croom 4/22/1739

Charles Driver, son of Edward Driver and Sarah, his wife, b. 12/26/1731

EXUM O. BRITT of Isle of Wight Co.
Owner: B. P. Chapman, Smithfield, Va.

BIRTHS

Exum O. Britt 2/2/1798
E. B. Britt 2/8/1831
Elizabeth Clarke 1/20/1802
Mary Eliza Britt 3/5/1832
J. E. S. A. Britt 1/9/1819
Nancy Preston Thomas 2/12/1831
Martha A. Britt 5/24/1820
John M. Exum Britt 10/22/1852
Mary Eliza Britt 7/11/1821

George W. Britt Jr. 10/31/1855
B. F. Britt 3/25/1823
Florence O. Britt 3/18/1858
George W. Britt 12/9/1824
Lewis N. Britt 10/2/1861
Thomas Norsworthy Britt 7/28/1826
Nancy May Britt 1/16/1868
John W. Britt 8/8/1828
Sarah E. Britt 1/20/1871

MARRIAGES

Exum Britt to Elizabeth Clarke 12/23/1817
Exum O. Britt to Mavenda Joyner 9/6/1829
George W. Britt to Nancy P. Thomas 5/1/1851

DEATHS

Elizabeth Clarke Britt 11/5/1828
John M. Exum Britt 10/10/1862
Exum O. BrLtt 9/8/1833
Lewis N. Britt 3/31/1863
Mary Eliza Britt 9/1/183-
Nancy May Britt 8/2/1866
Thomas Norsworthy Brltt 8/16/1828

George W. Britt Sr. 6/30/1875
John W. Britt 10/28/1842
R. D. Marshall 5/29/1866
John Clarke 11/16/1842
J. E. S. A. Marshall 1/31/1869
Thomas E. Shepard 7/27/1857, aged 15 yrs.

NATHAN CARR BIBLE of Isle of Wight Co.

Polly C. Carr, dau. of John and Nancy Carr, b. 12/3/1798

BIRTHS of Children of Nathan and Nancy Carr

Mary Elizabeth Carr 4/1/1818 -
James T. Carr 4/8/1825
Ann Matilda Carr 12/11/1819
Benjamin L. Carr 5/4/1828

Eliza Ann Carr 10/29/1821
Emaline Carr 6/1/1829
Sophia Jane Carr 1/30/1823

Polly C. Carr, dau. of John and Nancy, m. Jesse Holland 1/6/1815
Their son, Jesse Holland 10/24/1823-9/26/1826
Jesse Darius Holland 11/16/1826-7/6/1828

JOHN GIBBS BIBLE of Isle of Wight Co.
Owner: Mrs. J. D. Gray, Smithfield, Va.

BIRTHS of Children of John Gibbs and wife, Polly Driver
Patsy Gibbs 11/3/1805

Ralph Gibbs 4/14/1793
John Gibbs 8/3/1801
Nancy Gibbs 10/3/1795
Samuel Whitfield Gibbs 3/27/1805
Polly Gibbs 11/14/1797

Rachel Gibbs 11/30/1799
Polly Gibbs, wife of John, d. 11/3/1805
John Gibbs d. 4/20/1823

ARTHUR CHANNELL BIBLE of Isle of Wight Co.

Arthur Channell, son of Arthur and Mildred Channell, b. 2/18/1782 Margaret, dau. of Lemuel Bowden and Anne, b. 11/29/1780

BIRTHS of Children of Arthur and Margaret Channell
Arthur M. Channell 12/27/1806

William P. Channell 10/24/1804
Mary A. Channell 3/11/1811

Margaret Channell 2/10/1814
Jane Channell 8/29/1809

Richard B. Channell 3/26/1819
Polly Gibbs, dau. of John Gibbs and Polly Driver, his wife, b. 1/14/1797

MARRIAGES

Arthur Channell to Margaret Bowden 12/23/1803
Arthur Channell to Polly D. Gibbs 3/9/1824
John M. Pasteur to Emily F. Channell, dau. of Arthur and Polly, 12/21/1848
Adelbert Oswell Whitney to Maggie A. Channell 11/30/1869

BIRTHS of Children of Arthur and Polly Channell

George Franklin Channell 1/8/1826
John Channell 11/7/1832
Emily F. Channell 1/28/1828

Virginia Channell 5/6/1827
Cornelia Channell 6/23/1830
Margaret Anne Channell 8/16/1834

Arthur Otis Channell, son of George Franklin Channell and Emma R. Johnson, his wife, b. 9/22/1868
Arthur Otts Channell m. Bessie Morris 1/1896
Maggie Oswell Whitney, dau. of Adelbert O. and Maggie A. Whitney, his wife, b. 11/9/1870
Arthur M. Whitney, son of same, b. 10/1/1872
Clarence W. Whitney, son of same, b. 6/5/1875

DEATHS

Margaret Channell 11/30/1823, wife of Arthur Channell
Jane C., dau. of Arthur and Margaret Channell, 8/10/1831

Richard B., son of same, 9/14/1825
John G., son of Arthur and Polly Channell, 8/10/1842

(Arthur Channell Bible, DEATHS, contd....)

Arthur Channell 6/5/1838
Polly Driver Channell, wife of Arthur Channell, 10/7/1862, aged 65
Clarence Whitney, son of Adelbert and Maggie A. Channell,3/11/1876
George Franklin Channell 1/8/1897, aged 71 yrs.
Virginia Channell 2/10/1914, aged 76 yrs.
Cornelia Cutchin 5/21/1901
Maggie Batten 9/2/1905, wife of Ernest Batten

WILLIAM PLEASANTS' BIBLE

"The Lanier Family" by Mrs. William Anderson 1126 Kessler Parkway, Dallas, Texas

BIRTHS

William Pleasants 6/30/1759
Frances Pleasants, wife of William Pleasants, 1/18/1766

Thomas Pleasants 8/28/1788
Peyton Pleasants 6/27/1794
Polly Pleasants 10/16/1788
Gibson Pleasants 1791

Girl twins 4/22/1790
Sophronia Pleasants 10/30/1793
Washington Pleasants 3/5/1787?
Elizabeth Pleasants 6/15/1803

Elbert Clower, son of John and Polly Clower, 9/3/1800
Cynthia Clower 12/1813

Memorable Pleasants, son of Thomas and Mary Pleasants, 10/17/1809
Frances A. Pleasants 8/1812
Nancy Narcisey Pleasants 3/1815 ?
Hapta J. Conn ---

MARRIAGES

William Pleasants to Frances Flournoy 11/24/1785
Polly Pleasants to John Glower 6/11/1805
Thomas Pleasant 12/27/1808
Sophronia Newberry 1/19/1813
Washington Pleasants 12/9/1813
Peyton L. Glower to Rachel 8/3/1851
Samantha Glower 4/22/1811-1891 m. 1st John Burch; 2nd, Thomas Beckham, 3rd, Coleman Holmes, 4th, 7/31/1860 William Lewis (7/11/1791-1874)
Richard Burch to Jane
Richard Burch Jr. b. Brunswick 1755? Richard Burch b. 1783

BIRTHS

John Glower 3/16/1780
Polly Glower 10/18/1788
Samanthia Glower 4/22/1811-12/1/1891
Thomas P. Clower 1/26/181-

Sally Spoos? (Spencer) -/12/1820
Matilda Clower 5/26/18-6
William A. Spencer 3/22/1822

DEATHS

one twin girl 4/23/1790, the other twin girl 4/19/1790
Gibson Pleasants 9/17/1793 Peyton Pleasants 12/19/1814 Dicy Louisa Burkhalter 10/13/1854
Samanthia --- 6/--/--
James Lanier m. Clarissa Tillman
Cinderella Lanier b. 1817 (sIsters, Melissa and Elizabeth) m. John Wilson Brumfield.

(William Pleasants Bible, contd...)

BIRTHS of Children of John Wilson Brumfield and Cinderella

Ezekiel Brumfield 1839
John Brumfield 1844
Frances Brumfield 1841
William Brumfield 1845
Melissa Brumfield 1842

Louisiana Brumfield 1848
John Brumfield 1844
Candacia Brumfield 5/1850

JOHN CHAPMAN BIBLE
Virginia HIstorical Magazine

John Chapman, son of Charles Chapman and Ann, his wife, m. Frances Ward, dau. of Thomas Ward, 2/15/1794

BIRTHS of Children of John and Frances Chapman

Benjamin Chapman 2/8/1706, baptized 10th day following. James Chapman,
William Clarke and grandmother, Mary Clarke, witnesses. He d. 8/23/1723, aged 16 years
Joseph Chapman 11/13/1724. Henry Lightfoot, Hugh Giles and Sarah Davis, witnesses to baptism
Rachel Norsworthy Chapman 8/6/1722. Mary Forbes and William Norsworthy, witnesses to baptism
My wife, Frances Chapman, d. 7/22/1727, aged 29 yrs., and I was then married unto Mary Marshall, wid. and dau. of Thomas Bevan 12/28th the year following was born unto us a son named William, baptised May following 1730, with Thomas Bevan, Jr. George Norsworthy and Elizabeth Bevan, witnesses

My dau., Patience Chapman, m. Moses Wills 2/13/1723

BIRTHS of Children of Moses and Patience Wills

Mary Wills 513/1725
Ann Wills 11/29/1730
Sabre Chapman b. 9/22/1755, dau. of Joseph and Lydia Chapman. Witnesses to baptism-Joseph Haskins and Mrs. Rachel Chapman
John Chapman, son of Joseph and Lydia Chaman, b. 2/23/1763. John Whitfield and Samuel Barnes, witnesses.

ISAAC JONES BIBLE
Of Isle of Wight Co.

Isaac Jones b. Isle of Wight Co., Va. 11/4/1772 and his wife, Elizabeth 1/3/1769

BIRTHS of THEIR CHILDREN:

Martha B. Jones 11/15/1795
Wiley Jones 12/6/1806
Benjamin J. Jones 4/5/1797
Henry C. Jones 12/1/1808
Peter R. Jones 2/27/1799

Robert T. Jones 9/5/1811
William N. Jones 9/21/1800
Amelia Jones 4/27/1818
Leodicea Jones 10/6/1804

Lucy Ann Jones, wife of Robert T. Jones, 9/17/1817

BIRTHS of Children of Robert T. and Lucy Ann Jones

Roxanna E. Jones 10/26/1835
Lucy Ann C. Jones 9J22/1842
Martha B. Jones 9/25/1839

Peter Calvin Jones 12/23/1851
Benjamin C. Jones 5/13/1841

LANDON CARTER BIBLE of Loudoun Co.
Owner: Robert Corbin Carter Lafayette Co., Mississippi

Landon Carter m. Mildred Willis 2/15/1772

BIRTHS of THEIR CHILDREN:

Mary Champe Carter 9/15/1773-2/20/1774
Mildred Ann Byrd Carter 10/20/1774
Lucy Landon Carter 4/29/1776
Sarah Carter 8/10/1777-3/17/1805
Mildred Carter d. 10/20/1778

Mildred Ann Byrd Carter m. Robert Mercer 3/22/1792
Landon Carter m. Elizabeth Thornton 3/16/1782

BIRTHS of Children of Landon and Elizabeth Carter

Robert Charles-Carter 4/24/1783 at Cleve, sponsors at baptism: Robert Wormeley Carter, grandfather by maternal side to infant, George Carter of Corotoman as proxy, Landon Carter, son to R. W. Carter, George Carter, also son of R. W. C. and Landon Carter, father of the infant--

Winifred Travers Carter, grandmother of the infant, by Elizabeth, his mother as proxy, Catherine Carter and Anna Beale Carter, his aunts, Mildred Ann Byrd, Lucy Landon and Sarah Carter, three sIsters of the infant.

St. Leger Landon Carter 12/19/1785, baptised 1/11/1786 by Rev. R. Kenner, publicly baptised by Rev. John Lowe, 26 of same mo. Sponsors: Dr. David Morrow, George Catlet, proxy for William Lindsay and his father, Mrs. Frances Humphry Toy Fitzhugh, Miss Anne Fox and Mrs. Fanny fee by his mother, as proxy.

Eliza Travers Carter 8/31/1787 at Cleve, her sponors: Her father and mother, Thomas Ludwell Lee and his Lady, Mildred Ann Byrd, Lucy Landon and Sarah Carter, her three sIsters.

Thomas Otway Byrd Carter 7/10/1790 at Sabine Hall, baptised by Rev. Isaac William Giberne at Parish of Lunenburg; his sponsors: his father and mother, his grandfather, Robert W. Carter, his grandmother, Winifred Travers Carter, John Carter of Pittsylvania, William Currie Beale, his two brothers, Robert Charles and St. Leger Landon Carter, Mrs. Lucy Colston, her two. daus., Susan and Elizabeth Landon Colston, Harriet Beale of Chestnut Hill and his sIster, Eliza Travers Carter

Fanny Lee Carter 4/9/1792 at Cleve, baptised June following at Berry Hill by Rev. Mr. Buchan of Stafford Co.; sponsors: her father and mother, Mrs. Mary Lee, her uncle and aunt, Thomas Ludwell and Fanny Lee, Miss Lucinda Lee, Miss Charlotte Boynton and George Lee

Charles William Carter 4/12, baptised at W. church in St. Mary's parish and Co. of Caroline 6/22nd following (1794), by Rev. Abner Waugh; his sponsors: his father, by proxy, George Catlet, and his mother, his uncle, Mr. Reuben Beale, by proxy, Laurence Catlet, Eliz. Morrow and his two sIsters, Sarah and Eliza Travers Carter

Edward Carter 12/21/1797, baptised at Cleve by Rev. George Hartley Spierin of Parish of St. Asaph in Caroline Co. Sponsors: John Minor and Robert Mercer, his brothers in law, by their proxies, John Gobande and Rev. Mr. Spierin, his father, his brothers, Robert Charles, St. Leger Landon and Thomas Otway Byrd Carter, his sIsters, M. A. B. Mercer, Sarah and Eliza T. Carter and his cousins, Elizabeth Carter and Eliz. and Winifred Lee.

Anna Maria Carter 11/1/1799 at Cleve, baptised 1/6/1800 at Cleve by Rev. Abner Waugh of St. Mary's Parish, Caroline Co.; her sponsors: her father and mother, her sIsters, Sarah, Eliza Travers and Fanny Lee Carter, Per bros., Robert Charles, by the minIster as proxy and St. Leger Landon Carter, by his father, as proxy

(Landon Carter Bible continued...)

Son b. d. 4/21/1801

Robert C. Carter m. Harwar Beale, dau. of Reuben and Judith Beale of Beale's Farm, Madison Co., 4/4/1805

Eliz. Landon Carter 2/1/1806, baptized 5/3 at Cleve. Sponsors: Grandfather, Landon Carter; her uncles, St. L. Landon, Thomas Otway Byrd and Edward Carter; her grandmothers, Judith Beale and Elizabeth Carter; her aunts, Eliza Travers, Fanny Lee and Anna Marie Carter

St. Leger Landon Carter m. Elizabeth Ludwell Lee, dau. of Thomas Ludwell and Fanny Lee of Coton, Loudoun Co., Va. by Rev. Mr. Dunn 10/6/1808

DEATHS

Landon Carter of Cleve, King George Co., Va. 12/10/1811 at his mansion house, aged 61 yrs.
Reuben Beale of Chestnut Hill, Richmond Co., Va., 11/2/1802, aged 52 yrs.
Edward C. Carter, son of Landon of Cleve, 10/1/1818, aged 21 yrs.

Frances Lee Tidball, dau. of Landon and Elizabeth Carter of Cleve, d. at mansion of her husband, Josiah Tidball in Fauquier Co., Va. 4/29/1822

Anna Maria Carter, dau. of Landon and E. of Cleve, 10/30/1822, at Cleve, aged 23 yrs.
Elizabeth Carter of Cleve (wife of Landon) 9/12/1840, aged 82 yrs.
Robert C. Carter 8/18/1849 at Cleve, 66 yrs., 3 mos., 25 days
Olivia Hanson Carter, dau. of R. and H. Carter, d. at their residence, 8/8/1824, aged 13 yrs.

Landon St. Leger Carter, son of Robert C. and Harwar Carter, at Cleve, King George Co., Va. 10/15/1835, aged 28 yrs.

Judith Beale, dau. of Landon and Elizabeth of Sabine Hall, at her mansion in Madison Co., 6/18/1836, 87 yrs. Interred in Madison Emma Cleve Carter at Cleve, King George Co., Va. 8/8/1840, aged 13 yrs, 11 mos., 19 days

Harwar Carter, wife of R. C. Carter, at Cleve, 8/11/1840

MARRIAGES

Landon Carter of Cleve to Elizabeth Carter, then wid. of Peter Thornton, 3/16/1782
Reuben Beale of Chestnut Hill to Judith Carter of Sabine Hall 1/16/1773
Robert Charles Carter, son of Landon of Cleve, to Harwar Beale, dau. of Reuben and Judith, 4/4/1805
St. Leger Landon Carter, son of Landon of Cleve, to Elizabeth Lee, dau. of Thomas Lee of Loudoun,10/6/1808. Frances Lee Carter,dau of Landon and Elizabeth of Cleve, to Josiah Tidball, Fauquier, Cleve, 5/25/1820
Robert O. Carter, son of R. C. Carter, to Edmonia F. Corbin, dau. of Richard Randolph Corbin,
great nephew of Mrs. Judith Beale at Oakenham, the res. of Thomas W. Fauntleroy, Middlesex Co., Va. 9/30/1845

BIRTHS

Landon Carter of Cleve 7/11/1751 Elizabeth, his wife, 9/3/1759
Reuben Beale 2/1/1751 Judith, his wife, 10/28/1749
Robert Charles Carter, son of Landon and E., 4/24/1783
Harwar Beale, his wife, 2/23/1786
St. Leger Landon Carter, son of Landon and E., 12/10/1785
Elizabeth Ludwell Lee, his wife, 4/16/1787.
Eliza Travers Carter, dau. of Landon and E., 8/31/1787
Thomas Otway B. Carter, son of Landon and E., 7/10/1790
Fanny Lee Carter, dau. of Landon and E., 4/9/1792
Edward Carter, son of Landon and E., 12/21/1797
Anna Maria Carter, dau. of Landon and E., 11/1/1799

(Landon Carter Bible continued...)

BIRTHS of Children of Robert C. and H. Carter

Eliz. Landon Carter 2/1/1806 –
Landon St. Leger Carter 3/1/1808
Robert Otway Carter 1/3/1810
Olivia Hanson Carter 2/23/1812
Edward St. Orville Carter 5/11/1814

Mary Eleanor Carter 10/14/1816
Clarence Hervie Carter 10/17/1818
Flora Berkeley Carter 2/7/1821
Laura Montreville Carter 11/7/1823
Emma Cleve Carter 8/20/1826

BIRTHS of Children of R. O. Carter and Edmonia Fauntleroy

Carter Robert Corbin Carter
8/11/1846 LaFayette Co,,Miss
Edmonia Beverley Carter 10/3/1847
Otway Lane Carter 1/24/1849
Anna Fauntleroy Carter 10/7/1850

Note: "After last entry, four more children were born to Robert O. and E. F. Carter: St. Leger Landon Carter, Mary Harwar Carter, Charles Cleve Carter and Berkeley Carter. Lucien Beverley Howry of Washington, D. C."

GENERAL WILLIAM F. GORDON'S BIBLE of Albemarle Co., Va.

BIRTHS

James L. Gordon 10/31/1813
George Loyall Gordon 1/17/1929
Maria L. Gordon 12/2/1815-1/29/1848
Charles Henry Gordon 1/17/1829
Hannah Elizabeth Gordon 9/28/1817
John Churchill Gordon 3/2/1831
Reuben L. Gordon 1/15/1820

Alex.Tazewell Gordon 5/12/1833
William Gordon 3/6/1822-12/17/1822
Mason Gordon 9/17/1840
William F. Gordon 11/26/1823
Elizabeth Gordon 7/9/1826-6/21/1827

JAMES JOHNSTON BIBLE of Isle of Wight Co., Va.

James Johnston, son of Dr. Robert Johnston and his wife, Mary Ponsonby, m. Elizabeth Smith 9/20/1798

BIRTHS of Children of James and Elizabeth Johnston

Elizabeth Woodrop Johnston 11/8/1799
James Johnston d. 3/3/1805
Robert Jardine Johnston 9/2/1801-9/25/1804

Jane Deacon Johnston 9/5/1803-9/15/1805
Eliza Woodrop Johnston b. 11/8/1799 m. 2/11/1819
Lt. William Henry Cocke of U. S. Nancy b. 9/4/1791

Louisiana Susan Cocke, dau. of William Henry and Eliza, m. 8/12/1840 to Charles Benham Hayden, son of Julia and Norman Hayden

BIRTHS

Louisiana Susan Cocke 2/1821 Norfolk, Va.
Powhatan William Cocke 7/19/1822 Norfolk, Va.
Irene Hayden 8/1/1841 Smithfield, Va.
Louisiana Cocke Hayden 6/10/1843 Abingdon, Va.

Lt. William Henry Cocke killed 3/6/1823 by a cannon ball from the Morrow Castle fired at CT. S. Schooner Fox, of which he was commander. By order of the Secretary of Navy his remains were brought to this country and buried with the honours of war in new cemetery in Portsmouth, Va., 1832 Powhatan
William Cocke d. 9/19/1823
L. C. Hayden, wife of Charles, d. 7/18/1843 at Abingdon, Va.
Mrs. E. W. Cocke, consort of late Lt. William Cocke, d. Smithfield 5/26/1861, aged 61yrs.

JESSE WHITEHEAD BIBLE of Isle of Wight Co., Va.

Jesse Whitehead, son of Dempsey and Sarah Whitehead, b. 4/7/1818

Jesse Whitehead m. Eliza Ann Carr, dau. of Nathan Carr and Nancy, his wife, on 1/4/1844

BIRTHS of Children of Jesse and Eliza Ann Whitehead

William J. Whitehead 6/21/1845
Eva E. Whitehead 10/30/1856
Jesse T. Whitehead 5/28/1854
Sarah E. Whitehead 2/7/1847

Julius I. Whitehead 1/16/1859
Virginia T. Whitehead 1/7/1849
Ida C. Whitehead 8/16/1860

MARRIAGES

William j. Whitehead to Mollie J. Purvis 4/18/1865
Sarah E. Whitehead to Thomas W. Goring 1/10/1866
Virginia T. Whitehead to M. G. Digg s/9/1869
Eva E. Whitehead 1st to Welcome Leigh and after his death, 2nd to T. M. Henderson
Note: Jesse, Julius and Ida Whitehead d. in infancy

JOSEPH CONWAY SR. BIBLE
Owner: Mrs. Berry B. Brooks, Jr.
Epping Forest Manor, Memphis, Tenn

BIRTHS

Joseph Conway Sr. 12/14/1763
Samuel Conway 7/25/1799
Elizabeth Conway 9/1/1773
Ann Conway 9/26/1803
Waiter Conway 7/1/1793
James Conway 9/5/1805
John Conway 4/14/1795
Louisa, dau. of Samuel and Mourning Baxter Conway, 4/24/1840

Joseph Conway Jr. 8/22/1807
Fountain Conway 5/6/1797
Lucinda Conway 4/9/1814
Elizabeth Conway Jr. 9/19/1825
Joseph Conway Jr. 9/12/1827

DEATHS

Elizabeth Conway Sr. 9/30/1821
Joseph Conway Sr. 12/27/1830
Prestly Conway b. 12/1801-d. 9th mo. of his age
Elizabeth Conway b. ---
Polly Conway b. 12/22/1811-d. in her 15th mo.
Walter Conway 7/1/1793-5/16/1823
Samuel Conway 10/28/1870
Louisa Conway, wife of Frederick Bates Walton, 6/30/1895 St. Louis, Mo.
Cene Conway Bates, wife of Lucius Lee Bates, 4/26/1921, aged 88 yrs., 4 mos., 8 days

JOHN SIMS BIBLE of Hanover Co.
Owner: Mrs. Randolph Allen
4603 Forest Hill Ave., Richmond, Va.

John Lipscombe Slms, son of John Sims, 5/1799-12/28/1848
Louisa Ann Caroline Mills 11/6/1817-2/11/1862 m. 1/28/1834
BIRTHS of Children of John L. and Louisa Ann Sims Charles Francis Sims 2/15/1836
Elizabeth Edmona Frances Fowlkes Sims 3/12/1838
Lucian Mills Sims 12/25/1839

(John Sims Bible, BIRTHS, contd....)

Peter Lipscomb Sims 3/5/1841-4/16/1844
Benjamin Higgason Sims 1/10/1843
Robert Mortimer Sims 10/19/1845-7/25/1864
Benjamin H. Sims m. Virginia A. Swift 6/23/1870

BIRTHS of Children of Benjamin H. and Virginia Sims

Versal Aubrey Sims 6/14/1871
Mary Mosely Sims 3/13/1873
Odelia Carolinda Sims 10/25/1874
Adelaide Brown Sims 2/3/1876
Asa Higgason Sims 3/16/1878

Bennie Virginia Sims 11/10/1880
Reuben Mills Sims 2/18/1883
Ola Bernice Chetwynde Sims 4/22/1886
Alfred Elmore Sims 3/23/1890
Mortimer Sims 2/5/1893

MILLS-SIMS BIBLE of Hanover Co.
Owner: Mrs. Randolph Allen
4603 Forest Hill Ave., Richmond, Va.

Robert Mills, son of Robert Mills, b. 4/28/1743 m. 1/4/1767 Antess Hopkins b. 3/13/1748

BIRTHS of THEIR CHILDREN:

David Mills 12/1/--
James Mills 2/2/1783 Garland Mills 2/4/1772
Susannah
Mills 12/1/1780 John Mills 1/17/1774
Mary Mills 4/13/1785 Rice Mills 9/13/1775
Anstess Mills 10/17/1787
Edmund Mills 9/26/1778-4/25/1855 (m. 1838)
2nd wife of Edmund d. 5/12/1855
Louisa Anstess Sims, dau. of Lucean Sims, b. 3/2/1880
Edmund Mills, son of Robert, b. 9/26/1778 m. 4/3/1806
Frances Fowlkes Higgason b. 3/25/1789

BIRTHS of Children of Edmund and Frances Mills

Mary Colly Hopkins Mills 1/21/1807
Maria H. Mills 10/24/1819
Elizabeth Anne Wade Mills 3/9/1809
Robert Garland Mills 4/9/1822
Frances Isabella Mills 4/1/1811
Amanda Melina Mills 6/15/1824

Gabriel Higgason Mills 5/12/1813
Edmond B. Mills 8/20/1827
Andrew Lewis Mills 6/17/1815
Lucy Colly Mills 9/30/1831
Louisa Ann Caroline Mills 11/6/1817

DEATHS

Gabriel H. Mills 9/15/1814
Frances Fowlkes Mills 10/17/1834
Elizabeth A. W. Mills 9/2/1828

Amanda M. Mills 7/31/1848
Frances I. Mills 9/6/1828

YELVERTON PEYTON BIBLE
Kentucky HIstorical Society

Yelverton Peyton b. Stafford Co., Va. 11/20/1755-d. 1/23/1849
Anne Guffey Peyton, his wife, 3/1/1762-12/15/1848
Yelverton Peyton Jt. 12/17/1793-1/23/1849
Yelverton Peyton Jr. m. Sallie Ann Garvin 10/11/1836
Craven Peyton, son of Yelverton, 1/2/1799-9/13/1876
Margaret Moore Peyton, his wife, 11/26/-- - 4/23/1973
Mary Jane Peyton, dau. of Craven and Margaret Peyton, 1/28/1830-9/18/1901 m. Newland Jones 12/18/1849

BURWELL-STEPTOE BIBLE
Of Liberty, Bedford Co.
Owner: William McCreery Burwell

MARRIAGES

William McCreery Burwell b. 11/1/1809 to 11/4/1830
Frances Callaway Steptoe b. 8/6/1810
Catherine Burwell, dau. of William M. and Frances C. Burwell, to Dr. T. M. Bowyer of Botetourt
Co., Va., and their only child, Lilian Bowyer was b. at Liberty 12/13/1861
Mary Fanny Burwell to James Breckenridge of Botetourt Co., Va. 3/4/1862
Rosalie Burwell, dau. of William M. And Frances C. Burwell to Dr. Charles H. Todd of Ky., 2/1865

BIRTHS

William McCreery Burwell, the only surviving child of William A. and Letitia Burwell, 11/1/1809
at Mrs. Martha Burwell's in Botetourt Co., Va. (Note--W. A. Burwell was William Arm1stead Burwell, son
of Major Thatcher Burwell, Rev. War Soldier. W. A. Burwell served as private secretary to President Thomas Jefferson. He m.
Letitia McCreery of Va.)
Letitia McCreery Burwell 8/16/1831 at res. of Dr. William Steptoe in Bedford Co.. Va.
Catherine Steptoe Burwell 6/14/1833 Franklin Co., Va.
Mary Fanny Burwell 12/28/1839 Bedford Co., Va.
James Steptoe Buruell 9/8/1842, at Liberty, Bedford Co., Va. Rosalie Burwell 1/14/1845 at Liberty, Bedford Co., Va.

DEATHS

James Steptoe Burwell, son of William M. and Frances C. Burwell, 8/26/1843, aged 11 yrs., 2 mos., 18 days
Mary Fanny m. James Breckenridge of Botetourt Co., Va. and d. at Liberty 8/1862, aged 23 yrs.

JACKSON ESTES BIBLE of Orange Co.

Jackson Estes m. Susannah Corum 6/9/1836

BIRTHS

Susannah W. Estes 11/6/1815
Jackson Estes 12/15/1815 Madison Co., Ky.
Martha Estes 5/10/1837
Virginia Estes 3/27/1848
Anna Estes 12/5/1838
Henry Estes 4/19/1852
Lucinda Estes 2/22/1841
Jefferson Estes 11/25/1853
Madison Estes 12/25/1842
Willia Jane Estes 2/13/1855
Nancy Estes 7/17/1845
---Courtney Estes 4/5/1860
Maria Estes 1/12/1847

DEATHS

Maria Estes 3/14/1847
Lucinda White 7/24/1878
Jackson Estes 3/21/1899 at res. in Clinton Co., Mo., 1/2-mi. north of Starfield, aged 80 yrs., 2 mos.,27 days
Nancy Estes Fowler 4/21/1899 in Salt Lake City, Utah
Susannah Estes 11/4/1901 at res. of A. M. Creek, Clinton Co.. Mo.

HOLLADAY-DAY-KELLY BIBLE
Owner: Carroll Goodrich Smithfield, Virginia

BIRTHS of Children of Thomas R. and Edith Day

Ann Eliza Day 11/16/1816
Abraham Ballard Day 8/18/1823
Lydia Day 1/15/1818
Thomas Davis Day 3/19/1824
Laura Ballard Day 8/15/1820

Fanny Ridley Day 11/14/1827
Martha Ann Virginia Day 3/2/1822
Virginia Priscilla Day 9/24/1829
Joseph Holladay 7/10/1789

Elizabeth Charlton, wife of Joseph Holladay, 2/4/1793
Martha Ann Pinner 1811
Edith Ballard, wife of Thomas R. Day and Joseph Holladay, 12/4/1798
Thomas R. Day m. Edith Ballard, dau. of Lydia and Andrew Ballard 8/31/1815
Thomas R. Day d. 12/20/1829

MARRIAGES

Joseph Holladay to Elizabeth Charlton 2/20/1812
Joseph Holladay to Martha Ann Pinner 3/15/1831
Joseph Holladay to Edith Ballard Day 8/28/1836
Jacob Holland Kelly to Minerva W. Hancock 9/15/1829
Jacob H. Kelly to Elizabeth Eley 3/4/1834
Jacob H. Kelly to Susannah B. Carney 3/14/1834
Ezekiel P. Kelly to Mary C. Flynn 11/24/1858
Jacob Eley Kelly to Lucie Edith Ballard Holladay 1/12/1859
Ezekiel P. Kelly to Sally B. Phillips 8/18/1865
Ezekial P. Kelly to Mollie Williams 7/29/1869
Jacob Kelly, son of Jacob H. and Elizabeth Eley Kelly, b. 2/24/1836
Hugh H. and Ezekial P., sons- of Jacob H. and Susannah B. Kelly, b. 3/2/1839
Margaret Elizabeth, dau. of Jacob H. and Susannah B. Kelly, b. 11/1/1840
George T., son of Jacob H. and Susannah B. Kelly, b. 8/16/1842
Hening W., son of Jacob H. and Susannah B. Kelly, b. 1/25/1845

DEATHS

Minerva W. Kelly 4/26/1833, aged 21
Martha Susan Kelly 5/1871
Elizabeth fley Kelly 1/13/1837
Edith H. Kelly 10/16/1874
Susannah B. Kelly 5/14/1845, aged 45
Sally P. Kelly 5/1870
Fanny Day Kelly 6/4/1876
Mollie C. Kelly 1/1861

Lydia Day Kelly 5/19/1877
Sally B.Kelly 10/25/1867
Mollie P. Kelly 3/15/1870
Harry Kelly 1882
E. P. Kelly 10/1880
Elizabeth E. Kelly 3/13/1869
Lucy E. B. H.Kelly 2/21/1882

Joseph Holladay Kelly, son of Joseph Eley Kelly and L. E. B. Kelly, 1882

WILLIAM WALKER BIBLE

MARRIAGES

Wm Walker to Judith B. I. Shields 1/10/1810, by Rev. John Saunders
George Walker, son of above, to Rebekah Allen Warren, dau. of Doctor M. S. Warren, 1/10/1839 by Rev. A. Norris. Mary Chrlstian Walker to William A. Warren 6/16/1840
John L. Walker to Deborah Anne Ladd 2/14/1842

DEATHS

John Walker 9/30/1815
Littleberry Walker, son of John Walker, 9/30/1814

Nancy Walker, wife of J. Walker, 7/9/1814

(William Walker Bible continued...)
Nancy Walker, dau. of Nancy and John Walker, 1/12/1818

BIRTHS

Nancy Walker 7/9/1814 Judith B. I. Shields 10/15/1785
William Walker, Jr.6/16/1784
Ellen H--- Hill, dau. of Elizabeth Walker and Thomas Hill, 3/16/1833

Children of William and Judith Walker:

William Page Walker 1/15/1811 Mary Christiana Walker 10/23/1818
John Walker 11/9/1816 George Walker 8/8/1814
Mary U. P. Walker 9/10/1812

Elizabeth Warren, dau. of George and Rebeckah Allen Walker, 10/24/1840 at Warrenton, James City Co. Va.
Children of J. L. and Deborah Anne Walker:

Thomas Ledbetter Walker 11/19/1843 John Littlebury Walker 8/13/1845
Mary Susan Walker 8/27/1848

DEATHS

William Edward Walker, son of George and Rebecca A. Walker, 5/11/1846, 3 yrs., 8 mos.,29 das
James Robert Walker, son of George and R. A., 11/27/1857
Fanny Allen Walker, dau. of George and R. A., 5/20/1858, 30 days
J. L. Walker 6/1/1892
Rebecca A. Walker, wife of George A. Walker, 4/20/1890 at Swineyards, Charles City Co., Va.

MARRIAGES
George Walker, son of William & Judith Walker, m. Rebecca Allen Warren, dau. of Dr. Michael S. & Eliz. B. Warren, 1/10/1829
Richard Walker, son of George & Rebecca Walker to Mattie E. Bates of Norfolk, Va., 1/27/1881, Norfolk by Rev. J. B. Newton
BIRTHS of Children of George and Rebecca A. Walker
William Edward Walker 8/12/1842 at Swineyards, Charles City Co., Va., baptised 11/27/1842 by Rev. William T. Leavel, Upper Church
George Michael Walker 3/16/1844 at Swineyards, Charles City Co., Va.
Mary Christian Walker 11/1/1846 at Swineyards
Rebekah Allen Walker 11/10/1850 at Swineyards
Richard Wilcox Walker 3/6/1866 at Swineyards
Judith Bray Shields Walker 1/20/1860 at Swineyards

DEATHS

Thomas J. Walker 1/16/1811, aged 50 yrs., 11 mos., 19 days
Elizabeth Walker, wife of above, 24th of above mo. and year
George Walker 3/2/1882 at Swineyards, Charles City Co., Va.
Mattie Bates Walker, wife of R. Walker, 9/27/1882
Elizabeth Walker, wife of R. Walker, 9/27/1882
Richard W. McClennan 9/21/1882
William P. Walker, son of Wm and Judith, 2/27/1815, 1 mo., 22 days
Mary U. P. Walker 9/19/1818 (or 1816), 4 yrs., 9 days old
Judy B. I. Walker, wife of William Walker, 3/13/1820
William Walker, Jr. 1/19/1820

GEORGE MARKHAM BIBLE
Owner: Mrs. George Lyng Bryan, Leesburg, Florida

Col. Bernard Markham, eldest son of John and Catharine Markham, 1737-7/13/1802 Chesterfield Co., Va.
BIRTHS of Children of Bernard and Mary Markham
Martha Markham 2/28/1768 m. Efford Bently 1782-d. Wintington 1791 where she was interred
John Markham 1/20/1770 m. Lucy Champe Fleming 1/9/1794
Catharine Markham 12/30/1771-2/1776, bur. at Mr. William Harris in Manikin Town

(George Markham Bible, BIRTHS, contd....)

Bernard Markham 10/2/1774-8/1777, bur. in orchard where "I (Col. Bernard Markham) now live, at the Ware."
Mary Markham 12/31/1776 m. Linneus Boiling, son of Robert Belling of Buckingham, 12/17/1793
Elizabeth Markham 5/25/1779-3/1790
William Harris Markham 2/23/1781-3/1790
George Markham 2/6/1783 m. 5/9/1805 Elizabeth Evans, dau. of Dr. George Evans and Mary, his wife.
Judith V. Markham 7/9/1787 m. William Cooke of Ky.
Sarah Markham 2/1785-7/1786

THOMAS HEALY SR. BIBLE of Middlesex Co.
Owner: Mrs. Emma Campbell Wright
Rappahannock, Virginia

Thomas Healy Sr. b. 2/23/1746 m. Ann 11/3/1767

BIRTHS of Children of Thomas and Ann Healy

William Healy 213/1769
Elizabeth Healy 6/26/1774
Thomas Healy 4/2/1770

Ann K. Healy 2/15/1776
Edmund Healy 9/9/1772

Thomas Healy m. Hannah Dillard 7/5/1776 (she d. 2/9/1785)

BIRTHS of Children of Thomas and Hannah Healy

Sarah Healy 2/13/1777
Jane Healy 2/3/1781
Frances Healy 3/13/1777
Catherine Healy 2/20/1783-2/1788
Thomas Healy m. Sarah Mitchell 10/29/1785
Sarah Batchelder, dau. of John and Elizabeth, b. 6/7/1753

BIRTHS of Children of Thomas and Sarah Healy

George Healy 3/28/1787
Walter Healy 5/24/1792
James Healy 7/13/1789-9/1792
Robert Healy 7/25/1797
Edmund Healy d. 9/17/1791 by fall from riding in woods after deer

EDWARD THRUTSTON, JR. BIBLE of Nansemond Co., Va.

"6/13/1717 my father, Edward Thruston came from Boston to live with me Edward Thruston, Jr....I was married to my wife, Elizabeth, who was the dau. of Thomas Housden, Minlster of Upper Parish of Nansemond in Virginia. Our wedding day was 8/31/1706."

BIRTHS of Children of Edward Thruston, Jr. and Elizabeth

Mary Thruston 12/9/1707
Edmond Thruston 7/14/1717
John Thruston 10/24/1709
Susannah Thruston 7/30/1719

Elizabeth Thruston 4/8/1712
Perry Thruston 8/30/1721
Frane Thruston 1/7/1714
Thomas Thruston 12/4/1725

My dau., Franc Smith d. 8/21/1749, aged 34 yrs., 7th Jan. last
My grandson, Moses Robertson, b. 10/27/1742 and his slster, Frances Robertson b. 6/11/1744
Their mother, my dau., Susanna Robertson, d. 12/27/1748
Cornelius Calvert m. Elizabeth Thruston 5/5/1772.
Mrs. Elizabeth Calvert d. 1/18/1782.
My son, Thomas Thruston, d. 2/15/1738

(Bible of Edward Thruston, Jr. continued....)

Col. John Thruston aged 57 yrs. d. at Gloster Town in Va. 2/20/1766. By his wife, Sarah, relict of Hanes, had issue:

Charles Minn Thruston 11/6/1738
Elizabeth Thruston 4/27/1740 m. Col. Thomas Whiting at Gloster Sarah Thruston 4/27/1743 m. John Thornton of Hanover
Mary Thruston 5/17/1746 m. Hugh Walker of Gloucester Co.
John Thruston 5/20/1750
Frances Thruston 3/20/1752 m. Col. Wm Hubbard of Charlotte Co. Edward Thruston 7/12/1753-
6/24/1754 Jemima Thruston 12/18/1755-7/4/1756
Mildred Thruston 10/2/1756-9/30/1758
Robert Thruston 1/14/1759
Sarah, relict of Col. John Thruston d. 5/12/1786, aged 69 yrs. Elizabeth Thruston d. 1766
Mary Thruston d. since this date
John Thruston d. 1781 Frances Thruston d. abt 1780

Col. Charles Minn Thruston b. 11/6/1738 m. Mary Buckner, dau. of Col. Samuel Buckner of Gloucester Co., Va. (she d. 8/18/1765) in 1760, by whom he had 3 children: John b. 10/15/1761; Buckner b. 2/9/1764; Charles b. 8/3/1765. He m. 2/1766 Ann, dau. of Col. Alexander of Gloster and had children: Sarah Alex. b. 12/15/1766; Frederick b. 3/15/1770; Mary Buckner b. 7/31/1772; Francis b. 2/3/1774; Eliza Minn b. 4/6/1775; Alfred b. 5/14/1778; Eloise b. 3/23/1782; Sidney Ann b. 5/2/1783

Edmund Taylor b. 10/24/1785
John Thruston m. Elizabeth Thruston Whiting, dau of Col. Thomas Whiting of Gloster 10/13/1782
Buckner Thruston m. Jannett January, dau. of Peter January, 3/1795 in Ky.
Charles Thruston m. Frances O'Fallon, relict of Dr. James O'Fallon, dau. of John Clark of Ky. 1/20/1796
Sarah Thruston m. George Floerdew Norton of Va. 12/17/1784
Mary Thruston m. Col. Charles Magill 5/25/1792 of Winchester Frances Thruston m. Frederick
Conrad of Winchester, 4/25/1793 Elizabeth Thruston m. Henry Dangerfield 8/10/1794
Eloise Thruston m. Capt. Edmund Hanes Taylor of Ky.
Charles Thruston, son of Charles M. Thruston and Mary Buckner, d. 12/8/1800, aged 35 yrs., 4 mos. Sydney Anne Powell, dau. of Col. Charles M. Thruston, d. 9/12/1803

"I, John Thruston having recd this book from my father, Col. C. M. Thruston, I have thought proper to insert the births of my children. I was married as before mentioned to Eliza T. Whiting, dau. of Col. Thomas A. Whiting of Gloster, 13th Oct. 1782."

BIRTHS of Children of John Thruston and Eliza

Mary Buckner Thruston 8/14/1783
Catharine Thruston 9/19/1790
Elizabeth Taylor Thruston 2/13/1785
Thomas Whiting Thruston 11/6/1786
Sarah Thruston 11/8/1788
Fanny Badello Thruston 3/7/1795
Charles Minn Thruston 2/26/1793
Lucius Falkland Thruston 7/18/1799
Alfred Thruston 4/16/1797.
Col. John Thruston d. 2/19/1802, aged 41 yrs
Algernon Sidney Thruston b. 5/19/1801
Eliza T. Thurston

Eliza T. Fontaine, wid. of Capt. Aaron Fontaine, d. 7/2/1822

Mary Buck, Thruston, my dau., m. Thomas January of Lexington, Ky. 11/14/1799
Eliza T. Thruston, dau. of John Thruston and Elizn, his wife, m. Worden Pope of Louisville, Ky.,

(Charles Brent Bible continued...)

John Gunn Brent 12/6/1803
Susan Brent 12/9/1818
Mary Ann Brent 3/21/1806

On loose sheet or paper in Bible

Elizabeth Washington b. 2/2/1833
Mary Amelia Washington b. 2/7/1827
John Edward Washington b. 12/26/1828
(Line drawn thru name "Virginia Elizabeth" and "Caroline Matilda" entered above it).

FREDERICK BATES BIBLE of Goochland Co.
Owner: Mrs. Berry B. Brooks, Jr.
Epping Forest Manor, Memphis, Tenn

BIRTHS

Frederick Bates 6/23/1777. Goochland Co., Virginia
Nancy Ball 4/19/1802, Lancaster Co., Va.
Nancy Ball m. Frederick Bates 3/4/1819
Emily Caroline Bates 1/5/1820
Woodville Bates 7/29/1823
Lucius Lee Bates 3/19/1821
Fredcrick Bates 2/1/1826
Conway Bates 8/16/1856
Lucia Lee Bates 12/1863-9/3/1936
Samuel Gilbreath 1/3/1855-9/3/1936

DEATHS

Frederick Bates 8/4/1825, aged 49 yrs.
Woodville Bates 2/12/1840 at St. Charles College, aged 17 yrs.
Dr. Frederick Bates at his home opposite "Thornhill", 10/18/1862, aged 37 yrs.
Lucius Lee Bates d. at home near "Thornhill", 10/24/1898, aged 77 yrs., 7 mos., 7 days, bur. Thornhill.
Robert C. Ruby m. Nancy Opie Bates 2/1/1831
Robert C. Ruby b. 3/21/1796 Green Co., Tennessee
Nancy Opie Bates b. 4/19/1802 Lancaster Co., Virginia

BIRTHS

Caroline Jett Ruby 2/11/1833
John Ball Ruby 3/10/1837
Nancy Opie Ruby 4/8/1835
Robert Ashley Ruby 12/10/1839

DEATHS

Dr. Robert C. Ruby 5/30/1839, Columbus, Miss., aged 44 yrs.
Robert Ashley Ruby 8/29/1847 in Bon Homme, aged 9 yrs.
Rev. John S. Ball 4/12/1849, aged 76 yrs, his res. in Lincoln Co., Missouri
Nancy Opic Ruby, dau. of Rev. John S. Ball and who was 1st wife of Frederick Bates and after his death the wife of Dr. Robert C. Ruby, d. in St. Louis 3/16/1877, aged 75 yrs., bur. at "Thornhill" near the grave of her first husband
Lucius Lee Bates 10/24/1898 at his home near "Thornhill", aged 77 yrs., 7 mos., 7 days
Conway Bates d. 5/2/1934 at Iconton, Mo.

Notes: John S. Ball was the son of Jesse Ball and Agatha Conway, Jesse Ball was the son of James Ball and --- Smith, of Lancaster co., Virginia Agatha Conway was the dau. of Peter Conway and Betty Lee of Lancaster Co., Va. Nancy Opie, the wife or John S. Ball, was the dau. of Lindsey Opie (the son of Lindsey Opie of Northumberland Co., Va.) and Elizabeth McAdams, the dau. of Dr. McAdams, a native of Scotland, but married lived and died in Northumberland Co., Virginia.

JOSEPH HATCHETT BIBLE of Nottoway Co.
Owner: J. S. Hatchitt, Wichita Falls, Texas

Joseph Hatchett, son of Abraham Hatchett and Mary, his wife of Nottoway Co., Va., b. 12/8/1778
Elizabeth Hatchett, dau. of Jacob Berger of Pittsylvania Co., Va. b. 5/2/1781

BIRTHS of Children of Joseph and Elizabeth Hatchett

Pliny Hatchett 11/20/1804
Polley Farley Hatchett 2/5/1812
Sophia Hatchett 5/20/1806
Abraham ReMay Hatchett 10/18/1815

Livy Hatchett 3/3/1808
Jacob Berger Hatchett 11/10/1818
Logan Hatchett 1/22/1810
Leroy Cole Downey Hatchett 2/23/1821

Alalinda Persia Gale, dau. of Polley F. Gale, 10/28/1834
Angeline Sophia Gale, dau. of Polley F. Gale, 4/23/1838
Mary Eliza Loona Gale, dau. of Polley F. Gale, 10/26/1840
Martha Colesta Gale, dau. of Polley F. Gale, 5/6/1846
Mary E. Hatchett 9/1843
Margaret Remey Hatchett 11/13/1845
Harrison Pliny Hatchett Harris, son of John and Sophia Harris, 5/4/1844
Nary Frances Harris, dau. of John and Sophia Harris, 12/10/1846
Louisa E. Hatchett 10/1848

MARRIAGES

Joseph Hatchett to Elizabeth Berger 2/8/1804
Sophia Hatchett to John Harris 2/8/1827
Pliny Hatchett to Catherina Thornberry 2/23/1831

Polley F. Hatchett to Jarvis H. Gale 7/11/1833
Levy Hatchett to Margaret Ann Conn 8/10/1847
Leroy C. D. Hatchett to Maryann P. Adams 12/20/1846

BIRTHS

Livy S. Hatchett 8/31/1839 William F. Hatchett 12/19/1837

BIRTHS of Children of Sophia Harris

Joseph W. Harris 8/16/1829
James S. Harris 3/15/1839
Emily J. Harris 2/26/1831
Levy H. Harris 5/25/1841
Ann C. Harris 4/5/1833

Harrison P. H. Harris 6/4/1844
Nancy E. Harris 3/13/1835
Mary F. Harris 12/10/1846
Harriet h. Harris 3/3/1837
Sarah A. Harris 11/27/1849

DEATHS

Jacob Berger Hatchett 10/5/1823
Abraham ReMay Hatchett 7/19/1831
Logan Hatchett 1/1/1835
Polley P. Gale, dau. of Joseph and Elizabeth Hatchett, 9/18/1847

Elizabeth Hatchett, wife of Joseph, 10/22/1833
Joseph Hatchett 9/10/1857, aged nearly 79 yrs

Note: Sometimes spelling is Hatchitt.

JOHN T. McKEE BIBLE
Owner: O. B. Dunlap

John McKee b. 1707 m. Jane Logan 1/29/1744

BIRTHS of THEIR CHILDREN:

Mary McKee 6/11/1746

John McKee 12/17/1756-5/24/1761

(John McKee Bible continued...)

Mariam McKee 9/27/1747
William McKee 2/28/1759
William McKee 2/18/1750-7/28/1752
David McKee 12/25/1760
John McKee m. Rosannah Cunningham, his 2d wife, 12/12/1765
John McKee 10/27/1771, only child by 2nd marriage
John McKee, Jr. m. Susannah Simonds 6/14/1798
John McKee Jr. d. 12/1/1815 Susannah McKee d. 3/20/1815
Hugh Weir d. 7/14/1822 Wife, Mary McKee Weir d. 9/3/1822
James Logan McKee m. Jane Telford 6/6/1782
The only child by this marr. was John Telford McKee b. 4/14/1783
Jane Telford McKee 10/19/1754-4/30/1800, dau. of Alexander and Mary Telford
James Logan McKee m. Mrs. Nancy Scott, his 2nd wife, 1807
James Logan McKee d. 8/14/1832, aged 80 yrs, 5 mos.
John Telford McKee m. Nancy Hanna (b. 5/5/1779) 11/18/1806

James McKee 3/14/1752
Jane Logan McKee d. 717/1763

BIRTHS of Children of John Telford and Nancy McKee

Jane Teltord McXee 8/25/1807
Mary Susan McKec 3/7/1815
Samuel W. McKee 4/30/1809
Martha Hanna McKee 8/5/1811
John Telford McKee d. 4/30/1857
His wife, Nancy Hanna McKee, d. 4/23/1847
Samuel W. McKee m. Polly Ann Davidson 8/20/1834

BIRTHS of Children of Samuel W. and Polly Ann McKee

Nancy Hanna McKee 9/4/1835-
Sally Gilmore McKee 9/11/1845
Polly McKee 9/18/1837
James Gilmore McKee 6/15/1848
Lucinda J. McKee 10/4/1839
Elizabeth Samuella McKee 6/5/1850
John T. McKee 10/21/1841

Samuel Madison McKee 5/4/1853
Martha Davidson McKee 10/5/1843
Samuel W. McKee d. 1883
Polly Ann McKee, wife of Samuel W. McKee, d. 1/23/1860
Matthew Hanna Parry m. Jane Telford McKee 6/5/1831

BIRTHS of Children of Matthew H. and Jane T. McKee

Mary E. Parry 3/1832
Charlotte Parry 10/1/1841
Martha L. Parry 1/20/1834
John McKee Parry 8/1943
Nancy M. Parry 11/24/1835

Jane T. Parry 9/4/1845
Susan B. Parry 9/22/1837
Charles E. Parry 11/1852
Emma W. Parry 9/12/1839
Willis Richardson Parry ---

DANIEL SOUTHALL BIBLE of Amelia Co.
Owner:Emily Southall Lawrence, Murfreesboro,NC
.BIRTHS

Daniel, son of James and Elizabeth Southall of Amelia Co., Va., 8/9/1768
Julia. dau. of Seth and Leah Riddick, 6/23/1774

BIRTHS of Children of Daniel and Julia Southall

Sophia Riddick Southall 8/31/1795
Emma Hunter Southall 12/9/1803
John Wesley Southall 7/28/1797
James Southall 3/29/1806
Ann Rebecca Southall 11/26/1799

Sarah Eliza Southall 1/13/1808
Seth Riddick Southall 12/13/1801
Richard, son of Robert and Ann Johnston of New York,
Martha, dau. of John and Elizabeth Wheeler, 2/7/1758

(Daniel Southall Bible, contd....)

BIRTHS of Children of Richard and Martha Johnston

Richard Wheeler Johnston 2/11/1807
Julia Munroe Johnston 10/31/1808
Elizabeth Johnston 6/25/1810-1/10/1848

BIRTHS of Children of John W. and Julia M. Southall

Laura Rebecca Southall 2/11/1827
Julia Riddick Southall 12/20/1828
John Richard Southall 7/14/1831
Martha Frances Southall 9/14/1833, baptised by Rev. Thomas Crowder 2/8/1834
Mary Williams Southall 2/1/1843, baptised by Rev. G. W. Langhorne 2/1844

DEATHS

Laura Rebecca, dau. of John W. and Julia M. Southall, 5/7/1827
John or Richard, son of John W. and Julia M. Southall, 8/7/1832
Mary William Southall, dau. of John U. and Mary A. Southall, 8/31/1854, aged 11 7yrs., 7 mos.
Susan Emily Southall Lawrence, dau. of John W. and Mary A.
Southall, b. 10/12/1845, baptized by Rev. Thomas Crowder 2/1846, m. 8/27/1938

JOHN COATES BIBLE of Halifax Co.

BIRTHS

John Coatee, son of William and Mary Coatee, 2/9/1813
Edeline Frances Murrey 8/13/1822

DEATHS

Edeline Coates 12/23/1877

MARRIAGES

John Coates to Edeline Coffey 11/11/1846

JOHN BASS BIBLE
Owner: Richard E. Dyson, Box 3508
Tech Sta., Blacksburg, Virginia

John Bass, his book, b. 11/27/1738

BIRTHS of Children of John and Tabitha Bass

Martha Bass 4/17/17b2
Frances Bass --1/4/1770
Tabitha Bass 10/3/1763
John Bass 3/14/1772
Agnes Bass 5/23/1765
Edward Bass 4/24/1776
Elizabeth Bass 2/27/1767

Nancy Bass 11/20/1777
Mary Bass 8/24/1768
Lucy Bass 9/18/1781
Richard E. Dyson 11/19/1837
H. H. Dyson 12/29/1840
Harry H. Dyson 12/29/19--

Tabitha Dyson, wife of Thomas, d. 6/25/1845; her baby b. 5/9/1843
5/12th Thomas W. Dyson bid the last farewell 1856
E. R. Dyson d. 3/18/1945 at Medical College of Virginia
Tabitha Dyson d. 6/25/1841, her baby b. 5/9/1843

THACKER VIVION BIBLE
Of Spotsylvania and Orange Co.'s
Owner: Mrs. Walker Perish, Sr.

BIRTHS of Children of Thacker and Mary Vivion

Jane Vivion 1/7/1776
Virgil Vivion 12/16/1777
Polly Vivion 6/7/1771
Sally Vivion 11/25/1779
John Vivion 6/5/1773

Betsey Vivion 12/7/1781
Thacker Vivion 4/16/1775
Nancy Vivion 3/14/1784
William Walker 9/5/1765

Polly Vivion 6/7/1771 m. 11/20/1791
Their offspring, Virgil Walker, 9/14/1792

On flyleaf: (signatures) Thomas Walker, Edmund Byne, John Walker, William Walker, his hand and pen, b. 9/6/1765

DANIEL DODSON BIBLE of Dinwiddie Co.
Owner: Miss Bertha Dodson, Scottdale, Ga.

BIRTHS

Daniel Dodson 4/29/1769
Daniel Dodson 2/25/1848

Sarah Peters 1774
Sarah Dodson 7/30/1863

Daniel Dodson m. Sarah Peters 7/1792

BIRTHS of Children of Daniel and Sarah Dodson

Joshua Dodson 6/7/1794
Edmund Dodson 1/13/1796
John Peters Dodson 2/17/1806
Nancy Dodson 2/24/1798
William Dodson 3/1/1808

Lochy Dodson 2/14/1801
Constantine Dodson 1/19/1811
Elijah Dodson 2/24/1804
Stephen Dadson 1/28/1813

MUSE-HEALY BIBLE
Owner: Mrs. Emma Campbell Wright Rappahannock, Virginia

Anna F. M. Muse n. Carter Braxton of Windsor, Essex, 1/21/1818 by Bishop Moore.
Maria, my beloved dau. m. 7/12/1821 Walter Healey, by Mr. Montague.

BIRTHS of Children of Walter and Maria Healy

Augustus Healy 5/5/1822-8/4/1925, aged 3 yrs, 3 mos.
Anna Muse Healy 9/27/1824-8/8/1825, aged nearly 11 nos.
Martha Augusta Healy 8/8/1826
Walter Healy 8/21/1828
Tazewell Healy 3/21/1831-10/12/1831
Betty Muse Healy 9/3/1832
Thomas Healy 4/4/1835
Walter Healy 6/21/1835
Penny Healy 1/25/1838-10/14th
Elliot Muse Healy 1/8/1840

DEATHS

Father, Ellit Muse 2/2/1818, aged 40 yrs, 5 days
Grandson, Tayloe, 7/1/1821, 10 nos. old

Anna F. M. Braxton 3/19/1824
Mrs. Betty T. Muse 9/24/1832

JOHN KEMP BIBLE
Owner: Miss Lucy Kurtz, Winchester, Virginia

John Kemp, son of James and Elizabeth Kemp, b. 8/28/1742 m. Nancy North

BIRTHS of Children of John and Nancy Kemp

William Kemp 10/8/1775
Jan Kemp 1/22/1780
Elizabeth Kemp 7/14/1776
Mary Kemp 5/2/17-- - 8/23/1784

John Kemp 1/29/1779
Jesay Kemp 12/1/--
Maryan Doughtry 11/25/1818
Mary Ann Thomas Doughty 11/25/1818

William Boyd, his Book

James Boyd 5/16/1730
Nancy Boyd 10/20/1743
Jan Boyd 11/13/1741

John Boyd 11/8/1733
William Boyd 10/29/1745

GEORGE W. PURVIS BIBLE
Owner: Mrs. James Braxton Cash, 405 Monticello Blvd., Alexandria, Va.

MARRIAGES

Moses Boyd 10/20/1753
Mary Boyd 8/20/1737

---Boyd 12/21/1747
Elizabeth Boyd 11/1739

BIRTHS of Children of Thomas and Elizabeth Doughty

Nancy 1. Doughty 8/19/1800
Sally M. Doughty 3/6/1808
Martha L. Doughty 7/27/1805
Jane H. Doughty 2/8/1803
George W. Purvis to Martha A. Ikers 10/21/1823
Charlotte Davis Gray to James Braxton Cash of Br1stol, Va. 7/2/1939, Harrisburg, Va.
James Braxton Cash, Jr. to Lelitia Bivor of Have, England in Williamsburg, Va. 4/8/1967
James Braxton Cash, Jr. b. Columbia Hospital, Washington, D. C., 12/11/1941

William Doughty 6/17/1812
E. Doughty 1/27/1815

BIRTHS of Children of George W. and Martha Purvis

William A. Purvis l/id/1825-
John James Purvis 3/13/1836
Margaret F. Purvis 4/29/1827
George Winston Purvis 10/24/1838
Amanda Melvina Purvis 2/7/1829
Albert Alexander Purvis 1/5/1841
Sarah Elizabeth Purvis 5/4/1831

Martha Susan Purvis 7/12/1843
Mary Ann Purvis 11/3/1833
Geneva Louise
Neva Neva L. Denton b. 10/27/1873
Elizabeth Hendricks
Bessie H. Denton b. 8/12/1876
William S. Medrick 11/8/1899

Geneva Louise Denton m. Charles Winton Gray 10/19/1893

BIRTHS

Lewis Hedrick 2/7/1901
Ruth Hedrick 1/14/1906
Gilbert Denton Gray 1138/1899
Charlotte Davis Gray 4/26/1905
Lucille Elizabeth Gray 12/--
Amanda Melvina Purvis d. 5/17/1830
William A. Purvis killed at Petersburg 12/6/1864
Mrs Charles Winton Gray (Geneva) 10/27/1873-7/11/1955
William S. Hedrick 1871-5/25/56

Gilbert D. Gray d. 10/27/1954
Martha Archer Akers 9/16/1813-12/19/1877
George W. Purvis 8/1/1801-8/15/1878
Robert M. Denton d. 6/1/1914
Martha Susan Denton d. 8/22/1904
Charles Winton Gray 6/11/1405
Bessie H. Hedrick 4/15/1939
Louis W. Hedrick 11/8/1939
Rose L. Gray 3/14/1951

JOHN TAYLOR BIBLE
Owner: Mrs. Mary Blackwell

John Taylor, son of James and Mary Taylor, 11/18/1696-3/22/1780
Cstherine Pendleton, dau. of Phillip Pendleton and Isaballa,his
wife, 12/8/1699 m. to John Taylor 2/14/1716, d. 7/26/1774
Note: Cathecine Pendleton was a sIster to Judge Edmund Pendleton, dIstinguished jurIst of Virginia, and sIster to mother of
Gen. Edward P. Gaines, also sIster to the mother of Phillip P. and
James Barbour)

BIRTHS of Children of John and Catherine Taylor

Mary Taylor 5/30/1718-9/13/1757 Catherine Taylor 12/30/1719-11/4/1774
Ann Taylor 5/10/1721-8/10/1761 Edmund Taylor 5/12/1723
Isabella Taylor 6/26/1725 John Taylor 7/17/1727-10/26/1787
James Taylor 9/7/1729-9/26/1750 aged 21 yes,
Phillip Taylor 2/17/1732-9/7/1765
Elizabeth Taylor 7/9/1735
William Taylor 12/19/1735, baptised 1/18th-d. 11/5/1803
Joseph Taylor 2/19/1742, baptised 20th of same no.
William Taylor m. Elizabeth Anderson 7/28/1763

BIRTHS of Children of William and Elizabeth Taylor

Sarah Taylor 3/5/1766 Anderson Taylor 10/18/1761-1808
William Taylor 12/9/1770-12/26/1854 John Taylor 2/20/1773-1847
7/4/1739 I gave my dau., Catherine, in marriage to Moses Penn, who d. 11/4/1759
John Penn son of Moses and Catherine, 5/6/1740-9/14/1788. (He was one of the signers of the Declaration of Independence)
2/3/1735 I gave my dau., Mary, in marriage to Joseph Penn

BIRTHS of Children of Joseph and Mary Penn

--- 12/13/1736	Catherine Penn 3/11/1741
Moses Penn 12/3/1744	James Penn 8/12/174-
Joseph Penn 9/2/1738	Phillip Penn 2/6/1742/3
Elizabeth Pann 174-	Thomas Penn 4/25/174-

1/25/1750 I gave my dau., Isabella, in marriage to Samuel Hopkins

BIRTHS of Children of Samuell and Isabella Hopkins

Samuel Hopkins 4/9/1753 -	James Hopkins 7/27/1755-8/20/1758
John Hoptins 2/20/1762	Edmund Hopkins 2/27/1767
Catherine Hopkins 3/3/1755	Elizabeth Hopkins 10/30/1759
Mary Hopkins 3/13/1764	

BIRTHS of Children of Edmund and Ann Taylor

Lewis Taylor 8/17/1751	Frances Taylor 7/24/1771
Edmund Taylor 7/3/1763	Mary Taylor 12/3/1760
Richard Taylor 1/17/1753	John Taylor 12/4/1756
Eliza Taylor 1767	James Taylor 1763
Howell Taylor 10/16/1754	

BIRTHS of Children of James and Ann Taylor

John Taylor 12/19/1753 (Col. John Taylor of Caroline Co.)
Elizabeth Taylor 1/5/1796

(John Taylor Bible, contd......)

BIRTHS of Children of Phillip and Mary Taylor

Walker Taylor 11/9/1752-1/1---
Catherine Taylor 2/4/1754 (dead)
John Taylor, Jr. answered for Mary who was b. 12/14/1756 and died
Phillip Taylor 3/28/1759
Ann Taylor 3/20/1761
John Taylor 2/10/1763-8/1792
James Taylor 1/8/1765
12/25/1752 I gave my dau., Elizabeth, in marriage to James Lewis

BIRTHS of Children of James and Elizabeth Lewis

Catherine Lewis 11/21/1753
Charles Lewis 8/2/1760   James Lewis 8/28/1755   Mary Lewis 11/22/1762
John Lewis 10/10/1757
Capt. James Lewis d. 5/21/1764
Joseph Taylor b. 2/19/1742 and Frances Anderson, his wife b. 3/30/1743 and they m. 4/7/1763.
Great grandfather of Howell Lewis Taylor

BIRTHS of Children of Joseph and Frances Taylor

Elizabeth Taylor 10/32/1764
Mary Ann Taylor 9/24/1769
Thomas Taylor 7/18/1771
Joseph Taylor 8/14/1773, grandfather of F. L. Taylor
Lucy Penn Taylor 12/9/1782-8/22/1787
Frances Anderson Taylor 10/11/1786 m. 12/18/1804
John Somerville. Father of W. L. Somerville.

ALEXANDER P. HIGHT BIBLE
Owner: Ed Allen
Monticello, Virginia

Tilman Hight m. Elizabeth K. Holmes 1813, Rockbridge Co., Va.

THEIR CHILDREN::

BIRTHS

Alexander P. Hight 7/29/1814
Nancy H. Hight 1/7/1831
Eliza Jane Hight 2/14/1817
Rebecca F. Hight 12/23/1835
Julia Ann Hight 6/24/1819
David Hight 9/22/1833-4/5/1836
Mary M. Hight 6/2/1821
Ellen V. Hight 8/30/1837
Sarah W. Hight 4/6/1823
William H. Hight 5/5/1839
Peter J. Hight 4/15/1825
Caroline A. Hight 10/14/1842
George R. Hight 12/22/1827
Elizabeth Susan Hight 2/6/1846
Permelia M. Hight 3/3/1829

WILLIAM C. RICHARDS BIBLE
Owner: Mrs. Richard Joseph, Sr.
4101 Seminary Rd., Alexandria, Va.

William C. Richards b. 6/6/1817   Mary A. Morgen b. 9/18/1822

BIRTHS of Children of William C. and Mary Richards

Catherine Rebecca Richards 4/30/1851
Jane Morgan Richards 7/21/1854
Annie Cornelia Richards 3/6/1857
William Franklin Richards 8/11/1860
Archie C. Richards 12/7/-
Harry Burton Richards 1/11/1876
Burton M. Richards 7/25/1921
Glenn D. Richards 1/30/1927
Allen K. Richards 1/14/1923
David M. Richards 8/5/1934
Lucille R. Richards 5/21/1924
James C. Richards 7/1952

BIRTHS of Children of J. C. and Nellie Richards

Jennie M. Richards 12/15/1894 -
Willie F. Richards 1898
William B. Richards 11/29/1896

BIRTHS of Children of M. R. and Jennie Dwyer

Mary Jean Dwyer 3/27/1927 - - -
Elizabeth Ann Dwyer 10/1931
William Carlin Dwyer 4/25/1929
Margaret Ellen Dwyer 2/27/1933

MARRIAGES

William C. Richard to Mary A. Morgen 2/7/1950
Edgar Campbell to Jennie M. Richards 10/10/1882
John T. Wilkins to Kate R. Richards 11/10/1874
James C. Richards to Nellie Allen Draft 9/12/1893
Jennie Morgen Richards to Richard Joseph Dwyer 1/14/1922 by Rev. Lawrence Kelly at St. Mary's Parsonage
Alms Rebecca Davis to William Burton Richards 6/3/1920 by Rev. Reg1ster
Mazie May Simpson to William Burton Richards 2/5/1945

DEATHS

Mary A. Richards 4/20/1866
John Morgen Richards 7/4/1866
Nellie F. Richards 3/2/1877
Jennie M. Richards 7/4/1866
Hallie F. Richards 8/4/1898
William C. Richards 9/7/1901
Nellie Allen Richards 4/15/1943, wife of James Carlin Richards
Alma Rebecca Richards 1/16/1944, wife of William Burton Richards
James Carlin Richards 6/11/1950
Nellie Wallace Richards Groves (adopted by Nellie and James Carlin Richards) 8/1942

JOHN BACON BIBLE
Owner: J. Swigert Taylor Frankfort, Kentucky

BIRTHS of Children of Lyddall and Ann Bacon

John Bacon 3/10 1767
Langston-Bacon 3/30/1777

Lyddall Bacon 8/29/1775
Edmund Bacon 8/26/1780

MARRIAGES

John Bacon to Anna 11/13/1794
John Bacon to Elizabeth 5/31/1799
Elizabeth P. Bacon to B. H. Bryan 12/31/1839
Anne A. Bacon to Philip S. Fall 5/1/1821
Charles P. Bacon to Caroline Castleman 5/18/1821

Williamson W. Bacon to Anne Maria Noel 11/3/1824
John M. Bacon to Sarah Jane Haggin 3/29/1835
Richard A. Bacon to Elizabeth E. Terrill 4/15/1830
James V. Bacon to Alice Riggs 3/24/1836

BIRTHS of Children of John and Elizabeth Bacon

Anne A. Bacon 3/25/1800 - --
Richard Apperson Bacon 7/2/1809
Sally W. Bacon 3/24/1802
John Mosby Bacon 10/31/1811

Williamson Bacon 3/7/1804
Elizabeth P. Bacon 5/7/1814
James W. Bacon 3/22/1807
Albert Gallatin Bacon 12/8/1816

BIRTHS of Children of John and Anna Bacon

Charles P. Bacon 9/26/1795
James Bacon 7/9/1797
Amanda Bacon, dau. of Benedict and Susan, b. 11/7/1812
Maria C. Rouzee, dau. of Philemon and Agnes, b. 9/1808

BIRTHS of Children of W. U. Bacon

Maria Bacon 4/11/1826 - -
?Laura Bacon 2/1834
Anna Bacon 5/1/1828

Alice Bacon 8/12/1836
Sarah Cordelia Bacon 11/1830
Williamson Bacon 2/3/1844

James S1ster Fall, son of Philip S. and Anne Apperson Fall, b. 4/4/1822
John Bacon, son of Charles P. and Caroline M., b. 3/15/1822
James Haggin Albert Bacon, son of John M. and Sarah J., 1/30/1836 8/30/1837
Romulus Riggs Bacon, son of James W. and Alice, b. 12/31/1836
Alice E. Bacon, dau. of James W. and Alice, m. B. H. Blanton 1/15/1868
James W. Bacon Blanton, her son, b. 1/2/1869

DEATHS

Anne Bacon, wife of John, 7/15/1797, aged 24 yrs., 2 mos., few days James Bacon, son of John and Anne, 7/19/1797, aged 11 days
Susan Bacon, wife of Benedict Bacon, 3/30/1813
John Bacon 5/9/1817, aged 50 yrs., 2 mos.
John M., son of John and Elizabeth, 9/16/1843
Williamson, son of John and Elizabeth, 3/17/1845
Elizabeth, wire of John Bacon, 7/30/1849
Elizabeth (Bryan), dau. of John and Elizabeth Bacon, 10/15/1850 Charles P. Bacon, son of John and Anna, 9/17/1854
Albert Bacon, son of John and Elizabeth, was killed in battle 12/28/1861
James V. Bacon, son of John and Elizabeth, 10/1863
Richard A. Bacon son of John and Elizabeth, 10/1865
John Bacon, son of Charles, 9/26/1854
R. R. Bacon, son of James and Alice, 9/1868 Howard Bryan, son of Elizabeth, 8/30/1849

NICHOLAS TALIAFERRO BIBLE

Ann Hay Taliaferro b. 2/27/1760, private baptism by Rev. James Marye, Jr.-d. 3/2/1760
Nicholas Taliaferro m. Ann Taliaferro 11/3/1781 by Rev. James Stevenson. My beloved wife, Ann Taliaferro, was the dau. of Colonel John and Ann Taliaferro of "Dissington", was b. 4/7/1756d. 2/3/1798

BIRTHS of Children of Nicholas and Ann Taliaferro

Lucy Mary Taliaferro 8/6/1782, baptised by Rev. William Douglas 1/18/1783. Sureties: Winslow Parker, Mrs. Lucy May Thurston, Miss Ann Thurston, my wife and self

John Champe Taliaferro 10/12/1784, baptised by Rev. James Stevenson 4/27/1786. Sureties: John Grinnan, Joseph Stewart, Miss Frances Willis Stewart and his mother. He d. 2/26/1811
Matilda Battaile Taliaferro 9/30/1787, baptised by Rev. James Stevenson 8/24/1788. Sureties: John & Miss Ann Grinnan Mary Willis Taliaferro 8/11/1789, baptised by Rev. James Stevenson 11/15/1789. Sureties: John Stevens, Joseph Morton, Miss Elizabeth Taliaferro, Miss Ann Hay Taliaferro, and her mother. She d. 1/25/1797, bur. in Pa. where Gen. Braddock was defeated, Alleghany Co.

George Catlett Taliaferro 3/21/1792, baptised by Rev. Mr. Woodville 12/23/1794. Sureties: John Grinnan & wife, Lucy, myself
William Thornton Taliaferro 1/16/1795, baptised by Rev. Mr. O'Neal. Sureties: his grandfather who named him, Hay Taliaferro, Hay Taliaferro, Jr., his grandmother, mother and Miss Abby Gibson

Nicholas Taliaferro m. 2nd Miss Frances Blasingame, dau. of James and Mary Blasingame and had following children:

Carr Blasingame Taliaferro 8/13/1799-1806
Lawrence Washington Talfaferro 10/28/1800
Ann Patterson Taliaferro 10/29/1802-11/25/1803
James Hay Taliaferro 9/2/1804-8/18/1808
Nicholas Taliaferro 8/14/1806
Marshall Howe Taliaferro 3/9/1809
Frances Ann Talfaferro 11/9/1811

William Buckner b. 6/19/1780 m. Lucy Mary Taliaferro 6/26/1799.

BIRTHS of Children of William and Lucy Buckner

Philip Johnson Buckner 8/8/1800
Ann Whitaker Taliaferro Buckner 1/8/1803
Nicholas Taliaferro Buckner 6/29/1805

My bro., John Taliaferro, m. Ann Stockdell, dau. of Capt. John and Mary Stockdell of Orange Co.

BIRTHS of Children of John and Mary Taliaferro

Mary Taliaferro 6/17/1713 m. Robert Reynolds d. with her 1st child, which is called Thornton

Elizabeth Hay Taliaferro 5/4/1778
Lucy Mary Battaile Taliaferro 5/14/1780
William Taliaferro 3/23/1782
Sarah TalLaferro 2/20/1784
John Taliaferro 4/6/1786
Martha Taliaferro 1/22/1789
Ntcholas Hay Battaile Taliaferro 6/15/1793
Lawrence Wesley Taliaferro 8/5/1796

(Nicholas Taliaferro Bible, contd....)

Reglster of the names and ages (BIRTHS) of my negroes:

James 3/1756
Hannah 8/19/1786
Rachel 11/1773
Sarah 6/10/1773
Clemintina 2/1781
Batty 9/15/1788
Anthony 3/12/1784
Sally 7/10/1788
Billy 12/9/1785
Phil 8/5/1789
Daniel 1/12/1792
Joe 11/9/1806

Jenny 11/6/1794
Prissy 12/11/1808
Sharlotty 2/10/--
Caroline 9/28/1809
Ben 10/25/1798
Simon 9/2/1910
Nelly 1/5/1801
Henry 5/22/1811
Mary 3/12/1803 stillborn
Charles 1810
Lucy 8/11/1805

EDMUND BACON BIBLE
Owner: Mrs. Alexander Bacon

Edmund Bacon 10/11/1774-2/1819
Mary B. Hanley 2/25/1779 m. 11/3/1797 Edmund Bacon

BIRTHS of THEIR CHILDREN:

John R. Bacon 8/21/1798-10/2/1801
Edmund Bacon 2/29/1800
Samuel A. Bacon 1/29/1802-5/19/1802
William A. Bacon 5/16/1803-5/6/1808
Eliza B. Bacon 12/23/1804
Alexander B. Bacon 12/22/1806
Richardson Bacon 5/16/1808
Mary D. Bacon 3/20/1809
Susan H. Bacon 3/15/1811
Virginia P. B. Bacon 1/9/1813
Alice M. A. Bacon 6/18/1815
Sary Elizabeth Bacon 8/15/1817
Edmond R. H. Bacon 4/12/1828

JOHN REGIS ALEXANDER BIBLE
Owner: Mrs. J. K. Polk South, Jr.
High Street, Frankfort, Ky.

BIRTHS

John Regis Alexander 11/13/1793 Henrico Co., Va.
Andrew Jonathan Alexander 3/19/1796, Calfpasture
Charles Alexander 7/21/1798, Calfpasture
Marianne Alexander 12/30/1800, Calfpasture
James Robert Alexander 9/22/1803, Calfpasture
Apolline Alexander 10/15/1807, Calfpasture

William Alexander, son of John R. and Marian F. Alexander, 4/17/1820, Woodford Co., Ky.
James Robert Alexander 8/12/1822
Frances Agatha Alexander 7/12/1824

(John Regis Alexander Bible, BIRTHS, contd....)

Thomas Biddle Alexander 4/5/1827 John Begis Alexander 8/2/1829

DEATHS

Pierre Victoir Delaporte 7/30/1796, aged 17 yrs.
Made. Marianne Delaporte, aged 65 yrs., d. at Rockcastle 8/7/1811
William Alexander, son of Robert and Eliza, 8/1816
James Robert Alexander 10/8/1817
Marie Agatha Henriette Sophie Alexander, wife of Wm, 10/17/1817
William Alexander, aged 90 yrs., 1/10/1819 in Woodford Co., Ky.
Marianne Alexander 4/28/1819, aged 18 yrs.
Andrew J. Alexander-killed 12/1833 by machinery of steam sawmill Jane Alexander, dau. of A. J. and Mira Alexander, 10/1832
Eliza Jane Alexander, wife of John Regis Alexander and dau. of Elizabeth Brooks, 6/6/1901, aged 89 yrs, 25 days of being 90
John Begis Alexander, husband of Eliza Jane Brooks, 10/18/1883, age 89 yrs, 25 days of being 90
M. P. Alexander 8/1843

MARRIAGES

William Alexander to Marie Agatha Henrietta Sophie DeLaporte 11/12/1792
Robert Alexander to Eliza Richison Weiseger 10/2/1814
John R. Alexander to Marion Francis Campbell 5/14/1818
Charles Alexander to Martha M. Madison 12/4/1821
John Regis Alexander to Eliza Jane Van DeGraphe, nee Brooks, 1849

BIRTHS

William Alexander, son of Eliza and Robert, 8/6th, Frankfort, Ky.
Robert Andrew Alexander, son of J. Regis and Marian F. Alexander, 10/21/1833 at Roslin, Woodford Co., Ky.
Charles Williams Alrxander, son of J. R. and Marian F., 9/8/1837
John Campbell Alexander, son of J. Regis and E. J., 4/20/1852
Alice Seeley Alexander, dau. of John Campbell, 3/19/1898

MAJOR CLARK PENN BIBLE of "Nettie Ridge", Patrick Co.

MARRIAGES

Gabriel Penn to Jane Clark 2/6/1797
Samuel Martin to Ruth Penn 8/24/1827
Abram Penn to Cathrine Reid 2/26/1824
Josiah Ferris to Mary Penn 10/27/1825
Clack Penn to Mary M. Harris by Dr. Phillips 4/24/1826
Clark Penn to Barbara A. L. Penn by Rev. C. Taylor 6/21/1831
Abram Penn to Mary E. Thomas 6/26/1836
Clark Penn to Susan Clark 10/8/1548
Gabriel J. Penn to Susan E. Penn 10/7/1857 by Rev. C. H. Phillips
George W. Hilton to Sarah C. Penn 10/7/1858
Greensville Penn to Henrietta Cardwell 10/18/1836
George W. Hylton to Susan E. King 11/20/1873
John W. Fulton to Barbara A. Hylton 12/10/1885 by Rev. D. J. Traynham
George Bylton Fulton to Stella B. Correll of Illinois 9/7/1920
Annie Sue Fulton to J. Myron Clark 9/20/1926
William Penn Fulton to Virginia Clark 12/22/1939

(Major Clark Penn Bible, contd....)

BIRTHS

Gabriel Penn 11/14/1773
Greensville Penn 10/22/1810
Jane Clark 1/14/1780
Francts Jane Penn 5/31/1815
Clark Penn 12/7/1797
Mary M. Harris 7/29/1812
Ruth Penn 2/11/1800

William H. Penn 1/31/1827
Abram Penn 3/16/1803
James G. Penn 4/16/1829
Sarah Penn 12/11/1805
Barbara h. L. Penn 4/1/1809
Mary Penn 12/29/1807

BIRTHS of Children of C. and B. Penn

Abram Clark Penn 418/1832
Mary H. Penn 10/9/1839
Gabriel J. Penn 11/27/1836
Susan Kennerly 3/27/1805 George W. Hylton 9/7/1823
Ella Cathrine Penn, child of G. J. and S. E. Penn, 8/8/1858

BIRTHS of Children of G. W. and S. C. Hylton

Gabriel V. Hylton 9/2211863 Patrick Co.,Va.
Barbara A. and Clark P. Hylton 4/16/1865

BIRTHS of Children of John U. and Barbara A. Fulton

George Hylton Fulton 915/1886 Patrick Co., Va.
John Kelly Fulton 10/10/1887
Catharine Penn Fulton 5/17/1889
Hylton Harrison Fulton 6/7/1891
Barbara Anne, dau. of Annie Sue and Myron Clark 9/12/1930
Edward Fulton, son of Annie Sue and Myron Clark, 8/10/1933

Louise Barbara and Annie Sue Fulton 12/7/1895
William Penn Fulton 11/27/1899

DEATHS

Cant. Gabriel Penn 7/18/1818
Sallie Penn 4/6/1821
Cathrine, wife of A. Penn, 12/12/1824
Francts J., wife of P. P. Penn, 6/25/1833
Barbara A. L. Penn, wife of C. Penn, 6/30/1847
J. G. Penn 12/2/1829
Mary M. Penn 2/10/1830 W. H. Penn 9/28/1830
Francis, inf. dau. of P. P. P. and F. J. Penn, 7/13/1833
Abram Penn 12/15/1848
Abram C. Penn, son of C. and B. Penn, 4/30/1832
Clk. Penn 8/3/1858
Col. Abram Penn 6/26/1801 Gabr. V. Hylton 4/13/1864 Sarah C. Hylton 5/15/1865
Clark P.Hylton 6/6/1866
Nancy Hylton, wid. of Jm. W. Hylton, 3/7/1879
Valentine Hylton, son of Jeremiah W. and Nancy Hylton, 10/19/1821-6/12/1896
George W. Hylton, Sr. 8/12/1898
Susan E., wife of George W. Hylton, Sr., 10/1919
John Kelly Fulton, 2nd son of John W. and Barbara Ann Fulton, 9/22/1922
Catherine Penn Fulton, oldest dau. of John W. and Barbara Fulton, 2/22/1908, Farmville, Va.
Hylton Harrison Fulton, 3rd son of John W. and Barbara Fulton, 4/16/1910 at Bedford City, Va.
(R. M. Academy)John William Fulton, husband of Annie B Hylton Fulton 11/22/1927
Barbara Ann Hylton Fulton 12/29/1934

(Major Clark Penn Bible, DEATHS, contd....)

George Hylton Fulton 8/1/1955 at St. Petersburg, Fla., son of John W. and Barbara Ann Fulton, husband of Stella
William Penn Fulton, son of John W. and Barbara A. Fulton, 8/21/1968 in Stuart, Va.
Gabriel J. Penn, son of Clark Penn, 3/28/1905
Susan E. Penn, wife of Gabriel J. Penn, 5/31/1919--b. 12/4/1838 Ruth 8. Penn, sis ter of Barbara Penn (2d wife of Clark .ann) 3/18/1897--aged abt 84

JAMES GREEN BIBLE
Owner: Mrs. Grace Green Weir Mansassas, Virginia

I, James Green, son of Moses and Elizabeth Green, b. 1/11/1776 My wife, Mary, dau. of Rush and Joanna Marshall, b. 1/1/1786

BIRTHS of Children of James and Mary Green

Sally Green 1/12/1800
William Adams Green 5/13/1815
Alfred Green 11/15/1802
Richard Nelson Green 4/27/1817
Nancy Green 6/28/1805
Thompson Abner Green 2/13/1819 Betsy Green 3/28/1807
Mary Ellen Green 4/22/1822
Rush Marshall Green 6/15/1809
Lucy Amanda Green 12/27/1825
George Washington Green 5/15/1811
James Franklin Green 9/3/1828
Emily Ann Green 7/19/1813

James Thomas Green, only son of Alfred Green, 1/10/1833

BIRTHS of Children of James F. and Mary C. Green

Walter Brawner Green 7/20J1856
George W. Green 4~/311867
William Goodwin Green 9/14/1858
Mary C. Green 4/3/1867

Emily Ann Green 11/23/1860
Grace F. Green 4/25/1870
John S. Green 2/25/1863

DEATHS

Sally Green, dau. of James and Mary, 2/17/1818, aged 17 yrs, 3 mos., 15 days
Thompson Abner Green, son of James and Mary, 8/5/1824, aged 5 yrs., 5 mos., 23 days
Lucy Amanda Green, dau. of James and Mary, 9/26/1826, 8 mos., 29 days
Mary Ellen Green, dau. of James and Mary, 11/12/1829, aged 7 yrs., 6 mos., 23 days
Alfred Green, son of James and Mary,---
Rush Marshall Green, son of James and Mary, 3/13/1840, aged 30 yrs, 9 mos., 2 days
William Adams Green, son of James and Mary, 2/27/1841, aged 25 yrs., 10 mos., 15 days
Emily Ann Ferguson, dau. of James and Mary Green, 9/15/1843, aged 30 yrs, 1 mo., 27 days
George W. Green, son of James and Mary, 1/6/1866, 54 yrs., 7 mos., 25 days
Nancy Green, dau. of James and Mary, 11/2/1869, 64 yrs., 4 mos. James Green, son of noses and Elizabeth, 11/14/1850, aged 74 yrs, 9 mos., 3 days

Mary Green, wife of James Green and dau. of Rush and Joanna Marshall, 10/4/1862, aged 76 yrs., 9 mos., 4 days

Mary Catharine Green, wife of James F. Green, dau. of John and Julia Ann Strother, 3/20/1872, aged 36 yrs., 4 mos., 16 days
James Franklin Green 5/19/1892, aged 63 yrs., 7 mos., 16 days

(James Green Bible continued...)

Richard N. Green 5/8/1882, aged 65 yrs., 11 days Emily Ann Green Hopper 3/19/1938

MARRIAGES

I, James Green, son of Moses and Elizabeth Green, to Mary Marshall, dau. of Rush and Joanna Marshall, 9/10/1799
Alfred Green to Jane K. Doughty 3/13/1832 John Marshall to Betsy Green 3/15/1832
John D. Ferguson to Emily Ann Green 12/23/1834 George Green to Nancy Marshall 2/11/1840
Richard Nelson Green to Maryanne Ferguson 9/21/1841
James Franklin Green to Mary Catharine Strother 8/14/1855 William Goodwin Green to Virginia Estelle Gossom 4/14/1906
James Franklin Green to Sarah Obanon 10/30/1873
Sarah Obanon Green left James F. Green's house and him with her own free will and accord on 22nd day of July 1875
Milton Hopper to Emily A. Green 2/5/1880
Waiter B. Green to mary Julia Hanson 7/27/1880
John S. Green to Eliza J. Vaughn 11/28/1888
George W. Green to Florence E. Strother 12/12/1888
Samuel Tasker Weir to Grace Foster Green 10/18/1899

DABNEY WASHINGTON WALLER BIBLE
Owner: Raymond Waller

Thomas Waller, son of John and Agnes Carr Waller, 7/29/17322/10/1788, aged 55 yrs., 5 mos., 19 days m. Sarah Dabney.
Sarah Dabney, dau. of John and Sarah Ann Jennings Dabney, 10/2/1740-1/10/1822, aged 81 yrs., 3 mos., 8 days

BIRTHS of Children of Thomas and Sarah Waller

Mary Waller 2/26/1761-1850 m. Joseph Woolfolk
Mary Waller
Anna Waller 11/11/1762-8/5/1834
Agnes Waller 11/17/1764-L1/7/1817, aged 53 yrs. wanting 4 days
Sarah Waller 1/24/1764-3/22/1829, aged 62 yrs., 1 mo. 28 days
Carr Waller 3/12/1769-5/7/1843, aged 74 yrs.,
Dabney Waller 2/20/1772-6/6/1849, aged 77 yrs., 3 mos., 17 days m. Elizabeth Minor
Pomfrett Waller 5/8/1774-4/20/1814, aged 40 yrs. wanting 9 days
Dorothy Waller 3/31/1777-12/2/1838,aged 61 yrs., 7 mos., 2 days m. Rev. E. T. Rowzie
John Waller 2/10/1780-9/10/1842, aged 44 yrs, 7 mos.
Elizabeth Waller 3/2/1783-6/7/1872, aged 89 yrs., 3 mos., 5 days
Dabney Waller 2/20/1772-6/6/1849, aged 77 yrs., 3 mos., 17 days m. Elizabeth Minor

BIRTHS of Children of Dabney and Eliz. Minor Waller

Elizabeth Minor Waller 9/26/1768-1/7/1832, aged 62 yrs., 3 mos., 11 days
Thomas Carr Waller 7/29/1799, baptised 9/1st following by Rev. Jesse Lee-d. 10/25/1872, aged 73 yrs., 2 mos., 26 days

Sarah Minor Waller 11/15/1801, baptised 7/2nd following by Rev. William Kenyan-d. 11/18/1976, aged 73 yrs., 2 mo., 26 days

Dabney Washington Waller 1/1/1804, baptised 9/16th following by Rev. Hezekiah Arnold m. Caroline Pleasants 3/6/1827-d. 8/16/1880, aged 76 yrs, 8 mos., 16 days

Mary Ann Dabney Waller 5/2/1806, baptised 7/18th following by Rev. Samuel Stewart-d. 11/3/1862, aged 56 yrs., 6 mos. 1 day

Elizabeth Dabney Waller 4/11/1808, baptised 6/12th following by Rev. E. T. Rowzie m. Dr. H. S. E. Pollard-d. 5/1881

(Dabney Washington Waller Bible continued....)

Agnes Carr Waller 11/22/1810, baptised 4/10/1811 by Rev. E. T. Rowzie m. Pike Pollard-d. 3/15/1844, aged 33 yrs, 3 mos., 23 days John Mercer Waller 8/2/1814, baptised 3/15/1815 by Rev. E. T. Rowzie-d. 4/6/1876, aged 61 yrs., 8 mos., 4 days
Dabney Washington Waller 1/1/1804-8/16/1880 m. Caroline Pleasants 3/6/1827
Caroline Pleasants, dau. of Jordan and Elizabeth Tyler Pleasants 11/19/1805-12/28/1878

BIRTHS of Children of Dabney W. and Caroline Waller

Mary Elvira Waller 3/137/1829, baptised 8/15/1830 by Rev. Lewis Kidmore m. D. G. F. Suann 5/3/1846-8, 10/24/1860

Archibald Pinckny Waller 12/14/1830, baptised 8/21/1831 by Rev. E. R. Rowzie m. Miss Wilson-d. 7/26/1887

Elizabeth Pleasants Waller 1/12/1833, baptised by Rev. B. H. Johnson m. Dr. Edger McKenney 6/29/1851-d. 6/7/1909

George Washington Waller 9/7/1835, baptised by Rev. B. H. Johnson-d. 8/7/1913

Caroline Ann Waller 11/21/1837, baptised by Rev. B. H. Johnson m. T. T. Johnson 1/23/1856-d. 7/20/1896

Louisa Waller 3/14/1840-6/12/1840

Dabney Jordan Waller 6/29/1841, baptised 6/18/1843 by Rev. B. H. Johnson m. Annie Catherine Waddy, dau. of Sophia Pleasants and Garland Thompson Waddy 6/26/1867 m. 2nd wife, Alice C. Lee 10/29/1889-d. 4/12/1925

John Thomas Waller 8/24/1844, baptised by Rev. B. H. Johnson m. Anna Otelia Mann 11/12/1868

Judith Anna Waller 12/19/1846, baptised by Rev. B. H. Johnson (Method1st Church) m. George P. Goodlow 12/19/1876-d. 11/29/1902
Dabney Jordan Waller 6/29/1841 m. 1st Annie Catherine Waddy 6/26/1867

BIRTHS of Children of Dabney Jordan and Annie Catherine Waller

Caroline Waddy Waller 5/8/1868 at Oak Hill, Louisa Co., Va.
Kate Clarke Waller 9/21/1869 at Oak Hill, Louisa Co., Va. m. Lynn Purcell Chewning of Spotsylvania Co., Va. 11/25/1891 at Bethany Church, Caroline Co., Va.

Edward Pinckney Waller 3/21/1871 at Walnut Hill, Caroline Co., Va. m. Eula Young Spicer of Louisa Co. 4/3/1901-d. Frederick Hall, Louisa Co., Va. 2/28/1910

Rose Garland Waller 11/30/1872 at Walnut Hill, Caroline Co., Va. m. Frederick Lee Frazer of Spotsylvania Co.,Va. 1/23/1895 at Bethany Church, Caroline Co., Va.

Sophia Woodson Waller 7/17/1875 at Walnut Hill m. John Westly Hancock of Caroline Co., Va. 12/12/1899 at Bethany Church

George Tyler Waller 10/16/1877 at Walnut Hill m. William E. Dalton of Philadelphia, Pa. 8/1895

Dabney Jordan Waller, Jr. 3/22/1879 at Walnut Hill m. Minnie Lee of "Linstead Magna", Halesworth, England, 2/8/1905

Hampden Pleasants Waller 3/1/1882 at Walnut Hill m. Belle Wright Houck of Washington, D. C. 7/20/1911

Dabney Jordan Waller m. 2d 10/29/1889 Alice C. Lee of "Linstead Magna", Halesworth England

BIRTHS of Children of Dabney Jordan and Alice C. Waller

Roberta Lee Waller 8/16/1890 Walnut Hill m. Leland B. Anderson of Hanover Co., 10/29/1919
Raymond Minor Waller 6/21/1892 m. Mrs. Katharine Barkley Kendall 7/3/1920
Dorothy Vivian King Waller 7/13/1895 Walnut Hill, Caroline Co.
Rose Garland Waller, dau. of Annie Catherine Waddy and Dabney

(Dabney Washington Waller Bible contd...)

Jordan Wallet, m. 1/23/1895 Frederick Lee Frazer

BIRTHS of Children of Rose Waller and Frederick Lee Frazer

Ivarine-Jordan Frazer 11/11/1898 Washington, D. C. m. John Presser Harrison II, 10/15/1921

Kathryn Waller Frazer 1/17/1901 Washington, D. C. m. Gordon Wallace Yerby 12/29/1927

CHARLES GRANDVIEW FEILD BIBLE
Owner: Miss Jeanne Scott 322 N. McLean, Memphis, Tenn

Charles Grandison Feild, son of Alex and Feild, b. 2/22/1805 Mecklenburg, Virginia-d. 3/20/1845, Haywood Co., Tenn., aged 40 yrs, --- mos., 24 days

Annie Martha Steele, dau. of William and M. C. Steelrt, b. 4/1/1810 Dumfries, Virginia-d. 8/27/1837, Fayette Co., Tennessee, aged 27 yrs., 4 mos., 24 days

Jean Murray Feild, dau. of C. C. and A. M. Peild, b. 9/20/1830 Mecklenburg, Virginia, baptized by William Steel A. D. 1835-d. 7/4/1893 Lauderdale Co., Tennessee, aged 62 yrs., 9 mos., 14 days

Charles Grandison Feild, son of Alex S. and Jean M. Feild and Annie M. Steel, dau. of William and Mary C. Steel, were m. in Mecklenburg Co., Virginia

Henry Sanford, son of R. W. and Frances L. Sanford, m. Jean M. Feild, dau. of C. G. and A. M. Feild, 5/9/1849, Haywood Co., Tennessee

Henry Sanford, son of Robert W. and Frances, b. 12/1/1827 Covington, Tennessee, baptised by Rev. Samuel Williamson in 1837 d. 6/18/1885, Lauderdale Co., Tennessee

Mary Catharine Feild, dau. of C. G. and Ann M. Feild, b. Mecklenburg, Virginia 2/24/1833, baptised 1835 by Rev. William Steel-d. at her home in Lauderdale Co., Tennessee 2/7/1880, aged 46 yrs., 11 mos., 23 days

Charles Grandison Feild, son of C. G. and Ann M. Feild, b. Mecklenburg, Virginia 5/22/1835, baptised 1835 by Rev. William Steel-d. 3/5/1869 Shelby Co., near Memphis, Tenn., aged 34 yrs., 9 mos., 11 days

Robert Alexander FeiLd, son of C. G. and A. M. Feild b. 8/6/1837 Fayette Co., Tennessee

Francis Malcol;n Green, son of J. W. and Elizabeth Green m. Mary Catharine Feild, dau.of C. G. and A. M. Feild 11/16/1853 in TLpton, near Covington, Tennessee

Charles Grandison Fefld, son of V. G. and A. M. Feild m. Mary An Person 5/1857, dau. of W. and Lucy Person, Fayette Co., Tenn.

Robert Alexander Feild, son of C. G. and A. M. Feild m. Matilda Ann Jarrett, dau. of W. F. and H. Jarratt, 11/1859, Haywood Co., Tennessee

(Charles Grandview Feild Bible, contd....)

Williaetta Feild, dau. of C. G. and C. M. Feild, b. 4/26/1840 Haywood Co., Tenn., baptised by Mr. Alison.

Henry Alison Feild, son of C. G. and C. M. Feild, b. haywood Co., Tenn. 2/27/1842, baptised by M. Alison-d. 3/4/1922, Jonesboro, Ark., aged 80 yrs.

Thomas Blackburn Feild, son of C. G. and C. M. Feild, b. Haywood Co., Tenn. 8/1843, baptized by Mr. Alison-killed at Shiloh 4/7/1862, aged 19 yrs., 8 mos., -- days

P. R. B. Browne m. Williaetta Feild, dau. of C. G. and C. M. Feild, 12/1859 in Shelby Co., near Memphis, Tennessee

Henry A. Feild, son of C. G. and C. M. Peild m. Margaret Barrett, dau. of R. and M. Barrett in Covington, Tennessee
Charles Feild Sanford, son of H. and J. M. Sanford, b. Covington, Tennessee 2/23/1850, baptised by Mr. David Cummins

Mary Agnes Sanford, dau. of H. and J. M. Sanford, b. 2/12/1853 in Covington, Tennessee, baptised by Mr. D. Cummins

Robert Walker Sanford, son of 8. and J. M. Sanford, b. 9/18/1855, Covington, Tenn.-d. Tipton Co., Tenn. 7/26/1856

Charles F. Sanford, son of Henry and Jean M. Sanford, m. Mary Agnes Reese Jayroe, dau. of John Reese and Mary Agnes Jayroe, in Durhamville, Lauderdale Co., Tenn. 5/15/1878

William Carter Person, son of W. E. and M. A. (Jeffrey) Person m. Mary Agnes Sanford, dau. of H. and J. M. Sanford, Lauderdale Co., Tenn., 3/8/1876

Henry W. Sanford, son of H. and J. M. Sanford b. Tipton Co., Tenn. 7/25/1857?, baptized 1857? by Rev. Samuel Williamson-3. 6/21/1885

Edgar E. Sanford, son of H. and J. M. Sanford, b. Tipton Co., Tenn. 8/1/1839

Thomas L. Sanford, son of H. and J. M. Sanford, b. Tipton Co., Tenn., baptised by Rev. D. H. Cummins, d. Lauderdale Co., Tenn. 8/21/1880, aged 18 yrs., 9 mos., 3 days

Henry William Sanford, son of Henry and Jean Murray Sanford m. Susie Anthony ---

Jennie Wren Sanford, dau. of H. and J. M. Sanford, b. Tipton Co., Tenn. 8/25/1867, baptized 1868 by Rev. D. H. Cummins.

John Applewhiete Gren, son of J. M. and M. C. Green, b. Covington, Tenn. 6/29/1855-d. 12/17/1855, 3 mos., 18 days

Annie Jean Malcolm Person, dau. of W. E. and M. C. Person, b. Tipton CO., Tenn. 7/2/1863, baptised 9/20/1870 by Mr. A. Cage - d. 9/28/1870, Tipton, Tenn., aged 7 yrs., 2 mos., 26 days

Joe Manley Scott, son of J. M. and Melvina Scott m. Jennie Wren Sanford, dau. of Henry and Jean Murray Sanford 12/27/1777, Lauderdale Co., Tenn.

CAPT. THOMAS PENN BIBLE
Poplar Grove, Patrick Co.

MARRIAGES

Thomas Penn to Martha Leath 11/26/1805; m. 2nd time to Mary C. Kennerly 12/25/1819

Martha A. C. Penn to J. N. Zentmeyar 9/15/1847
Eliza A. Penn to Samuel W. Hairston 10/26/1848
George W. Penn to Mary A. Penn 7/30/1854
Sarah R. Pann to Dr. R. D. Hay 6/12/1857
Lucinda S. Penn to James A. Penn 9/23/1857
William A. Penn to Mary L. Smithee 8/10/1865

Joseph G. Penn to Ruth Shelton 12/6/1866
Mary Elizabeth Penn to John Edd Foster 12/1/1866
Martha Susan Penn to William Moore Tatum 12/18/1890
Thomas Penn b. 6/15/1781
Martha Leath b. 4/15/1790
Mary Kennerly b. 10/16/1803

BIRTHS of Children of Thomas and Martha Penn

Peter L. Penn 3/31/1806
Andrew Jackson Penn 3/27/1811
Columbus F. Penn 11/1/1808

BIRTHS of Children of Thomas and Mary C. Penn

Martha Ann Catharine Penn 8/9/1820
George Washington Penn 10/16/1822
Lafayette Penn 11/9/1824
Eliza Penn 12/14/1826
Sarah Ruth Penn 9/9/1829

Joseph Abram Goodman Penn 2/10/1832
Lucinda Susan Penn 10/13/1834
Thomas Greensville Penn 1/15/1838
William Alexander Penn 7/7/1840
John S. Penn 12/4/1842

BIRTHS of Children of George W. and Anna Penn

Edmund Penn 4/3/1852
Bella Penn 11/26/1857-6/1863

Mary Ann Penn 4/16/1854

BIRTHS of Children of Lucinda S. and James A. Penn

Thomas Penn 7/16/1858
Mary C. Penn 9/11/1863
James Penn 1/6/1380

Inf. dau. 4/16/1868-6/1868
Joseph Penn 11/23/1861

BIRTHS of Children of William Alexander and Mary I. Penn

Mary Elizabeth Pann 8/20/1866 at Poplar Grove
Thomas Bennatte Penn 3/25/1868 at River Band
Martha Susan Penn 8/13/1870

Ellen Maxwell Penn 10/20/1872

BIRTHS of Children of John Edd and Lizzie Penn Foster

Hallie Ethel Foster 10/6/1887   William Penn Foster 5/1/1891   John Edd Foster, Jr. 4/2/1889

DEATHS

Martha Penn, wife of Thomas, 8/28/1816   Lafayette Penn 11/13/1829
Dr. Peter L. Penn 5/22/1835 in Talladega Co., Ale.
Thomas Penn 3/29/1858
John S. Penn 10-/27/1861 of typhoid fever at Lewisburg while in Confederate service
Columbus Penn in Fayette Co., Texas

(Capt. Thomas Penn Bible, DEATHS, contd...)

William Alexander Penn 6/21/1887
George W. Penn 8/27/1867
Jackson Penn 3/27/1877
Martha Penn, wife of Jackson Penn, 6/14/1887
Mary C. Penn 6/1885
Thomas G. Penn 6/1885
Mrs. Eliza Hairston, dau. of Mary C. and Thomas Penn, 1/1/1900
Mrs. Sarah Hay 1898
Mrs. M. A. Zentmeyer 11/1897
Mrs. Susie Penn Tatum 2/11/1926

BIRTHS

Francis Penn 1/9/1735
Abraham Penn 12/27/1743-6/26/1801
George Penn 12/12/1737
William Penn 4/9/1746
Philip Penn 6/27/1739
Moses Penn 1/13/1748
Gabriel Penn 7/17/1741

BIRTHS of Children of Abraham Penn

George Penn 1/6/1770
Thomas Penn 6115/1781
Lucinda Penn 9/3/1771
Abraham Penn 3/14/1783
Gabriel Penn 11/14/1773
James Penn 1/31/1785

Horatio Penn 11/14/1775
Luvenia Penn 4/3/1787
Polley Penn 7/1/1777
Edmond Penn 1/8/1789
Greensville Penn 5/16/1779
Philip Penn 3/5/1792

MOODY HOLLEMAN BIBLE
Owner: Jack Leaan Hollemen
813 Southern Ave., Hettiesburg, Miss.

BIRTHS

Moody Holleman, son of Wilson and Elizabeth (Moody) Holleman,
12/28/1784, Surry Co., Va.
Margaret Holleman, dau. of Francis and Mary Brown, 12/24/1794
Note: Margaret Brown was m. 1st to David or Denial Butler-had two children)
Mary Ann Butler 12/25/1814, dau. of David or Daniel and Margaret Butler

BIRTHS of Children of Margaret Brown and Moody Holleman

Alexander Holleman 2/6/1821
Wilson Hollaman 9/6/1822
Jeremiah Holleman 10/2/1824
George Washington Holleman 2/16/1826
Patrick Henry Holleman 12/9/1827

Caroline Holleman 6/14/1829
John Wesley Holleman 5/30/1831
Emeline Holleman 3/22/1833
Feliciana Holleman 1/15/1835
Louretta Holleman 3/4/1837

DEATHS

Moody Holleman 10/15/1865, Gainesville, Mississippi
Margaret Hollaman 4/16/1880 at Gainesvilla, Mississippi
John Wesley Holleman, grandfather of Mrs. Eunice Holleman St. John

JOSEPH WEST BIBLE

Joseph West b. 1/8/1775
Harriet Hetley West b. 5/5/1789
Joseph West m. Harriet Hetley 3/12/1807

BIRTHS

Margaret Hall West 2/19/1808
Mary Hall West 5/25/1819
Eliza West 10/17/1809
Amanda Minerva West 6/27/1821
Prudence Harris West 5/2/1812
Elizabeth Ann West 8/1/1824
Elias Jackson West 11/11/1814
Harriet Louisa West 5/29/1827
Martin Volney West 7/15/1817

BENNETT MOSELEY BIBLE

BIRTHS

Bennett Williamson Moseley 3/2/1780
Elizabeth Winston Moseley 6/10/1783

THEIR CHILDREN:

Hanry Winston Moseley 5/19/1802 at Fincastla, Va.
Bennett W. Moseley 5/2/1804 at Pincastle, Va.
Mary Malinda Moseley 1/6/1806 at Fincastla, Va.
John Moseley 11/8/1807 at Fincastla, Va.
George Cabel Moseley 12/1/1808 at Fincastla, Va.

MARRIAGES

Hanry W. Moseley to .Jane Leyburn, Lexington, Va., by Dr. George Baxter
Mary Melinda Moseley to A. W. Campbell at Otteeburn, Va. by Father Mitchell, Bedford Co.
George Cabell Moseley to Mary Whitlock at Fancy Farm, Bedford Co., Va. 12/17/1835 by Rev. J. O. Mitchell
Elizabeth Winston Moseley to Dr. George W. Layburn 10/27/1936 by Rev. A. W. Campbell, near Dr. Moseley's, Bedford Co.

DEATHS

Bennett Williamson Moseley 7/17/1805
John Moseley 2/8/1808
Dr. Bennett Williamson Moseley 9/30/1811 at Fincastle, Va., bur.
In burial ground of Presbyterian Church
Mary M. Campbell 9/17/1855 at Inglesida, buried there
Elizabeth Moseley 7/26/1856 at Tngleside, res. of George Cabell Moseley, buried there
Funeral serman preached there, Sabbath, July 27, by her son-in-
law, George W. Leyburn

JOHN CLARK BIBLE
Owner: B. M. Clark, San Benito, Texas
MARRIAGES

John Clark to Mary Moore 2/21/1767
Their first son, John Clark, Jr. to Susannah Henderson, dau. of
John Henderson, 11/15/1791
Son, Micajah Clark to Sarah Henderson, dau. of John Henderson 12/1/1788,
Dau., Mary Clark to David Clark, son of Christopher Clark, 12/1794

(John Clark Bible, MARRIAGES, contd....)

Dau., Elizabeth to M. Morton 12/2/1819
Dau., Judith Clark to Samuel Moormen, son of Zachariah Moorman, 3/2/1796
Son, Jamy Clark to Maria McCalla, dau. of Andrew McCalla, 3/1808
Son, Edward B. Clark to Margaret Madden 11/14/1815
Son, William Clark to Elizabeth H. Winston, dau. of George Winston of Richmond, 11/10/1818

BIRTHS

John Clark, son of Micajah Clark, 12/26/1745
Mary Moore, dau. of John Moore, 1/1/1748

THEIR CHILDREN:

John Clark 6/2/1768
Tucker Woodson Clark 3/8/1779
Micajah Clark 12/31/1769
Elizabeth Clark 3/12/1781
Mary Clark 1/12/1772
Martha Clark 5/9/1783

Judith Clark 3/27/1774
James Clark 7/10/1785
Matthew Clark 4/13/1775
Edward Bowling Clark 3/3/1788
3/3/1788 Mary Clark 3/13/1777
William Clark 1/24/1790

Sarah Shuster, dau. of Philip Schuster, 2/18/1788
Edward B. Clark, son of John Clark, 3/3/1788
Margarat Horton Maddux, dau. of William Maddux, 7/25/1796

BIRTHS of Children of Edward B. and Margaret H. Clark

John Tucker Clark 10/10-11816
Thomas Craven Clark 9/20/1826
Mary Evalina Clark 2/22/1818
Micajah Snowden Clark 2/7/1829

William Maddux Clark 2/1/1820
James Martin Clark 9/6/1822
Edward Granville Clark 8/17/1824

DEATHS

Mary Moore 1720-5/14/1814, aged 94 yrs.
John Clark 6/2/1768-4/2/1848, aged 79 yrs., 10 mos.
Susannah Clark 1775-3/7/1840
Margaret H. Clark 7/25/1796-10/30/1864, 68 yrs., 3 mos., 5 days
Mary Clark 1/12/1772-10/1775
Matthew Clark 4/13/1776-same mo.
Martha 5/9/1783-4/27/1786
John Clark 12/26/1745-4/2/1819, aged 73 yrs., 3 nos., 7 days
William Clark 1/24/1790-2/15/1822
Mary Clark 1/1/1748-11/5/1830, aged 82 yrs., 10 mos., 4 days
 Edward 8. Clark 3/3/1788 8/10/1835, aged 46 yrs., 5 mos., 7 days
Mary Clark 3/13/1777-11/1831, aged 54 yrs., 4 mos.
James Clark 7/10/1785-11/10/1837, aged 52 yrs., 4 mos.
Micajah Clark 12/31/1769-9/21/1845, aged 75 yrs., 8 mos., 21 days
Tucker W. Clark 3/8/1779-2/14/1847, aged 67 yrs., 11 mos., 6 days
Sarah Clark 1766-5/18/1847
John J. Clark, son of Edwerd B. Clark, b. 10/10/1816
His wife, Sarah A. Hinchee, dau. of John T. Hinchee, b. 8/29/1816 They were m. 7/26/1839, and had following children:

BIRTHS of Children of John J. and Sarah A. Hinchee Clark

Margaret Elizabeth Clark 5/29/1840-1/10/1841
Mary Eliza Clark b. 1/7/1842
Edward Bowling Clark b. 10/16/1843
Sarah Catharine Clark b. 6/10/1845
Amanda Evalina Clark b. 3/26/1847

John Tucker Clark b. 4/13/1849
James Barley Clark 6/29/1851-6/6/1852
Micajah Marshall Clark b. 5/7/1853
Virginia Emeline Clark 6. 2/3/1856

(John Clark Bible, contd....)

Sarah A. Clark, wife of John T. Clark, d. 2/18/1861, aged 44 yrs., 5 mos., 20 days
John Tucker Clark d. 9/17/1872, aged 55 yrs., 11 mos., 29 days

Sarah Cathrine Clark, wife of Lloyd B. Hughes, d.8/1878
Edward Bowling Clark d. ---

Amanda E. Clark b. 3/26/1847 n. V. N. White 7/1/1869
Volney Napoleon White b. 1/20/1842

Claude Marshall White, son of V. N. and A. E. White b. 7/2/1872
Volney Napoleon White d. 10/14/1895, aged 53 yrs., 8 mos., 6 days

TIMOTHY BROWN APPLIN BIBLE

BIRTHS

Timothy Brown Applin 11/13/1760
Ann Wyman 3/24/1762 m. Timothy Brown Applin 1/9/1783
Anna Applin 7/13/1783
Benjamin Redman Applin 10/6/1785-10/6/1785
Benjamin Redman Applin 8/7/1786
Rebecca Applin 4/4/1791
Sabrina Applin   11/3/1793
Philinda Applin   7/17/1796
Abigail Applin   8/27/1799
Elizabeth Applin 6/17/1801
Wessen Timothy Applin 11/16/1806

WILLIAM HENRY MOSELEY BIBLE of Bedford Co.

BIRTHS

William   Henry Moseley   9/19/1844

Catherine Turner 9/26/1844-7/8/1912

Mary D. Moseley 9/21/1867 Bedford Co., Va.

Frank T. Moseley 4/1/1870 Bedford Co., Va.

Clara L. Moseley 1/5/1872 Bedford Co., Va.

Cabell Moseley 9/19/1873 Bedford Co., Va.

Arthur Moseley 7/29/1875 Bedford Co, Va.

Estelle Moseley 7/17/1878 Bedford Co., Va.

Sarah V. Moseley 11/18/1880 Bedford Co., Va.

Edmund N. Moseley 2/14/1883 Bedford Co., Va.

Henry B. Moseley 10/2/1885 Bedford Co., Va.

William Henry Moselay 10/3/1890 Bedford Co., Va.-10/17/1922

William Henry Moseley m. Catherine Turner 12/4/1867

CHRISTIAN PETERS BIBLE
From: Rev. War Pension #S5898

Chrlstian Peters b. 10/16/1760 Rockbridge Co., Va. d. 10/18/1837 Peterstown, Va m. Anna Katharine Fudge b. 3/3/1766 Rockingham Co., Va. - d. 7/25/1839 Peterstown, Va.

BIRTHS of Children

Conrad Lewis Peters 3/14/1786 m. Clara Snidow
John Peters 2/27/1788 m. 1st Cynthia Ann Clark, 2d, Eliza Spangler
Jacob Peters 1/8/1791 m. Elizabeth Shumate
Mary Peters 5/20/1793 m. Thomas Dunn
Elizabeth Peters 6/15/1795 m. John Symms
Rhoda Peters 8/3/1798 m. Charles Spangler
Nancy Peters 9/4/1801 m. Elias Hale
Sarah Peters 6/14/1804 m. George Spangler

GEORGE NOLAN BIBLE
Owner: Regina Holloman Rt. 1, Temple, Ga.

BIRTHS

George Nolan 1733 in Virginia
Peyton Nolan 1793 in Wilkes Co., Ga.
Sallie Moseley 1808 in Wilkes Co., Ga.
Stephen B. Pace 1775 in Virginia
Mary Bohannon 1781 in Virginia
Henry Terrell Nolan 12/10/1825, Walton Co. Ga.
Mary Ann Jane Pace in Grady, now Spalding Co Ga., 3/20/1828 W. Nolan 9/1862, Heard Co., Ga., near Walnut Hill

MARRIAGES

Stephen B. pace 1798 to Mary Bohannon in North Carolina
Peyton Nolan 1820 to Sally Moseley, Walton Co., Ga.
John Pace 6/7/1827 to Mary Jane McDaniel, Fayette Co., Ga.
Henry Terrell Nolan to Mary Ann Jane Pace 1853, Aiken, S. C.
William Henry Nolan to Luana Lane 1/1/1888, Heard Co., Ga., at Walnut Hill

WILLIAM PENDLETON HERNDON BIBLE
From: Rev. War Pension #S9575

William Pendleton Herndon b. 2/29/1764 Albemarle Co., Va.
His wife, Mary Rucker, b. 3/2/1767-d. Greene Co., Va. 2/26/1836

BIRTHS of THEIR CHILDREN:

Thomas Herndon 11/28/1785
Rachel Herndon 8/27/1797
Edward Herndon 5/13/1787
William Herndon 1/29/1799
James Herndon 1/23/1789
Henry Herndon 9/9/1800
Ezekiel Herndon 12/7/1790
Manson Herndon 6/29/1802
Elizabeth Herndon 6/6/1792
Joel Herndon 7/29/1804
Mary Pendleton Herndon 5/2/1794
Thomas Herndon 6/29/1807
Abner Herndon 1/22/1796

JOHN WINSTON SR. of Louisa Eatonton, Ga.
Owner: Mrs. Reuben A. Garland, At

John Winston Sr. of Louisa Co., Va. m. Miss Patsey Bickerton (from England) and had children:

Patsey Winston m. Col. Kellis
R. W. Barbara Winston m. Dr. Robert Barret
Betsey Winston m. Tarlton Payne
William Winston
Ailsey Winston m. Harry Pendleton

Joseph Winston m. Rebecca Johnston
James Winston m.
Sallie Marks Bickerton Winston m. Nancy Smelt
John Winston, Jr. m. Mary Johnson

BIRTHS

John Winston, Jr. 10/14/1757
Nicholas I. Winston 12/13/1789
Mary Johnson 8/31/1763
Maria T. Winston 3/21/1793
Thomas Winston 10/11/1781
Martha C. Winston 1/30/1798

John Winston 5/1/1783
Barbara O. Winston 10/1/1799
William O. Winston 10/21/1785
Thomas Winston 10/11/1781
Bickerton Winston 4/3/1788
Ann A. Tinsley 4/29/1788

BIRTHS of Children of Thomas Winston and Ann A. Tinsley

John T. Winston 2/4/1806
Thomas I. Winston 2/19/1813
Reuben T. Winston 12/25/1819
Joseph B. Winston 12/25/1807
George H. Winston 3/5/1815
Sarah A.E. Winston 8/28/1810
Mary I. Winston 6/23/1817
Susan C. Alford 8/16/1786
Ann E. Ervin 8/25/1838
Thomas W. Erwin, Jr. 4/15/1836
S. E. Eliza Irvin 8/25/1838
Thomas Winston Ervin, Thomas U. Erwin's first child, 6/16/1857
George W. Erwin; Thomas W. Erwin's second child, 11/29/1858

MARRIAGES

John Winston to Mary Johnson 12/7/1780
Thomas Winston to Ann A. Tinsley 8/20/1804
Thomas Winston to S. C. Gilliam 6/3/1824
Sarah A. E. Winston to Dr. A. Means 12/25/1827
Mary I. Winston to H. F. Erwin 12/23/1834

John T. Winston to Mercy A. Davison 10/1/1850
Thomas W. Erwin to Catherine M. Whitaker 1/29/1850
O. D. Winston to Miss M. G. Lyon 2/19/1861
Jacob U. F. Little to Miss A. E. Ervin 1/26/1864
Dr. Thomas A. Means and Miss Powell 2/11/1864

DEATHS

William O. Winston 7/13/1794, 8 yrs.
Mary I. Ervin 11/24/1844
John Winston, Jr. 4/28/1800, 43 yrs.
John T. Winston 12/29/1854
Mary Winston 11/22/1823
Martha C. Anderson 2/26/1857
Bickerton Winston 7/25/1822, 35 yrs.

Thomas Winston, Sr. 12/12/1864
John B. Winston 12/23/1846
Barbara Willis in La.
Ann A. Winston 1/5/1820
Reuben T. Winston 10/8/1841
Joseph Bickerton Winston in La.

George Hendree Winston 12/4/1887, near West Point, Ga.
Ann Eliza Erwin Little 7/30/1919, Atlanta, Ga., b. West Point

WILLIAM HOUGH BIBLE
Of Loudoun County
Owner: Miss Ivie B. Hough

716 Reservoir St., Baltimore, Md.

William Hough b. 11/24/1744 Loudoun Co., Va.-d. 2/18/1815, m. Eleanor Htte 1766
BIRTHS of THEIR CHILDREN:
John Hough 9/9/1767 m. Jane Braden
Joseph Hough 10/10/1770-5/15/1806
Thomas Hough 7/23/1772 m. Margaret Skinner
Samuel Hough 7/6/1774 m. Zoubbide Skinner
Elizabeth Hough 12/11/1777-5/22/1848 m. John Schooley
Sarah Hough 7/27/1779-2/20/1851 m. Daniel Stone
Ann H. Hough 12/25/1781-8/23/1863
William Hite Hough 12/23/1783 m. 1st Ann Steer, 2nd, Mary Ann Chalmers, 3rd, Eliza Neill Brown
Eleanor Hough 1/25/1786 m. Richard Chilton
Benjamin Hough 1/23/1788 m. 1st Mary Williams, 2nd, Elizabeth Orrison, 3rd, Rachel Lambert
Amasa Hough 6/23/1790 m. Ann E. Bond

THOMAS ADAMS BIBLE
From: Rev War Pension #W4111

Thomas Adams b. Fluvanna Co., Virginia 1758 m. Sally Ford 10/14/1786

BIRTHS of THEIR CHILDREN:

Elizabeth Adams 7/13/1787 -
Richard C. Adams 6/24/1798
Mourning Adams 2/8/1789
Abner Adams 3/16/1800
Thomas F. Adams 6/5/1791

John Adams 5/30/1801
James B. Adams 3/25/1795
Nicholas Adams 7/2/1804
Calvin Adams 3/9/1797

THOMAS HARRIS, SR. BIBLE
Owner: Mrs. Reuben A. Garland
Atlanta, Georgia

Thomas Harris Sr. b. 6/4/1739 Mary Baker Harris b. 5/5/1744
Thomas Harris Sr. m. Mary Baker 4/20/1763

BIRTHS

Elizabeth Harris 7/30/1764
Justus Harris 4/14/1773
Samuel Baker Harris 12/30/1765
Eli Harris 8/18/1775
Martha Harris 9/29/1767
Thomas McCall Harris 10/10/1777
Margaret Harris 8/9/1769
Gabriel Harris 8/4/1780
Sarah Harris 2/3/1772
Lovel? Clark Harris 2/24/1784
Ann Hall Brodnax, wife of Eli Harris, b. 5/11/1785

ALBIN PASTEUR DEARING BIBLE
Owner: Mrs. Marion Dearing Lawrence, Athens, Ga

Albin Pasteur Dearing, son of William and Eliza Jane, b. 12/29/1821
Eugenia Emily Dearing, dau. of Thomas NapLer and Sarah Sherwood Hamilton, b. 4/26/1826
Eugenia E. Hamilton m. Albin P. Dearing 11/21/1844
John Dearing, grandfather of A. P. Dearing, m. Ann Jett of Virginia, lived and died Culpepper Co., Va.

Children of William and Eliza J. Dearing

John T. A. Dearing m. E.F. Stone
Eliza Margaret Dearing m. T. H. Harden Mary Dearing - d. in childhood
William E. Dearing m. C. E. Stovall Albin P. Dearing m. Eugenia E. Hamilton
James W. Dearing d. childhood
Alfred L. Dearing m. Marcella Jones Marion A. Dearing m. F. W. Pickens Indiana E. Dearing m.
J. J. Dearing Joseph S. Dearing d. in Mexican War
St. Clair Dearing
Emma F. Dearing - d. childhood

MARRIAGES

Emery Speer to Sallie Dearing, dau. of Albin P. Dearing and Eugenia E. Dearing 9/8/1869
William D. Dearing to Heleo A. McCay 12/18/1883
Marion E. Dearlng to R. B. Lawrence 8/25/1886
Thomas Hamilton Dearing to Edith Goodwin 12/29/1869
Eugenia Dearing Speer to William Aubrey 8/25/1892
Anne Middleton Spear to Howard Burr
Sally Dearing Speer to Matt Howland Signor 3/10/1900
Lulie Hamilton Speer to Samuel Forder Crecelius 3/14/1901
Frank Hamilton Dearing to Pauline Heyward 4/1900
Marion Sherwood Speer to Andrew Hasell Heyward 5/10/1903
Louise Hamilton Dearing to Thomas C. Myers 11/3/1909
Munro Goodwin Dearing to Julia M. Daniel 4/22/1914
Katherine Graham Dearing to George Munro Goodwin 6/1915
Harry Timrod Gearing to Lillie Heyward Lynah 1916
Robert Brashear Lawrence to Elsie Collins 1923
Eugenia Dearing Lawrence to William Tyler Ray 12/3/1927
Robert McCay Dearing to Katherine Godfrey

DEATHS

John Godfrey Dearing 1/6/1883
Albin Eugene Dearing 3/18/1913
Munro Goodwin Dearing 12/10/1930
Eugenia Dearing Speer Aubrey 7/3/1936 Anne Hiddleton
Speer Burr Anderson ---

THOMAS HAMILTON DEARING BIBLE

Thomas Napier Hamilton, son of James and Anne Fox Napier Hamilton, 2/3/1798-11/7/1858 m.
Sarah Sherwood Bugg, dau. of Sherwood and Sarah Ann Jones Bugg, 10/28/1797-3/11/1796

BIRTHS

Thomas Hamilton Dearing 7/21/1848 Sarah Jane Dearing 1/31/1851
Marion Eugenia Dearing 3/18/1853 Albin Pasteur Dearing 9/9/1855
William Dearing Dearing 12/28/1859 John Alfred Dearing 4/26/1866

(Thomas Hamilton Dearing Bible, BIRTHS, contd....)

Eugenia Dearing Speer, dau. of Emery and Sarah Jane Dearing Speer, 10/1/1570
Albin Eugene Dearing, son of Thomas Hamilton and Edith Goodwin Dearing, 2/23/1871
Anne Middleton Speer 5/26/1872
Hunro Goodwin Dearing 2/1/1873
Marion Sherwood Speer 5/11/1874
Frank Hamilton Dearing 10/28/1874
Sally Dearing Speer 5/4/1875
Harry Timrod Dearing 8/6/1877
LulLe Hamilton Speer 9/26/1877
John Godfrey Dearing 6/30/1881
Robert McCay Dearing 1/3/1885, son of William Dearing and Helen McCay Dearing
Looise HamiltoN Dearing 8/30/1887
Frances Efffngham Lawrence 1/5/1890
KatherLne Graham Dearing 5/9/1890, dau. of Thomas Hamiltoo and Edfth G. Dearing
Robert Brashear Lawrence, Jr. 11/4/1891
Eugene Dearing 10/6/1889. William D. and Helen M. D.
Helen McCay Dearing 7/29/1893
Eugenia Hamilton Dearing 6/1/1897, dau. of John Alfred and Richie Dearing

DEATHS

William Dearing 6/3/1853
Eliza Jane Dearing 5/21/1880
Albin Pasteur Dearing 5/29/1885
Eugenia Emily Hamilton Dearing 12/26/1912
Thomas Hamilton Dearing 10/8/1890
Sallie Dearing Speer 8/3/1879
John Alfred Dearing 2/26/1903
Edith St. John Goodwin Dearing 4/26/1928
William Dearing Dearing 2/13/1933
Albin Pasteur Dearing, Jr. 10/8/1933
Frances Effingham Lawrence 12/21/1896
Robert Brashear Lawrence, Sr. 11/9/1929

ROBERT LEONARD BARNES BIBLE
Of Richmond, Virginia
Owner: Mrs. Russell B. Gladding
179 Gamont Drive, Decatur, Ga. 30030

Robert Leonard Barnes of Richmond Va. m. Alice Gertrude Hardy of Richmond, Va. 2/9/1876 at res. of her father, J. C. Hardy, by Rev. C. C. Bittings and George H. Ray, Witnesses: George Napier Thomson, William A. Neal and numerous friends

BIRTHS

Robert Leonard Barnes 9/4/1350
Alice Gertrude Barnes 12/24/1859
Inez Gertrude Barnes 11/13/1877
Alice Lillian Barnes 6/10/1880
Robert Hardy Barnes 4/3/1883
Julia Gay Barnes 3/14/1885
Elwood Dance Barnes 11/22/1887 Aubrey Leonard Barnes 1/3/1991 Horace Collingsworth
Barnes 3/18/1893 Leonard Hartley Barnes 4/22/185
Ruth Barnes 12/31/1900
Lucille Audrey Barnes 1/28/1902

(Robert Leonard Barnes Bible, contd....)

MARRIAGES

J. Stuart Hopkins to Alice Lillian Barnes 6/10/1903
Samuel H. Templeton to Inez Gertrude Barnes 4/28/1909
Elwood Dance Barnes to Nannie Myrtle Adams 6/9/1909
R. Lester Hudgins to Julia Gay Barnes 11/29/1911
Horace C. Barnes to Laura Harper 12/18/1915, Jacksonville, Fla., First Bapt1st Church by Rev. W. A. Hobson, Pastor
Dr. Humie Lee Horton and Lucille Audrey Barnes 4/17/1924 at Grove Ave. Bapt1st Church by
Rev. Samuel H. Templeton
Robert Hardy Barnes to Eve Virginia Agnew 1/25/1917, Huntington, W., Va., by Dr. Cary F. Moore

DEATHS

Aubrey Leonard Barnes 8/11/1892 Leonard Hartley Barnes 7/3/1896
Ruth Barnes 12/31/1900
Horace Collingsworth Barnes 12/21/1916, Jacksonville, Fla.
Robert Hardy Barnes 2/17/1930
J. Stuart Hopkins 10/16/1930
Robert Leonard Barnes 10/21/1936
Alfce Gertrude (Hardy) Barnes 11/9/1937
Dr. Robert Lester Hudgins 7/2/1929
Sarah Frances (Dance) Hardy 12/28/1907
Dr. Humie Lee Horton 10/27/1938, Raleigh, N. C.

BIRTHS of Grandchildren

Robert Leonard Hopkins 3/25/1910
Dorothy Barnes 7/31/1910
Gertrude Barnes Templeman 10/21/1910
Alice Gertrude Hopkins 7/13/1912
Inez Frances Templeman 7/12/1914
Elwood Dance Barnes, Jr. 3/9/1916
Sarah Frances Hudgins 8/11/1916
Horace C. Barnes, Jr. 10/13/1916, Jacksonville, Fla.
Samuel Huntington Templeman 11/30/1916

Sallie Moore Barnes 7/15/1918
Robert Hardy Barnes, Jr. 12/25/1919
Myrtle Virginia Barnes 9/13/1919
Andrew Leonard Barnes 4/19/1921
Ruth Matilda Templeman 3/12/1920
Julia Audrey Hudgias 2/25/1924
Lucille Audrey Horton 11/21/1930
Humie Zebbie Lee Horton 10/17/1933

JAMES FORD BIBLE
From: Rev. War Pension #W8820

James Ford (Faure) Sr. b. Manakin Town, Henrico Co., Va. 1708-d. 1810 Buckingham Co., Va. m. Ann Bondurant 1710-12/17/1751 Henrico Co., Va.

BIRTHS of Children

Marie Ford 9/2/1730
Rachel Ford 8/27/1739
Judith Ford 9/6/1732
James Ford Jr. 3/14/1743
Pierre Ford 1/11/1734
Ruth Ford 2/14/1745
Magdeline Ford 8/20/1736
Boaa Ford 6/23/1748
Anne Ford 2/24/1738

MARRIAGES

Marie Ford to James Agee Anne Ford to Rev. Rene' Chastain
James Ford, Jr. to Sally Burit Ruth Ford to Nathaniel Maxey

LAWSON H. DANCE BIBLE of Richmond
Owner: Gertrude Templeton Gladding
179 Lament Drive, Decatur, Ga. 30030

"This is my grandfather's Bible given to me by my mother, his only child. He was married three times. His first wife was Rebecah Young, my mother's mother. His second wife was Kate Wallace. his third wife was Catherine McQuin. My mother, Sarah Frances, married James C. hardy when she was seventeen years old. My father was from Spartanburg, S. C. and was a student here at Richmond College when he met my mother. He was an orphan - both parents dieing when he was quite young."
/s/Gertrude Hardy Barnes

MARRIAGES

L. H. Dance to Rebecah Young 4/14/1835
Kate Wallace, 2nd wife
L. H. Dance to C. A. McQuin 11/10/1857 by Rev. Dr. Hoge

BIRTHS

Lawson H. Dance 1813
Children of L. H. Dance and Rebecah: Sarah F. Dance 8/29/1836
Benjamin H. Dance 9/23/1843 Martha Ann Dance 11/25/1846

GEORGE WASHINGTON GLADDING BIBLE
Of Accomack County
Owner: Russell B. Gladding
179 Lament Drive, Decatur, Ga. 30030

BIRTHS

George W. Gladding 1/12/1807
Betty Whatley 3/25/1808
Maelcha Wilkerson, dau. of John and Elizabeth Wilkerson, 4/12/1818
Children of George W. and Milchey Gladding:
Elizabeth Gladding 8/30/1839
John Thomas Gladding 1/18/1843
Emily Ann Gladding 2/7/1841
Betsy Thomas Gladding 6/4/1845

DEATHS

Hetty Gladding 1/2/1837
John Thomas Sledding 4/16/1945
Tully Gladding 9/24/1837
Milchey Gladding 9/12/1851

Elizabeth Gladding 8/30/1839
George W. Gladding 6/23/1854
Mary Ann Gladding 12/2/1840

J. H. THORNTON BIBLE
Owner: James Day Thornton, Huntsville, Alabama

J. M. Thornton 4/22/1822-8/10/1889 m. 4/27/1844
Lucinda Thornton 4/11/1826-1/21/1887 m. 4/27/1844
W. A. Thornton 8/4/1845 m. 11/14/1867
Mary E. Thornton 11/1/1847-3/12/1922
John M. Thornton 3/27/1849 m. 3/10/1875
P. L. Thornton 2/4/1851-12/1/1925 m. 12/19/1875
Robert D. Thornton 1/4/1853-11/27/1923 m. 12/2/1874
R. B. Thornton 11/11/1854
James B. Thornton 11/4/1856

(J. M. Thornton Bible, contd....)

Thomas H. Thornton 8/27/1858-11/1881
Laura G. Thornton 6/30/1862-6/27/1923
Charles H. Thornton 11/7/1846 m. 10/18/1865
F. M. Thornton d. 1/13/1863, a member of 8th Tenn. Regt., wounded in side and leg, d. at Rome, Ga.
Reuben Thornton, Sr. d. 2/8/1867 of inflammation of the brain,aged 66 yrs., 5 mos., 27 days
Mary Thornton d. 11/25/1865, with the dropsy

THOMAS FAUNTLEROY BIBLE
Owner: Juliet Fauntleroy, Alta VIsta, Va.

Thomas Fauntleroy b. Essex Co., Va. 1760-1765, d. Middlesex Co., Va. 2/10/1820, lived in Essex and Queen Co.-s, Va. during the Revolution. In 1796 he m. Isabell Lorimer in Middlesex Co., Va.

BIRTHS of THEIR CHILDREN:

Hannah Elizabeth Fauntleroy 6/26/1797-12/25/1814
Isabella Lorimer Fauntleroy b. 9/19/1798 m. 5/4/1819
James C. Wiatt John Fauntleroy b. 11/16/1799 m. Rebecca Parke Farley Corbin
Thomas Waring Fauntleroy b. 3/7/1801 m. Juliet
Muse Henly Catherine Moore Fauntleroy b. 8/7/1802 m. Richard Randolph Corbin William
Lawson Epuphroditus Waring Fauntleroy b. 8/7/1804 m. Kitty Carter Corbin
Mary Lorimer Fauntleroy b. 4/3/1806 m. Charles C. Curtis
Sarah Tomlin Fauntleroy 6/1/1808-10/10/1817
George Lorimer FauntLeroy b. 1/24/1810 m. his cousin, Apphia Bushrod Fauntleroy
Apphia Bushrod Fauntleroy b. 6/19/1811 m. John I. Adams
Martha Payne Waring Fauntleroy b. 1/11/1817 m. George Lewis Willis Judith Tomlin Fauntleroy b. 5/21/1815 m. Robert Cunningham Caldwell

WILLIAM STARK BIBLE of York Co.
Owner: Charles Stark, Overwharton Parish

BIRTHS

William Stark 1733, Chief Justice of York Co.
James Stark 1717, and his wife, Catherine, d. 1750, m. 1746

BIRTHS of Children of James and Catherine Stark

James Stark 12/21/1747
Sarah Ann Stark 11/25/1749
Lydia Stark 6/30/1748
Jeremiah Stark 6/11/1750-1824
Jeremiah Stark m. 2nd Mary King 1759-1831

JOSHUA STONE BIBLE of Pittsylvania Co.
Owner: Mrs. W. S. Frazier, Alta VIsta, Va.

Joshua Stone b. abt 1725 in Maryland, near Ft. Tobacco-d. 1822 Pittsylvania.Co., Va, m. Mary Coleman, b. 1730-d. after 5/20/1822

BIRTHS of THEIR CHILDREN:

William H. Stone 1750
Samuel C. Stone 1757 Mary C. Stone 1752
Colamen Stone 1759 John Stone 11/25/1754
Joshua Stone 1/62
Thomas C. Stone 1756 Polly Stone 1763

(Joshua Stone Bible, contd....)

Mary C. Stone m. 10/2/1777 Robert Harrison
John Stone m. 1st 10/2/1777 Dollie Hoskin, d. 4/4/1808, m. 2nd in
1807, Lucy Hoskin
Joshua Stone m. Mary Hoskin Polly Stone m. William Terry

EDMUND FITZGERALD BIBLE
Owner: Ethel Hancock, Alta V1sta, Va.

Edmund Fitzgerald b. on board a vessel in mid-ocean in 1742-d. 1845. (His family left Ireland on account of oppression, migrated to New York, later settling near the Peaks of Otter in Belford Co., Va. They finally settled in Pittsylvania Co., Va. in 1774).

Edmund Fitzgerald m. 1774 Mildred Payne 1752-1872

BIRTHS of THEIR CHILDREN:

Reuben Fitzgerald 1112111777
Edmund Fitzgerald 5/1/1788
Nancy Fitzgerald 6/16/1780
William Fitzgerald 5/21/1791
James Fitzgerald 12/13/1782
Samuel Fttzgersld 8/5/1794
Elizabeth Fitzgerald 6/2/1785
Elizabeth Fitzgerald m. 1803 James Hoskins Stone, d. 1865 Edmund Fitzgerald m. Polly Cooke
William Fitzgerald m. 1812 Sarah Jones, d. 1868
Samuel Fitzgerald m. 1826 Emily Anderson, d. 1862

CHARLES CALLAWAY BIBLE of Bedford Co.
Owner: Mrs. James Lewis Arthur (decd)

Charles Callaway b. 6/7/1752 Virginia-d. 1827 Bedford Co., Va. m. Judith Early Pate, wid. Of John Pate and dau. of Colonel Jeremiah Early and his wife, Sarah Anderson Early

BIRTHS of Children of Charles and Judith Callaway

Joel Callaway 9TT5J1769
Charles Callaway 9/4/1781
Archilles Callaway 2/13/1771
Judith Callaway 7/22/1783
William Callaway 6/12/1772
John Callaway 8/21/1785

Sarah Callaway 6/11/1775
Frances Callaway 8/6/1777
James Callaway 9/12/1777
Henry Callaway 5/23/1792
Polly Callaway 10/17/1779

Sarah Callaway m. John Anderson b. 11/19/1797

COLONEL JEREMIAH EARLY BIBLE of Bedford Co.
Owner: Mrs. James Lewis Arthur Alta V1sta, Virginia (decd)

Colonel Jeremiah Early b. Culpepper Co., Va. 1730-d. 1779 Bedford Co., Va. m. 1st Sarah
Anderson (d. 1764)

BIRTHS of THEIR CHILDREN:

Jacobus Early 11/16/1750
Jinny Early 1/2/1761
Judith Early 3/9/1752
Jeffry Early 8/19/1762
Jeremiah Early 9/27/1754
Jubal Early 4/12/1764

Joseph Early 2/27/1756
Sally Early 4/15/1766
John Early 9/15/1757
Abner Early 12/21/1767
Elizabeth Early 2/2/1759
Judith Early m. 1st John Pate, 2nd, Charles Callaway

THOMAS CARTER BIBLE
Of "Green Rock" Pittsylvania Co.
Owner: Mrs. George Stone, Danville, Virginia

Thomas Carter b. Lancaster Co., Va. 11/27/1734-d. Pittsylvania Co., Va. 7/15/1817, m. 7/10/1765 Winifred Hobson 7/7/1745 12/3/1831 Cumberland Co., Va.

BIRTHS of THEIR CHILDREN:

Joanna Carter 8/15/1766-7/1809
Jeluthan Carter 3/22/1779
Elizabeth Carter 6/21/1768
Lawson Hobson Carter 6/3/1781
Jesse Carter 11/30/1770
Christopher Lawson Carter 2/7/1784-10/7/1860
Sarah Carter 2/17/1773-12/23/1805
Edward Carter 3/8/1775-9/18/1847
Dale Miller Carter 3/17/1786
Thomas Carter 4/8/1777-10/1852
_____ 9/8/1796

Rawley Williamson Carter 3/8/1788-10/18/1847 m. 1809 Anne Jennings Robertson 1790-abt 1847

JEREMIAH STARK of Stafford Co.
Owner: Mrs. A. H. Gunter
P. O. Box 375, Mineral Wells, Texas

Jeremiah Stark 1750/2-1824 m. 1773 Mary King 1759-1831

BIRTHS of THEIR CHILDREN:

Charles Stark 1774-1838 m. 1801
Charity Stark James Stark 1775
Rachel Stark 1788 Naomi Stark 1778
Lydia Stark Phoebe Stark 1780

Mary Stark 1795
Leah Stark 1782
Ruth Stark 1798
Charles Stark 1774-1838 m. 1801 Kezia Cannon, d. 1850

BIRTHS of Children of Charles and Kezia Stark

Samuel Cannon Stark 1801-1829
Isaac Stark 1810
Jeremiah Pennington Stark 1803
Lydia Stark 1812
James Harvey Stark 1806
Elizabeth Otison Stark 1815
Mary King Stark 1808
Sarah Ann Stark 1817
James Harvey Stark b. 1806 m. 1832 Mary Ann Cargile 1818-1896
Mary King Stark b. 1808
Abbeville, S. C. m. James Mattison

MRS. WILLIAM D. DANTZLER
Ft. Eustis, Virginia

Ruby Beatrice Duggan b. 6/5/1907 m. 8/10/1933 William Daniel Dantzler b. 11/11/1910, Ct., USA, Ft. Eustis, Virginia

William D. Dantzler, Jr. b. 12/6/1935
Robert Carroll Dantzler b. 1937
Ruby Catherine Dantzler b. 1943

JEREMIAH OSBORN of Augusta Co.
Owner: Samuel Osborn, North Carolina

Jeremiah Osborn m. Mary Newman, dau. of John Newman

THEIR CHILDREN:

Reuben Osborn
Jonathan Osborn
Joseph R. Osborn
John Osborn 10/27/1770-11/2/1849 m. 1790 Jane Claypool 2/18/176910/8/1834, dau. of James and Margaret Claypool of Augusta Co., Va.
Jeremiah Osborn Jr. 12/24/1772-6/15/1857 m. Anne Blythe b. 3/27/1771

THOMAS HEALY BIBLE
Owner: Mrs. Emma Campbell Wright
Rappahannock, Virginia

Children of Thomas Healy by 1st wife:

William Healy 5. 2/3/1769 m. Elizabeth Br1stow 12/24/1791
Thomas Healy b. 4/2/1770 m.
Frances Montague 5/6/1797
Edmund Healy 9/9/1772-9/17/1791
Elizabeth Healy b. 6/26/1774 m. Gabriel Jones 12/13/1792
Ann K. Healy b. 2/15/1776 m.
Thomas Montague 4/1795

Children of Thomas Healy by 2nd wife:

Sarah Healy b. 2/13/1777 m. William Nelson Stiffe 1/28/1796
Frances Healy b. 3/13/1779 m.
William Robinaon 2/28/1799 Jane Healy b. 2/3/1781 m. William C. Blakey 1/28/1802
Catherine Healy 2/20/1783-2/1788

Children of Thomas Healy by 3rd wife:

George Healy b. 4/28/1787
James Healy 7/13/1789-9/1792
Welter Healy b. 5/24/1792 m. 1st 11/7/1815 Juliet Tayloe Corbin, 2nd, 7/12/1821, Maria Muse
Robert Healy b. 7/25/1797 m. Anna Owen

Note: Marriage dates are from Marriage Bonds, Middlesex Co., Va., with exception of Walter Healy.

ALEXANDER LEFTWICH BIBLE
Owner: Mrs. Clara Snyder , Alta Vista, Virginia

MARRIAGES

Alex and Sally Leftwich 1/8/1818
Jacob H. Anderson to Jane Leftwich 3/15/1847 by Rev. James Barberry
William C. Smith to Pauline Leftwich 2/9/1847 by Rev. William Ward
Edward M. Clayton to Eliza Ann Leftwich 12/8/1857, by Rev. William H. Mathews
John C. Jones to Mary Matilda Leftwich 11/16/1958 by Rev. William H. Mathews
Thomas Leftwich to Ann M. Smith 12/23/1858 by Rev. Eldridge Andrews
Thomas W. Anthony to Ellen F. Leftwich 4/21/1864 (or Nov.) by Rev. William H. Mathews
John S. Leftwich to Jennie Smith 11/13/1866 by Rev. Milton Bishop

(Alexander Leftwich Bible continued...)

BIRTHS

Alexander Leftwich 8/28/1796 Sally Leftwich 2/27/1798

BIRTHS of THEIR CHILDREN:

Thomas Leftwich 11/11/1818
Wm Alexander Leftwich 11/13/1829
Sarah Jane Leftwich 12/2/1820
Mary Matilda Leftwich 6/25/1832
Eliza Ann Leftwich 2/17/1823

John Smith Leftwich 10/22/1834
Samuel Leftwich 7/11/1825
Ellen Frances Leftwich 12/18/1836
Paulina Leftwich 10/2/1827
James Clayton Leftwich 3/20/1839

Eliza Samuel and Ann Ralph Leftwich, twin sons of William C. and Pauline Smith Leftwich, 1/17/1852
Mary Elizabeth Leftwich 8/6/1855, dau. of William C. and Pauline Smith Leftwich
Thomas R. Clayton, son of Edward N. and Eliza Ann Clayton, 3/10/1857
Alexander Leftwich, son of John C. and Mary M. Jones, 10/6/1859
Polly Alexander, dau. of William C. and Pauline Smith, 3/19/1868

DEATHS

Samuel Leftwich, son of Alexander and Sally, 7/2/1826
Ann Ralph, dau. of William C. and Pauline Smith Leftwich, 7/6/1852
Mary Matilda Jones, wife of John E. Jones and dau. of Alexander and Sally Leftwich 10/3/1861
James C. Leftwich, son of Alexander and Sally, 6/10/1863 from a gun shot reed at Kelly's Ford, March 1863
Samuel Smith 2/19/1845, aged 84 yrs., at Clifton
Sallie Leftwich, wife of Alexander, 2/13/1885
Alexander Leftwich 9/11/1882, aged 91 yrs.
Eliza A. Clayton 1/21/1900
Thomas R. Clayton 2/20/1898
Pauline C. Smith 4/22/1900

THOMAS CALLAWAY BIBLE
Owner: Mrs. Clara Snyder, Alta VIsta, Virginia

BIRTHS

Thomas Callavay 1712 William Callaway 1714
Francis Callaway
Richard Callaway
James Callaway, the youngest of these three brothers
Their two slsters were Elizabeth and Ann, (but several brothers and perhaps slster died younger)
William Callaway Sr. m. 1/8/1735 Elizabeth Tilley

BIRTHS

James Callaway 12/25/1735
Charles Callaway 6/28/1754
John Callaway 6/10/1738
Joseph Callaway 12/16/1856
William Callaway, Jr. -/28/1740

Milly Callaway 6/5/1759
Elizabeth Callaway 6/18/1743
Sena Callaway 12/8/1761
Mary Callaway 1/6/1741

DEATHS

Charles Callaway Jr. 6/30/1827

Judith Callaway, his wife, 2/23/1814

BIRTHS

John Pate Callaway 10/29/1767
Joel Callaway 9/15/1769
Archilles Callaway 2/13/1771
William Callaway 6/12/1773

Sarah Callaway 6/14/1775-6/4/1848
James Callaway 9/12/1777
Polly Callaway 10/17/1779-1817

(Thomas Callaway Bible, contd....)

Charles Callaway 9/4/1781-2/1/1854
Judith Callaway Jr. 7/22/1773-5/29/1848
John Callaway 8/21/1785-8/22/1831
Flaney Callaway 5/23/1792
Francis Callaway 8/16/1787-11/16/1846

COLONEL JOHN CALLAWAY BIBLE
Of Bedford and Campbell Counties
Owner: Frank Hewitt
Asheville, North Carolina

John Callaway 6/10/1738-1/28/1820 Campbell Co,, Va. m. 1st, 1760 Tabitha Tate, 2nd, 1768 Agatha Ward

Children of John Callaway and his 2nd wife, Agatha Ward:

James Callaway 2/16/1761-1787
Elizabeth Callaway 4/20/1763-1804
William Callaway 10/11/1769-2/27/1808
John W. Callaway 7/27/1771-9/17/1795
Matilda Callaway 4/8/1774-11/10/1795
Anna Callaway 11/6/1776-12/29/1776
David Callaway 1/26/1776-12/6/1813
Henry Green Callaway 5/7/1781-12/6/1817 m. Ann Callends
Sarah Callaway 11/27/1783-2/1/1808
Peggy Callaway 6/12/1786-6/17/1811
William Callaway m. 1794 Doshea Callaway 8/8/1768-6/17/1822
Their dau., Sarah Ann Callaway 12/9/1801-4/3/1831 m. 10/26/1826
John Hewitt d. 2/9/1835
Their son, Dr. Richard Newton Hewitt 8/7/1827-11/9/1908 m. 10/25/1849
Frances Dorothea Michie 6/14/1928-5/30/1890
Their dau., Margaret Elizabeth Hewitt, resides Evington, Campbell Co., Va.

CAPTAIN ROBERT COBBS
Of Bedford and Campbell Counties
Owner: Claudine Hutter
122 Harrison St., Lynchburg, Virginia

Robert Cobbs b. 3/2/1754 Louisa Co., Va.-d. 5/2/1829 in Campbell Co., Va. at his home "Plain Dealings", bur. at home, which is located 2 miles from Durham Railroad, 6 miles from Brookneal, Campbell Co.

Anne G. Poindexter, his wife, dau. of John poindexter (Rev. War Soldier) of Louisa Co., Va.-d. 1842, bur. beside her husband

BIRTHS of THEIR CHILDREN:

Louisa Cobbs
John polndexter Cobbs 5/27/1785 m. Jane Garland
Mary Lewis Cobbs 6/11/1757 m. M. William Armistead
Robert Lewis Cobbs 12/25/1789
William Cobbs 3/2/1792 m. Marian Stannard Scott Samuel Cobbs 7/14/1796
Sarah White Cobbs 2/12/1738 m. William C. McAll1ster
Charles Lewis Cobbs 3/12/1800 m. Anne Scott
Anne Elizabeth Cobbs 1902 m. Joel Motley
Meriwether Lewis Cobbs 3/4/1805

PATRICK HENRY'S BIBLE
Owner: Mrs. W. R. Rierson
Rainbow's End Alta VIsta, Virginia

Patrick Henry 5/29/1736-6/6/1799 m. 1st Sarah Shelton (had 6 children)- Martha m. Colonel John Fontaine; John; William; Anne m. Judge Spencer Roane; Elizabeth m. Philip Aylett; and Edward Patrick Henry m. 2nd Dorothea Dandridge, granddau of Gov. Alexander Spotswood (had 10 children).

Dorothea Dandridge Henry m. George D. Winston
Sarah Henry m. Robert Campbell, bro. of poet, Thomas Campbell
Martha Catherine Henry m. Edward Henry
Patrlck Henry m. Elvira Cabell
Fayette Henry
Alexander Spotswood Henry m. Pauline J. Cabell
Nathaniel Henry m. Virginia Woodson
Richard Henry - d. infancy
Edward Winston Henry m. Jane Yuille
John Henry m. Elvira McClelland

Children of Nathaniel Henry and Virginia Woodson:

Patrick Henry William Henry
Mary Henry
Lucy Henry
Martha Catherine Henry m. Charles Terrell Ward

Children of Charles Terrell Ward and Martha Catherine Henry:

Virginia Ward
Anselm Ward
Robert Henry Ward 3/17/1834-10/24/1894 m. 4/7/1861
Susan Lynch Deering 3/6/1838-9/27/1892

They had 9 children:

Charles Lynch Ward 6/7/1861-7/5/1863
James Dearing Ward 10/24/1864-12/22/1888
Robert Chalmers Ward 11/12/1866-2/20/1884
Charles Henry Ward 12/12/1868-8/20/1889
Mary Elizabeth Ward 3/29/1871-7/11/1901
Anselm Lynch Ward 1/16/1873

Infant son 7/29/1875-4/2/1875
Susan Virginia Ward 4/30/1876
William Patrick Ward 11/16/1877-11/5/1903
Anselm Lynch Ward m. 5/16/1894

Nathalie Floyd Otey and had 9 children: Mallie, Mary, Lynch, Lucy, Floyd, Susan, Dorothea. Virginia, and Petey Otey Ward
Susan Virginia Ward m. 7/25/1907 William Covington Rierson 4/8/1871-4/24/1928

BENJAMIN WALLER BIBLE of Williamsburg
Owner: Juliet Fauntleroy
Alta VIsta, Va.

Judge Benjamin Waller b. 10/1/1716 Spotsylvania Co., Va. m. 1/2/1740 Martha Hell 7/2/1728-8/9/1780

BIRTHS of THEIR CHILDREN:

Martha Waller 11728/1741 m. 1767 William Tayloe
Robert Waller 7/16/1749-10/4/1749
Benjamin Waller 12/3/1750-~/71/1751
Mary Waller 7/14/1752 m. 2/16/1751 John Tayloe Corbin
John Waller 7/25/1753 m. 9/1774 Edith Page
Dorothy Elizabeth Waller 9/2/1755 m. 1/13/1774 Henry Tazewell

(Benjamin Waller Bible, contd....)

Anne Waller 2/29/1756 m. 4/18/1773 John Boush
Benjamin Carter Waller 12/24/1757 m. 2/1778 Catharine Page
Clara Waller 9/2/1759 m. 1st 2/20/1779 Edward Travis, 2nd, Mordecai Booth
William Waller 2/16/1762 m. 11/30/1785
Elizabeth Macon of Hanover Co., Va.
Robert Hall Waller 1/7/1764 m. 3/5/1789
Camm-- ? Daughter (Mrs. Smith)
Frances Waller 4/6/1766-1767

HENRY STUART BIBLE
Owner: Mamie Donalson, Bainbridge, Ga.

Her Mother's Family, James Stuart of Virginia Mary Stuart m. 2/26/1796

BIRTHS of Children of Henry and Betsy Stuart

Giles Stuart 11/22/1796
Henry Stuart 3/26/1802

James Stuart 11/26/1798

BIRTHS of Children of James and Coley Stuart (m. 4/17/1821)

Ann Elizabeth Stuart 3/13/1822
Andrew Jackson Stuart 8/17/1828
Frances J. Stuart 9/2/1823
Lois Lunsford Stuart 7/29/1830

Henry Dabney Stuart 4/8/1825
William Randolph Stuart 7/31/1833
Giles O. Stuart 12/4/1826
James Goodwin Stuart 9/1/1835

DEATHS

Coley Robinson Chiles Stuart 12/14/1876
Henry Stuart m. Elizabeth Richardson.

William Randolph Stuart 12/11/1879

THEIR CHILDREN:

James Stuart m. Coley Robinson Chiles
Ann Elizabeth Stuart m. Reuben Donalson, son of John and Agnes Peel Donalson; Jane
Goodwin Stuart m. Dabney Chiles
John Goodwin m. Mary Robinson (cousin of George the III)
William Donalson m. Rachel Chiles (had George and Rachel)
William Donalson, bro. of John who m. Agnes Peel
Ann Elizabeth Stuart m. Reuben Donalson

NANCY BOYKIN BIBLE of Southampton Co.
Owner: Mrs. J. D. Renfroe, Massee Apts, Macon, Ga.

MARRIAGES

Nancy Virginia Boykin of Southampton Co., Va. to Alexander Saunders 11/15/1806, surety-Simon Boykin
Nancy Virginia Boykins Saunders (wid. of Alex Saunders) to Dr. John Saunders 3/20/1819, John and Simon Boykin, sureties

BIRTHS of Children of Nancy and Alexander Saunders

Thomas Jefferson Saunders 7/4/1809, Southampton Co., Va.
Simon Hardy Saunders, Southampton Co., Va.
Alexander Saunders, Southampton Co., Va.

BIRTHS of Children of Nancy Boykin Saunders and George Bartlett
Medora, Charlie, Eugene, Lucian (b. Ga. m. Ann Eliza Lyon), and Virginia Bartlett b. Ga.
Alexander Saunders, Jr. m. Ann Broughton and had 15 children:

(Nancy Boykin Bible, contd....)

Simon, Louisa, Nannie, Eliza, Lucian (twins that were never named), Jennie, Willie, Alexander and Mollie
Thomas Jefferson Saunders had one son - Job C. Saunders (d. Civil War, aged of 47 yrs. m. 1st Eliza Atkinson - had Cornelius J. Saunders b. 12/22/1834; m. 2nd Elizabeth Boyle Patterson and had children - Job C., Simon, Troy, Jane A., Nancy Virginia, Mary, Catherine, Ann Eliza, Susan Penelope, Sarah and Alice Tallulah

Nancy Virginia Saunders m. W. A. Elder, Jr. and had - Leila, Irene, Eugene, Rose, Effie and Beatrice

Susan Penelope Saunders m. Isaac Slaughter and had: Thomas K., Lizzie, Fannie and Viola

Allie Tallulah m. 1st O. P. Health 8/23/1885, 2nd, B. A. Green, 4/17/1917

Simon Hardy Saunders m. 4 times: 1st, Susan Bryan (one son, John), 2nd, Ann Eliza Lyon, 3rd, Sarah Slaton, 4th, Victoria Hill

Nunnally (widow, two children: Snow and Shellis?)

W. A. Elder, Jr. m. Cynthia Barlow
W. A. Elder, Jr. m. Nancy Virginia Saunders 4/27/1869
Nancy Virginia Saunders, wife of W. A. Elder, b. 9/26/1844
T. J. Saunders d. 2/28/1900
Thomas J. Saunders and Elizabeth B., dau. of Job C. Patterson, m. 6/14/1838
Thomas J. Saunders b. 7/4/1809
Nancy V. Saunders, dau. of T. J. and E. B., m. W. A. Elder, Jr. 4/27/1869
Elizabeth B. Saunders, wife of T. J., b. 4/1/1821

Note: Dr. John Saunders and Nancy Virginia Saunders bur. at old Saunders homestead, several hundred yards off State route 16, east of Jackson, Ga. on road landing to Indian Springs, near Mr. Woodie Higgins place. Inscription: "John Saunders, b. October 2, 1782 in South Hampton Co., Va., d. Butts Co., Ga. Dec. 10/1842."

THOMAS CARLETON BIBLE
Owner: Mrs. Jesse Bone, Milledgeville, Georgia

Thomas Carleton, son of Thomas and Sarah, b. 2/15/1752 in Charles City Co., Virginia m. 1st 10/28/1773 Elizabeth Hyde 2/10/1751-1/19/1775, 2nd, Martha Finch b. 3/17/1755

BIRTHS

John Hyde Carleton 12/24/1774, son of Thomas and Elizabeth

Children of Thomas and Martha Carleton:

Sarah Carleton 9/17/1776
Brothers Carleton 6/27/1778
Thomas and Martha Carleton 6/27/1778
Thomas Carleton 3/4/1780
Elizabeth Carleton 1/21/1782
Martha Carleton 10/9/1783
Rebecca Finch and Susanna Finch Carleton 2/15/1785
Senry Carleton 3/5/1786
Polley Carleton 3/10/1785

Martha Carleton, wife of Thomas, delivered with a dead child (girl) 12/19/1789

Martha Carleton, wife of Thomas, was second time delivered of dead child (boy) 6/16/1791

(Thomas Carleton Bible, contd....)

"Thomas Carleton and family moved to Georgia (Wilkes Co.) where we arrived the 9th of May 1792"

"Thomas Carleton and family moved to Greene Co. the 16th of November 1792 and settled on Beaverdam Creek"

Martha Carleton was a third time delivered of a dead child (boy) 11/29/1793
Nancy Carleton, dau. of Thomas and Martha, 9/4/1797
Betsy Allen Carleton, dau. of Martha, 9/22/1807

DEATHS

Brothers Carleton 7/29/1797
John Hyde Carleton, son of Thomas and Elizabeth, 10/15/1798, Savannah, Ga.
Thomas Carleton, Sr. 6/20/1818, aged 67 yrs.
Martha Carleton, wife of Thomas, 10/24/1810. Her funeral preached 2/24/1911 by Rev. L. Pierce, a respectable Methodlst preacher, of which Society she was and had been a member for several years. Betsy Allen Carleton, dau. of Martha, 4/21/1813. Her funeral preached by Rev. John Dingier 6/16/1814, a Baptlst preacher
John Allen, who m. Elizabeth Carleton, dau. of Thomas and Martha,
"Thomas Carleton and family moved on the Academy 4/30/1799"

MARRIAGES

Thomas Carleton, Jr. to Lydia Carleton 12/16/1803
Rebecca F. Carleton to Devereaux Jarrett 4/12/1808
Henry Carleton to Nancy Moore 4/27/1808
Polly Carleton to John Cunningham 3/23/1809
Martha Carleton, dau. of Thomas and Martha, to Edward Butler 11/19/1815
Devereau Jarrett b. 3/9/1773 in Yorktown County, Virginia
"Thomas Carleton and family moved to Morgan Co., Ga. 29th January 1810, near Madison"

REUBEN COOK BIBLE
Owner: Mrs. Sanders Upshaw, Social Circle, Georgia

Reuben Cook b. Hanover Co., Virginia 1740-d. in Major Washington's army during the Revolution.
John Cook, son of Reuben, 12/11/1769-11/18/1846
Mary Alexander (John Cook's 2nd wife) 8/27/1785-9/27/1864 m. 2/25/1310 John Cook

BIRTHS of Children of John and Mary A. Cook

Willie Cook 11121/1816 - -
Mary Cook 6/24/1820
George Cook 6/5/1812
John Cook 9/27/1822
Reuben Cook 9/26/1813
Mourning Cook 4/11/1825
Lucy Cook 4/24/1815

Elizabeth Cook 5/20/1827
James Cook 9/17/1816
Eliza Jane Cook 10/25/1829
Diana Cook 6/23/1818
Wm Alexander Cook 11/30/1833
James Cook m. 1/1/1851
Sarah Hamilton Oliver 6/19/1830-4/9/1895

BIRTHS of Children of James and Sarah H. Cook

James Hamilton Cook 10/26/1831
Walter Cook 5/28/1861
Luther Alexander Cook 1/27/1853
Sidney Oliver Cook 5/28/1862
Reuben Andrew Cook 5/6/1854

Robert Lee Cook 2/2/1867
Charles Edward Cook 3/17/1859
James Thomas Cook 7/12/1856
Sallie Cook 6/27/1869

(Reuben Cook Bible, contd....)

Reuben A. Cook d. 8/16/1912 m. 4/16/1879 Willie Blasingame b. 6/6/1862

BIRTHS of Children of Reuben A. and Willie B. Cook

Ethel Vests Cook 111911880- -
Neva Alline Cook 12/5/1888
Ina Alberta Cook 1/28/1882
Mabel Cook 12/24/1894
Ruby Augusts Cook 11/21/1884
Mary Dean Cook 4/25/1896
Edna Willie Cook 12/5/1888
Ruby A. Cook m. 6/1/1909
Sanders Upshaw b. 9/29/1874
Laurie Upshaw b. 5/1/1910

JOSEPH COOPER BIBLE
Owner: Mrs. Ellen Heath Cooper
2008 Wynnton Drive, Columbus, Ga.

Joseph Cooper ca 1767-6/22/1819
Milton Cooper 6/3/1799-1/19/1828 m. 3/30/1819
Caroline M. Evans 10/1/1799-7/28/1823
Alexander H, Cooper 1/18/1820-10/10/1844 m. 1st Ann Elizabeth Billups 9/1/1825-4/17/1845, m. 2nd, 7/11/1848 Eliza Cassandra Harris b. 11/2/1830
Milton Warren Cooper, son of Alexander H. and Eliza C. Cooper, b. 7/4/1849, Muscogee Co., Ga.
Thomas Evans b. ca 1760 Dublin Ireland,-d. 11/26/1817
Martha Crenshaw b. 2/4/1773 Lunenburg Co., Virginia

BIRTHS of Children of Thomas and Martha C. Evans

Eliza Evans 4/1/1795 Baltimore, Maryland
James Evens 4/5/1797-9/13/1797
Caroline Evens 10/1/1799-7/28/1823
Sophia Evens 2/4/1802

Ann Evens 7/9/1804-8/9/1804
Thomas C. Evans 8/22/1806
Mart R. Evens 4/23/1809
Martha Evans 8/29/1811

Father and mother of Martha Crenshaw:

Robert Crenshaw
Wife, Elizabeth Beauford m. ca 1750 on Rappahannock River, Virginia

Buckner Beasley m. 5/2/1832 Martha M. E. Evens

BIRTHS of Children of Buckner and Martha M. E. Beasley

Thomas M. Beasley 3/6/1836 -
John Beasley 10/20/1838
Mary Antolnett Beasley 2/7/1841-8/14/1842
Sarah Caroline Beasley 4/24/1843
Buckner Massilon Beasley 9/30/1845-

John William Cooper b. 10/19/1893
Maggie Baggett b. 5/6/1900
John William Cooper m. 11/16/1919
Maggie Baggett.

THEIR CHILDREN:

Susie Eleanor Cooper b. 2/14/1923
John William Cooper, Jr. b. 2/26/1930

FREDERICK THOMPSON BIBLE of Brunswick Co.
Owner: Ray Thompson
RFD 2, Eatonton, Georgia

Frederick Thompson b. 9/16/1763 Brunswick Co., Virginia m. 12/28/1784 Nancy Coker

BIRTHS of Children of Frederick and Nancy Thompson

James Thompson 11/8/1785
Alexander Thompson 2/26/1794
David Thompson 1/19/1787-4/26/1857
Charlotte Thompson 3/16/1796
Nancy Thompson 8/25/1788
Elizabeth Thompson 3/29/1798

John Thompson 2/24/1790
Faithy Thompson 6/6/1802
Lucy Thompson 1/24/1792
David Thompson m. 10/28/1810
Drucilla Camp

BIRTHS of Children of David and Drucilla Thompson

James R. Thompson 10/13/1811
John F. Thompson 12121/1824
Nancy Thompson 12/13/1813
John F. Thompson 12/21/1824
Eliza Thompson 1/28/1816
Drucilla Thompson 3/1/1827
Faithy Thompson 5/7/1816

Alfred Parks Thompson 1/8/1833
Susana Thompson 9/28/1820
Mary Caroline Thompson 12/10/1834
Violet Thompson 11/22/1822
Lucy Adeline Thompson 8/19/1837

ROBERT MANSFIELD BIBLE of Orange Co.
Owner: Mrs. James C. Gentry, Atlanta, Ga.

Robert Mansfield b. 12/19/1762 m. 5/4/1785 Albemarle Co., Va. Mourning Clark b. 10/27/1763

BIRTHS of THEIR CHILDREN:

Mildred Martin Mansfield 5/11/1786
Elizabeth Clark Mansfield 10/12/1788
Nancy Harrison Mansfield 7/25/1789
William Hearndon Mansfield 10/2/1790
Pleasant Fountain Mansfield 1/16/1793
James Wilkerson Mansfield 3/18/1794
Mary Lewis Mansfield 10/17/1795

Sarah Homes Mansfield 9/4/1797
Susannah Ware Mansfield 6/12/1799
Thomas Martin Mansfield 11/17/1801
Robert Clark Mansfield 11/12/1804
Joseph Allen Mansfield 6/25/1806
Micajah Willis and Beverly Winston Mansfield 4/13/1808 (twins)

DEATHS (from Bible of J. R. Gentry (burned)

Mourning Clark Mansfield 3/18/1831
Robert Mansfield 10/1/1833

MARRIAGES

Mildred Martin MansEield to Dr. John Taliaferro, Orange Co., Va.
Elizabeth Clark Mansfield to Joseph Snell in Orange Co., Va.
Nancy Harrison Mansfield to Isaac Graves, Jr., 9/14/1826, Orange Co., Va.
William Hearndon Mansfield to Salina Eddins 1/1/1818, Orange Co.
James Wilkerson Mansfield to Mildred Clark 11/18/1813, Orange Co.
Mary Lewis Mansfield to Henry James Clark 12/27/1815, Orange Co.
Susannah Ware Mansfield to Richard Duritt Austin 2/21/1826
Robert Clark Mansfield to Sarah E. Beatty 10/19/1830
Joseph Allen Mansfield to Susan Ann Lindsay 3/24/1835, Orange Co.
Thomas Martin Mansfield to Cassandra Paxton Orbison 1/1/1827, Rockbridge Co., Va.

THOMAS MARTIN MANSFIELD BIBLE of Franklin Co.
Owner: Mrs. Everett E. Bawsel, Atlanta, Ga.

"Mrs. Thomas Martin Mansfield was dau. of Thomas Orbison b. 2/1782 and his wife, Jane Moore, b. 2/1782. her grandmother was Miss Kirkpatrick, wife of John Moore, bur. at Old Monmouth Church in Va. Her mother was Jane Moore of Rockbridge Co., Va. 2/27/1782-2/22/1860. Her father, John Moore, had one bro., James Moore

Their father, John Moore came from Scotland and settled in Rockbridge Co., Va. His wife was Miss Adams of Mass., a relative of John Quincy Adams, the President."

Thomas Martin Mansfield b. 11/17/1801 m. 1/1/1827 Cassandra Paxton Orbison

BIRTHS of THEIR CHILDREN:

Charles Fenton Mercer Mansfield 9/23/1829
Mary Jane Mansfield 10/21/1831
Robert Thomas Mansfield 9/19/1833
John William Mansfield 3/17/1835
Mildred Mourning Mansfield 1/27/1837
Samuel Allen Mansfield 8/1/1839
James David Mansfield 3/23/1842
Henry Clay Mansfield 4/24/1844
Emma Campbell Mansfield 3/13/1847
Rebecca Maud Mansfield 9/18/1849

MARRIAGES

Mary Jane Mansfield b. 10/21/1831 m. 2/1851 John Rice Gentry b. 5/5/1827
Mildred M. Mansfteld b. 1/27/1837 m. 5/11/1869 Chr1stain W. Booze

Mortuary

RobertThomas Mansfield 7/1/1862, killed at Malvern Hill
John William Mansfield 6/5/1862, fatally wounded in the war
Emma Campbell Mansfield 6/23/1862 of dyptheria
Henry Clay Mansfield 6/30/1862 fatally wounded
Rebecca Maud Mansfield 7/6/1862 of dyptheria
Samuel Allen Mansfield 12/6/1862 exposure in the war
James David Mansfield 7/3/1863 killed at Gettysburg
Thomas Martin Mansfield 11/11/1874

TALLIE V. JOLLY JONES BIBLE of Loudoun Co.
Owner: Mrs. J. Doyle Jones, Jackson, Georgia

BIRTHS

Vincent Sanford 4/17/1777 Loudoun Co., Va.
Benjamin Sanford 11/26/1771 Loudoun Co., Va.
Jeremiah Sanford, Jr. 9/30/1765 Loudoun Co., Va.
Daniel Sanford 1/28/1778 Loudoun Co., Va.
Mildred Washington Sanford 7/13/1781 Loudoun Co., Va.
Thomas Sanford 12/24/1783 Loudoun Co., Va.
Jeremiah Sanford, Sr., 11/4/1739 Loudoun Co., Va.

MARRIAGES

George, Speaks to Martha Giles 10/16/1830
Nancy Virginia Jolly to W. R. Parker 1/23/1867
Elizabeth Jane Jolly to Larkin Davis Lee
1/21/1840 Lucy Jane Lee to William Henry Maddox 7/15/1880

DEATHS

Elizabeth Jane (Jolly) Lee 10/8/1860 Larkin Davis Lee 3/27/1906
Henry S. Lee 5/26/1887

(Tally V. Jolly Jones Bible, contd....)

BIRTHS

Joseph Jolly 4/13/1540 Butts Co., Ga.
Emma William Dickson 2/16/1849 Hancock Co., Ga.
William Dickson Jolly 5/9/1869 Butts Co., Ga.
Jesse Thomas Jolly 9/24/1880 Butts Co., Ga.
Tallie Virginia Jolly 4/17/1884 Jackson, Ga.
Joseph Howard Jolly 10/27/1897 Jackson Co., Ga.
Mildred Carolyn Jolly 1/9/1900 Jackson Co., Ga.

MARRIAGES

William Crawford Dickson to Caroline E. Palmer 8/15/1843 in Hancock Co., Ga.
Joseph Jolly to Emma William Dickson 12/6/1866 Butts Co., Ga.
William Dickson Jolly to Menla Ham 11/1/1896 Butts Co., Ga.
Tallie Virginia Jolly to James Doyle Jones 4/12/1911 Jackson, Ga.
Mildred Carolyn Jolly to Ralph C. Vaughn 5/15/1919 Atlanta, Ga.

CAPTAIN MAY BURTON, JR. BIBLE
of Orange County
From: Rev. War Pension

Application of Benjamin Burton, for heirs of May Burton, Jr.

Capt. May Burton, Jr. m. 9/29/1776 Martha Head, dau. of Benjamin

BIRTHS

Lucy Burton 4/28/1778 m. James Collins

Fanny Burton 2/6/1780 m. Baldwin M. Buckner

Elizabeth Burton 6/17/1781

Benjamin Burton 6/22/1784

Hannah Burton 6/30/1786 m. Alexander Bradford

Jarth Burton 9/9/--- m. 1st Blakey, 2nd John Webb

Sarah Burton 5/9/1790 m. 11/11/1811 Melton

Peggy Burton 2/13/1792 m. Douglass

Martha Burton 5/31/1794 m. 1st Edward Shipp, 2nd, James Craie of Augusta Co., Ga.

Harriet Burton 2/27/1797

Mary Mariah Burton 10/10/1798 m. Smith Eddins

Note: May Burton, Jr., was son of May Burton Sr. and Hannah Medley, dau. of John and Eleanor Medley of Middlesex Co., Va.

May Burton, Sr. was son of John Burton of Caroline Co. (d. 1735).

JOHN ASHBY BIBLE of Fanquier Co.
Owner: Martha Ann Ashby (decd)
DAR Records, Ga. State Archives

John Ashby 4/1/1743-4/5/1915, aged 75 yrs., 5 days Mary Ashby 1750-4/26/1826, aged 76 yrs.

BIRTHS of Children of John and Molley Ashby

Martha Ann Ashby 1/5/1770
Betsy Ashby 9/10/1782
Dolly Ashby 1/25/1772
Tomson Ashby 3/31/1785
Samuel Ashby 8/17/1773
Son b. & d. 3/28/1787
John Ashby 9/9/1775
Turner Ashby 8/31/1789
Nimrod Ashby 10/7/1778
Marshall Ashby 11/8/1798
William Ashby 12/19/1780

MARRIAGES

John Tutt to Betsy Ashby 2/1803 by Rev. James Thompson

"Copied from an English Prayer Book containing a New Version of The Psalms of David presented at the Court at Kensington, December 3rd 1696."

"Ashby Prayer Book owned by Fatsy (Martha) Ann Ashby of Fauquier Co., Va. She married William Withers."

"The above mentioned Prayer Book is now the property of Mr. and Mrs. Thomas Purse of Savannah, Georgia."
Thomas Purse, son of Laura Ashby Purse Laura Ashby, dau. of Marshall Ashby

JOHN AND KESIAH JOBSON BIBLE
Of Warden's Cross Rd., Princess Anne Co.

BIRTHS

Daniel Jobson 6/28/1788
Francis W. Jobson 12/12/1798
John S. Jobson 9/30/1790
Robert M. Jobson 12/18/1801

William Jobson 5/12/1793
Batson M. Jobson 4/15/1804
Joseph Jobson 6/13/1796

JOHN LEWIS BIBLE of Pittsylvania Co.
DAR Records, Ga. State Archives

John Lewis m. Mildred Shelton, Pittsylvania Co., Va. 9/26/1793

BIRTHS of THEIR CHILDREN:

Lucinda Lewis 7/24/1794
Chloe Spencer Lewis 1/12/1810
Charles Woodson Lewis 8/21/1796
Temple Lewis 1/23/1812
James Mansfield Lewis 2/22/1799
Thos. Anderson Lewis 6/12/1914
John Marshall Lewis 3/19/1801

Elizabeth P. Lewis 6/23/1816
William Lewis 7/23/1803
Augustine Lewis 3/10/1818
David Pannill Lewis 9/25/1805
Arch Stewart Lewis 5/2/1820
Nancy Grasty Lewis 11/29/1807
Chrisehana Caroline Lewis 7/7/1822

ROBERT COWAN PENN of Bedford Co.
Owner: Mrs. Thomas G. Read, Rt. 2, Evington, Virginia

Note: His home, St. Helena, located about 7 miles south of Liberty (Bedford), Va.

MARRIAGES

Robert C. Penn to Lucinda Steptoe 6/15/1814 Julia Penn to Nelson Crawford in Alabama
Virginia Penn to Dr. Charles Snow in Alabama
Alfred Penn to Evelyn S. Bradfute 9/11/1838, Lynchburg, Va.
Elizabeth Penn to William B. Harris 1815 Matilda Penn to Isaac Patrick 5/17/1815
Margaret Penn to --- Shortridge 1822, in Alabama

Children of R. C. and Lucy Penn

Frances L. Penn to David Rodes 5/1jJ1846, at St. Helena, Bedford Co., Va.
Bettie Penn to Hezekiah Jordan 11/7/1850

BIRTHS

Robert C. Penn 2/19/1789 at "The Grove", east of New London

Ada Augusta, 1st child of Elizabeth J. and Hezekiah T. Jordan, 9/11/1851, at "St. Helena". Bedford Co.

Imogene, 2nd child of Elizabeth J. and Hezekiah T. Jordan, 12/8/1833 at "St. Helena", Bedford Co., Va.

John J. Jordan 7/11/1837-9/26/1890, aged 23 yrs.
James Steptoe Penn, 1st child of Robert and Lucy Penn, 3/20/1817
Frances Louise Penn b. 1/21/1818
Lafayette Penn 8/5/1820
Elizabeth Johnson Penn b. 10/9/1822
Margaret Penn b. 4/3/1828

DEATHS

James S. Penn 11/9/1854 at St. Helena, Bedford Co., Va., at res. of his parents, James S. Penn, aged 39 yrs.

Robert C. Penn 7/2/1856 at St. Helena, Bedford Co., Va., aged 67

Mrs. Lucinda Penn, wid. Of Robert C. Penn, 7/10/1878, at her res.in Bedford Co., Va., aged 84 yrs

Bettie Johnson Jordan, consort of Thomas Hezekiah Jordan, 3/17/1912, in Lynchburg, Va., aged 90 yrs.
James Penn, Sr., 2/1823, New Orleans, aged 58 yrs.
James Penn, Jr., killed on Missouri River by Ricogee Indians in Spring of 1823, aged 25 yrs.
William Penn 1522, at St. Stevens, Alabama, aged 22 yrs.
Isaac Patrick 1823, Tuscaloosa, Alabama
James Steptoe, Sr. 2/9/1826 at his res. (Federal Hill) near New London in Campbell Co., 75 yrs.

Margaret Penn, 3rd dau. of Robert and Lucy Penn, 8/19/1828, at our res. (St. Helena) in Bedford Co., Va., aged 4 mos., 19 days
Cab'l Penn 1/18/1830, his mother's near Tuscaloosa, Ale., 35 yrs
Betsy Harris 9/1832, Winchester, Tenn.
Alfred Penn 1875
Mrs. Sarah Penn, aged 80 yrs., at the Glebe in Amherst Co., Va., 1/22/1826

Margaret Penn 12/15/1831, Tuscaloosa, Alabama, aged 62 yrs., the mother of Robert, Gabriel, James, etc.
Matilda Patrick, dau. of late James Penn, Esq., relict of late
Isaac Patrick, 1834, Tuscaloosa, Ala.

Lafayette Penn, son of Robert and Lucy Penn, aged 19 yrs., 1840, in Fincastle, 4/29th

FRANCIS MERIWETHER BIBLE
Owner: J. B. Jenkins, Albany, Georgia

Francis Meriwether b. 10/31/1737 m. Martha Jameson (ca 1765)

BIRTHS of THEIR CHILDREN:

Thomas Meriwether 1766 m. Rebecca Matthews
Valentine Meriwether 1768 m. Barbara Crosby
Mary Meriwether 1770 m. William Barnett
Elizabeth Meriwether 1772 m. William Matthews
Mildred Meriwether 1774 m. Joel Barnett
Margaret Meriwether (Peggy) 1776 m. John A. Bradley
D. Nancy Meriwether 1778 m. William Glenn
Lucy Merivether 1780 m. Grover Howard
Sarah Meriwether 1782 m. James Olive
Nicholas Meriwether 1784 (lived Montgomery, Ala.)

DEATHS

Francis Meriwether 1/2/1803
Martha Jameson Meriwether, wife of Francis Meriwether, 5/29/1818
Margaret J. Meriwether Bradley, wife of Dr. John A. Bradley, 3/14/1819

JOHN HUMBER, JR. BIBLE
Of "Air Hill", Goochland County

Note: The plantation "Air Hill" was located 35 miles north of Richmond, Virginia. Bible published in 1752

BIRTHS of Children of John Humber, Jr.

Charles Humber 1/22/1758-3/30/1758
Chrlstian Humber 4/26/1759-10/23/1761
Mary Humber 3/31/1761-d. infancy
John Humber 1/6/1764-1/30/1765
Elizabeth Humber 1/26/1765 m. Mr. Mangum
Lucy Humber 10/9/1765 m. Mr. Pleasants
John Humber 8/7/1770 (removed to Alabama)
Judith Humber 6/9/1775 m. Edward Cox, Jr.
William Humber 2/23/1778 (removed to North Carolina)
Charles Chrlstian Humber 5/27/1781
Robert Chrlstian Humbar 6/6/1783 (removed to Monticello, Georgia)
Mary Chrlstian Humber 2/19/1786
Edward Humber 2/14/1790
William Hutson Humber, son of William, 1/17/1804
Thomas Cole Humber, son of Charles Chrlstian Humber, 1/5/1802

MATHEW WILLS BIBLE of Amelia Co.
From Bible of J. Bolyer, Sr. (1795) Ga. DAR Records, Nancy Hart Chapter

BIRTHS

Mathew Wills, husband of Elizabeth Wills, 12/1752 Elizabeth Abney, wife, 6/14/1763

THEIR CHILDREN:

Patsy Wills 2/12/1785
Francis Wills 12/7/1790
Nancy Wills 11/8/1786

Isabella Wills 12/22/1792
James Wills 9/17/1789-6/1795

(Matthew Wills Bible, contd....)

Matthew Wills, their father, d. 6/24/1795
John Bolyer m. Eliiabeth Wills 10/1795.

THEIR CHILDREN:

Sophia Bolyer 8/8/1796-1/1800
John Bolyer, Jr. 3/3/1798
Susannah Maria and Elizabeth Bolyer, twins, 9/22/1802
Susannah Maria Bolyer, twin dau., d. 6/27/1804
Sarah Bolyer 7/28/1804
Henry Bolyer 4/9/1808
Anna Abney Bolyer 10/24/1810
William Morris m. Elizabeth M. Bolyer 8/6/1820.
Elizabeth Sarah Ann Morris, their dau., 5/21/1821-6/29,'1821
John Bolyer Sr. b. 11/10/1768
Elizabeth Bolyer, his wife, b. 6/14/1763

CAPT. THOMAS LEE BIBLE

"I am the son of Richard Lee and Judith Steptoe", b. 12/3/1729, Northumberland County, Virginia"
His wife, Mary Bryan of North Carolina

BIRTHS of THEIR CHILDREN:

Thomas Lee 12/9/1761
Lewis Lee 1772
John Lee 5/10/1763
Zilpha Lee 1/3/1773
William Lee 11/15/1764
Willis Lee 1775
Richard Lee 4/3/1766
Winnifred Lee 1778
James Lee 10/20/1768
Edward Lee 1779
Needham Lee 11/4/1770
Anna Lee 1781

SION AND PRISCILLA HUNT BIBLE
In back of Robert Patron Eberhardt Bible
Ga. DAR Records, Georgia State Archives

BIRTHS

Sion Hunt 2/1/1798-2/11/1875
Priscilla Hunt 10/24/1803-8/16/1846
Sarah Hunt 5/10/1810-7/3/1875
James J. Hunt 12/21/1830-Winchester, Virginia 7/25/1863
Mary Elizabeth Hunt 6/15/1833-9/22/1844
Frances Jane Hunt 9/26/1834-1918
Benjamin Thornton 2/10/1837-7/31/1862 Richmond, Virginia
Reuben Smith 4/8/1838
T. W. Harrison 1/18/1841-7/4/1862 Richmond, Virginia
Dozier Calloway 10/4/1842-10/4/1864
Richmond, Virginia Daniel Crumlay 12/14/1844
Emma Priscilla 4/9/1846

WILLIAM P. HENRY BIBLE

William P. Henry b. 2/4/1796 in Virginia-d. 3/18/1833 Forsyth, Georgia m. 6/17/1821 Sarah Lucy Beck 4/3/1803-2/4/1881
John P. Henry 6/12/1822-10/27/1822
William Benson Henry 3/24/1825 m. 12/19/1850
Martha Elizabeth Wall b. 3/27/1834
Sarah Ann Ofelfa Henry 4/19/1827 m. 2/16/1843 Amos L. Vail
Beverly Allen Henry 2/20/1829
m.10/14/1852 Mary Hamilton Lewis
Benjamin Cabaniss Henry 11/4/1830 m. 8/15/1860 R. Dankins

WILLIAM HARDING BIBLE of Northumberland County
Owner: Mrs. Betty (Hiram) Herding
Wicomico Church, Virginia (decd)

William Herding m. Sally Sutton 6/14/1792 by Rev. John Bryant

BIRTHS of Children of William and Sally Harding

Hiram Herding 3/23/1793 m. 1st 1815 Millicent Cockrill, 2nd, 1826 Ann Ball Convey
Thomas Everett Hardtng 9/15/1795 m. 1st 9/28/1815 Rebecca Herding, 2nd, 2/19/1822, Mary G. Harding
William Harding 10/8/1787 m. 8/13/1818 Mrs. Sally Cockrill
Sally Coppedge Harding 9/6/1799 m. 8/19/1817 Thomas Harvey
Eliza Harding 5/17/1801 m. 3/2/1830 Edward Cole
John Hopkins Herding 2/6/1803 m. 1st 3/1825 Elizabeth Downing, 2nd, 1828, Josephine Lemoine
Hopkins Harding 3/13/1S05-d. 6 mos. after
Cyrus Harding 4/7/1807 m. 1st Mrs. Julia Anderson, 2nd, Bettie Carter
James Herding 12/3/1809 m. Frances Maclemaw

JOHN ROUNTREE BIBLE
Found in Second-Hand Book Store
by: Mrs. E. L. Bigham 3415 Scott St., San Francisco, Calif

BIRTHS

John Rountree 1/15/1805-1/24/1891 Thaddeus Rountree 5/24/1837
Mary Lane 1839
Peary Rountree 5/12/1841-1/30/1902 Martha Ann Rountree 6/9/1843
Lydia Maria Rountree d. 5/24/1858, aged 40 yrs.

JESSE CORN BIBLE
From: Rev. War Pension #W909

BIRTHS

Jesse Corn 10/31/1753
Nancy Corn 2/17/1763

Elizabeth Corn 12/4/1780 m. Richard Sharp, Sr.

John Adam Corn 1/26/1783
William Corn 1/1/1756
Jesse Corn 3/11/1787
Mary Corn 8/8/1789 m. James Sharp
Samuel Corn 4/10/1792 Suckey Corn 12/16/1794

Nancy Corn 4/1/1797 m. George McCutcheon

(Jesse Corn Bible, contd....)

George Corn 9/30/1799
Dicea Corn 1/11/1803

Note: Nancy Corn, widow of Jesse, applied for pension 6/26/1841, Franklin Co., Tenn. She thinks her late husband commenced the war in Albemarle Co., Va. After their marriage 2/1780 he was wounded on Yadkin, afterwards a cripple. He was called Major Corn and was preacher in Clinton Co., Ky. until he moved to Patrick Co., Va.

Jesse Corn m. Nancy Hancock, dau. of John, in Albemarle Co. Va. 2/1780. Jesse Corn d. 3/5/1909 Patrick Co.. Va., and Nancy d. at home of her dau., Mary, near Winchester, FrankLin Co., Tenn., 6/17!1848.

VINCENT SANFORD BIBLE
Of Loudoun County
Owner: Mrs. Tallie (Jolly) Jones Jackson, Georgia

BIRTHS

Vincent Sanford 4/17/1727
Daniel Sanford 1/28/1778
Benjamin Sanford 11/26/1777
Mildred Sanford 7/13/1781
Jeremiah Sanford Jr. 9/30/1765
Thomas Sanford 12/24/1783
Jeremiah Sanford, Sr. 11/4/1739-8/1/1825 (Greensboro, Ga.)

CHARLES DEVEREAUX BIBLE
DAR Records, Georgia State Archives

Charles Devereaux m. 10/7/1766 Nancy Woods in Virginia

BIRTHS of Children (all b. in Va.)

Elizabeth Devereaux 12/7/1767
Archibald Devereaux 8/20/1775
William Devereaux 3/15/1769
John Devereaux 9/7/1777

James Devereaux 10/7/1771
Nancy Devereaux 11/16/1779
Samuel Devereaux 12/7/1773
Charles J. Devereaux 3/7/1782

Samson S. Steele m. 10/18/1784 Elizabeth Devereaux

BIRTHS of Children

Samuel Sanders Steele 1/27/1786
Eliza Steele 7/1/1797
Nancy Steele 8/14/1788
John Steele 10/1/1800

James Devereaux Steele 1/29/1791
Emily Steele 6/16/1803
Polly Steele 5/19/1793
Lavinia Steele 8/13/1807

JOHN McMULLEN BIBLE
Owner: Mrs. J. B. Tillman, Quitman, Ga.

BIRTHS

John McMullen 5/3/1808
Nancy Rountree NcMullen 10/25/1814
John McMullen m. Nancy Rountree 10/4/1832
Jane McMullen 1833-4/15/1853, aged 19 yrs., 7 mos., 24 days, m. 9/20/1849 William McMillan
Nannie Mullen 1/17/1846 m. 10/25/1865 Clayton R. Denmark

(John McMullen Bible, contd....)

Virginia McMullen 9/1/1847-8/31/1876 m. 12/20/1866 Thomas Arrington
Eli McMullen 7/28/1840-1/3/1862, Centerville, Virginia
Clinton McMullen 7/3/1844-
Caroline McMullen 6/21/1852-5/30/1876 m. 6/5/1873 J. M. Hart

ISAAC FOSTER BIBLE
Owner: James R. Foster of "Glenville"The Plains, Virginia

BIRTHS

Redmond Grigsby, son of James and Susannah, 4/19/1721
Robert Foster, son of William, 10/7/1711
William Foster, son of William, 7/15/1714
Isaac Foster 7/2/1719
George Foster 8/14/1723
Susannah Purcell, dau. of Redmond Grigsby, 4/1750
Mary Davis, dau. of R. Grigsby, 6/1752
Redmond Grigsby, son of R. Grigsby, 3/1775
Catherine Stewart 1773
Dorcas Foster 1777
Robert Foster d. 2/22/1768
William Foster d. 4/10/1779
George Foster d. 1/3/1778 of smallpox
Daniel Foster m. Ann R. Cundiff 12/19/1816

Issue:

Elizabeth Mary Foster 9/21/1819 William P. Foster 12/31/1820
Anna Maria Daniel Foster 10/10/1822 unmarried child 10/19/1818
Redmond Grigsby, Sr. 4/15/1721-10/6/1809
Daniel Foster, son of james and Elizabeth, d. 10/3/1822, aged 33 yrs.
Redmond Foster d. 6/12/1828
James Foster, son of Robert, 1/1750-9/10/1800 m. 5/15/1772
Elizabeth Foster 1/12/1775-5/21/1837
Children of James and Elizabeth Foster
Mary Foster 4/3/1773 m. Elijah Wyatt
Mildred Foster 11/16/1775 m. James Munday
Isaac Foster (our grandfather) 4/16/1778-2/7/1837
James Foster 11/3/1780
Redmond Foster 8/15/1783-6/12/1848 m. 12/24/1839 Margaret Williams
Susannah Foster 9/3/1786 m. Cornelius Gaines-d. 10/12/1824
Daniel Foster 9/10/1789-10/30/1822
Thomas Foster 2/28/1792-d. 11/4/1865 Warrenton
Silas Foster 3/11/1795

MARRIAGES

Isaac Foster b. 4/10/1778 to Priscilla Hunton b. 6/10/1779 on 2/28/1805
William Foster to Sarah Lucelia Hunton 8/13/1834

BIRTHS of Children of Isaac and Priscilla Foster

Judith Keith Foster 8/22718--
John Hunton Foster 10/27/1811
James William Foster 11/7/1807
Thomas Redmond Foster 4/2/1817
Mary Elizabeth Foster 2/19/1810

(Isaac Foster Bible, contd....)

DEATHS
John Hunton Foster, son of Isaac, 11/26/1832, aged 21
Isaac Foster 2/7/1837, aged 59 yrs.
Judith K. Foster 5/3/1840, aged 33 yrs., 8 mos., 12 days Priscilla Hunton of "Whitevood", relict of Isaac Foster, 10/16/1R59,a ged 80 yrs., 4 mos.
James William Foster 4/10/1866, aged 58 yrs.
Mary Elizabeth Foster 7/11/1890, aged 80 yrs.
Thomas Redmond Foster 2/1896, aged 77 yrs.
Daniel Foster, son of James, 10/31/1822, aged 33 yrs., in Prince William Co., Va.
James Hunton, son of late William, 11/14/1823, aged abt 60 yrs. Susannah Caines, wife of Cornelius Gaines and dau. of James and Elizabeth Foster, 10/13/1824
Margaret Hampton 8/6/1826, Reed 49 yrs.
John Hampton 7/1826
Thomas Bunton 10/27/1826, age supposed abt 54
Owen? Thomas 12/29/1828
Mary Bunton Brown, wife of John Brown, 12/15/1829, aged 62 or 63 Nancy Boynton Thomas 4/11/1833, aged abt 61 yrs.
Eppa Hunton d. a few days before Mrs. Thomas
Mary Grigsby Davis 1/18/1831, near her 80th yr.
Frances Elizabeth Hunton 10/17/1824
Elizabeth Foster of "Foston" 5/20/1837, aged 83 yrs.
William Hunton of Fairfax 7/6/1836, aged 70 yrs.

BENJAMIN INGRAM BIBLE of Brunswick County
Owner: Mrs. Frank S. Bean Putnam Co., Georgia

Benjamin Ingram, son of John, m. 12/27/1756 Elizabeth Nelms, dau. of William and Elizabeth Nelms

BIRTHS of THEIR CHILDREN:

Nancy Ingram 9/27/1757
Benjamin Ingram 8/6/1767
Mary Ingram 12/3/1759
Paulina Ingram 4/22/1769
Elizabeth Ingram --/22/1763
John Ingram 9/22/1773
Charles Ingram 9/22/1765
Presley Ingram 5/19/1777

REDMOND GRIGSBY BIBLE
The Plains, Fanquier County
Owner: James R. Foster, The Plains, Virginia

BIRTHS

Redmond Grigsby, Sr., son of James Grigsby, 4/15/1721-10/6/1509

Children of Redmond Grigsby:

Susannah Purcell Grigsby 4/1750
Redmond Grigsby 3/1775
Mary Davis Grigsby 6/1752
Catherine Stewart Grigsby 1773
Dorcas Foster Grigsby 1777
Mary Grigsby Davis d. 1/18/1831, nearly 80 yrs. old.
Elizabeth Foster 1754 of "Foston"-5/20/1837, aged 83 yrs

JOHN T. W. READ BIBLE
Owner: Miss Daisy Read Rt. 2, Evington, Virginia

MARRIAGES

John T. W. Read to Elizabeth Alexander 12/25/1808
Ann Isabella Read to Frederick G. Peters 9/6/1827 by Rev. Nicholas Cobbs
Nathan Reid, Jr. to Eliza A. Read 3/3/1830 by Rev. N. E. Cobbs
William A. Read to Mary Jane Hall 9/.11/1974 by Rev. W. T. Rice
Robert A. Read to Frances Ann Pendleton 11/5/1834 by Rev. Mr. Bowmen
John T. W. Read to Eliza Douthat 2/4/1835 by Rev. William S. Read
Samuel Read to Theresa Samantha Arnold 5/3/1843 by Rev. Cleland Nelson
John T. U. Read to Rebecca Pryer 1/15/1846 by Rev. Isaac Cocerin

BIRTHS

Elizabeth Read, dau. of Robert Alexander and Nancey, 2/16/1787
Ann I. A. Read 9/24/1809
William A. Read 9/12/1814
Elizabeth A. Read 3/1/1811
Samuel Read 2/15/1817
Robert A. Read 9/11/1812
William Read, son of Jones Read, 7/27/1777
Nancy Read, dau. of Jones Read, 3/8/1779

DEATHS

Edmund Read 2/27/1826, aged 46 yrs.
Elizabeth Read, wife of Samuel Read, 3/27/1829
Samuel Read 1/28/1831
William C. Read, son of Samuel Read, 9/21/1833
Elizabeth Read, wife of John T. W. Read, 1/10/1833
Eliza Read, wife of John T. W. Read, 5/30/1844
Dr. John T. W. Read, son of William and Joanna Read, 8/27/1852

WILLIAM N. BRUCE BIBLE
Owner: Mrs. Sallie Gaines, Bainbridge, Ga.

William N. Bruce m. Sarah Ann Williams 3/23/1850
Sarah Ann (Williams) Bruce d. 6/18/1853, aged 20 yrs., 8 mos., 24 days, second dau. of W. Williams. She was buried beside her mother at Fowlstown Church.
William N. Bruce m. in Cleveland, Caroline Co., Va. by Rev. W. Grice to Mary Susan Bates, dau. of William D. Bates 7/24/1857

BIRTHS

William N. Bruce 10/13/1811, 6 miles north of Cheraw, S. C.
Mary Susan Bates 12/4/1831 in Caroline Co., Virginia
Louisa Powell ---
Lucy Estelle Bruce 5/4/1858
Mary Susan Bruce 4/23/1853
George William Bruce 8/3/186?
Robert Lee Bruce 4/24/1864 .John Potter Bruce 6/9/1866
Charles Potter Bruce 2/5/1869-named for his grandfather living at Darlington, S. C. and his great-grandmother of Guilford, N. C.
Sarah Bruce 10/26/1872
Mary Susan Bruce m. O. B. Floyd 3/14/1881
Lucy Estelle Bruce m. Benjamin Griffin 2/12/1885
Sallie Bruce, 8th child of William N. Bruce, m. William A. Gaines 11/13/1902
John Potter Bruce d. 7/10/1884 William A. Gaines d. 1/8/1926, aged 83 yrs
Mary Susan Bruce d. 12/29/1816, aged 85 yrs., 24 days

JAMES O. HENRY BIBLE
Owner: Johnnie 8. Hendren Smith
(d. 1959)

BIRTHS

James O. Henry 4/4/1832
V. Henry 6/2/1865
Y. E. Hendre 11/9/1836
S. Henry 5/22/1868
F. A. A. Henry 10/31/1856
Henry 11/29/1872
S. E. T. Henry 4/22/1858
B. Henry 3/12/1876
A. F. E. Henry 1/11/1863

DEATHS

James O. Henry 11/15/1899
S. Henry 10/9/1914
Mrs. M. E. Henry 2/12/1909
N. A. Henry 4/9/1874

F. A. Henry 12/8/1938
F. E. Henry 3/28/1933
E. V. Henry 8/26/1881
S. E. T. Henry 12/1932

MARRIAGES

James O. (Oliver) Henry to M. E. (Martha Eleanor) Hendren (b. 11/9/1836) on 9/26/1855

DANIEL ALLEN BIBLE
From Simmons Bible
Owner: George Smith

Daniel Allen, son of James, b. 9/12/1728 Hanover Co., Virginia-d. 1807 Cumberland Co., m. 1st Miss Harrison.

BIRTHS of Children

Moses Allen - d. onboard prison ship in Charleston, prisoner during Revolutionary War
Frances Allen - d. aged 18
Priscilla Allen m. Mr. Wilson
Benjamin Allen m. M. S. Hill
Elizabeth Allen m. Mr. Smith
Anns. Allen m. Mr. Anderson
Anne Allen m. 1st Mr. Watson, 2nd, Mr. Claybrook
Cary Allen m. Miss Fleming
Sarah Allen m. Mr. Snoddy Pstsey Allen m. Mr. Smith
Daniel Allen m. 2nd, the widow of Joseph Hill, Johanna Read, dau. of William Read of Bedford County, Virginia.
Johanna had by her 1st husband Joseph Hill: Thomas, William, Elizabeth, Joicy and Joseph Hill.
Zella Allen, dau. of Daniel and Johanna, m. Mr. Penick Polly Allen, dau. of Daniel and Johanna,
m. Mr. Smith Daniel A. Allen, son of Danial and Johanna, m. Lucy Watts

BIRTHS of Children of Anthony Carnett Smith, son of Polly, 1/25/1809-2/1/1891

Charles A. Smith 2/26/1849-9/4/1865
Emma C. Smith 10/22/1859
Cary A. Smith 6/2/1850-2/2/1852
Robert L. Smith 6/20/1861
Mary E. Smith 12/13/1851-2/21/1852
Ida V. Smith 11/7/1863
Wesley A. Smith 3/26/1853

Addie Smith 7/20/1865
S. Hull Smith 11/25/1854
Eleanor Smith 12/20/1867
Martha J. Smith 10/23/1856
S. Hattie Smith 12/17/1869
Garnett D. Smith 5/8/1858

ABRAHAM WOOD BIBLE

BIRTHS

Abraham Wood 3/31/1739
Parents: Mary LaDu (Marie LaDoux) 3/24/1744

BIRTHS of Children

Levi Wood 11/3/1766
John Wood 4/28/1777
Anne Wood 8/18/1768
Abraham Wood 7/11/1780
Joseph Wood 5/25/1770

Betsy Wood 11/4/1783
Mary Wood 9/12/1772
Judith Wood 2/7/1784
Nathaniel Wood 6/11/1774
Gabriel Wood 9/9/1786

LITTLETON THEODORE PETERSON HARWELL BIBLE
Owner: Mrs. C. P. Harwell, Godfrey, Georgia

"This Bible the property of L. T. P. Harwell. On my death I give it to my son, Renaldo and wish it not to be sold by him. In the event of his deat, I wish it to go to my son, Littleton Manson (Harwell) and not parted with my either." 3/27/1834 /s/ Littleton L. P. Harwell.

BIRTHS

Littleton Theodore Peterson Harwell, son of Ishmael and Lucy F. Harwell, 10/12/1802, Dinwiddie Co.
Martha Sylvian HarwelL, wife of L. T. P. Harwell, 7/29/1804, dau. of Capt. Ltttleberry and Sarah Robinson of Greenvtlle Co., Va.

Children of Littleton T. P. and Martha Harwell

Renaldo Peterson Harwell 1/20/1829
Littleberry Harwell 2/17/1830
Littleton Hanson Harwell 4/27/1831
Rebecca Roe Harwell 12/16/1833

Lucy Finey Harwell 11/4/1836
Lewis Ishmael Harwell 10/14/1838
Martha Virginia Harwell 4/29/1851
Mary Estelle Harwell 10/14/1839

Isaac Walker, son of Seaborn I. and Lucy F. Walker, 7/21/1858
Ellar Margarie, dau. of L. M. and Adeline Harwell, 8/20/1858
Littleton Harwell Walker, son of S. I. and I. F. Walker, 3/14/1816

MARRIAGES

Littleton T. P. Harwell-Martha L. Nesbit 10/4/1827 at Major Isaac R. Waltons, Morgan Co., Ga
Littleton M. Harwell to Adeline Campbell 2/1855
Seaborn I. Walker to Lucy Finey Harwell 12/11/1855
Even H. Lawrence to Mary E. Harwell 12/1/1859, Evansville, Ga.
Julius E. Lawrence to Lula E. Cunningham 3/8/1881, Homer, Ga.

DEATHS

Richard Dunortmes, 2nd son of L. M. and M. M. Harwell, 9/27/1874, aged 7 yrs., 1 mo., 14 days
Littleberry Ishmael Harwell, 4th son of Littleton and Martha Harwell, 10/l4th, St Helms, Claiborn Parish, La., aged 37 to a day
Littleberry Harwell 3/18/1830, aged 23 days
Rebecca P. Harwell, dau. of Littleton and Martha, 9/29/1843, aged 9 yrs., 6 mos., 25 days.
Martha S. Harwell, wife of Dr. L. T. P. Harwell, 2/28/1853, Evansville, Morgan Co., Ga., aged 48 yrs., 6 mos., 28 days
Littleton L. P. Harwell, my father, b. Dinwiddie Co., Virginia 10/12/1801 and d. Morgan Co., Ga. 8/10/1864
Lucy Finey Harwell, my mother, 7/6/1824, the dau. of William and Mary Parkam of Brunswick Co., Virginia, aged 43 yrs., 25 days. She was b. 1/15/1781
Ishmael Harwell, my father, 1/10/1838, the son of Ishamel and Mary Harwell of Dinwiddie Co., Virginia, he was b. 1770, aged 68 yrs.

SAMUEL COCKE BIBLE
Owner: Tucker Cocke Saleat, Virginia

MARRIAGES

Samuel Cocke 1st to Elizabeth Shepherd 9/14/1796; 2nd to Susannah Woodson 10/7/1802
Sarah C. F. Cocke to Alfred Latham 4/6/1814
Polly A. Cocke 12/26/182- to Caleb Hopkins
John S. Cocke to Polleny E. Woodson 11/26/1821
Benjamin W. Cocks to Sabina W. Henley 5/22/1823
Portina S. Cocke to A. Mitchell 11/28/1826
Harriet E. Cocke to Francis Hague 3/13/182-
Hartwell F. Cocke to Miss Godden 6/17/182-
Cathrine Latham to William P. Hopkins 9/7/1843
Thomas M. Cocke 2nd 8/15/1843 to Susannah Woodson
Charles S. Cocke to Honoria Hopklns 11/21/1866

BIRTHS

Samuel Cocke 1/19/1771
Sylvester P. Cocke 2/14/1810
John S. Cocke 2/26/1798
Richard F. Cocke 4/20/1812
Polly A. Cocke 3/14/1800
James M. Cocke 1/14/1816
Benjamin W. Cocke 11/22/1803
Thomas M. Cocke 7/31/1818
Samuel H. Cocke 1/4/1807
Hartwell F. Cocke 11/12/1821
Perlina S. Cocke 5/1/1808
Sanford P. Cocke 5/10/1823

Sarah E. Cocke 4/2/1824, was John E. Cocke's 1st dau. Sarah E. Mitchell 11/10/1827

William Hague 8/13/1828, was Francis Hague's 1st son Charles S. Cocke 8/29/1840

Joseph R. Cocke 2/2/1842

James M. Cocke and Sarah A. Cocke, his wife,

Anna R. Cocke, dau. of E. R. and M. A. Cocke, 9/26/1866 1st son of E. R. and M. A. Cocke, 5/7/1868

DEATHS

Susannah Cocke, wire of Samuel Cocke, 3/18/1854, she was b. 5/22/1781
The mother of Samuel Cocke 4/13/1826, aged 74 yrs. The father of Samuel Cocke 5/28/1828, aged 84 yrs.
Benjamin Woodson 10/28/1808. His wife, Sarah Woodson, 11/3/1817
Benjamin W. Cocke 1/20/1839
Samuel Cocke 4/12/1844 Sarah A. Cocke 10/10/1844
Thomas Y. Cocke 3/13/1846 Joseph Lewis 4/9/1843
Sanford B. Cocke 11/5/1852
Susan Cocke, wid. of Ssmuel, 3/18/1854
H. F. Cocke 7/27/1865
Harriet E. Cocke, wife of Thomas Hague,
Joseph R. Cocke 10/14/1870
James Rufus Cocke, son of James M. and Sallie Abbie, 10/14/1870 Charles S. Cocke, son of
James M. and Sally Abbie, 3/8/1913, aged 72 yrs.
James M. Cocke 12/1892, aged 76 yrs.
R. F. Cocke 1885
Sylvester Pleasant Cocke's wife was Mary Ellen Pleasant

JAMES L. COMBS BIBLE of Fauquier Co.
Owner: Mrs. Leon Albert Warren
The Marlborough, Washington, D. C.

MARRIAGES

John L. Combs to Francis A. Welch 2/18/1858
Virginia Elizabeth Combs to Leon Albert Warren 4/24/1911

BIRTHS

Ada Patterson Combs 1/6/1859
Cathartne Cochran Combs 2/7/1870
Dixie Lee Combs 7/17/1861
Fannie McGill Combs 2/18/1873
Jane Linton Combs 8/2/1864
Paul Combs 5/8/1875
Beverly Brook Combs 8/22/1867
Virginia Elizabeth Combs 7/28/1876
Luther M. Welch 9/1/1827
John N. Welch 10/1830
Frances Ann Welch 11/28/1832
John Linton Combs 8/11/1827

DEATHS

Dixie Lee Combs, dau. of John L. and Fannie Combs, 5/2/1873, aged 12 yrs.
Crawford C. Combs 8/1870, aged 46 yrs.
Burr Combs 4/16/1876, aged 79 yrs.
John Linton Combs 3/14/1878, aged 51 yrs.
Catharine A. Combs 3/19/1888, aged 83 yrs., wife of Burr Combs
Luther M. Welch 12/16/1893, aged 67 yrs.
Frances A. Combs 12/31/1907, aged 76 yrs.
Ada Patterson Combs 9/2/1919
Janie Combs Foley 9/14/1918
Beverly Brook Combs 8/10/1933
Fannie McGill Combs, infant dau. of John L. and Fannie, 4/20/1873

DAVID STOVER BIBLE
Of Shenandoah Valley

David Stover m. Elizabeth, dau. of Jacob Strickler, and granddau. of Abraham Strickler.

BIRTHS of Children of David and Elizabeth Stover Daniel Stover 12/29/1785

Samuel Stover b. Shenanodah Co., Va. m. 9/3/1807 Mary, dau. of Johann Balsec and Sarah Dieterich, d. 8/27/1837
David Stover Mary Stover
Elizabeth Stover Ann Stover
Barbara Stover 11/1787 Shenandoah Co., Va. m. 9/4/1806 Philip Munch
Catherine Stover m. 12/19/1812 Jacob Springer
Mary Magdalena Stover m. 9/25/1817 Isaac James

JOHN DAVIS' BIBLE of Washington Co.
Owner: Mrs. Ivie T. McNees
212 Myrtle Ave., Johnson City, Tenn.

"D. O. Bradley's Book bought at John Corry's sale. The Confession of Faith, The Larger and Shorter Catechisms, with the ScriptureProofs at Large, etc....Of Public Authority in the Church of Scotland. Printed in the year MDCCLXVLII (1768)."

(John Davis Bible, contd....)

BIRTHS

John Davis 10/14/1743
Nathaniel Davis 1/20/1771
Mary Davis 2/14/1743
Mary Davis 5/16/1773

Sarah Davis 7/9/1767
Esbel Davis 8/24/1775
Hannah Davis 2/9/1769
Robert Davis 4/26/1778

WILLIAM MURPHEY BIBLE
From: Rev. War Pension #W9580

BIRTHS of Children of William Murphy and Rachel (Henderson)

John Craford Murphy 10/16/1782
Keturah B. Hurphy 4/9/1796
Mary Hedges Murphy 6/22/1784
Francis Menafee Murphy 5/23/1798
Marthy Hedges Murphy 5/29/1786
Sarah Barton Murphy 1/4/1803
Elizabeth Barton Murphy 4/16/1788

David Henderson Murphy 6/12/1802
William Ecclos Murphy 5/8/1790
----enderson Murphy 9/-
Delilah Sarah Murphy 5/14/1792
youngest child 5/6/1806
James Henderson Murphy 5/19/1794

Note: William Murphy applied for pension 5/7/1833, St. Francis Co., Mo., stating he was b. 3/12/1759 in PLttsylvania Co., Va. He d. 11/2/1833, St. Francis Co., Mo. 4/7/1841 Rachel Murphy, widow, applied, stating that she was b. 11/15/1764 (Rachel Henderson) and that she m. William Murphy 1/26/1782 in Green Co., Tenn.

WILLIAM S. WILKERSON BIBLE of King George County
Owner: Mrs. William B. Pratt (decd) 5213 14th St., Washington, D. C.

MARRIAGES

William S. Wilkerson to Peggy 2/25/1813
Burkett Pratt to D. Maria 12/15/1874 at her uncle's (T. B. Reamy) by Rev. W. L. D. Moncure (Baptist)

BIRTHS

Dona Leslie Ford, dau. of Oscela and Rowland Ford and granddau. of W. Burkett Pratt and Dona Maria, his wife, 5/19/1904
William B. Pratt, son of Burkett and Mary A. E. Pratt, 3/19/1551
William O. Humphries, son of John F. and Caroline Humphries, 4/2/1857
William S. Wilkerson 2/17/1784
And Margaret, his wife, 12/9/1794
And W. S. Wilkerson and Peggy, his wife. Son, John Newman Wilkerson 2/8/1815 and was christened by Rev. Mr. Thornton, a Methodlst preacher at a camp meeting 2 miles below Matter Bridge

HAMILTON DUNBAR BIBLE
Owner: Mrs. Robert Lykins, Tollesboro, Ky

Hamilton Dunbar b. 5/28/1752 m. 1/14/1808 Delilah Sparks who was b. 1/1/1792

BIRTHS of THEIR CHILDREN:

John Collins Dunbar 12/8/1808
David Dunbar 2/4/1820
Ann Dunbar 11/21/1810
George F. Dunbar 8/3/1822
Gracy Dunbar 12/6/1812
Johannah Dunbar 7/4/1825
Agness A. Dunbar 8/22/1815
John Sparks Dunbar 12/6/1827
William Willson Dunbar 11/16/1817

(Hamilton Dunbar Bible continued...)

MARRIAGES

Gracy Dunbar 4/23/1829 to Mr. Murray
George F. Dunbar to Cstharine 7/28/1842 by Rev. Stone
J. S. Dunbar to Lucy P. Dudley 3/12/1850
Ann Dunbar to Peter L. Bryant 7/16/1837 by Rev. G. R. Bruce   John 2. Cox to Nancy Dunbar 4/3/1830 by Rev, James A. Casko   David Dunbar to Nancy J. Dougherty 9/12/1848

BRYANT BIBLE
(Inside above Bible)

Bayley D. Bryant m. Mary C. Dale 8/14/1860 by Rev. F. F. Johns
Edward Hamilton Bryant 9/30/1861
Bayley Dale Bryant, son of Bayley D. Bryant and Mary, b. 8/6/1864
Minnie Ann Elizabeth Bryant b. 11/9/1873
Edward H. Bryant m. Jane D. Farrow 3/23/1882 by Rev. W. T. Benton

DEATHS

John Collins Dunbar 1/29/1810
Delilah Dunbar 8/14/1828
Gracy Murray 4/25/1833
Hamilton Dunbar 6/28/1835 of cholera, aged 53 yrs.
Johannah Fristo 5/10/1866
George F. Dunbar 7/13/1872
Charles N. Bryant 6/28/1876-1/7/1877
John S. Dunbar 6/14/1886, aged 56 yrs.
America Angelius Bryant 10/20/1853
Bailey D. Bryant 3/20/1839-3/27/1880
Mary C. Bryant 2/12/1883, aged 38 yrs.
Peter Bryant 10/23/1885, aged 73 yrs.
Annle D. Bryant 7/19/1894
Edward Hamilton Bryant 11/8/1931

JAMES AND JERUSHA ALEXANDER BIBLE
From: Rev. War Pension #W8322

BIRTHS

James Alexander 2/28/1756
William Alexander 10/17/1785
Jerusha Alexander 4/17/1755
Polly Alexander 8/29/1789
John T. Alexander 5/2/1777

Nelson Alexander 3/1/1791
Willis Alexander 8/28/1797
James Alexander, Jr. 11/9/1778
Benjamin Alexander 12/6/1783

Note: Jerusha Alexander, wid. of James, applied for pension 1838, Boone Co., Ky. aged 83, stating she m. soldier 4/10/1776 in Orange Co., Va. and that her husband d. 4/10/1817 Boone Co., Ky.

WILLIAM S. B. HENRY BIBLE
Owner: Mrs. Nellie Waldenmaier, Washington. D. C.

"Presented bo Lucy Brokenbrough Henry by her affectionate husband, Aug. 11, 1886."

MARRIAGES

Wm S. B. Henry of Gloucester County, Va. to Lucy B. Daningerfield of Matthews County, Va. 2/13/1851 at Sleepy Hollow by George W. Carriway, Rector of Chr1st Church in Matthews Co.,
Va. Witnesses: Alex Dudley, J. H. Henry. John S. Henry to Emma Cauby 7/9/1877
Mary Beal Henry to J. R. Kelsey 3/28/1882

(William S. B. Henry Bible, MARRIAGES, contd....)
William D. Henry to Sarah E. Frazer 6/24/1884

BIRTHS

John Scarborrough Henry 10/28/1852 at Free Welcome, Gloucester Co., Va.
William Daingerfield Henry 3/29/1855 at Sunny Deli, Richmond Co., Va.
Mary Beal Henry 6/13/1856 at same place
Georgina Henry 12/20/1858 at Shelly (or Shelby), Richmond Co., Va.
Lucy Moore Henry 3/17/1859 at Shelly
Charles Spottiswood Henry 7/9/1861 at Shelly
Ann Elizabeth Benry 8/20/1869 at Shelly
Ludwell Braxton Henry 10/29/1867 at Stony Hill in Westmoreland Co. Sarah Leigh Henry 3/7/1869 at Oakland in Lancaster Co.
Infant son d. at birth at Stomy Hill
Infant dau. d. at birth at Kelmarnock in Lancaster Co., Va.

DEATHS

Infant dau. stillborn 12/4/1851, Free Welcome, Gloucester Co.,Va. Infant son d. at birth 11/19/1868
Sarah Leigh Henry 8/17/1869 at Oakland, Lancaster Co., Va. Ludwell Braxton Henry 3/3/1878 in Washington City, O. C.
Georgina Henry 9/3/1863 at Shelly, Richmond Co., Va.
Charles Spottisvood Henry 7/23/1862, Richmond Co., Va.
Infant dau. d. at Kilmarnock 8/16/1872, Lancaster Co., Va.

A Temperance Pledge signed by the following: W. S. B. Henry, John S. Henry, W. D. Henry, Herbert Henry, W. D. Henry, Jr., Lucy Brokenbrough Henry, Mary Beal Henry, Lucy Moore Henry, Bessie Braxton Henry and Mary Henry.

SOLOMON AND DOROTHY QUARLES BIBLE
Owner: Waller Quarles Terry
King William C. H., Virginia

Bettie, dau. of Solomon and Dorothy Quarles, b. 10/9/1750
Solomon Quarles d. 1/24/1774
Dorothy Quarles b. 7/21/1776
Judith Quarles, dau. of Waller Quarles and Keziah Ellet, his wife, b. 12/27/1809
Susan A. Quarles, dau. of above, b. 12/27/1809
Susanna E. Quarles dau. of above, b. 1812 m. Alexander Bond

WILLIAM AND MARY WATSON BIBLE
From: Rev. War Pension #W8044 of Jacob Lewis
Children of William Watson and Mary Parker Watson

Francis Watson 6J15/1814, aged 14
William Watson 8/2/1814, aged 10
David Watson 2/27/1814, aged 8
Nancy Watson 8/11/1814, aged 6
Mary Watson 2/11/1814, aged 4
Prudence Watson 11/18/1813, aged 2
Son b. 9/10/1814

Note: Jacob Lewis applied for pension 1/19/1833, Tyler Co., Va., was b. Berkeley Co., Va. 4/15/1755-d. 6/23/1840 or 6/29/1843 Tyler Co., Va. Mary Levis, widow, applied for pension 4/1/1853, aged 17, Tyler Co., Va. Mary Parker m. 1st William Watson 1796 or 1797 in Greene Co., Pa., 2nd, 12/17/1816 Jacob Lewis by William Well, Esq., Tyler Co., Va.

CHRISTOPHER SIPPEL BIBLE
Owner: Harry D. Hill
4231 Brook Rd., Richmond, Va.
Written in German script:

Johannes Mathes Stroher 1748 Jacob Frederici--- 1782

On flyleaf: Christopher Sippel

9/2/1775 the Coed God gave me a little dau. and we named her Elizabeth. her godparents were: Johannes Harbach and his wife.

Remainder of Record in English:

John Peter Nye m. above Elizabeth 8/15/1796
I had a son b. 4/24/17987, John Richard Nye 3/24/1799
George Washington Nye 5/2/1801
Jefferson Nye-5/3/1801, bur. 5/4/1801   9/2/1805
Griseldah Malinday Nye
7/6/1809
James Madison Nye
J. P. Nye

John Peter Nye m. Eliza Sippel 8/15/1796 and his son, John Richard Nye, b. 4/24/1797 Wythe Toune:
3/18/1799 b. George Washington Nye
6/7/1816 Jn. P. Nye struck with the dead palsey
6/19/1826 Jn. P. Nye was struck second time with the dead palsey which removed him from this world on the 21st.

Note: Bible acquired by owner from his aunt, Nancy Umbarger Hill who d. 7/1939, formerly property of Delilah Umbarger.

DANIEL AND BARBARA MILLER BIBLE
From: Rev. War Pension #W18512

Record in German Prayer Book, "Daniel Miller, his book."

BIRTHS

Prisley Miller 1/18/1785
Jackson Miller 9/3/1797
Elizabeth Hiller 7/15/1787
Thos Jefferson Miller 9/6/1803
Polly Miller 2/9/1790
Evelina Miller 2/7/1805
Morgan Alexander Miller 7/2/1792
Alphard Miller 11/16/1806

Note: Daniel Miller applied for pension 10/4/1819, aged 64 yrs., Fayette Co., Pa.; wife Barbara, aged 61 in 1820 and living with them was their widowed dau. and her four children, oldest about 6. 4/30/1824 Daniel Miller transferred his pension to Winchester, Va. 10/22/1838, Barbara Miller, aged 81, widow, Winchester, Frederick Co., Va. stated she m. after Rev. War, moved to Uniontown, Pa. where they lived 10 yrs., then back to Winchester.

Soldier d. 11/24/1825 Winchester, Va. 7/1839 William Seems, aged 56, states he m. Elizabeth Miller, b. 7/15/1787, dau. of Daniel Miller and s1ster, Prisley Miller, b. 1/18/1785.

NICHOLAS AND MARY CRENSHAW BIBLE
Owner: Mrs. Thomas M. Galey Owensboro, Kentucky

BIRTHS of Children of Nicholas and Mary (Carr) Crenshaw

William Crenshaw 3/26/1755
Waller Crenshaw 5/26/1786
Elizabeth Crenshaw 3/8/1757
Millie Crenshaw 5/14/1788
John Crenshaw 6/21/1759
Betsy Crenshaw 6/25/1790
Ann Crenshaw 12/3/1762
Garland Crenshaw 12/10/1792
Susanna Crenshaw 10/20/1767
Dabney Crenshaw 9/29/1794
David Crenshaw 6/6/1771
Susan Crenshaw 3/10/1796
Sarah Crenshaw 8/21/1778
Anderson Crenshaw 8/10/1798

BIRTHS of Children of John Crenshaw (b. 1759) and Mildred (Milly) Thompson, dau. of William Thompson of Albemarle Co., Va.
Thompson Crenshaw 3/16/1782 –
Lucy Crenshaw 11/13/1783

JOHN NELSON BIBLE
From: Rev. War Pension #S5414

BIRTHS

Thomas Maudnit Nelson 9/27/1782 John Nelson 3/31/1784-2/18/1827
Robert Nelson 1/30/1787
Hugh Nelson 11/22/1788-2/25/1830
Nancy Carter Nelson 9/27/1790
William Nelson 7/31/1792
Mary Nelson 3/16/1794-4/20/1795
Nathaniel Nelson 4/9/1796 at Oak Hill
Caroline Matilda Nelson 12/27/1798-4/5/1802
Sarah Nelson 8/14/1802-11/25/1802
Anna Matilda Nelson, dau. of William Nelson, 11/15/1817
Nancy C. Kemon, wife of E. Kemon, d. 5/24/1831

Note: Mrs. Nancy Carter Nelson applied for pension 11/15/1837 Mecklenburg Co., Va. Stating she (Nancy Carter) was m. to John Nelson 7/25/1781 in the Chapel of William and Mary College and her husband d. 2/18/1827.
3/21/1838 Robert Greenhow's affidavit, Richmond, Va. stated that Secretary Nelson of York had two sons - Thomas and John. The older son m. Sally Carey, the oldest dau. of Wilson Miles Carey and she d. soon after birth of her son, Carey Nelson. The second son, John, a Major in the State Cavalry, m. 1780 or 1781 Nancy Carter of Williamsburg, Va. 4/9/1881 Halifax Co., Va. Mrs. Woodson Hughes writes that her grandfather was Major John Nelson of Mecklenburg Co., Va. and his brother was Gov. and Gen. Thomas Nelson, signer of the Declaration of Independence. Her father was William Nelson, a soldier in War of 1812 and his brother, Major Thomas Nelson, also in War of 1812

GEORGE D. GLENN BIBLE
Owner: Edward Keyser Page Co., Pennsylvania

BIRTHS

George D. Glenn 1/2/1797 Holly Forge, Cumberland Co., Pa.1/5/1862, aged 55 yrs., 3 days
Nancy Glenn 7/10/1799 Shenandoah Co., Va.-6/S/1878, aged 80 yrs., 10 mos., 28 days, m. 6/14/1821
David G. Glenn 3/23/1822 at Isabella Furnace, Shenandoah Co., Va. William H. Glenn 10/8/1820 at Isabella Furnace, Va.-9/21/1900 Mary Ann Glenn 10/16/1825 at Isabella Furnace, Va.-1/21/1897

(George D. Glenn Bible continued....)

Eliza Jane Glenn 1/30/1826 at Isabella Furnace-1/21/1897
Maria Louisa Glenn 8/11/1830 at Isabella Furnace, Va.-11/21/1892 Mark Thomas Glenn 6/10/1833,Isabella Furnace, Page Co., 2/20/1864 Cecilia Glenn 1/16/1836 m. 5/12/1852 James Bumgarner George Hiram Glenn 3/24/1838 Page Co., Va.-8/23/1864
Note: Shenandoah Co. later Page Co., Va. David Glenn removed in 1830 to Indiana.
Grandchildren of George D. Glenn: Edward Keyser and s1ster. Mrs. Keyser, Nancy Ann (Grove) was dau. of David Grove and granddau. of Marcus Grove.

JANE RIDING THORNLEY BIBLE of Charlottesville
Owner: Mrs. John Cooke Grayson Charlottesville, Virginia

On flyleaf: Jane Thornley

Note: Mrs. Grayson was given these records from an old Prayer Book, which copy was given her by her cousin, Mary Amelia Smith, dau. of William Smith ("Extra Billy"), twice Governor of VA. Aaron Thornley and Catherine, his wife, m. 4/9/1772

BIRTHS of THEIR CHILDREN:

Enoch Thornley 2/6/1773-4/1778
William Thornley 1/2/1775-2/27/1837
Judith Berry Thornley 5/31/1777-2/28/1788
Frances Ann Thornley 9/8/1779
Elizabeth Thornley 11/18/1781
Jean Thornley 9/26/1783

Mary Matilda Thornley 1/27/1786 T
homas Berry Thornley 2/17/1788
Judith Ann Thornley 2/17/1788
Catherine Thornley 7/22/1790
Lucy Thornley 1/25/1793

MARRIAGES

William Thornley to Jane 12/22/1796
Emily Thornley, dau. of William and Jane, to Hazelwood Parish, son of Stephen and Catherine, 3/15/1821
Ann Eliza Thornley, dau. of William and Jane, to Bland Dangerffeld, son of William Henry, 9/2/1824
Jane Thornley, dau. of William and Jane, to Thomas J. West, son of Ellis West and Charity, his wife, 5/11/1830
Aaron Thornley, son of Wm and Jane, to Mary M. Buckner, dau. of Thomas and Lucy,5/14/1833
William Thornley, son of William and Jane, to Sarah P. Boulware, dau. of Mark and Lucy, 12/20/1838
James Thornley, son of William and Jane, to Catherine C. White, dau. of Jesse and Helen, 4/16/1850 in town of Charlottesville
John Thornley, third son of William and Jane, to Mary Downes, 1st dau. of Nathaniel and Bose Pearce Downes in Baltimore 4/2/1856 Caroline Virginia Thornley, dau. of William and Jane, to George C. Omohundro, son of John Omohundro and Nancy Crank, 10/5/1858

BIRTHS:

William Thornley, son of Aaron and Catherine, 1/2/1775
Jane Riding, dau. of George T. and Winney Riding, 6/18/1780

BIRTHS of Children of William and Jane Riding

Thornley Emily Thornley 1/10/1797
Catherine Thornley 8/6/1310
Ann Eliza Thornley 10/25/1800
William Thornley 3/15/1813
Aaron Thornley 4/23/1803
John Thornley 8/27/1316
Maria Thornley 12/9/1805
James Thornley 10/20/1818
Jane Thornley 1/6/1808
Caroline Virginia Thornley 9/11/1822

(Jane Riding Thornley Bible, BIRTHS, contd....)

James P. Thornley, son of James and C. C., 2/28/1851, Fredericksburg, Va.
Catherine Jane Farish, dau. of Hazlewood and Emily, 3/23/1822 Sarah Jane, dau. of Bland and
Ann Eliza Dangerfield, 8/6/1825 Lucy Jane, dau. of William and Sarah Thornley, 11/11/1839
George, son of George C. and Caroline Virginia Omohundro, 5/6/1860
Carrie, dau. of George C. and Caroline Virginia Omohundro, 2/6/1865
Clarence, son of John and Mary Dovnes Thornley, 2/1/1857, N. Y. John, son of John and Mary
Downes Thornley, 2/8/1858, Baltimore, Maryland

DEATHS

Catherine Thornley, dau. of William and Jane, 3/8/1814
Hazlewood Farish, husband of Emily Farish, formerly Emily Thornley, 9/12/1821
Aaron Thornley, father of William, 7/29/1821
William Thornley, Sr. 2/27/1837 on Island of St. Croix
Winifred, wife of Aaron Thornley, Sr., 7/28/1842
Maria, dau. of Wm Thornley, Sr. and Jane, 9/10/1856,Charlottesville, Va., bur. Maplewood Cem.
Bland Dangerfield 12/1843
Mary Downes Pearce 4/22/1861 Morristown, New Jersey
Jane Thornley, wife of Thomas J. West, 9/6/1864 in City of Richmond, Virginia
Jane, relict of William Thornley, Sr., 6/12/1865 in Charlottesville, Va., bur. Maplewood Cemetery
John, infant son of John Thornley and Mary Downes Pearce, his wife, 2/10/1859,Baltimore, Md.
John T., son of Jane and T. J. West, 9/3/1863 in Richmond, Va. Clarence, son of John and Mary Downes Thornley 7/21/1873 in Charlottesville, Va.
Aaron, son of William and Jane Thornley, 4/8/1880
Emily Parish, dau. of William and Jane Thornley, 4/16/1881
Anna Eliza Dangerfield, dau. of William and Jane Thornley, 3/3/1882 in Baltimore, Maryland
Julian Thornley, son of John and Julian H. Payne Thornley, 12/21/1912 in N. Y. City

JOHN THORNLEY BIBLE
Owner: Dr. John Thornley, U. S. N

BIRTHS

John Thornley, son of William and Jane, 8/27/1816, in King George Co., Va.

Mary Downes Pearce, dau. of Nathaniel and Rosetta Pearce, 10/3/1831, in City of Baltimore, Maryland 2/1/1857

John, son of John and Mary D. Thornlcy, 2/8/1858, Baltimore, Md. JuLia Henrietta, dau. of

Josiah Smith Payne and Isabella J. Rolando Payne, 9/19/1835, Charleston, South Carolina

Josiah Payne, son of John and Julia H. Thornley, 7/17/1867 Julian, son of John and Julia H. Thornley, 12/25/1868

Jane Alding, dau. of John and Julia H. Thornley, 9/2/1570, Charlottesville, Va.

John, son of John and Julia H. Thornley, 10/28/1876

Maria Julia Grayson, dau. of Jane Riding Thornley and her husband, John Cooke Grayson of
Culpepper, Va., 5/17/1894 in Culpepper, Va.

Sarah Mason Cooke Grayson, dau. of Jane Riding Thornley and John Cooke Grayson, 10/30/1895, Culpepper, Va.
John Thornley Grayson, son of Jane Riding Thornley and John Cooke Grayson, 10/27/1897, in Pulaski City, Va.

(John Thornley Bible, contd....)

MARRIAGES

John Thornley to Mary Downes Pearce 4/2/1856, Baltimore, Maryland
John Thornley to Julia H. Payne 10/4/1866, Emmanuel Church, Baltimore, Maryland
Jane Riding Thornley, dau. of Dr. John Thornley,
O. S. N., and his wife, Julia Henrietta Payne of Charleston, S. C., to John Cooke Grayson, son of Dr. John Cooke Grayson of "Salubria", Stevensburg, Culpepper Co., Va. and his wife, Lens Pettus (widow Walton), in St. Michael's Church, Charleston, South Carolina, 6/14/1893, by Dr. Trappier, Bector. Witnesses: Josiah Payne Thornley, bro. of the bride, and John Strode Barbour, best man Sarah Mason Cooke Grayson, dau. of John Cooke and Jane Riding Thornley Grayson, his wife, to Lewis Benjamin Johnson of Albemarle Co., Va., 1920

DEATHS

Julia H. Payne, 2nd wife of John Thornley, Sr. 1/23/1885 in Charlottesville, Va., bur. Greenwood Cemetery, N. Y.
Isabella Rolando Payne, widow of Josiah Smith Payne of Charleston, S.C., d. Charlottesville, Va. 12/4/1884, bur. Greenwood Cemetery, N. Y.
John Thornley, Sr., son of William and Jane Riding Thornley, 11/1887 in Charlottesville, Va., bur. Greenwood Cemetery, N. Y.
Julian Thornley, son of John and Julia H. Thornley, 12/21/1912 in N. Y., bur. Greenwood Cemetery

WILLIAM AND ELIZABETH ANDERSON BIBLE
From: Rev. War Pension #W5204

MARRIAGES

Foster Anderson to Sarah Billingsley 11/29/1801
Jacob Callahan to Jenny Anderson 12/11/1817
William B. Williby to Elizabeth Anderson 12/24/1822
William L. Anderson to Eudocia M. Hill 2/2/1825 by Wm H. Gray
Susannah Anderson to Hugh McCain 12/16/1802
Lewis Anderson to Elizabeth Guest 12/17/1812
Richard Anderson to Polly McKlin 5/3/1816
Richard Anderson to Huldah Simons 12/31/1822

BIRTHS

William Anderson, Sr. 3/2/1763
Elizabeth Anderson 5/8/1799
Polly Anderson 2/22/1787
William L. Anderson 5/24/1802
Lewis Anderson 9/14/1789
Lovey Anderson 3/8/1806
Jenney T. Anderson 8/27/1793
Eudocia M. Anderson 1/30/1807
Richard Anderson 10/28/1796
Mary Elizabeth Anderson 11/16/1825
William Isaac Anderson 7/4/1827
Jane Katharine Anderson 8/7/1829
Martha Ann Anderson 2/29/1632

Note: Elizabeth Anderson applied for pension as widow of William, stating her maiden name was Elizabeth Lewis and she m. 5/18/1786. William Anderson d. 10/25/1837.

JACOB CONRAD BIBLE
Owner: Flora L. Ward, Pasadena, California

BIRTHS

(First) Jacob Conrad 1/17/1744
Peter Conrad Sr. 11/20/1777
Ann Currence Conrad, Peter's wife, 10/16/1780 They m. 9/7/1802
Peter Conrad's Family
Nancy Conrad
Elizabeth Conrad m. David Salsberry 1/20/1803
Sarah Conrad m. Joseph Wamsley b. 11/10/1804
Phoebe Conrad m. Jeremiah Couger b. 2/8/1806
Alloy Conrad m. Daniel Wamsley b. 11/20/1807
John B. Conrad m. Mary Wilson b. 5/13/1809
Diannah Conrad m. Lewis Couger
b. 10/15/1810 Marish Conrad m. Isaac Dodrell b. 7/23/1811
Polley Conrad m. Thomas Curtis b. 2/23/1813
Barbra Conrad
Jacob Conrad m. Ann Bailey b. 12/8/1815
Rachel Conrad
Peter Conrad m. Elsey Arbigast b. 12/2/1817
Syrena Conrad m. Marshall Clark b. 10/8/1820
Barbara Conrad 4/11/1822-4/25/1899
Ann Conrad 2/25/1825-5/20/1919
L. C. Conrad 11/11/1827-9/19/1919

WILLIAM AND POLLY JENNINGS BIBLE
Of Prince Edward County
From: Rev. War Pension #W27144

BIRTHS of Children of William and Polly Kidd Jennings

Martin Jennings 11/6/1787
Salley Jennings 2/10/1801
Nancy Jennings 9/4/1789
Webb Jennings 5/11/1802
Elizabeth Jennings 1/1/1792
Wm Calvin Jennings 6/20/1803
Allen Jennings 12/28/1794

Robert Jennings 4/18/1808
Nancy Allen Jennings 3/11/1796
Lucrecy Jennings 5/12/1810
William K Jennings 7/19/1798
Sophy Jennings 5/27/1812
James W. Jennings 12/31/1813

DEATHS

Sophy Jennings 6/6/1812
Sarah W. Smoot 1/12/1842
John B. Smoot 7/12/1840

MARRIAGES

James W. Jennings to Mary Bevell 8/4/1836
Sally W. Jennings 12/30/1820 to John B. Smoot 3/4/1795-7/12/1840

Note: William Jenning. appied for pension 10/16/1832, Lincoln Co., Tenn; was from Prince Edward Co. r Va.; in 1836 pension transferred to Shelby Co., Alabama. Soldier d. 7/17/1840

Polly Jennings, widow, applied j/3/1843, stating she was b. Polly Kidd on 1/14/1771 and m. William Jennings 1/18/1787. In 1851 Mrs. Polly Jennings lived in Claiborne Parish, La. With her son, James W. Jennings and his family.

CAPTAIN SAMUEL BROWN BIBLE
Owner: Mrs. Lennoe S. Drew, Bogalusa, Louisiana

MARRIAGES

Samuel Brown to Judy Cottrell 7/26/1801
Samnel Brown to Ann Cottrell
Samuel Brown to Sarah C. Bowles 12/1825
Elizabeth C. Brown (dau. of Samuel Brown) to Dr. R. S. Cauthorn (b. 1805 Essex Co., Va.) 10/24/1833
Overton C. Brown (son of Samuel Brown) to Lucy W. Bowles 12/31/1840

BIRTHS of Children of Samuel Brown and Judy Cottrell

Maria S. Brown 6/15/1802
Sarah A. S. Brown 6/11/1811
Matilda W. Brown 2/10/1804
Catherine C. Brown 2/10/1813
Harriet W. Brown 9/23/1805

Elizabeth C. Brown 9/24/1814
George W. Brown 9/3/1807
Overton C. Brown 10/21/1817
Melinda W. Brown 7/1/1809

DEATHS

Samuel Brown 1771-3/10/1847
Catherine C. Brown 2/20/1813
His mother, 10/7/1820
Sarah A. S. Brown 4/15/1820 1st wife, 2/10/1823
Maria S. Brown 9/5/1820

2nd wife, 3/14/1825
Matilda W. Brown 6/5/1819 3rd wife, 8/14/1841
Harriet W. Brown 2/6/1826
Melinda W. Brown 12/2/1816
George W. Brown 11/5/1828

WILLIAM HERNDON BIBLE
Of Greene County
From: Rev. War Pension #S9575
BIRTHS

William Herndon, son of Edward and Mary, 2/29/1764

Mary Herndon 3/2/1767
Thomas Herndon 11/28/1785
Abner Herndon 1/22/1796
Edward Herndon 5/13/1787
Rachel Herndon 8/25/1797
James Herndon 1/23/1789
William Herndon 1/29/1799
Ezekiel Herndon 12/7/1790

Henry Herndon 9/9/1800
Elizabeth Herndon 6/6/1792
Manson Herndon 6/29/1802
Mary Herndon 5/2/1794
Mary Herndon d. 2/26/1835
Joel Herndon 7/27/1804
Thomas Herndon 6/29/1807

Note: William Herndon applied for pension 6/12/1845, Greene Co., Virginia, stating he was b. 1764, Albemarle Co., Virginia.

THOMAS AND HANNAH LEWIS BIBLE
From: Rev. War Pension #W9124

BIRTHS

Thomas Lewis 5/3/1755
Hannah Lewis 3/13/1766
Francis Lewis 3/3/1786
Sarah Lewis 4/10/1805
William Lewis 9/10/1786
Acy Lewis 3/4/1808
John Lewis 1/22/1789
Belinda Lewis 3/14/1811
Mary Lewis 8/5/1790

John Cox Lewis 11/15/1925
Margaret Lewis 12/12/1791
Nancy B. Lewis 11/1827
Nancy Lewis 4/8/1793
Thomas Lewis 7/23/1827
Gardiner Hopkins Lewis 11/8/1801
Henry Lewis 3/4/1828
Edmond B. Lewis 8/5/1803
James Cox Lewis 5/2/1829

(Thomas and Hannah Lewis Bible, contd....)

Note: Thomas Lewis applied for pension 8/8/1833, Morgan Co., Kentucky, stating he was b. 5/3/1755, was drafted in Washington Co., Virginia and in 1782 moved to Dick's Rivet, Ky. Soldier d. 8/9/1849. Hannah Lewis, widow, applied for pension 1/28/1850, stating she was Hannah Hopkins and m. Thomas Lewis in Washington Co., Virginia 3/3/1784 by Thomas Wolsey, a Baptist minister.

CORNELIUS M. VANDEVANTER BIBLE
Owner: William C. S. Thomas
Washington, D. C.

BIRTHS

Cornelius M. Vandevanter 9/28/1806
Sarah Jane Lampkin 7/10/1823
Lucy Elizabeth Vandevanter Diva--- 5/1/1842
Isaac C. Vandevanter 4/11/1844
James William Vandevanter 7/5/1846
Rodney Washington Vandevanter 4/18/1849
Mary Eliza Vandevanter 2/10/1852
Maurice Grimsley Vandevanter 12/1/1854
Hattie May Vandevanter 2/4/1859
Blanche Lilliam Vandevanter 4/28/1862
Ann M. Vandevanter 1/1/1865

DEATHS

Mary Eliza Vandevanter 10/19/1858, aged 6 yrs., 8 mos., 9 days Ann M. Vandevanter ---
C. M. Vandevanter 12/27/---
S. J. Vandevanter --I. C. Vandevanter ---
Lucy Elizabeth White 12/26/1912, in Philadelphia, Pa., aged 70 yrs, 7 mos., 25 days
J. William Vandevanter ---
Maurice Vandevanter ---

JAMES AND MARTHA RICHIE BIBLE
Of Lunenburg County
From: Rev. War Pension #R8795

BIRTHS of Children of James and Martha Richie

David Richie 11J14/1781(or 1783)
Lewis Richie 4/14/1808
Martha Richie 11/5/1804
Mary Richie 10/1/1809
James Richie 1/6/1806
Master Richie 4/7/1812

DEATHS

Hannah Richie 10/30/1831
Lewis Richie, son of David and Hannah, 8/16/1823
James Richie, son of David and Hannah, 9/21/1832

Note: James Richie applied for pension 8/28/1832, Smith Co., Tenn, stating he was b. 1754 and was from Lunenburg Co., Virginia. Soldier d. 3/6/1836 Smith Co.,Tenn. Widow, Martha Richie, applied 12/9/1842, aged 86, Weakley Co., Tenn. She m. James Richie 6/20/1774 in Lunenburg Co., Virginia by parson James Craig. They had seven children, 311 of whom died in infancy except David. Martha d. 6/10/1847.

ROBERT LEE BRANSCOME BIBLE of Roanoke

Robert Lee Branscome 12/7/1863 Carroll Co., Va.-7/7/1927 Roanoke, Va.
Elizabeth Alice Hylton 2/7/1867 Carroll Co., Va.-6/30/1888 Carroll Co., Va. m. 2/2/1882
BIRTHS of Children of Robert Lee and Elizabeth Alice Branscome
Dora AdaBranscome 2/2/1883
Anna Lee Branscome 1/3/1887
Nancy Jane Turner 10/24/1863 Bedford Co., Va.-9/18/1940
Robert Lee Branscome m. Nancy Jane Turner 10/1889

BIRTHS of Children of Robert Lee and Nancy Jane Branscome

Nancy Lee Branscome 2/3/1896-9/27/1966
Robert Linden Branscome 10/19/1896-12/15/1971 Albemarle Co., Va.
William Alva Branscome 8/7/1900-12/7/1969 Omaha, Nebraska
Dora Ada Branscome m. 1/21/1908 Henry Prince Burnett
BIRTHS of Children of Dora Ada and Henry Prince Burnett
Dorothy Lee Burnett 12117/1908 Wise Co., Va.
Margaret Burnett 5/31/1912 Wyoming Co., W. Va.
Nancy Elizabeth Burnett 6/10/1921 Grayson Co., Va.
Anna Lee Branscome m. 6/15/1909 John Vanderslice Barnes
BIRTHS of Children of Anna Lee and John V. Barnes
Janet Elizabeth Barnes 5/30/1910 Roanoke
Co., Va. Lois Cordelia Barnes 4/20/1912
Anna Frances Barnes 7/10/1914
Alice Branscome Barnes 3/5/1916
John Vanderslice Barnes, Jr. 10/6/1923
Robert Linden Branscome m. 9/1/1920 Annie Laura Davis

BIRTHS of Children of Robert L. and Annie Laura Branscome

Anna Lee Branscome 5/19/1921
Robert Linden Branscome, Jr. 12/21/1923
William Alva Branscome m. 2/7/1921 Ray Cubbage
Ray Cubbage Branscome d. 9/20/1968 Omaha, Nebraska
William Alva Branscome m. 9/22/1934 Robert Elmer Peterson

BIRTHS of Children of William Alva and Robert Elmer Peterson

Dorothy Lee Peterson 11/1/1935 Denver, Colorado
Charlotte Bay Peterson 5/20/1938 Shelby Co., Tenn.
Norma Jean Peterson 2/14/1941 Shelby Co., Tenn.
Margaret Burnett m. 12/23/1951 .Marshall Keith Arey
BIRTHS of Children of Margaret and Marshall K. Arey
Susan Call Arey 2J10/1953 Norfolk, Va.
Marsha Burnett Arey 4/25/1966 Norfolk, Va.
Nancy Elizabeth Burnett m. 2/5/1949 Russell Frank Frazier
BIRTHS of Children of Nancy E. and Russell F. Frazier
Nancy Elizabeth Frazier 5/25/1951 Henrico Co., Va.
Frances Burnett Frazier 6/5/1953 Henrico Co., Va.
Janet Elizabeth Barnes m. 8/5/1929 David McCarty Armstrong

(Robert Lee Branscome Bible continued...)

BIRTHS of Children of Janet E. and David Armstrong

Janet Ann Armstrong 3/3/1931
David McCarty Armstrong, Jr. 7/15/1933

Lois Cordelia Barnes m. 11/27/1936
Meredith Sanders Urick

BIRTHS of Children of Lois C. and Meredith S. Urick

Meredith Sanders Urick, Jr.-12/25/1941
John William Urick 12/5/1947

Anna Frances Barnes m. 7/23/1933 Hampton Barnett Deyerls

BIRTHS of Children of Anna Frances and Hampton Deyerle

Sue Deyerle 5731/1934
Judith Deyerle 8/5/1940 F
Frances Deyerle 7/7/1937

Alice Branscome Barnes m. 11/29/1939 Stuart Austin Taylor

BIRTHS of Children of Alice and Stuart Taylor

Nancy-Stuart Taylor 10/811940 John Warwick Taylor 12/30/1946
Stuart Austin Taylor d. 10/1/1958 Henrico Co., Va.
John Vanderslice Barnes, Jr. m. 3/20/1948 Mary Augusts Cox. One son: John Vanderslice Barnes b. 1/31/1955
Anna Lee Branscome m. 4/21/1944 Arthur Frank Bunton

BIRTHS of Children of Anna Lee and Arthur F. Bunton

Anne Davis Buntin 6/8/1955
Robert Franklin Bunton 12/7/1957

Dorothy Lee Peterson m. 2/6/1954
Robert Earl Banker

BIRTHS of Children of Dorothy Lee and Robert E. Banker

David Christopher Banker 3/2/1956 Knox Co., Tenn
Dana Burnett Banker 11/5/1963 Hillsboro Co., Fla.

Elizabeth Banker 6/24/1968 Hillsboro Co., Fla.
Charlotte Ray Peterson m. 10/5/1957 Finis Dixorl Carrell

BIRTHS of Children of Charlotte R. and Finis D. Carrell

Catherine Ray Carrell 7/2211958 Shelby Co., Tenn
Elizabeth Ann Carrell 9/29/1959 Shelby Co., Tenn.
Jeanne Hylton Carrell 9/28/1961 Santa Rosa Co., Fla.

Nora Jean Peterson m. 8/22/1964
Henry Roby Lesesne

BIRTHS of Children of Norms Jean and Henry R. Lesesne

Margaret Lucy Lesesne 8/17/1969 Orange Co., N. C.
Henry Roby Lesesne, Jr. 12/9/1971 Orange Co., N. C.

Janet Ann Armstrong m. 8/26/1950 Murray Gilbert Ashman

BIRTHS of Children of Janet Ann and Murray Gilbert Ashman

Ellen Murray Ashman-(8/23/1952
David William Ashman 8/13/1964
Elizabeth Ann Ashman 6/1/1951

Murray Gilbert Ashman, Jr. 8/5/1958
David McCarty Armstrong m. 12/28/1954 Faye Sours

BIRTHS of Children of David and Faye Armstrong

Janet Faye Armstrong 5/31/1958
John William Urick, killed in action in Vietnam 5/3/1967. Unmd. Meredith Sanders Urick, Jr. m. 9/29/1960 Harriet Puryear

David McCarty Armstrong 12/30/1961

BIRTHS of Children of Meredith and Harriet Urick

Lois Alana Urick 5/4/1961
Alan Dennis Urick 7/9/1962

Sue Deyerle m. 8/18/1956
William Branford Roane

Children: William Bradford Roane, Jr. 3/8/1960 and Mary Susan Roane 4/11/1963

(Robert Lee Branscombe Bible, MARRIAGES, contd....)

Frances Deyerle m. 9/26/1959 Elbert Bearst Rosne.
Children: Matthew Hearst Roane 12/12/1964 and Hampton Bradford Roane 3/11/1966
Judith Deyerle m. 11/27/1963 Charles L. Windham, Jr. Children: Baylor Charles Windham 12/29/1967 and Anna Lane Windham 7/7/1969
Nancy Stuart Taylor m. 10/17/1959 Eugene Christopher Smith III. Children: Christopher Stuart Smith 8/21/1960, Nancy Claiborne Smith 1/12/1963, Rebecca Alice Smith 4/4/1964 and Laura Taylor Smith 5/21/1968
John Warwick Taylor m. 4/17/1971 Patricia Anne Martorano. Child: Jason Stuart Taylor 11/4/1971
John Vanderslice Barnes Sr. d. 10/4/1938 Roanoke Co., Va. Henry Prince Burnett d. 4/28/1957 Grayson Co., Va.

FRANCIS BIAS BIBLE
Rosslyn, Arlington County

BIRTHS of Children of Francis and Sarah Bias

John F. Bias 9/11/1846
Dolly Elizabeth Bias 5/8/1852
Murray Alexander Bias 8/16/1848
Sarah Virginia Bias 7/5/1854
Lucinda Bias 5/2/1850
Mary Louisa Bias 3/2/1856

BIRTHS of Children of Wm H. and Sarah Toler

David C. Toler 12/13/1863   Charles S. Toler 1/11/1866

DEATHS

Dolly Eliez Beth Bias 4/8/1856
Francis Bias 1/8/1857
Sarah Hellen Bias 3/15/1911 at her home in Rosslyn, Va. Lucinda Griffin 12/12/1915, aged 65 yrs.
Murray Alexander Bias 1/26/1916, aged 68 yrs.

THOMAS W. SCOTT BIBLE of "Wildwood", Charlotte Co.
Owner: Mrs. Herbert Preston Henderson
Chantilly, Rt. 2, Keysville, Virginia

Thomas W. Scott m. Ruth J. Watkins 11/16/1865

BIRTHS

Ruth Josephine Watkins 11/19/1840 Thomas Watkins Scott 4/17/1844
William C. Scott 8/16/1856, baptised by M. H. Brown Frank Elfreth Scott 2/10/1863
Mary E. Scott 4/22/1869, baptised by M. H. Brown Ella K. Scott 4/27/1870
Carrie E. Scott 4/20/1872, baptised by M. H. Brown Martha Van neter Scott 5/12/1875 at "Wildwood" Ruth Josephine Scott 7/5/1876 at "Wildwood" Thomas W. Scott, Jr. 2/6/1878 at "Wildwood"
Joel Morton Scott 11/25/1879 at "Wildwood"
Frank Ben Watkins Scott 5/6/1881 at "Wildwood"

DEATHS

Frank Elfreth Scott 2/25/1868 Ella G. Scott 7/2/1870
Joe Morton Scott (in infancy) Mama 2/17/1894 (Ruth Josephine Scott)
Martha Henry Scott 11/2/1895, aged 81 yrs. (Mother of Thomas Watkins Scott)

HUTCHINS BURTON SR. BIBLE

The ages of Hutchins Burton Sr. and his wife and all

THEIR CHILDREN:is as followeth

Hutchins Burton Sr. 4/9/1694
Ann Burton 12/7/1731
Susannah Burton 5/17/1700
Charles Burton 5/4/1734
Samuel Burton 9/25/1710
Robert Burton 12/4/1736
Drury Burton 11/1721
Susannah Burton 1/15/1738
Hutchins Burton Jr. 9/25/1723
Richard Burton 2/5/1740
David Burton 6/25/1725
Julius Burton 10/22/1742
William Allen Burton 7/25/1727
Nowell Burton 4/27/1729
William Price, Sr., now of Pittsylvania Co., Va. was b. Henrico Co., near City of Richmond, Va., 9/3/1730
Susannah Burton b. near same place 1/15/1738
The aforesaid William and Sarah m. 3/29/1752, aforesaid county

Offspring:

Sarah Price 1/8/1754
Daniel Price 8/27/1766
Susannah Price 3/26/1756
Robert Price 10/6/1768
Elizabeth Price 5/13/1758
Maraday Price 6/1/1770
John Price 3/25/1760

Molly Price 5/4/1772
William Price 3/2/1762
Nancy Price 3/15/1774
Cutburd Price 6/13/1764
Patsy Price 6/1/1776
Major Peice 1779

Name written on one of leaves - Julius Burton, 5/10/1763
Mary Watson Hines b. 10/1744

In 1754 someone computed Hutchin Burton, Sr. as 60, subtracting 1694 from 1754.
David Allen is 15 years old on May --Banner Guinn d. 1/20/1755 - George King

JACOB WEAVER BIBLE
Owner: Mrs. Arthur Wiseman
Greenville, Virginia

BIRTHS

Jacob Weaver 1/1/1813
Rebecca Weaver 5/4/1820

Children:

John C. Weaver 2/27/1843
David B. Weaver 12/11/1852
Sarah S. Weaver 4/9/1845

Alexander Franklin Weaver 7/4/1856
Jacob W. Weaver 8/31/1848
Mary Elizabeth Weaver 12/14/1858

DEATHS

Jacob W. Weaver 5/26/1894, aged 81 yrs. Alexander Franklin Weaver 11/27/1862
John C. Weaver 4/5/1865
Rebecca Weaver 3/25/1889, aged 68 yrs.

JOSEPH BRIDGER HODSDEN BIBLE
Owner: Mrs. Robert Edmond Hodsden
Chuckatuck, Virginia

Joseph Bridger Hodsden, son of William Hodsden and wife, Sarah, 3/29/1776-11/19/1815 in Isle of Llight Co., Va. m. 1.1/23/1799 Mary Pasteur 2/12/1780-10/9/1837. Her mother, Honour Pasteur 17553/16/1805 "Thomas Hill, Ejus Libri, A. D. 1720"

BIRTHS

Henry Hodsden 9/30/1800-10/21/1800
Sally Bridger Hodsden 11/22/1801-5/5/1836
Mary Wilson Hodsden 4/30/1804
Robert Hstton Hodsden 11/23/1806-6/18/1836
John Goodrtch Hodsden 4/21/1809-10/4/1805
Joseph Bridger Hodsden, Jr. 11/29/1811
Martha Pasteur Hodsden 4/24/1814-5/1/1814
Elizabeth Davis Hodsden 7/8/1815-7/31/1815
Julia Ann Hodsden 7/1/1816-1827

Joseph Bridger Hodsden, Jr. 11/29/1811-7/15/1877 m. 6/7/1338 Mary Mears Lawrence 1/12/1817-2/28/1865

Julia Ames Hodsden 4/8/1839-6/30/1893
Clara Hodsden 1/7/1841-4/28/1851
Emma Hodsden 3/19/1843-4/20/1851
Wilfred Hodsden 2/9/1845-1/28/1925
Robert Bruce Hodsden 2/8/1847-3/10/1906
Joseph Bridger Hodsden III 3/12/1849-9/22/1867
Emma Hodsden 2/3/1853-2/21/1896
William Hodsden 1/14/1853-2/20/1896

GEORGE F. HOSICK BIBLE
Owner: Ted Rudolph Hosick

Husband - George F. Hosick 11/29/1854
Wife - Susan S. Rudolph 6/=5!1858 m. 5/6/1894

Children:

Maisie Phee Hosick 5/14/1895
Mary June Hosick 6/11/1897
Teddy Rudolph Hosick 9/14/1900

MARRIAGES

Mary June Hosick 5/29/1917 to Hal L. Houke
Ted Rudolph Hosick 2/19/1924 to Eunice Pauline Thomas

DEATHS

George F. Hosick, father, 5/30/1918 Susan S. Hosick 2/2/1931

JOHN R. CARSON BIBLE
Of Isle of Wight County

John R. Carson b. 8/27/1760 Isle of Uight Co., Va. m. 2/9/1791 Betsey b. 12/17/1772

BIRTHS

Barbara Carson 3/15/1795
Meridith Carson 12/31/1803
Robert Holland Carson 2/10/1797
Richard Carson 9/16/1806
Betsey Carson 9/23/1799
Samuel Carson 11/16/1809
Andrew Carson 1/11/1801
Ann Mariah Carson 11/26/1810
John R. Carson, son of Richard and Lydia, b. 10/22/1807, lived east. of Carrsville, Isle of Wight Co., Va. m. 4/5/1838 Martha Ann Edwards b. 4/16/1822

BIRTHS

Robert D. Carson 2/24/1842
Margaret Jane Carson 2/1/1845-11/19/1925 m. George Washington Johnson
Darious U. Carson 10/1/1848
James R. Carson 8/17/1850
Elizabeth A. Carson 12/7/1852

WILLIAM PORTER BIBLE of Nansemond County
Owner: Albert Dunston Johnson, Windsor, Va.

William Porter, 12/16/1762-11/8/1825, son of John and Betty, lived e. of Carrsville, Nansemond Co., Va., m. Mary Foulk, 2/28/1763-8/30/1857 dau. of John and Esther Foulk.
Joseph Porter 8/19/1787-10/26/1834
Margaret Porter 10/16/1789-12/1/1815
William Porter Jr. 4/11/1792-5/21/1806
Zachariah Porter 5/28/1794
Edna Porter 3/23/1796
Lydia Porter L0/28/1798-4/15/1844, 1st wife of Albert B. Johnson Mary Porter 7/28/1801
Anne Porter 5/6/1804

JAMES HOAGLAND BIBLE of Loudoun County
From: Rev. War Pension #28044

BIRTHS

Henry Hoagland 5/13/1726
Leah, his wife, 2/11/1725
Henry and Leah Hoagland m. 4/12/1749
Anny Hoagland 4/6/1751
Derrick Hoagland 5/11/1758
Agneys Hoagland 9/23/1752
James Hoagland 5/9/1760
John Hoagland 10/14/1754
Mary Hoagland 5/1/1762
Daniel Hoagland 9/17/1756

Note: James Hoagland applied for pension 8/13/1832, Loudoun Co., Va., mentions his father's Bible, owned by his sister Ann Hough who m. Isaac Hough, Somerset Co., N. J.

GARRET VAN METER BIBLE of Hampshire County

Garret Van Meter m. 4/3/1757 Ann.

BIRTHS of THEIR CHILDREN:

Isaac Van Meter 12/10/1757 -
David Van Meter 7/24/1762
Henry Van Meter 10/20/1759
Jacob Van Meter 5/19/1764
Henry Van Meter 5/9/1761
Abraham Van Meter 1/22/1766
Ann Van Meter 4/15/1768
Jacob Van Meter b. Ft. Pleasant, Hampshire Co., Va. 5/19/1764-8. 9/1/1829 m. Tabitha Inskeep b. Hampshire Co. 3/11/1767, dau. of Joseph and Hannah Inskeep, d. 9/27/1851

BIRTHS of THEIR CHILDREN:

Hannah Van Meter 1/14/1791
Anne Van Meter 4/1/1793
Isaac Van Meter 9/24/1794
Solomon Van Meter 4/3/1796-1/3/1818
Rebeckah Van Meter 10/7/1797-5/2/1798
Rebeckah Van Meter 5/2/1799
Joseph Inskeep Van Meter 5/28/1802-1/7/1805
Joseph Inskeep b. 5/10/1733, wife, Hannah b. 10/15/1737

Benjamin Franklin Van Meter 1/11/1803-1/1805
Abraham Van Meter 9/24/1804
Garret Van Meter 4/20/1806
Susanna Van neter 12/12/1807
Sarah Inskeep Meter 9/26/1810

BIRTHS of THEIR CHILDREN:

William Inskeep 2/11/1759
Tabitha Inskeep 3/11/1767
Mary Inskeep 7/25/1761
Hannah Inskeep 4/10/1769

Elizabeth Inskeep 2/3/1763
Joseph Inskeep 5/10/1771
Amelia Inskeep 2/25/1765

STITH BOLLING SPRAGINS BIBLE of Halifax Co.
Owner: Mrs. Samuel Hamilton Spragins
2622 N. Calvert St., Baltimore, Maryland

"The Spragins Family Bible. Whoever may get possession of this Bible--will please notify some member of the family and oblige S. B. Spragins 1903".

"Melchijah Spragins. Mr. Spragins was b. near Huntsville, Ala. 5/1/1831 and d. at his home near Drapersville, Mecklenburg Co., Va. 11/14/1899. In 1870 he m. Sue Martin of Madison, Rockingham Co., N. C., with whom he lived happily to the day of his death. He joined the Presbyterian Church in middle life and held his membership at the Concord Church until that church was dissolved by the Presbytery.....W. W. Royal."

Stith B. Spragins m. Eliza A. Green 12/30/1824
Stith B. Spragins d. 5/8/1839, aged 43 yrs.
Eliza Apperson Spragins d. 12/19/1889, aged 90 yrs.
Charlotte E. B. Spragins 4/20/1826-7/18/1885, aged 59 yrs.
Rebecca S. Spragins 2/15/1828-1/10/1892, aged 64 yrs.
Stith B. Spragins 10/3/1829-7/5/1904
Melchijah Spragins 5/1/1831-11/14/1899, aged 68 yrs.
Louisa Seigniora Spragins 7/23/1833-4/9/1896, 63 yrs
Virginia Spragins 3/17/1835
Marston G. Spragins 2/19/1837-10/8/1896, aged 60 yrs
Lucy E. Spragins 9/10/1838-12/8/1889, 51 yrs.

(Stith Bolling Spragins Bible continued....)

Children's MARRIAGES

Rebecca S. Spragins to Dr. G. O. Rogers of Boydton, Va. 11/12/1856
Rebecca S. Rogers to Peter Manson King, Mecklenburg Co., Va. 12/21/1863
Slith B. Spragins to Bettie A. Hamilton, West River, A. 4. Co., Md., 5/29/1866
Melchijah Spragins to Susan Eva Martin 9/20/1870, Rockingham Co., M. C.
Lucy Elizabeth Spragins to Thomas LeidwelL Bennett of Mecklenburg Co., Va. 12.23.1873
Marston Green Spragins to Louisa James Puff (d. 10/9/1896) of Brunswick Co., Va. 5/24/1876

BIRTHS

Elizabeth Hamilton Spragins, dau. of Stith B. and Bettie A., 7/26/1867-1878
LouLsa Duval Spragins 11/19/1869
Stith Bolling Spragins Jr. 6/2/1872
Samuel Hamilton Spragins 8/23/1875
Melchijah Spragins 12/10/1877
Stith Bolling Spragins, son of Melchijah and Sue E. Spragins, 10/26/1872-d. st birth
Stith Bolling Spragins, son of Marston Green and Louisa James, 2/26/1877
Rebecca Stith Spragins 7/8/1878
Lucy Lee Bennett, dau. of Thomas L. and Lucy E. Bennett 6/20/1877
Virginia Spragins Bennett 4/4/1879
Peter Manson King Jr. 4/2/1870-10/19/1871
Wright King 2/14/1872-6/19/1876

ALEXANDER BOLLING BIBLE of Prince George County
Owner: Mrs. Samuel Hamilton Spragins
2622 N. Calvert St., Baltimore, Maryland

On flyleaf: "Samuel Davies to Mrs. Susannah Bolling as a small token of gratitude for her kindness."

BIRTHS

Alexander Bolling 3/12/1721
Susanna Bolling 6/16/1728
Alexander and Susanna Bolling m. 12/23/1745

BIRTHS of Children of Alexander and Susanna Bolling

Elizabeth Bolling 6/24/1747
John Bolling 10/13/1756-11/9/1759
Robert Bolling 3/24/1751
Alex Bolling 12/2/1761
Stith Bolling 5/11/1753

Susanna Bolling 12/5/1764
Alex Bolting Sr. d. 6/11/1767
Ann Bolling 3/31/1755
Sally Bolling 3/25/1766

Elizabeth Boiling m. Peter Jones 4/6/1769
Peter Jones d. 1/18/1771
Elizabeth Jones, dau. of Alex and Susan Bolling, m. Chris. Manlove 11/24/1771
Jane Manlove, dau. of Chris. and Elizabeth, b. 10/8/1772
Robert Bolling m. Franky Green 5/10/1772
John Bolling, son of Robert and Franky, b. 3/10/1773
Frances, wife of Robert Bolling, d. 3/15/1773
Sally Bolling d. 6/17/1773
John Bolling, son of Robert and Pranky, d. 5/1/17--
Rebecca Bolling Manlove 4/24/1774-7/8/17--
Thomas Bolling Manlove b. 11/4/1776
Eliza Manlove d. 11/23/1776
Stith Bolling m. Charlotte Edmunds 10/10/1776
Rebecca B. Bolling, dau. of Stith and Charlotte, b. 2/16/1778 m.

(Alexander Belling Bible, contd....)

Melchijah Spragins, son of Lieut. Thomas Spragins of Halifax Co., Va. From this marriage were two children: Stith Bolling and Melchijah who settled with their mother in Alabama near Huntsville

Robert Bolling m. Clara Bland, widow, 12/18/1779
Eliz Yates Belling, dau. of Robert and Clara Belling Alex Bolling, son of Stith and Charlotte Bolling

Note: Included in Bible is newspaper clipping of speech of Senator Daniel of Virginia to Senate on behalf of Henry S. Wellcome, an American residing in England, a portrait of Pocahontas, which hands at Bollin Hall in Norfolk, England, the former seat of the Rolfe family...Senator Daniel reviewed h1story of Pocahantos and her marriage in 1613 to John Rolfe, her chrIstian name "Rebecca" and sudden death at Gravesend, England 3/16/17, aged 22. Pocahontas left a son, Lieut. Thomas Rolfe who returned to Va. and m. Jane Poythress and their dau., Jane, the granddau. of Pocahontas, became 1st wife of Col. Robert Belling (1646-1709). By this union was b. a son, John Bolling....Col. Robert Belling m. 2nd Anne Stith, dau. of Major John Stith and Jane, his wife.

The original owners of this Bible, Alexander Bolling and his wife and cousin, Susanna Belling, were both grandchildren of Colonel Robert Belling by his second wife, Anne Stith.

STEPHEN CALLOWAY BIBLE
Callaway Family Assn Journal, 1984, P. 67

BIRTHS

Ballenger Calloway 8/17/1837
Mary E. Ball 4/25/1842
Stephen Calloway 9/9/1884
Mollie Calloway 8/---
Mary Calloway 4/25/1842 (Mary E. Ball)
Richard T. Calloway 5/14/1892
Carrie Bell Calloway 7/9/1886
Nancy Calloway 10/15/1876
Lucy Calloway 3/13/1874
Charles Calloway 3/19/1860
Ella Calloway 12/21/1860
James Calloway 1/28/1863
Margaret Calloway 12/15/1865
George Calloway 12/28/1867
John Calloway 10/18/1888
John M. Murphy 9/19/1898
Ballenger Calloway d. 12/29/1914, aged 78
Mary E. Calloway d. 3/3/1916, aged 73
John Murphy d. 10/8/1949
Charles B. Calloway, son of Charles J., b. 3/17/1860
Mary Howard Calloway b. 2/6/1865
Charles B. Calloway b. 5/24/1909 m. Icie Fee Calloway b. 6/25/1915

BIRTHS of Children of Charles B. and Icie Calloway

Sudie Mae Calloway 7/27/1934 m, Jimmie Gene Baker b. 7/26/1933.

Children:

Daniel Lee Baker b. 7/18/1955 m. Mary Ann Powers b. 7/27/1056 (they have on dau., Audry Laine Baker b. 1/29/1983)
Linda Lou Baker b. 5/25/1956
Timothy Lyle Baker b. 9/20/1859 m. Candice Aston Baker b. 10/1/1960

(Stephen Colloway Bible, contd....)

Coleida Calloway b. 1/5/1937 m. Harry K. Campbell b. 3/9/1936. One child: Harry Trever Campbell b. 10/2/1958
Clara Aline Calloway b. 1/25/1940 a. Charles P. Howard b. 12/13/1931. Two Children:
Beatrice Aline Howard b. 2/26/1961 m. Deny Allen Visnoski b. 2/5/1959
Charles P. Howard Jr. b. 3/16/1965
Theodore 8. Calloway b. 12/4/1942 m. Kay Frances Billings b. 5/30/1942. Two Children:
Theodore R. Calloway Jr. b. 6/22/1966 and Carrie Ann Calloway b. 10/27/1975
Icie Lillian Calloway b. 9/3/1944 m. Ronald G. Berg b. 3/13/1940. Three Children:
Matraca M. Berg b. 2/3/1964 Lois Berg b. 5/20/1967
Eric Callaway Berg b. 10/11/1971
Charles B. Calloway Jr. b. 7/5/1946 m. Betty Gayle Hackler b. 5/23/1945. Two Children:
Susan Michelle Calloway b. 10/5/1970
Jennifer Lynne Calloway b. 1/19/1973
Will Calloway, son of Charles J. Calloway, b. 3/17/1860
Mary Soward Calloway b. 2/6/1865
Will Calloway b. 7/19/1882 m. Clementine Campbell b. 8/14/1885

THEIR CHILDREN:

Shirley Calloway Payne b. 6/8/1912
Laura Calloway Cagna 2/22/1908-6/4/1976
Eula Calloway Clemeos b.1/10/1910
Cecil Calloway b. 1/22/1914
Lens Calloway Howard b. 7/14/1917
Frank Calloway b. 8/9/1906-2/25/1970 m. Hazel Quinn b. 5/13/1912.

THEIR CHILDREN:

Carlos F. Calloway b. 6/15/1944 m. Molly McCloud b. 11/30/1947.
They have four children: Edith Arlene Calloway b. 12/28/1966
Collin T. Calloway b 1/20/1969.
Janie B. Calloway b. 2/19/1971
Chrlsts L. Calloway b. 6/6/1973
Sharon Calloway Haywood b. 8/21/1947, dau. of Frank and Hazel Calloway

ROGER THOMPSON BIBLE
Owner: Nicholas W. Thompson. Bedford County, Virginia

Roger Thompson b. 12/5/1750 m. 9/4/1781 to Mary White (b. 1761)

BIRTHS of THEIR CHILDREN:

Mary Thompson 11/27/1782 m. Richard Franklin
Nicholas Thompson b. 3/9/1784
Elizabeth Thompson 9/19/1785 a. John Ballard
Sarah Thompson 11/26/1786 m. Samuel Ward
William Thompson 4/25/1788 a. Elizabeth Ward
Nathaniel Thompson 12/5/1789 m. Temperance
Crenshaw John Thompson 9/26/1792-3/21/1810
David Thompson 1/3/1801 m. Polly Crenshaw
Joseph Thompson 5/23/1804-11/6/1812
Susannah Thompson 12/16/1807 m. William Ward

THOMAS THORNTON BIBLE Of Richmond County

Owner: Mrs. Cora Craft Tignall, Georgia

"Bible is to be given to Frank Warren, Tignall, Georgia" Dated at Concordla, Georgia

BIRTHS

Thomas Thornton 4/11/1742

Children of Thomas Thornton:

Sarah Thornton 9/2/1768
Betsy W. Thornton 12/29/1807
Prior Thornton 4/27/1770
Memorable Thornton 1/7/1810
Susannah Thornton 4/11/1772
Eppy White Thornton 5/22/1811
Elizabeth Thornton 12/4/1773

John M. Thornton 10/10/1813
John Thornton 12/14/1775
Salley Thornton 5/20/1816
Martha Thornton 12/22/1777
Mark Thornton 12/31/1819
David Thornton 12/1/1779
Elsabad Thornton 9/28/1806

DEATHS

Thomas Thornton 5/20/1820
Elizabeth Thornton Warren 1872

BIRTHS of Children of John Thornton

Middleton Thornton 11/36/1799
Micajah Thornton 7/3/1809
Sarah Thornton 1/4/1802

Benajah Thornton 12/15/1811
Polley Thornton 4/9/1804

MARRIAGES

David Thornton to Lucy K. White (2nd wife)
Lucy R. White Thornton 2/23/1787-1/25/1837

ADAM JAMES HANDY BIBLE of Stuart
Owner: Mrs. Charlie W. Moorefield
Stuart, Virginia

Adam James Handy d. 3/19/1941
Mrs. A. J. Handy (Lucille Hill) d. 5/23/1927

Children of Mr. and Mrs. A. J. Handy

Martha Bula Handy m. Joe Martin b. 1/1807-1895
Maggie Tee Handy m. John Martin (b. d. Amelia, Va., bur. Little Flock Baptist Church
Lillie Belle Handy m. Milliard Gunter b. 3/2/1885
Mary Donis Handy m. Frank Bohannon b. 7/27/1888
Louisa Anna Handy m. Jim Dalton b. 4/23/1882
Lucy Lee Handy m. Charlie Moorefield b. 6/3/1893

Mr. and Mrs. Adam James Handy bur. Russell Creek Primitive Bapt1st Church, Patrick Co., Near Stuart, Va.

DEATHS

Rev. Davis Hill 6/10/1890
William Davis Handy bur. Russell Creek Cemetery, Stuart, Va.
Abe Esters Handy 3/6/1915

ABRAM ERNEST HANDY BIBLE of Stuart, Va.

Abram Ernest Handy of Stuart, Virginia m. Leila Alice Watkins of Lawsonville, North Carolina 6/23/1902 at Salem, Virginia, by Charles K. Bell

BIRTHS

Abram Ernest Handy 1/22/1879
Wm. Edger Handy 5/23/1910
Lelia Alice Watkins 9/23/1883
Ralph Waldo Handy 5/23/1911
Stafford Odell Handy 6/1/1903

Abram Ernest Ha:ldy Jr. 8/15/1915
Wilbour Ernestene Handy 9/20/1904
Phillip Watkfns Handy 7/25/1918
Kenneth Earl Handy 2/25/1906
Ann Clark Handy 7/18/1926

MARRIAGES

Stafford Odell Handy to Louise Bransford Ballou 10/28/1929, Va.
Wilbour Ernestene Handy to William L. Cunningham 10/1/1932, Elktown, Md.
Wm. Edger Handy to Vergie Harris 10/16/1935, Va.
Kenneth Earl Handy to Mary Williams Jones 3/21/1921, Va.
Ralph Waldo Handy to Buth Marie James 4/28/1845, Memphis, Tenn. Phillip Watkins Handy to Barbara Humbert 9/5/1946, Va.
Douglas Quentin Handy to Doris Meade Ray 1/26/1947, Washington, DC. Ann Clark Sandy to
Charles Herman Droste 8/9/1947, Portsmouth, Va. A. Ernest Handy, Jr. to Eleanor Thomas, Shaker Heights, Ohio

DEATHS

Abram Ernest Handy Sr. 9/11/1951, Lynchburg, Va., bur. Stuart, Va at Peter's Creek Church Cem.
Stafford Odell Handy 3/26/1950, bur. Lynchburg, Va.
Lelia Alice Handy 12/1964, Nursing Home, Bedford,Va., bur. Stuart, Va., Peter's Creek Cem.
Darien Smith Watkins 6/24/1957-7/7/1920
William L. Cunningham 9/16/1937

JONATHAN HENKEL BIBLE
Owner: J. O. Henkle
526 University Dr., Starkville, Miss

Note: Rev. Phillip Henkel's diary in German library at Lenoir Rhyne College, Hfckory, N. C., records he baptised five children in 1821 of Jonathan Henkel at home of Joseph Henkel, Chester, South Carolina. James L. Henkel remained in Chester.

BIRTHS

Jonathan Henkel 5/9/1785
John Henkel 9/21/1820
Mary Henkel 10/15/1788
Lou A. Henkel 12/9/1822
William Henkel 7/13/1808
Martha Henkel 5/25/1825

Elizabeth Henkel 1/23/1811
Mary Henkel 7/25/--
James L. Henkel 12/15/1813
Jonathan L. Henkel Jr. 9/10/1834
Albert Henkel 12/6/1816

DEATHS

Jonathan Henkel 9/25/1846, 61 yrs, 5 mos., 17 days
Mary Henkel 3/5/1853, 64 yrs., 17 days
William Henkel 4/21/1863 Martha Burch 4/17/1867
John Henkel, son of Jonathan, 7/15/1841, 20 yrs, 7 mos., 23 days

James L. Henkel 6/20/1858,45 yrs., 7 days
J. L. Henkel 12/6/1051 at Manassas, Virginia
James A. Burch m. Martha Henkel 12/14/1843
James M. Taland m. Jane E. Henkel 11/23/1843

BIRTHS

James A. Burch Sr. 11/12/1816
Savannah Burch 2/26/1855
James A. Burch 11/12/1849
Jonathan C. Burch 5/17/1857
Mary Virginia Burch 8/6/1851

Elisha Burch 1/28/1859
Eliser America Burch 4/6/1853
Sarah E. Burch 11/6/1864

THOMAS MASON'S BIBLE
Owner: B. F. Mason

George Turner, maternal grandfather of Turner Mason and greatgrandfather of W. L. Mason, 1695-10/26/1777
Elinor Turner, maternal great-grandmother of William Lowe Mason, wife of George Turner, 1699-1779
Thomas Mason, father of Turner Mason, 3/7/1722-1769
Elizabeth Turner, dau. of George and Elinor Turner and wife of Thomas Mason, 10/1/1733-10/6/1784

BIRTHS of Children of Thomas Mason

Peter Mason 9/13/1751
Turner Mason 1/27/1754-5/18/1843
Martha Mason 10/26/1756
Thomas Mason 12/19/1758
Susana Mason 12/26/1760
James Mason 11/27/1762
Turner Mason, father of William Lowe Mason, m. 1st 2/1776 Elizabeth Burns and had three children as follows:

James Mason 8/15/1777-8/27/1777
Joseph Mason 9/11/1778-11/11/1779
Mary Mason 1/19/1781-7/23/1785

Elizabeth Mason, 1st wife of Turner Mason, d. 12/27/1783

MARRIAGES

Turner Mason to Miss Mary Lowe 12/15/1785. His second wife.

BIRTHS of Children of Turner and Mary Mason

William Lowe Mason 1011/1786 Halifax Co., North Carolina 12/12/1863 at Buckeye, Laurens Co.,Ga., his home

Turner Mason 2/8/1789-9/16/1807
Sarah Mason 12/14/1790-6/10/1794
Martha Mason 10/31/1792-1/30/1803
Turner Mason 11/30/1795-10/4/1796
Susan Mason 8/28/1797-2/19/1853
Betsey Lowe Mason 8/9/1799-7/16/1801
James Mason 6/30/1801-12/14/1860
Polly Mason 3/5/1803-9/1804
David and Daniel Mason 2/17/1805

DEATHS

David Mason 9/29/1812
Daniel Mason 2/20/1830
Rebecca Mason b. 9/10/1808 dead
Mary Ann Mason 7/9/1811-4/17/1856

Note: Turner Mason served as a Lieutenant in the American Revolution

WESLEY BURDINE BIBLE
Of Henry County
Owner: Mrs. Edwin M. Standefer
737 Goodlett, Memphis, Tenn.

BIRTHS

Samuel Burdine, my grandfather, 5/27/1745
Mary Burdine, my grandmother, 7/1/1754
John Burdine, my father, 1/7/1772
Susannah Burdine, my mother, 4/23/1779
Wesley Burdine 10/4/1811
Sarah Burdine, my wife, 7/25/1797
Addison H. Burdine 10/5/1823
Mandone T. Burdine 5/26/1825
Melissa E. Burdine 5/27/1827

Adilla T. Burdine 8/3/1829
James C. Burdine 12/17/1831
Mary Jane Burdfne 9/1/1834
Judith V. Burdine 10/23/1837
Joannah A. Burdine 8/19/1840
Nancy N. Burdine 9/22/1834
Counsel W. McCullen 5/14/1866
Fannie May McCullen 11/13/1873
Ira McCullen 1/11/1895

MARRIAGES

John Burdine to Susannah Tarrant 9/8/1793?
Wesley Burdine to Sarah Standefer 12/22/1822
Melissa Burdine to George Fellworth 1/16/1865
James C. Burdine to Nancy M. Parchman
1/26/1854 William Tears to Judith Burdine 1/10/1861
---- Burdine to --- 11/15/185-

WOODSON MOSBY BIBLE of Henrico County
Owner: Mrs. Jennie Mosby B. Cochran
Olive Branch, Mississippi

BIRTHS

Benjamin Mosby, husband of Sallie A. Mosby, 9/9/1819
Sallie A. Mosby, wife of Benjamin Mosby, 9/18/1817

BIRTHS of Children of Benjamin and Sallie A. Mosby

May Pauline Mosby 3/30/1840
Robert Overton Mosby 6/6/1841
Eugenia Pollydora Mosby 10/13/1842
Matthew Woodson Mosby 12/19/1843
Samuel Anderson Mosby 2/4/1845
Nathaniel Anderson Mosby 5/3/1846

Virginia Anderson Mosby 5/26/1848
John Stout Mosby 4/4/1850
Thomasin Price Mosby 5/30/1851
Thomas Price Mosby 7/19/1853
William Overton Mosby 9/7/1854
Philip Woodson Mosby 9/17/1855

MARRIAGES

Benjamin Mosby to Sarah Ann Woodson 5/15/1839
Samuel A. Morby to Joelliert A. Massey
2/13/1866 Matthew Woodson to Paulina Woodson 10/19/1816

DEATHS

Samuel A. Mosby 1/7/1888
Philip Woodson, 8th son of Benjamin and Sallie A. Mosby, 11/25/1899

(Woodson Mosby Bible, contd....)

BIRTHS of Children of Matthew and Paulina Woodson

Sarah A. Woodson 9/18/1817
John Royal Woodson 12/28/1822
Mary J. Woodson 4/26/1819
Jane Eliza Woodson 3/6/1825

Phillip Stephen Woodson 9/3/1820
Paulina Woodson 3/10/1827
Matthew Woodson 4/15/1779

Paulina Woodson, wife of Matthew, 7/7/1793
Matthew Woodson, youngest child of above, 1/28/1829

DEATHS

Mary J. Woodson, 2nd dau. of Matthew and Paulina, 9/29/1819
Matthew Woodson, youngest child of above, 2/2/1829, age abt 5 days
Paulina Woodson, 4th dau. of above, 4/13/1832
Jane Eliza Woodson, 3rd dau. of above, 12/3/1833, aged 9 yrs.
Matthew Woodson, husband of Paulina, 7/9/1828

ROBERT M. BONDURANT BIBLE
Virginia State Library

MARRIAGES

Robert M. Bondurant to Pamelia Moseley, dau. of Peter, 11/11/1824 Mary A. J. Bondurant to B. F. Nurrell 6/8/1840
P. M. Bondurant to L. B. Hillfard 4/5/1854
John M. Bondurant to Rebecca R. Owen 8/30/1857
Ida May Bondurant to A. G. Smith 4/1/1880
Bessie Bondurant Smith to T. E. Campbell 4/26/1904

BIRTHS

Robert M. Bondurant 4/9/1801

Pamelia A. Bondurant 4/13/1801

THEIR CHILDREN:

Mary A. J. Bondurant 11/3/1825
Robert M. Bondurant 1/10/1831
Edward Bondurant 10/10/1826

John U. Bondurant 10/18/1833
Peter M. Bondurant 5/29/1829
Sarah Adeline Bondurant 12/19/1837

Joseph W. Bondurant, son of Robert and Margaret W., 6/23/1848
Infant son of A. G. and Ida May Smith 7/30/1893-8/10/1893
Pearson Owen, son of A. G. and Ida M. Smith, 11/15/1894
Adorian George, son of A. G. and Ida M. Smith, 4/2/1897
Cornelius, son of A. G. and Ida Smith, 3/2/1899
Ida May, dau. of Rebecca B. and John M. Bondurant, 12/14/1858
Bessie Bondurant Smith, dau of Ida May and A. G., 3/27/1881
Lilburne Mason, dau. of A. G. and Ida May Smith, 8/28/1882
Mary Ella, dau. of A. G. and Ids May Smith, 6/26/1884
Thomas Dillard, son of A. C. and Ida May Smith, 7/26/1887
John W., son of A. G. and Ida M. Smith, 8/14/1889
Ida George, dau. of A. G. and Ida M. Smith, 8/23/1891

DEATHS

Robert M. Bondurant 4/16/1866
Mary A. J. Murrell 1/26/1855, aged 30 yrs
Pamelia A. Bondurant 2/26/1845, aged 44 yrs
Edward Bondurant 7/16/1827

Robert M. Bondurant 7/17/1832
Sarah Adeline Bondurant 11/26/1845
Cornelius, son of A. G. and Ida May Smith, 10/26/1906

PHILIP WILLIAM GUTHRIE BIBLE of Floyd County
Owner: Mrs. William Bell Guthrie
7704 Dartmoor Rd., Richmond, Va. 23229

MARRIAGES

Philip William Guthrie to Nancy Susan Burnett 1/26/1860
William Henry Willis to Laura Guthrie 5/30/1878
Charles Luther Guthrie, son of Philip and Nancy, to Annie Rebecca Morris 10/8/1912
Charles Luther Guthrie to Etta Mabel Bell 10/14/1916
Charles Luther Guthrie, Jr. to Dorothy Elizabeth Ayer 1/28/1945 by Capt. Will E. Arnold, Chaplain, 0. S. A., Leghorn, Italy, in Club House of 37th Bn. Q. M., 5th Army
William Bell Guthrie to Mary Milam Foster 3/31/1951 by Rev. Barney W. Ashby, Trinity Church, Lexington, Va.
Charles Luther Guthrie, Jr. to Lothaine Anne Arloga 7/7/1962 at Weisbagea, Germany
Laura Isabelle Guthrie to William Henry Willis 5/30/1878

BIRTHS

Philip William Guthrie 6/6/1836-11/23/1906 Burnett and his wife, Judith Slaughter Burnett
Nancy Susan Guthrie 8/26/1837-9/8/1904, dau. of Berveridge Austin
Laura Isabelle Guthrie 10/1/1863 Floyd Co., Va.-9/21/1879
Edward Bennett Willis 9/10/1879, son of William Henry and Laura Wills, Floyd Co., Va.
Ella Rusabell Guthrle 2/21/1869-3/14/1877, aged 8 yrs., 24 days
George William Austin Guthrie 8/22/1875-3/21/1877, aged 1 yr., 7 mos.
Charles Luther Guthrie 7/17/1879 Floyd Co., Va.
Dorothy Elizabeth Ayer Guthrie 6/3/1911
Charles Luther Guthrie, Jr. 1917, son of Charles and Etta Guthrie William Bell Guthrie 7/9/1922
Nancy Elizabeth Guthrie 3/6/1946 Richmond, Va., dau. of Charles and Dorothy Guthrie
Baby boy Guthrie 10/25/1948-10/25/1948, son of Charles and Dorothy Mary Milam Foster 11/2/1923 Brookneal, Va.
Charles Foster Guthrie 2/12/1959 Richmond, Va., son of William Bell Guthrie and Mary Foster Guthrie
Etta Mabel Bell 4/29/1890
Charles Luther Guthrie III 6/14/1964, Wiesbaden, Germany (USAF), son of Charles and Lothaine Guthrie

DEATHS

Annie Morris Guthrie d. 7/5/1913
Isabel Guthrie Willis 9/21/1879
Ella Rosabell Guthrie 3/14/1871
George William Austin Guthrie 3/21/1877
Nancy Susan Burnett Guthrie 9/8/1904
Philip William Guthrie 11/23/1906
Annie Morris Guthrie 7/5/1913, 1st wife of Charles Luther Guthrie
William Henry Willis 1/22/1932
Leilia Goodson Willis 3/11/1934, wife of Edward Bennett Willis
Edward Bennett Wills 5/27/1938, son of William Henry and Laura Guthrie Willis
William Silas Guthrie 8/23/1946 (1st cousin of Charles Luther Guthrie)
Dorothy Ayer Guthrie 10/8/1958
Charles Luther Guthrie 2/21/1967
William Bell Guthrie 3/13/1971

Memoranda, 1/15/1922, Ancestors of Charles Luther Guthrie

Father's parents: (Parents of Philip William Guthrie)

William Guthrie 5/22/1809-9/10/1892
Isabel Williams Guthrie 8/6/1809-2/5/1892

(Philip William Guthrie, Bible, contd....)

Father's grandparents: (Parents of William Guthrie) Benjamin Guthrie d. 1/16/1853
Sarah Bradley Guthrie d. 11/13/1853

Mother's parents: (parents of Nancy Susan Burnett Guthrie)
Beveridge Austin Burnett 9/11/1811 Patrick Co., Virginia - 10/31/1890 Carroll Co., Virginia
Judith Slaughter Burnett 8/19/1816 Patrick Co., Va. - 11/5/1886 Carroll Co., Virginia

Mother's grandparents: (Parents of Beveridge Austin Burnett) Valentine Burnett b. ca 1789 Patrick Co., Va.-d. ca 1844 Patrick Co., Va. (son of Obadiah Burnett)

Agnes Hughes Burnett d. after 1844 Patrick Co., Va., dau. of Beveridge Hughes

Parents of Judith Slaughter Burnett:

Dandridge Slaughter d. 1844 Patrick Co., Va.

Susan Handy (Palmer) Slaughter d. 4/8/1854 Patrick Co., Va. (she 1st m. a Palmer and was a widow when she m. Dandridge Slaughter)

Charles Luther Guthrie, Jr. joined Trinity M. E. Church South 12/12/1926. Rev. C. C. Bell, Pastor, Petersburg, Va.

Charles Luther Guthrie joined Market St. Church by letter from Holston Conference 2/17/1906, Rev. W. H. Edwards.

Etta Bell Guthrie joined Trinity Church 3/27/1932. Dr. J. Murray, Pastor, Petersburg, Va.

Dorothy Ayer Guthrie joined Trinity Church 4/21/1946 by letter from St. James Episcopal Church, Springfield, Mass., Rev. Oakey Wilburn

Notes: William Guthrie, son of Benjamin Guthrie (d. 1/16/1853) and his wife, Sarah Guthrie (d. 11/13/1853) was b. 5/21/1809 near Boon Mill in Franklin Co., Va. His father soon after the birth of William, moved with his family and settled in the Pine Creek Section of Floyd Co., Va. where William Guthrie was reared. 1/21/1834 he m. Isabel Williams (8/6/1809-2/5/1892) and soon thereafter moved to Burke's Forkon west end of Floyd Co. where he was a well-known farmer until his death on 9/10/1892.

His family of children were:

Elizabeth Jane Guthrie 6/6/1836-11/23/1908
Philip William Guthrie 2/22/1838-
Sarah Amanda Guthrie 12/27/1840-11/26/1862
Martha Ann Guthrie 12/27/1840-11/26/1862
James Henry Guthrie 12/6/1842-1/15/1917
John H. Guthrie 4/21/1845-11/1/1862
Thomas T. Guthrie 2/1/1850-11/22/1863
Mary Emily Guthrie 7/1/1852-
Benjamin Joseph Guthrie 7/1/1854-1/19/1855

THOMAS AND MARY POSEY BIBLE
The Historical Foundation Archival Agency of Presbyterian Church of U. S. (Southern)
"Thornton-Posey 1773"

MARRIAGES

George Thornton to Mary Alexander 10/9/1773 (Stafford Co., Va., St. Paul's Perish) by Rev. William Stewart
Mary Alexander Thornton to Thomas Posey 1/22/1784
Charles B. Foote to Sarah E. Hall 4/3/1851
William J. Whiteman to Fanny Hall 6/24/1851
John Posey to Lucy Frances Thornton 1/25/1798
Mary H. Posey to James Hall 2/1823
Thomas L. Posey to Lure Campbell 7/13/1826
Frederick A. Jones to Eliza Easton
Lloyd T. Posey to Georgianna T. Posey
William T. Posey to Eliza Jane Dixon 5/10/1829
Dr. Alexander H. Posey to Jane S. Dixon 1/8/1846
Addison C. Posey to Mary M. Hickey 3/25/1886
John B. Cabell to Martha Ann Posey 4/25/1839
Addison T. Posey to Sarah A. Redman 10/31/1840

WILLIAM B. HENDERSON BIBLE
The HIstorical Foundation Archival Agency of Presbyterian
Church of U. S. (Southern)

MARRIAGES

William B. Henderson b. 9/7/1787 to 9/27/1816
Marry Barry b. 9/22/1795
Margaret M. Henderson to Robert C. Hiett 12/23/1840
John Henderson to Nancy I. Berry 9/16/1841
Marry E. A. Henderson to Charles O. Force --- 6/25/1844
Lawson P. Henderson to Talitha C. Hiett 10/10/1849
Charles W. Henderson to Sarah C. Harris 10/1/1856
Alice E. Henderson to W. O. McWhorter 12/24/1860
Andrew J. Henderson to Matilda Foster 6/19/1862
James F. Henderson to Virginia Helborn (or Melborn) 9/7/1864 in Petersbur, Va.
Harriet L. Henderson to Robert L. Mackey 6/18/1868
Rebecca Jane Handerson to Hugh G. Williams 2/18/1873
H. L. Mackey to Josiah Reynolds 11/18/1879

REV. WILLIAM JOHNSON of Bedford Co
.Owner: William T. Johnson
Moneta, Virginia

BIRTHS

Thomas Johnson 13/5/1770
Sally Johnson 5/17/1778

THEIR CHILDREN:

Francis Johnson 4/27/1797
Thomas Johnson 1/31/1809
Patsy Johnson 1/13/1800
Sallie Johnson 6/6/1812
Nancy Johnson 5/27/!1802

Robert Johnson 1/12/1814
William Johnson 10/25/1804
Joseph Johnson 12/31/1816
George Johnson 11/10/1806
Elizabeth Jane Johnson 3/24/1819

PHILIP JOHNSON BIBLE
Owner: Mrs. Vernon Gomez
4603 Cliffstone Cove
Austin, Texas 73735 (Bible burned)

Philip Johnson 12/14/1766-1849

Children of Philip and Mary Broughton Johnson

Philip Johnson m. Mollie, lived in North Carolina
Maria Johnson m. Mr. Arms, lived in North Carolina
Judith Johnson m. Edwin Palmer. Halifax Co., Virginia
Susan Johnson m. Elijah Hull, Hallfax Co., Virginia
Thomas Johnson m. Diana Roberts Chandler 6/5/1833, Halifax Co.,Va.
Mary Johnson m. Mr. Taylor
Willis Chandler 1771-9/10/1847 m. 6/20/1802 Halifax Co.,Va. Rebecca Hill (d. 3/30/1834)

Children of Willis and Rebecca Hill Chandler

Dian Roberta Chandler m. Dr. Thomas Johnson of "Greenway", Halifax Co., Va.
Jane Chandler m. Mr. Moseley Rowena Chandler m. Mr. Williams Ryle Chandler

ISRAEL STANDEFER BIBLE of Henry Co.
University of Texas, Austin, Texas

Israel Standefer, his Book

Israel Standefer, son of Israel and Susannah, b. 11/8/1781
Naomi StandeEer, dau. of William and Jemima, 2/10/1794-10/9/1843
Israel and Naomi Standefer m. 1/12/1815

BIRTHS of Children of Israel Standefer

Polly Standefer 1/7/1807
James Stuart Standefer 4/22/1807?

BIRTHS of Children of Israel and Naomi Standefer

Jemima Standefer 3/5/1817
Susannah Standeler 5/3/--
Abraham Porter Standefer 3/23/1819

Nancy Lamb? Standefer 4/1/1833
Naomi Standefer 8/3/1828
Israel Skelton Standefer 10/22/---

BIRTHS

James Standefer, son of John and Margaret, 10/1715
Israel Standefer, son of James and Martha, 11/13/1740
Mary Standefer, dau. of Israel and Susanna, 9/13/1767
Jesse Standefer 1/11/1770
Skelton Standefer 4/12/1772
Martha Standefer 1/28/1775
--- Standefer ---

DEATHS

James Standefer, son of John and Margaret, 9/1807
Israel Standefer 10/19/1822

Israel Standefer Jr. 10/28/1852
Martha Johnson, formerly Martha Standefer, 12/23/1817

MARRIAGES

Susanna Standefer, formerly Susanna Heards, b. 3/22/1750
Phebe Frost b. 1/23/1771

(Israel Standefer Bible, MARRIAGES, contd....)

Israel Standefer to Phebe Frost 1/7/1798
Israel Skelton Standefer to Elizabeth Frances Conover 1/14/1874
Susanna Frances Standefer, son. of I. S. and E. F., b. 7/28/1876
Abraham Mills Standefer, son of I. S. and E. F., b. 12/10/1873
Susannah Standefer, wife of Israel Standefer, d. 5/31/1795
Susanna Frances Standefer, dau. of I. S. and Elizabeth Frances, d. 10/16/1391
Abraham Mills Standefer, son of I. S. and E. F., d. 9/20/1900

BIRTHS

William Standefer 10/13/1786
John Standefer 7/1801
Stephen Standefer 11/28/1788
Micajah Standefer 6/1/1804
Susanna Stsndefer 4/18/1791
Elijah Standefer 11/30/1806
Thomas F. Standefer 3/28/1799
--- Standefer --

DEATHS

William Standefer 8/29/1861 Joshua Standefer 6/1810
Stephen Standefer 1/15/1821
The next portion mostly blotted out:
--------, wife of -----------,   9/12/1720
---fon and ---- 1715
Ro----dau. of J. and C., b. 8/11/1717
George Chamberlaine, son of Thomas Chamberlaine, b. 12/27/1720(1725?)
Benjamin Defon, son of William and Mary Defon, b. 9/1713 Edmond Defon, son of William and Mary Defon, b. 3/30/1721

Mary Norington, dau. of J. N. and Elizabeth Norington, b. 3/1711 Elizabeth Norington, dau. of John and Elizabeth Norington, b. 4/1714
Francis Norington, son of John and Elizabeth Norington, b. 6/1718
(marked through) Margarett Durham, wife of James Durham, d. 11/6/1720
Joseph Taylor, son of Abraham and Sarah Taylor, b. 10/9/1720 James A. Watkins, son of Samuel and Mary Watkins, b. 11/1751 (written over the date of 1717 or 1721)
William Watkins, son of Samuel and Mary Watkins, b. 1720
Martha Watkins, dau. of Samuel and Mary Watkins, 1/13/1723
----dau. of------, b. 1728
 Demofs, son of D----- Demofs, b. -/22/1736

MARRIAGES

Samuel Willson to Rebecca Smithson 1729
James Standeford m. Martha Watkins 10/1737

BIRTHS of Children of Samuel and Rebecca Willson

Aquilla Willson 3/1731
Samuell Willson 4/1733
Sarah Willson 4/14/1729
Hannah Willson 10/1734
William ---uhardson, son of Thomas ---uhardson and Sarah, b. 4/11/1733

ALSA PACE BIBLE

Alsa Pace m. Miss Rhoda Jarvis 9/22/1816

BIRTHS of Children of Alsa and Rhoda Pace

Burrell H. Pace 6/28/1817
Elizabeth Pace, twin, 6/1/1831
Bennett R. Pace 7/11/1819
Justinia P. Pace, twin, 6/1/1831
Laurianna Pace 12/12/1822
Alsa C. Pace 11/4/1833

Minerva Pace 10/10/1824
Jasper N. Pace 9/30/1835
Edward I. Pace 12/6/1826
Cornelius R. Pace 7/30/1837
Abner W. Pace 6/16/1829
Edwin J. Pace 1/29/1842

Elizabeth M. Rainey, dau. of D. and Laurianna Rainey, b. 11/27/1836
Martha E. Rainey, dau. of D. and Laurianna Rainey, b. 4/24/1840
Edmund Pace, son of John and Sarah, 2/29/1764
Sarah Pace, wife of Edmund Pace and dau. of David and Ann Walker, b. 8/1766
Also Pace, son of Edmund and Sarah Pace, b. 30/30/1796
Rhoda Jarvis, now wife of Alsa Pace and dau. of Reziah Jarvis and Elizabeth, b. 3/6/1796

DEATHS

Rev. Edmund Pace 8/28/1834   Sarah Pace, wife

WILLIAM HENRY PATMAN BIBLE
Hitory of Cass County (Ga.)

6/4/1839 David Lucas of Montgomery Co., Va. m. Susan T. Richards of Fauquier Co., Va.
Memoranda - Mule colt age - Roda, mule colt was folded the 10 day May 1907

BIRTHS

William Henry Patman 5/27/1844
Mary Rosabell Patman 5/25/1853
David Elias Patman 1/27/1874
Birdie Willie Patman 8/25/1879

Joseph Augustus Patman 7/26/1886
Linda Jane Patman 1/18/1892
Terisa Lousinda Patman 5/4/1870-10/15/1877

DEATHS

David Elias Patman 11/29/1898, killed by a wagon running over him and breaking his neck

James Perryman Lathem 7/10/1907
Ben Lathem's boy's death
Birdie Willie Lathem 10/31/1925
Gladys Lathem 8/24/1925

Mary Rosabelle Patman 11/12/1927, aged 74 yrs.
William Henry Patman 1/18/1935
John E. Harris 1/24/1919 Ida's husband's death

MARRIAGES

David Elias Patman to Maggie May Smith 1/27/1895
William Henry Patman to Mary Rosabell Lucas 7/4/1867

B. P. Lathem to Birdie Patman 1/25/1898
Joseph A. Patman to Rate Harris 12/1/1907

DEATHS

David Lucas 10/9/1896   Elias Bell Patman 1/15/1893, my father's death
Susan Terisa Lucas 4/13/1899
Augustus L. Patman 2/18/1894, killed by a shingle machine - my brother's death

BIRTHS:

D. E. Patman 1/27/1874   Callie May Patman 7/17/1896
Maggie Patman 6/16/1878

WILLIAM HENDREN BIBLE
Owner: Mrs. Robert L. Cox
626 McConnell Street Memphis, Tennessee 38112

William Hendren, his Bible Gregory Glascock, his Book

BIRTHS of Children of Gregory Glascock

Sarah Glascock 11//1729
Travers Glascock 10/5/1730
William Glascock 5/28/1730
John Glascock 12/28/1738

Gregory Glascock 1/25/1731/2
Grace Glascock 9/1/1741
Jesse Glascock 5/10/1733

BIRTHS of Children of William and Sarah Hendren

George Hendren 10/1790
Synthea Hendren 9/16/1802
Peggy Hendren 2/16/1792
Richard J. Hendren 8/11/1805
Elijah Hendren 2/16/1794
Stephen Hendren 9/12/1807
Oliver Hendren, son of John and Margaret, 9/11/1759
Brantley Bryan Hendren 11/23/1776

Ambrose Hendren 5/23/1796
Solomon Hendren 9/12/1807
Sarah Hendren 7/25/1798
Eli Hendren 11/21/1811

BIRTHS of Children of William and Sarah Taylor

Milley Taylor 1/28/1762 --
Sharot Taylor 1776
Reggey Taylor 10/1768

George Taylor 1779
Nancy Taylor 1772
Berthey Taylor

On flyleaf: William Deadman, his hand and pen

John and Mary Glascock   William Hendren   John

WILLIAM BROWNE BIBLE
Owner: William Randolph
Surry County, Virginia

"Given under our hands at Cedar Fields in Surry County, February 21, 1823. Witnesses: John Faulcon, William Randolph, John Hunnicutt, Sr. Recorded March 24, 1823. Surry County Deed Book 7, Page 2."
Ann, dau. of William and Lucy Taylor, b. 11/26/1752 William Browne m. Ann Taylor 1/8/1771

BIRTHS of THEIR CHILDREN:

Mary Browne 10/21/1771-11/15th, aged 3 weeks, 3 days
Henry Browne 2/5/1773-10/13th, aged 8 mos., 8 days
Hannah Edwards Browne 4/19/1775-11/6/1776, aged 18 mos., 27 days
William Taylor Browne 1/18/1778
Robert Browne 11/21/1780-9/18/1783, aged 2 yrs, 9 mos., 28 days
Anne Browne 3/11/1783
William Browne, son of Henry and Hannah, d. 1/5/1786
Ann Browne, wife of William, d. 6/21/1786
William Taylor Browne d. 5/26/1801, aged 22 yrs, 11 mos., 8 days

JOHN STREET BIBLE of New Kent County

BIRTHS of Children of John Street and Hannah Waddy Street

John Street, Jr. 1735
Joseph Street 2/12/1737

Anthony Waddy Street 10/16/1741-1/22/1809

(John Street Bible, BIRTHS, contd....)

Sarah Street 1743
Mary Street 1745
Frances Street 1747
Baptised in the Episcopal Church

MARRIAGES

John Street of New Kent County to Hannah Waddy, dau. of Anthony Waddy and Ann Parke, his second wife (ca 1734). He was a surveyor of New Kent County and tobacco inspector

John Street, Jr. to Frances Parke, New Kent Co.

Anthony W. Street the elder, to Mary Stokes. He was vestryman and church warden of Cumberland Parish for many years.

Waddy Street to Elizabeth Smith. (He was lieutenant colonel in War of 1812, 73rd Regt.)
David Street to (1st) his cousin, Mary Stokes, dau. of Capt. Peter Stokes, 2nd, Mary Scott, dau. of Lt. William Scott (4th Va. Continentals, State Line).

Sarah Montfort Street to 1st John Smith, 2nd, Adam Bell, son of Colonel George Bell

Anthony Street, Jr. to Mary Smith, dau. of Major Robert Smith Joseph Montfort Street to Eliza M. Posey, dau. of General Thomas Posey, Rev. War. (Gen. Posey was Governor of Indiana 1813-1816)

Notes: William Street was Clerk of Deep Run Chapel (Henrico Co.) ca 30 yrs. and paid 1700 pds. of tobacco annually for reading the prayers.

David Street was church warden and vestryman for many years. He was presiding justice 43 yrs. Anthony Street appointed lieutenant colonel of 73rd Regt. in 1786, commissioned lieutenant of the county in 1787; in House of Representatives 1783-5, Lunenburg Co., Va. John Street m. Miss Harris.

THEIR CHILDREN: were Judge William Street of Alabama and Dr.

Montfort Street of North Carolina
William B. Street never married.

Joseph Montfort Street was Indian agent, Prarie du Chien, many years; Brig-Gen. in State Militia, Illinois (Black Hawk War) John Thomson Street represented Lunenburg Co. in House of Delegates 1822-1842.

Sarah Stokes Street m. Dr. William H. Jameson, moved to Madison Co., Tenn.
David Anthony Street m. Mary Degrafenriedt Woodson 11/1828, moved to Madison Co., Tenn.
Peter W. Street m. Susan Marion Scott, dau. of Lt. William Scott Welter Scott, Jr. served as Capt. in Revolution
Lucy Ann Street m. William H. Stokes
James Parke Street m. Sallie Williams
Waddy Street, C. S. A., 9th Va. Cavalry, m. Martha S. Forrest
Susan Frances Street m. Dr. John T. Merryman. Their dau., Margaret E. Merryman, m.
William Alexander Neal

Lt. Colonel Waddy Street (War 1812), son of Colonel Anthony Street and Mary Stokes, m. Elizabeth Smith, dau. and widow Nune McGeehee and 1st wife of James Smith. He m. 2nd, Ann Parke Street, s1ster of Col. Waddy and dau. of Col. Anthony Street. Dau. of Col. Waddy Street

Mary Ann Street m. her cousin, Edward Montford Jones. Their dau., Ann Parke Jones, m. Edward Chambers Craig, grandson of Rev. James Craig and Mary Terry.

DAVID STREET BIBLE of Lunenburg County

David Stokes, the elder, 10/23/1707-9/12/1794
Sarah Stokes Sr. (formerly Sarah Montfort), wife of said David Stokes, 2/3/1717-4/9/1800
William Stokes, son of David and Sarah, 10/10/1735-179- (m. Sarah Wade, dau. of Robert Wade, Sr. of Halifax Co., Va. 4/19/1759)

BIRTHS-

Ann Wade 10/11/1737 (m. Robert Wade, Jr. of Halifax Co., Va.) Elizabeth Herring 8/30/1740
Molley Street 8/20/1743-11/7/1802, aged 59 yrs., 2 mos., 18 days
David Stokes Jr.3/18/1745-12/9/1797
Sarah McCullach 12/19/1748-
Susanna Stokes 9/23/1753
Jane Jones 3/24/1751-8/1828
John Stokes 3/20/1756-10/12/1790
Peter Stokes 10/25/1758-2/1825
Montfort Stokes 3/12/1762

Sarah Stokes, Jr., wife of Peter Stokes, 5/24/1765-7/2/1827 m. 4/26/1781 Peter Stokes
Anthony Street, the elder, father of David, 10/16/1741-1/22/1509, aged 68 yrs., 3 mos., 6 days
Waddy Street b. 2/12/1768 (bro. of David Street)
John Street (bro. of David Street) 4/7/1773-12/1841
Sarah M. Smith (s1ster of David Street) b. 4/24/1775
Anthony Street, Jr., bro. of David, b. 5/16/1777
William B. Street, bro. of David, 10/14/1778-1818
Ann Parke Smith (s1ster of D. Street) 12/25/1780-2/7/1815 Joseph Montfort Street (bro. Of David Street) 12/18/1782-1840 (m. Eliza M. Posey, dau. of Colonel Thomas Posey)
John Stokes, bro. of Sarah Street, wife of David Street, b. 2/11/1784
Joseph Street (bro. of Anthony, the elder) b. 12/17/1737
William Street (bro. of Anthony, the elder) b. 12/20/1739 Robert Smith, Sr. 8/8/1761-183-
(father of Mary Scott Street, wife of Anthony Street)

Ages of John and Elizabeth (Scott) Haynes' Children, sis. of Mary Scott Street, wife of David:-

Elizabeth-Haynes 6/22/1805 (decd)William Scott Haynes 8/1/1807
Henry Haynes 10/22/1809 Mary T. Haynes 12/12/1811
Malcolm Decatur Haynes 2/15/1815 (decd)Harriet Amanda Haynes 4/2/1816
Susan Marion Haynes 1/14/1818 John Haynes 7/3/1821 James M. Haynes 2/10/1824

MARRIAGES

David Street to Sarah M. Stokes 10/16/1798 by Rev. John Cameron (Sarah was dau of Capt. Peter Stokes)David Street to Mary Scott 9/7/1813 by Rev. Charles Price of Bedford County (Mary was dau of Lt. William Scott)

BIRTHS

David Street 4/21/1770 Sarah S. Street 3/14/1782
John Thomson Street, son of David and Sarah, 9/2/1799
Peter William Street, son of David and Sarah, 11/13/1801-8/1849
Mary Stokes Street, dau. of David and Sarah, 3/15/1803
(John Thomson, Peter William and Mary Stokes Street all baptised by Rev. John Cameron)
Sarah Smith Street, dau. of David and Sarah, 1/23/1805
David Anthony Street, son of David and Sarah, 1/29/1807
Lucy Ann Street, dau. of David and Sarah, 5/30/1809
Joseph Montfort Street, son of David and Sarah, 4/30/1811
Mary Scott, now Mary Street, wife of David Street, b. 5/12/1792

(David Street Bible, contd....)

BIRTHS of Children of David and Mary S. Street

James Parke Street 6110/1814, baptised by Rev. Charles Price
Elizabeth Abbott Street 12/9/1815, baptised by Rev. Charles Price
Mary Stokes Street 10/28/1817
Waddy Street 3/7/1821, baptised by Rev. Charles Price
Susan Frances Street 7/2/1828, baptised by Rev. John Phillips, Episcopalan, d. 2/8/1895
Susan Frances Street m. Dr. John Thomas Merryman 2/28/1854.

Two children born to them:

Mary Scott Merryman (deed in infancy), and Margaret Elizabeth Merryman b. 11/8/1857
Susan F. Cheatham (nee Street) d. 2/8/1895 in Crewe, Virginia, aged 67 yrs
.
Waddy Street d. 5/8/1895 at his home in Richmond, Va., aged 75
Mary Stokes Street d. 8/26/1804, aged 1 yr, 5 mos., 11 days
Sarah Stokes Street, wife of David, d. 5/10/1811, aged 29
yrs., 1 mo., 26 days. She died....leaving a child 11 days old (Joseph Montfort Street)
Joseph Montfort Street d. 3/5/1812, aged 10 mos., and days old
Mary Stokes Street d. 6/12/1819, aged 8 mos., dau. of David and Mary Street
Elizabeth Abbott Street, dau. of David and Mary, d. 3/22/1821, aged 15 yrs., 3 mos., 14 days
Susan M. (Scott) Street d. 11/2/1853
Lucy Ann Stokes, formerly Street, dau. of David Street, d. 11/2/1831, aged 22 yrs, 6 mos.
David Henry Stokes, son of William S. Stokes and Lucy Ann Stokes, d. 5/22/1833, aged 1 yr., 6 mos.
Sarah Smith Jamerson, formerly Street, d. 5/15/1850 in Madison Co.,Tenn. (m. Dr. William H.Jamerson)
John T. Street, son of David, d. 10/23/1846, aged 47 yrs, 1 mo., 21 days
David Street d. 5/3/1849, aged 79 yrs., 12 days. His funeral was preached by Rev. Thomas E.
Locke from Job, 10 verse, 14 chapter Peter W. Street d. 8/11/1849, aged 48 yrs.
David Anthony Street d. 5/11/1856, aged 49 yrs.
Anthony Waddy Street 10/16/1741-1/22/1809

Register of BIRTHS of Mrs. Elizabeth Scott's Children

Ursuly Goode Scott 6/7/1785 m. Alexander Price
Elizabeth Scott 12/19/1786 m. John Haynes
Polly (Mary) Scott 5/12/1792 m. David Street
Leneas Scott 8/10/1798
Susan Marion Scott 4/14/1801 m. Peter Street

William Scott m. Elizabeth Wade 5/20/1784 in Chesterfield Co., Va.
William Scott, Uncle of Mary Scott Street, b. 1/30/1755/6
Walter Scott, uncle of Mary Street, b.Walter Scott, Sr., father of William b.
Sarah Baynie Stokes, dau. of William S. Stokes and Lucy Ann Stokes b. 11/28/1838
Reglster of BIRTHS of William H. and Sarah Jamerson's Children
William H.Jamerson 2/20/1824 David Clement Jamerson 3/20/1825
Joseph D. Jamerson 11/15/1828 John Richard Jamerson 10/3/1826
Martha Elizabeth Jamerson 2/3/1833 Sarah Stokes Jamerson 4/10/1830
Virginia Jamerson 1839

Waddy Street, son of David and Mary, m. Martha Forrest 5/29/1855 in Lunenburg Co. Va
by Rev. Mathew Dance. Margaret Elizabeth Merriman. William Alexander Neal
4/12/1917.St. Paul's Church, Lunenburg Co., Va.

TIMOTHY THARP BIBLE Of Southampton County
Found in "Loose Papers"
Southampton County Court House

BIRTHS

Betty Tharp 5/19/1733
Temperance Tharp 2/6/1749
Mary Tharp 8/19/1735
Sylvia Tharp 2/10/1752
Patty Tharp 8/19/1738

Timothy Tharp 4/6/1755
Lucy Tharp 7/26/1741
William Tharp 11/25/1758
Peterson Tharp 11/25/1745

Martha Jones, the mother of the above named children, was b. 2/20/1716

Note: Name spelled Tharp and Thorp

THOMAS SCOTT BIBLE of Caroline Co.
Owner: Mrs. Anna M. Scott (1894)
Mrs. Florence Henry, Brooklyn, N. Y.

Thomas Scott, son of James, b. St. Mary's Parish, Caroline Co., Virginia 6/15/1718 m. 11/2/1742 Martha Uilliams, dau. of Rice Williams and Frances, his wife.

BIRTHS of Children of Rice and Frances Williams

Frances Williams 12/2/1721
Martha Williams 5/2/1727

Ann Williams 12/2/1723

BIRTHS of Children of Thomas and Martha Scott

Rice Scott 8/12/1743
Samuel Scott 3 14/1754
Frances Scott 6/27/1745
William Scott 12/15/1756

John Scott 10/19/1747
Robert Scott 12/30/1758
James Scott 2/17/1752

MARRIAGES

Thomas Scott to Martha Williams 11/2/1742
Frances Scott, dau. of Thomas and Martha, 12/30/1766 to James Gatewood, son of Dudley and Sarah Gatewood
Thomas Scott, Jr. to Isabel, his wife, 8/1/1767

DEATHS

Isabel Scott, wife of Thomas, 5/20/1770 Martha Scott, wife of Thomas, Sr., 4/8/1777

MARTIN NALLE BIBLE
Owner: Mrs. P. W. Iden

Martin Nalle 12/7/1777-12/2/1843, aged 66 yrs.   Thomas Barbour d. 5/16/1825
Nelly M. Barbour Nalle 3/10/1785-7/3/1826, aged 42 yrs.
(Note: of Orange Co. Thomas and Mary were parents of Gov. James Barbour, Judge Philip Pendleton Barbour and Nelly Barbour whose marriage on 9/15/1809 to Martin Nalle is recorded in Orange Co., Va. records. Thomas Barbour was a Member of the Conventions of 1774-1775)
Mary Barbour d. 7/3/1826, aged 74 yrs.

BIRTHS of Children of Martin and Nelly B. Nalle

Lucy Mary Nalle 8/15/1810 m. 12/15/1831 Richard H. Willis
Richard Thomas Nalle 9/7/1811 m. Ellen Ann Hooe 2/22/1837
Sarah Elenora Nalle 12/1/1812 m. Garret H. Scott 2/14/1831
Ann Frances Nalle 1/21/1314 m. John C. Hansbrough 9/4/1832

(Martin Nalle Bible, contd....)

James Barbour Nalle 4/7/1815-1/6/1832, aged 17 yrs.
Philip Pendleton Nalle 5/27/1816 m. Elizabeth Wallace 5/28/1843
Cordelia Nalle 8/31/1817 m.
Joseph Hiden 5/5/1836
Lucetta T. Nalle 5/8/1819 m. George Booten 12/1/1846
Martinette Nalle 12/15/1820 m. Blucher
W. Hansbrough 6/21/1838 Edmonia P. Nalle 8/27/1822 m. William Major 3/22/1842
Benjamin Johnston Nalle 4/4/1824
Jane S. Nalle 12/5/1825 m. Edward M. Clark 9/8/1847
Martin Nalle m. 2nd 12/13/1831 Elizabeth Mallory (no issue)

ARTHUR LANDON DAVIES' BIBLE
Owner: Mrs. L. L. Chapman, Smithfield, Va.

BIRTHS of Children of Arthur L. Davies and Elizabeth Whiting, his 1st wife

Ann Bowyer Clayton Davies 3/13/1797
Catherine Elizabeth Davies 11/4/1798
Emily Nicholss Davies 11/22/1800
William Henry Davies 11/6/1802
Walter Davies 4/13/1807
Alfred Boyle Davies 7/8/1804
Algernon Sidney Davies 1/24/1910
Lucy Elvira Davies 10/30/1819, dau. of Arthur L. Davies and his 2nd wife, Lucy Clayton

DEATHS

A dau. of Arthur L. Davies and Elizabeth Whiting, his 1st wife, not baptised, on 8/5/1803
Catherine E. Davies, dau. of same, 2/18/1813
Elizabeth Whiting Davies, 1st wife of Arthur t. Davies, and dau. of Christopher and Catherine Pryer, 4/18/1813
Lucy Elvira Davies, dau. of Arthur L. and Lucy C. Davies, his 2nd wife, 8/20/1822, aged 2 yrs, 9 mos., 20 days
Lucy Clayton Davies, 2nd wife of Arthur L. Davies, 10/19/1823, aged 47 yrs.
Arthur L. Davies 4/25/1840, aged 67 yrs., 6 mos., 9 days

MARRIAGES

Henry Landon Davies to Ann Clayton 1/15/1767

BIRTHS of THEIR CHILDREN:

Nicholas Clayton Davies 1769 m. Elizabeth Crawford
Arthur Landon Davies 1770 m. Miss Pryer
Catherine Elizabeth Davies 1772 m. Francis Thornton i'leriwether Samuel Boyle Davies 1774 m. Elizabeth McCulloch
Editha Davis 1777 m. Rev. Charles Clay Henry Ann Davies 1780-1843
Lybg m. Dr. John Jordan Cabell TamerlaLn Whiting Davies d.1843 m. James Smith Payne

REV. ANDREW TRIBBLE BIBLE

Frances T. Tribble b. 9/3/1769 m. Michael Stoner 9/30/1753-9/3/1814
Samuel Tribble b. 12/30/1771 Thomas Tribble b. 6/13/1776
Peter Tribble b. 10/8/1773 m. 10/8/1793 Polly Boone who d. 9/14/1831
Nancy Tribble b. 11/6/1778 m. 4/1794 David Chenault
Sally B. Tribble 2/9/1781-2/2/1810 m. 3/7/1799 David Crews
Silas Tribble 6/3/1783-11/18/18h2 m. 10/30/1809 Jerusha White

(Rev. Andrew Tribble Bible continued...)

Andrew Tribble b. 12/2/1785 m. 6/24/1810 Lucy Boone
Mary Tribble b. 3/29/1788 m. 12/23/1806 Joseph Stephenson; their son, James M. Stephenson, d. 9/1809
John Tribble (Gen.) b. 8/15/1790 m. 1st Martha White. Had several children. Martha d. 6/10/1850. Gen. Tribble m. 2nd Sally Coffee who d. 1/3/1865
Patsey Tribble b. 3/7/1794 m. 10/5/1812 Jacob White
Dudley Tribble b. 5/1/1797 m. 1/21/1819 Matilda H. Tevis (b. 1/10/1805), parents of James P. Tribble, Dudley Tribble (of Richmond, Ky., Robert G. Tribble, etc.

BIRTHS of Children of Sally Burrus (9/30/1753-12/15/1830)

Roger Burrus 4/18/1769 m. 1/14/1790 Cynthia Mills b. 9/19/1772

BIRTHS of Children of Roger and Cynthia Burrus

Nathaniel Burrus 1112011790 -
FrancesBurrus 9/8/1797
Mary Ann Burrus 5/30/1800
Henry Trandy Burrus 9/23/1793
Peggy Burrus 1/25/1794
Sally Ellen Burrus 11/14/1801

Roger Burrus 12/11/1795
Cynthia Mills Burrus b. 2/15/1805 m. 3/25/1824
Robert Ray (bro. of Gabriel Kay who m. Anna
Andy Mason, granddau. of Henry Tandy)

BIRTHS

Charles Mills Burrus 2/19/1807
Rebecca Massie Burrus 6/19/1814
Virginia Banks Burrus 5/26/1811
Cynthia Burrus d. 1/26/1853, aged 80 yrs.,

Celia Ann Burrus 6/20/1809
Mildred Thompson Burrus 2/13/1815
Roger Burrus Sr. d. 9/30/1826, aged 57 yrs., 5 mos. 12 days

JOHN C. PRYOR BIBLE

MARRIAGES

John C. Pryer to Betsy A. Tyler 7/18/1798
Betsy A. Pryer, dau. of John C. and Betsy A. Pryer, to Dr. John J. Semple 1/8/1824
John C. Pryer to Maria Smith Crawford 5/31/1827
Maria Emily Pryer, dau. of John C. and Betsy A. Pryer, to Alfred B. Davies 22-1934
Martha Christiana Pryer, dau. of John C. and Betsy A. Pryor, to George William Sample 2/1836

BIRTHS

John A. Pryor 6/9/1800 at Greenway
Mary Catherine Pryer 2/15/1802
Anne Countis Tyler Pryor 4/25/1803 in Gloucester
Betsy A. Pryer 10/18/1808 in Gloucester
Maria Emily Pryer 3/31/1813
Martha Chritiana Pryer 12/1611817 in Williamsburg
William Clayton Pryer 11/29/1820 in Williamsburg
Maria Elizabeth Semple, dau. of John T. and Betsy A. Semple, 12/13/1825 in Hampton
John C. Pryor, son of John C. and Maria S. Pryer, 5/19/1830 in Hampton
Skaife Whiting Pryer, son of John C. and Maria S. Pryer, 1/19/1830

DEATHS

Mary Anne Catharine Pryer 5/4/1802 John A. Pryer 8/11/1802
Anne Counti Tyler Pryer 11/1820, while on visit to her Uncle, Dr. Wat Tyler
Betsy P. Pryer 10/31/1824, aged 44
John C. Pryer, son of John C. and Maria S. Pryer, 10/4/1824

(John C. Pryer Bible, BIRTHS, contd....)

Mary Eliza Semple 8/1/1828 in Hanover
William C. Pryer 1/26/1833
Elizabeth Crawford, dau. of Maria S. Pryor by her 1st husband, 10/2/1836, aged 16 yrs.
Betsy A. Semple, wife of Dr. John 'i. Semple, at "Lombardy", in James City Co., 6/24/1840, aged 31
Maria S. Pryer, wife of John C. Pryer, 7/2/1840, aged 49 yrs.
Col. John C. Pryer 1/4/1846 in Hampton, aged 67 yrs.
Maria Emily Davies 3/2/1850, aged 37 yrs., wife of Alfred B. Davies, dau. of John C. Pryer
Harriet Anne Pryer, dau. of John C. and Maria S. Pryer, at her uncle's, Robert Armistead, on 7/27/1853, aged 22 yrs.

BIRTHS of Children of Alfred B. Davies

Arthur Pryer Davies 11/28/1834
Christiana Elizabeth Davies 9/20/1836
William Henry Davies 8/12/1838
Emily Landon Davies 3/13/1842
Alfred B. Davies 4/9/1846

Account written 8/30/1860 by Mrs. Maria Edwards, dau. of John B. Seawell and Maria Henry Tyler, dau. of Judge John Tyler:

"Elizabeth Armi s tead Tyler (dau. of Judge John Tyler) m. .Tohn Clayton Pryor of Gloucester, d. 1824. Her children were: Anne Contesse who died lamented by all at 17, unmarried.

Elizabeth Armistead married to her cousin john T. Semple, Marfa Emily married her cousin Alfred B. Davies of Gloucester, William, who died young, and Christiana who married Judge Semple's son by second marriage, Dr. George William Semple, of Hampton."

MATTHEW FONTAINE MALTRY BIBLE
Recollections of a Virginian By Gen. Dabney H. Maury, P. 179

"In 1860 this Bible was taken to England when grandfather went to see about the copyrights of his new edition of the Physical Geography of the Sea.

In Sept. 1862 he was ordered to England by the Confederate Government on a 'special service'. It was then that his 'Sweet Molly' lent him the Bible which he had used in 1860 and had given to her.

In April 1863 he learned of the disappearance of his son, John, at Vicksburg. In May 1865 he was returning with his young son, Matthew, Jr., who sailed with his father from
Charleston, S. C. to England in 1862."

Notes of the inside cover:

M. F. Maury Bowden, Esq., Sunday, 10 April 1863

"My Bible bought for this trip to England in the Bossange LLbraire, New York from New York 27 October 1860.

"Sailed from New York 27 Oct. 1860, arrived in Plymouth 13 Nov. 1860"

"Wortley Hall Eng. 8 April 1863. Before rising this morning reed a letter 28 Feb. from Richmond saying my brave and noble boy, John H., a charming youth of 20 had been missing from his post since 27 January. He was Lt. on the staff of Major General D. H. Maury in the West. He was beloved by all who knew him. Mostly lovely in character and comely too, he was very previous to the hearts of his parents."

(Matthew Fontaine Maury Bible, contd.....)

"My precious boy, Lt. John H. Maury, C. Army, was b. Fredericksburg, Va., 10/21/1842. He was a good son.
"England, 1863....The pencil underscoring in this Bible are my Father's. Mary M. Werth."
M. F. Maury at sea 11/4/1860
"My sweet Molly lent me this in Sept. 1862. Shall I see her sweet face again? Let us hope.
1865."

HENRY LEWIS' BIBLE of Brunswick County
Owner: Henry W. Lewis
address unknown

BIRTHS

Charles Stuart Lewis 1/1/1818
Ashton Lewis 9/27/1823
Louisa Gray Lewis 9/30/1819
Richard Edwin Lewis 4/22/1827
Henry Lewis 5/29/1821

Note: These BIRTHS of younger children are from the Plantation Cemetery, Woodstock, Brunswick Co., Va.:

Benjamin Lewis 6/30/1829
James Edmund Lewis 5/26/1834
Joseph Warner Lewis 5/18/1833
Note: Dr. Henry Lewis m. Frances Gibbons Stuart

THOMAS JEFFERSON BIBLE
Of Henrico County

"This Bible is owned by Thomas Jefferson of Henrico County, Va. and prior to him ownership of Thomas Jefferson, son of John Jefferson, the emigrant, 1612."

BIRTHS of Children of Thomas and Mary Jefferson

Judith Jefferson 8/30/1698
Feild Jefferson 3/16/1702
Thomas Jefferson 9/24/1700

DEATHS

The soul of my dear bro., Thomas Jefferson, 2/14/1723, he being in
voyage on board "The Williamsburg", Capt. Isham Randolph, Cammander to Virginia
The soul of my dear father, Thomas Jefferson, 2/18/1735, 53 yrs. he soul Of my dear wife, Mary
Frances Jefferson 2/26/1750, aged 44 yrs. /s/ Feild Jefferson
The soul of my dear father, Feild Jefferson, 2/10/1765, 62 yrs. The soul of my dear bro.,

Thomas Jefferson, 12/5/1783 /s/ P.F.J. The soul of my dear father 1/1/1794

The soul of my dear mother 5/7/1828 /s/S.A.J.

The soul of Thomas Jefferson 2/14/1814
The soulof William Allan Jefferson 8/19/1814
The soul of Elizabeth Jefferson 10/19/1814

BIRTHS

Peter Jefferson 2/29/1707
Peter Feild, son of Feild and Mary Frances Jefferson, 3/14/1735 Elizabeth, wife of Peter Feild
Jefferson and dau. of Samuel Allan and wife, Martha Allan, 12/7/1739

(Thomas Jefferson Bible, contd.....)

Peterfeild Jefferson m. Elizabeth Allan 5/30/1762

BIRTHS of Children of Peterfeild and Elizabeth Jefferson

Feild Jefferson 4/1/1763
Frances Jefferson 1/11/1772
Wm Allan Jefferson 12/14/1764
Judith Jefferson 1/7/1774
Archer Jefferson 5/4/1766
Samuel Allan Jefferson 3/24/1776
Thomas Jefferson 3/21/1768
Alexander Jefferson 7/31/1779
John Jefferson 2/23/1770
Elizabeth Jefferson 9/2/1785
Martha Feild Jefferson 4/7/1781

MARRIAGES

Sanuel Allan Jefferson to Betsy Ann Jefferson 6/20/1803
John Jefferson, son of Feild Jefferson and Mary Frances, to Elizabeth Broome, dau. of Dr. Thomas Broome of London, England, 3/28/1763 by Rev. Robert McClawson

Samuel Jefferson, son of Peterfeild Jefferson and his 1st cousin, Elizabeth Ann Jefferson, dau. of John R. Jefferson and wife, Elizabeth Broome, 6/20/1803

James Hopkins Jefferson, son of Samuel A. Jefferson, b. 10/30/1819 and m. his mother's great-niece, Kittle Jefferson, dau. of John Pinkard Jefferson and S. F. S. Brown-Jefferson and who was a great-granddau. of John Jefferson and wife, Elizabeth Broome Jefferson and J. H. J. and Kittle J. were m. 11/27/1858

JAMES GORDON BIBLE o Lancaster County
Owner: J. Newton Gordon Lynchburg, Virginia

James Gordon m. 3/28/1742 Miss Millicent Conway, youngest dau. of Col. Edwin Conway of this county
Ann Gordon b. 3/29/1743
We had a son b. 4/15/1745-d. 18th.
Ann Conway, wife of Col. Edwin Conway and dau. of Col. Hack of Northumberl?nd Co.-d. 8/28/1747, aged 50 yrs. old
Agatha Gordon 10/19/1746-9/8/1747
Sarah Gordon 12/10/1747-
My dear wife d. 2/2/1747/8, aged 20 yrs.

I was married 11/12/1748 at Col. Arm1stead Churchill's to Miss Mary Harrison, youngest dau. of Hon. Nathaniel Harrison of Surry County

BIRTHS

James Gordon 8/2/1750 at Col. Arm1stead Churchill's Mary Gordon 7/17/1752
Hannah Gordon 1/29/1754-13/18.1757 Elinor Gordon 11/27/1755-7/17/1756
John Gordon 4/11/1757-8/17/1757
My dear child Sally d. 6/7/1758, aged 11 yrs. Elizabeth Gordon 8/6/1758
My dau., Ann, m. 6/9/1759 to Richard Chichester of this county We had a dead dau. b. 9/9/1760
Sarah Gordon 5/6/1762-8/5/1762
Nathaniel Gordon 8/28/1763-
Col. Edwin Conway d. 10/3/1763, aged 82 yrs. Millicent Chichester b. 3/13/1765

(James Gordon Bible, contd....)

My dear dau., Chichester, d. 4/20/1766, aged 23 yrs.
John Gordon b. 10/9/1765
Col. James Gordon d. 1/2/1768, aged 54 yrs.
Mrs. Mary Gordon d. 5/13/1771
James Gordon, son of above James and Mary, m. 6/30/1774 to Miss Ann Payne, dau. of Col. John Payne of Goochland County

BIRTHS

Mary Smith Gordon 9/17/1776
Ann Smith Gordon 7/26/1786
James Harrison Gordon 6/18/1779
Janetta Gordon 4/4/1793
Addison Gordon 2/14/1789
John Matthews Gordon 3/25/1781
Samuel Baldwin Gordon 7/23/1784
My dear little Samuel Baldwin d. 10/29th
Addison, 3 yrs, old, d. 9/15/1792
Mary Smith Gordon m. 6/6/1793
Nathaniel Waddel, 2nd son of Rev. Mr. James Waddel, by
Rev. Mr. Levis Lunceford
Janetta Gordon d. 8/28/1794, 16 mos., 24 days old
My dear bro., Col. James Gordon, d. 9/29/1794, aged 45 yrs.
My very dear dau., Mary Smith Waddel, d. aged 20 yrs, 3/10/1746 at Rev. Mr. James Waddell's home in Louisa Co., Va.
Ann Gordon, wife of above Col. James Gordon, 10/7/1758-3/16/1798
John M. Gordon m. 12/15/1804 Agnes Scott, dau. of Major Samuel Scott of Campbell

Family of John M. Gordon

John M. Gordon b. 3/25/1781 –
Agnes W. Scott b. 2/25/1787
Agnes W. Scott 2/25/1787
John M. Gordon, the 2nd son of Col. James Gordon and Agnes W. Scott, 2nd dau. of Haj. Samuel Scott, m. 12/16/1804 by Rev. William P. Martin at Major Scott's in Campbell.

BIRTHS of Children of John M. and Agnes W. Gordon

Ann Belinda JamesGordon 11/10/1805 Louisa Payne Gordon 9/28/1808
Martha Jane Gordon 1/1/1811 James Beverly Gordon 7/11/1815-12/10/1811
Agnes Maria Gordon 4/17/1816 Caroline Scott Gordon 7/16/1817
Samuel Gordon 12/9/1820 John Calvin Gordon 4/8/1823
James Newton Gordon 5/19/1825 We had a son b. 4/28/1828-d. same night

MARRIAGES

Louisa Payne (afterwards called Maria Louisa) Gordon, 2/11/1829 to Elias Ogden of Abingdon, by Rev. William S. Reid
Ann B. Gordon to Hugh White of Abingdon 10/12/1835, by Rev. Jacob O. Mitchell at our residence in Lynchburg
John M. Gordon, our dear father, d. 5/16/1840, aged 60 yrs.
Agnes Maria Gordon d. 4/29/1851
Ann B. White, wife of Hugh White, Esq. (of Liberty), d. 8/7/1851...leaving a husband and five little children....
James Newton Gordon m. Edwina Gordon Moon of Halifax Co. 5/22/1851 by Rev. John Scott of the Presbyterian Church
Samuel Sordon m. Miss ---- of Texas in 1549. His wife died short time afterwards in Oregon
Caroline Scott Gordon d. 7/8/1870 at Campbell Court House, aged 53 yrs. She was member of the Second Presbyterian Church of Lynchburg

(James Gordon Bible, contd....)

Hugh White d. 5/25/1872 at Warm Springs in N. C., member of Presbyterian Church, aged about 70

Eliza Ogden d. 10/11/1874 at Osher Point, La. For many years he was a ruling elder in the Presbyterian Church at Abingdon, Virginia. His age was 78 yrs.

Marissa Jane Gordon d. 11/8/1875, aged 65 yrs., at res. of her bro., John M. Gordon in City of Lynchburg.

James Newton Gordon d. at 1023 Jackson St., Lynchburg, Va., 4/15/1888, bur. in Presbyterian Church at Lynchburg.

The following were his children: the 1st was b. d. 6/1852, Armistead,
Imogene Stanard b. 1/28/1856, Mary Elizabeth, John Newton 8/14/1859 10/30/1898 at his home in Barton Heights, Richmond, Va.; Rate Blanks b. 6/26/1864 and Elvira Moon b. 8/2/1868. All b. Lynchburg, Va. Imogene Stanard m. William Minnegerode, son of Rev. Dr. Charles Minnegerode (Rector of St. Paul's Church, Richmond, Va.),

John Newton m. Ida Bowers (dau. of A. J. Bowers of Richmond, Va. 11/16/1887.

Kate Blanks m. Dr. William S. Gordon, son of James Gordon of Richmond, Va., on 10/16/1890.

Elvira Moon m. Alfred Randolph Carrington, son of Col. Henry Alexander Carrington of Charlotte Co., Va., 12/15/1891)

BIRTHS of Children of John Newton and Ida B. Gordon

Kathleen Gordon 4/4/1890
John Newton Gordon 7/19/1891
Alexander Terrell Gordon 7/26/1893

John Newton Gordon, father of above children, d. after lingering illness....was a Deacon formerly in Westminster Presbyterian of Lynchburg and latterly of Grace Street Presbyterian Church of Richmond, Va. Funeral services conducted by Rev. Dr. Jere Witherspoon and Rev. Mr. Christman (Episcopal Minister in Barton Heights) in Grace St. Church 10/31/1898, interment in Hollywood in A. J. Bower's section.

Loose Papers inside Bible: Our Line from Rob Roy
Roy Roy McGregor
Agnes McGregor
Thomas Roy
John Beverly Roy m. Ann Waller
Ann Roy, his dau., m. Major Samuel Scott after the American Revolution

THEIR CHILDREN: were:

Belinda Roy, Agnes Waller, Aphira Beverly, Emily Williams,
Beverly Roy, Samuel McGregor and Marion Stanard
Belinda m. James Moseley
Agnes m. John Mathews Gordon Aphira m. William Rose
Emily m. Patrick Philip Barton Beverly m. Almira Anderson
Samuel m. Camilla Payne
Marion m. William Cobb

DASEY SOUTHALL BIBLE
Owner: W. R. Shelton Atlee's, Hanover Co., Va.

Dasey Southall m. Edith 1/26/1720-1/2

BIRTHS of THEIR CHILDREN:

Stephen Southall 11/17/1722-
William Southall 3/16/1732-3
Philip Southall 7/10/1726
Turner Southall 7/25/1736
James Barret Southall 10/20/1726
Philip Southall, son of Dasey and Edith, d. 12/12/1759
Dasey Southall d. 6/28/1767
Turner Southall d. 4/27/1791, aged 55 yrs., 8 mos.
Callam Jones d. 3/20/1808, aged 40 yrs.
Turner Southall m. Martha 2/3/1756

BIRTHS of Children of Turner and Martha Southall

Stephen Southall 6/16/1757
William Southall 1/4/1759-10/13/1759
Ann Southall 11/2/1760
William Southall 4/27/1765
Philip Southall 5/5/1763
Pleasant Southall 7/27/1767

Polina (Pauline?) Southall 5/20/1769
James Barrett Southall 9/27/1772
Cynthia Southall 4/12/1777
John Southall 12/12/1777
John Southall 12/12/1777
Elizabeth Southall 6/19/1779

Martha Southall, wife of Turner Southall, d. 3/3/1781
Edith Southall d. 1/20/1782, aged 92 yrs.
Philip Southall, son of Turner, d. 10/27/1790, aged 27 yrs, 6 mos. Turner Southall d. 4/27/1791, aged 55 yrs, 8 mos.
Stephen Southall, son of Turner, d. in Richmond, 3/12/1799
--- Jones d. 10/14/1819, aged 31 yrs.
Ann Southall, dau. of Turner Southall, m. 1st John Shelton, m. 2nd, Capt. Peter Foster, and d. 6/8/1830
Martha Wood, wife of Stephen Southall, b. 3/12/1768
Philip Turner, son of Stephen Southall and Martha Wood, his wife, b. 4/12/1791 in Goochland
Frances Wilson Southall, wife of Philip Turner Southall, b. 11/10/1801 in Prince Edward Co., Va.

BIRTHS of Children of Philip Turner Southall and Frances Stephen Osborne

Southall 12/16/1816, Prince Edward Co., Va.
Philip Francis Southall 4/6/1822
William Valentine Southall 9/1820-9/1821

BIRTHS of Children of Philip Turner Southall and Elizabeth Anthony

Webster Southall 5/5/1827 Lucy Henry Southall 6/12/1830
Joseph Wells Southall 6/12/1833 Giles M. Southall 7/18/1835
Frank W. Southall 6/1/1837 Valentine Wood Southall 10/9/1839
John Turner Southall 12/30/1841, Amelia Co. William Wood Southall 10/9/1844, Amelia Co.
Edward Henry Southall 5/13/1848
Stephen Southall, son of Col. Turner Southall of Fairfield, Henrico, and father of Philip Turner Southall, d. at Richmond 3/2/1799
Martha, mother of Philip Turner Southall, d. Washington, D. C., 9/30/1834
Frances W. Southall, wife of Philip Turner Southall, d. 7/22/1833 in Prince Edward Co., Va.
Osborne Lockett, father of Frances W. Southall (1st) wife of Philip Turner Southall, b. Amelia Co., Va. 5/19/1769-d. 10/11/1836 Prince Edward Co., Va.

(Dasey Southall Bible, contd,...)

Anthony Webster, father of Elizabeth (2nd) wife of Philip Turner Southall, b. 6/1/1770-d. suddenly 12/20/1836 Philip Turner Southall m. Frances W. Lockett 11/10/1815 Philip Turner Southall m. Elizabeth Webster 11/18/1824

BIRTHS

William Goode 10/25/1761
Robert Goode, son of above, 9/21/1789
Mary H. Loper, wife of above, 9/15/1801
LouLsa Goode, dau. of above, 2/21/1819
Eliza Jane Goode dau. of above, 5/17/1821 Barnwell D1strict, South Carolina

BIRTHS of Children of Philip Turner Southall and Eliza Philip

Francis Southall 5/29/1849
Philip Turner Southall 5/18/1851 Robert Goode Southall 12/26/1852
Stephen Osborne Southall 5/15/1858 Mary Eliza Southall 11/10/1860

MARRIAGES

Robert Goode to Mary H. Loper 1/30/1817
John R. Woodridge to Louisa Goode 10/18/1839
Philip Francis Southall to Eliza Jane Goode 12/16/1845 Robert Goode to Martha Childress 11/21/1833

RALEIGH CARTER BIBLE
Owner: Mrs. Ellen H. Abbott

BIRTHS of Children of Thomas and Sarah Carter

Judith Carter 7/6/1735
Millicent Carter 8/9/1743
Raleigh Carter 1/1/1737
George Carter 10/4/1745
Lucy Carter 2/22/1739
Sarah Carter 11/25/1748
William Carter 5/27/1741
Leanna Carter -/26/1751
Alcy (Alice) Carter, dau. of Thomas and Ann Carter, b. 6/26/1753.
Thomas Griggs b. 10/11/1746 and m. Alcy Carter 10/8/1772

SARAH TAYLOE WASHINGTON BIBLE
Owner: Mrs. Susan Latane Oak Grove, Virginia (1932)

Inside cover: Sarah Tayloe, 1786

BIRTHS of Children of Hen. George Plater, Esq. of Maryland

Rebecca Plater 8/8/1731
Anne Plater 10/31/1732
George Plater 11/8/1735-2/10/1742?
Elizabeth Plater 8/7/1742-d.---

BIRTHS of Children of John and Elizabeth Tayloe

William Tayloe 7/8/1716-5/8/1726
John Tayloe 5/28/1721, and Betty Tayloe, 1/2 hr. later, twlns
Anne Corbin Tayloe 8/25/1728
John Tayloe m. Rebecca, dau. of Hon. George Plater, Esq. of Maryland, 7/11/1747 and d. 4/28/1779, and his lady 1/22/1787

(Sarah Tayloe Washington Bible, contd....)

Elizabeth, dau. of John Tayloe and Rebecca, b. 1/17/1752 and m. Francis Lightfoot Lee, Esq. 5/25/1769. She d. 1/7/1797 and Col. Lee 1/17/1797

Anne Corbin (Tayloe) b. 7/7/1753 and m. Thomas Lomax, Esq. 5/25/1773. He d. Mary Tayloe 5/1/1775-10/16/1755

Eleanor Tayloe b. 10/16/1756 m. Ralph Wormley, Esq. 11/19/1772. He d. 1/19/1806. Mrs. Wormley d. 2/23/1815

Mary Tayloe b. 10/28/1759 m. Mann Page, Esq. 4/18/1776. He d. 3/22/1803

William Augustine Washington m. Sarah Tayloe 5/11/1799
Sarah Tayloe Washington, dau. of above, b. 4/14/1800, her sponsors were: Ralph Wormley, John Tayloe, Bickwith Butler, Mrs. Eleanor Wormley, Mrs. Fitzhugh, Mrs. Tayloe, Mrs. Elizabeth Spotswood and Miss Anne Aylett Washington

4/12/1803 Mrs. Washington was delivered a son who lived only a few hours

William Augustine Washington, son of William Augustine and Sarah Tayloe Washington, b. 8/30/1804. His sponsors were: Rev. Mr. Davis, Charles Wayman, Bushrod Washington, Churchill Blackburn, Miss Marian M. Page, Catherine Lomar and Miss Charlotte Thornton
Ann Aylet Robinson, dau. of William Aug. Washington and Jane, his 1st wife, d. 9/12/1804
Mrs. Elizabeth Spotswood d. 10/20/1814 Gen. Alexander Spotswood d. 12/20/1818

William Augustine Washington m. Juliet Elizabeth, dau. of Samuel Bayard, dau. of Samuel Bayard, Esq. of New Jersey, 10/7/1823. 6/26/1830 he d. st Haywood, Virginia

Juliet Elizabeth b. 3/4/1806

Their 1st child b. at Samuel H. Smith's near Washington City 7/28/1824 and lived only two days
Martha Washington b. 1/2/1826, baptised 9/3/1826. Her sponsors: Hen. Bushrod Washington, Needham L. Washington, Daniel Carmichael, Samuel J. BSrard, Benjamin F. Stuart, Mrs. Susan V. Bradford, Miss Caroline S. Bayard:-she d. 2/21/1828, aged 2 yrs, 1 mo., 20 days

William Augustine Washington b. 9/1/1830 at Princeton, New Jersey, baptised by Rev. Mr. Lewis P. Bayard

Sarah Washington d. at Princeton, new Jersey 9/3/1834, aged 70

Julia Augusta Washington m. 11/19/1855 to Dabney C. Wirt and d. 4/24/1888. She was bur. At Haywood 4/30/1888
Julie E. Washington d. at Campbellton 12/16/1865, aged 59 yrs., 8 mos., 12 days, bur. At Haywood 12/22/1865

BIRTHS

William Augt. Washington 11/25/1757
Jane Washington, his wife, 6/20/1759 m. 9/25/1777 Hannah Bushrod Washington 8/7/1778-5/1797 Augustine Washington 6/15/1783-2/9/1798
Ann Aylett Washington 2/11/1783-9/12/1804

Mrs. Ann 4. Robinson, aged 21 yrs., d. at house of Dr. Rose in Alexandria on llth inst., the amiable consort of William Robinson of Westmoreland....
Bushrod Washington b. 4/4/1785 m. 8/1806 Miss Henrietta Spotswood

(Sarah Tayloe Washington Bible, contd....)

Corbin Aylett Washington 5/11/1787-11/1788
George Corbin Washington b. 8/20/1789 m. 9/1/1807 Miss Eliza R. Beall of George Town.

Mrs. Jane Washington d. at Sweet Springs 8/16/17.91
William Augustine Washington m. Mary Lee, his 2nd wife, 7/10/1792 Mary Lee 7/28/1764-11/2/1795, aged 30 yrs, 3 mos., 25 days William Aug. Washington m. Sarah Tayloe, his 3rd wife, 5/11/1799
Sarah Tayloe, his wife, b. 3/5/1765
Sarah Tayloe Washington, his 1st child, b. 4/14/1800 William Augt. Washington Jr. b. 5/30/1804

Colonel William Augt. Washington 11/25/1757-10/2/1810, aged 53 yrs. His remains deposited in vault at Mount Vernon near those of his illustrious relative and amiable daughter on 10/4/1810

Mann Page, Esq. d. 22nd inst. at his seat, Mannsfield, aged 51 yrs. after a long and painful illness....(1803)
Betty d. 5/13/1784, aged 63
Ann C. Tayloe d. 9/17/1784, aged 56
Catherine Tayloe 10/10/1761-12/22/1789 m. Landon Carter, Esq. 2/5/1780. he d. 8/30/1820
Sarah Tayloe b. 3/5/1765 m. William Augt. Washington, Esq. 5/11/1799. He d. 10/2/1810
John Tayloe b. 9/3/1771, youngest of twins, m. Miss Ann Ogle of Maryland 10/4/1792
Jane Tayloe 3/25/1774-5/10/1816 m. Robert Beverly, Esq. 5/26/1791.

MARRIAGES

Lawrence and Sarah Tayloe Washington at Haywood, Va. 10/26/1819 Henry A. Washington and Cynthia Beverly Tucker 7/8/1852 at Williamsburg, Virginia
John T. Washington to Mary Ashton 6/10/1850, Washington City George Washington (3rd son of Sarah and Lawrence) to Sally Massie 12/1/1852 in Warrenton
Betty Washington and John E. Wilson 10/22/1850
Mary W. Washington and Walker Washington 12/29/1856
Richard Washington and Ellen Carter 6/28/1859 in St. Lukes Church at Hartings, Minnesota
William A. Washington and Sallie A. James 9/19/1860 at old Florence, S. C.

BIRTHS

Lawrence Washington 2/26/1791
Sarah Tayloe Washington 4/14/1800

BIRTHS of THEIR CHILDREN:

Henry Augustine Washington 8/24/1820
John Tayloe Washington 12/20/1822 George
Washington 7/24/1825
Richard Washington 6/21/1827
Mary West Washington 10/13/1828
Sarah Ashton Washington 8/17/1831
William Augustine
Washington 3/5/1838
Lawrence Washington 5/1/1839
Elizabeth Washington 11/23/1838
Robert James Washington 9/16/1841
Lloyd Washington 11/2/1846

(Sarah Tayloe Washington Bible, contd....)

DEATHS

Sarah Ashton Washington 1/2/1832, aged 4 mos., 14 days
Henry Augustine Washington 2/28/1858, son of Lawrence and Sarah T. Washington, aged 38 yrs., in City of Washington, by accidental discharge of an air-gun
Sarah Tayloe Washington, dau. of John T. and Mary, 4/5/1857
Orlando Fairfax, son of George and Sally Fairfax, 10/21/1858
Lucy B. Washington, dau. of Henry and Cynthia Washington, b. 7/22/1854 and lived only 8 days
Sarah Augustine Washington, 2nd dau. of Henry and Cynthia, 12/26/1856-10/1/1862

BIRTHS of Children of John Tayloe and Mary Washington

Sallie Tayloe Washington 8/9/1852
Mary Ashton Washington 6/14/1858

BIRTHS of Children of George and Sally Washington

Orlando Fairfax Washington 11l/18/1853
Henry Augustine Washington 10/1856
Effy Washington 12/17/1858-12/24/1858, having lived 7 days
Susan, dau. of Betty and John E. Wilson, b. 9/9/1957
Lawrence Augustine, son of Mary W. and Walker Washington, b. 11/9/1857
Henrietta Washington, dau. of John and Betty Washington Wilson b. 3/20/1859
Lawrence Gibson, son of Richard and Ellen Washington. b. 6/2/1860 at Hartings, Minnesota
George W. b. 5/1862; a dau. d. 8/5/1862

BIRTHS

Lawrence Washington 2/26/1791 Sarah Tayloe Washington 4/14/1800
Lawrence and Sarah m. 10/26/1819. They had ten children:

Henry Augustine Washington b. 8/24/1820 m. 7/8/1852 Cynthia B. Tucker. They had two children, both died infants

John Tayloe Washington b. 12/20/1822 m. 6/10/1850 Mary D. Ashton. They had four children: Sarah T. 5/4/1857-4/5/185-; John b. 8/7/1852; Mary A. b. 6/1858; and Richard Henry b. 3/22/1862.

George b. 7/24/1825 m. 1st 12/1852 Sally Massie. They had 5 children: Orlando T. 11/18/1853-d. --- ; Henry Augt. b. 10/1857; Effie d. infant; George b. 5/1861 and Edgar C. b. 1867

Richard b. 6/21/1827 m. Ellen Center 6/28/1857. Had two children: Lawrence Gibson b. 62/1860 and Mary W. b. 8/5/1862

Mary W. Washington b. 8/13/1928 m. Walker Washington 12/17/1856. They had 5 children: Lawrence Augustine b. 11/1857; Walker b. 11/1860; Richard b. 1862; two dau s. d. infants;

William Augustine b. 3/4/1833 m. Sally A. James 9/19/1860. They had two daus., Julia and Leasy?, /s/ William Ethel Claire Lawrence b. 5/1/1836-single

Elizabeth b. 11/23/1838 m. John E. Wilson 10/22/1856. They had 6 children: Susan b. 9/9/1857; Henrietta b.3/26/1859; John F. b. 8/1860; William b. 2/1862; Lawrence W. b. 5/1966; Sarah T. b. 11/1867-d. following June Robert J. b. 9/16/1341 - 10/1867 Bettie P. Wirt. They had one child: Selma b. 4/16/1570 Lloyd b. 11/2/1844-single

(Sarah Tayloe Washington Bible, contd....)

DEATHS

Henry A. 2/28/1858   John T. 5/18/1864   Richard 6/6/1853

Note: This record made by Law. Washington, Sr. and continued by his dau., Betty Washington Wilson, 3/1892

William Augustine Washington d. 9/4/1889 San Diego, California, bur. Stockton California 9/6th.
George Washington d. 1869, Alexandria, Va.

Lawrence Washington Dr. d. at Wakefield, the res. of J. E. and Betty (Washington) Wilson 3/15/1875, bur. Campbellton 3/17th

Sarah Tayloe Washington d. at Wakefield 12/20/1886, bur. at Campbellton 12/22/1886

ROBERT TUCKER BIBLE of Norfolk County
Owner: Miss Otelia Harvie Mattoax, Virginia

Robert Tucker m. Joanna Corbin, dau. of Gawin and Martha Corbin in King and Queen Co., Va., 5/17/1739 by Rev. Mr. William Phillips

BIRTHS of THEIR CHILDREN:

FrancesTucker 4/6l1740, baptised 5/17th-d. 21st of sd month

Robert Tucker 9/14/1741, baptised 7 days after by Rev. Mr. Moses Robinson. Godfathers: Robert Dinwiddie, Esq., Edward Hack Moseley and Godmothers were: Mrs. Eliza and Susan Thurston

Martha Tucker 2/9/1742/3, baptised 8th after by Rev. Mr. Charles Smith. Godfathers and Godmothers were: Edward Hack Moseley, Samuel Boush, Jr., Mrs. Frances Phripp and Margret Walker

Joanna Tucker 4/12/1774, baptised 16th of said month by Rev. Mr. Charles Smith. Godfathers: Capt. William Gordon of his Majesty's Sloop Hound (by proxy) and John Tucker. Godmothers: Mrs. Frances Nelson and Mary Moseley. Died young.

John Tucker 12/29/1745, baptised 1/17th by Rev. Mr. Charles Smith. Godfathers: John Tucker and Capt. Policarpus Taylor. Godmother: Mrs. Mary Moseley. Died 7/1/1746.

Sarah Tucker 10/13/1747, baptised day after by Rev. Mr. Charles SmFth. Godfather: Edward Hack Moseley. Godmothers: Mrs. Frances Nelson and Chrlstian Loyde. (She m. John Taylor whose only dau. m. James Heron of Richmond)

Mary Tucker 1/2/1748/9, baptised 2/30th by Rev. Mr. Charles Smith. Godfather: Mr. Moseley. Godmother: Mrs. Moseley
Martha Tucker 1/11/1750/51, baptised same mo. by Rev. Mr. Charles Smith. Godfsther: Edward Hack Moseley. Godmothers: Mrs. Moseley and Mrs. Perkins.

Frances Tucker 3/21/1751/52, baptised 30th of same month by Rev. Mr. Charles Smith. Godfathers: Edward Hack Moseley and Christopher Perkins. Godmothers: Mrs. Moseley and Mrs. Perkins.

Elizabeth Tucker 5/4/1753, baptised 11th of same month by Rev. Mr. Charles Smith. Godfathers: Edward Hack Moseley and Francis Farley, Esq. Godmothers: Mrs. Moseley and Mrs. Hansford. Elizabeth d. 7/4/1754.

(Robert Tucker Bible, contd....)

Gawin Corbin Tucker 1/31/1755, baptised 20th of Feb. by Rev. Charles Smith.
Godfathers; John Norton and Col. Gawin Corbin.
Godmothers; Mrs. Nelson and Miss Sarah Smith.

Courtney Tucker 4/30/1756, baptised by Rev. Mr. Charles Smith.
Godfathers: Capts. Mariot
Arbuthnot and Charles Stuart.
Godmothers; Mrs. Courtney Norton and Joanna Tucker.

Ann Tucker 8/27/1757, baptised by Rev. Mr. Charles Smith.
Godfather: Dr. Archibald Campbell.
Godmothers: Mrs. Mary Streep and Joanna Tucker, Jr.

John Tucker 1/16/1759, baptised by Rev. Mr. Charles Smith 2/11th. Godfathers; Godfrey Malbone and John Tucker. Godmothers: Mrs. Malbone and Mrs. Frances Nelson.

Alice Tucker 5/15/1760-7/21/1761

John Pulman Tucker 1/18/1762, baptised --- 1762. He d. 7/22/1762.

Richard Tucker 7/20/1763, baptised by Rev. Thomas Davis.
Godfathers: Dr. John Ramsey and Robert Tucker, Jr. Godmother: Sarah Tucker.
He died some few hours after his birth.

Carolina Henrietta Tucker 3/16/1765, baptised 6/1st by Rev. Mr. James Pasteur.
Godfathers: Thomas Newton and Robert Tucker, Jr.
Godmothers: Mrs. Carolina Henrietta Bedford, in Barbadoes, by proxy, and Mrs. Sarah.

"The above is the family record of Colonel Robert Tucker of Norfolk who was the grandfather of Mrs. John G. Blair's mother.

It is copied from the original in the hand-writing of Colonel Tucker - for Mrs. Harvie his great-great-grand-daughter.

Norfolk, July 31, 1858. /s/ Tazewell Taylor."

COLONEL WILLIAM EDMONDS BIBLE
Of Fauquier County
Owner: Emma B. Belt

William Edmonds m. Elizabeth Blackwell 3/17/1764 by Rev. James Craig

BIRTHS

William Edmonds, Jr. 5/10/1765; James Bell, Franke Bell and Hannah Blackwell, godfathers and godmothers

Franke Edmonds 8/1/1766; Samuel Blackwell, James Blackwell, Anne Pickett and Anne Edmonds, godfathers and godmothers

Sarah Edmonds 10/4/1767; Sarah Blackwell and Rev. James Craig, godfather and godmother. Died 12/17/1828

Elias Edmonds 11/10/1768; Elias Edmonds, Jr., Bennitt Price, Mrs. Billy Edmonds and Judith Price, godfathers and godmothers. Died

Mary Edmonds 4/17/1770; Col. William Blackwell, Joseph Fantleroy, Mrs. Elizabeth Blackwell and Judith Edmonds, godfathers and godmothers. Died 6/1887

Elizabeth Edmonds 6/2/1771; Francis Attswell, Thomas Keith, Judith Hubbard and Betty Edmonds, godfathers and godmothers. Died 4/16/1778

Betty Edmonds 2/20/1778; Hancock Lee, Joseph Blackwell, Elizabeth Hewitt, Susannah Yates, godfathers and godmothers

John Edmonds 6/6/1775; John Blackwell, son of Joseph, George Pickett, Miss Betty Edmonds and Frankey Edmonds, godfathers and godmothers

Lucy Edmonds 5/10/1777; John Barker, godfather, Elizabeth, her mother, godmother

James Edmonds 2/16/1778; William Ed. and Elizabeth, father and mother to the above, godmother and godfather

Catey Edmonds 2/20/1781; William Edmonds, Jr., godfather, nancy Taylor and Elizabeth Taylor, godmothers

Judith Edmonds 12/28/1783; Robert Green, godfather

Susannah Ellza Green 1/9/1789

Robert Green 2/28/1790

---The above were the two oldest grandchildren of William Edmonds, whose oldest dau., Frankey, m. her cousin, R. Green (Note by grandson, Gust. R. B. Horner, Surg. U.S.N. 2/27/1848)--

Names of servants of William Edmonds of Fauquier Co., Va

Manuel
Dick
Hannah James
Anthony
Myma Daniel
Franke
Dinah Harry
Cati
Agga
Toney
Jane
Grace
Sam
Willey
William Ben Ben
Phillis
Abram Phill
Fanny

CATHERINE WEST BIBLE
Owner: Mrs. Tabitha Joynes Hance
Baltimore, Maryland

DEATHS

Lt. Col. John West 5/27/1703
Mrs. Matilda West 1/3/1721

BIRTHS

John Snead 1/7/1707
Thomas Snead 12/21/1708
Charles Snead m. Catharine 1/7/1711

BIRTHS of Children of Charles and Catharine Snead

Huldah Snead 3/1/1712/13, christianed the 15th-d. 4/30/1713
Charles Snead 8/26/1714-2/18/1720
John Snead 2/3/1715, chrIstianed 3/18th
Smith Snead 1/13/1718
Charles Snead, the 2nd, 11/13/1723-2/23/1724
Capt. Charles Snead, the Elder, d. 4/30/1727
Catharine Snead d. 2/19/1750

BIRTHS of Children of John Snead, Accomack

Charles Snead 12/26/1741
Thomas Snead 11/28/1752
John Snead 3/10/1743-3/23/1777
Scarborough Snead 11/23/1758

Catharine Snead 7/25/1756
Anne Snead 9/1/1746
Mary Snead 1/25/1749
Tully Snead 7/10/1753

Mrs. Catharine Snead d. 2/19/1750
John Snead d. 9/15/1780
Scarborough Snead d. 12/7/1780
Thomas Snead, son of John, d. 3/20/1787

BIRTHS of Children of John Wise

John Wise 3/8/1745
Charles Wise 6/19/1759
Solomon Wise 6/6/1748
Peggy Wise 11/11/1761
William Wise 11/16/1750
Peggy Wise, mother of aforesaid children, b. 9/5/1726
Nancy S. Wise, dau. of Solomon and Mary, d. 3/10/1806
Solomon Wise d. 1/25/1820

George Wise 10/8/1765
Elizabeth Wise 9/11/1754
Nancy Wise 3/17/1769
Henry Wise 2/6/1756

BIRTHS

Trefania Wise 4/11/1777
Nancy Selmon Wise 7/13/1789
John Wise 9/5/1780-10/12th
Polly Wise 2/18/1783

Peggy Wise 7/6/1786
Margaret Wise d. 11/30/1781
John Wise d. 12/8/1781
John Sparrow b. 12/17/1706

Elizabeth Sparrow b. 9/12/1708

REV. WILLIAM DOUGLAS BIBLE
Owner: W. Mac Jones (1929)

I was b. 8/3/1708
I was married 11/27/1835 Peggy Douglas b. 9/2/1737 My wife was b. in fall 1715
Dr. William Hunter d. 10/2/1766, aged 33, my wife's Broyr. Dr. Joseph Hunter d. 8/21/1759, my wife's cousin
Broyr. James Douglas d. 5/1/1760, aged 52

(Rev. William Douglas Bible, contd....)
Slster Elizabeth Douglas d. 6/15/1759, aged 47-1/2
Broyr James Hunter d. 2/15/1758
Broyr. John Douglas d. 11/1/1761, aged 64
My fayr William Douglas d. - , aged 77
My moyr. Grishild McLeand d.   aged 70
My slster Mary d. aged 21, married
My slster Janet d. aged 20 unmarried
My slster Margaret 1703-5/1766?
My fayr in law, James Hunter d. 12/16/1771, aged 84
My wife, Nicholas Hunter, b. Glencairn Parish Nithsdale, Scotland, 9/1715--came to Virginia 10/6/1757 was seized with palsy Oct. 19 and d. Dec. 31/1781.../s/Will Douglas

My 2nd wife, Elizabeth Burrows, b. 6/9/1755 married to me 12/21/1782, aged 27 and I was then 74

BIRTHS

Lucy Ware 7/20/1774
Bettie's Harry 9/23/1794
Chiles Terrel and Mary Douglas a son, John Hunter, 9/8/1784
Will Douglas Merriwether 11/2/1761
Thomas Merriwether 4/24/1763
Nicholas Hunter Merriwether 1/9/1765
Charles Merriwether 8/12/1766

Francis Thornton Merriwether 11/5/1768
Elizabeth Merriwether 2/24/1771
Tibble, a son, 7/31/1785, called Dick
Negro Dinah's child, Pattie 1/6/1787
Negro, Bettie's son, Warwick 5/16/1787
James Douglas, John's son, m. 1773
Ju: Douglas, John's son, had a son, William, 5/1784

Niece, Peggie Heron, d. aged 23, June 15 '62
Her mother, my slster, d. aged 47 1/2 June 15 '59
Her fayr my broyr in law d. Feb. 10 '89
Her broyr. Sam Heron d. Oct. 26 '85
Granddau. Bettie bore her child called Peggie Douglas--for her mother July 31 '91
Thomas Merriwether m. Ann Minor 7/27/1791. She was b. 12/14/1771
Grandson, Nicholas, his child, Ann Overton, b. 2/22/1792
Will Collon of Auchenchain d. aged 84 5/1788
Grandson Thomas had a son Richard born 5/11/1792
Slster Elizabeth Hunter's son, James Smith was b. 1/14/1761
Charles Merriwather m. Lydia Laurie 11/14/1791
Nickolas Hunter and Bettie Lewis child Nicholas Hunter b. 10/1/1789
Many Walker, Bettie Lewis child b. 3/25/1793
Lydia Laurie d. 4/5/1793
Me: Merriwether and Beckie Terrell a son Walker Gilmour b. 2/9/1794
Thomas Merriwether and Ann Minor a son 4/20/1794
Henry Landon Merriwether b. 3/19/1794
Will Hunter my wife's uncle d. 11/14/1758
Francis Merriwether m. 6/2/1793
Cath: Eliza Davis in Amelia Co. and a son b. 3/19/1794
My grandson Nickle m. 2/26/1787 aged 22 yrs. to Rebekah Terrell aged 23 yrs.
Nickle's negro Dinah had Nannie b. 6/1/1787
My broyr James son William m 12/12/1786
Violet's child Randie b. 10/10/1757
Tibbie's child Suckie b. 1/3/1788

WILLIAM SYDNOR BIBLE of Lunenburg Co.
Owner: Lucy Gwathmey Fleet

Lafayette Co., Missouri (decd)
"This Bible is the property of William Sydnor, Lunenburg."

MARRIAGES

William Sydnor to Sarah Garland 3/5/1778
William Sydnor to his 2nd wife, Elizabeth Cros, 1/27/1795
Ann Sydnor, dau. of William and Sarah, to Thomas Blackwell 1793
Elizabeth Taylor Sydnor, dau. of William and Sarah, to William Trueheart 10/1799
Amanda Trueheart, dau. of William and Elizabeth, to Burwell Starke 4/15/1828
Burwell Starke to Ann Baylor Hatchett, dau. of William Hatchett, 3/14/1839
Burwell Starke to Fanny Lewis Hatchett, dau. of William Hatchett, 7/29/1853

BIRTHS of Children of Fortunaus Sydnor, an Englishman, and

Joanna, his wife
Ruth Sydnor 4/11/1671
Joan Sydnor 8/2/1678
Fortunatus Sydnor 11/8/1673

William Sydnor 11/13/1680
Ruth Sydnor 8/24/1676
Anthony Sydnor 1/18/1682

BIRTHS of Children of Fortunatus and Ruth Syndor, his wife

William Sydnor 2/26/1699
Joanna Sydnor 278/1709 Judith Sydnor 5/6/1705
Anthony Sydnor 1/18/1711

Fortunatus Sydnor 1/23/1707
Elizabeth Sydnor, wife of Anthony Sydnor, b. 3/2/1722

BIRTHS of Children of Anthony and Elizabeth Sydnor

Fortunatus Sydnor 1/30/1737/8
William Sydnor 4J27/1752
John Sydnor 3/19/1739/40
Bettey Sydnor 2/11/1755
Ann Sydnor 9/9/1757
Joseph Sydnor 10/17/1749
Judith Sydnor 4/16/1745

Ruth Sydnor 1/1/1760
Susanna Sydnor 5/27/1747
Anthony Sydnor 5/27/1762
Fanny Mitchell Sydnor 11/19/1766
Catharine Sydnor 1/3/1742/3
Sarah Sydnor, wife of William Sydnor, b. 10/3/1752

BIRTHS of Children of William and Sarah Sydnor

Ann Sydnor 2/18/1779
Elizabeth Taylor Sydnor 11/8/1780
Elizabeth Cross, 2nd wife of William Sydnor, b. 1741

Burwell Starke b. 5/27/1806
Amanda, his wife, b. 12/31/1809

BIRTHS of Children of Burwell and Amanda Starke

Elizabeth Taylor Starke 3/27/1831
Alfred Lewis Starke 4/13/1835

William Thomas Starke 3/5/1833
Amanda Trueheart Starke 4/20/1837

BIRTHS of Children of Burwell and Ann B. Starke

Edwin Temple Starke 7/20/1840
Edward BrookeStarke 9/17/1846
Virginia Burwell Starke 7/18/1843

James Newton Starke 10/4/1847
Judson Starke 11/21/1844

DEATHS

Fortunatus Sydnor 1722 Anthony Sydnor 10/1759
William Sydnor 1/23/1751
Fortunatus Sydnor 3/14/1750
Joanna Sydnor d. y. Anthony Sydnor 10/5/1779

Fortunatus Sydnor 2/12/1781
Judith Sydnor 3/1778
Susanna Sydnor 3/5/1766

(William Snydnor Bible continued...)

Fanny Mitchell Sydnor 10/27/1769
Ann Sydnor 10/23/1793
Sarah Sydnor, 1st wife of William Sydnor, 1/7/1789
Elizabeth Sydnor, 2nd wife of William Sydnor, 10/1/1815

BIRTHS of Children of B. and Fanny L. Starke

Mary Ann Starke 5/17/1854 –
Robert Lee Starke 8/10/1861
William Gwathmey Starke 4/24/1858

Lucy Gwathmey Starke 9/28/1863
Lewis Newton Starke 11/1/1859
Americus Hatchett Starke 9/4/1865

DEATHS

Amanda Starke, wife of Burwell Starke and dau. of William Trueheart, 7/10/1837, aged 27 yrs.
Ann Baylor, 2nd wife of Burwell Starke and dau. of Elder William Hatchett, 3/3/1851, aged 33
Amanda Trueheart, 5th child of Burwell and Amanda Starke, 7/20/1837, aged 4 months
Alfred Lewis Starke, son of Burwell and Amanda, 7/18/1855, aged 21 yrs.
James Newton Starke, son of Burwell and Ann Baylor Starke, 1/13/1855, aged 9 yrs.
Mary Ann Starke, 1st dau. of Burwell and Fanny L., 5/17/1854 5/9/1855
William Gwathmey Starke, 1st son of Burwell and Fanny Lewis Starke, 4/24/1858-10/2nd, aged 5 mos., 8 days
Americus Hatchett Starke, son of B. and Fanny L. Starke, 10/16/1890, aged 24-1-12
Fanny L., wife of Burwell Starke, 7/28/1891, aged 67-5-6
Burwell Starke 7/16/1895, aged 89-1-19

EDWARD GARLAND SYDNOR BIBLE of Hanover Co.
Owner: Mrs. W. P. Robinson, Danville, Va.

BIRTHS

Edward Garland Sydnor 10/15/1769 Hanover Co., Virginia
Sarah White, his wife, 12/14/1775 (m. 1/18/1800)

THEIR CHILDREN:

William B. Sydnor 10/12/1800
George W. Sydnor 3/4/1810
Edward Sydnor 12/12/1801
John S. Sydnor 7/24/1812
Elizabeth Garland Sydnor 12/12/1803

Dau. b. & d. 3/1815
William B. Sydnor (2nd) 3/26/1806
Thomas White Sydnor 6/1/1816
Frances Ann Sydnor 4/26/1808

MARRIAGES

Edward Garland Sydnor to Sarah White 1/18/1800
Edward Sydnor to 1st Margaret W. Cowley 1/15/1824
William Barrett to Sarah Thomas Austin 6/18/1829
John Seabrooke to Sarah C. White 12/22/1830
Edward to Sarah E. Ladd 12/2/1834,
2nd marriage Thomas White to 1st Sarah L. M. Chapin 10/15/1840
Thomas White to 2nd Blanche McClanahan 12/11/1845

DEATHS

Elizabeth White 12/14/1815, aged 82
Ann Sydnor 1/1817

Ann White 7/13/1818, aged 63
Elizabeth Garland Sydnor 3/15/1821, aged 17

Note: William Sydnor of Hanover Co. m. Bessie Ann Garland, widow of William Thompson and dau. of Edward Garland and Jane Jennings. Susanna, her dau. by Thompson m. Peter Tinsley.
William Sydnor was father of Edward Garland Sydnor

JAMES TAYLOR BIBLE
Owner: John Moore Taylor Hamilton
Meridian, Mississippi (1926)

James Taylor, the Elder, m. Mary Gregory 8/10/1682
James Taylor II m. Martha Thompson 2/23/1699
Erasmus Taylor m. Jane Moore 10/13/1749
John Taylor, son of Erasmus, m. Anne Gilbert 9/6/1786

John Moore Taylor, son of John and Anne, m. Anne Foote, dau. of William Foote, 3/26/1811
Anne Gilbert Taylor, dau. of John M. and Anne, m. F. A. W. Davis 1/17/1837
Sigismunda Mary Taylor, dau. of John M. and Anne, m. Oscar Hamilton 11/10/1844
Felix H. G. Taylor, son of John M. and Anne, m. Medora E. Davis 1/29/1846
John Noore Taylor m. Mrs. Caroline E. Thurman 12/24/1851
Felix H. G. Taylor, son of John M. and Anne, m. Anne Troup Carter, 10/30/1854
Ages of Children of James Taylor, the Elder

Jane Taylor 12/21/1668
SarahTaylor 6/30/1676
James Taylor 3/14/1675
The above children by his 1st wife who d. 9/22/1680, and he m. his 2nd wife, Mary Gregory, 8/10/1682
Ages of Children of James Taylor and Mary

Anne Taylor 1/2/1685
Edmund Taylor 7/5/1690
Mary Taylor 6/29/1688

John Taylor 11/18/1696
James Taylor, the Elder, d. 4/30/1698

The 2nd James Taylor m. Martha Thompson 2/23/1699

BIRTHS

Frances Taylor 8/30/1700
Tabitha Taylor 3/2/1713
Martha Taylor 1/27/1701
Erasmus Taylor 9/5/1715
James Taylor 3/20/1704

Hannah Taylor 3/15/1718
Zachary Taylor 4/17/1707
Milley Taylor 12/11/1724
George Taylor 2/11/1711

Jane Moore b. 12/22/1728 m. Erasmus Taylor

BIRTHS of Children of Jane and Erasmus Taylor

Milley Taylor 12/15/1751 - -
John Taylor 10/26/1760
Frances Taylor 12/16/1753
Robert Taylor 4/29/1763
Elizabeth Taylor 9/22/1755
Jane Taylor 3/2/1766
Lucy Taylor 12/13/1757

Anne Gilbert b. 6/13/1769 m. John, the son of Erasmus Taylor and Jane Moore

BIRTHS of Children of John and Anne Taylor Ann Taylor 8/411787

Felix Taylor 8/19/1797
William Taylor 3/21/1795
John Moore Taylor 6/28/1788
Felix Haywood Taylor 10/21/1800

Gilbert Dade Taylor 11/18/1791
Maria Taylor 10/9/1803
Anne Foote b. 3/17/1788 m. John M. Taylor

BIRTHS of Children of Anne and John M. Taylor

Anne Gilbert Taylor 1/28/1812
Felix H. G. Taylor3/28/1822
William F. Taylor 12/27/1813
John William Taylor 10/20/1824

Maria Eliza Taylor 11/1/1815
Sigismunde Mary Taylor 9/8/1827
Felix H. G. Taylor 2/21/1818
Matilda Foote Taylor 9/19/1833
Third son 5/8/1820

Medora Davies b. 6/22/1528 m. Felix H. G. Taylor, son of John M. and Ann Taylor

BIRTHS of Children of F. H. G. and Medora Taylor

John Anthony Taylor 8/1847 - -
Ann Taylor 12/18/1851
Emma Aldridge Taylor 7/27/1849
Medora Taylor 4/9/1853
Anne Troupe Carter, 2nd wife of F. H. G. Taylor, b. 6/14/1827

DEATHS

James Taylor, Elder's 1t wife 9/23/1680
James Taylor the Elder 9/10/1698
James Taylor II 1/23/1730
Martha, his wife, 11/19/1702
Erasmus Taylor 12/1794
Ann, dau. of John and Ann Taylor, 8/21/1787
Felix Taylor 2/17/1799
Felix H. G. Taylor 1822
Maria Taylor 10/1/1804
William Taylor 1/1822
Jane Taylor, wife of Erasmus, 9/1812
Third son of J. M. Taylor and Ann, 5/19/1820
Maria Eliza Taylor 9/20/1820
F. H. G. Taylor 5/8/1821
William F. Taylor 10/1/1822
Ann, wife of John Taylor, Elder, 12/1823
John William Taylor, son of John M., 12/9/1825
John Taylor, Elder 8/6/1826
Matilda Foote Taylor, dau. of J. M. and Anne, 4/6/1836
Ann G. Davis 10/29/1837

Anne Taylor, dau. of William Foote and wife of John M. Taylor, 5/5/1847
John Anthony Taylor 6/20/1850
Ann Taylor 1/1/1852
Medora E., wife of F. H. G. Taylor 4/27/1553
John Moore Taylor, Jr. 8/1854
John Moore Taylor, Sr. 2/28/1856

Note: John Moore Taylor, son of Capt. John Taylor and wife, Anne Gilbert, was b. at "Greenfield", Orange C. H., Va., 6/28/1788. He moved to Huntsville, Ala. abt 1812; was Judge of Ala. Supreme Ct. 1825-1834. Later d. on his plantation near Delhi, La. 2/28/1856.

WILLIAM AND MARTHA WALLER TAYLOR BIBLE
of Lunenburg Co.
Owner: Rev. Edward Watts Gamble, Selma, Alabama

William Taylor m. Martha Waller 3/15/1767 by Rev. James Horoches

BIRTHS:

Benjamin Taylor 1/16/1768
Daniel Taylor 3/27/1769
Martha Taylor 10/15/1770
Waller Taylor 12/7/1775
William Waller Taylor 6/25/1772-10/2/1773, aged abt 16 mos.
Thomas Taylor 5/3/1774

Edmund Francis Taylor 3/12/1787
Richard Taylor 3/15/1778
John Taylor 2/18/1780
Robert Taylor 2/2/1782
William Henry Taylor 1/25/1784
Lewis Littlepage Taylor 5/29/1788

(Bible of William and Martha Waller Taylor continued....)

DEATHS

My bro., Thomas Taylor, d. 12/23/1773, aged 33 yrs.
Robert Taylor 12/18/1800, aged 18 yrs. 10 mos.
My dau., Martha Wells 1/18/1909, aged 8 yrs., and abt 3 mos.
My mother, Alice Taylor, 11/9/1787, aged 81 yrs.
My sIster, Martha Moore, 3/11/1800, aged 67 yrs
My bro. Richard Sqr Taylor 10/--
My sister, Frances Anderson, 12/23/1808, aged 47 (67?) yrs.

END

Abbie, Sallie 227
Abney, Elizabeth 216
Adams, Abner 195
Adams, Anna 84,85
Adams, Calvin 195
Adams, Charles Brandt 85
Adams, Chloe 85
Adams, Edward 43
Adams, Elizabeth M. 85
Adams, Elizabeth Marshall 85
Adams, Fannie 85
Adams, Francis 84,85
Adams, George 85
Adams, Harriet 85
Adams, Harriet V. 85
Adams, James B. 195
Adams, Joanna M. 85
Adams, John 5,195
Adams, John I. 200
Adams, John Quincy 212
Adams, Littleton 84,85
Adams, Littleton Turner 85
Adams, Mary Ann 85
Adams, Maryann P. 170
Adams, Mourning 195
Adams, Nannie Myrtle 198
Adams, Nicholas 195
Adams, Oscar Judson 153
Adams, Richard C. 195
Adams, Richard T. 153
Adams, Sarah 5
Adams, Susan Thomas 85
Adams, Thomas 85,195
Adams, Thomas F. 195
Adams, Thomas Marshall 85
Adams, Willis 84,85
Adarns, Elizabeth 5,84,85,195
Adarns, Harriet W. 85
Addams, Joseph M. C. 31
Addams, Samuel M. C. 31
Adkins, W. H. 19
Agee, James 198
Agnew, Eva Virginia 198
Aiken, Jane 4
Akers, Martha A. 174
Akers, Martha Archer 174
Alexander, A. J. 181
Alexander, Alice Seeley 181
Alexander, Andrew Jonathan 180
Alexander, Ann 166
Alexander, Apolline 180
Alexander, Benjamin 230
Alexander, Charles 180,181
Alexander, Charles William 181
Alexander, Colonel 166
Alexander, Eliza 181
Alexander, Eliza Jane 181
Alexander, Elizabeth 222
Alexander, Frances Agatha 180
Alexander, James 230
Alexander, James Robert 180,181
Alexander, James, Jr. 230
Alexander, Jane 181
Alexander, Jerusha 230
Alexander, John Campbell 181
Alexander, John R. 180,181
Alexander, John Regis 180,181
Alexander, John T. 230
Alexander, Lucy 284

Alexander, M. F. 181
Alexander, Marian F. 180,181
Alexander, Marianne 180,181
Alexander, Marie Agatha Henriette Sophie 181
Alexander, Mary 102,209,257
Alexander, Mira 181
Alexander, Nelson 230
Alexander, Polly 230
Alexander, R. B. 116
Alexander, Richard
Alexander, Robert 181
Alexander, Robert Andrew 181
Alexander, Thomas Riddle 181
Alexander, W. T, 284
Alexander, William 180,181,230
Alexander, William Seay 116
Alexander, Willis 230
Alford, Elizabeth 18
Alford, Susan C. 194
Alfred, Prince Doctor 8
Alison, Mr. 187
Allan, Elizabeth 269,270
Allan, Martha 269
Allan, Samuel 269
Allen, Emmett Lewis 55
Allen, Fayett 41
Allen, Frances 223
Allen, George C. 55
Allen, George Tavvener 95
Allen, James 223
Allen, James C. 39
Allen, James Henderson 95
Allen, John 209
Allen, John Daris 95
Allen, John I. 55
Allen, John N. 39
Allen, John Shelby 55
Allen, Lawrence Berkley 55
Allen, Lucy Davis 95
Allen, Mary 126
Allen, Mary A. 39
Allen, Mary Caroline 95
Allen, Mary G. 55
Allen, Moses 223
Allen, Newman 39
Allen, Patsey 223
Allen, Polly 223
Allen, Priscilla 223
Allen, S. J. 39
Allen, Sallie W. 55
Allen, Sarah 223
Allen, Sarah Jane 39
Allen, Susan Frances 95
Allen, Thomas 95
Allen, Anne 223
Allen, Benjamin 223
Allen, Benjamin Fuller 148
Allen, Berkley 55
Allen, Bettie L. 55
Allen, Cary 223
Allen, Daniel 223
Allen, Daniel A. 223
Allen, David 25,243
Allen, Drury 127
Allen, E. F. 39
Allen, Earl 55
Allen, Eleanor Henderson 95
Allen, Eliza Mildred 95
Allen, Elizabeth 223

Allen, Elizabeth F. 39
Allen, Emmett L. 550
Allen, Erwin Forrest 95
Allen, Thomas Catlett 95
Allen, Zella 223
Allin Laryderdale 116
Ambler, Sarah 107
Amen, Ann Eliza 76
Amen, Daniel 76
Amen, Ella Neville 76
Amen, Frank 76
Amen, Hester 76
Ames, George C. 129
Ames, George Chrlstian 130
Ames, James L. 73
Ames, Margaret 130
Ames, Zeribabel 130
Amiss, Sarah 13,18
Ammen, Constance 76
Amnen, Eliza 76
Amnen, Emma Zulema 76
Amy, Elarsha Burnett 240
Amy, Margaret 240
Amy, Marshall Keith 240
Amy, Susan Gain 240
Anderson, Almira 272
Anderson, Anne 223
Anderson, Anne Middleton Speer B.196
Anderson, Charles 32
Anderson, Dabney M. 54
Anderson, Dorothy 41
Anderson, Edward 49
Anderson, Elizabeth 21,175,236
Anderson, Emily 201
Anderson, Eudocia M. 236
Anderson, Foster 236
Anderson, Frances 22,176,288
Anderson, Henry 32
Anderson, Jacob H. 203
Anderson, Jane Katharine 236
Anderson, Jenney T. 236
Anderson, Jenny 236
Anderson, John 201
Anderson, Leland B. 185
Anderson, Lewis 236
Anderson, Louisa R. Y. 48
Anderson, Lovey 236
Anderson, Martha Ann 236
Anderson, Martha C. 194
Anderson, Mary Elizabeth 236
Anderson, Polly 236
Anderson, Richard 236
Anderson, Sarah 133,201
Anderson, Sophia Ertine 73
Anderson, Susannah 236
Anderson, Theosia 32
Anderson, Virginia M. 52
Anderson, William Isaac 236
Anderson, William L. 236
Anderson, William, Sr. 236
Andrews, Ann H. 91
Andrews, Eldridge, Rev. 203
Andrews, Robert, Rev. Mr. 119
Anrdstead, Howard L. 50
Anthony, Susan 26
Anthony, Thomas W. 203
Apperson, Ada Byron 82
Apperson, Leer M. 73
Applin, Abigail 192
Applin, Anna 192

Applin, Benjamin Redrnan 192
Applin, Elizabeth 192
Applin, Philanda 192
Applin, Rebecca 192
Applin, Sabrina 192
Applin, Timothy Brown 192
Applin, Wessen Timothy 192
Arbigast, Elsey 237
Arbuthnot, Mariot, Capt. 279
Archer, Fanny Book 60
Archer, J. R. 60
Archer, Mary B. 47
Archer, Polly Eliza 47
Archer, Sallemaud 47
Archer, Susan Nine 47
Archer, Virginia Susan 47
Archer, Wilbur 47
Archer, Alexander 47
Archer, Alexander Boisseau 47
Archer, Ann Bett 47
Archer, Benjamin Hatcher 47
Archer, Burke 47
Archer, Calvln 47
Archer, Eliza A. 47
Archer, Eliza F. 34
Armistead, Alice M. 50
Armistead, D. L. 50
Armistead, Drury L., Jr. 50
Armistead, Elizabeth Ann 50
Armistead, Elizabeth D. 50
Armistead, Elvira L. 50
Armistead, Fanny 62
Armistead, James 40
Armistead, James A., Jr. 50
Armistead, Janes A. 50,70
Armistead, John 70
Armistead, John H. 70
Armistead, Lucie J. 50
Armistead, Martha Burwell 70
Armistead, Mary S. 50
Armistead, Mattie Sue 50
Armistead, Polley 70
Armistead, Robert 268
Armistead, Robert P. 50
Armistead, Thomas 138
Armistead, Thomas S. 70
Armistead, William S. 70
Armitage, Ethel Rogers 72
Armstrong, Ambrose 79
Armstrong, David 241
Armstrong, David McCarty 240
Armstrong, David McCarty III 241
Armstrong, David McCarty, Jr. 240
Armstrong, Elizabeth Garnett 79
Armstrong, Ellis 79
Armstrong, Fanney 79
Armstrong, Faye 241
Armstrong, James Richards 79
Armstrong, Jane Ann 241
Armstrong, Janet Ann 240
Armstrong, Janet E. 240
Armstrong, Janet Faye 241
Armstrong, John 79,80
Armstrong, Joseph Noel 79
Armstrong, Kills 79
Armstrong, Mary 79
Armstrong, Phanney 79
Armstrong, Polly 79
Armstrong, William 79
Arnold, Ann 91,92

Arnold, Ann E. E. 91,92
Arnold, C. A. 91
Arnold, C. V. 92
Arnold, Catherine V. 91
Arnold, Charles A. 91
Arnold, Charles G. 91
Arnold, E.W. 91
Arnold, Edwin 92
Arnold, Elisha 91
Arnold, Elvira A. 91
Arnold, Endly W. 91,92
Arnold, George A. 91
Arnold, Hartwell 91
Arnold, Henry W. 91
Arnold, Hezekiah, Rev. 184
Arnold, Isaac 91,92
Arnold, Isaac M. 91
Arnold, John J. 91
Arnold, Joseph D. 91,92
Arnold, Martha W. 91
Arnold, Mary W. 91,92
Arnold, Narcissus M. 91
Arnold, Richard H. 91
Arnold, Silvanus J. 91
Arnold, Susan E. 91
Arnold, Will E. 255
Arres, Margie B. 150
Arrington, Thomas 220
Arthur, Caleb 5
Arthur, Dosia 5
Arthur, Larkin 5
Arthur, Lilly Ann 5
Arthur, Melindah 5
Arthur, Nenah 5
Arthur, Sally 5
Arthur, Thomas 5
Arthur, Willis 5
Arthur, Winnifred 5
Ash, Elizabeth 84
Ashby, Betsy 214
Ashby, Dolly 214
Ashby, Harvey W., Rev. 255
Ashby, John 214
Ashby, Laura 314
Ashby, Marshall 214
Ashby, Martha Ann 214
Ashby, Mary 214
Ashby, Molley 214
Ashby, Nimrod 214
Ashby, Patsy Arm 214
Ashby, Samuel 214
Ashby, Tanscn 214
Ashby, Turner 214
Ashby, William 214
Ashman, David William 241
Ashman, Ellen Murray 241
Ashman, Jane Ann 241
Ashman, Murray Gilbert 241
Ashrrtln, Elizabeth Ann 241
Ashton, Burditt W. 226
Ashton, C. H., Jr. 226
Ashton, Charles H., Jr. 226
Ashton, Charles H., Sr. 226
Ashton, Elizabeth Jacksgn 226
Ashton, John 226
Ashton, Mary D. 277
Ashton, Mary M. 226
Ashton,, Mary 276
Asolea Clark 14
Atkins, Mary 71

Atkinson, Eliza 208
Atkinson, Mamie P. 41
Attswell, Frands 280
Aubrey, Eugenia Dearing Speer 196
Aubrey, William 196
Austin, Berveridge 255
Austin, C. E. 153
Austin, C. M. 153
Austin, John R. 153
Austin, Mary 153
Austin, Mary E. 153
Austin, Nancy Susan 255
Austin, Richard 211
Austin, Sarah Thomas 286
Austin, William F. 153
Avery, Nellie Lcuise 132
Ayer, Dorothy Elizabeth 255
Aylett, Ann 110
Aylett, Elizabeth 131
Aylett, John 131
Aylett, Mary Macon 104
Aylett, Philip 70,206
Aylett, William 131
Bacon, John M. 178
Bacon, Albert Gallatin 178
Bacon, Alexander B. 180
Bacon, Alice 178
Bacon, Alice E. 178
Bacon, Alice M. A. 180
Bacon, Allen Stokes 126, 127
Bacon, Amanda 178
Bacon, Anna 178
Bacon, Anne 126
Bacon, Anne A. 178
Bacon, Bacon 126
Bacon, Benedict 178
Bacon, Caroline M. 178
Bacon, Charles P. 178
Bacon, Drury A. 127
Bacon, Drury A., Capt. 126
Bacon, Drury Allen 126,127
Bacon, Edmond R. H. 180
Bacon, Edmund 178,180
Bacon, Edmund C. 127
Bacon, Edmund Currnins 126
Bacon, Edmund Parks 126
Bacon, Eliza B. 180
Bacon, Elizabeth 126,178
Bacon, Elizabeth P. 178
Bacon, James 178
Bacon, James Haggin Albert 178
Bacon, James Lawrence 126,127
Bacon, James W. 178
Bacon, John 178
Bacon, John Mosby 178
Bacon, John R. 180
Bacon, Josephus Carter 127
Bacon, Langston 126,127,178
Bacon, Laura 178
Bacon, Lucy 126
Bacon, Lyddall 127,178
Bacon, Lyddall, Colonel 126
Bacon, Lyddall, Jr. 126
Bacon, Maria 178
Bacon, Mary 126,127
Bacon, Mary Ann 125,127
Bacon, Mary D. 180
Bacon, Mary J.127
Bacon, Mary Jane 127
Bacon, Mildred Balmy Carter 126,127

Bacon, Moseley, Mrs. 127
Bacon, Nancy 126
Bacon, Nancy A. M. 127
Bacon, Nancy Aris 125,127
Bacon, Nathaniel 126,127
Bacon, R. R. 178
Bacon, Richard 126
Bacon, Richard A. 178
Bacon, Richard Apperson 178
Bacon, Richard Parkes 125,127
Bacon, Richardson 180
Bacon, Robert Carter 126
Bacon, Romulus Riggs 178
Bacon, Sally W. 178
Bacon, Samuel A. 180
Bacon, Sarah 126
Bacon, Sarah Cordelia 178
Bacon, Sarah J. 178
Bacon, Sary Elizabeth 180
Bacon, Susan 178
Bacon, Susan H. 180
Bacon, Susannah 126
Bacon, Thomas A. 127
Bacon, Thomas Alexander 127
Bacon, Thornas Alexander
Bacon, Virginia 126,127
Bacon, Virginia P. B. 180
Bacon, W. W. 178
Bacon, William A. 127,180
Bacon, William Allen 126
Bacon, Williamson 178
Bacon, Williamson W. 178
Bafret, Mary 53
Bagby, Rev. A. 83
Bagby, Sarah Jane 83
Baggett, Meggie 210
Bagly, Richard 110
Bailey, A. C., Mrs. 123
Bailey, Andrew 123
Bailey, Andrew, Jr. 120
Bailey, Andrew, Sr. 120,121,123
Bailey, Ann 237
Bailey, Bettie A. 123
Bailey, Daniel E. 123
Bailey, Daniel E., Capt. 124
Bailey, Daniel Edwin 120
Bailey, Harriette 123
Bailey, John Green 120
Bailey, Joseph 146
Bailey, Joseph H. 146
Bailey, Joseph R. 123
Bailey, Joseph Richard 120
Bailey, Julia A. 123
Bailey, Mary A. 122
Bailey, Mary A., Mrs. 121
Bailey, Mary Am Zorada 120
Bailey, Mary nn Green 120
Bailey, Mildred Maranda 120
Bailey, Obedience Green 120
Bailey, Peter R. 123
Bailey, Peter Renard 120
Bailey, Richard C. 93
Bailey, Seleuda Harriette Janette 120
Bailey, Thomas 146
Bain, George A., Rev. 140
Baker, Albert Riflin 100
Baker, Andrew Ellis 100
Baker, Audry Laine 248
Baker, Bushrod W. 100
Baker, Candice Aston 248

Baker, Clemmentina R. 38
Baker, Cliveous Albert 100
Baker, Daniel Lee 248
Baker, Elizabeth 141
Baker, George 18
Baker, George Peter 18
Baker, Henry 18
Baker, Herman Cliveous 100
Baker, Jacob 18
Baker, Jimmie Gene 248
Baker, John P. 38
Baker, Joseph 18
Baker, Joseph Hart 99
Baker, Joseph, Jr. 18
Baker, Judith T. 100
Baker, Linda Lou 248
Baker, Margaret 18
Baker, Peter 18
Baker, Susie Mae 248
Baker, Timothy Lyle 248
Baldwin, Samuel 271
Ball, Abigail 94
Ball, Allce 94
Ball, Amanda 94
Ball, Anliza Henerson 94
Ball, Ann Liza 94
Ball, Cad Welinder 94
Ball, Calvin 94
Ball, Colonel 102
Ball, Conwellsee 94
Ball, Davis Henry 94
Ball, Elizabeth 94
Ball, Emily 94
Ball, Fanny, Mrs. 102
Ball, Francis Marion 94
Ball, George Wesley 94
Ball, Isaac 94
Ball, Isaac Munson 94
Ball, James 133
Ball, James Wesley
Ball, Jesse 169
Ball, John Henry 94
Ball, John Maurice 94
Ball, John S., Rev. 169
Ball, John Wesley 94
Ball, Johnath 94
Ball, Jonathan Jones 94
Ball, Lucy Jane 94
Ball, M. Dulaney 103
Ball, Mary 133
Ball, Mary Amanda 148, 149
Ball, Mary E. 248
Ball, Mary Magdalene 94
Ball, Nancy 169
Ball, Naomi 94
Ball, Sallie A. 132
Ball, Sarah 94, 133
Ball, Sarah Isabel 94
Ball, William Pinkney 94
Ball, Willie May 94
Ball, Zachariah 94
Ballard, Andrew 163
Ballard, Edith 163
Ballard, Frances Elizabeth 85
Ballard, John 249
Ballard, Lydia 163
Balle, James Barbour 266
Balling, Alex 247
Balling, Alexander 247,248
Balling, Eliz Yates 248

Balling, John 247
Ballon, Louise Bransford 251
Balser, Johann 228
Balyer, Elizabeth M. 217
Banlster, Anne Blair 60
Banlster, Anne, Mrs. 60
Banlster, Augusta 60
Banlster, Eliza Thompson 60
Banlster, Henry Tudor 60
Banlster, J. B. 60
Banlster, James Coraway 60
Banlster, John 60
Banlster, Martha
Banlster, Robert Jones 60
Banlster, Theodoric Blair 60,61
Banlster, Thomas Yelverton 60
Banlster, Virginia Peyton 60
Bandy, Cary 46
Bandy, Elihu 46
Bandy, Elizabeth 46
Bandy, Horsha 46
Bandy, James 46
Bandy, Martha 46
Bandy, Nancy 46
Bandy, Phebe Chrlstian 46
Bandy, Polly 46
Bandy, Richard 46
Bandy, Robert Dodson 46
Bandy, Thomas 46
Banker, Blair Elizabeth 241
Banker, Dana Burnett 241
Banker, Dorothy Lee 241
Banker, Robert Earl 241
Banks, Deborah 11
Banks, Jane 11
Banks, Mary Abigail 11
Banks, Richard, Capt. 11
Banks, Ruth 11
Barbour Phillip P. 175
Barbour, James 175
Barbour, James, Gov. 265
Barbour, John Strode 236
Barbour, Mary 265
Barbour, Nelly 265
Barbour, Philip Pendleton, Judge 265
Barbour, Thomas 265
Baret, William Ovlertan 53
Barker, Jchn 280
Barksdale, Fanny Peyton 60
Barksdale, Marlarna Elizabeth 60
Barksdale, W. T, 60
Barlow, Barbara Ann 8
Barlow, Cynthia 208
Barlow, Fannie E. 8
Barlow, Frances E. 8
Barlow, George D. 8
Barlow, James E. 8
Barlow, James W. 8
Barlow, James Willie 8
Barlow, John Matthew 8
Barlow, Mary Elizabeth 8
Barlow, Sally A. 8
Barnedge, E. W. S. 110
Barnedge, L. N. 110
Barnedge, Noble 110
Barnes, Alice Branscane 240 ,241
Barnes, Alice Gertrude 197
Barnes, Alice Gertrude Hardy 198
Barnes, Alice Lillian 197,198
Barnes, Ann 109

Barnes, Anna Frances 240,241
Barnes, Anna Lee 240
Barnes, Aubrey Leonard 197,198
Barnes, David Christopher 241
Barnes, Dorothy 198
Barnes, Elwood Dance 197,198
Barnes, Elwood Dance, Jr. 198
Barnes, Gertrude Hardy 199
Barnes, Horace Collingsworth 197,198
Barnes, Inez Gertrude 197,198
Barnes, Jane Elizabeth 240
Barnes, John V. 240
Barnes, John Vanderslice 111,241
Barnes, John Vanderslice 240
Barnes, John Vanderslice, Sr. 242
Barnes, Julia Gay 197,198
Barnes, Leonard Hartley 197,198
Barnes, Lois Cordelia 240
Barnes, Lucille Audrey 197,198
Barnes, Myrtle Virginia 198
Barnes, Robert Hardy 197,198
Barnes, Robert Hardy, Jr. 198
Barnes, Robert Leonard 197,198
Barnes, Ruth 197,198
Barnes, Sallie Moore 198
Barnes, Samuel 156
Barnett, Joel 216
Barnett, William 216
Barney, John H. 132
Barren, Cynthia A. 152
Barret, Barbara 54
Barret, Barbara W. 54
Barret, Barbara Winston 53,54
Barret, Charles Nelson 53
Barret, David Bullock 53
Barret, Elizabeth I. 53,54
Barret, Elizabeth Lewis 54
Barret, Fatsy H. 53
Barret, James Winston 54
Barret, Jdn Y. 54
Barret, John Winston 54
Barret, John Yates 54
Barret, Lewis 54
Barret, Mary O. 54
Barret, Mary Overton 54
Barret, Nancy 53
Barret, Nancy Bullock 53
Barret, Nancy C. 54
Barret, Nancy Coleman 54
Barret, Nelson Berkley 54
Barret, Robert 54
Barret, Robert B. 54
Barret, Robert Bullock 53
Barret, Robert Lewis 53,54
Barret, Robert, Dr. 194
Barret, Robert, Sr. 54
Barret, Sary Jane 53
Barret, W. 0. 53
Barret, William Overton 54
Barrett, Ann C. 53
Barrett, Bryan 58
Barrett, Elizabeth 58
Barrett, flary Arme 58
Barrett, George 58
Barrett, Henry 58
Barrett, Jane Sndth 58
Barrett, John Smith 58
Barrett, M. 187
Barrett, Margarat 187
Barrett, Mary Ann Foster 58

Barrett, Milton 58
Barrett, R. 187
Barrett, Robert Foster 58
Barrett, Robert Lewis 63
Barrett, William 286
Barrett, William Augustine 63
Barry, Marry 257
Barslan, Elise Ruth 10
Bartlett, Charlie 207
Bartlett, Eledora 207
Bartlett, Eugene 207
Bartlett, George 207
Bartlett, Lucien 207
Bartlett, Nancy Boykin Saunders 207
Bartlett, Virginia 207
Barton, Addie Maude 92
Barton, Arthur L. 92
Barton, Byron 92
Barton, Byron Lemon 92
Barton, Earl 92
Barton, Elaud 92
Barton, Emma 92
Barton, Era 92
Barton, Isaac 92
Barton, Isaac C. 92
Barton, Patrick Phillip 272
Barton, Pearl 92
Bartrxl, T. C. 92
Baskerville, Anne M. 64,65
Baskerville, Betsey Fatan 65
Baskerville, Betsey P. 64,65
Baskerville, Delha P. 64,65
Baskerville, Emma Virginia 65
Baskerville, George 64
Baskerville, George D. 64,65
Baskerville, George D., Jr. 65
Baskerville, Isabella 64
Baskerville, Isabella H. 65
Baskerville, John 65
Baskerville, John W. 64,65
Baskerville, Lucy C. 64,65
Baskerville, Mary Eaben 65
Baskerville, Mary Williams 65
Baskerville, Mary Willis 65
Baskerville, Roberta P. 64,65
Baskerville, Ruth 65
Baskerville, Sally D. 65
Baskerville, Sally D. 65
Baskerville, Sally T. 65
Baskerville, Sally Turner 65
Baskerville, William J. 65
Baskerville, William Wharton 65
Bass, Agnes 172
Bass, Anthary 34
Bass, Archard 47
Bass, Arme 34
Bass, Chrlstoptr?r 47
Bass, Cicillia 47
Bass, Colin 48
Bass, Eckard 34,47,172
Bass, Edward Wesley 48
Bass, Ezebath 172
Bass, Frances 48,172
Bass, Henry 48
Bass, Hester 47
Bäss, Humphrey 34
Bass, John 34,48,172
Bass, Joseph 47,56
Bass, Martha 47,48,172
Bass, Martha Eveline 48

Bass, Mary 47,48,172
Bass, Mary Louisa 48
Bass, Matoaca 48
Bass, Montes 55
Bass, Nancy 172
Bass, Nathaniel 34
Bass, NesMt A. 55
Bass, peter 47
Bass, Richard Royall 48
Bass, Sarah E. 56
Bass, Tabitha 172
Bass, Thomas 47
Bass, William 34,47,48
Bass, William Edward 48
Bass, William, Jr. 48
Bassett, Alfred 62
Bassett, Amette Lewis 63
Bassett, Anna Maria 61,131
Bassett, Anna Maria Dandridge 61,62
Bassett, Anna Virginia 63
Bassett, Annette L. 63
Bassett, Benjamin M. 63
Bassett, Betty Burwell 63
Bassett, Betty Carter 62,63
Bassett, Elizabeth 60,61
Bassett, Ella Moore 63
Bassett, Frances 61
Bassett, Frances Carter 61
Bassett, George 61
Bassett, George Anna Maria 63
Bassett, George W. 63
Bassett, George Washington 62,63
Bassett, Hannah 60
Bassett, Henry Alfred 62
Bassett, Joanna 60
Bassett, John 61,63
Bassett, John Burwell 62
Bassett, John Churchill 62
Bassett, Judith Carter 62
Bassett, Judith Frances Carter 63
Bassett, L. Frames Carter 63
Bassett, Lewis 60
Bassett, Lucy 60
Bassett, Martha 60
Bassett, Mary 60
Bassett, Mary Burnet 63
Bassett, Nathaniell 60
Bassett, Virginia 61,62
Bassett, William 60,61,62
Bassett, William 60,61,62
Batchelder, Elizabeth 165
Batchelder, John 165
Batchelder, Sarah 165
Bateman, Elizabeth 28
Bates, Conway 169
Bates, Endly C. 152
Bates, Endly Caroline 151,169
Bates, Frederick 169
Bates, Gene Conway 160
Bates, Lucia Lee 169
Bates, Lucius Lee 160,169
Bates, Mary Susan 222
Bates, Mattie T. 164
Bates, Nancy 112
Bates, Nancy Onie 169
Bates, William D. 222
Bates, Woodville 169
Batten, Ernest 155
Batten, Maggie 155
Bauldin, Elizabeth 142

Bauldin, Margaret 141,142
Bauldin, William 141,142
Bayard, Caroline S. 275
Bayard, Juliet Elizabeth 275
Bayard, Samuel 275
Bayard, Samuel J. 275
Baylor, Alexander Gait 66
Baylor, Ann 67,286
Baylor, B. H. 66
Baylor, Betsey 62
Baylor, Eliza L. 65
Baylor, Eliza Lewis, Mrs. 66
Baylor, Elizabeth Todd 62
Baylor, Ellen Augustus 66
Baylor, F., Miss 62
Baylor, Frances 62,65,66
Baylor, Frances Courtenay 62,66
Baylor, George D. 65
Baylor, George Daniel 66,66
Baylor, George Marie 66
Baylor, George Robert 66
Baylor, John Norton 66
Baylor, John, 62,65,66
Baylor, Julia Ann 66
Baylor, Lewis 66
Baylor, Louisa Henrietta 66
Baylor, Mary A. E. 66
Baylor, Susanna Frances 62,66
Baylor, Thomas Wiltshire 66
Baylor, W. I. 66
Baylor, W. L., Dr. 65,66
Baylor, Warner Lewis 66
Bayly, Ann D. 67
Bayly, Ann Drummond 67
Bayly, Elizabeth Wharton 67
Bayly, Henry C. 67
Bayly, Henry Curtis 67
Bayly, Jane 67
Bayly, Jane O. 67
Bayly, John Cropper 67
Bayly, Margaret P. 67
Bayly, Richard Drummond 67
Bayly, Rosy 67
Bayly, Sally C. 67
Bayly, Samuel 67
Bayly, Thomas H. 67
Bayly, Thomas M. 67
Bayly, William P. 67
Bayne, Delia C. 122
Bayne, Lawrence Pope 122
Bayne, Patterson 122
Bayne, Richard 122
Bayne, Susan 122
Bayne, Washington 122
Bayne, William 122
Bayoe, George H. 122
Baytle, Charles 122
Beadles, A. P. 63
Beadles, Cecilia Alice 63
Beadles, Dianna Am 63
Beadles, George W. R. 63
Beadles, Hazletine Mary William 63
Beadles, James E. 63
Beadles, John 63
Beadles, Lealila kancis 63
Beadles, Mareens Judson 63
Beadles, Tanasia C. 63
Beadles, Tharas Newton 63
Beale, Harriet 157
Beale, Hartasr 158

Beale, Judith 158
Beale, Reubin 157,158
Beale, Tavener 108
Beale, William Olrrie 157
Beall, aornas 50
Beall, Colon Peter 50
Beall, Eliza R. 276
Beall, George, Colonel 50
Beall, H. A. 50
Beall, Harriett Am 50
Beall, John Peter 50
Beall, John Thomas 50
Beall, Thomas Peter 50
Beaman, Cullen 68
Beaman, Gearge Munroe 68
Beaman, Huldeth 68
Beaman, John 68
Beaman, John C. 68
Beaman, John Crowder 68
Beaman, John Cullen 68
Beaman, John Wesley 68
Beaman, Joseph Thomas 68
Beaman, Martha M. 68
Beaman, Martha Moore 68
Beaman, Mary 68
Beaman, Mary Ann 68
Beaman, May 68
Beaman, William P. 68
Bear, Ella D. 47
Bear, John K. 46,47
Bear, Nancy C. 46,47
Bear, Sallie W. 47
Bear, Sally Warren 47
Beard, Agnes 80
Beard, Elizabeth 80
Beard, Elizabeth A. 50
Beard, Jam 80
Beard, Jesse 80
Beard, John, Capt. SO
Beard, Josiah 0. 50
Beard, Katherine 80
Beard, Lucretia 50
Beard, Margaret 80
Beard, Margaret A. 50
Beard, Margaret Am 50
Beard, Mary 80
Beard, Sabina 80
Beard, Samuel 0. 50
Beard, Samuel 50,80
Beard, Sarah Jane 50
Beard, Thomas 80
Beard, William Ryneck 80
Beasan, William 218
Beasley, Buckner 210
Beasley, Buckner Massilon 210
Beasley, John 210
Beasley, Martha M. E. 210
Beasley, Mary Antoinett 210
Beasley, Sarah Caroline 210
Beasley, Thomas M. 210
Beauford, Elizabeth 210
Beazley, Eliza Ann 79
Beazley, Ellis Armstrong 79
Beazley, Ephraim 79
Beazley, James Benjamin 79
Beazley, Mary Elizabeth 79
Beazley, Polly 79
Beazley, Richard 79
Beazley, Richard Edward 79
Beck, Sarah Lucy 218

Beckner, Lucien 167
Beckner, Lucien 168
Bedford, Carolina Henrietta 279
Bedford, Mary 71
Beell, Elizabeth Ridgeley U)
Beetty, Sarah E. 211
Belcher, Sarah Jam 284
Belk, Theodosia 142
Bell, Able 51
Bell, Adam 262
Bell, amrnas Pennell 76
Bell, Charles K. 251
Bell, David 51
Bell, Elizabeth 51
Bell, Esther 51
Bell, Etta Mabel 255
Bell, Fanny B. 76
Bell, Farnry 76
Bell, Francis 51
Bell, Franke 280
Bell, George, Colonel 252
Bell, Hemy kanklin 76
Bell, Henrietta B. 76
Bell, Henrietta Susan 76
Bell, Henry F. 75
Bell, James 51,280
Bell, Jane 76
Bell, Johanna S. 75
Bell, John 51
Bell, John Hendren 51
Bell, Joseph W. 76
Bell, Juulianna Susan 76
Bell, Mary 128
Bell, Nancy 51
Bell, Nathan E. 73
Bell, Rebecca 51
Bell, Sarah 141
Bell, Seth 75,76
Bell, Thomas P. 75
Bell, William 51
Bellamy, Rebecca 15
Bellamy, William 15
Belling, Alex Sr. 247
Belling, Am 247
Belling, Elizabeth 247
Belling, Frances 247
Belling, Franky 247
Belling, Helen Wilma 2
Belling, Mary Elizabeth 2
Belling, Mary Louisa 2
Belling, Rebecca B. 247
Belling, Robert 165 ,247 ,248
Belling, Robert, Cdlonel 248
Belling, Sally 247
Belling, Stith 247,248
Belling, Susanna 248
Belling, Susannah 247
Belling, Thomas 2
Belling, Thomas, Jr. 2
Belling, William, Colonel 2
Bennett, J. H., Rev. 48
Bennett, Mary 91
Bennett, Thomas Leidwell 247
Bennett, Virginia Spragins 247
Bennett, Vivian 25
Bentley, John Ambler 49
Bentley, Mary Ann 49
Bently, Efford 164
Berg, Eric Callaway 249
Berg, Lcds 249

Berg, Matraca 249
Berg, Ranald G. 249
Berger, Elizabeth 170
Berger, Jacob 170
Berkeley, Benjamin Pasco, 58
Berkeley, Betty Landoa 57
Berkeley, C. 57
Berkeley, Carter 57
Berkeley, Carter Nelson 57,58
Berkeley, Catherine Frances 57
Berkeley, Catherine Robinson 57
Berkeley, Catherine Spotswood 57,58
Berkeley, Catherirre S. 57
Berkeley, Charles Carter 57
Berkeley, Cornelia Leigh 48
Berkeley, Edmund 57
Berkeley, Elizabeth W, 58
Berkeley, Elizabeth W. C. 57
Berkeley, Jacquelin A, 57
Berkeley, Julia 58
Berkeley, Kidder Randolph 57
Berkeley, L. C, 58
Berkeley, Landon Carter 58
Berkeley, Landonia Carter 57
Berkeley, Lewis 57,58
Berkeley, Louisa Carter 58
Berkeley, Lucy Am 57
Berkeley, Lucy Burwell 57
Berkeley, Lucy Mary 58
Berkeley, Lucy S. 58
Berkeley, Lucy Thweatt 58
Berkeley, Mary E. 58
Berkeley, Mary Nelson 57,58
Berkeley, Mary Randolph 57
Berkeley, Nelson 57,58
Berkeley, Nelson William 58
Berkeley, Park Farley 57
Berkeley, Parke F. 57
Berkeley, Parke Julian 58
Berkeley, Parke Parley 58
Berkeley, Peyton Randolpb 57
Berkeley, Robert 58
Berkeley, Robert Carter 57,58
Berkeley, Sally Nelson 57
Berkeley, Sarah 57
Berkeley, Sophia Carter 58
Berkeley, Susan Elizabeth 58
Berkeley, William 57
Berkeley, William Henry 57
Berkeley, William Randolph 57
Berkley, Lucy 57
Berkley, Mary 57
Berrey, Berry Slaughter 69
Berrey, Daniel Fischer 69
Berrey, David Burnam 69
Berrey, David S. 69
Berrey, Emma D. 69
Berrey, Grace Woodward 69
Berrey, James Hay 69
Berrey, Lelia S. 69
Berrey, Mary Slaughter 69
Berrey, Ray 69
Berrey, Winnie Doris 69
Berry, Charles B. 47
Berry, Juriah 39
Berry, Nancy I. 257
Betts, Calvln 42
Betts, Mollie 42
Betts, Sidney Branch 42
Bevan, Elizabeth 156

Bevan, flary 156
Bevan, Tharras 156
Bevan, Thomas, Jr. 156
Bevell, Mary 237
Beverley, William P. 102
Beverly, Robert 276
Bfckley, Frances 84
Bias, Dolly Elizabeth 242
Bias, Dolly Ellez Beth 242
Bias, Francis 242
Bias, John F. 242
Bias, Lucinda 242
Bias, Mary Louise 242
Bias, Murray Alexander 242
Bias, Sarah 242
Bias, Sarah Hellen 242
Bias, Sarah Virginia 242
Bick, William James 35
Bickerton, Patsey 194
Bickham, Thomas 155
Bickley, Caroline Matilda 84
Bickley, Charles 86
Bickley, Hannah 84
Bickley, Humphy Caleb 84
Bickley, John 84
Bickley, Joseph 84
Bickley, Mary 84
Bickley, Munphrey 84
Bickley, Sarah 84
Bickley, William 84
Bigelow, Agnes 85,86
Bigelow, Agnes M. 86
Bigelow, Agnes N. 57
Bigelow, Archibald Nisbet 85,86
Bigelow, Fannie 86
Bigelow, Isabella B. 85
Bigelow, Jane E. 85
Bigelow, Jane Elizabeth 86
Bigelow, Joseph 57,85,86
Bigelow, Robert William 86
Bigelow, Woodbury B. 85
Bilbo, Martha 78
Billings, Kay Frances 249
Billingsley, Sarah 236
Billups, Ann Elizabeth 210
Billups, Peter, Rev. 113
Bird, William 4
Bishop, Ann V. 120
Bishop, Ann V. 96
Bishop, Milton, Rev. 203
Bittings, C. C., Rev. 197
Black, Mary 90
Blackburn, Churchill 275
Blackburn, Jean 113
Blackburn, Nancy 33
Blackwell, Elizabeth 280
Blackwell, Hannah 280
Blackwell, Janes 280
Blackwell, Jdn 280
Blackwell, Joseph 280
Blackwell, Samuel 280
Blackwell, Sarah 280
Blackwell, Thomas 285
Blair, Eliza T. Peachy 61
Blair, John B., Mrs. 279
Blair, Join 61
Blair, Mary 61
Blaisdell, Susan 38
Blaisdell, Thomas 38
Blake, Elizabeth 16

Blaker, David 168
Blaker, Fenuxl 168
Blaker, Harriet 168
Blaker, James 168
Blaker, Jane 168
Blaker, Jey 168
Blaker, John 168
Blaker, Lucinda 168
Blaker, Mary 168
Blaker, Matilda 168
Blaker, Peter 168
Blaker, Sarah 168
Blaker, Susanna 168
Blakey, Jarth 122
Blakey, William C. 203
Bland, 151llian Preston 18
Bland, Clara 248
Bland, Robert E. 152
Bland, Tila Mae 18
Blanks, J. R. 41
Blanks, Kate 272
Blanton, Arm Elizabeth 100
Blanton, Bettie L. 55
Blanton, Betty L. 55
Blanton, C. H. 55
Blanton, Emmet Todd 100
Blanton, George Goodloe 55
Blanton, George W. 55
Blanton, Isla C. 55
Blanton, James R. 55
Blanton, Julian A. 55
Blanton, Laura 0. 55
Blanton, Mary 55
Blanton, Mary A. 100
Blanton, Mary J. 55
Blanton, Nettie S. 55
Blanton, Richard 55
Blanton, Richard Alfred 100
Blanton, Sallie H. 55
Blanton, Sarah 55
Blanton, Sarah H. 55
Blasingame, Frances 179
Blasingame, James 179
Blasingame, Mary 179
Blasingame, Willie 210
BlcMey, Jam 84
Blount, Annie M. 16
Blunt, Ann 49
Blunt, Nora Louise 23
Blvor, Letitia 174
Blythe, Anne 203
Bmaddus, Lucy Virginia 77
Bnun, Charles Lee 125
Boggs, Hugh C., Rev. WI
Bohannan, Frank 250
Bohannon, Mary 193
Boiling, Charlotte 247
Boiling, William 2
Bolton, Annie 11
Bolton, Caswell I. 11
Bolton, Joseph C. 10,11
Bolton, Martha Lightfoot 136
Bolyer, Anna Abney 217
Bolyer, Elizabeth 217
Bolyer, Henry 217
Bolyer, John 217
Bolyer, John, Jr. 217
Bolyer, John, Sr. 217
Bolyer, Sarah 217
Bolyer, Sophia 217

Bolyer, Susannah Maria 217
Bond, Ann E. 195
Bondurant, Amanda Harding 22
Bondurant, Angeline Judith 22
Bondurant, Ann 198
Bondurant, Benjamin 25
Bondurant, Bessie 254
Bondurant, Darby 25
Bondurant, David 25
Bondurant, E. P. 26
Bondurant, Ebmrd Poindexter 26
Bondurant, Edward 254
Bondurant, Elizabeth 26
Bondurant, Elizabeth M. 26
Bondurant, George Perkins 22
Bondurant, Ida May 254
Bondurant, J. M. B. 26
Bondurant, Jacob Jades 26
Bondurant, Jacob M. 26
Bondurant, James Agee 25
Bondurant, James F. 26
Bondurant, Jams 25
Bondurant, John B. 26
Bondurant, John M. 254
Bondurant, John W. 254
Bondurant, Joseph 25
Bondurant, Joseph Alexander 22
Bondurant, Joseph R. 26
Bondurant, Joseph W. 254
Bondurant, Marcia L. Moseley 22
Bondurant, Margaret W. 254
Bondurant, Martha M. 26
Bondurant, Mary 25
Bondurant, Mary A. J. 254
Bondurant, Mary Am 25
Bondurant, P. M. 254
Bondurant, Pamelia A. 254
Bondurant, Peter M. 254
Bondurant, Polley 25
Bondurant, Rebecca 25
Bondurant, Robert Leander 26
Bondurant, Robert M. 254
Bondurant, Salley E. 25
Bondurant, Samuel 25
Bondurant, Samuel R. 26
Bondurant, Sarah Adeline 254
Bondurant, Sarah Eliza 22
Bondurant, Thomas 25
Bondurant, Thomas Leigh 22
Bondurant, Thomas M. 22
Bondurant, William Arthur 22
Bondurant, William M. 25
Bone, Melinda B., Mrs. 116
Bonner, Eliza Ann 111
Bonner, Martha 111
Bonner, Minerva W. 111
Book, Fanny 60
Booker, Arm 15
Booker, Blanche Redwood 76
Booker, Elizabeth Julia 73
Booker, Letty 15
Booker, Thomas 15
Boom, Polly 266
Boone, Lucy 267
Booten, George 266
Booth, Abner 10
Booth, Adah 10
Booth, Ann 9,10
Booth, Daniel 10
Booth, Elizabeth 10

Booth, George 10
Booth, Henry S. 10
Booth, Isaac 10
Booth, Jemimah 10
Booth, keelove 10
Booth, Mordecai 207
Booth, Thomas 66
Booth, Zillah 10
Booze, Chr1stian W. 212
Boswell, Richard C. 73
Boulware, Lucy 234
Boulware, Mark 234
Boulware, Sarah P. 234
Boush, John 207
Boush, Samuel, Jr. 278
Bowden, Elizabeth 15
Bowden, M. F. Maury 268
Bowden, Margaret 154
Bower, A. J. 272
Bowers, A. J. 272
Bowers, Ida 272
Bowers, William V., Rev. 2
Bowie, Emma L. 11
Bowie, James W. 11
Bowie, James William 10
Bowles, Lucy W. 238
Bowles, Sarah C. 238
Bowman, Eleanor Blanche 10
Bowman, George Price 10
Bowman, J. Price 10
Bowman, J. R., Rev. 45
Bowman, Rev. Mr. 222
Bowman, Richard Batcher 10
Bowman, Samuel Theodore 10
Bownan, Moffett Halley 10
Bowyer, Ann 283
Bowyer, T. M., Dr. 162
Boyd, Elizabeth 174
Boyd, James 174
Boyd, Jan 174
Boyd, John 174
Boyd, Katharine 20
Boyd, Kathryn Ann 20
Boyd, Mary 174
Boyd, Moses 174
Boyd, Nancy 174
Boyd, William 174
Boyd, William Spotswood 117
Boykin, H. E. 142
Boykin, John 207
Boykin, Nancy Virginia 207
Boykin, Simon 207
Boynton, Charlotte 157
Braaddus, John Prince 77
Bracken, Rev. Mr. 119
Braddock, General 179
Bradford, Alexander 122,213
Bradford, Swan V. 275
Bradfute, Evelyn S. 215
Bradley, D. 0. 228
Bradley, John A. 216
Bradley, John A., Dr. 216
Bradley, Margaret J. Meriwether 216
Bragg, Amanda Melvira Fitzwallen 17
Bragg, Ann Elizabeth 17,18
Bragg, Eliza 18
Bragg, Eliza Anne 17
Bragg, Elizabeth Janis 17
Bragg, Emma Hudsan 17

Bragg, Emma K. 18
Bragg, Evans 17,18
Bragg, Francis R. 17
Bragg, Gabriel James 17
Bragg, James F. 17
Bragg, James W. 17,18
Bragg, Lucy Am 17
Bragg, Lucy Rudisille 17
Bragg, Margaret 17
Bragg, Mary E. 17
Bragg, Philip E. 17
Bragg, Philip Evans 17,18
Bragg, Phillip T. 17
Bragg, Sarah Wade 17
Bragg, Susan Prances 17
Bragg, Thomas 17
Bragg, William C. 17
Bragg,Thomas E. G. 17
Branch, Aaron 8. 55,56
Branch, Aaron H., Mrs. 56
Branch, Aunt Monty 56
Branch, Cabel B. 55,56
Branch, Lilly L. 55
Branch, Lucian M. 55,56
Branch, Martha E., Mrs. 56
Branch, Mary E. 55,56
Branch, Robert H. 55
Branch, Robert R. 55,56
Branch, Sarah E. 55
Branch, Sarah J. 56
Branch, Stanley 8. 55,56
Branch, Thermuthis 55,56
Branch, Virginia Royster 55
Branch, Virginius R. 55,56
Brandon, Jessie 11
Brandon, John G. 11
Brandon, Nancy 11
Brandon, Polly 11
Brandon, Sary S. 11
Branscombe, Robert Lee 240
Branscome, Anna Lee 240,241
Branscome, Annie Laura 240
Branscome, Data Ada 240
Branscome, Elizabeth Alice 240
Branscome, Nancy Jam 240
Branscome, Ray Cubbage 240
Branscome, Robert Linden 240
Branscome, Robert Linden, Jr. 240
Branscome, William Alva 240
Braseltcn; Daniel 141
Braselton Carter 61
Braselton, Amos 141
Braselton, Elizabeth 141
Braselton, Green 141
Braselton, Hannah 141
Braselton, Hannah, Jr. 141
Braselton, Henry 141
Braselton, Jacob, Jr. 141
Braselton, Job 141
Braselton, Joel, Sr. 141
Braselton, John 141
Braselton, Mary 141
Braselton, Polly 61
Braselton, Rebecca 141
Braselton, Reutea 141
Braselton, Sarah 141
Braselton, William 142
Braxton, Anna F. M, 173
Braxton, Carter 173
Bray, Joseph 66

Bray, Julia Am 66
Brazeal, W, H, 56
Breckenridge, James 162
Brent, Catherine Mom 168
Brent, Charles 168
Brent, Charles Innis 168
Brent, Eliza 168
Brent, Emala Frances 168
Brent, Henry 168
Brent, John Gunn 168
Brent, Mary Am 168
Brent, Rachel More 168
Brent, Sally 168
Brent, Susan 168
Brete, Mildred 144
Brick, Mary 51
Bricker, Allen 51
Bricker, Christopher 51
Bricker, Eunice 51
Bricker, John 51
Bricker, Margaret 51
Bricker, Melissa 51
Bricker, Orpha 51
Bricker, Rebecca 51
Bricker, Sarah 51
Bricker, Truman 51
Bricker, William 51
Bright, Elianna M. J, 106
Bright, Francis Peyton 106
Bright, Jane Sinclair Jennings 106
Bright, Robert Anderson 106
Bright, S, F. B. 106
Bright, Samuel Francis 106
Bright, Susan H. 106
Bright, Susan Hannah 106
Brightwell, Martha 35
Bristow, Elizabeth 203
Britt, B. F. 153
Britt, E. B. 153
Britt, Elizabeth Clark 153
Britt, Exum 0. 153
Britt, Florence 0, 153
Britt, George W. 153
Britt, George W., Jr. 153
Britt, J. E. S. A. 153
Britt, John M. Exum 153
Britt, John W. 153
Britt, Lewis N. 153
Britt, Martha A. 153
Britt, Mary Eliza 153
Britt, Nancy May 153
Britt, Sarah E. 153
Britt, Thomas Norsworthy 153
Broaddus, A, W. 77
Broaddus, A. T. 77
Broaddus, Alexander Preston 77
Broaddus, Alexander Woodford 77
Broaddus, Alexander Woodford 77
Broaddus, Andrew, Rev. 77
Broaddus, Archibald Thomas 77
Broaddus, Attaway Miller 77
Broaddus, Attie Miller 77
Broaddus, Ellen 61
Broaddus, F. E. 77
Broaddus, John P. 77
Broaddus, John William 77
Broaddus, Junius M. 77
Broaddus, Lena Madison 77
Broaddus, M. R. 77
Broaddus, Matilda Haile 77

Broaddus, Mattie H. 77
Broaddus, Mordecai 77
Broaddus, Narmie P. 77
Broaddus, Preston 77
Broaddus, Roland F. 77
Broaddus, Roland Falconer 77
Broaddus, S. A. 77
Broaddus, S. M. 77
Broaddus, Sarah Ann Miller, Mrs. 77
Broaddus, Sarah Elizabeth 77
Broaddus, Susie S. 77
Broaddus, Alexander Woodford, Jr. 77
Broaddus, Attaway Miller, Miss 77
Broadnax, Martha 283
Broane, Thomas, Dr. 270
Brochax, Martha 283
Brockett, Mary Virginia 71
Brocks, Catherine 30
Brodnax, Am Hall 195
Brodnax, Ann 283
Broecldus, Sarah A. 77
Broeddus, Mordecai Redd 77
Brooke, Catherine 109
Brooks, Ann (Nancy) 30
Brooks, Berry Boswell 152
Brooks, Berry Boswell, Jr. 152
Brooks, Eliza Jam 181
Brooks, Elizabeth 30,181
Brooks, Elvira Anna 27
Brooks, Frances 30
Brooks, James 30
Brooks, Jotn 30
Brooks, Virginia Feild Walton 152
Brooks, Virginia Walton 152
Brooks, William 33
Brooks, William C. 30
Broome, Elizabeth 270
Broughton, Ann 207
Broun, Ann Lee 124
Broun, Edwin 125
Broun, Edwin Conway 124
Broun, Elizabeth 125
Broun, George 124
Broun, George McA. 125
Broun, Harriet 124,125
Broun, Jane Ann 125
Broun, Janetta 124,125
Broun, Margaret 124
Broun, Sarah Elizabeth 125
Broun, Thomas 124,125
Broun, Thomas 125
Broun, Thomas Kennerly 125
Broun, William 124,125
Brown, Anne Ludwell 119
Brown, Arm1stead 39
Brown, Catherine C. 238
Brown, Cynthia 141
Brown, Daniel 39
Brown, Daniel, Jr. 39
Brown, Daniel, Sr. 39
Brown, Elizabeth 39
Brown, Elizabeth C. 238
Brown, Frances 8. 39
Brown, Francis 88,189
Brown, George McAdam 124
Brown, George W. 238
Brown, Gustavus, Dr. 4
Brown, Harriet W. 238
Brown, James, Jr. 119
Brown, John 221

Brown, John H. 39
Brown, John H., Jr. 39
Brown, John McClintick 141
Brown, Judy 238
Brown, Lucy 39
Brown, M. H. 242
Brown, Margaret 189
Brown, Maria S. 238
Brown, Mary 141
Brown, Mary 189
Brown, Mary Arm 39
Brown, Mary Hunton 221
Brown, Matilda W. 238
Brown, Mr. 124
Brown, Nancy S. 27
Brown, Overton C. 238
Brown, Richard 39
Brown, Russel 39
Brown, Samuel, Captain 238
Brown, Sarah A. S. 238
Brown, Susannah 88
Brown, Thomas C. 39
Brown, Walter A. 39
Brown, Walter A., Sr. 39
Brown, William 39
Browne, Anne 261
Browne, Betty Carter 61
Browne, Charles Potter 222
Browne, Elizabeth 141
Browne, Hannah 261
Browne, Hannah Edwards 261
Browne, Henry 261
Browne, Mary 261
Browne, P. F. Doc 67
Browne, P. R. B. 187
Browne, Robert 261
Browne, Sally C. 67
Browne, William 261
Browne, William Taylor 261
Brown-Jefferson, S. F. S. 270
Bruce, G. R., Rev. 230
Bruce, George William 222
Bruce, Hannah E. 120
Bruce, John Potter 222
Bruce, Lucy Estelle 222
Bruce, Mary I. 120
Bruce, Mary Susan 222
Bruce, R. H. 56
Bruce, Robert Lee 222
Bruce, Sallie 222
Bruce, Sarah 222
Bruce, Sarah Arm Williams 222
Bruce, William N. 222
Brumfield, Candacia 156
Brumfield, Cinderella 156
Brumfield, Ezekiel 156
Brumfield, Frances 156
Brumfield, John 156
Brumfield, John Wilson 155,156
Brumfield, Louisiana 156
Brumfield, Malissa S. 149
Brumfield, Melissa 156
Brumfield, William 156
Brunskill, Rev. Mr. 110
Bryan, B. H. 178
Bryan, Elizabeth 178
Bryan, Howard 178
Bryan, Mary 217
Bryan, Susan 208
Bryant, America Angeline 230

Bryant, Annie D. 230
Bryant, Bayley D. 230
Bryant, Bayley Date 230
Bryant, Charles N. 230
Bryant, Edmund H. 230
Bryant, Edward Hamilton 230
Bryant, Mary 230
Bryant, Mary C. 230
Bryant, Minnie Ann Elizabeth 230
Bryant, Peter 230
Bryant, Peter L. 230
Buchan, Rev. Mr. 157
Buchanan, Mary Green 123
Buck, Lucy W. 37
Buckner, Ann Whitaker Taliaferro 179
Buckner, Baldwin M. 122,213
Buckner, Edmund Taylor 166
Buckner, Eliza Minn 166
Buckner, Elizabeth 143
Buckner, Eloise 166
Buckner, Francis 166
Buckner, Lucy 179
Buckner, Mary 166
Buckner, Mary M. 234
Buckner, Nicholas Taliaferro 179
Buckner, Philip Johnson 179
Buckner, Samuel, Colonel 166
Buckner, Sidney Am 166
Buckner, William 179
Bucknrer, Alfred 166
Bugg, Sarah Ann Jones 196
Bugg, Sarah Sherwood 196
Bugg, Sherwood 196
Bullock, Alice 111
Bullock, J. J., Rev. 128
Bullock, Mary 110
Bums, Elizabeth 252
Bundick, Sarah 150
Bunton, Anna Lee 241
Bunton, Anne Davis 241
Bunton, Arthur Frank 241
Bunton, Robert Franklin 241
Burch, Arthur Wilmer 149
Burch, Elisha 251
Burch, Ellser America 251
Burch, Frances Cletena 149
Burch, James A. 251
Burch, James A., Sr. 251
Burch, Jane 155
Burch, John 155
Burch, John R. 149
Burch, Jonathan C. 251
Burch, Lena Leota 149
Burch, Lewis B. 149
Burch, Martha 251
Burch, Mary Rebecca 149
Burch, Mary Virginia 251
Burch, Oscar Monroe 149
Burch, Richard 155
Burch, Richard, Jr. 155
Burch, Rosa A. 149
Burch, Sarah E. 251
Burch, Savarmah 251
Burch, Thomas E. 149
Burch, Walter V. 149
Burch, Weston J. 149
Burch, William V. 149
Burch, Wiltan E. 149
Burdine, Addison H. 253
Burdine, Adilla T. 253

Burdine, James C. 253
Burdine, Joannah A. 253
Burdine, John 253
Burdine, Judith 253
Burdine, Judith V. 253
Burdine, Mandone T. 253
Burdine, Mary 253
Burdine, Mary Jane 253
Burdine, Melissa 253
Burdine, Melissa E. 253
Burdine, Nancy N. 253
Burdine, Sarah 252
Burdine, Sarmel 253
Burdine, Susannah 253
Burdine, Wesley 253
Burford, Anne 145
Burgess, B., Rev. 125
Burgess, EdkkVd 39
Burgess, Elizabeth F. 39
Burgess, Littleton J. 42
Burit, Sally 198
Burkhalter, Dicy Louisa 155
Burnell, William McCreery 162
Burnet, Am C. 284
Burnet, Jchn 284
Burnet, Mary 61
Burnett, Agnes Hughes 256
Burnett, Beveridge Austin 256
Burnett, Dora Ada 240
Burnett, Dorothy Lee 240
Burnett, Henry Price 242
Burnett, Henry Prinae 240
Burnett, Judith Slaughter 255,256
Burnett, Margaret 240
Burnett, Nancy Elizabeth 240
Burnett, Nancy Susan 255
Burnett, Obadiah 256
Burnett, Valentitle 256
Burns, William C. 146
Burr, Hacrard 196
Burret, Paul H. 54
Burroughs, Eliza 132
Burrows, Elizabeth 282
Burrus, Celia Ann 267
Burrus, Charles Mills 267
Burrus, Cynthia Mills 267
Burrus, Frances 267
Burrus, Henry Trandy 267
Burrus, Mary Ann 267
Burrus, Mildred Thompson 267
Burrus, Nathaniel 267
Burrus, Peggy 267
Burrus, Rebecca Massfe 267
Burrus, Roger 267
Burrus, Roger, Sr. 267
Burrus, Sally 267
Burrus, Sally Ellen 267
Burrus, Virginia Banks 267
Burton, Ann 25,243
Burton, Benjamin 122,213
Burton, Charles 25,243
Burton, David 26,243
Burton, Drury 243
Burton, Elizabeth 122,213
Burton, Fanny 122
Burton, Fanny 213
Burton, Hannah 122
Burton, Hannah 313
Burton, Harriet 213
Burton, Harriett 122

Burton, Hutchins 25,243
Burton, Hutchins, Sr. 243
Burton, James 122,213
Burton, Julius 26,243
Burton, Lucy 122,213
Burton, Martha 122
Burton, Mary Mariah 122,213
Burton, May, Jr., Captain 213
Burton, May, Sr. 213
Burton, Nowell 26,243
Burton, Peggy 122,213
Burton, Richard 26 ,243
Burton, Robert 26,243
Burton, Samuel 26,243
Burton, Sarah 122,213
Burton, Susannah 26,243
Burton, William Allen 26,243
Burwell, Alice Williams 130
Burwell, Am Price 130
Burwell, Anrdstead 135
Burwell, Catherine 162
Burwell, Catherine Steptoe 162
Burwell, Elizabeth Ann 130
Burwell, Frances C. 162
Burwell, Francis Page 130
Burwell, George Washington 130
Burwell, James Steptoe 162
Burwell, Jdn Perrin 130
Burwell, John Blair 135
Burwell, Letitia 162
Burwell, Lewis 130
Burwell, Mary Blair 130
Burwell, Mary Famy 162
Burwell, Nathaniel 130
Burwell, Peter B. Whiting 130
Burwell, Rosalie 162
Burwell, William Kennon 130
Burwell, William M. 162
Butler, Bickwith 275
Butler, David 189
Butler, Margaret 189
Butler, Mary Ann 189
Butts, A. B. C. 225
Butts, A. I. 225
Butts, Alice 225
Butts, Benjamin 3,225
Butts, Benjamin Kirby 3,225
Butts, Betsy Eleanor. 3
Butts, C. L. 225
Butts, Catherine 225
Butts, Daniel 3,225
Butts, David Edward 3,225
Butts, E. A. 225
Butts, Eliza 3,225
Butts, Elizabeth LeGay 3,4,225
Butts, Ellza Clements 3,225
Butts, Fanney 225
Butts, Fanny 225
Butts, Farnrle Lewis 4
Butts, Francis 3
Butts, Frwces 225
Butts, Hull J. 225
Butts, James 3,225
Butts, James I. 225
Butts, James Indn 3,225
Butts, James, Sr. 225
Butts, Jatn 3,225
Butts, Jchn Floyd 3
Butts, John F. 225
Butts, John L. 225

Butts, K. S. 225
Butts, Keziah 4
Butts, Keziah Simmons 3
Butts, Lewis 3,225
Butts, Lucy 3,225
Butts, M. E. 225
Butts, Matt Calvert 3,225
Butts, Molley (Mollie) 3,225
Butts, Parker 3,225
Butts, Patsy Eleanor 225
Butts, Peter 3,225
Butts, Rebecca 3,4,225
Butts, Richard Henry 3,4,225
Butts, Sallie 3
Butts, Sallie Simmons 225
Butts, Samuel 3,4,225
Butts, Samuel, Captain 225
Butts, Sarah 225
Butts, Simnons 3,225
Butts, Thornas 3,225
Butts, Washington 3,225
Butts, William 3,225
Byars, Sarah 144
Byne, Edmund 173
Bynes, Patience 84
Byrd, Mildred Ann 157
Byrd, Thomas Otway 158
Cabell John Jordan, Dr. 266
Cabell, Elvira M6
Cabell, Pauline J. 206
Cage, A. 187
Cagna, Laura Calloway 249
Cain, John 143
Cain, Lucinda 143
Caines, Rev. Mr. 106
Caldwell, David, Rev. 63
Caldwell, Robert Cunningham 200
Calhoun, John T. 47
Callahan, Jacob 236
Callaway, Ann 204
Callaway, Anna 205
Callaway, Archilles T01,204
Callaway, Charles 201,204,205,248
Callaway, Charles, Jr. 204
Callaway, Dasha 205
Callaway, David 205
Callaway, Elizabeth 204,205
Callaway, Flaney 225
Callaway, Frances 201,204
Callaway, Francis 205
Callaway, Henry Green 21)5
Callaway, Jal 201,204
Callaway, James 201,204,205
Callaway, John 201,204
Callaway, John 205
Callaway, John Pate 204
Callaway, John W. 205
Callaway, John, Colonel 205
Callaway, Joseph 204
Callaway, Judithi 201,204,205
Callaway, Mary 204
Callaway, Matilda 205
Callaway, Milly M4
Callaway, Peggy 205
Callaway, Polly 201,204
Callaway, Richard 204
Callaway, Sarah 201,204,205
Callaway, Sarah Am 205
Callaway, Sena 204
Callaway, Thomas 204

Callaway, Will 249
Callaway, William 204
Callaway, William M.,204,205
Callaway, William, Jr. 204
Callaway,, Henry 201
Callenda, Ann 205
Callis, Mary Ermine 34
Calloway, Ballenger 248
Calloway, Carlos F. 249
Calloway, Carrie Ann 249
Calloway, Carrie Bell 248
Calloway, Cecil 249
Calloway, Charles B. 248
Calloway, Charles B., Sr. 249
Calloway, Charles J. 248,249
Calloway, Christa L. 249
Calloway, Clara Alice249
Calloway, Coleih 249
Calloway, Collin T. 249
Calloway, Dozier 217
Calloway, Edith Arline 249
Calloway, Ella 248
Calloway, Frank 249
Calloway, George 248
Calloway, Hazel 249
Calloway, Icie Fee 248
Calloway, Icie Lillian 249
Calloway, James 248
Calloway, Jernifer Lynne 249
Calloway, Jmie B. 249
Calloway, John 248
Calloway, Lucy 248
Calloway, Mallie 248
Calloway, Margaret 248
Calloway, Mary E. 248
Calloway, Mary Howard 28,249
Calloway, Nancy 248
Calloway, Stephen 28 ,249
Calloway, Sudie Mae 248
Calloway, Susan MtcheTle 249
Calloway, Theodore R. 249
Calloway, Theodore R., Jr. 249
Calver, Elizabeth 165
Calvert, Cornelius 165
Camden, Athy 7
Camden, Edward Norgrove 7,8
Camden, Ethel Claudine 7
Camden, Janes Lewis 7
Camden, Lillian Belle 8
Camden, Little Athy 7
Camden, Lucy Campbell 7
Camden, Lucy M. 7,8
Camden, Margarett Ovedia 7,8
Camden, Mrs. C. C. 8
Camden, Sallie C. 7
Camden, Sally Davis 7
Camden, W. L. 8
Camden, Walker L. 7
Camden, William Wray 7
Cameron, John, Rev. 263
Cameron, John, Rev. 263
Camm, Ann 111
Camm, John 110
Camm, John, Rev. Mr. 119
Camm, Mary 110,111
Camm, Richard 111
Camm, Sarah 111
Camn, Elizabeth 110
Camp, Drucilla 211
Campbell, A. W., Rev. 190

Campbell, Alexander 36
Campbell, Andrew 36
Campbell, Archibald 36
Campbell, Archihald, Dr. 279
Campbell, Betty 20
Campbell, Caroline 46
Campbell, Caroline Alice 47
Campbell, Clementine 249
Campbell, Darcas 46,47
Campbell, Darcas Ellen 47
Campbell, Edgar 47
Campbell, Elizabeth 36,46
Campbell, Harry K. 249
Campbell, Harry Trever 249
Campbell, James 36,56
Campbell, Jane 36
Campbell, Jane 36,181
Campbell, John H. 46,47
Campbell, Lavinia 46
Campbell, Luro 257
Campbell, Margaret 46
Campbell, Mary 36
Campbell, Mary C. 7
Campbell, Mary M. 190
Campbell, Nancy 36,46
Campbell, Nancy C. 47
Campbell, Robert 36,206
Campbell, Samuel 26
Campbell, Sarah 36
Campbell, Susan 119
Campbell, T. E. 254
Campbell, Thomas 206
Campbell, W. L. 7
Campbell, William 36
Campbelll, Marion Francis 181
Campell, Adellne 224
Cannaday, Armie 17
Cannaday, Asa Howard 17
Cannaday, E. C. 17
Cannaday, Frank W. 17
Cannaday, Julia A. 17
Cannaday, Julian 17
Cannaday, Kate 17
Cannaday, Linnie 17
Cannaday, T. 17
Cannaday, T. H. 17
Cannaday, Tazewell H. 17
Cannaday, William Foster 17
Cannday, Iva Ella 17
Cannon, Jdn W. 117
Cannon, John F. 117
Cannon, Kennan Page Overbey, Mrs. 117
Cannon, Kennon Page Overbey 117
Capen, Edward Albert 226
Carber, Sarah 70
Cardwell, Henrietta 181
Carey, Sally 233
Carey, Wilson Miles 233
Cargile, Mary Am 202
Carletan, Henry 208
Carletan, Nancy 209
Carletcn, Thomas, Sr. 209
Carleton, Betsy Alien 209
Carleton, Elizabeth 2C8,209
Carleton, John Hyde 2C5,209
Carleton, Lydia 209
Carleton, Martha 209,209
Carleton, Polley 208
Carleton, Polly 209
Carleton, Rebecca F. 209

Carleton, Sarah 208
Carleton, Susannah Finch 208
Carleton, Thomas 208,209
Carleton, Thomas, Jr. 209
Carlis, Jeremiah 101
Carlton, Herbert, Rev. 83
Carmichael, Daniel 275
Carney, Susannah 163
Carpenber, Am Eliza F. 283
Carpenter, Sarah E. 39
Carpenter, Thomas P., Dr. 69
Carr, Agnes 13
Carr, Alexander Walter 5
Carr, Ann MatFtda 154
Carr, Anne Watkins 5
Carr, Benjamin L. 154
Carr, Charles Nelson 5
Carr, Cynthia 5
Carr, Elijah Walker 5
Carr, Eliza Ann 154,160
Carr, Emaline 154
Carr, Ethan 154,160
Carr, F., Mrs. 5
Carr, Florida Cynthia 5
Carr, Frances C. 5
Carr, Frances Selina 5
Carr, Frances Susan 5
Carr, James 13
Carr, James I. 154
Carr, Jane 5
Carr, Jernima 13
Carr, Joanna 13
Carr, Joel 13
Carr, John 154
Carr, Mary Ann Selina 5
Carr, Mary Eliza 5
Carr, Mary Elizabeth 154
Carr, Nancy 154,160
Carr, Polly C. 153
Carr, Selina Agnes 4
Carr, Sophia Jane 154
Carr, Susan Agnes 5
Carr, Susanaah 5
Carr, Temperance 13
Carr, Tharras D. 5
Carr, Thomas Walker 5
Carr, Thomas, Colonel 4
Carr, William 5
Carr, William A. 4,5
Carr, William Bacon 5
Carr,Thomas 5
Carrell, Catherine Ray 241
Carrell, Charlotte Ray 241
Carrell, Elizabeth Ann 241
Carrell, Finis Dixon 241
Carrell, Jeanne Hylton 241
Carrington, Alfred Randolph 272
Carrington, Ann Blair 33
Carrington, Henry AlexanQr 272
Carriway, George W. 230
Carson, Andrew 245
Carson, Ann Mariah 245
Carson, Barbara 245
Carson, Betsey 245
Carson, Darious W. 245
Carson, Elizabeth A. 245
Carson, James R. 245
Carson, John R. 245
Carson, Margaret Jane 245
Carson, Meridith 245

Carson, Miss 105
Carson, Richard 245
Carson, Robert D. 245
Carson, Robert Holland 245
Carson, Samuel 245
Carson, T. M., Rev. 23
Carter, Abigail 100
Carter, Alcy 274
Carter, Ann 274,283
Carter, Ann B. 283,284
Carter, Ann Bowyer 283
Carter, Anna Beale 157
Carter, Anna Fauntleroy 159
Carter, Anna Maria 157,158
Carter, Anne Troop 287
Carter, Anne Troupe 288
Carter, Berkeley 159
Carter, Bettie 218
Carter, Bettie M. 19
Carter, Betty 61
Carter, Catherine 157
Carter, Catherine Spotswood 57
Carter, Charles Cleve 159
Carter, Christopher Lawson 202
Carter, Clarence Harvie 159
Carter, Dale Miller 202
Carter, E. F. 159
Carter, Edmonia Bewrley 159
Carter, Edmonia F. 158
Carter, Edmonia Fauntleroy 159
Carter, Edward 157,158,202
Carter, Edward C. 158
Carter, Edward Phillpot 22
Carter, Edward St. Orville 159
Carter, Eliz. Landan 158
Carter, Eliza Travers 157
Carter, Elizabeth 157,158,202
Carter, Ellen 276
Carter, Emna Clew 158,159
Carter, Fanny Lee 157,158
Carter, Flora Berkeley 159
Carter, Frances Lee 158
Carter, George 157,274
Carter, Harwar 158,159
Carter, Henry Ann C. 283
Carter, James 22
Carter, James Drew 22
Carter, James Drew Virginius 22
Carter, Jeluthan 202
Carter, Jesse 202
Carter, Joanna 202
Carter, John Hill 61
Carter, John M. 283,284
Carter, John Michel 283
Carter, Jonathan Melter 100
Carter, Judith 18,274
Carter, Julia 58
Carter, Landon 58,61,157,158,276
Carter, Landon St. Leger 159
Carter, Laura Montreville 159
Carter, Lawson Hobson 202
Carter, Lucy 274
Carter, Lucy Emily 283
Carter, Lucy Landon 157
Carter, Marco Bozzaris 283,284
Carter, Mary Ann 127
Carter, Mary Ann J. 100
Carter, Mary Champe 157
Carter, Mary Eleanor 159
Carter, Mary Harwar 159

Carter, Melzer 100
Carter, Mildred Ann Byrd 157
Carter, Millicent 274
Carter, Mollie 22
Carter, Mollie Magdeline 22
Carter, Nancy 233
Carter, Olivia Hanson 158,159
Carter, Otway Lane 159
Carter, R. O. 159
Carter, R. C. 158
Carter, R. W. 157
Carter, Raleigh 274
Carter, Rawley Williamson 202
Carter, Rev. Mr. 119
Carter, Robert C. 158,159
Carter, Robert Charles 157,158
Carter, Robert Corbin 159
Carter, Robert O. 158
Carter, Robert Otway 159
Carter, Robert W. 157
Carter, Robert Wormeley 157
Carter, Rosa 22
Carter, Sallie 133
Carter, Sallie Ann Peable 22
Carter, Sarah 157,202,274
Carter, St. Leger Landon 157,158,159
Carter, Thomas 202,283
Carter, Thomas Otway Byrd 157,158
Carter, Wallis Marion 100
Carter, William 274
Carter, William Fetter 100
Carter, Winifred 202
Carter, Winifred Travers 157
Cary, Elizabeth 138,139
Cary, Hannah 138,139
Cary, Martha Catherine 78
Cary, Mary 139
Cary, Miles 138,139
Cary, Nathaniel 139
Cash, Barnett 137
Cash, James Barton 174
Cash, James Braxton, Jr. 174
Casko, James A., Rev. 230
Cason, Ann Sophia 44
Cason, Benjamin 44
Cason, William James 44
Cassell, Deborah 11
Castleman, Caroline 178
Catlet, George 157
Catlet, Lawrence 157
Cauby, Emma 230
Cauthorn, R. S., Dr. 238
Cdlloway, Mary 248
Cenden, Lillie Bell 7
Center, Ellen 277
Chadwick, Rhoda 105
Cluletm, Brothers 208,209
CrIffin, Fayette 103
Cuter, Charles William 157
Cuter, Ellenorah Hassentine 100
Cuter, Leanna 274
Dillard, John W., Dr. 23
Dillard, John William 23
Dillard, Joseph 137,139
Dillard, Joseph Henry 138
Dillard, Judith 137,139
Dillard, Lucy Myra 43
Dillard, Mahala R. 137
Dillard, Mahala Roberson 137
Dillard, Mary Anne 138

Dillard, Mary E. J. 137
Dillard, Mary Elizabeth 138
Dillard, Mary Ellen Judith 137
Dillard, Mary J. 138
Dillard, O. D. ,138
Dillard, Orgon Duvall 137
Dillard, Oscar P. 138
Dillard, Paulina E. 137,138
Dillard, Paulina Smith 137
Dillard, Robert Franklln 138
Dillard, Sophia F. 138
Dillard, Sukey 139
Dillard, Susan Ann 137
Dillard, Thomas P. 137
Dillard, Virginia Pettus 138
Dillard, William Walker 138
Dillard, William Warner 138
Dillard, William White 23
Dillard,Thomas Pettus 177
Dillion, ChrIstian 18
Dillon, Jackson 9
Dingler, John, Rev. 209
Dinwiddie, Robert 278
Dismore, Olive 143
Dixon, Eliza Jane 257
Dixon, Jane S. 257
Dnnbar, Delilah 229 ,230
Dobbins, Allie 17
Dobbins, E. L. 16
Dobbins, E. L. 17
Dobbins, Edward E. 17
Dobbins, Edward L. 16
Dobson, John T. 113
Dodd, Thaddeus 146
Dodrell, Isaac 237
Dodson, Constantine 173
Dodson, Daniel 173
Dodson, Edmund 173
Dodson, Elijah 173
Dodson, John Peters 173
Dodson, Joshua 173
Dodson, Lochy 173
Dodson, Nancy 173
Dodson, Sarah 173
Dodson, Stephen 173
Dodson, William 173
Donaldson, Caroline 101
Donaldson, Katherine 101
Donalson, Agnes 207
Donalson, Agnes Peel 207
Donalson, George 207
Donalson, John 207
Donalson, Reuben 207
Donalson, William 207
Doty, Hanah 90
Dougherty, Nancy J. 230
Doughtry, Maryan 174
Doughty, E. 174
Doughty, Elizabeth 174
Doughty, Jane H. 174
Doughty, Jane R. 184
Doughty, Martha L. 174
Doughty, Mary Ann Thomas 174
Doughty, Nancy B. 174
Doughty, Sally M. 174
Doughty, Thomas 174
Doughty, William 174
Douglas, Elizabeth 282,283
Douglas, James 281,282
Douglas, John 282,283

Douglas, John Hunter 282
Douglas, Margaret 282,283
Douglas, Mary 30,282
Douglas, Nath. Heron 283
Douglas, Patsie Seldon 283
Douglas, Peggie 282
Douglas, Peggy 122,281
Douglas, Will 283
Douglas, William 282
Douglas, William, Rev. 179,281
Douglass, Elizabeth 30
Douglass, Jane 30
Douglass, Mary 30
Douglass, Nancy M. 30
Douglass, Peggy 213
Douglass, Sarah 30
Douglass, William 30
Douglass, William, Jr. 30
Douglass, William, Sr. 30
Douthall, Edith 273
Douthat, Eliza 222
Dowell, Mary 143
Downes, Mary 234
Downes, Nathaniel 234
Downes, Rose Pearce 234
Downing, Elizabeth 218
Dozier, Emily H. 101
Draft, Nellie Allen 177
Draper, Birdie 9
Draper, Charles L. 152
Draper, E. J., Miss 9
Draper, Emma J. 9,19
Draper, Emma Jane 11
Draper, John Harrison 11
Draper, Letitia Annanda 11
Draper, Letitia Annanda Scott 11
Draper, Martin 11
Draper, Mary G. 11
Draper, Mary Peyton Walton 152
Draper, Roberta Susan 19
Driver, Charles 153
Driver, Edward 153
Driver, Polly 154
Driver, Sarah 153
Droste, Charles Herman 251
Drummond, Elizabeth 89
Drummond, William 89
Dudley, ALex 230
Dudley, Lucy P. 230
Dugan, Elizabeth Ann 148
Dugan, John 148
Dugan, Lucy L. 148
Dugan, Margaret C. 148
Dugan, Marthy E. 148
Dugan, Mary J. 148
Dugan, Nancy 148
Dugan, Robert 148
Duggan, Ruby Beatrice 202
Duke, Betsey Park 65
Duke, Betsy P. 65
Duke, Emre 116
Duke, James L. 64,65
Duke, James Lawrence 65
Duke, Mary Ransom 64,65
Duke, Mildred Wirt 133
Dumkum, Mary I. 100
Dunbar, Agness A. 229
Dunbar, Ann 229,230
Dunbar, Catharine 230
Dunbar, David 229,230

Dunbar, George F. 229,230
Dunbar, Gracy 229 ,230
Dunbar, Hancock, Rev. Mr. 110
Dunbar, HAnnilton 229,230
Dunbar, J. S. 230
Dunbar, Johannah 229
Dunbar, John Collins 229,230
Dunbar, John S. 230
Dunbar, John Sparks 229
Dunbar, Rev. Mr. 111
Dunbar, William Willson 229
Dunn, Ernest 9
Dunn, Maggie 9
Dunn, Thares 193
Dupuis, Jane 115
Durham, James 259
Durham, Margarett 259
Durrett, Abigail 100
Durrett, Albert Albea 99,100
Durrett, Ann Lewis 100
Durrett, Braxton Byrd 100
Durrett, Charles Lewis 100
Durrett, E. V. 100
Durrett, Elliott V. 100
Durrett, Elliott Vermanet 100
Durrett, Harvey John Thomas 100
Durrett, Jonathan 99,100
Durrett, Jonathan J. 100
Durrett, Jonathan Jackson 100
Durrett, Judith T. 100
Durrett, Judith Terrell 10
Durrett, Kate Baker 100
Durrett, Laurence Blanton 100
Durrett, Maria L. 100
Durrett, Martha E. 100
Durrett, Martha Ellen 100
Durrett, Mary A. J. 100
Durrett, Mary Ann Johnson 100
Durrett, Mary Elizabeth 100
Durrett, Mary Virginia 100
Durrett, Nancy 100
Durrett, Oscar Fitzwallen 100
Durrett, Polly H. 99,100
Durrett, Robert Henry 100
Durrett, Susan E. 100
Durrett, William 0. 100
Durrett, William Hines 99
Durrett, Williamn Albert 100
Dutton, Mary 168
Dwyer, Elizabeth Arm 177
Dwyer, Jennie 177
Dwyer, Margaret Ellen 177
Dwyer, Mary Jean 177
Dwyer, Richard Joseph 177
Dwyer, William Carlin 177
Dyer, Mary C. 120
Dyke, Dorothey E. 108
Dyke, Elizabeth 108
Dyke, James 108
Dyke, Richard L. 108
Dyson, E. R. 172
Dyson, H. H. 172
Dyson, Harry H. 172
Dyson, Richard E. 172
Dyson, Tabitha 172
Dyson, Thomas W. 172
Earle, Amanda A. 116
Earley, Abner 2
Early, Abner 201
Early, Bishop 284

Early, Elizabeth 201
Early, Jacobus 201
Early, Jeffry 201
Early, Jeremiah, Colonel 201
Early, Jinny 201
Early, John 201
Early, Joseph 201
Early, Jubal 201
Early, Judith 201
Early, Sally 201
Early, Sarah Anderscn 201
Easton, Ellza 257
Eastwood, Rev. Mr. 283
Eblen, J. W. 22
Eblin, Grace Maudine Goodwin 22
Edans, Mary Jane 135
Eddins, Salina 211
Eddins, Sndth 213
Edmonds, Anne 280
Edmonds, Betty 280
Edmonds, Billy, Mrs. 280
Edmonds, Catey 280
Edmonds, Elias 280
Edmonds, Elias, Jr. 280
Edmonds, Franke 280
Edmonds, Frankey 280
Edmonds, Jars 280
Edmonds, John 280
Edmonds, Judith 280
Edmonds, Lucy 280
Edmonds, Sarah 280
Edmonds, Thomas W. R. 99
Edmonds, William Ed. 280
Edmonds, William, Colonel 280
Edmonds, William, Jr. 280
Edmonds. Elizabeth 280
Edmondson, Angeline V. F. 91
Edmondson, Ann E. E. 92
Edmondson, C. R. 91
Edmondson, Charles R. 91
Edmondson, E. E. 91
Edmondson, Joseph H. 91
Edmondson, Martha 91
Edmondson, Martha V. E. 91
Edmondson, V. F. 91
Edmunds, Annerica 99
Edmunds, Charlotte 247
Edmunds, Cornelia 99
Edmunds, Ealine Louise 99
Edmunds, Edward R. 99
Edmunds, Edwin S. 99
Edmunds, Edwin Short 99
Edmunds, Eliza H. 99
Edmunds, Eliza Kennon 99
Edmunds, Eliza Randolph 99
Edmunds, George M. 99
Edmunds, Jack B. F. 99
Edmunds, John 99
Edmunds, Marguerite 99
Edmunds, Martha A. E. M. 99
Edmunds, Martha A. E. M. J. S. 99
Edmunds, Martha Short 99
Edmunds, Thomas 99
Edmunds, Thomas M. I. 99
Edmunds, Thomas McAfee II 99
Edmunds,Thomas M. 99
Edwards, Thomas Theodore 149
Edwards, Alice Tallietha 118,149
Edwards, Ann 132,133
Edwards, Anna Elizabeth 71

Edwards, Annericus A., Doctor 133
Edwards, Annericus AdAnns 133
Edwards, Betsy 8
Edwards, Bosto 8
Edwards, Boston Alexandra 8
Edwards, Cardle Perlina 8
Edwards, Caroline 8
Edwards, Carrie 8
Edwards, Core Perlina 8
Edwards, Doctor P. 8
Edwards, Elijah Rall 149
Edwards, Elizabeth Ann 133
Edwards, Etta Frances 8
Edwards, Etta Virginia 149
Edwards, F. M., Rev. 35
Edwards, G. M. 149
Edwards, George M. 149
Edwards, George McIntosh 149
Edwards, George S. 148,149
Edwards, Georgia Ware 149
Edwards, Hemy Shelton 148,149
Edwards, Isaac 8
Edwards, James 8
Edwards, James M. 8
Edwards, John Luke 8
Edwards, John Sumner 149
Edwards, Joseph 8
Edwards, Joseph C. 133
Edwards, Joseph Chirn 133
Edwards, Joseph M. K. 8
Edwards, Lirwood 81
Edwards, Louise Virginia 149
Edwards, Margaret Ball 149
Edwards, Maria 268
Edwards, Martha Ann 245
Edwards, Mary 8
Edwards, Mary A. 149
Edwards, Mary C. 8
Edwards, Mary Cornelia 148,149
Edwards, Mary Hope 149
Edwards, Mary Virginia 8
Edwards, May E. 148, 149
Edwards, Priscilla 135
Edwards, Robert 132,133,135
Edwards, Robert Andrew 135
Edwards, Robert Ann 132
Edwards, Robert E. Lee 135
Edwards, Rosa Lee 8
Edwards, Rosa Lee 8
Edwards, Sallie 8
Edwards, Sally Sands 149
Edwards, Sarah 8,133
Edwards, Sarah Bdll 133
Edwards, Sarah Frances 148,149
Edwards, Sarah Howorth 133
Edwards, Thomas 133
Edwards, Thomas Andrew 132,133
Edwards, Thomas McAfee 11 199
Edwards, William 8
Edwards, William Henry 149
Edwards, William, Sr. 132
Egglestan, Mary E. 69,71
Elbeck, Henry, Rev. Mr. 119
Elcan, Junius H. 283
Elder, Beatrice 208
Elder, Effie 208
Elder, Eugene 208
Elder, Irene 208
Elder, Leila 208
Elder, Nancy V. 208

Elder, Rosa 208
Elder, W. A., Jr. 208
Eldridge, Ann M. 48
Eldridge, Thomas 48
Eliot-Newman, Nell 128
Elkin, Dorcas 32
Elkin, Elizabeth 32
Elkin, James 32
Elkin, Jean (Jane) 32
Elkin, Katharine 32
Elkin, Luvica 32
Elkin, Martha 32
Elkin, Mary 32
Elkin, Nancey 32
Elkin, Rhoda 32
Elkin, Sibbo 32
Elkin, Thomas B. 32
Elkin, William 32
Elkin, Zacheus 32
Elkln, James 32
Elktn, William Terry 32
Ellet, Keziah 231
Ellett, Daniel, Capt. 34
Ellett, Elizabeth T. 34
Ellington, John 91
Elliott, W., Rev. 113
Ellis, Henry 93
Ellis, J. L. 19
Ellis, Martha R. B. 93
Ellis, Susan C. 42
Emerson, Louisa S. 54
Emory, Bishop 48
Empie, Rev. Dr. 63
Erwin, Ann E. 194
Erwin, Ann V. 116
Erwin, George W. 194
Erwin, H. F. 194
Erwin, Mary I. 194
Erwin, S. B. 116
Erwin, S. E. Eliza 194
Erwin, Thomas W., Jr. 194
Erwin, Thomas Winston 194
Erwln, A. E., Miss 194
Eskridge, Allucius 3. 132
Eskridge, Allucius Jett 132
Eskridge, Ann 132
Eskridge, Ann E. 132
Eskridge, Ann Elizabeth 132
Eskridge, Ann H. 132
Eskridge, Betty 132
Eskridge, Elizabeth Baker 132
Eskridge, Mary C. 132
Eskridge, Mary Qdar 132
Eskridge, Robert E. 132
Eskridge, Robert Edwards 132
Eskridge, William 132
Eskridge, William, Jr. 132
Eskridge, William, Sr. 132
Estes, Anm 162
Estes, Courtney 162
Estes, Henry 162
Estes, Jackson 162
Estes, Jefferson 162
Estes, Lucinda 162
Estes, Madison 162
Estes, Maria 162
Estes, Martha 162
Estes, Nancy 162
Estes, Susannah W. 162
Estes, Virginia 162

Estes, Willia Jane 162
Evans, Thomas, Rev. 167
Evans, Ann 210
Evans, Caroline 210
Evans, Caroline M. 210
Evans, Eliza 210
Evans, Elizabeth 165
Evans, George 165
Evans, James 210
Evans, Martha 210
Evans, Martha C. 210
Evans, Martha M. E. 210
Evans, Mary 165
Evans, Matt R. 210
Evans, Sophia 210
Evans, Thomas 210
Evans, Thomas C. 210
Fair, J. Y., Dr. 45
Fairfax, Orlanlo 277
Fairfax, Sally 277
Fall, Anne Apperson 178
Fall, James Slater 178
Fall, Philip S. 178
Faris, Ella A. 73
Farish, Catherine 234
Farish, Catherine Jane 235
Farish, Emily 235
Farish, Hazlewood 234,235
Farish, Stephen 234
Farley, Francis 278
Farmer, Bertha 101
Farmer, David Thomas 12
Farmer, Elizabeth Ellen 12
Farmer, Eugenia Jackson 12
Farmer, Henry 12
Farmer, James K. Polk 12
Farmer, Louisa 12
Farmer, Louisa J. 12
Farmer, Martha Ann 12
Farmer, Sally Henry 12
Farmer, Susan Emily 12
Farrar, Pattie 127
Farris, Eliza A. 146
Farrow, Jane D. 230
Faster, Hattie Funds 16
Faulcon, John 261
FaunfLeroy, Mary Lorimer 200
Fauntleroy, Thomas Waring 167
Fauntleray, Isabella Lorimer 200
Fauntleroy, Appirfa Bushrod 200
Fauntleroy, Catherine Moore 200
Fauntleroy, George Lorimer 200
Fauntleroy, Hannah Elizabeth 200
Fauntleroy, John 200
Fauntleroy, Judith T. 200
Fauntleroy, Martha Payne Waring 200
Fauntleroy, Sarah Tomlin 200
Fauntleroy, Thomas 200
Fauntleroy, Thomas Waring 200
Fauntleroy, Thonras W. 158
Fauntleroy, William Lawson Epuphroditus Waring 200
Feild, A. M. 186,187
Feild, Alex 186
Feild, C. G. 186,187
Feild, Charles Grandview 186,187
Feild, Charles Grandison 186
Feild, Henry A. 187
Feild, Henry Alison 187
Feild, Jean Murray 186
Feild, Mary Catharine 186

Feild, Robert Alexander 186
Feild, Thomas Blackburn 187
Feild, Virginia 152
Feild, Williaetta 187
Fellworth, George 253
Feree, Leah 18
Ferguson, Emily Ann 183
Ferguson, Emma V. 64
Ferguson, John D. 184
Ferguson, Maryanne 184
Ferris, Josiah 181
Few, Ignatius 4
Field, Mary C. May 54
Fields, Carmen Erselle 71
Fife, William, Rev. Mr. 119
Finch, Martha 208
Finch, Rebecca 208
Finch, Tyree G. 127
Findley, John 56
Finks, A. N. 69
Finks, Alexander Newton 69
Finks, Alexander, Capt. 69
Finks, Alice Ola 71
Finks, Clarles S. 71
Finks, David Lee 69
Finks, Edna Lee 71
Finks, Edna Lee Hamilton 71
Finks, Emmet C. 69
Finks, Emmett L. 69
Finks, Emmett Lester 69
Finks, Frances B. 71
Finks, Frances Story 69
Finks, Fred Neal 69
Finks, Fred Neale 69
Finks, Fred W. 69
Finks, Genevieve Constance 71
Finks, Helen Elizabeth 69
Finks, Henry L. 69
Finks, Henry Linwood 69
Finks, John Beverly 71
Finks, John H. 69,71
Finks, Judith F. 69
Finks, Juriah 39
Finks, Lewis 39
Finks, Lewis Fisher 39
Finks, Lewis Franklin 71
Finks, Louis Lozano 69
Finks, Lula Clyde 69
Finks, Mark F. 39
Finks, Mary Eve 39
Finks, Ola E. 71
Finks, Percy N. 71
Finks, Robert Lyrm 71
Finks, Robert N. 71
Finks, Robert Newton 71
Finks, Ruth L. 71
Finks, Sallie Eggleston 71
Finks, Sallie Lewis 69
Finks, Virginia Frances 71
Finks, William Preston 39
Finley, Elizabeth 27
Finley, Elizabeth 27
Fishback, John N. 85
Fisher, James, Rev. 18
Fisher, Sarah Jane 284
Fitzgerald, Edmnd 201
Fitzgerald, Elizabeth 201
Fitzgerald, James 201
Fitzgerald, Mildred 201
Fitzgerald, Nancy 201

Fitzgerald, Reuben 201
Fitzgerald, Rev. 24
Fitzgerald, Samuel 201
Fitzgerald, William 201
Fitzhugh, Alexander 105
Fitzhugh, Colonel 105
Fitzhugh, Dennis 105
Fitzhugh, Edda 104
Fitzhugh, Elizabeth Henry 104
Fitzhugh, Frances Hhrmphry Eqr 157
Fitzhugh, John 105
Fitzhugh, Lafayette Henry 105
Fitzhugh, Lucy 105
Fitzhugh, Lucy Redd 104
Fitzhugh, Mary Macon, Mrs. 104
Fitzhugh, Mrs. 275
Fitzhugh, Patrick Henry 104
Fitzhugh, Philip 104
Fitzhugh, Philip Aylett 105
Fitzhugh, Thadeus 105
Fleming, Lucy C. 164
Fleming, Mary A. 78
Flerning, Miss 223
Flippen, Mary 142
Flournoy, David 123
Flournoy, Elvenia E. 55,56
Flournoy, Frances 155
Floyd, 0. B. 222
Fluke, Nannie 127
Flynn, Mary C. 163
Fodcs, Sabra 23
Fogle, Thomas W. 20
Foley, Janie Combs 228
Fontaine, Eliza T. 166
Fontaine, John, Colonel 206
Foote, Alexander HAnnilton 284
Foote, Anne 287
Foote, Charles B. 257
Foote, Charles Hayward 284
Foote, Elizabeth 284
Foote, Elizabeth Washington 284
Foote, Hayward 284
Foote, Helen Elizabeth 284
Foote, Helen Maria 284
Foote, Henry S. 284
Foote, Richard 284
Foote, Richard Stuart 284
Foote, Richard Zach 284
Foote, Sallie 284
Foote, Sarah Stuart 284
Foote, William 287,288
Foote, William Hayward 284
Foote, William Stuart 284
Forbes, Lorna Doone Hubard 24
Forbes, Mary 156
Force, Charles 0. 257
Ford, A. C., Dr. 115
Ford, Ann 198
Ford, Anna 32,198
Ford, Boaz 198
Ford, Dona Leslie 229
Ford, James, Jr. 198
Ford, JAnnes 198
Ford, Jennetta M. 115
Ford, Judith 198
Ford, Magdeline 198
Ford, Marie 198
Ford, Mary E. 128
Ford, Oscela 229
Ford, Pierre 198

Ford, Rachel 198
Ford, Rowland 229
Ford, Ruth 198
Ford, Sally 195
Forrest, Martha 264
Forst, M. A. 129
Foster, A. 16,17
Foster, Agnes 16
Foster, Anna Maria Daniel 220
Foster, Annie 17
Foster, Asa 16,17
Foster, Bettie 16
Foster, Bettie Ridinger 16
Foster, Daniel 220,221
Foster, Dorcas 220
Foster, E. A. 16,17
Foster, Earle 16
Foster, Edgar 16
Foster, Edgar A. 16 ,17
Foster, Eliza 16
Foster, Elizabeth 16 ,220,221
Foster, Elizabeth Mary 220
Foster, Ewindwina 16
Foster, Gabriel 16,17
Foster, George 16,17,220
Foster, George F. 16
Foster, George P. 17
Foster, George W. 17
Foster, George William 16
Foster, Hallie Ethel 188
Foster, Harry Holland 17
Foster, Hattie F. 16
Foster, Hugh 16
Foster, Isaac 16,220,221
Foster, James 223,221
Foster, James William 220,221
Foster, John 16
Foster, John 17
Foster, John Edd 188
Foster, John Edd, Jr. 188
Foster, John Hinton 221,221
Foster, Judith K. 221
Foster, Judith Keith 220
Foster, Julia Ann 16
Foster, Julianna 16
Foster, Larkin 16,17
Foster, Larkin Alice 16
Foster, Lillie L. 16
Foster, Lizzie 16
Foster, Lizzie Blake 16,17
Foster, Lizzie Pem 188
Foster, Maida Ruth 16
Foster, Margaret R. 17
Foster, Mary 16 ,220
Foster, Mary Ann 58
Foster, Mary Elizabeth 220,221
Foster, Mary J. 16
Foster, Mary Jane 16
Foster, Mary MilAnn 255
Foster, Matilda 257
Foster, Mattie Martha 16
Foster, Mattie W. 16
Foster, Mildred 220
Foster, Nancy 16
Foster, Oney 16
Foster, Orpha 16,17
Foster, Pattie L. 16
Foster, Pattie Lee 16
Foster, Paul Harris 17
Foster, Peter, Capt. 273

Foster, Priscilla 220
Foster, Priscilla Hunton 221
Foster, Robert 220
Foster, Silas 220
Foster, Susannah 220
Foster, Thomas 220
Foster, Thomas Redmond 221,221
Foster, William 16,17,220
Foster, William P. 220
Foster, William Penn 188
Foulk, Mary 245
Fountaine, Martha 136
Fountaine, P. H. 136
Fowler, Nancy Estes 162
Fox, Anne 157
Fox, Eleanor 65,66
Fox, Eliza Lewis 65,66
Fox, John 65,66
France, Alma 18
France, Sarah J. 19
France, Waldon S. 19
France, Walton Stephen 18
Frances, Aine Lovette 18
Frances, Rufus P. 19
Frances, Verna M. 18
Frances, Verna Mae 18
Francis, Betsey Bennet 86
Francis, C. W. 7
Francis, Elizabeth 86
Francis, George Leake 87
Francis, Hasten 86
Francis, Jares Matterson 86
Francis, John 86,87
Francis, John Andrew 87
Francis, Joseph 86
Francis, Mariah 86
Francis, Mary 86
Francis, Melchezedick 86
Francis, Micajah 86
Francis, Nancy Fisher 86
Francis, Nancy Ruth Ella 87
Francis, Polley 86
Francis, Presley 86
Francis, Rebecca 86
Francis, Rebecca Green 86
Francis, Salley Cammel 86
Francis, Sarah 86
Francis, Tan 86
Francis, Walter Lee 87
Francis, William 86
Francis, William Madison 87
Franklin, Richard 249
Franklln, Mary 26
Fraser, Alexander 95
Fraser, Betsy 95
Fraser, Caroline 95
Fraser, Edwin 95
Fraser, Frederick 95
Fraser, Frederick R. 95
Fraser, Harriet M. L. 95
Fraser, John W. 95
Fraser, Martha T. 95
Fraser, Mary Ann 95
Fraser, Robert 95
Fraser, Robert B. 95
Frazer, Frederick Lee 183,180
Frazer, Frederick, Rev. 185
Frazer, Ivarine Jordan 186
Frazer, Kathryn Waller 186
Frazer, Sarah E. 231

Frazier, Frances Burnett 240
Frazier, Nancy E. 240
Frazier, Nancy Elizabeth 240
Frazier, Russell Frank 240
Freeman, Ann 33
Freeman, Cavil H. 90
Freeman, Elizabeth 90
Freeman, George W. 90
Freeman, Howell 89,90
Freeman, Howell, Sr. 90
Freeman, James 3
Freeman, John R. 90
Freeman, Jordan L. 89,90
Freeman, Martha Ann 90
Freeman, Mary 90
Freeman, Mary Ann 89,90
Freeman, Nancy 33
Freeman, Sylvanus 90
Freeman, Thanes M, 89
Freeman, William P. 90
Freeman, William R. 89,90
Freemen, Frances 89,90
French, Merrill 81
Friend, Ann Catherine 140
Friend, Ann Stevenson 139
Friend, Ann Woodson 139
Friend, Charles Edward 140
Friend, Charles Nathaniel 140
Friend, Charles W. 140
Friend, Frances 139
Friend, George William 140
Friend, Martha 140
Friend, Martha Maria 139
Friend, Robert Craig 140
Friend, Sarah 139
Friend, Sarah Frances 140
Friend, Thomas 139
Friend, Thomas Henry 140
Friend, William 139
Friend, William Craig 139
Fristo, Johannah 230
Frost, J. M. 129
Frost, Joseph Lemon 129
Frost, Phebe 258,259
Frseman, Pleasant M. 90
Fudge, Anna Katherine 193
Fulkerson, AbrAnn 12
Fulkerson, Caty Van Hook 12
Fulkerson, Dinah 12
Fulkerson, Frederick DeBaugh 12
Fulkerson, Hannah DeBaugh 12
Fulkerson, Jacob Van Hook 12
Fulkerson, James 12
Fulkerson, John 12
Fulkerson, Mary 12
Fulkerson, Peter 12
Fulkerson, Thomas 12
Fulton, Annie Sue 181,182
Fulton, Barbara A. 182
Fulton, Barbara Ann 182,183
Fulton, Barbara Ann Hylton 182
Fulton, Betsey 87
Fulton, Catherine Pem 182
Fulton, George Henry 87
Fulton, George Hylton 181,182
Fulton, Hugh 87
Fulton, Hylton 182
Fulton, Hylton Harrison 182
Fulton, James Reid 87
Fulton, John 87

Fulton, John Kelly 182
Fulton, John W. 181,182,183
Fulton, John William U32
Fulton, Louise Barbara 182
Fulton, Nancy Ann 87
Fulton, Orlando 87
Fulton, Robert Campbell 87
Fulton, Sally 87
Fulton, Stella 183
Fulton, William Penn 181,182
Gaines, Cornelius 220,221
Gaines, Edmund P., General 175
Gaines, Pattie Venable 45
Gaines, Sallie Garlick 45
Gaines, Susannah 221
Gaines, William A. 222
Gale, Alalinda Persia 170
Gale, Angeline Sophia 170
Gale, Jarvia H. 170
Gale, Martha Colesta 170
Gale, Mary Eliza Leona 170
Gale, Polley F. 170
Gamble, Esther 51
Gamble, Polly 118
Gamble, Robert 118
Gamble, Robert Porter 118
Gannon, J. W. 117
Garland, Bessie Arm 286
Garland, Edward 286
Garland, Elizabeth 41
Garland, Sarah 285
Garnett, Ellen Augusta 66
Garrard, Eliza M. 284
Garrard, Henry 284
Garretson, B. Carter 62
Garretson, Isaac 62
Garrett, Gary 25
Garrett, Isaac 25
Garrett, Polley 25
Garth, A. G. 129
Garth, Albert G. 129
Garth, M. A. 129
Garth, Mary Elizabeth 129
Garvin, Sallie Ann 161
Gatewood, Dudley 265
Gatewood, James 265
Gatewood, Sarah 265
Gayle, Mary 33
Gayle, Matthew 33
Geddy, C. Texie 98
Gee, Charles 51
Gee, Henry 51
Gee, James 51
Gee, John 51
Gee, Rachel 51
Gee, Rebecah 51
Gee, Sarah 51
Gee, Thomas 14
Gee, Thomas H. 14
Gentry, John Rice 212
George, Enoch, Rev. Bishop 125
Gibbs, John 154
Gibbs, Nancy 154
Gibbs, Patsy 154
Gibbs, Polly 154
Gibbs, Polly D. 154
Gibbs, Polly Driver 154
Gibbs, Rachel 154
Gibbs, Ralph 154
Gibbs, Samuel Whitfield 154

Gibson, Abby 179
Gibson, Ann C. 284
Gibson, C. J., Rev. 65
Gibson, Calvin 94
Gibson, Charles 94
Gibson, Dallas 94
Gibson, James 94
Gibson, John 11,394
Gibson, John 111
Gibson, Melvin 94
Gibson, Rev. Mr. 49
Gibson, Sarah 94
Gibson, Walter 4Y,
Giddings, G. P., Rev.
Gilberne, Isaac William, Rev. 157
Gilbert, Anne 287,288
Gilbreath, SAnnuel 169
Giles, Hugh 156
Giles, Martha 212
Gill, Ann F. 91
Gill, Charles H. 92
Gill, Emily W. 92
Gill, James R. 92
Gill, Joseph P. 92
Gill, Martha V. 92
Gill, Mary E. 92
Gill, Rosella A. 92
Gill, Samuel F. 92
Gill, William F. 92
Gilliam, Ann 49
Gilliam, Anny 49
Gilliam, Anny Ann 49
Gilliam, Eliza Bates 49
Gilliam, John 49
Gilliam, John W. 49
Gilliam, John William 49
Gilliam, John William Russell 153
Gilliam, Joseph Peterson 49
Gilliam, Louisa Samuel 49
Gilliam, Maria Randolph 49
Gilliam, Mary 49
Gilliam, Roberta Clara Pocahontas 49
Gilliam, S. C. 194
Gilliam, Samuel 49
Gilliam, Sarah E. 93
Gilliam, Susan 49
Gilliam, Susan Bolling 49
Gilliam, Susannah Bolling 49
Gilliam,Thaddeus W. 153
Gilliland, M. D. 13
Gilliland, Mary Eliza 49
Gilliland, Richard M. 93
Gilmer, Elizabeth Anderson 133
Gilmer, Frank 133
Gilmer, George 132
Gilmer, George Anna 133
Gilmer, George C. 133
Gilmer, George Walker 133
Gilmer, Georgeanna 133
Gilmer, James N. 133
Gilmer, Leanna D. 133
Gilmer, Lucy 110
Gilmer, Maria Walker 133
Gilmer, Martha Jane 133
Gilmer, Sarah E. 133
Gilmer, Sarah Eliza 133
Gilmer, Zachariah Lee 133
Gilmour, Walker 282
Gladding, Betsylthomas 199
Gladding, Elizabeth 199

Gladding, Emily Ann 199
Gladding, George W. 199
Gladding, George Washington 199
Gladding, Hetty 199
Gladding, John Thomas 199
Gladding, Mary Ann 199
Gladding, Milchey 199
Gladding, Tully 199
Glascock Gregory 261
Glascock, Graham 261
Glascock, Gregory 261
Glascock, Jesse 261
Glascock, John 261
Glascock, Mary 261
Glascock, Sarah 261
Glascock, Travers 261
Glascock, William 261
Glass, Mary S., Mrs. 128
Glenn, Cecilia 234
Glenn, David 234
Glenn, David G. 233
Glenn, Eliza Jane 234
Glenn, George D. 233,234
Glenn, George HirAnn 234
Glenn, Maria Louisa 234
Glenn, Mark Thomas 234
Glenn, Mary Ann 233
Glenn, Nancy 233
Glenn, William 216
Glenn, William H. 233
Gneen, Mary P. 99
Gobande, Jotn 157
Godden, Miss 227
Godfrey, Katherine 196
Godon, Blanche Redwood 76
Godon, Ella Neville 76
Godrin, Nancy, Mrs. 76
Godwin, Constance 76
Godwin, Eliza Ammen 76
Godwin, Harriet 76
Godwin, James 76
Godwin, Martha M. 76
Godwin, Mary Hopkins 76
Godwin, Thomas G. 76
Godwln, James A. 76
Godwln, Nancy 76
Goodall, Peter C. 71
Goodall, Edward 70
Goodall, James 70
Goodall, James A. 71
Goodall, John 70
Goodall, Junior Turner 70,71
Goodall, Lattitia 71
Goodall, Lodowick 70,71
Goodall, Mary 70.71
Goodall, Mildred 70
Goodall, Nancy 70
Goodall, Nancy G. 71
Goodall, Peter Copeland 70
Goodall, Rhoda G. 71
Goodall, Thomas 70
Goodall, Turner 70
Goodall, Turner L. 71
Goodall, William M. 71
Goode, Eliza Jane 274
Goode, Louisa 274
Goode, Robert 274
Goode, William 274
Goodloe, Aquilla 55
Goodloe, Aquilla J. 55

Goodloe, Elizabeth 55
Goodloe, Sarah H. 55
Goodlow, George P. 185
Goodwin, Edith 196
Goodwin, George Munro 196
Goodwin, John 207
Goodwin, Mary Elizabeth Coleman 49
Goodwin, Rev. Mr. 110
Goolesley, Anne Harrison 119
Goolesley, Francis 119
Goolesley, George 119
Goolesley, Susan 119
Goolesley, William 119
Goolsley, Anne 119
Goolsley, BenjAnnin 119
Goolsley, Carey 119
Goolsley, Elizabeth 119
Goolsley, Frances 119
Goolsley, George 119
Goolsley, Lucy 119
Goolsley, Martha 119
Goolsley, Samuel Beall 119
Goolsley, Sarah Carey 119
Goosley, William 119
Gordon, Addison 271
Gordon, Agatha 270
Gordon, Agnes Maria 271
Gordon, Alex. Tazewell 159
Gordon, Alexander Terrell 272
Gordon, Ann 270,271
Gordon, Ann B. 271
Gordon, Ann Belinda James 271
Gordon, Ann Smith 271
Gordon, Annelia Colernan 112
Gordon, Arm1stead 272
Gordon, Caroline L. 38
Gordon, Caroline Scott 271
Gordon, Charles Henry 159
Gordon, Chilcester 271
Gordon, Clarissa 38
Gordon, Clementina Amanda 38
Gordon, Clementina R. 38
Gordon, Elizabeth 38,159,270
Gordon, Elizabeth Ann 38
Gordon, Elizabeth G. 38
Gordon, Ellen 270
Gordon, Emily Ann 38
Gordon, George Loyall 159
Gordon, Hannah 38,159
Gordon, Hannah Elizabeth 159
Gordon, Hannah Maria 38
Gordon, Henry Ladd 38
Gordon, Ida B. 272
Gordon, Imogene Stanard 272
Gordon, James 270,271,272
Gordon, James 38
Gordon, James 38
Gordon, James Beverly 271
Gordon, James Harrison 271
Gordon, James L. 159
Gordon, James Newton 271,272
Gordon, Janetta 271
Gordon, John 270,271
Gordon, John Calvin 271
Gordon, John Churchill 159
Gordon, John M. 271,272
Gordon, John Mathews 272
Gordon, John Matthews 271
Gordon, John Newton 272
Gordon, Kathleen 272

Gordon, Louisa Payne 271
Gordon, Marcia Lovejoy 38
Gordon, Maria L. 159
Gordon, Maria Louisa 271
Gordon, Marissa Jane 272
Gordon, Martha Jane 271
Gordon, Mary 270,271
Gordon, Mary Elizabeth 272
Gordon, Mary L. 38
Gordon, Mary Ladd 38
Gordon, Mary Smith 271
Gordon, Mason 159
Gordon, Nathaniel 270
Gordon, Reuben L. 159
Gordon, Rufus 38
Gordon, Rufus L. 38
Gordon, Ruth A. 38
Gordon, Sallie S. 38
Gordon, Sally 270
Gordon, Samuel Baldwin 271
Gordon, Samuel Gordon 271
Gordon, Sarah 270
Gordon, Sarah Floyd 38
Gordon, Simeon L. 38
Gordon, Simeon Ladd 38
Gordon, William 38,159
Gordon, William F. 159
Gordon, William S., Dr. 272
Gordon, William, Capt. 278
Gordon, William, Sr. 38
Gordoner, John 14
Goring, Thomas W. 160
Gosney, Mary 84
Gossip, Hannah Temple 111
Gossips, Catharine White 110
Gossips, Christopher 110
Gossips, Elizabeth Beverley 110
Gossips, Francis Orill 110,111
Gossips, Junior 110
Gossips, Mary Watkins 111
Gossips, Sarah Gwathmey 111
Gossom, Virginia Estelle 184
Graham, Catherine 4
Graham, Duncan 4
Graham, Elizabeth 4
Graham, Jean 4
Graham, John 4
Graham, Margaret 4
Graham, Martha O. 25
Graham, Mary 4
Graham, Robert 4
Graham, Walter 4
Graham, William 4
Gratton, Robert 110
Graves, Ann 142
Graves, David 142
Graves, Elizabeth Holland 142
Graves, Harrison Andersonville 142
Graves, Isaac, Jr. 211
Graves, John Washington 142
Graves, Richard Evermont 142
Graves, Zerelda 142
Gray, Charles Winton 174
Gray, Charlotte Davis 174
Gray, Geneva 174
Gray, Gilbert D. 174
Gray, Gilbert Denton 174
Gray, Lucille Elizabeth 174
Gray, Rose L. 174
Graybill, Theodosia E. 10

Grayson, Benjamin 4
Grayson, Jane Riding Thornley 235,236
Grayson, John Cook 235
Grayson, John Cook 236
Grayson, John Thornley 235
Grayson, Lena 236
Grayson, Maria Julia 235
Grayson, Mrs. 234
Grayson, Sarah Mason Cooke 235,236
Greathouse, Anna 99
Green, A. G. 72
Green, A. P. 121
Green, Albert 73
Green, Albert G. 72
Green, Albert G., Jr. 73
Green, Albert Gallatin 73
Green, Albert Gallatin, Jr. 73
Green, ALfred 183,184
Green, Allie Tallulah 208
Green, Ann Philemen 121
Green, Anny 121
Green, Anny Clay 121
Green, B. A. 208
Green, Berryman Davis 73
Green, Betsy 183,184
Green, Carlos Berrymman 73
Green, Charles Richard 121
Green, Coalman 121
Green, Cornelia S. 73
Green, Cornelia Stuart 73
Green, Croxson 121
Green, Don Carlos 73
Green, Duff 141
Green, Eliza A. 246
Green, Elizabeth 125,183,184,186
Green, Elizabeth Julia 73
Green, Ella Amantha 73
Green, Ella S. 73
Green, Ella Saline 732
Green, Emily Ann 183,184
Green, F. 121
Green, Frances Veola 73
Green, Francis Malcolm 186
Green, Franky 247
Green, George 125,184
Green, George W. 183,184
Green, George Washington 183
Green, Gideon Flournoy 73
Green, Grace F. 183
Green, Grace Foster 184
Green, Gressett 121
Green, Hannah 141
Green, Ira N. 120
Green, J. C. 187
Green, J. W. 186
Green, James 183,184
Green, James C. 121
Green, James Croxson 121
Green, James F. 183
Green, James Franklin 183,184
Green, James Thomas 183
Green, Jceeph G. 120
Green, Jdn 121
Green, Jesse Davis 121
Green, John Applewhite 187
Green, John Parish 73
Green, John R. 121
Green, John Randolph 121
Green, John S. 183,184
Green, John Thomas 121

Green, Joseph Gressett 121
Green, Letty 121
Green, Lucy Annanda 183
Green, M. C. 187
Green, Mary 183
Green, Mary Ann 120
Green, Mary Arm Mildred 121
Green, Mary C. 183
Green, Mary Catharine 183
Green, Mary Ellen 183
Green, Mary Lou 72
Green, Mary Louise 72,73
Green, Mildred 121
Green, Mildred Davis 121
Green, Mollie Lou 59
Green, Moses 183,184
Green, Nancy 121,183
Green, Nancy Flournoy 73
Green, Nannie Read 73
Green, Pailim Elizabeth 73
Green, Pauline E. 73
Green, Polly Ann 121
Green, Rebecca 121
Green, Rebecca Anne 120
Green, Richard N. 184
Green, Richard Nelson 183,184
Green, Robert 280
Green, Robert L. 12
Green, Rush Marshall 183
Green, Sally 183
Green, Sarah 121
Green, Sarah Catherine 73
Green, Sarah E. 72
Green, Sarah Scott 73
Green, Susannah Eliza 280
Green, Thomas E. 73
Green, Thomas Embro 73
Green, Thomas Hope 73
Green, Thompson Abner 183
Green, Walter B. 184
Green, Walter Brawner 183
Green, William 121
Green, William AdAnns 183
Green, William Booker 73
Green, William Davis 121
Green, William Goodwin 183,184
Green, William Scott 73
Green,Thomas Crymes 121
Greene, Elizabeth B., Mrs. 14
Greene, Rev. 7
Greenhow, Robert 233
Greenway, Margaret 48
Greenway, Martha 48,49
Gregory, Fendall 283
Gregory, Jares, Rev. 45
Gregory, Mary 287
Greshem, James 95
Grice, W., Rev. 222
Grider, Rebecca 147
Griffin, BenjAnnin 222
Griffin, Cyrus 103
Griffin, Cyrus Anstruther 103
Griffin, Henry Stuart 103
Griffin, J. L. C. G. 103
Griffin, J. S. D. 102
Griffin, James Lewis Corbin 103
Griffin, Jane Hester 103
Griffin, John 103
Griffin, John Mercher 103
Griffin, Julia Aq 103

Griffin, Ludnda 242
Griffin, Mary 114
Griffin, Mary Lcuise 103
Griffin, Mary Stuart 103
Griffin, Mary, Mrs. 103
Griffin, S. S. 103
Griffin, S., Mrs. 103
Griffin, Sarah 103
Griffin, Thomas Stuart 103
Griffin, Thomas, Major 103
Griggs, Thomas 274
Grigsby, James 220,221
Grigsby, R. 220
Grigsby, Redmond, Sr. 220
Grigsby, Susannah 220
Grigsby, Susannah Purcell 220,221
Grinnan, Ann 179
Grinnen, John 179
Grlffin, Lady Chr1stina 103
Grlffin, S. S. G. 103
Grlffin, Samuel Stuart 103
Grlgsby, Catherine Stewart 221
Grlgsby, Dcrcas Foster 221
Grlgsby, flary Davis 220,221
Grlgsby, Redmond 220,221
Grove, Mary Ann 234
Groves, James S. 148
Groves, Nellie Wallace Richards 177
Grubbs, Joseph A. 116
Grundy, Polly 115,116
Guest, Elizabeth 236
Guill, Elizabeth 41
Guill, Joseph 41
Guinn, Hanner 243
Guinn, Harmer 26
Gunter, Milliard 250
Guthrie, Anne Mcorrls 255
Guthrie, Annie Morris 255
Guthrie, Benjamin Joseph 256
Guthrie, Charles 255
Guthrie, Charles Foster 255
Guthrie, Charles Luther 255,256
Guthrie, Charles Luther III 255
Guthrie, Charles Luther, Jr. 255,256
Guthrie, Dorothy 255
Guthrie, Dorothy Ayer 255,256
Guthrie, Dorothy Elizabeth 255
Guthrie, Elizabeth Jme 256
Guthrie, Ella Rosabell 255
Guthrie, Etta 255
Guthrie, George William Austin 255
Guthrie, Isabel Williams 255
Guthrie, Jares Henry 256
Guthrie, John H. 256
Guthrie, Laura Isabelle 255
Guthrie, Lorraine 255
Guthrie, Lrura 255
Guthrie, Martha Ann 256
Guthrie, Mary Emily 256
Guthrie, Mary Foster 255
Guthrie, Nancy 255
Guthrie, Nancy Elizabeth 255
Guthrie, Nancy Susan 255
Guthrie, Nancy Susan Burnett 255,256
Guthrie, Philip 255
Guthrie, Philip William 255,256
Guthrie, Sarah 256
Guthrie, Sarah Annanda 256
Guthrie, Sarah Bradley 256
Guthrie, Thomas T. 256

Guthrie, William 255.256
Guthrie, William Bell 255
Guthrie, William Silas 255
Gwathmey, Philadelphia 111
Gwathmey, Richard 110 Ann 270
Haagland, Jaroes 245
Hack, Colornel 270
Hackler, Betty Gayle 249
Hague, Francis 227
Hague, Harriet E. 227
Hague, William 227
Hahkins, Mary Ann Susan 98
Haile, E. 77
Haile, Elizabeth 77
Haile, R. G., Capt. 77
Haile, Richard 79
Haile, Robert G., Capt. 77
Haile, Sallie M. 77
Haile, Sallie Matilda 77
Haile, Susan A. 79
Hairston, Eliza 189
Hairston, SAnnuel W. 188
Hale, Elias 193
Hall, Ann 143
Hall, Anna Maria 106
Hall, Anne A. 129
Hall, Bartlett 128
Hall, Dr. 105
Hall, Elizabeth 106
Hall, Farmy 257
Hall, Frederick 185
Hall, James 257
Hall, James V. 75
Hall, Jane 106
Hall, John 143
Hall, Jonathan Jones 94
Hall, Lucy 25,101,143
Hall, Lucy C. 65
Hall, Lucy Cuthbert 65
Hall, Margaret 106
Hall, Martha 206
Hall, Martha Gladys 12,13
Hall, Mary Jane 222
Hall, Nathaniel Ingraham 226
Hall, Robert R. 64,65
Hall, Sabine 61
Hall, Sarah E. 257
Hall, Sarah R. 52
Hall, Thomas 25
Hall, Thomas, Colonel. 106
Halley, Lucy 10
Ham, Menla 213
Hamblen, Elizabeth 118
Hamblen, Louisa Sidney 118
Hamblen, Thomas 118
Hamblen, William Matterson 118
Hamilton, Anne Foc 196
Hamilton, Bettie A. 247
Hamilton, Eugenia E. 196
Hamilton, James 196
Hamilton, Jane 167
Hamilton, Leonora 167
Hamilton, Oscar 287
Hamilton, Sallie J. 117
Hamilton, Sarah Sherwood 196
Hamilton, Thomas 197
Hamilton, Thomas Napier 196
Hamlet, A. C. 123
Hamlet, Elizabeth Ann 117
Hamlett, Andrew Jackson 71

Hamlett, Francis Marian 71
Hamlett, James 71
Hamlett, John Elliott 71
Hamlett, Joseph James 71
Hamlett, Josephine 71
Hamlett, Margaret Ann 71
Hamlett, Maria Louisa 71
Hamlett, Mary Jane 71
Hamlett, Susan Elizabeth 71
Hamlett, Wiley Norflett Blunt 71
Hamme, Caroline 41
Hammer, Rev. 7
Hammond, Catherine 97
Hammond, Chrlstena 97
Hammond, Daniel 97
Hammond, Daniel Louis 97
Hammond, Elizabeth 97
Hammond, Elvira 97
Hammond, Elvira Adalim 97
Hammond, Eva Rose 97
Hammond, Francis W. 98
Hammond, Hamilton Jefferson 97
Hammond, Henry 97
Hammond, Henry Oliver 97
Hammond, Jacob 97
Hammond, Janes 97
Hammond, Lily Mary 97
Hammond, Marie Angeline 97
Hammond, Mary 97
Hammond, Mary E. 97
Hammond, Minerva Jane 97
Hammond, Paul 97
Hammond, Peter 97
Hammond, Peter Horatio 97
Hammond, Rebecca M. 97
Hammond, Rebecca S. 97
Hammond, Samuel 97
Hammond, Samuel J. 97
Hammond, Samuel Sheplar 97
Hammond, Sylvanus 97
Hammond, William Harrison 97
Hamonsly, Mr. 123
Hampton, John 221
Hampton, Margaret 221
Hancock, John 219
Hancock, John Westly 185
Hancock, Minerva W. 163
Hancock, Nancy 219
Hancock, Susan 146
Hand, Sarah 94
Handy, A. Ernest, Jr. 251
Handy, Abe Esters 250
Handy, Abram Ernest 251
Handy, Abram Ernest, Jr. 251
Handy, Adam James 250
Handy, Ann Clark 251
Handy, Douglas Quentin 251
Handy, Kenneth Farl 251
Handy, Leila Alice 251
Handy, Lillie Belle 250
Handy, Louisa Anna 250
Handy, Lucille Hill 250
Handy, Lucy Lee 250
Handy, Maggie Tee 250
Handy, Martha Wila 250
Handy, Mary Doris 250
Handy, Phillip Watkins 251
Handy, Ralph Waldo 251
Handy, Stafford Odell 251
Handy, Wilbcur Ernestene 251

Handy, William Davis 250
Handy, William Edgar 251
Hanger, Catherine F. 29
Hankins, Alice Browne 98
Hankins, Alloe 98
Hankins, Ann 93
Hankins, Archer 98
Hankins, Catharine Texanna 98
Hankins, Clarinda 93
Hankins, Elizabeth 93
Hankins, G. A., Dr. 98
Hankins, George 98
Hankins, George A. 98
Hankins, George Archer W
Hankins, Harriet 98
Hankins, Harriet A. 98
Hankins, Harriet Ann 98
Hankins, John 93
Hankins, Lorenda 93
Hankins, Margret 93
Hankins, Mary 93,98
Hankins, Mary A. S. 98
Hankins, Nannie V. 98
Hankins, Reynolds 98
Hankins, Richard 93
Hankins, Robert 93
Hankins, Robert Evilman 93
Hankins, Sarah 93
Hankins, Sarmel 93
Hankins, Scuthy S. 98
Hankins, Southy 98
Hankins, Southy Savage 98
Hankins, William 93
Hankins, William Edwin 98
Hankins, William N. 98
Hankins, William Nathaniel 98
Hanks, Richard 36
Hanley, Mary B. 180
Hanna, Mary 171
Hannerson, David Clement 264
Hannold, Elizabeth 97
Hanrom, Frances 132
Hansbrough, Blucher W. 266
Hansbrough, John C. 265
Hansford, Mrs. 278
Hanson, Julia 184
Harbach, Johannes 232
Harcum, Frances H. J. 132
Harcum, William 132
Hardaway, JAnn 131
Hardaway, Joseph E. 143
Harden, T. H. 196
Harding, Cyrus 218
Harding, HirAnn 218
Harding, John Hopkins 218
Harding, Josephine Lemoine 218
Harding, Mary G. 218
Harding,Thomas Everett 218
Hardy, ALLoe Gertrude 197
Hardy, Ann 10
Hardy, J. C. 197
Hardy, James C. 199
Hardy, Sarah Frances 199
Haring, Sally Coppedge 218
Harper, Laura 198
Harper, Martha W. 91
Harper, Mary M. 91
Harris, Adolphus Washington 127
Harris, Ann C. 170
Harris, Anne Marion 127

Harris, Betsy 215
Harris, Caroline R. W. 127
Harris, Charles Henry 37
Harris, Charlotte Corde 127
Harris, Daniel H. 37
Harris, Daniel Hunt 37
Harris, Elenar Vancleave 37
Harris, Eli 195
Harris, Eliza Cassandra 210
Harris, Elizabeth 195
Harris, Emily J. 170
Harris, Gabriel 195
Harris, H. C. 61
Harris, Hannah Stewart 37
Harris, Harriet A. 170
Harris, Harrison P. H. 170
Harris, Harrison Pliny Hatchett 170
Harris, Innis T. 37
Harris, Irene Todd 37
Harris, James LaFayette 127
Harris, James S. 170
Harris, John 170
Harris, John 37
Harris, John E. 260
Harris, John F. 37
Harris, John Fowler 37
Harris, John M. 37
Harris, Joseph W. 170
Harris, Justus 195
Harris, Kate 260
Harris, Livy H. 170
Harris, Lovel Clark 195
Harris, Margaret 195
Harris, Martha 195
Harris, Martha JAnn Eloise 127
Harris, Mary 83
Harris, Mary B. in
Harris, Mary Baker 195
Harris, Mary F. 170
Harris, Mary FrAnnes 170
Harris, Mary J. 182
Harris, Mary M. 181
Harris, Mary Magdeline 127
Harris, Miss 262
Harris, Nancy E. 170
Harris, Robert Edward 127
Harris, Robert H. 127
Harris, Samuel Baker 195
Harris, Samuel, Rev. 2
Harris, Sarah 195
Harris, Sarah A. 170
Harris, Sarah Ann 37
Harris, Sarah C. 257
Harris, Sarah Smed 37
Harris, Sophia 170
Harris, Stephen P. 127
Harris, Thomas McCall 195
Harris, Thomas, Sr. 195
Harris, Vergle 251
Harris, Virginia Bacon 127
Harris, William 164
Harris, William B. 215
Harris, William S. 37,127
Harris, William SAnnuel 127
Harris, William Sneed 37
Harrison, Ann 135
Harrison, BenjAnnin 119,135
Harrison, Bur 109
Harrison, Burr 109
Harrison, Elizabeth 119

Harrison, Hannah 119
Harrison, Harriett 33
Harrison, I. W. 217
Harrison, James 33
Harrison, Joel 33
Harrison, John C. 33
Harrison, John Prosser II 186
Harrison, Joseph 33
Harrison, Kitty 33
Harrison, Lovell 33
Harrison, Ludwell 119
Harrison, Mary 119,270
Harrison, Mary Foster 33
Harrison, Milly 33
Harrison, Miss 223
Harrison, Nathaniel 119,135
Harrison, Nathaniel, Hm. 270
Harrison, Peter Cole 119
Harrison, Robert 201
Harrison, Sarah 109
Harrison, Susannah 119
Harrison, Thompson M. 33
Harrison, William, Rev. 138
Harriss, Ben 61
Harriss, Ph--- 61
Harriss, Pheby 61
Harriss, Wilber 61
Harrox, James, Hon. 135
Hart, Andrew 100
Hart, J. M. 220
Hart, Joseph, Rev. 7
Hart, Marie Lou 100
Hart, Mary Ann Johnson 100
Hart, Sephas 84
Hart, William H., Rev. 98
Hartwell, Ann 107
Hartwell, Mary 107
Hartwell, William 107
Harvey, Andrew IshAnn 123
Harvey, Elizabeth Ann 133
Harvey, Elizabeth Jordan 123
Harvey, John W., Jr. 123
Harvey, John William 123
Harvey, Joseph Daniel 123
Harvey, Mildred M. 123
Harvey, Robert Hester 123
Harvey, Thomas 133,218
Harvey, Thomas C. 123
Harwell, Adeline 224
Harwell, Ellar Margarie 224
Harwell, Elvira A. 92
Harwell, Ishmael 224
Harwell, L. M. 224
Harwell, L. T. p, 224
Harwell, Lewis Ishmael 224
Harwell, Litfleberry 224
Harwell, Littleberry Israel 224
Harwell, Littleton L. M. 224
Harwell, Littleton M. 224
Harwell, Littleton Theodore Peterson 224
Harwell, Lucy F. 224
Harwell, Lucy Finey 224
Harwell, M. M. 224
Harwell, Martha S. 224
Harwell, Martha Sylvian 224
Harwell, Martha Virginia
Harwell, Martha Virginia 224
Harwell, Mary Estelle 224
Harwell, Rebecca P. 224
Harwell, Renaldo 224

Harwell, Renaldo Peterson 224
Harwell, Richard 91
Harwell, Richard Dunortmes 224
Hasick, George F. 244
Haskell, Decca S. 133
Hatchell, Abraham 170
Hatchell, Mary 170
Hatcher, 3. Watson 10,11
Hatcher, Cora O. 11
Hatcher, Julian Guy 10
Hatcher, Margery 96
Hatcher, Mary B. 47
Hatcher, Sidney Watson 10,11
Hatchett, AbrahAnn ReMay 170
Hatchett, Ann Baylor 285
Hatchett, Elizabeth 170
Hatchett, Fanny Lewis 285
Hatchett, Joseph 170
Hatchett, Leray Cole Downey 170
Hatchett, Leroy C. d. 170
Hatchett, Livy 170
Hatchett, Logan 170
Hatchett, Louisa E. 170
Hatchett, Margaret Remey 170
Hatchett, Mary E. 170
Hatchett, Polley F. 170
Hatchett, Polley Farley 170
Hatchett, Polly 170
Hatchett, Sophia 170
Hatchett, William 285
Hatchett, William, Elder 286
Hatding, Eliza 218
Hatrhett, Jacob Berger 170
Hauck, Belle Wright 185
Hawell, L. I. P., Dr. 224
Hawell, Rebecca Roe 224
Hawkins, Rosa B. 117
Hay, Elizabeth 138
Hay, Elizabeth Cary 138
Hay, Helena 138
Hay, James 138
Hay, John 138
Hay, Peter 138
Hay, R. D., Dr. 188
Hay, Sarah 189
Hay, William 138
Hay, Willie 138
Hayden, Charles 159
Hayden, Charles BenhAnn 159
Hayden, Hannah 143
Hayden, Irene 159
Hayden, Julia 159
Hayden, L. C. 159
Hayden, Louisiana Cocke 159
Hayden, Norman 159
Haynes, Elizabeth 263
Haynes, Elizabeth Scott 263
Haynes, Harriet Annanda 263
Haynes, Henry 263
Haynes, James M. 263
Haynes, John 263,264
Haynes, Malcolm Decatur 263
Haynes, Mary T. 263
Haynes, Susan Marion 263
Haynes, William Scott 263
Haynie, Ann 133
Hays, Rebecca 82
Haywood, Sharon Calloway 249
Hazelrigg, Francis 90
Hazelrigg, John W. 90

Hazelrigg, Lucy J. 90
Head, BenjAnnin 213
Head, Martha 213
Heakle, Joseph 251
Health, Allie Tallulah 208
Health, O. P. 208
Healy, Ann 165
Healy, Anna Muse 173
Healy, Augustus 173
Healy, Betty Muse 173
Healy, Catherine 165,203
Healy, Edmund 165 ,203
Healy, Elizabeth 165,203
Healy, Elllot Muse 173
Healy, Fanny 173
Healy, Frances 165,203
Healy, George 165,203
Healy, James 165.203
Healy, Jane 165,203
Healy, Juliet Muse 167
Healy, Juliet Tayloe 167
Healy, Julle Tayloe 167
Healy, Martha Augusta 173
Healy, Robert 165,203
Healy, Sarah 165,167,203
Healy, Sarah Elizabeth 167
Healy, Tazewell 173
Healy, Thomas 167,173,203
Healy, Thomas, Sr. 165
Healy, Walter 165,167 J73,203
Healy, William 165,203
Heards, Susanna 258
Hedley, Maria 173
Hedley, Martha 131
Hedly, Ann K. 165,203
Hedrick, Besie H. 174
Hedrick, Lewis 174
Hedrick, Louis W. 174
Hedrick, William S. 174
Heidelberg, S. F., Mrs. 46
Heidelberg, S. Franklin 46
Helms, John 9
Hendersan, Nancy A. 284
Henderson, Adallne McCutchen 52
Henderson, Alice E. 257
Henderson, Andrew J. 257
Henderson, Charles W. 257
Henderson, Elizabeth 284
Henderson, Elizabeth A. 53
Henderson, George 284
Henderson, Harriet L. 257
Henderson, Harvey 53
Henderson, James F. 257
Henderson, Janes L. 53
Henderson, John 190
Henderson, John A. 53
Henderson, John McClung 52
Henderson, John V. 257
Henderson, Joseph 52
Henderson, Lavinia Ellen 53
Henderson, Lawson P. 257
Henderson, Margaret M. 257
Henderson, Mary E. A. 257
Henderson, Mary F. 150
Henderson, Mary S. 53
Henderson, Nancy Cummins 52
Henderson, Nicholas Kinney 53
Henderson, Rachel 229
Henderson, Rebecca Jane 257
Henderson, Rev. Mr. 119

Henderson, Roberbls 53
Henderson, Robert 52
Henderson, Rodney Boys 53
Henderson, Rosanna Rachel 53
Henderson, Sally 52,150
Henderson, Sarah 190
Henderson, Sarah Susan 53
Henderson, Shelton Jones 52
Henderson, Susannah 190
Henderson, T. M. 160
Henderson, Tabitha S. 53
Henderson, William 150
Henderson, William B. 257
Henderson, William Harvey 53
Hendetson, Martha Ruth 23
Hendon, Abner 193,238
Hendon, Edward 193,238
Hendre, M. E. 223
Hendren, Annbrose 261
Hendren, Elijah 261
Hendren, Eli 261
Hendren, George 261
Hendren, John 261
Hendren, Margaret 261
Hendren, Martha Eleanor 223
Hendren, Oliver 261
Hendren, Peggy 261
Hendren, Richard J. 261
Hendren, Sarah 261
Hendren, Solomon 261
Hendren, Stephen 261
Hendren, Synthea 261
Hendren, Thantlery Bryan 261
Hendren, William 261
Hendrick, John T., Rev. 85
Hendricks, Elizabeth 174
Hendron, Sophia 33
Henkel, Elizabeth 251
Henkel, Jane E. 251
Henkel, John 251
Henkel, Jonathan 251
Henkel, Jonathan L., Jr. 251
Henkel, Lou A. 251
Henkel, Martha 251
Henkel, Mary 251
Henkel, Phillip, Rev. 251
Henkel, William 251
Henkle, Ada 20
Henley, Bartholomow 131
Henley, Frances Dandridge 131
Henley, George 131
Henley, John Dandridge 131
Henley, Leonard 131
Henley, Robert 131
Henley, Sabina W. 227
Henley, Samuel 131
Henley, William 131
Henly, Juliet Muse 200
Henry, A. F. E. 223
Henry, Alexander Spotswood 206
Henry, Ann Elizabeth 231
Henry, Anne 206
Henry, Benjamin Cabaniss 218
Henry, Bessie Braxton 231
Henry, Charles Spottiswood 231
Henry, Dorothea Dandridge 206
Henry, E. V. 223
Henry, Edward 206
Henry, Edward Winston 206
Henry, Eliza G. 99

Henry, Elizabeth 206
Henry, F. A. A. 223
Henry, Fayette 206
Henry, Georgina 231
Henry, Herbert 231
Henry, J. B. 223
Henry, J. H 230
Henry, James 0. 223
Henry, John 206
Henry, John S. 230,231
Henry, Jotn P. 218
Henry, Lucy 206
Henry, Lucy Brockenbrough 230~231
Henry, Lucy Moore 231
Henry, Ludwell Braxton 231
Henry, Martha 206
Henry, Martha Catherine 206
Henry, Mary 206,231
Henry, Mary Beal 230,231
Henry, N. A. 223
Henry, Nattreniel 206
Henry, O. S. 223
Henry, Patrick 206
Henry, Richard 206
Henry, S. E. T. 223
Henry, Sarah 206
Henry, Sarah Ann Ophelia 218
Henry, Sarah Leigh 232
Henry, Virginia 206
Henry, W. D., Jr. 231
Henry, W. S. B. 231
Henry, W. W. B. 231
Henry, William 206
Henry, William D. 231
Henry, William Daingerfield 231
Henry, William P. 218
Henry, William S. B. 230
Herding, Hopkins 218
Herding, James 218
Herding, Sally 218
Herding, William 218
Herkel, Albert 251
Herkil, James L. 251
Herndon, Elizabeth 193,238
Herndon, Ezekiel 193,U8
Herndon, Frost HirAnn 142
Herndon, Henry 193,238
Herndon, James 193,238
Herndon, Joel 193,238
Herndon, Manson 193,238
Herndon, Mary 238
Herndon, Mary Pendleton 193
Herndon, Rachel 193,238
Herndon, Thomas 193,238
Herndon, William 193,238
Herndon, William Pendleton 193
Herny, Beverly Allen 218
Heron, James 278
Heron, Peggie 282
Heron, Sam 282
Herring, Elizabeth 83
Hester, Maria L. 100
Hetley, Harriet 190
Hewit, Richard, Rev. 119
Hewitt, Elizabeth 280
Hewitt, John 205
Hewitt, Margaret Elizabeth 205
Hewitt, Richard Newton, Dr. 205
Heyward, Andrew Hasell 196
Heyward, Pauline 196

Hickay, Mary M. 257
Hicks, Absalom 6
Hicks, Ekthe Carolim 6
Hicks, Eliza 6
Hicks, Elizabeth 6
Hicks, Harris 6
Hicks, James Williams 71
Hicks, John 6
Hicks, Joseph John 6
Hicks, Mary 6
Hicks, Peyton 6
Hicks, Polly 6
Hicks, Preston 81
Hicks, Robert 6
Hicks, Temperance 6
Hicks, William 6
Hiden, Jane 6
Hiden, Joseph 266
Hider, J. C., Rev. 142
Hiett, Robert C. 257
Hiett, Talitha C. 257
Higgason, Frances Fowlkes 161
Higginbotham, Aaron 140
Higginbotham, Absalom 140
Higginbotham, Absalom, Jr. 140
Higginbotham, Absalom, Sr. 141
Higginbotham, Alexander B. 140
Higginbotham, Ann 140
Higginbotham, Benjamin G. 140
Higginbotham, Betty Ann 140
Higginbotham, Clara G. 140
Higginbotham, Daniel 123
Higginbotham, Elizabeth 140,141
Higginbotham, Elizabeth C. J. 137
Higginbotham, Jack 140
Higginbotham, James 140
Higginbotham, James 141
Higginbotham, Johannah 140
Higginbotham, John 140
Higginbotham, John J. 140
Higginbotham, John, Capt. 114,123
Higginbotham, Judith 137
Higginbotham, Mary 140,141
Higginbotham, Mary C. 140
Higginbotham, Nancy 140
Higginbotham, Nancy Croxton 140
Higginbotham, Paul 140,141
Higginbotham, Rachel 139
Higginbotham, Rufus A. 140,141
Higginbotham, Sallie 140
Higginbotham, Sarah A. 141
Higginbotham, Thomas 114,140
Higginbotham, William 140
HigginbothAnn, A. L. 141
HigglnbothAnn, Tirzah 114
Hight, Alexander P. 176
Hight, Caroline A. 176
Hight, David 176
Hight, Eliza Jane 176
Hight, Elizabeth Susan 176
Hight, Ellen V. 176
Hight, George R. 176
Hight, Julia Ann 176
Hight, Mary M. 176
Hight, Mary M. 176
Hight, Nancy H. 176
Hight, Permelia M. 176
Hight, Peter J. 176
Hight, Rebecca F. 176
Hight, Sarah W. 176

Hight, Tilman 176
Hight, Vivian H. 176
Hightower, Ann 143
Hill, Richard G. 48,49
Hildebrand, Anna 152
Hill, Ann 40
Hill, Ann M. 48,49
Hill, Berryman J. 48,49
Hill, Berryman Jones 48,49
Hill, Betty Ann 140
Hill, Blantan M. 40
Hill, Blanton M. 40
Hill, Davis, Rev. 250
Hill, Dolley 32
Hill, E. H. 49
Hill, Edna 13
Hill, Eliza Applin 87
Hill, Eliza Jane 137
Hill, Elizabeth ,39,223
Hill, Ellen H. 164
Hill, Eudocia M. 236
Hill, George 32
Hill, Grace 8,49
Hill, Hampton W. 40
Hill, Henrietta 32
Hill, Humphrey 110
Hill, James A. 40
Hill, James Greenway 49
Hill, James Robert 48,49
Hill, Johanna 223
Hill, John 32
Hill, Joicy 223
Hill, Joseph 223
Hill, Louisa Roberta 49
Hill, Luce 32
Hill, Malinda 40
Hill, Margaret 48
Hill, Margaret Elizabeth 48,49
Hill, Martha D. 48
Hill, Martha Emma 48,49
Hill, Martin 32
Hill, Mary 48
Hill, Mary Ann 20
Hill, Mary Jane 48
Hill, Mary Jones 45,49
Hill, May 32
Hill, Miles 40
Hill, Miss 223
Hill, Molly 32
Hill, Nancy 32
Hill, Nancy Umbarger 232
Hill, Powhatan 49
Hill, Rebecca 258
Hill, Richard 48
Hill, Richard, Dr, 49
Hill, Robert G, 48
Hill, Robert Greenway 49
Hill, Rowland 49
Hill, Salley 32
Hill, Susan Ann Bragg 49
Hill, Tabitha 40
Hill, Thomas 110,164,223,224
Hill, Thomas E. 49
Hill, William 223
Hill,Edward Harvie 49
Hillinrd, L B 254
Hinchee, John T. 191
Hinchee, Sarah A. 191
Hines, Abner 100
Hines, Mary E. 100

Hines, Mary Watson 24,243
Hire, Elelinda 88
Hire, Polly 88
Hitchcock, Georgia A. 3
Hite, Abraham 88
Hite, Ann 88
Hite, Ann Hance 88
Hite, Benjamin 88
Hite, Benjamin Gabriel 88
Hite, Benjamin Rawlings 88
Hite, Betsey 88
Hite, Charles Lewis 88
Hite, Eleanor 195
Hite, Elizabeth Ann 88
Hite, Francis Asbury 88
Hite, Gaberilla 88
Hite, Gabriel 88
Hite, Henry Clay 88
Hite, Isaac 108
Hite, Isaac, Major 108
Hite, Jacob 888,108
Hite, James 88
Hite, John 88
Hite, John 88
Hite, John Wesley 88
Hite, Margaret Rebecca 8
Hite, Margaret Strawther 88
Hite, Meliday 88
Hite, Nancy Sarah 88
Hite, Peggy 88
Hite, Sally 88
Hite, Samuel 88
Hite, Samuel Charles Lewis 88
Hite, Sarah 88
Hite, Strawther 88
Hite, Susan harriett 88
Hite, Susanna 88
Hite, William 88
Hite, William Eberly 88
Hoagland, Agneys 245
Hoagland, Anny 245
Hoagland, Daniel 245
Hoagland, Derrick 245
Hoagland, Henry 245
Hoagland, John 245
Hoagland, Leeh 245
Hoagland, Mary 245
Hobson, W. A. Rev. 198
Hobson, Winifred 202
Hodges, Nancy 99,100
Hodsden, Clara 244
Hodsden, Elizabeth Davis 244
Hodsden, Emma 244
Hodsden, Henry 244
Hodsden, John Goodrich 244
Hodsden, Joseph Bridger 244
Hodsden, Joseph Bridger, Jr. ZWe
Hodsden, Julia Ann 244
Hodsden, Julla Annes 244
Hodsden, Martha Pasteur 244
Hodsden, Mary Wilsm 244
Hodsden, Robert Bruce 244
Hodsden, Sally Bridger 244
Hodsden, Sarah 244
Hodsden, Wilfred 244
Hodsden, William 244
Hodsden, William Wirt 244
Hodson, Robert Hattan 244
Hoge, Rev. Dr. 199
Hoggard, Margie 75

Holan, Frances 70
Holgh, Isaac 245
Holgh, Sarah 195
Holladay, Anna 44
Holladay, Catherine 44
Holladay, James Lewis 44
Holladay, Joseph 163
Holladay, Lewis 44
Holladay, Lucie Edith Ballard 163
Holladay, Polly Boxley 44
Holladay, Rebecca 44
Holladay, William, Capt. 44
Holland, Anny 142
Holland, C. L. 19
Holland, Elizabeth 142
Holland, Fatsy 142
Holland, Jesse 154
Holland, Jesse Darius 154
Holland, John 142
Holland, Jonas M. 142
Holland, Judy 142
Holland, Nancy 142
Holland, Polly 142
Holland, Polly C. 154
Holland, Susanna 142
Holland, Theodosia 142
Holland, William P. 59
Holleman, Alexander 189
Holleman, Caroline 189
Holleman, Elizabeth Moody 189
Holleman, Fellciana 189
Holleman, Jerendah 189
Holleman, John Wesley 189
Holleman, Louretta 189
Holleman, Moody 189
Holleman, Panick Henry 189
Holleman, Wilson 189
Hollernan, Ceorge Washington 189
Hollernan, Emeline 189
Hollerran, Margaret 189
Holley, Harrison W. 40
Holliday, Catherine 84
Holliday, Elizabeth 33
Holmes, Coleman 155
Holmes, Elizabeth K. 176
Holt, Mary 28
Holt, Ruth A. 38
Homer, Gust. R. B. 280
Honnold, Elizabeth C. 97
Honnold, Hamilton J. 97
Honnold, James 97
Honnold, Julla Ann 97
Honnold, Lucinda 97
Honnold, Martha 97
Honnold, Rebecca M. 97
Honnold, Richard 97
Honnold, SAnnuel 97
Honnold, Sarah 97
Hope, Ellen Ann 265
Hope, May E. 148
Hopkins, Alioe Gertrude 198
Hopkins, Antess 161
Hopkins, Caleb 227
Hopkins, Catherine 21,175
Hopkins, Edmund 21,175
Hopkins, Elizabeth 21,175
Hopkins, Hanoria 227
Hopkins, Isabella 175
Hopkins, Isabella Taylor 21
Hopkins, J. Stuart 198

Hopkins, James 21,175
Hopkins, John 21,175
Hopkins, Lavinia B. 47
Hopkins, Mary 21,175
Hopkins, Robert Leonard 198
Hopkins, Samuel 21,175
Hopkins, William P. 227
Hopklns, Richard, Rev. Mr. 119
Hopktns, Hannah 239
Hopper, Emily Ann Green 184
Hopper, Milton 184
Horoches, James, Rev. 288
Horton, Humie Lee, Dr. 198
Horton, Humie Zebbie Lee 198
Horton, Lucille Audrey 196
Hosea, John 23
Hosea, John Jefferson 23
Hosea, Nancy Jefferson 23
Hosea, Nancy T. Jefferson 23
Hosea, Sabra Jane 23
Hosick, Maisie Phee 244
Hosick, Mary June 244
Hosick, Susan S. 244
Hosick, Teddy Rudolph 244
Hoskin, Dollie 201
Hoskin, Mary 201
Hoskins, Bernard 66
Hough, Ann 245
Hough, Ann H. 195
Hough, Annasa 195
Hough, BenjAnnin 195
Hough, Eleanor 195
Hough, Elizabeth 195
Hough, Jdn 195
Hough, Joseph 195
Hough, SAnnuel 195
Hough, Thomas 195
Hough, William 195
Hough, William Hite 195
Houke, Hal L. 244
Houke, Mary June 244
Housden, Elizabeth 165
Housden, Thomas 165
Housewright, C. A. 45
Housewright, Maria Louisa 24
Howard Beatrice Allen 249
Howard, Charles P. 249
Howard, Charles P., Jr. 249
Howard, Grover 216
Howard, Lem Calloway 249
Howard, Thomas H. 50
Howe, Mollie E. 22
Howell, Elizabeth 6
Howry, Lucian Beverley 159
Hubard, Edmund Wilcox 24
Hubard, Elizabeth 136
Hubard, James 136
Hubard, John 136
Hubard, John E., Dr. 24
Hubard, John Eppes 24
Hubard, LorAnn Doom 24
Hubard, Margaret 136
Hubard, Mary 136
Hubard, Matthew 136
Hubard, William 136
Hubbard, BenjAnnin 111
Hubbard, Judith 280
Hubbard, Lucy 9
Hubbard, William, CdLoml 166
Hudgins, Julia Audrey 198

Hudgins, R. Lesher 198
Hudgins, Robert Lester, Dr. 198
Hudglns, Sarah Frances 198
Hudsan, Elizabeth Anderson 133
Hudson, Addisan P. 18
Hudson, Ann 133
Hudson, Christopher 132
Hudson, Elizabeth A. 133
Hudson, Elizer B. 17
Hudson, Emns K. 18
Hudson, Sarah 133
Huff, Louisa James 247
Huff, P. F. 16
Hughes, Beveridge 256
Hughes, Lloyd B. 192
Hughes, Martha 116
Hughes, Moses B. in
Hughes, William S. 137
Hughes, Woodson, Mrs. 233
Hughlett, Elizabeth B. 132
Hughlett, Elizabeth Baker 132
Hughlett, William Eskridge 132
Hughlett, Yarrett 132
Hull, Elijah 1,258
Humber, Charles 216
Humber, Charles Chrlstian 216
Humber, Chrlstian 216
Humber, Edward 216
Humber, Elizabeth 216
Humber, John 216
Humber, John, Jr. 216
Humber, Judith 216
Humber, Lucy 216
Humber, Mary 216
Humber, Mary Chrlstian 216
Humber, Thomas Cole 216
Humber, William 216
Humber, William Hutson 216
Humbert, Barbara 251
Humphries, Caroline 229
Humphries, John F. 229
Humphries, William D. 229
Hunnicutt, Jchn, St. 261
Hunt, Benjamin V. 37
Hunt, Daniel 37
Hunt, Eleanor Eyre 37
Hunt, Elener 37
Hunt, Elizabeth 37
Hunt, Frances Jane 217
Hunt, Isha Van Cleve 37
Hunt, James 84
Hunt, James J. 217
Hunt, Jane 84
Hunt, Jane S. 37
Hunt, Jane Smith 37
Hunt, Mary Elizabeth 217
Hunt, Priscilla 217
Hunt, Ralph 37
Hunt, Sarah 217
Hunt, Sim 217
Hunt, William 37
Hunter, Adeline V. 53
Hunter, Charles 283
Hunter, Edward E. 24
Hunter, Elizabeth 282
Hunter, James 282
Hunter, Janet 283
Hunter, Joseph, Dr. 282
Hunter, Nicholas 282
Hunter, Sarah M. 53

Hunter, Will 282
Hunter, William, Dr. 281
Hunton, Eppa 221
Hunton, Frances Elizabeth 221
Hunton, James 221
Hunton, Priscilla 221
Hunton, Thomas 221
Hunton, William 221
Hurrber, Robert Chr1stian 216
Hurt, Berry 18
Hurt, Calvin 18
Hurt, Cynthia 18
Hurt, Fannie Craig Mitchell 18
Hurt, James 18,84
Hurt, Margeret 18
Hurt, Meredith 18
Hurt, Polly 18
Hurt, Rhoda 18
Hurt, Stephen 18
Hurt, Washington 8
Hurt, William 84
Hurt, Zachariah 18
Hutcheaan, Annie 68
Hutchens, Belle 284
Hutchenson, Elizabeth 68
Hutchescn, Mary M. 68
Hutcheson, Ann J. 68
Hutcheson, Chiles 68
Hutcheson, Elizabeth C. 68
Hutcheson, Frances A. 68
Hutcheson, Jemimah 68
Hutcheson, John 68
Hutcheson, Martha R, 68
Hutcheson, Mary 68
Hutcheson, Nancy 68
Hutcheson, Rebecca i. 68
Hutcheson, Richard 68
Hutcheson, Sarmel 68
Hutcheson, Susannah C. 68
Hutcheson, William 68
Hyde, Elizabeth 208
Hyde, Lucy Goddard 152
Hylton, Barbara A. 181,182
Hylton, Clark 182
Hylton, Clark P. 182
Hylton, Elizabeth AUoe 240
Hylton, G. W. 182
Hylton, Gabr. V. 182
Hylton, Gabriel V. 182
Hylton, George W. 181,182
Hylton, George W., Sr. 182
Hylton, Jeremiah W. 182
Hylton, Nancy 182
Hylton, S. C. 182
Hylton, Sarah C. 182
Hylton, Susan E. 182
Hylton, Valentine 182
Ingle, Annette Lewis 63
Ingle, Inban E., Rev. 63
Ingram, Benjamin 221
Ingram, Charles 221
Ingram, John 221
Ingram, Lela 117
Ingram, Mary 221
Ingram, Nancy 221
Ingram, Paulina 221
Ingram, Presley 221
Ingram, Sarah M. 42
Inskeep, Annelia 246
Inskeep, Elizabeth 246

Inskeep, Hannah 246
Inskeep, Joseph 246
Inskeep, Mary 247
Inskeep, Tabitha 246
Inskeep, William 246
Irby, Anne 36
Irby, Betsey 36
Irby, John 36
Irby, Joseph 36
Irby, Joseph K. 36
Irby, Joshua 36
Irby, Nancey 36
Irby, Thomas Kendrick 36
Irby, William 36
Irgram, Elizabeth 221
Jackson, A. U. 96
Jackson, Annie E. 85
Jackson, Auguster M. 96
Jackson, C. M. 96
Jackson, Charles M. 96
Jackson, D. C. 46
Jackson, D. C., Mrs. 46
Jackson, Edna E. 44
Jackson, Eliza W. 105
Jackson, Emily Stith 120
Jackson, Ephraim 120
Jackson, Ephraim W. 120
Jackson, Frederick M. 120
Jackson, George 85
Jackson, Green 96,120
Jackson, Hannah E. M. 120
Jackson, Lillie D. 46
Jackson, Lucretia 120
Jackson, Lucretia Catherine 120
Jackson, Martha Green 120
Jackson, Mary 85
Jackson, Mary Jones 120
Jackson, Nancy Aris, Mrs. 127
Jackson, O. P. 96
Jackson, P. O. 96
Jackson, Rebecca 120
Jackson, Rebecca A. 120
Jackson, Rebecca Ann 120
Jackson, Rebecca R. 120
Jackson, Robert T. 120
Jackson, Robert T. 96
Jackson, Robert Tucker 120
Jackson, T. E. 96
Jackson, T. L. 96
Jackson, Temperance 120
Jackson, Thomas Jonathan (Stonewall) 69
Jackson, W. G., Rev. 67
Jackson, W. L. 96
Jackson, Wilbur L. 85
Jackson, William L. 120
Jackson, William Lucas 96,120
Jackson, Zena 96
Jackson,, W. L., Jr. 67
Jamerson, John Richard 264
Jamerson, Joseph D. 264
Jamerson, Martha E1izabeth 264
Jamerson, Sarah 264
Jamerson, Sarah Smith 264
Jamerson, Sarah Stokes 264
Jamerson, Virginia 264
Jamerson, William H, 264
James, Isaac 228
James, Nannie 98
James, Ruth Marie 251
James, Sallie A. 276

James, Sally A. 277
Jameson, William 8., Dr. 262
January, Peter 166
Jarnesaz, Martha 216
Jarratt, H. 186
Jarratt, Mortilda Am 186
Jarratt, W. F. 186
Jarrell, Catberirre 101
Jarrett, Devereaux 209
Jarvis, Elizabeth 260
Jarvis, Reziah 260
Jarvis, Rhoda 260
Jefferis, Georella B. 66
Jefferson, Alexander 270
Jefferson, Archer 270
Jefferson, Betsy Ann 270
Jefferson, Elizabeth 269,270
Jefferson, Elizabeth Arm 270
Jefferson, Elizabeth Broane 270
Jefferson, Feild 259 ,270
Jefferson, Frances 42,270
Jefferson, George 41
Jefferson, Hannah 23
Jefferson, Isaac P. 23
Jefferson, James F. 23
Jefferson, James Hopkins 270
Jefferson, John 23,269,270
Jefferson, John Pinkard 270
Jefferson, John R. 270
Jefferson, John W. C. 23
Jefferson, Judith 269,270
Jefferson, Kittie 270
Jefferson, Martha Elizabeth 41
Jefferson, Martha Feild 270
Jefferson, Mary 269
Jefferson, Mary Frances 269,270
Jefferson, Nancy T. 23
Jefferson, Peter 269
Jefferson, Peter Feild 269
Jefferson, Peterfeild 270
Jefferson, Peterfeild 270
Jefferson, Polly V. 23
Jefferson, Richard 23
Jefferson, Samuel 23,270
Jefferson, Samuel A. 270
Jefferson, Samuel Allan 270
Jefferson, Samuel Y. 23
Jefferson, Sarah P. 23
Jefferson, Thomas 269,270
Jefferson, Unicy 23
Jefferson, Warren 23
Jenkins, Abraham 35
Jenkins, Addie N. 35
Jenkins, Addie Nicolas 35
Jenkins, be D. 35
Jenkins, Benjamin 35
Jenkins, Betty Young 35
Jenkins, Charles V. 35
Jenkins, Clara 35
Jenkins, H. Y. 35
Jenkins, Henry 35
Jenkins, Henry J. 35
Jenkins, Henry T. 35
Jenkins, James 35
Jenkins, Jene W 35
Jenkins, Louis 35
Jenkins, Magg B. 35
Jenkins, Mamie E. 35
Jenkins, Martha, Mes. 35
Jenkins, Mary E. 35

Jenkins, Patsy 146
Jenkins, Patsy 35
Jenkins, Pattie 35
Jenkins, Pkuy 35
Jenkins, R. B. 35
Jenkins, Sally J. 35
Jenkins, Sarah Ann 35
Jenkins, Thomas James 35
Jenklns, Nathaniel A. 35
Jennings, Elizabeth 237
Jennings, James W. 237
Jennings, Jane 286
Jennings, Jane Sinclair 106
Jennings, Lucrecy 237
Jennings, Martin 87
Jennings, Nancy 237
Jennings, Nancy Allen 237
Jennings, Polly 237
Jennings, Polly Kidd 237
Jennings, Robert 237
Jennings, Salley 237
Jennings, Sally Y. 237
Jennings, Sophy 237
Jennings, Webb 237
Jennings, William 237
Jennings, William Calvin 237
Jennings, William L 237
Jerdone, Anne 144,145
Jerdone, Earnest 145
Jerdone, Elizabeth 104,144
Jerdone, Ellen 144
Jerdone, Ellen 145
Jerdone, Francis 144,145
Jerdone, Isabella 144
Jerdone, James 145
Jerdone, John 144,145
Jerdone, Maria 145
Jerdone, Maria C. 145
Jerdone, Mary 144
Jerdone, Polly 145
Jerdone, Sarah 144,145
Jerdone, William 144,145
Jerdone, William M, 145
Jeter, Florence Yates 52
Jeter, Ruby Rivers 52
Jeter, V. E. 52
Jett, Ann 196
Jett, Ann Elizabeth 132
Jett, Elizabeth 132
Jett, Thomas 8,132
Jobson, Batson M. 214
Jobson, Daniel 214
Jobson, Francis V. 214
Jobson, John 214
Jobson, John S. 214
Jobson, Joseph 214
Jobson, Kesiah 214
Jobson, Robert M. 214
Jobson, William 214
John, Camm 111
John, Pearlie V. 18
Johns, Alvin France Sutherlin 18
Johns, Clara 35
Johns, Lenora S. 35
Johns, Milton 18
Johns, P. P., Rev. 230
Johns, Pearl M 18
Johns, Preston 19
Johns, Roscoe Morrell 18
Johnson, A. R. 152

Johnson, Albert B. 245
Johnson, Ann 84
Johnson, B. 8., Rev. 185
Johnson, Elizabeth 84
Johnson, Elizabeth Jane 257
Johnson, Elizabeth Woodrop 15
Johnson, Emma R. 154
Johnson, Francis 257
Johnson, Gecrge Washington 24
Johnson, George 67
Johnson, Jane 125
Johnson, Joseph 257
Johnson, Judith 1, 258
Johnson, Julia Munroe 172
Johnson, Lewis Benjamin 236
Johnson, Lydia 245
Johnson, Maria 258
Johnson, Marie 1
Johnson, Martha 258
Johnson, Mary 1,84,194,258
Johnson, Mary 6. 33
Johnson, Mary Broughton I,258
Johnson, Milton B. 19
Johnson, Mollie 1,28
Johnson, Nancy 257
Johnson, Oliver 81
Johnson, Phebe 84
Johnson, Philip 1,25
Johnson, Robert 171
Johnson, Robert 257
Johnson, S. H., Rev. 74
Johnson, Sallie 257
Johnson, Sally 257
Johnson, Sarah 89
Johnson, Susan 1,258
Johnson, T. T. 185
Johnson, Thomas 1,257,258
Johnson, Thomas 1,257,258
Johnson, Thomas, Dr. 1
Johnson, Wiley 81
Johnson, William 257
Johnson, WIlliam, Rev. 35,257
Johnston, Ann 171
Johnston, Eliza Woodrop 159
Johnston, Elizabeth 19,172
Johnston, James 159
Johnston, Jane Deacon 159
Johnston, Martha 172
Johnston, Rebecca 194
Johnston, Richard 171,172
Johnston, Richard Wheeler 172
Johnston, Robert Jardine 19
Johnston, Robert, Dr 159
Jolley, Samuel G. 8
Jolly, Elizabeth Jane 212
Jolly, Jesse Thomas 213
Jolly, Joseph 213
Jolly, Joseph Howard 213
Jolly, Mildred Carolyn 513
Jolly, Nancy Virginia 212
Jolly, Tallie Virginia 213
Jones , Robert C. 65
Jones, Albert C. 64,65
Jones, Alexander Leftwich 204
Jones, Amelia 156
Jones, Amsted 74
Jones, Ann 33
Jones, Ann Elizabeth 82
Jones, Ann M. Bakserville 65
Jones, Ann Minge 65

Jones, Ann Minger 6
Jones, Ann Parks 262
Jones, Anne 106
Jones, Armsted 74
Jones, B. 142
Jones, Benjamin C. 156
Jones, Benjamin J. 156
Jones, Betsy Ann 33
Jones, Branch 41
Jones, Callam 273
Jones, D., Mrs. 42
Jones, Edward Montford 262
Jones, Eli 33
Jones, Elizabeth 33,94,127,143,156,247
Jones, Fanny, Mrs. 102
Jones, Frances 106,130
Jones, Frederick A. 257
Jones, Gabriel 29
Jones, Henry C. 156
Jones, Isaac 156
Jones, James 33,142
Jones, James Doyle 213
Jones, Jane 263
Jones, John C. 203,204
Jones, John E. 204
Jones, John Holland 142
Jones, Laines 106
Jones, Lane 106
Jones, Leodicea 156
Jones, Leonard 3
Jones, Lucy Ann 6,156
Jones, Lucy I. 146
Jones, Marcella 196
Jones, Margaret 33
Jones, Martha 106,265
Jones, Martha B. 156
Jones, Mary 33
Jones, Mary Ann 65
Jones, Mary M. 204
Jones, Mary Williams 251
Jones, Nancey 33
Jones, Newland 161
Jones, Orlando 106
Jones, Orpha 16
Jones, Patsy 257
Jones, Peg 33
Jones, Peter 247
Jones, Peter Calvin 156
Jones, Peter R. 156
Jones, Polly Ann 142
Jones, RdLando 106
Jones, Robert T. 156
Jones, Roberta Park 65
Jones, Roscoe Morrell 19
Jones, Roxanna E. 156
Jones, Sarah 33,281
Jones, Sinthey 74
Jones, Strawther 182
Jones, Susan 41,42
Jones, Susan E. 188
Jones, Susannah 33
Jones, Tallie V. 212
Jones, Thomas 40,143
Jones, Thomas J. U. 142
Jones, V. B. 28
Jones, W. Y. 74
Jones, Wiley 33,156
Jones, William 33,18
Jones, William D., Rev. 99
Jones, William V. 82

Jordan, Ada Augusta 215
Jordan, Amy 145
Jordan, Bettie Johnson 215
Jordan, Brittain 145
Jordan, Bruce 29
Jordan, Burrell 145
Jordan, C. J. 29
Jordan, Edna Wilson 29
Jordan, Elizabeth J. 215
Jordan, George 145
Jordan, Green H. 145
Jordan, Hezekiah 215
Jordan, Hezekiah T. 215
Jordan, Imogene 215
Jordan, James T. 59
Jordan, John 145
Jordan, John J. 215
Jordan, Lucy 143
Jordan, Mary 34, 145
Jordan, P. A. 29
Jordan, Patience 145
Jordan, Patience 145
Jordan, Susannah 145
Jordan, Theodore Miller 8
Jordan, Thomas Hezekiah 215
Jordan, Winifred 145
Joynder, Paulina Dillard 138
Joyner, Cassandra B. 133,139
Joyner, Mavenda 153
Joyner, Oscia Ella 138
Joyner, Peter H. 137,138,139
Justice, D. 31
Justice, Elizabeth 31
Justice, Join 31
Justice, Nancy 31
Justice, Patsey 31
Justice, Polley 31
Justis, Allen 31
Justis, David 91
Justis, Elizabeth 31
Justis, Henry 31
Justis, Jemima 31
Justis, John 31
Justis, Judith 31
Justis, Justinian 91
Justis, Kezie 31
Justis, Major 31
Justis, Pattey 31
Justis, Phrame 31
Justis, Priscilla 31
Justis, Stephen 31
Justis, William 31
Karr, William L. 53
Kate May Moseley 24
Kay Richard 79
Kay, Christopher 79
Kay, Edward 79
Kay, Elizabeth 79
Kay, Elizabeth Jane 79
Kay, Gabriel 267
Kay, James 79
Kay, John 79
Kay, Lucy Ann 79
Kay, Polly 79
Kay, Robert 267
Kay, Sarah 79
Kay, William 79
Keaton, Morttie 8
Keith, Thomas 238
Kellam, Betsey 129

Kellam, John 129
Kellam, Margaret 129
Kellis, P. V., Colonel 194
Kelly, Alexander D. 137
Kelly, Alexander 137
Kelly, Charles W. 78
Kelly, E. P. 163
Kelly, Edith H. 163
Kelly, Elizabeth 6,137
Kelly, Elizabeth E. 163
Kelly, Ezekiel P. 163
Kelly, Farmy 137
Kelly, Farny Day 163
Kelly, George L. 78
Kelly, George P. 137
Kelly, George T. 163
Kelly, George V. 78
Kelly, Harry 163
Kelly, Hening P. 163
Kelly, Henry 0. 137
Kelly, Hugh H. 163
Kelly, Jacob Eley 163
Kelly, Jacob Holland 163
Kelly, James 137
Kelly, James 137
Kelly, James V. 137
Kelly, James W.. 137
Kelly, James Y. 76
Kelly, John 137
Kelly, John D. 50
Kelly, John P. 137
Kelly, John Thomas 76
Kelly, Jonathan 137
Kelly, Joseph Holladay 163
Kelly, L. E. B. 163
Kelly, Lawrence 177
Kelly, Lucy E. B. H. 163
Kelly, Lydia Day 163
Kelly, Margaret Elizabeth 163
Kelly, Mary Ann 137
Kelly, Mary C. 78
Kelly, Mary C. W
Kelly, Minerva V. 163
Kelly, Minerva V. 163
Kelly, Mollie C. 163
Kelly, Mollie P. 163
Kelly, Molly 137
Kelly, Nancy 137
Kelly, Penelope 137
Kelly, Peter C. 137
Kelly, Sally 137
Kelly, Sally B. 163
Kelly, Sally P. 163
Kelly, Spicer 137
Kelly, Spicer Y. 137
Kelly, Susan 137
Kelly, Susannah B. 163
Kelly, Thomas C. 137
Kelly, Thomas C. 137
Kelly, Thomas Conway 137
Kelly, Walter P. W
Kelly, William T. 137
Kelsey, J. B. 230
Kemon, E. 233
Kemp, Elizabeth 174
Kemp, Isabella 56
Kemp, Jan 171
Kemp, Jessy 174
Kemp, John 174
Kemp, Mary 174

Kemp, William 174
Kemper, Nancy 147
Kendall, Katherine Barkley 185
Kendall, Nancy 150
Kendall, Sarah C. B. 150
Kendall, William 150
Kennedy, Alexander 64,65
Kennedy, Ann 5
Kennedy, Aralinta 5
Kennedy, Cyrus 5
Kennedy, Delha Park 65
Kennedy, James 5
Kennedy, Jefferson 5
Kennedy, Jesse 34
Kennedy, John 5
Kennedy, Josiah 5
Kennedy, Mary 5
Kennedy, Sidney Manson 34
Kennedy, Sophia 5
Kennedy, Susan 34
Kennedy, Thomas H. 34
Kennedy, Tully 5
Kennedy, William 5
Kenner, B., Rev. in
Kennerly, Mary 188
Kennerly, Mary C. 188
Kennerly, Susan 182
Kennings, Allen Alien 237
Kennnon, Rhode 105
Kennon, Charles 105
Kennon, Charles H. 18
Kennon, Charles Henry 105
Kennon, Eliza 18
Kennon, Eliza W. 105
Kennon, Elizabeth Rebecca 105
Kennon, Elizabeth V. 105
Kennon, Erasmus 105
Kennon, James 105
Kennon, Judith 130
Kennon, Lewis 105
Kennon, Lewis Willis 105
Kennon, Lucy 105
Kennon, Lucy Page 117
Kennon, Mary 105
Kennon, Mary B. 18
Kennon, Mildred L. 105
Kennon, Mildred Susan 18
Kennon, Nancy 105
Kennon, Nancy Millie 18
Kennon, Oswell B 105
Kennon, Patsey 18
Kennon, Rachel 43
Kennon, Rebecca 18
Kennon, Richard 18
Kennon, Robert Poe 105
Kennon, Sally 18
Kennon, Thomas 43
Kennon, William 18
Kenyan, William 184
Kerr, Alexander 109
Kerr, Ann 109
Kerr, Bazillac 109
Kerr, Elizabeth 109
Kerr, Fanny L. Newell 109
Kerr, Frances Ann McNeill 109
Kerr, Frankey 109
Kerr, Isabella 109
Kerr, James 109
Kerr, James Sadler C. 109
Kerr, John 109

Kerr, John H. McNeill 109
Kerr, John, Sr. 109
Kerr, Lucy 109
Kerr, Martha 109
Kerr, Mary 109
Kerr, Mary I. I. 109
Kerr, Nancy 109
Kerr, Sarah 109
Kerr, Solomon 109
Kerr, Susannah 109
Kesterson, Chloe 32
Kesterson, George 32
Kesterson, Mary 32
Key, Sally 79
Keyser, Mrs. 234
Kidd, Attie M., Mrs. 77
Kidd, Polly 237
Kidd, William B. 77
Kidmore, Lewis, Rev. 185
Killegrew, Elizabeth 15
Killegrew, George 15
Killegrew, Mildred 14
Killegrew, Molly 14
Killegrew, Rebecca 15
Killegrew, William 14,15
Kimball, Selascha A. 116
Kimborough, Rose 46
Kinckle, Rev. Mr. 283
King, E. Y. 49
King, George 243
King, J. B. 49
King, Joseph 0. 49
King, Joseph Waverly 49
King, Mary 200,202
King, Peter Manson 24
King, Peter Manson, Jr. 247
King, Rev. 115
King, Wright 24
Kinsolving, O. A., Rev. 67
Kirby, Bennett 111
Kirby, Bennett T. 111
Kirby, Charlotte 111
Kirby, Charlotte DeBerry 148
Kirby, Dorothy 111
Kirby, Eliza Ann 111
Kirby, Frances 111
Kirby, John
Kirby, John A. 111
Kirby, John Munford 112
Kirby, John Munford Walker 111
Kirby, John, Capt. 111
Kirby, Lucy V. 111
Kirby, Lucy Walker 112
Kirby, Lula P. 111
Kirby, Mary 111
Kirby, Minerva V. 111
Kirby, Samuel T. 111
Kirby, Thomas 111
Kirby, William 111
Kirby, William R. 111
Kirkland, Mary A. 29
Kirkland, Mary 29
Knor, Franklin 78
Knot, Mary 134
Koontz, C. D. 16
Kosterson, Nancy 32
Kyle, V. B. 118
Lacy, Agnes J. 83
Lacy, Archibald 83
Lacy, Edmund B. 83

Lacy, John Bacon 83
Lacy, John S. 83
Lacy, Junietta Constance 83
Lacy, Juriah 8
Lacy, Mary Juriah Elizabeth S3
Lacy, Salley Henry 83
Lacy, William Archibald 8
Ladd, Deborah Anne 163
Ladd, Hannah 38
Ladd, Sarah E. 28
LaDoux, Merle 2Z4
LaDu, Mary 224
Lafayette, Marquis de Lafayette, General 225
Lake, Clarence T. 42
Lambert, Rachel 195
Lamm, E. C. 19
Lampkin, Sarah Jane 239
Land, Pattie H. 52
Landon, Mary Banks 114
Landon, St L. 158
Lane, Luana 193
Lane, Martha 106
Lane, Mary 218
Langhorne, G. W., Rev. 172
Lanier, Cinderella 18
Lanier, Elizabeth 155
Lanier, James 155
Lanier, Melissa 155
Latham, Alfred 227
Latham, Cathrine P7
Lathem, B. P. 260
Lathem, Ben 260
Lathem, Birdie Willie 260
Lathem, Gladys 260
Lathem, James Perryman 260
Lattany, Lewis, Rev. 110
Lauck, William C. 69
Lauger, Ethel 99
Laurie, Lydia 282
Law, Fanny 4
Law, John 126
Law, Sarah 126
Lawrence, Eugenia Dearing 196
Lawrence, Even H. 224
Lawrence, Frances Effingham 197
Lawrence, Julius E. 224
Lawrence, Mary Mears 244
Lawrence, Robert Brashear 196
Lawrence, Robert Brashear, Jr. 197
Lawrence, Robert Brashear, Sr. 197
Lawrence, Susan Emily Southall 172
Lay, Charlotte 0. 18
Laycack, James Blaker 168
Laycock, Charles Fenton 168
Laycock, James William 168
Laycock, Lucy Elen 168
Laycock, Martha Lane 18
Laycock, Mary Elizabeth 168
Laycock, Mortilda 168
Laycock, Samuel l68
Laycock, Sarah Mortilda 168
Leach, J. H. C., Rev. 35
League, Ann 28
League, Archer 28
League, Benjamin 28
League, Berry 28
League, Candace 28
League, Casandra 28
League, Drusilla 28
League, Edward 28

League, Elizabeth 8
League, George 28
League, George B. 28
League, Harriett 28
League, Isham 28
League, James 28
League, James 28
League, Jane P. 28
League, Joab 28
League, Joel 28
League, Joshua 28
League, Lucy 28
League, Mary 28
League, Nary 28
League, Nathan 28
League, Oney 28
League, Rachel 28
League, Robert 28
League, Sallie 28
League, Ursilla 28
League, William 28
Leather, Elizabeth 18
Leathers, Elizabeth Ferguson 128,129
Leathers, Joseph 18,129
Leathers, Peter Ferguson 129
Leavel, William T., Rev. 164
Lee, Alice C. 184
Lee, Ann Catharine 84
Lee, Ann Mc 84
Lee, Anna 217,240
Lee, Anne Corbin 275
Lee, Bailey 284
Lee, Betty 84,169
Lee, Charles 125
Lee, Colonel 275
Lee, Daniel Chichester 84
Lee, Doddridge Chicester 84
Lee, Edward 217
Lee, Eliz. 157
Lee, Eliz. 157 158
Lee, Elizabeth 158
Lee, Elizabeth G. 125
Lee, Elizabeth Jane 212
Lee, Elizabeth Ludwell 158
Lee, Fanny 157,158
Lee, Francis Lightfoot 275
Lee, George 157
Lee, James 217
Lee, John 217
Lee, John Hancock 84
Lee, Judith 125
Lee, Larkin Davis 212
Lee, Lewis 217
Lee, Lucinda 157
Lee, Lucy Jane 212
Lee, Mary 157
Lee, Mary K. 84
Lee, Minnie 185
Lee, Needham 217
Lee, Richard 217
Lee, Richard Kendall 84
Lee, Sarah 125
Lee, Sarah McCarty 84
Lee, Sarah, Mrs. 125
Lee, Sinah Ellen
Lee, Thomas 158,217
Lee, Thomas, Capt. 217
Lee, William 217
Lee, William Lancelot 84
Lee, Willis 217

Lee, Winifred 157
Lee, Winnifred 217
Lee, Zilpha 217
Leftwich, Alexander 203,204
Leftwich, Ann Ralph 204
Leftwich, Eliza Ann 203,204
Leftwich, Eliza Samuel 204
Leftwich, Ellen F. 203
Leftwich, Ellen F. 203
Leftwich, Ellen Frances 204
Leftwich, James
Leftwich, James C. 204
Leftwich, James Clayton 204
Leftwich, James T. 40
Leftwich, Jane 2
Leftwich, Jane 203
Leftwich, John O. 40
Leftwich, John S. 203
Leftwich, John Smith 204
Leftwich, Mary Elizabeth 204
Leftwich, Mary Mortilda 203,204
Leftwich, Pauline 203,204
Leftwich, Pauline Smith 204
Leftwich, Sally 203,204
Leftwich, Samuel 204,204
Leftwich, Sarah E. 40
Leftwich, Sarah Jane 204
Leftwich, Susan A. 40
Leftwich, Thomas 203,204
Leftwich, William Alexander 204
Leftwich, William C. 204
Leftwich, William P. 40
Legrand, Evaline G. 68
Legrand, James A. 68
Legrand, John T. 68
Legrand, Thomas S. 68
Leigh, Welcome 160
Leith, Benjamin C. 42
Leith, Margaret L. 42
Lemon, Amelia 129
Lemon, Elizabeth A. 128
Lemon, Elizabeth Amelia 129
Lemon, George Washington 129
Lemon, James Cavin 129
Lemon, James, Jr. 129
Lemon, James, Sr. 129
Lemon, Joseph 129
Lemon, Joseph Francis Marion 129
Lemon, Joseph I. 128,129
Lemon, Joseph Isabella Francis 129
Lemon, Joshua L. 129
Lemon, Joshua Leathers 129
Lemon, Margaret A. 129
Lemon, Margaret Ann 129
Lemon, Mary Jane 129
Lemon, Nancy C. 233
Lemon, Thomas 129
Lemon, William T. 129
Lemon, William Thomas 129
Lerathers, Joseph 129
Lesesne, Henry Roby 241
Lesesne, Henry Roby, Jr. 241
Lesesne, Margaret Lucy 241
Lesesne, Norma Jean 241
Lester, Archibald 14
Lett, Rev. Mr. 62
Leverett, Abraham 100,101
Leverett, Almeda 101
Leverett, Alminda 100
Leverett, Ann 100,101

Leverett, Catharine 100
Leverett, Gideon 100,101
Leverett, Jeremiah 100,101
Leverett, John 100
Leverett, Malitta 100,101
Leverett, Maria 100
Leverett, Mariah 101
Leverett, Marian 100
Leverett, Mary E. 101
Leverett, Myrtilla 100
Leverett, Thomas 100
Lewis, Acy 238
Lewis, Arch Stewart 214
Lewis, Ashton 269
Lewis, Augustine 214
Lewis, Belinda 238
Lewis, Benjamin 269
Lewis, Betsy, Mrs. 102
Lewis, Bettie 282
Lewis, Bettie Burnet 63
Lewis, Catherine 22,176
Lewis, Charles 22,176
Lewis, Charles Stuart 269
Lewis, Charles Woodson 214
Lewis, Chloe Spencer 214
Lewis, Chrisehana Caroline 214
Lewis, David Pannill 214
Lewis, Dorcas 145
Lewis, Edmond B. 238
Lewis, Elizabeth 21,22,66,176,145,236,283
Lewis, Elizabeth Didamia 145
Lewis, Elizabeth P. 214
Lewis, Fannie 3
Lewis, Francis 238
Lewis, Gardiner Hopkins 238
Lewis, George Washington 145
Lewis, Hannah 238,239
Lewis, Henry 238,269
Lewis, Henry William 145
Lewis, Henry, Dr. 269
Lewis, Howell 105
Lewis, J. M., Rev. 48
Lewis, Jacob 231
Lewis, James 21,22,176
Lewis, James Cox 238
Lewis, James Edmund 269
Lewis, James, Capt. 176
Lewis, John 22,176,214,238
Lewis, John Cox 238
Lewis, John Jefferson 145
Lewis, John Marshall 214
Lewis, Joseph 227
Lewis, Joseph Martin 145
Lewis, Joseph Warner 269
Lewis, Judith 63
Lewis, Leearne D. 133
Lewis, Lottie H. 127
Lewis, Louisa Gray 269
Lewis, Lucinda 214
Lewis, Margaret 2,238
Lewis, Mary 22,176,231,238
Lewis, Mary Anne F. 137
Lewis, Mary Handltca 218
Lewis, Nancy 238
Lewis, Nancy B. 238
Lewis, Nancy Grasty 214
Lewis, Richard Ectrin 269
Lewis, Robert 63
Lewis, Sallie 103
Lewis, Sara Ann Elizabeth 145

Lewis, Sarah 80,103,238
Lewis, Temple 214
Lewis, Thomas 238,239,283
Lewis, Thomas Anderson 214
Lewis, Thomas D. 12
Lewis, Walker 7
Lewis, William 78,145 ,214 ,238
Lewis, William L. 145
Lewls, James Mansfield 214
Leyburn, Jane 190
Leyhurn, George W., Dr. 190
Liggan, Robert 81
Liggan, Sarah Elizabeth 81
Light, Agnes 13
Light, Elizabeth 13
Light, Joanne 13
Light, Joel 13
Light, John, Sr. 13
Light, Mary 13
Light, Sarah 13
Light, Stephen 13
Light, Tabitha 13
Light, Temperance 13
Light, William 13
Light, Winifred 13
Lightfoot, aillen A. 101
Lightfoot, Allen 101
Lightfoot, Anderson 101
Lightfoot, Aseneth 101
Lightfoot, Catherine 101
Lightfoot, Collin 101
Lightfoot, Edwin 101
Lightfoot, Edwin B. 101
Lightfoot, Elizabeth 101
Lightfoot, Frank Qyde 101
Lightfoot, Henry 156
Lightfoot, Thomas H. 101
Lightfoot, James 101
Lightfoot, James T. 101
Lightfoot, John A. 101
Lightfoot, John Richard 101
Lightfoot, John W. 101
Lightfoot, Margaret Caroline 101
Lightfoot, Peterson B. 101
Lightfoot, Sarah 101
Lightfoot, Thomas 101
Lightfoot, W. T. 101
Lightfoot, William 101
Lightfoot, William C. 101
Ligon, Elizabeth K. 46
Ligon, Lizzie Kimborough 46
Ligon, Richard 43
Ligon, Willian 43
Lill1ston, Deidanda 89
Lill1ston, John 89
Lily, Martha Peyton 60
Lily, W. B. 60
Lindsay, Susan Ann 211
Lindsay, William 157
Lipely, Polly H. 100
Lippincott, Caroline 90
Lipscomb, James Hill 113
Little, Ann Eliza Erwin 194
Little, Jacob W. F. 194
Littleberry, Capt 224
Littleberry, Martha Sylvian 224
Littleberry, Sarah 224
Littleberry, Sarah 224
Littleton, Askar, Rev. 35
Litton, Charity 52

Locke, Thomas E., Rev. 264
Lockett, Osborne 273
Lockett, Frances W. 274
Lockridge, Emily M. 116
Logan, Alexander 128
Logan, Fearl Jctns 19
Logan, Jane 170
Logan, Stonewall Jackson 18
Lomar, Catherine 275
Lomax, Thomas 275
London, Ann Eliza 140
London, Daniel Higginbotham 114
London, Eliza Ann 114
London, Frances Ann 114
London, Franes Jane 114
London, H. 123
London, John 114
London, John James 114
London, Tirzah 114
London, W. A. 123
London, William A. 123
London, William Augustus 114
Looney, Nancy Mariah 53
Looper, Polly 91
Loper, Mary H. 274
Lorimer, Isabell 200
Love, James, Colonel 2
Love, Mary 2,3
Loves, Haysten 86
Loves, Nancy 86
Loves, Richard 86
Loving, E. W. 20
Loving, Elljah 20
Loving, Gincey 20
Loving, J. C. 23
Loving, Matilda A. 20
Lovvorn, Elijah 20
Lovvorn, Thomas R. 20
Lovvorn, William R. 20
Low, Samuel, Rev. 125
Lowe, John, Rev. 157
Lowry, Edmond 102
Lowry, Fran. 102
Lowry, Jane 102
Lowry, John 102
Lowry, Mary Hallier 102
Lowry, Nancy 102
Lowry, Robert 102
Lowry, Thomas 102
Lowry, William 102
Loyde, William 102
Lozano, Mildred L. 69
Lucas, David 260
Lucas, Eliza 225
Lucas, Mary Rosabell 260
Lucas, Rebecca R. 120
Lucas, Susan Terisa 260
Luck, Child 7
Luckett, Elinor 109
Ludwell, Thomas 157,158
Lunceford, Lewis, Rev. Mr. 271
Lyle, Matthew, Rev. 141
Lynah, Lillie Heyward 196
Lyon, Ann Ellza 208
Lyon, M. L., Miss 194
Maben, David 57
Maben, Jane B. 57
Maben, John R. 30
Mabry William Fielden 9
Mabry, Absalom 9

Mabry, Arrerica 9
Mabry, Charles 9
Mabry, Churchwell 9
Mabry, Greenberry 9
Mabry, Henry 9
Mabry, Lucy 9
Mabry, Samuel 9
Mabry, Samuel, Jr. 9
Mabry, Sarah 9
Mabry, Sarah 9
Macaulay, Alexander 104,144
Macaulay, Elizabeth 104
Macaulay, Francis 104
Macaulay, John 104
Macaulay, Patrick 104
Macaulay, Patrlck, Dr. 106
Macauley, Alexander 104
Mackey, Robert L. 257
Macknamara, Gabriel S. 73
Maclemaw, Frances 218
Macnortan, W., Rev. 113
Macon, Ann 107
Macon, Ann 107
Macon, Ann Elizabeth 107
Macon, Ann Elizabeth 107
Macon, Elizabeth 107,207
Macon, Flary Cary 107
Macon, Gideon. 107
Macon, Hannah 107
Macon, Hartwell 107
Macon, Henry 107
Macon, John Augustine 107
Macon, Joseph 107
Macon, Judy 107
Macon, Lucy 107
Macon, Lucy Scott 107
Macon, Martha 107
Macon, Mary 107
Macon, Mary Hartwell 107
Macon, Mary Smith 107
Macon, Miles 107
Macon, Miles Selden 107
Macon, Rebecca 107
Macon, Sarah 107
Macon, Sarah 144
Macon, Thomas 107,108
Macon, William H. 107
Macon, William Hartwell 107
Macon, Williw 107
Maddox, William Henry 212
Maddux, Margaret Horun 191
Maddux, William 191
Madisan, Nelly 108
Madison, Ambrose 108
Madison, Arm 110
Madison, Caflett 108
Madison, Elizabeth 108
Madison, Frances 108
Madison, Frances Taylor 108
Madison, Francis 108
Madison, James, Sr. 108
Madison, James, Sr., Colonel 18
Madison, John 110
Madison, Martha M. 181
Madison, Nelly Conway 108
Madison, Reubin 108
Madison, Sarah 108
Madison, William 108
Magill, Charles, Colonel 166
Major, William 266

Malbone, Godfrey 279
Mallory, Elizabeth 266
Malone, Catharine 89
Maness, Isham 18
Maness, Laura Agnes 18
Maney, Sam B., Dr. 73
Mangum, Elizabeth 216
Mangum, Lucy 127
Manlove, Elizabeth 247
Manlove, Jane 247
Manlove, Olris 247
Manlove, Rebecca Bolling 247
Manlove, Thomas Bolling 247
Mann, Anna Otelia 185
Mansfield, Beverly Winston 211
Mansfield, Charles Fenton Mercer 212
Mansfield, Elizabeth Clark 211
Mansfield, Emma Campbell 212
Mansfield, Henry Clay 212
Mansfield, James David 212
Mansfield, James Wilkerson 211
Mansfield, John William 212
Mansfield, Joseph Allen 211
Mansfield, Mary Jane 212
Mansfield, Mary Lewis 211
Mansfield, Mildred Martin 211
Mansfield, Mildred Mourning 212
Mansfield, Mourning 211
Mansfield, Mourning Clark 211
Mansfield, Nancy Harrison 211
Mansfield, Pleasant Fountain 211
Mansfield, Rebecca Maud 212
Mansfield, Robert 211
Mansfield, Robert Clark 211
Mansfield, Robert Thomas 212
Mansfield, Samuel Allen 212
Mansfield, Sarah Homes 211
Mansfield, Susannah Ware 211
Mansfield, Thomas Martin 211,212
Mansfield, William Hearndon 211
Marberry, James, Rev. 203
Marion, Joseph Francis 129
Markham, Bernard, Colonel 164,165
Markham, Catharine 164
Markham, Elizabeth 165
Markham, George 164,165
Markham, John 164
Markham, Judith V. 165
Markham, Mary 165
Markham, Sarah 165
Markham, William Harris 165
Marks, Sallie 194
Marktram, Martha 164
Marshall, B. L. 19
Marshall, D. E. 19
Marshall, J. E. S. A. 153
Marshall, Joanna 183,184
Marshall, Join 184
Marshall, Mary 156,183,184
Marshall, Nancy 184
Marshall, R. D. 153
Marshall, Rush 183,184
Marshall, William 107
Martia, James H. 148
Martin, Abner 146
Martin, Adam 147
Martin, Barnet 151
Martin, Benjamin 147
Martin, Benjamin H. 147
Martin, Benjamin K. 148

Martin, Betsey 147
Martin, Caroline R. 148
Martin, Charlotte de 149
Martin, Christopher C. 40
Martin, David 147
Martin, Edmund D. 148
Martin, Elizabeth 146,147
Martin, Elizabeth W. 151
Martin, Emily A. 148
Martin, Ephraim 146
Martin, George 146
Martin, George J. 146
Martin, Henry 147
Martin, James 11., Jr. 148
Martin, Jane 146,147
Martin, Jehoida 147
Martin, Joe 250
Martin, Joel 146
Martin, John 146,147,250
Martin, John S., Rev. 76
Martin, Jonathan P. 147
Martin, Joseph 146
Martin, Julia E. 148
Martin, Lemuel K. 149
Martin, Letty 147
Martin, Lewis 147
Martin, Lucinda 147
Martin, Martha 146
Martin, Mary 146,147
Martin, Mary Louisa 48
Martin, Mary M. 147
Martin, Mary Susan Chandler 81
Martin, Melvina F. 148
Martin, Mildred 151
Martin, Minerva E. C. 152
Martin, Nancy 147
Martin, Nancy A. 147
Martin, Nathan 147
Martin, Nathan 147
Martin, Patsy 146
Martin, Paty 146
Martin, Rebekah 147
Martin, Robert N. 147
Martin, Salley 146
Martin, Samuel 181
Martin, Sarah 146
Martin, Stephen 146
Martin, Sue 246
Martin, Susan Eva 247
Martin, Susannah 146
Martin, Ursula 151
Martin, Virginia Lafayette 149
Martin, William 146
Martin, William Franklin 82
Martorano, Patricia Anne 242
Martorano, Patricia Anne 242
Mary, Elizabeth 163
Marye, James, Jr., Rev. 179
Marye, James, Rev. 102
Mashy, Robert Overton 253
Mason, Anma Andy Mason 267
Mason, Betsey Lowe 252
Mason, Daniel 252
Mason, David 252
Mason, Elizabeth 25
Mason, James 252
Mason, Lena B. 10
Mason, Martha 252
Mason, Mary Ann 252
Mason, Peter 252

Mason, Polly 252
Mason, Rebecca 252
Mason, Susan 252
Mason, Susana 252
Mason, Thomas 252
Mason, Turner 252
Mason, W. L. 252
Mason, William Lowe
Mass, Pattie, Mrs. 24
Massey, Joelliert A. 253
Massie, Margaret B. 17
Massie, Mary 89,90
Massie, Sally 276,277
Massie, Thomas 89
Maston, Sarah 90
Mathews, Philip 35
Mathews, William, Rev. 203
Matthews, Rebecca 216
Matthews, William 216
Mattison, James 202
Maury, Abraham 102
Maury, Abraham 102
Maury, D. H., Major General 268
Maury, John 268
Maury, John H., I,t. 269
Maury, Matthew Fontaine 268
Maury, Molly 268,269
Maury, Mortthew, Jr. 268
Maxey, John 25
Maxey, Nathaniel 198
Maxey, Sampson 25
Maxey, Sampson 25
May, Cornelia Lomax 12
May, Pattie R. 116
Mayby, Joseph 9
Mayfield, Joseph E. 150
Mayfield, William T. 54
McAdam, Charles 124
McAdam, Hugh 124
McAdam, James 124
McAdam, Jane 124
McAdam, Janetta 124
McAdam, John 124
McAdam, Joseph 124
McAdam, Robert 124
McAdam, Sarah Ann 124
McAdams, Dr. 169
McAdams, Elizabeth 169
McAfee, E. S. E. 99
McAfee, George 99
McAfee, George G., Rev. 99
McAfee, Georgia 99
McAfee, Hannah 167
McAfee, Sally 99
McAfee, Sarmel 167
McAfee, William, Sr. 168
McAlexander Millie 10
McAlexander, Adah 10
McAlexander, Anna 9,10
McAlexander, Elizabeth 9
McAlexander, Isaac R. 10
McAlexander, Lanrlna 9
McAlexander, Margaret 10
McAlexander, Margaret 10
McAlexander, Milly 0
McAlexander, Nancy 10
McAlexander, Reuben R. 10
McAlexander, Reubin 10
McAlexander, William 9,10
McAlexander, Wlrke 10

McAllister, Mrs. 101
McCain, Hugh 236
McCalla, Andrew 191
McCalla, Maria 191
McCarty, A. P. 118
McCarty, Absalom P. 118
McCarty, Andrew R. 118
McCarty, Anne 118
McCarty, Benjamin 118
McCarty, Darby 118
McCarty, Ehoch 118
McCarty, Elizabeth 118
McCarty, Hannah 118
McCarty, I. J. Thomas 118
McCarty, Isaac 118
McCarty, James 118
McCarty, James, Jr. 118
McCarty, Jares P. 118
McCarty, John 118
McCarty, John C. 118
McCarty, Jonathan 118
McCarty, Leah 118
McCarty, Lydia 118
McCarty, Martha 118
McCarty, Mary 118
McCarty, Rachel 118
McCarty, Robert K. 118
McCarty, Sarah 118
McCarty, Thomas J. 118
McCarty, Thomas Jefferson 118
McCarty, William 118
McCarty, William L. 118
McCarty, William, Sr. 118
McCaw, James Brown 119
McCaw, William R., Dr. 119
McCay, Helen A. 196
McClanahan, Blanche 286
McClawson, Robert, Rev. 270
McClelland, Elvira 206
McClernan, Richard W. 164
McCloud, Molly 249
McClung, Hannah 52
McClure, Frank E. 92
McClure, Maud Barton 92
McCorkle, Jane 30
McCorkle, Samuel 30
McCown, Frames Elizabeth 23
McCown, Oswald Stuart, Dr. 23
McCown, Oswald Stuart, Jr. 23
McCown, Oswald W., Dr. 23
McCrae, George 283
McCuen, D. E. 115
McCuen, D. Elwood 115
McCuen, George Elwood 115
McCuen, Rosalie 115
McCullach, Sarah 263
McCullen, Counsel W. 253
McCullen, Fannie May 253
McCullen, Ira 253
McCulloch, Elizabeth 266
McCutchen, Nancy Lavinia 53
McCutcheon, George 218
McDaniel, James W. 12
McDonald, Mary 5
McEffinger, Caroline 46
McElrath, James Metthew 145
McElrath, John 145
McElrath, John Augustus 145
McElrath, Margaret Lula 145
McElrath, Nancy Jane 145

McElrath, Sarah Ann 145
McElrath, William Joseph 145
McElrath, WilMorth C. 145
McGee, Mary 25
McGeehee, Mary 262
McGregor, Agpes 272
McGuen, Edwin Burke G. 115
McGuffin, Katie 29
McGuire, E. C., Rev. 63
McGuire, John, Rev. 63
McKee, David 170
McKee, Elizabeth Samuella 171
McKee, James 170
McKee, James Gilmore 171
McKee, James Logan 171
McKee, Jane 167
McKee, Jane Telford 171
McKee, John 170,171
McKee, John T. 170,171
McKee, John Telford 171
McKee, John, Jr. 171
McKee, Lucinda J. 171
McKee, Marine 170
McKee, Martha Davidson 171
McKee, Martha Hanna 171
McKee, Mary 170
McKee, Mary Susan 171
McKee, Nancy 171
McKee, Nancy Hanna 171
McKee, Pally 171
McKee, Polly Ann 171
McKee, Sally Gilmore 171
McKee, Samuel Madison 171
McKee, Samuel W. 171
McKee, Susannah 171
McKee, William 170
McKeehan, Allie Lee 132
McKenney, Edgar, Dr. 185
McKlin, Polly 236
McKse, Jane Logan 170
McLauflin, Rev. 41
McLeand, Grishild 282
McMillan, William 229
McMillen, Nancy Rountree 219
McMillen, Virginia 220
McMillin, Mary 147
McMullen, Jane 219
McMullen, Ccaroline 220
McMullen, Clinton 220
McMullen, Eli 220
McMullen, John 219
McNamara, Alice A. 74
McQuin, C. A. 199
McQuin, Catherine 199
McVean, J., Rev. 105
McWhorter, W. 0. 257
Meade, William, Rev. 67
Meaders, Benjamin, Rev. 40
Meanly, Mary 81
Means, A., Dr. 194
Means, Thomas A., Dr. 194
Mears, J. E., Sr., Dr. 81
Mebane, Mary Isabella 109
Mecaulay, Sarah 104
Medley, Eleanor 213
Medley, Hannah 213
Medley, John 213
Melborn, Virginia 257
Melton, Sarah 122,213
Melvin, Elizabeth W. 67

Melvin, Fanny Mayo 67
Melvin, Henry Bayly 67
Melvin, James 67
Melvin, Katherine Custis 67
Melvin, Margaret Cropper 67
Melvin, Mary Wharton 67
Melvin, Peggy Cropper 67
Melvin, Robert W. 67
Melvin, Samuel 67
Mend, Catherine 139
Mend, Charles Woodson 140
Mend, Chsrles Washington 139
Menefee, Jean 168
Mercer, Hugh, Colonel 103
Mercer, Louisa, Mrs. 103
Mercer, M. A. B., Mrs. in
Mercer, Robert 157
Meriklether, Valentine 216
Meriwefher, Mary 216
Meriwether, Charles, Dr. 2
Meriwether, D. Nancy 216
Meriwether, Elizabeth 216
Meriwether, Francis 216
Meriwether, Francis Thornton 266
Meriwether, Lucy 216
Meriwether, Margaret 216
Meriwether, Martha Jameson 216
Meriwether, Mildred 226
Meriwether, Nicholas 216
Meriwether, Sarah 216
Meriwether, Thomas 216
Merrill, Rasalie SindLaLr 109
Merriman, Margaret Elizabeth 264
Merriwether, Ann Overton 282
Merriwether, Charles 282
Merriwether, Douglas 283
Merriwether, Elizabeth 282,283
Merriwether, Francis 282
Merriwether, Francis Thornton 282
Merriwether, Henry Landon 282
Merriwether, Mc 282
Merriwether, Mc. Hunter 283
Merriwether, Nicholas Hunter 282,283
Merriwether, Thomas 282
Merriwether, Will Douglas 282,283
Merryman, Elizabeth 141,142
Merryman, John 142
Merryman, John T., Dr. 262
Merryman, John Thomas 142
Merryman, John Thomas, Dr. 141,264
Merryman, Margaret Bauldin 142
Merryman, Margaret Elizabeth 142,264
Merryman, Mary E. 93,142
Merryman, Mary Elizabeth 141
Merryman, Mary Flippen 142
Merryman, Thomas F. 141,142
Merryman, William J. 142
Merryman, William James 141
Merryman,, Margaret E. 262
Merrynoan, Mary Scott 141,142,264
Merryrmin, Thomas 142
Michel, Jane 284
Michel, Thomas 284
MicNe, Frances Dorothea 205
Milby, Betsy 129,130
Milby, Ilcstci Walter 129,130
Milby, John 129
Milby, John Kellam 129,130
Milby, Katharirre 130
Milby, Racbel 129

Miles, George Robert 150
Miller, Alphard 232
Miller, Ann D. 67
Miller, B. M., Rev. 67
Miller, Barbara 232
Miller, Benjamin M., Rev. 67
Miller, Daniel 232
Miller, Elizabeth 232
Miller, Ellza, Mrs. 92
Miller, Evans 44
Miller, Evelina 232
Miller, George 44
Miller, Henry 44
Miller, Jacklein 232
Miller, James 28
Miller, John 44
Miller, John Prince 77
Miller, John Willis 44
Miller, Martha E. 55
Miller, Mary 44
Miller, Morgan Alexander 232
Miller, Mortilda 44
Miller, Peninnah 44
Miller, Philip Evans 44
Miller, Polly 232
Miller, Prisley 232
Miller, Reuben 44
Miller, Sarah 28,52
Miller, Thomas 28
Miller, Thomas Evans 44
Miller, Thomas Jefferson 232
Miller, William 44
Miller, William Harrison 44
Mills, Amanda Melina 161
Mills, Andrew Lewis 161
Mills, Antess 161
Mills, Betty Burwell 63
Mills, Cynthia 267
Mills, David 161
Mills, Edmond B. 161
Mills, Edmund 161
Mills, Elizabeth Ann Wade 161
Mills, Frames Isabella 161
Mills, Frances 161
Mills, Gabriel Higgason 161
Mills, Garland 161
Mills, James 261
Mills, John 161
Mills, John, Rev. 144
Mills, Louisa Ann Caroline 160,161
Mills, Lucy Colly 161
Mills, Maria H. 161
Mills, Mary 161
Mills, Mary Colly Hopkins 161
Mills, Rice 161
Mills, Robert 161
Mills, Robert Garland 161
Mills, Ronald 63
Mills, Susannah 161
Mims, Eliza A. 47
Minge, Anna Mercer 114
Minge, Benjamin Carter 114
Minge, Christiana 114
Minge, Collier Harrison 114
Minge, David 114
Minge, Elizabeth Harrison 114
Minge, George William Hunt 114
Minge, James 114
Minge, John 114
Minge, John, M. D. 114

Minge, Margaret Adams 114
Minge, Mary Griffin 114
Minge, Sally Harrlson Steward 114
Minge, Sarah 114
Minge, William Henry 114
Minnegerode, Charles, Rev. Dr. 272
Minnegerode, Elvira 272
Minnegerode, William 272
Minor, Am 282
Minor, Carrie 30
Minor, Charles 110
Minor, Edward 110
Minor, Elizabeth 184
Minor, Frank 110
Minor, Franklin 110
Minor, George Gilmer 110
Minor, Hugh 110
Minor, John 157
Minor, John Skinner 110
Minor, Lucy Walker 110
Minor, Martha Divers 110
Minor, Mary 2
Minor, Mary Louisa 109,110
Minor, May Louisa 110
Minor, Peter 110
Minor, Peter Carr 110
Mitchell, A. 227
Mitchell, Arthur Glenn 16
Mitchell, Carol Patra 16
Mitchell, Charles T. 63
Mitchell, Dora Glen 16
Mitchell, Fannie Craig 18
Mitchell, George W. 16
Mitchell, J. D., Rev. 190
Mitchell, Jacob D., Rev. 271
Mitchell, James William 16
Mitchell, Mary J. 16,17
Mitchell, Minnie May 16
Mitchell, Mitchell F. 16
Mitchell, Sarah 165
Mitchell, Sarah E. 227
Mitchell, W. F. 17
Mitchell, William 16
Mitchell, William T. 17
MoCarty, Rachel B. 118
MoGregor, Roy Roy 272
Moncure, W. L. D., Rev. 229
Monroe, Jesse, Rev. 33
Montagoe, Mr. 173
Montague, Frances 203
Montague, Howard W., Rev. 77
Montague, Thomas 203
Moody, Andrew 56
Moomaw, Henry E. 53
Moon, Edwina Gordon 271
Moon, Elvira 272
Moonaw, Mary C. 53
Moore, Bishop 173
Moore, Cary F., R. 198
Moore, Isaac R. 20
Moore, Jane 212,287
Moore, Jennie L. 96
Moore, John 191,212
Moore, Martha 288
Moore, Mary 167,190,191
Moore, Nancy 209
Moore, William 102
Moorefield, Charlie 250
Moorman, Judith 191
Moorman, Samuel 191

Moorman, Zachariah 191
More, Jane 78
Morefield, Anna S. 41
Morgan, Mary A. 177
Morris, Ann 3
Morris, Annie Rebecca 255
Morris, Bessie 154
Morris, Catherine 3
Morris, Charles 2,3
Morris, Edward W. 2
Morris, Edward Watts 2
Morris, Elizabeth 2
Morris, Elizabeth Dabney 2,3
Morris, Elizabeth W. 2
Morris, John 3
Morris, John D. 2
Morris, John Dabney 2
Morris, John, Dr. 2
Morris, Mary 3
Morris, Mary Louise 2
Morris, Mary W. 2
Morris, Mary Watts 2
Morris, Richard 2,3
Morris, Richard, Jr. 2
Morris, Richard, Judge 3
Morris, Susannah Dabney 3
Morris, Sylvanus 3
Morris, Sylvanus W. 2
Morris, Sylvanus William 2
Morris, William 2,3,217
Morris, William, Sr. 2
Morrison, Margaret 12
Morrow, David, Dr. 157
Morrow, Elizabeth 157
Morrow, James Franklin 24
Morse, Stepren N. 38
Mort, Abraham 56
Mort, Anna Maria 56
Mort, Catherine 56
Mort, Eliza Francis 56
Mort, Elizabeth 56
Mort, Henry 56
Mort, Jeremiah 56
Mort, John 56
Mort, Mary Ann 56
Mort, Mary Elin 56
Mort, Mehaly Jane 56
Mort, Soffia 56
Mort, William Davis 56
Morthes 232
Morton, Elizabeth 191
Morton, Joseph 179
Morton, M. 191
Morton, Robert Alexander 59
Morton, Sally A. 59
Mosby, Benjamin 253
Mosby, Eugenia Pollydora 253
Mosby, Matthew Woodson 253
Mosby, May Pauline 253
Mosby, Nathaniel Anderson 253
Mosby, Phillip Woodson 253
Mosby, Sallie A. 253
Mosby, Samuel A. 253
Mosby, Samuel Anderson, 253
Mosby, Thomas Price 253
Mosby, Thornasin Price 253
Mosby, Virginia Anderson 253
Mosby, William Overton 253
Moseley, Maryan 29
Moseley, Adeline 29

Moseley, Alexander 24
Moseley, Alexander Trent 24
Moseley, Alfred 29
Moseley, Andrew J. 29
Moseley, Arthur 24,192
Moseley, Benjamin 29
Moseley, Bennett 190
Moseley, Bennett W. 190
Moseley, Bennett Williamson 190
Moseley, Cabell 192
Moseley, Carrie Trent 24
Moseley, Clara L. 192
Moseley, Edmund N. 192
Moseley, Edward Hack 278
Moseley, Elizabeth 190
Moseley, Elizabeth Montgomery 24
Moseley, Elizabeth Winston 190
Moseley, Emily 29
Moseley, Estelle 192
Moseley, Florence Lucille 24
Moseley, Frank T. 192
Moseley, George 29
Moseley, George Cabell 190
Moseley, Hardaway 29
Moseley, Harriet 29
Moseley, Hattie Heath 24
Moseley, Henry B. 192
Moseley, Henry Winston 190
Moseley, James 272
Moseley, Jane 258
Moseley, John 29,190
Moseley, Joseph 29
Moseley, Kate May 24
Moseley, Lucy Page 24
Moseley, Marcia I. 22
Moseley, Martha 29
Moseley, Mary 278
Moseley, Mary 29
Moseley, Mary Ann R. 25
Moseley, Mary D. 192
Moseley, Mary Melinda 190
Moseley, Monroe 29
Moseley, Mortimer 29
Moseley, Mr. 1
Moseley, Nannie Meredith 24
Moseley, Nicholas B. 24
Moseley, Nicholas Bocock 24
Moseley, Pamelia 254
Moseley, Perkins 24
Moseley, Peter 254
Moseley, Sallie 193
Moseley, Sarah V. 192
Moseley, Sargie 29
Moseley, Velina 29
Moseley, Virginia 29
Moseley, William 29
Moseley, William Henry 192
Mosely, Henry W. 190
Mosey, Woodson 253
Mosley, Salley C. 25
Moss, James L. 91
Mosty, John Stout 253
Mottley, Robert Courtney 18
Mottley, Robert Courtney, Jr. 18
Mountjoy, C. H., Mrs. 55
Mowatt, Jessie E. 12
Moyers, James Poage 27
Mudock, Mary Penelope 152
Mullen, Nernde 219
Mullins, James 15

Mullins, Solomon 15
Munch, Barbara 228
Munch, Philip 228
Munday, Ben H. 79
Munday, Elizabeth 79
Munday, James 220
Munday, Johnson 79
Munday, Robert Armstrong 79
Munday, Silas N. 151
Munday, Silas Y. N. 151
Muphy, Elizabeth Barton 229
Murdock, Ann E. 153
Murdock, Ann Ellen 152
Murdock, Anne Austin 152
Murdock, Caroline 152
Murdock, Elizabeth J. 153
Murdock, Elizabeth Jane 152
Murdock, James Samuel 152
Murdock, Mary P. 153
Murdock, Minerva E. C. 152,153
Murdock, Robert 152
Murdock, Thomas Punket 152
Murdock, W. I. 152
Murdock, William 152
Murdock, William Morgan 152
Murphey, William 229
Murphy Sarah Barton 229
Murphy, David Henderson 229
Murphy, Delilah Sarah 229
Murphy, Francis Menagee 229
Murphy, James Henderson 229
Murphy, John Craford 229
Murphy, John M. 248
Murphy, Keturah B. 229
Murphy, Marthy Hedges 229
Murphy, Mary Hodge 229
Murphy, Rachel 229
Murphy, William Ecclos 229
Murray, Edelim Frances 172
Murray, Gracy 230
Murray, James 84
Murrell, B. F. 254
Murrell, Mary A. J. 254
Murrow, Frank Trent 24
Murrow, Rachel Talbot 24
Muse, Anna F. M. 173
Muse, Betty T. 173
Muse, Elatia 173,203
Mussen, Bluford 78
Mussen, Catherine 78
Mussen, William Lewis 78
Myers, D. DeLos 16
Myers, E. D. 16
Myers, John W. 141
Myers, Naida Foster 16
Myers, Pattie L. 16
Myers, Thomas C. 196
Nalle, Am Frances 265
Nalle, Benjamin Johnston 266
Nalle, Cordella 266
Nalle, Edmonia P. 266
Nalle, Jam S. 266
Nalle, Lucetta T. 266
Nalle, Lucy Mary 265
Nalle, Martin 265
Nalle Martinette 266
Nalle, Nelly B. 265
Nalle, Nelly M. Barbour 265
Nalle, Philip Pendleton 266
Nalle, Richard Thomas 265

Nalle, Sarah Elenora 265
Name, Frederick 127
Nash, Amanda Malone 89
Nash, Catharine 89
Nash, Lavinia A. 89
Naton, Courtenay 62,66
Neal, Agnes 13
Neal, Alexander Thomas 13
Neal, Charles Alexander 141,142
Neal, Daisy Merryman 141,142
Neal, Elizabeth Merryman 141,142
Neal, Frances Alma 141,142
Neal, James H. 13
Neal, Margaret Ann 141,142
Neal, Temperance 13
Neal, Virginia Montfort 141,142
Neal, William A. 197
Neal, William Alexander 141,142,264
Neal, William Bernard 141,142
Neale, Nancy 137
Nelms, Elizabeth 221
Nelms, William 221
Nelsan, Secretary of York 233
Nelson, Ann Sage 226
Nelson, Anna Matilda 233
Nelson, C. V. 92
Nelson, Carey 233
Nelson, Caroline Matilda 233
Nelson, Cleland, Rev. 222
Nelson, Frances 278,279
Nelson, Francis P. 57
Nelson, Hugh 233
Nelson, Jane 84
Nelson, John 233
Nelson, John, Major 233
Nelson, Mary 233
Nelson, Mrs. 279
Nelson, Nancy Carter 233
Nelson, Nathaniel 233
Nelson, Robert 233
Nelson, Sarah 233
Nelson, Thomas Gov/Gen. 233
Nelson, Thomas Maudnit 233
Nelson, William 233
Nesbitt, Martha L. 224
Nevius, America 99
Nevius, H. V. D. 99
New, Anne Marie 64
New, Annie M. 64
New, Frances 64
New, Francis L. 64
New, Francis Samuel 64
New, Jane Josephine 64
New, Mary E. 64
New, Samuel F. 64
New, Samuel Frayser 64
New, Sarah Jane 64
New, T. R. 64
New, Theophilus 64
New, Theophilus R. 64
New, William T. 64
New, William Theophilus 64
Newberry, Sophronia 155
Newbill, Nathaniel Park 48
Newman, John 203
Newman, Mary 203
Newton, J. B., Rev. 164
Newton, Thomas 279
Nichol, James 99
Nichol, Martha Eliza 99
Nichols, John 142
Nicholson, George 107
Ninnally, Victoria Hill 208
Nisbet, Agnes 56
Nisbet, Agnes Miller 85
Nisbet, Archibald 56,86
Nisbet, David 56,86
Nisbet, Davis 57
Nisbet, Isabella 56,86
Nisbet, Isabella K. 57
Nisbet, Isabella Kemp 56,86
Nisbet, Janet 56
Nisbet, Richard 86
Nisbet, Robert 56,57
Nisbet, William 56,86
Noel, Alberta 39
Noel, Anne Elaria 178
Noel, Berkley 39
Noel, Berkley Muscoe 39
Noel, Catherine 39
Noel, Charles Muscoe 39
Noel, Elmer M. 39
Noel, Grace D. 39
Noel, Irene 39
Noel, James R. 39
Noel, Janis L. 39
Noel, Maria 39
Noel, Mary C. 39
Noel, Richard L. 39
Noel, Susannah S. 39
Nolan, George 193
Nolan, Henry Terrell 193
Nolan, Peyton 193
Nolan, W. H. 193
Nolan, William Henry 193
Noland, A. M. Preston Wellford 110
Noland, Ann Whiting 110
Noland, Anna Lloyd 110
Noland, Burr P. 109
Noland, Burr P. 110
Noland, Catherine 110
Noland, Catherine M. Powell 109
Noland, Catherine Y. 110
Noland, Charles Minor 110
Noland, Elizabeth W. L. 110
Noland, Frank M. 110
Noland, Kate Y. 109
Noland, Lloyd 109,110
Noland, Lucy 110
Noland, M. L. 110
Noland, Mary Louisa 110
Noland, Noble B. 110
Noland, Philip 109
Noland, Preston Wellford 109
Noland, R. Gratton, Rev. 109
Noland, R. W. N. 109,110
Noland, Rate Wellford 110
Noland, Richard William 110
Noland, Robert Gratton 109,110
Noland, Thomas 109
Noland, Thomas Lloyd 110
Norington, Elizabeth 259
Norington, Francis 259
Norington, J. N. 259
Norington, Mary 259
Norris, A., Rev. 163
Norsworthy, George 156
Norsworthy, William 156
Northcross, Alexander Campbell 24
Northcross, Elizabeth 25

Northcross, Hannah 24 ,25
Northcross, Hannah L. 25
Northcross, Hetty 25
Northcross, J. M. 24,25
Northcross, James 24,25
Northcross, John M. 25
Northcross, John Meglamre 24,25
Northcross, Maria 25
Northcross, Mary 24
Northcross, Matt 24
Northcross, N. N. 25
Northcross, Nelms 25
Northcross, Northern 24
Northcross, Richard 24,25
Northcross, Sarah 25
Northcross, Sarah L. 25
Northcross, Sarah Larrison Oates 24
Northcross, Sarah Margery 24
Northcross, Thomas 24,25
Northcross, Walter Scott 24
Norton, Courtney, Mrs. 279
Norton, Frances 65
Norton, George 62
Norton, George Floerdew 166
Norton, Henry 62
Norton, John 62,279
Nowlin, Robert, Rev. 46
Nunn, Birdie Draper 9
Nunn, Draper 9
Nunn, Emma J. 19
Nunn, Emna Jane 9
Nunn, Frank 9
Nunn, Huldah 9
Nunn, J. H. 19
Nunn, J. Wesley 19
Nunn, John W. 19
Nunn, John Wesley 19
Nunn, Joseph H. 19
Nunn, Joseph Henry 19
Nunn, Lillie B. 19
Nunn, Lillie Belle 19
Nunn, Martha A. 19
Nunn, Martha Ann 19
Nunn, Mary V. 19
Nunn, Mary Virginia 19
Nunn, Robert S. 19
Nunn, Sarah J. 19
Nunn, T. M. 19
Nunn, Thomas Martin 19
Nunn, Virginia 9
Nunn, W. R. 19
Nunn, Wesley Irvin 9
Nunn, William Oferall 9
Nunn, William R. 9,19
Nunn, William Riley 9,11
Nunnilee, Harvard 72
Nurm, Sarah Jam 19
Nye, Elizabeth 232
Nye, George Washington 232
Nye, Griseldah Malinday 232
Nye, Ida P. 232
Nye, J. P. 232
Nye, James Madison 232
Nye, Jefferson 232
Nye, John peter 232
Nye, John Richard 232
Oakes, Mary 84
Oakes, Rachael 84
Oakes, Sarah 25
Oakes, Sarah Larrison 24

Obanon, Sarah 184
Obenshain, Albert Sidney 10
Obenshain, Alonzo Waskey 10
Obenshain, Anne B. 10
Obenshain, Annie Bell 10
Obenshain, Annie E. 11
Obenshain, Blanche L. 10
Obenshain, Boyce P. 10
Obenshain, Boyce Putney 10
Obenshain, Cora M. 10
Obenshain, Emma L. 10
Obenshain, Halley Eidson 10
Obenshain, Ida Shockley 11
Obenshain, James T. 10,11
Obenshain, James Thomas 10
Obenshain, Louisa 10
Obenshain, Lucy 11
Obenshain, Lucy B. 10
Obenshain, Lucy Beale 10
Obenshain, Ptucus D. 10,11
Obenshain, Samael 10,11
Obenshain, Sidney J. 11
Obenshain, Z. Taylor 10,11
Obenshain, Zachary 10
O'Brien, E. K. 64
Odey, Nathalie Floyd 206
O'Fallen, Frances 166
O'Fallen, James, Dr. 166
Offutt, Alexander 128
Offutt, Alexander, Sr. 129
Offutt, Am 128,129
Offutt, Baruch 128
Offutt, Clarence L. 128,129
Offutt, E. A. 129
Offutt, E. N. 129
Offutt, Elisha 128
Offutt, Elizabeth 128
Offutt, Elizabeth M. 128,129
Offutt, Enoch 128
Offutt, Ezra 128
Offutt, Ezra N. 128
Offutt, H. C. 128
Offutt, Henry C. 128
Offutt, James 128
Offutt, James D. 128
Offutt, James M. 128
Offutt, Jart 128
Offutt, Joseph Ev-Alex. 128
Offutt, Joseph F. 128
Offutt, Keziah 128
Offutt, Laura V. 128
Offutt, Laura Verlinda 128
Offutt, Margaret 128
Offutt, Marion Ezra 128
Offutt, Mary 128
Offutt, Mary Edmonia 128
Offutt, Nathaniel 128
Offutt, Priscilla 128
Offutt, Rezin 128
Offutt, Samuel 128
Offutt, Sara 128
Offutt, Verlina 128
Offutt, Verlinda 128
Offutt, William C. 128,129
Offutt, William M. 128
Offutt, William Macgi. 128
Offutt, William P. 129
Offutt, Willian 128,129
Offutt, Z. C. 128
Offutt, Zachariah C. 128

Ogden, Elias 271
Ogden, Eliza 272
Ogg, Clara Frances 80
Ogle, Ann 276
Oknohmdro, George 235
Olive, James 216
Oliver, Mary D. 111
Oliver,, Sarah Hamiltan 209
Ollerbey, Mary Alice 117
Olsen, Patsy 121
Omohmdro, Caroline Virginia 235
Omohundro, Carrie 235
Omohundro, George C. 234-235
O'Neal, Rev. Mr. 179
Opie, Lindsey 169
Opie, Nancy 169
Orbison, Cassandra Paxton 211
Orbison, Ihanas 212
Orbison, Jane Mocre 212
O'Rear Mary 87
O'Rear, Benjamin 87
O'Rear, Daniel 87
O'Rear, Elizabeth 0. 87
O'Rear, Enoch 87
O'Rear, Jeremiah 87
O'Rear, Jesse 87
O'Rear, John 87
O'Rear, Margaret 87
O'Rear, William 87
Orme, Nancy 50
Orme, William John 50
Orrison, Elizabeth 195
Osbaurn, Louisa Jane 12
Osborn, Jam 203
Osborn, Jeremiah 203
Osborn, Jeremiah, Jr. 203
Osborn, John 203
Osborn, Jonathan 203
Osborn, Joseph R. 203
Osborn, Mary 203
Osborn, Reuben 203
Osbourn, Thomas 12
Outer, John 157
Outten, Fanny B. 75
Ovens, Charles Edward 148
Ovens, Sarah Prances Edrards 149
Overbey, Alice Camille 117
Overbey, Anna N. 117
Overbey, Anna Nelson 117
Overbey, Edwin Willams 117
Overbey, Kennon 117
Overbey, Lucy Kennan 117
Overbey, R. C. 117
Overbey, Robert C. 117
Overbey, Robert Camillus 117
Overbey, Rosalie 117
Overton, Barbara 54
Owen, Ann 44
Owen, Anna 203
Owen, Doctor 62
Owen, Elva 43
Owen, Rebecca R. 254
Paage, Rebecca Am 27
Pabwn, D. E. 260
Pace, Abner W. 260
Pace, Alsa 260
Pace, Alsa C. 260
Pace, Also 260
Pace, Bennett R. 260
Pace, Burrell H. 260

Pace, Cornelius R. 260
Pace, Edmund 260
Pace, Edward I. 260
Pace, Edwin J. 260
Pace, Elizabeth 260
Pace, Jasper N. 260
Pace, John 193,260
Pace, Justinia P. 260
Pace, Laurianna 260
Pace, Mary Ann Jane 193
Pace, Minerva 260
Pace, Rhode 260
Pace, Sarah 260
Pace, Stephen 8. 193
Padget, Henry, Rev. 125
Page, Catharine 207
Page, Gabriel H. 138
Page, Judith 206
Page, Laura 2
Page, Mam 275,276
Page, Marian M. 275
Page, Paulous Marion 138
Page, Susan 138
Palmer, Caroline E. 213
Palmer, Edwin 1,258
Palmer, H. C. 79
Paple, Ann 271
Paple, Caroline B. 75
Pardnran, Nanry M. 253
Paris, Andrew Bailey 122
Paris, Bettie C. 124
Paris, Charles Craddock 122
Paris, John Clark 122
Paris, Josiah 122,124
Paris, Julia Ellen 122
Paris, Louisa Catharine 122
Paris, Mary Elizabeth Cardwell 122
Paris, Matt 124
Paris, W. B. 122
Paris, William Richard 122
Paris, Wyatt B. 121
Paris, Wyatt B., Sr. 122
Paris, Wyatt Branch 122
Parkam, Lucy Finey 224
Parkam, Mary 224
Parke, Anne 262
Parker, Chloe 84
Parker, George 99
Parker, John 33
Parker, Mary 231
Parker, W. R. 212
Parker, Winslow 179
Parkham, William 224
Parrish, Mattie E. 50
Parrott, Anna S. 115,116
Parrott, C. S. 116
Parrott, Charles Shelton 116
Parrott, Elizabeth 116
Parry, Charles E. 171
Parry, Charlotte E. 171
Parry, Emma W. 171
Parry, Jane T. 171
Parry, Jane T. McKee 171
Parry, John McKee 171
Parry, Mary E. 171
Parry, Matthew Hanna 171
Parry, Nancy M. 171
Parry, Susan B. 171
Parry, Willis Richardsan 171
Parsons, Nancy 150

Parts, John 52
Pasteur, Emily F. 154
Pasteur, Honour 244
Pasteur, James, Rev. Mr. 279
Pasteur, John M. 154
Pate, John 201
Pate, Judith Early 201
Patman, Augustus L.260
Patman, Birdie Willie 260
Patman, Callie May 260
Patman, David Elias 260
Patman, Ellas Bell 260
Patman, Ida Jam 260
Patman, Joseph A. 260
Patman, Joseph Augustus 260
Patman, Maggie 260
Patman, Mary Rosabell 260
Patman, Terisa Lousinda 260
Patman, William Henry 260
Patrick, Isaac 225
Patrick, Matilda 215
Patron, Margie M. 73
Patterson, Elizabeth B. 208
Patterson, Elizabeth Boyle 208
Patterson, Job C. 208
Patterson, Maggie S. 74
Patton, John P. 54
Payne, Ann O. 75
Payne, Barbara W. 75
Payne, Camilla 272
Payne, Catherine G. 115
Payne, Elizabeth W. 75
Payne, Ella Susan 115
Payne, Emily C. 75
Payne, George B. 115
Payne, George M. 115
Payne, Harriet 283
Payne, Henrietta 235,236
Payne, Ida 115
Payne, Isabella J. 235
Payne, Isabella Rolando 236
Payne, James Smith 266
Payne, Jane 137
Payne, Jane C. 75
Payne, John W. 75
Payne, John, Colonel 271
Payne, Josiah Smith 235,236
Payne, Julia H. 236
Payne, Lizzie R. 46
Payne, Mamie Carol 10
Payne, Marion L. 115
Payne, Martha 136
Payne, Mary T. 75
Payne, Mildred 201
Payne, Nellie 46
Payne, Pollie G. 75
Payne, R. W. 46
Payne, Robert Withers 46
Payne, Rosa Kimbrough 46
Payne, Rosalie 115
Payne, Sallie Pean 115
Payne, Shirley Calloway 249
Payne, Susan M. 115
Payne, Susan Scoff 46,283
Payne, Tarlton 194
Payne, Tarlton F. 75
Payne, Virginia Morton 115
Payne, W. L. 46
Payne, Walter L. 46
Payne, Walter Ligon 46

Payne, Walter T. 46
Payne, Walter Tazewell 46
Payrre, G. B. 115
Peace, William W. 52
Peace, Willis H., Rev. 34
Peach, Anne Ban1ster 60
Peach, Mary Blair 61
Peachy, Ann Bann1ster 61
Peachy, Augusta Ban1ster 61
Peachy, Eliza T. 61
Peachy, Eliza Thompson 61
Peachy, John Blair 60
Pearce, Daniel 54
Pearce, Mary Downes 235,236
Pearce, Nathaniel 235
Pearce, Rosetta 235
Peck, Catherine Am 53
Pectn, Elizabeth 21,175,215
Pedigo, Joseph 19
Pedigo, Lovina Am 19
Pedigo, Lovirra 19
Pedon, Alex 283
Peel, Agnes 207
Pemberton, Elizabeth 84
Pemberton, John 84
Pendleton, Catherine 21,175
Pendleton, Edmund, Judge 175
Pendleton, Frances Ann 222
Pendleton, Harry 194
Pendleton, Isabella 21,175
Pendleton, Jchn 111
Pendleton, Philip 21,175
Penick, Zella 223
Penn, Abraham 189
Penn, Abram 181,182
Penn, Abram C. 182
Penn, Abram Clark 182
Penn, Abram, Colonel 182
Penn, Alfred 215
Penn, Andrew Jackson 188
Penn, Anna 188
Penn, B. 182
Penn, Barbara A. L. 181,182
Penn, Bells 188
Penn, Bettie 215
Penn, C. 182
Penn, Catherine 21,175,182
Penn, Catherine G. 115
Penn, Clark 182
Penn, Clark, Major 181,182,183
Penn, Columbus 188
Penn, Columbus F. 188
Penn, Edmund 115,188,189
Penn, Eliza 188
Penn, Eliza A. 188
Penn, Elizabeth Johnson 215
Penn, Ella Cathrlne 182
Penn, Ellen Maxwell 188
Penn, F. J. 182
Penn, Frances L. 215
Penn, Francis 182,189
Penn, Francis J. 182
Penn, Francis Jaw 182
Penn, G. J. 182
Penn, Gabriel 181,182,189,215
Penn, Gabriel J. 181,182,183
Penn, Gabriel, Capt. 182
Penn, George 21,189
Penn, George W. 188
Penn, George Washington 188

Penn, Greensville 181,182,189
Penn, Horatio 189
Penn, J. B. 182
Penn, Jackson 189
Penn, James 21,175,188,189,215
Penn, James A. 188
Penn, James G. 182
Penn, James Jr. 215
Penn, James S. 215
Penn, James Sbeptoe 215
Penn, James, Sr. 215
Penn, Jane 115
Penn, John 21,175
Penn, John S. 188
Penn, Joseph 21,175,188
Penn, Joseph Abram Goodman 188
Penn, Joseph G. 188
Penn, Julia 215
Penn, Lafayette 188
Penn, Lafayette 215
Penn, Lucinda 189,215
Penn, Lucinda Susan 188
Penn, Lucy 215
Penn, Luvenia 189
Penn, Margaret 215
Penn, Martha 189
Penn, Martha A. C. 188
Penn, Martha Ann Catharine 188
Penn, Martha Leath 188
Penn, Martha Susan 188
Penn, Mary 21,175,181,182
Penn, Mary A. 188
Penn, Mary Ann 188
Penn, Mary C. 188,189
Penn, Mary Elizabeth 188
Penn, Mary H. 182
Penn, Mary L. 188
Penn, Mary M. 182
Penn, Matilda 215
Penn, Moses 11,21,175,189
Penn, Newville 24
Penn, P. P. 0. 182
Penn, P. P. 182
Penn, Peter L. 188
Penn, Phillip 21,175,189
Penn, Polley 189
Penn, R. C. 215
Penn, Robert 215
Penn, Robert Cowan 215
Penn, Ruth 182
Penn, Ruth B. 183
Penn, S. E. 182
Penn, Sallie 182
Penn, Sarah 182,215
Penn, Sarah C. 181
Penn, Sarah R. 188
Penn, Sarah Ruth 188
Penn, Susan E. 181,183
Penn, Thomas 21,175,188,189
Penn, Thomas Bennette 188
Penn, Thomas G. 189
Penn, Thomas Greensville 188
Penn, Thomas, Capt. 188,189
Penn, Virginia 215
Penn, W. H. 182
Penn, William 189,215
Penn, William A. 188
Penn, William Alexander 188
Penn, William H. 182
Peon, Frances Louise 215

Peon, Lucinda S. 188
Perkins, Christopher 278
Perkins, Elrs. 278
Perkins, Sara T. 148
Perkins, W. H. 148
Perkinson, Martha 35
Perry, James M. 120
Perry, Sophia F. 137
Persca, W. E. 187
Person, Annie Jean Malcolm 187
Person, Lucy 186
Person, M. A. (Jeffry) 187
Person, M. C. 187
Person, Mary An 186
Person, W. 186
Person, William Carter 187
Peters, Ann Isabella 222
Peters, Anna Katharine 193
Peters, Chrlstian 193
Peters, Conrad Lewis 193
Peters, Elizabeth 193
Peters, Frederick G. 222
Peters, Jacob 193
Peters, Joel, Rev. 40
Peters, John 193
Peters, Mary 193
Peters, Nancy 193
Peters, Rhode 193
Peters, Sarah 173,193
Petersan, Norma Jean 240,241
Peterson, Charlotte Ray 240,241
Peterson, Dorothy Lee 240,241
Peterson, Robert Elmer 240
Peterson, William Alva 240
Pett, Rev. Mr. 65
Pettit, C. A. 64
Pettitt, Margaret 67
Pettus, Lena 236
Peyton, Anne Guffey 161
Peyton, Craven 161
Peyton, Margaret Moore 161
Peyton, Martha 60
Peyton, Mary Jane 161
Peyton, Virginia 60
Peyton, Yelverton 161
Peyton, Yelverton, Jr. 161
Phillips, Dr. 181
Phillips, John, Rev. 264
Phillips, Sallie B. 163
Phillips, William, Rev. Mr. 278
Phipp, Frances 278
Pickens, F. W. 196
Pickett, Anne 280
Pickett, George 280
Pickett, George E., Capt. 114
Pierce, Ellen 20
Pierce, John A. 20
Pierce, John K. 73
Pilkinton, Bettie W. 42
Pinner, Martha Ann 163
Pitchford, E. F. 91
Pitt, Miss 62
Pittman, Wlllliamson H. 167
Pittrnan, James 43
Pitts, Emily 146
Pitts, Emily G. 146
Pitts, Malissa 128
Pitts, Nancy 146
Plater, Anae 274
Plater, Elizabeth 274

Plater, George 274
Plater, George, Hen. 274
Plater, Rebecca 274,275
Pleas, Hazel L. 42
Pleasaats, Sophronia 155
Pleasant, Mary Ellen 227
Pleasants, Elizabeth 155
Pleasants, Elizabeth Sler 185
Pleasants, Frances 155
Pleasants, Frances A. 155
Pleasants, Gibson 155
Pleasants, Jordan 185
Pleasants, Lucy 216
Pleasants, Mary 155
Pleasants, Memorable 155
Pleasants, Nancy Narcisey 155
Pleasants, Peyton 155
Pleasants, Polly 155
Pleasants, Qsroline 184,185
Pleasants, Sarah Ann 112
Pleasants, Sophia 185
Pleasants, Thomas 155
Pleasants, Washington 155
Pleasants, William 155
Pledge, A. Tenperance 231
Plunket, Willis R. 137
Poage, Ann 27
Poage, Annette Margaret 27
Poage, Betsy 27
Poage, Cyrus 27
Poage, Elizabeth 27
Poage, George W. 80
Poage, James 27
Poage, James B. 27
Poage, Jane 27
Poage, John 27
Poage, Mary Virginia 27
Poage, Nancy S. 27
Poage, Polly 27
Poage, Rachel Cameron 80
Poage, Robert G. 27
Poage, Thomas 27
Poage, Thomas C. 27
Pocohantos, 248
Poindexter, Anne G. 205
Poindexter, John 205
Poindexter, Mary Stevens 15
Pollard, Caleb D. 40
Pollard, Charles W. 66
Pollard, Elizabeth 84
Pollard, Elizar Jane 40
Pollard, Frances C., Mrs. 66
Pollard, George James 40
Pollard, H. S. E., Dr. 184
Pollard, Hezekiah 84
Pollard, Jam 136
Pollard, Jemima 40
Pollard, Mary M. 256
Pollard, Pike 185
Pollard, Robert 111
Pollard, Thomas 84
Pollard, Virginia Frances 40
Pollard, William 84
Ponsanby, Mary 159
Pope, Austin 122
Pope, Caty 122
Pope, Ectrin Robertson 122
Pope, Eliza T. Thurston 166
Pope, Elliott 121
Pope, Gabrilla 122

Pope, Henry 131
Pope, John 121,131
Pope, John B. 122
Pope, Kitty 121
Pope, Lawrence 121
Pope, Lawrence B. 122
Pope, Maire 131
Pope, Patsey 121
Pope, Penelope 121,122
Pope, Rockey 122
Pope, Sallie 121
Pope, Susan 121
Pope, William 131
Pope, William Bayne 122
Pope, Worden 166
Porter, Anne 245
Porter, Edna 245
Porter, Flary 245
Porter, John 245
Porter, Joseph 245
Porter, Lydia 245
Porter, Margaret 245
Porter, Petty 245
Porter, Sarah J. 55
Porter, Thomas W. 35
Porter, William 245
Porter, William, Jr. 245
Porter, Zachariah 245
Posey, Addison 102
Posey, Addison C. 257
Posey, Addison T. 257
Posey, Alexander 102
Posey, Alexander H., Dr. 257
Posey, Eliza M. 262
Posey, Eliza M. 263
Posey, Eliza Maria 102
Posey, Fayette 102
Posey, Georgianna T. 257
Posey, John 102
Posey, John 257
Posey, Lloyd 102
Posey, Lloyd T. 257
Posey, Martha Ann 257
Posey, Mary 257
Posey, Mary H. 257
Posey, Mary, Mrs. 102
Posey, Sarah Ann T. T. 102
Posey, Sarah Ann Thornton Taliaferro 102
Posey, Thomas 102,257
Posey, Thomas L. 257
Posey, Thomas, Colonel 263
Posey, Thomas, General 102,262
Posey, Thornton Alexander 102
Posey, William Churchill 102
Posey, William T. 257
Potter, John 134
Potter, Sarah 134
Potts, Mary Jam 12
Powell, A. W. P. 109
Powell, Ann Whiting 109,110
Powell, Anna Lloyd 109
Powell, Catherine Mary 109
Powell, Eugene Cole, M. D. 64
Powell, Eugene Cole, Mrs. 65
Powell, L. N. 109
Powell, Levin 109
Powell, Louisa 222
Powell, Miss 194
Powell, Nancy 96
Powell, Purr 109

Powell, Sara Ella 109
Powell, Sarah 110
Powell, Sidney Anne 166
Powers, Mary Ann 248
Poythree, Jane 248
Pqrtin, Harriet 60
Pratt, Dona Maria 229
Pratt, Frank C., Dr. 72
Pratt, Louise Catherine Rogers 72
Pratt, Mary A. E. 229
Pratt, W. Burkett 229
Pratt, Whitcome E. 24
Pratt, William B. 229
Price, Agpes 69
Price, Alexander 264
Price, Bennitt 280
Price, Charles A. 64
Price, Charles, Rev. 142,263,264
Price, Cutburd 26,243
Price, Daniel 26,243
Price, Elizabeth 26,243
Price, James, Rev. 113
Price, Jane Chapman 125
Price, John 26,243
Price, Judith 280
Price, Katie 80
Price, Major 25,243
Price, Maraday 26,243
Price, Molly 26,243
Price, Nancy 26,243
Price, Nathaniel W. 125,126
Price, Patsy 26,243
Price, Robert 25,243
Price, Sarah 25,243
Price, Susannah 26,243
Price, Susannah Smith 125
Price, Thomas 80
Price, William 26,243
Price, William, Sr. 26,243
Priddy, Charles W. 93
Priddy, Cornelia F. 93
Priddy, Elizabeth E. 93
Priddy, Frances Ann 93
Priddy, J. G. 93
Priddy, Jan D. 93,142
Priddy, John Gustevil 93
Priddy, Joseph S. 93
Priddy, Lucy A. 93
Priddy, Lucy Alma 93
Priddy, Margaret Arm 93
Priddy, Martha R. B. 93
Priddy, Mary E. 93
Priddy, Mary Helen 93
Priddy, Mary M. 93
Priddy, Nancy D. Frances 93
Priddy, Robert 93
Priddy, Robert T. 93
Priddy, Robert W. 93
Priddy, Sarah E. 93
Priddy, Sarah Eliza 93
Priddy, Thomas G. 93
Priddy, William K. 93
Priest, Sarah Am 33
Province, Mary Eugenia King 1
Pruit, Lottie 27
Pryor, Anne Contesse 268
Pryor, Arrcle Countis Tyler 267
Pryor, Betsy A. 267
Pryor, Catherine 266
Pryor, Christiana 268
Pryor, Christopher 266
Pryor, Elizabeth 266
Pryor, Elizabeth Arm1stead 268
Pryor, Harriet Anne 268
Pryor, Jan C. 267,268
Pryor, John C., Colonel 258
Pryor, John Clayton 268
Pryor, Maria Emily 267,268
Pryor, Maria S. 267,268
Pryor, Martha Christiana 267
Pryor, Mary Anne Catharine 267
Pryor, Mary Catherine 267
Pryor, Miss 266
Pryor, Rebecca 222
Pryor, Skaife Whiting 267
Pryor, William 268
Pryor, William C. 268
Pryor, William Clayton 267
Ptilby, Gilbert 129,130
Ptsbty, Winfield S. 9
Pulliam, Winifred 44
Purse, Laura Ashby 214
Purse, Thomas 214
Purvis, Albert Alexander 174
Purvis, Amanda Melvina 174
Purvis, Geneva Louise 174
Purvis, George W. 174
Purvis, George Winston 174
Purvis, John James 174
Purvis, Margaret F. 174
Purvis, Martha Susan 174
Purvis, Mary Ann 174
Purvis, Mollie 3. 160
Purvis, Sarah Elizabeth 174
Purvis, William A. 174
Puryear, Harriet 241
Puryear, Richard R. 73
Qilloway, Richard T. 248
Quarles, Benjamin 1W,
Quarles, Dorothy 231
Quarles, Frances 144
Quarles, Francis W. 144
Quarles, Judith 231
Quarles, Keziah 231
Quarles, Solomon 231
Quarles, Susan A. 231
Quarles, Susan Ann 144
Quarles, Susanna E. 231
Quarles, Thomas D. 144
Quarles, Waller 231
Quick, Lou 20
Quinn, Hazel 249
Ragsdale, Mildred Anne 144
Rails, Charles 52
Rails, Charles Thomas 52
Rails, Edward 0. 52
Rails, George A. 52
Rails, George Alexander 52
Rails, Jare 52
Rails, John W. 52
Rails, John Williams 52
Rails, Luther N. 52
Rails, Luther Nathaniel 52
Rails, Margaret Sophia 52
Rails, Maria 52
Rails, Mary Anderson 52
Rails, Sarah 52
Rails, Sarah Endly 52
Rails, Sophia M. 52
Raines, Elizabeth Judkins 31

Rainey, D. 260
Rainey, Elizabeth M. 260
Rainey, Laurianna 260
Rainey, Martha E. 260
Ramsey, Daniel 28
Ramsey, Elizabeth 28
Ramsey, Ella 92
Ramsey, John, Dr. 279
Ramsey, M. K. 92
Randolph, Bathurst 60
Randolph, Betty 57
Randolph, Elizabeth W. 75
Randolph, Isham, Capt. 269
Randolph, James 75
Randolph, Mary 60
Randolph, William 261
Rankin, L. W. 96
Rarkin, Helena 138
Ratcliffe, C. S., Dr. 99
Rawlings, Benjamin, Dr. 88
Rawlings, James WI
Rawlings, King 88
Rawlings, Rebecca 44
Rawlins, Ann 88
Rawls, George Norton 52
Ray, Agnes Waller 272
Ray, Amy 90
Ray, Ann 272
Ray, Aphira Beverly 272
Ray, B. B. 90
Ray, Belinda 272
Ray, Benjamin B. 90
Ray, Benjamin H. 90
Ray, Beverly 272
Ray, Biddy 90
Ray, Doris Meade 251
Ray, George A. 90
Ray, J. C. 90
Ray, J. C. 91
Ray, James K. P. 90
Ray, James P. K. 90
Ray, James Polk 91
Ray, John Beverly 272
Ray, John C. 90
Ray, John H. 90
Ray, Joseph L. 90
Ray, Leonard 90,91
Ray, Leonard R. 90
Ray, Leonard, St. 91
Ray, Magness L. 90
Ray, Marion Stanard 272
Ray, Martha A. 91
Ray, Martha Jane 90
Ray, Mary 90
Ray, Mary k 91
Ray, Nancy 90
Ray, Polly 40,91
Ray, Polly Ann 93
Ray, R. 91
Ray, Rebecca 90
Ray, Richard 8. 79
Ray, S. J. 91
Ray, Theney D. 90
Ray, Washington N. 90
Ray, William 196
Read, Annatha 150
Read, Arm I. A. 222
Read, Asa R. 150
Read, Edmund 222
Read, Eliza A. 222

Read, Elizabeth 222
Read, Elizabeth A. 222
Read, Elizabeth C. 26
Read, George Rodgers 150
Read, Gladys E. 150
Read, Joanna 222
Read, Johanna 223
Read, John 149,150
Read, John T. W. 222
Read, Jones 222
Read, Jones. 150
Read, Kathryn Ames 150
Read, Kendall Agnes 150
Read, Margie B. 150
Read, Mary F. 150
Read, Mary Irene 150
Read, Nancey 222
Read, Nancy 222
Read, Ray IM
Read, Richard 150
Read, Robert A. 222
Read, Robert Alexander 222
Read, Samuel 222
Read, Sarah Elizabeth 150
Read, William 222,223
Read, William A. 222
Read, William C. 222
Read, William K. 150
Read, William Kendall 150
Read, William S., Rev. 222
Reasoner, Elizabeth 97
Redd, Elizabeth T. 34
Redd, Samuel 34
Redman, Sarah A. 257
Reese, Martha 95
Reeves, R. L., Dr. 101
Reid, Ann 87
Reid, Cathrine 181
Reid, Clara 59
Reid, Felix 101
Reid, Jare 87
Reid, Nathan, Jr. 222
Reid, William S., Rev. 271
Rennie, Frarde 112
Rerae, Chastain, Rev. 198
Reynelds, Elizabeth 125
Reynolds, Harriet 96
Reynolds, Josiah 257
Reynolds, Robert 179
Reynolds, Thomas 179
Rice, Adelinoa Wyatt 111
Rice, Azuleka 111
Rice, Clay S. 111
Rice, Elizabeth 109
Rice, James W. 111
Rice, John B. 111
Rice, Lucy Kirby 111
Rice, Lucy McGruder 111
Rice, Lucy T. Kirby 112
Rice, Mary J. 112
Rice, Mary S. 111
Rice, Paul 111
Rice, Rev. Mr. 24
Rice, Robert 111
Rice, Robert R. 111
Rice, Robert Richie 112
Rice, S. T. 111
Rice, S. T. K. 112
Rice, W. T., Rev. 222
Rice, William 111

Richards, Allen K. 177
Richards, Alma Rebecca 177
Richards, Annie Cornelia 177
Richards, Burton M. 177
Richards, Catherine Rebecca 177
Richards, David M. 177
Richards, Glenn D. 177
Richards, Hallie F. 177
Richards, Harry Burton 177
Richards, James C. 177
Richards, James Carlin 177
Richards, Jane Morgan 177
Richards, Jennie M. 177
Richards, Jennie Morgan 177
Richards, John Morgan 177
Richards, Kate R. 177
Richards, Lucille R. 177
Richards, Mary A. 177
Richards, Nellie 177
Richards, Nellie Allen 177
Richards, Nellie F. 177
Richards, Susan T. 260
Richards, William B. 177
Richards, William Burton 177
Richards, William C. in
Richards, William Franklin 177
Richardsan, Robert B. 98
Richardson, Elizabeth 207
Richardson, Elizabeth T. 98
Richardson, Francis W. 144
Richardson, H. B. M. 98
Richardson, Harriet A. 98
Richardson, John B. 144
Richardson, R. B., Dr. 98
Richerson, Agnes 144
Richerson, Alfred Pleasants 144
Richerson, Anderson 144
Richerson, Ann Ellza Frances 144
Richerson, Carrie 30
Richerson, Charlotte Blatterman 144
Richerson, Edward Motier 144
Richerson, Elizabeth H. 144
Richerson, Frances W. 144
Richerson, Gracey B. 144
Richerson, Holt 143,144
Richerson, Holt C. 144
Richerson, Holt, Colonel 143
Richerson, James 144
Richerson, Jane P. Brete 144
Richerson, John A. 144
Richerson, John Brete 144
Richerson, John Holt 144
Richerson, Maria Louisa 144
Richerson, Mary Evans 144
Richerson, Mary Jane Frances 144
Richerson, Mildred 144
Richerson, Mildred Dungleson 144
Richerson, Ragsdale Anderson 144
Richerson, Susanna 143,144
Richerson, Susanna W. 144
Richerson, William West 144
Richeson, Andrew 30
Richeson, Andrew J. 30
Richeson, Andrew Jackson 30
Richeson, Ernest 30
Richeson, J. S. 30
Richeson, James Douglass 30
Richeson, James S. 30
Richeson, Kathleen Temple 30
Richeson, Lucy Anna 30

Richeson, M. Kabe 30
Richeson, Mary Catherine 30
Richeson, Nancy M. 30
Richeson, Nannie L. 30
Richeson, William 30
Richeson, William A. 30
Richie, David 239
Richie, Hannah 239
Richie, James 239
Richie, Lewis 239
Richie, Martha 239
Richie, Mary 239
Richie, Master 239
Richs, Archie C. 177
Rickman, C. C. 12
Rickman, Calvin Calaway 12
Rickman, Christine Briggs 13
Rickman, Eunice Arzelia 13
Rickman, Grace Maddry 13
Rickman, Harriet Azilla 12,13
Rickman, Harriet Noami 12,13
Rickman, John Edwin 12,13,33
Rickman, Joseph W. 12
Rickman, Joseph Wiley 12,13
Rickman, M. Lee 12
Rickman, Martha Jane 12,13
Rickman, Mary 12
Rickman, Mary Nelson 13
Rickman, Miles Lee 12,13
Rickman, Narcissa E. 12
Rickman, Narcissa Elizabeth 12,13
Rickman, Philip R. 12
Rickman, Philip Riley 12,13
Rickman, Royal Grams 13
Rickman, Royal Graves 12
Rickman, Sarah Emeline 12,13
Rickman, Theodosia Arzilla 12,13
Rickman, Thomas Merit Fuller 12
Rickman, Thomas Merritt Fuller 13
Rickman, Willada Hall 13
Rickman, William R. 12
Rickman, William Riley 12,13
Rickman, William Villines 13
Ricknan, John E. 12
Riddick, Julia 171
Riddick, Leah 171
Riddick, Seth 171
Riding, George I. 234
Riding, Jane 234
Riding, Winney 234
Ridinger, Bettie C. 16
Ridout, F. A., Rev. 76
Ridout, James Winchester 76
Riersan, William Covington 206
Rieves, Floyd 16
Rieves, Mary 95
Riggs, Alice 178
Riggs, Matilda 33
Rishe, James 84
Roach, E. W. 123
Roane, Frances 242
Roane, Hampton Bradford 242
Roane, Mary Susan 241
Roane, Matthew Hearst 242
Roane, Spencer, Judge 206
Roane, William Bradford, Jr. 241
Roane, William Branford 241
Roarre, Elbert Hearst 242
Roberson, Elizabeth Jane 131
Roberson, Joseph 54

Roberts, Catherine 30
Robertson, Anna 42
Robertson, Anne Jennings 202
Robertson, Camel 42
Robertson, Cole 42
Robertson, Ede 42
Robertson, Elizabeth C. 42
Robertson, Frances 165
Robertson, Hugh 42,43
Robertson, Jemima 42
Robertson, John 43
Robertson, Moses 165
Robertson, Moses, Capt. 102
Robertson, Polly 42
Robertson, Richard 43
Robertson, Salley 43
Robertson, Stuart 43
Robertson, Susannah 42,43
Robertson, Thomas 43
Robertson, William 42
Robertson, William Albert 42
Robins, Andrew 142
Robinson, Ann A. 275
Robinson, Anthony 135
Robinson, Anthony, Major 134
Robinson, Braxton 48
Robinson, Diana 134
Robinson, George III 207
Robinson, Margaret 49
Robinson, Martha Dixon 49
Robinson, Martha Dixon Hill 48,49
Robinson, Mary 207
Robinson, Mary Elizabeth Mary Ann 225
Robinson, Moses, Rev. Mr. 278
Robinson, Rachel 134,135
Robinson, Sarah 224
Robinson, William 203,275
Robinson, Wright 48,49
Robson, Sudsn B. 17
Rodes, David 215
Rodgers, Abel 149,150
Rodgers, Abel R. 150
Rodgers, America J. 92
Rodgers, America Jane 92
Rodgers, Edward 64
Rodgers, Elizabeth 149,150
Rodgers, Elvira 64
Rodgers, Emily 150
Rodgers, Emma 92
Rodgers, Enoch 150
Rodgers, Frances 64
Rodgers, Isaac Newton Hyram Lafayette 64
Rodgers, John 149,150
Rodgers, John H. 64
Rodgers, Louisa Adalaide 92
Rodgers, Margaret Annatha 150
Rodgers, Margaret Annatha Parsons 150
Rodgers, Marion 64
Rodgers, Martha Emily 92
Rodgers, Nancy Angaline 92
Rodgers, Nancy B. 92
Rodgers, Peggy Smith 150
Rodgers, Richard 149,150
Rodgers, Robert 149,150
Rodgers, Samuel H. 92
Rodgers, Sarah 150
Rodgers, Sarah Jane 64
Rodgers, Smith 150
Rodgers, Stephen T. 64
Rodgers, Tabitha 149,150

Rodgers, William B. 64
Rodgers, William Benjamin 64
Rodgers, William T. 64
Rodges, Asa J. 150
Rogers, O. O., Dr. 247
Rogers, Ada Lee 72
Rogers, Charlotte Embrer 72
Rogers, Chules 38
Rogers, Clifton Paul 72
Rogers, Colerman W. 72
Rogers, E. F. 1
Rogers, Edna 95
Rogers, Edward W. 72
Rogers, Ethel June 72
Rogers, Ida Collins 72
Rogers, Ida Ruth 72
Rogers, Louise Catherine 72
Rogers, Mary 1
Rogers, Mary L. 38
Rogers, Robert 95
Rogers, Robert Sterling 72
Rogers, S. T. 72
Rogers, Sallie Am 1
Rogers, Stephen T. 72
Rogers, Stephen Virginius 72
Rogers, Thomas Sidney 72
Rogers, William Stuart 72
Rolfe, John 248
Rolfe, Rebecca 248
Romy, Mary King 25
Rose, Dort Robert H. 108
Rose, Willian 272
Rosey, Willia A. 150
Roudesill, Frances 17
Rountree, John 218
Rountree, Lydia Maria 218
Rountree, Martha Ann 218
Rountree, Nancy 219
Rountree, Peary 218
Rountree, Thaddeus 218
Rouzee, Agnes 178
Rouzee, Maria L. 178
Rouzee, Philemon. 178
Rowsie, William B., Rev. 140
Rowzie, E. T., Rev. 184,185
Roy Emily Williams 272
Roy, Samuel McGregor 272
Roy, Thane 272
Royal, W. W. 246
Royall, John M. 85
Royster, Nancy C. 141
Ruby, Caroline Jett 169
Ruby, John Ball 169
Ruby, Nancy Opie 169
Ruby, Robert Ashley 169
Ruby, Robert C. 169
Rucker, Mary 193
Rucker, S. B. 30
Rudersill, Lucy 17
Rudisille, Frances 18
Rudisille, Lucy 18
Rudolph, Susan S. 244
Rushing, Elizabeth 90
Rushing, Mark 90
Rust, Bushrod, Dr. 122
Rust, Cornelia L. 85
Rust, Delia C. 122
Sadth, Eliz. W. 109
Sag, Elizabeth 226
Sage, Ann 226

Sage, Catherine 226
Sage, Charles 226
Sage, Ester 226
Sage, Ezekiel 225
Sage, James 226
Sage, Lovice 2;16
Sage, Lovice Ott 226
Sage, Margret 226
Sage, Mary 226
Sage, Sampson 226
Sage, Samuel 226
Sage, William 226
Sale, Rev. Mr. 283
Salsberry, David 237
Sammis, Charlotte Embrer Rogers 72
Sammis, Theodore A., Sr. 72
Sanders, Elizabeth M. 26
Sanders, Hubbard 26
Sanders, Sarah C. 12
Sandidge, Anderson 140
Sandidge, Benjamin 140
Sandidge, Elizabeth 140
Sandidge, Mary C. 140
Sandifer, James 36
Sandifer, Martha 36
Sandifer, Martha Ann 36
Sandifer, Robert 36
Sandridge, Anna 44
Sandridge, Austin 44
Sandridge, David, Sr. 44
Sandridge, Elizabeth 44
Sandridge, Larkin 44
Sandridge, Sophia 44
Sandridge, Winifred 44
Sandridge, Zacharias 44
Sanford, Benjamin 212,219
Sanford, Charles F. 187
Sanford, Charles Feild 187
Sanford, Daniel 212,219
Sanford, Edgar E. 187
Sanford, Elildred 219
Sanford, Frances 186
Sanford, H. 187
Sanford, Henry 186,187
Sanford, Henry W. 187
Sanford, Henry William 187
Sanford, J. M. 187
Sanford, Jean M. 187
Sanford, Jean Murray 187
Sanford, Jennie Wren 187
Sanford, Jeremiah, Jr. 212,219
Sanford, Jeremiah, Sr. 212,219
Sanford, Mary Agnes 187
Sanford, Mildred Washington 212
Sanford, Robert W. 186
Sanford, Robert Walker 187
Sanford, Thomas 212,219
Sanford, Thomas L. 187
Sanford, Vincent 212,219
Sankey, Richard, Rev. 141
Saunderland, B., Rev. 82
Saunders, Alexander 207,208
Saunders, Alexander, Jr. 207
Saunders, Alice Tallulah 208
Saunders, Allie Tallulah 208
Saunders, Ann Eliza 208
Saunders, Catherine 208
Saunders, Cornelius J. 208
Saunders, E. B. 208
Saunders, Edward Claiborne 45

Saunders, Eliza 208
Saunders, Elizabeth B. 208
Saunders, fray 208
Saunders, Jane A. 208
Saunders, Jennie 208
Saunders, Job C. 208
Saunders, John 207,208
Saunders, Katherine Anne 45
Saunders, Lcuisa 208
Saunders, Lucian 208
Saunders, Martha 143
Saunders, Martha Stith 143
Saunders, Mary 208
Saunders, Mollie 208
Saunders, N. M., Jr. 45
Saunders, Nancy V. 208
Saunders, Nancy Virginia 208
Saunders, Nancy Virginia Boykin 207
Saunders, Nannie 208
Saunders, Nathaniel M. 45
Saunders, Nathaniel Morris, Jr. 45
Saunders, Nathaniel Morris, Sr. 45
Saunders, Pattie Gaines 45
Saunders, Sarah 208
Saunders, Shellis 208
Saunders, Simon 208
Saunders, Simon Hardy 207,208
Saunders, Snow 208
Saunders, Stith 143
Saunders, Susan Penelope 208
Saunders, T. J. 208
Saunders, Thomas J. 208
Saunders, Thorns Jefferson 207,208
Saunders, Willie 208
Savage, Am 112
Savage, Harriet 98
Savage, Harriet Reynolds 96
Savage, Mary A. Susan 96
Savage, Mary Ann Susan 98
Savage, Mary L. 98
Savage, Nathaniel Littleton 96
Savage, Samuel Griffin 150
Savage, Southy Littleton 96
Savage, Thorns Lytt 96
Savage, William Reynolds 96
Sawyer, M. R. 177
Saxe, Anna M. 45
Sayre, Burwell Bassett 62
Sayre, Edward 62
Sayre, John Bassett 62
Sayre, Philip LudweT1 62
Sayre, Samuel William 62
Sayre, Stephen 62
Sayre, William 62
Scarburgh, Americus 134
Scarburgh, Dorothy Wainhouse 134
Scarburgh, Edmund 134
Scarburgh, Edmund, Colonel 106
Scarburgh, Elizabeth 134
Scarburgh, Margrate 134
Scarburgh, Mary 134
Scarburgh, Matilda 134
Scarburgh, Mitchell 134
Scarburgh, Mitchell, Jr. 134
Schooley, John 195
Schuster, Philip 191
Scott, Agnes 271
Scott, Agnes W. 271
Scott, Carrie E. 242
Scott, Elizabeth 107,264

Scott, Ella G. 242
Scott, Ella K. 242
Scott, Elviza Cuthbert 65
Scott, Frank Ben Watkins 242
Scott, Frank Elfreth 242
Scott, Garret H. 265
Scott, Isabel 255
Scott, J. M. 187
Scott, James 265
Scott, James, Rev. Mr. 4
Scott, Joe Manley 187
Scott, Joe Morton 242
Scott, Joel Morton 242
Scott, John 107,265
Scott, Leneas 264
Scott, Letitia Amanda 11
Scott, Lucy 107
Scott, Marree 265
Scott, Martha 265
Scott, Martha Henry 242
Scott, Martha Van Meter 242
Scott, Mary 2,141,142,262,263
Scott, Mary E. 242
Scott, Melvina 187
Scott, Nancy 171
Scott, Polly 264
Scott, Rice 265
Scott, Robert 265
Scott, Samuel 265
Scott, Samuel, Major 271,272
Scott, Sarah Elizabeth 73
Scott, Susan Marion 262,264
Scott, Thomas 265
Scott, Thomas W. 242
Scott, Thomas Watkins 242
Scott, Thomas, Jr. 265
Scott, Thomas W., Jr. 242
Scott, Ursuly Goode 264
Scott, Walter, Jr. 262
Scott, Walter, Sr. 264
Scott, William 254,265
Scott, William C. 242
Scott, William, Lt. 262,263
Scotts, Elizabeth 86
Scotts, Frank 86
Seabrooke, John 286
Sears, John 6
Sears, Temperance 6
Seaton, George M. 96
Seaton, Hiram 96
Seaton, James P. 96
Seaton, John M. 96
Seaton, Margery 96
Seaton, William 96
Seawell, Elizabeth 113
Seawell, John B. 268
Seawell, Maria 268
Seawell, Overton 113
Seay, Amanda A. 115
Seay, Ann V. 115
Seay, Anna S. 116
Seay, Annie S. 116
Seay, Annie V. 116
Seay, Carole Ann 116
Seay, Charles T. 116
Seay, Charles Thomas, Dr. 116
Seay, Elizabeth G. 115
Seay, Elizabeth M. 115,116
Seay, Emne Duke 116
Seay, Felix G. 115

Seay, Felix Grundy 116
Seay, George G. H. 115
Seay, George Green H. 116
Seay, George W. 115,116
Seay, James G. 115,116
Seay, James Gordon 115,116
Seay, John R. 115.L16
Seay, John G. 115,116
Seay, John Richard 116
Seay, Joseph I. 116
Seay, Lou Ella 116
Seay, Marion 116
Seay, McElrath 145
Seay, Melinda B. 116
Seay, Melvina G. 115,116
Seay, Michel J. 116
Seay, Moses A. 115
Seay, Patrick Thomas 116
Seay, Polly 115,116
Seay, Salascha Annie 116
Seay, Samuel 115,116
Seay, Samuel R. 116
Seay, Sarah Maria 145
Seldon, Hannah 107
Semple, Betsy A. 268
Semple, George William 267,268
Semple, John T. 268
Semple, John T., Dr. 268
Semple, Maria Elizabeth 267
Semple, Mary Eliza 268
Sendridge, David 44
Seward, Clifton Elliott 108
Seward, Dorothey E. 108
Seward, Eldrid Benson 108
Seward, Elizabeth Eunice 108
Seward, Henry Lewis 108
Seward, James Vernon 108
Seward, John, Rev. 125
Seward, Peter E. 108
Seward, Peter Elliott 108
Seward, Richard Hamilton 108
Seward, Weston W. 103
Sewart, Clara Brooke 108
Shackleford, ? 44
Sharon, Frances A. 40
Sharp, James 101,218
Sharp, Richard, Sr. 218
Sheasrt, Alma France 19
Shell, Charles W. 148
Shell, Daniel Asbury 147
Shell, Dorothea 147,148
Shell, Dorothea L. 147,148
Shell, Elizabeth 147
Shell, Elizabeth A. 147
Shell, Herman 147
Shell, James E. 147
Shell, Jane E. 147
Shell, John Fletcher 148
Shell, Lemmon 147,148
Shell, Martha 147
Shell, Mary A. 147
Shell, Nancy 147.148
Shell, Nancy L. 147
Shell, Precious 148
Shell, Thomas 147,148
Shell, Thomas H. 147
Shell, William B. 147
Shelton, Elizabeth 84
Shelton, John 273
Shelton, Mildred 214

Shelton, Ralph 84
Shelton, Ruth 188
Shelton, Sarah 206
Shepard, Thomas E. 153
Shephenson, Joseph 267
Shepherd, Elizabeth 227
Shepherd, Harriet A. 12
Sheppard, John 134
Sheppard, Martha Estelle Marshall 152
Shield, Mrs. 62
Shield, Sam, Rev. Mr. 119
Shields, Judith B. I. 163,164
Shipley, Mary L. 135
Shipman, Sarah 90
Shipp, Edward 223
Shirley, Mary A. 111
Shockley, Ida 10
Shore, Ann Elizabeth 22
Shore, Frances 22
Shore, Joseph T. 22
Shore, Robert Belling 22
Shore, Sarah Ann Virginia 22
Shore, Taylor 22
Shore, Thomas William 22
Shore, William 22
Short, Amanda C. 78
Shortridge, Margaret 215
Shumate, Elizabeth 193
Shumate, Elizabeth A, 47
Shumate, Lillian V. 19
Shuster, Sarah 191
Signor, Platt Howland 196
Simcoe, Rev. 74
Simmons, Ben 225
Simmons, Keziah 3
Simmons, Sallie 3,225
Simmons, Spratly 3
Simmos, Elizabeth ZL5
Simms, Huldah 236
Simonds, Susannah 171
Simpson, Mazie May 177
Sims, Adelaide Brown 161
Sims, Alfred Elmore 161
Sims, Asa Higgason 161
Sims, Benjamin H. 161
Sims, Bernie Virginia 161
Sims, Charles Frathcis 160
Sims, Elizabeth Edmona Franoes Fowlkes 160
Sims, John 160
Sims, John Lipscanbe 160
Sims, Louisa Ann Caroline 160
Sims, Louise Antess 161
Sims, Lucean 161
Sims, Lucian Mills 160
Sims, Mary Mosely 161
Sims, Mortimer 161
Sims, Odelia Carolinda 161
Sims, Ola Bernioe Chetwynde 161
Sims, Peter Lipscomb 161
Sims, R.Higgason 161
Sims, Reuben Mills 161
Sims, Robert Mortimer 161
Sims, Versal Aubrey 161
Sims, Virginia 161
Sippel, Christopher 232
Sippel, Elizabeth 232
Sippel, Elize 232
Skiles, Mary 80
Skinner, Margaret 195
Skinner, Zoubbide 195

Slaton, Sarah 208
Slaughter, Bettie Florence 69
Slaughter, Dandridge 256
Slaughter, Daniel F. 69
Slaughter, Fannie 208
Slaughter, Isaac 208
Slaughter, Lelia Stewart 69
Slaughter, Lizzie 208
Slaughter, Susan Handy Palmer 256
Slaughter, Susan Penelope 208
Slaughter, Thomas K. 208
Slaughter, Viola 208
Sloane, Henry 126
Slyder, William T. 76
Smelt, Nancy 194
Smi\th, Anthony Garnett 223
Smith, A. G. 254
Smith, Addie 223
Smith, Alfred 1
Smith, Alfred Lee 1
Smith, Algernon Sidnrey 41
Smith, Alla May 1
Smith, Allen 132
Smith, Ann 70,77
Smith, Ann C. SO
Smith, Ann Cunningham 81
Smith, Ann Farlie 80,82
Smith, Ann M. 203
Smith, Ann Parke 263
Smith, Anna Maria 52
Smith, Annie F. 82
Smith, Annie Farlie 82
Smith, Archie Columbus 1
Smith, Augustus 70
Smith, Batty 131
Smith, Bessie Bondurant 254
Smith, C. T. 64
Smith, Carbin 1
Smith, Caroline B. 77
Smith, Caroline Cagernan 77
Smith, Cary A. 223
Smith, Charles 223
Smith, Charles Claborn 41
Smith, Charles, Dr. 41
Smith, Charles, Rev. Mr. 278,279
Smith, Christopher Stuart 242
Smith, Cordelia Cunningham 80
Smith, Cornelius 254
Smith, David 58
Smith, David C. 1
Smith, Delaware John 81
Smith, E. E. 42
Smith, Earnest Dewitt 1
Smith, Edward Oscar 52
Smith, Eleanor 223
Smith, Eliza E. 42
Smith, Eliza Edmonds 41
Smith, Eliza Georgiana 80
Smith, Elizabeth 38,58,70,159,223,262
Smith, Elizabeth Garlard 126
Smith, Elizabeth W. 109
Smith, Emiline 128
Smith, Emma C. 223
Smith, Errma Belle 42
Smith, Ethel Virginia 81
Smith, Eugene Christopher 111242
Smith, Franc 165
Smith, Frances Ann Bagby 42
Smith, G. 42
Smith, Garnett D. 223

Smith, George C. 1
Smith, George Edward 52
Smith, George Lewis 41,42
Smith, George Lewis 41,42
Smith, Georgianna 80,81
Smith, Gregory 70
Smith, H. H. 1
Smith, H. Rev. 113
Smith, Harriet 84
Smith, Hattie E. 1
Smith, Hattie O. 1
Smith, Hattie Opelia 1
Smith, Henry Cox 41
Smith, Henry H. 1
Smith, Ida 1
Smith, Ida George 254
Smith, Ida May 254
Smith, Ida V. 223
Smith, J. K., Dr. 99
Smith, James 262,282
Smith, James Alexander 77
Smith, James Lesley 1
Smith, James Mumford 42
Smith, Jane 70
Smith, Jane Eliza 52
Smith, Jennie 203
Smith, John 58,70,262
Smith, John Augustus 70
Smith, John G. 80,81
Smith, John Grosjean 81
Smith, John, Rev. 119
Smith, Joshua 41,42,76,77
Smith, Joshua Branch 41
Smith, Josiah 58
Smith, Larkin 80,81
Smith, Laura Taylor 242
Smith, Lelia Alice 42
Smith, Lewis Oliver 80
Smith, Lucy Cooke 70
Smith, M. A. 74
Smith, M. C., Mrs. 81,83
Smith, Maggie Mae 1,260
Smith, Margaret Aurelia 80,82
Smith, Margaret C. 80
Smith, Margaret Farlie 80,81
Smith, Mark Stokes 41
Smith, Martha 104
Smith, Martha J. 223
Smith, Martha Jane 77
Smith, Mary 70,262
Smith, Mary Amelia 234
Smith, Mary Ella 254
Smith, Mary Fleming 81
Smith, Mary Jacqueline 70
Smith, Mary S. 42
Smith, Mildred 70
Smith, Morata 1
Smith, Mrs. 207
Smith, Nancy Claiborne 2
Smith, Nannie 18
Smith, Nellie 1
Smith, Ola 69
Smith, Olive F. 77
Smith, Olive Francis 77
Smith, Opal Lee 1
Smith, Patsey 223
Smith, Pauline 204
Smith, Pauline C. 204
Smith, Pearson Owen 254
Smith, Peteronelia 77

Smith, Peteronelia Susan 77
Smith, Phoebe 18,19
Smith, Polly 223
Smith, Polly Alexander 204
Smith, R. G. 74,82
Smith, Ransom 6
Smith, Rebecca Alice 242
Smith, Reuben 217
Smith, Richard 41
Smith, Richard G. 81,82
Smith, Richard Graves 80
Smith, Robert Chapel 77
Smith, Robert H. 81
Smith, Robert Harrison 80
Smith, Robert L. 223
Smith, Robert St. Patrick 82
Smith, Robert, Major 262
Smith, Robert, Sr. 263
Smith, Rogers Morris 1
Smith, Rose Wilnette 81
Smith, S. A. 1
Smith, S. Hattie 223
Smith, S. Hull 223
Smith, Samuel 204
Smith, Samuel G. 41
Smith, Samuel H. 275
Smith, Sarah 52,70,77,107,279
Smith, Sarah A. 41
Smith, Sarah Emily 52
Smith, Sarah M. 263
Smith, Stephen 18,19
Smith, Susan 41,42
Smith, Thomas 14
Smith, Thomas Dillard 254
Smith, Thomas Gregory 70
Smith, Thomas W. 42,52
Smith, Thomas Wise 42
Smith, Thomas, Rev. 70
Smith, Wesley A. 223
Smith, William 52,58,234
Smith, William C. 80,203,204
Smith, William Campbell 81
Smith, William Campbell Code 80
Smith, William Cunningham 81
Smith, William Wesley 41
Smithee, Mary L. 188
Smithson, Rebecca 259
Smoot, John B. 237
Smoot, Sarah W. 237
Snead, Anne 281
Snead, Catharine 281
Snead, Charles 281
Snead, Charles H. 41
Snead, Charles, Capt. 281
Snead, Eller 41
Snead, Huldah 281
Snead, John 281
Snead, Mary 281
Snead, Reset B. 41
Snead, Scarborough 281
Snead, Smith 281
Snead, Thomas 281
Snead, Tully 281
Sneed, Sarah A. 77
Snell, Joseph 211
Snider, Catherine 76
Snider, Harriet 76
Snider, Henry 76
Snider, William 76
Snidow, Clara 193

Snoddy, Sarah 223
Snow, Charles, Dr. 215
Somerville, Frances 176
Somerville, John 22,176
Somerville, W. L. 176
Southall, Ann 273
Southall, Ann Rebecca 171
Southall, Anthony Webster 273
Southall, Cynthia 273
Southall, Daniel 171
Southall, Dasey 273
Southall, Edward Henry 273
Southall, Elianna Maria Jerdane 106
Southall, Elizabeth 171,273,274
Southall, Emna Honoer 171
Southall, Frances W. 273
Southall, Frances Wilson 273
Southall, Frank W. 273
Southall, Giles M. 273
Southall, James 171
Southall, James Barret 273
Southall, John 273
Southall, John D., Rev. 49
Southall, John Richard 172
Southall, John Turner 273
Southall, John W. 172
Southall, John Wesley 171
Southall, Joseph Wells 273
Southall, Julia 171
Southall, Julia Riddick 172
Southall, Julla M. 172
Southall, Laura Rebecca 172
Southall, Lucy Henry 273
Southall, Martha 273
Southall, Mary Williams 172
Southall, Paullae 273
Southall, Philip 273
Southall, Philip Francis 273,274
Southall, Philip Turner 273,274
Southall, Pleasant 273
Southall, Robert Goode 274
Southall, Sarah Eliza 171
Southall, Seth Riddick 171
Southall, Sophia Riddick 171
Southall, Stephen 273
Southall, Stephen Osbotne 273,274
Southall, Turner 273
Southall, Turner, Colonel 273
Southall, Valentine Wood 273
Southall, William 273
Southall, William Valentine 273
Southall, William Wood 273
Southell, Martha Frances 172
Southell, Mary Eliza 274
Spangler, Charles 193
Spangler, Eliza 193
Spangler, George 193
Sparks, Delilah 229
Sparrow, Elizabeth 281
Sparrow, John 281
Speaks, George T. 212
Speer, Anne Middleton 196,197
Speer, Emery 196,197
Speer, Eugenia Dearing 196.197
Speer, Marion Sherwood 196,197
Speer, Salite Dearing 197
Speer, Sally Dearing 196,197
Speer, Sarah Jane Dearing 197
Speer, Wie Hamilton 197
Speiden, Marian E. 122

Speiden, William 122
Spencer, Elizabeth 69
Spencer, Frances 69
Spencer, George 69
Spencer, James A. 69
Spencer, John 69
Spencer, John R., Capt. in
Spencer, John, Rev. 24
Spencer, Mary Ann 127
Spencer, Nancy A. H. 127
Spencer, Sarah 69,70
Spencer, Sharp 69,70
Spencer, Sharp, Sr. 70
Spencer, Susannah 69
Spencer, Thomas 69
Spencer, William 69,70
Spencer, William A. 155
Spicer, Eula Young 185
Spierin, George Hartley, Rev. 157
Spiller, Colin C. 133
Spoos, Sally 155
Spotswood, Alexander, General 275
Spotswood, Alexander, Governor 206
Spotswood, Dcrothea 135
Spotswood, Elizabeth 275
Spotswood, Henrietta 275
Spotts, John, Rev. 80
Spragins, Bettie A. 247
Spragins, Charlotte E. 8. 246
Spragins, Eliza Apperson 246
Spragins, Elizabeth Hamilton 247
Spragins, Louisa Duval 247
Spragins, Louisa Seigniora 246
Spragins, Lucy E. 246
Spragins, Lucy Elizabeth 247
Spragins, Marston G. 246
Spragins, Marston Green 247
Spragins, Melchijah 246,247 ,248
Spragins, Rebecca S. 246,247
Spragins, Rebecca Stith 247
Spragins, S. 8. 246
Spragins, Samuel Hamiltcn 247
Spragins, Stith Belling 246,247
Spragins, Stith Belling, Jr. 247
Spragins, StLth B. 246,247
Spragins, Sue E. 247
Spragins, Thomas 248
Spragins, Virginia 246
Spring, Lovina A. Nunn 19
Srrdth, Mary E. 59–80,223
Stamps, Elizabeth 90
Stamps, Nancy 90
Stamps, Rebekah 90
Stamps, Sanford 90
Standefer, Abraham 258
Standefer, E. F. 259
Standefer, Elljah 259
Standefer, I. S. 259
Standefer, Israel 258,259
Standefer, Israel Skelton 258,259
Standefer, James 258,259
Standefer, James Stuart 25R
Standefer, Jemima 258
Standefer, Jesse 258
Standefer, John 258,259
Standefer, Joshua 259
Standefer, Margaret 258
Standefer, Martha 258
Standefer, Mary 258
Standefer, Micajah 259

Standefer, Nancy Lamb 258
Standefer, Naomi 258
Standefer, Paul 258
Standefer, Sarah 253
Standefer, Skelton 258
Standefer, Stephen 259
Standefer, Susanna Frances 259
Standefer, Susannah 258,259
Standefer, Thomas F. 259
Standefer, William 258, 259
Stark, Catherine 200
Stark, Charity 202
Stark, Charles 202
Stark, Elizabeth Otisan 202
Stark, Isaac 202
Stark, Isaac 202
Stark, James 203,202
Stark, James Harvey 202
Stark, Jeremiah 202
Stark, Jeremiah Pennington 202
Stark, Kezia 202
Stark, Leah 202
Stark, Lydia 200,202
Stark, Mary 202
Stark, Mary King 202
Stark, Naomi 202
Stark, Phoebe 202
Stark, Rachel 202
Stark, Ruth 202
Stark, Samuel Camon 202
Stark, Sarah Ann 200,202
Stark, William 200
Starke, Alfred Lewis 285,286
Starke, Amanda 285.286
Starke, Amanda Truebeart 285,286
Starke, Americus Hatchett 286
Starke, Ann B. 285
Starke, Ann Baylor 286
Starke, B. 286
Starke, Burwell 285,286
Starke, Edward Brooke 285
Starke, Edwin Temple 285
Starke, Elizabeth Taylor 285
Starke, Fanny L. 286
Starke, James Newton 285,286
Starke, Judson 285
Starke, Lewis Newton 286
Starke, Lucy Gwathmey 286
Starke, Mary Ann 286
Starke, Robert Lee 286
Starke, Virginia Burwell 285
Starke, William Gwathmey 286
Starke, William Thomas 285
Starkey, Evie 41
Starkley, Leila G. 41
Stebbens, Sarah Sophia 3
Steel, Annie M. 186
Steel, Annie Martha 186
Steel, M. C. 186
Steel, Mary C. 186
Steel, William 186
Steel, William, Rev. 186
Steele, Eliza 219
Steele, Emily 219
Steele, James Devereaux 219
Steele, John 219
Steele, Lavinia 219
Steele, Nancy 219
Steele, Polly 219
Steele, Samson S. 219

Steele, Samuel Sanders 219
Steer, Ann 195
Steger, S. B. 124
Stephens, Rev. Mr. 102
Stephenson, James M. 267
Stephenson, Joseph 167
Steptoe, Frances Callaway 162
Steptoe, James, Sr. 215
Steptoe, Judith 217
Steptoe, Lucinda 215
Steptoe, William, Dr. 162
Stevens, James E. 10
Stevens, John 179
Stevens, Lucy 11
Stevenson, James, Rev. 179
Steward, Ann 284
Stewart, Andrew 134
Stewart, Catherine 220
Stewart, Ed Dorsey 18,19
Stewart, Frances Willis 179
Stewart, Joseph 179
Stewart, Joseph 179
Stewart, Mary 134
Stewart, Samuel, Rev. 184
Stewart, W. P. 284
Stewart, William, Rev. 102,257
Stith, Ann 101,143
Stith, Anne 248
Stith, Benjamin 101,143
Stith, Buccner 143
Stith, Catharille 143
Stith, Drury 143
Stith, Edmund 143
Stith, Elizabeth 143
Stith, Elizabeth Buckner 101,143
Stith, Emily 120
Stith, Griffin 143
Stith, Henry 143
Stith, Jane 248
Stith, Jesse J. 143
Stith, John 101.143
Stith, John C. 143
Stith, John, Major 248
Stith, Joseph 101,143
Stith, Katherine 101
Stith, Lucy 101,143
Stith, Lucy, Sr. 143
Stith, Martha 101,143
Stith, Martha Ann 143
Stith, Mary 101,143
Stith, Mary Ann 143
Stith, RIchard 101,143
Stith, Richard, Sr. 143
Stith, Susan 143
Stith, Thomas 101,143
Stith, William 101,143
Stith, William Nelson 203
Stith, William, Sr. 143
Stockdell, Ann 179
Stockdell, John, Capt. 179
Stockdell, Mary 179
Stockwell, Abi R. 45
Stockwell, Anna M. Saxe 45
Stockwell, Benajah L. 45
Stockwell, David S. 45
Stockwell, Godfrey E. 45
Stockwell, Harriet S. 45
Stockwell, Hermit 0. 45
Stockwell, Joseph 45
Stockwell, Joseph M. 45

Stockwell, Lucy 45
Stockwell, Maloma 45
Stockwell, Mary A. 45
Stockwell, Mathew J. 45
Stockwell, Samuel S. 459
Stokes Lucy Ann 264
Stokes William S. 264
Stokes, David 263
Stokes, David Henry 264
Stokes, David, Jr. 263
Stokes, John 263
Stokes, Lucy Ann 264
Stokes, Mary 262
Stokes, Montfort 263
Stokes, Peter 263
Stokes, Peter, Captain 262,263
Stokes, Polly 126,127
Stokes, Sarah Haynie 254
Stokes, Sarah M. 263
Stokes, Sarah, Jr. 263
Stokes, Sarah, Sr. 263
Stokes, Susannah 263
Stokes, William H. 262
Stokes, Willian 263
Stone, Coleman MO
Stone, Daniel 195
Stone, Dolly C. 59
Stone, E. F. 196
Stone, John 201
Stone, Joshua 200,201
Stone, Lucy J. 19
Stone, Mary C. M3,201
Stone, Nancy 68
Stone, Polly 200,201
Stone, Thomas C. 200
Stone, William 8. 200
Stoner, Michael 266
Stones, James Hoskins 201
Story, J. F. 69
Story, Judith Frances 69
Stovall, C. E. 196
Stover, Ann 228
Stover, Barbara 228
Stover, Daniel 228
Stover, David 228
Stover, Elizabeth 228
Stover, Mary 228
Stover, Mary Magdalena 228
Stover, Samuel 228
Strange, Owen 34
Stratton, Laura V. 75
Streep, Mary 279
Street, Ann Parke 262
Street, Anthony 263
Street, Anthony W. 262
Street, Anthony Waddy 261,264
Street, Anthony, Colonel 262
Street, Anthony, Jr. 262,263
Street, David 141,142,262,263
Street, David Anthony 262,263,264
Street, Elizabeth Abbott 264
Street, Frances 262
Street, Hannah Waddy 261
Street, James Parke 141
Street, James Parke 262,264
Street, John 261,262,263
Street, John T. 264
Street, John Thomson 262,263
Street, John, Jr. 261,262
Street, Joseph 261,263

Street, Joseph M., General 102
Street, Joseph Montfort 262,263,264
Street, Lucy Ann 262,263,264
Street, Mary 262,264
Street, Mary Ann 262
Street, Mary S. 264
Street, Mary Scott 142,263,264
Street, Mary Stokes 263,264
Street, Molley 263
Street, Montfort, Dr. 262
Street, Peter W. 262,264
Street, Peter William 263
Street, Sarah 262,263
Street, Sarah Montfort 12
Street, Sarah S. 263
Street, Sarah Smith 263
Street, Sarah Stokes 262,264
Street, Susan Frances 141,142,262,264
Street, Susan M. Scott 264
Street, Waddy 141
Street, Waddy 262,263,264
Street, Waddy, Lt. Colonel 262
Street, William 262,263
Street, William B. 262,263
Street, William, Judge 262
Strickler, Abraham 228
Strickler, Annely 85
Strickler, Daniel 85
Strickler, David 85
Strickler, Elizabeth 228
Strickler, Jacob 228
Strickler, Maria 85
Strickler, Samuel 85
Strotfier, John 183
Strother, F. A. , Rev. 9
Strother, Florence E. 184
Strother, Julia Ann 183
Strother, Mary Catharine 183,184
Stuart, Andrew Jackson M7
Stuart, Ann Elizabeth 207
Stuart, Benjamin F. 275
Stuart, Betsy 207
Stuart, Charles, Chapt. 279
Stuart, Coley 207
Stuart, Coley Robinson Chiles 207
Stuart, Elizabeth 207
Stuart, Frances Gibboas 269
Stuart, Frances J. 207
Stuart, Giles 0. 207
Stuart, Giles 207
Stuart, Helen Gibbon 284
Stuart, Henry 207
Stuart, Henry Dabney M7
Stuart, James 207
Stuart, James Goodwin 207
Stuart, Jane Goodwin 207
Stuart, John 4
Stuart, Lois Lunsford 207
Stuart, Mary 207
Stuart, William Randolph 207
Stuart, William, Rev. 284
Sugget, Mary 68
Sutherlin, Solomon 18,19
Sutherlin, Verna M. 19
Sutton, Sally 218
Sydnor, Ann 285,286
Sydnor, Anthony 285
Sydnor, Betsey 285
Sydnor, Catharine 285
Sydnor, Edward 286

Sydnor, Elizabeth 285,286
Sydnor, Elizabeth Garland 286
Sydnor, Elizabeth Taylor 285
Sydnor, Fanny Mitchell 285~86
Sydnor, George W. 286
Sydnor, Joan 285
Sydnor, Joanna 285
Sydnor, John 193
Sydnor, John 285
Sydnor, John S. 286
Sydnor, Joseph 285
Sydnor, Jubith 285
Sydnor, Ruth 285
Sydnor, Sarah 285,286
Sydnor, Susanah 286
Sydnor, Susanna 285
Sydnor, Thomas White 286
Sydnor, William 285,286
Sydnor, William B. 286
Sydnot, Frances Am 286
Syndnor, Edward Garland 286
Syndor, William 286
Syrtnor, Fortunatus 285
Tabb, Dianna 134
Tabb, Sarah 103
Taland, James M. 251
Taliaferro, Ann 179
Taliaferro, Ann Hay 179
Taliaferro, Ann Patterson 179
Taliaferro, Carr Blasingame 179
Taliaferro, Elizabeth 179
Taliaferro, Elizabeth Hay 179
Taliaferro, George Catlett 179
Taliaferro, Hay 179
Taliaferro, Hay, Jr. 179
Taliaferro, James Hay 179
Taliaferro, John 179
Taliaferro, John Champe 179
Taliaferro, John, Colonel 179,284
Taliaferro, John, Dr. 211
Taliaferro, Lawrence Washington 179
Taliaferro, Lawrence Wesley 179
Taliaferro, Lucy Mary 179
Taliaferro, Lucy Mary Battaile 179
Taliaferro, Marshall Howe 179
Taliaferro, Mary 179
Taliaferro, Mary Willis 179
Taliaferro, Matilda Battaile 179
Taliaferro, Nicholas 179
Taliaferro, Nicholas Hay Battaile 179
Taliaferro, Sarah 179
Taliaferro, William 179
Taliaferro, William Thornton 179
Tallaferro, Frances Ann 179
Talor, Martha Waller 288
Tandy, Henry 267
Tarr, Ann 109
Tarrant, Susannah 253
Tate, Tabitha 127,205
Tatum, Susan Penn 189
Tatum, William Moore 188
Tayloe, Am C. 276
Tayloe, Anne Corbin 275
Tayloe, Catherine 276
Tayloe, Eleanor 275
Tayloe, Elizabeth 274,275
Tayloe, Jane 276
Tayloe, John 274,275 ,276
Tayloe, Mary 275
Tayloe, Sarah 275,276

Tayloe, William 206,274
Taylor Howell Lewis 176
Taylor, Abraham 259
Taylor, Alice 241,288
Taylor, Am 175,176,261,288
Taylor, Anderson 175
Taylor, Ann 287
Taylor, Anne 287
Taylor, Anne Gilbert 287
Taylor, Benjamin 288
Taylor, Berthey 261
Taylor, C., Rev. 181
Taylor, Catherine 175,176
Taylor, Daniel 288
Taylor, Davis Littlepage 288
Taylor, Edmund 175,287
Taylor, Edward Francis 288
Taylor, Edward Hams, Capt. 166
Taylor, Elaria 287,288
Taylor, Eliza 175
Taylor, Elizabeth 139,175,176,280,287
Taylor, Emma Aldridge 288
Taylor, Erasmus 287,288
Taylor, F. H. B. 288
Taylor, F. L. 176
Taylor, Felix 287,288
Taylor, Felix H. G. 287
Taylor, Felix Haywood 287
Taylor, Frances 198,175,176,287
Taylor, Frances Anderson 176
Taylor, George 261,287
Taylor, Gilbert Dade 287
Taylor, Hannah 237
Taylor, Howell 175
Taylor, Isabella 175
Taylor, J. M. 288
Taylor, Jam 287,288
Taylor, James 111,175,176,187,188
Taylor, James II 287,288
Taylor, Jason Stuart 242
Taylor, John 175,261,278,287,288
Taylor, John Anthony 288
Taylor, John M. 287
Taylor, John Moore 287
Taylor, John Moore, Jr. 288
Taylor, John Moore, Sr. 288
Taylor, John Warwick 241,242
Taylor, John William 287,288
Taylor, John, Capt. 288
Taylor, John, Colonel 175
Taylor, John, Jr. 176
Taylor, Joseph 175,176,259
Taylor, Lewis 175
Taylor, Lucy 261,286
Taylor, Lucy Penn 176
Taylor, Maria Eliza 287,288
Taylor, Martha 287,288
Taylor, Mary 175,176,258,287
Taylor, Mary Am 176
Taylor, Matilda Foote 287~88
Taylor, Medora 288
Taylor, Medora E. 288
Taylor, Milley 261,287
Taylor, Nancy 261,280
Taylor, Nancy Stuart 241,242
Taylor, Pl-dllip 175,176
Taylor, R. D. 92
Taylor, Reggey 261
Taylor, Richard 138,175,288
Taylor, Richard Sqr 288

Taylor, Robert 287,288
Taylor, Sarah 175,259 ,261,287
Taylor, Sharlot 261
Taylor, Sigismunda Mary 287
Taylor, Stuart 241
Taylor, Stuart Austin 241
Taylor, Tabitha 287
Taylor, Tazewell 279
Taylor, Thomas 176,288
Taylor, Walker 176
Taylor, Waller 288
Taylor, William 175,261,287,288
Taylor, William F. 287,288
Taylor, William F. 288
Taylor, William Waller 288
Taylor, Zachary 287
Tazewell, Henry 206
Tears, William 253
Telford, Alexander 171
Telford, Jam 171
Telford, Mary 171
Temple, Ann 110,111
Temple, Joseph 110,111
Temple, Samuel 105
Temple, William 107,111
Templeton, Gertrude Barnes 198
Templeton, Inez Frances 198
Templeton, Ruth Matilda 198
Templeton, Samuel H. 198
Templeton, Samuel H., Rev. 198
Templeton, Samuel Huntington 198
Terrel, Miles 282
Terrell, Backie 282
Terrell, Rebekah 282,283
Terrill, Elizabeth E. 178
Terry, Mary 262
Terry, William 201
Tevis, Matilda H. 267
Thackara, O. P., 115
Tharp, Betty 265
Tharp, Lucy 265
Tharp, Mary 265
Tharp, Patty 265
Tharp, Peterson 265
Tharp, Sylvia 265
Tharp, Temperance 265
Tharp, Timothy 265
Tharp, William 265
Thomas, D. W. 91
Thomas, Eleanor 251
Thomas, Eunice Pauline 244
Thomas, Lou Ella 116
Thomas, Mary 132
Thomas, Mary E. 181
Thomas, Mary W. 92
Thomas, Nancy Hunton 221
Thomas, Nancy P. 153
Thomas, Nancy Preston 153
Thomas, Owen 221
Thompsan, Susana 211
Thompson, Alexander 211
Thompson, Alfred Parks 211
Thompson, Charlotte 211
Thompson, David 211,249
Thompson, Drucilla 211
Thompson, Eliza 211
Thompson, Elizabeth 211,249
Thompson, Faithy 211
Thompson, Frederick 211
Thompson, James 211

Thompson, James R. 211
Thompson, James, Rev. 214
Thompson, John 211,249
Thompson, John F. 211
Thompson, John Herbert 142
Thompson, Joseph 249
Thompson, Lucy 211
Thompson, Lucy Adeline 211
Thompson, Maria W. R. 167
Thompson, Martha 287
Thompson, Mary 249
Thompson, Mary Caroline 211
Thompson, Mildred 233
Thompson, Nancy 211
Thompson, Nathaniel 249
Thompson, Nicholas 249
Thompson, Phill. 102
Thompson, Roger 249
Thompson, Sarah 249
Thompson, Susannah 249
Thompson, T. G. Pnstt 115
Thompson, Violet 211
Thompson, William 233,249,286
Thomson, George Napier 197
Thoniley, Julia H. 235,236
Thornberry, Catherine 170
Thornley, Aaron 234,235
Thornley, Ann Ellza 234
Thornley, C. C. 235
Thornley, Caroline Virginia 234
Thornley, Catherine 234,235
Thornley, Clarence 235
Thornley, Elizabeth 234
Thornley, Endly 234,235
Thornley, Fnach Berry 234
Thornley, Frances Arm 234
Thornley, James 234
Thornley, Jane 234,235
Thornley, Jane Riding 234,235~236
Thornley, Jares P. 235
Thornley, Jean 234
Thornley, John 234,235,236
Thornley, John, Dr. 236
Thornley, John, Sr. 236
Thornley, Josiah Payne 235
Thornley, Judith Ann 234
Thornley, Judith Berry 234
Thornley, Julian 235,236
Thornley, Julian H. Payne 235
Thornley, Lucy 234
Thornley, Maria 234,235
Thornley, Maria Julia 235
Thornley, Mary D. 235
Thornley, Mary Downes 235
Thornley, Mary Matilda 234
Thornley, Sarah 235
Thornley, Thoma Berry 234
Thornley, William 234,235,236
Thornley, William, Sr. 235
Thornley, Winifred 235
Thornly, Lucy Jane 235
Thorntoa, Robert D. 199
Thornton, Benajah 250
Thornton, Benjamin 217
Thornton, Betsy 102
Thornton, Betsy W. 250
Thornton, Charles H. 200
Thornton, Charlotte 275
Thornton, David 250
Thornton, Elizabeth 157,158,250

Thornton, Elsabad 250
Thornton, Eppy White 250
Thornton, F. M. 200
Thornton, Francis, Jr. 102
Thornton, George 102,257
Thornton, J. M. 199
Thornton, James B. 199
Thornton, John 166,250
Thornton, John Alexander 102
Thornton, John M. 199,250
Thornton, John Washington 102
Thornton, Laura 0. 200
Thornton, Lucinda 199
Thornton, Lucy Frances 102,257
Thornton, Lucy K. White 250
Thornton, Mark 250
Thornton, Martha 250
Thornton, Mary 102,200
Thornton, Mary Alexander 102,257
Thornton, Mary E. 199
Thornton, Melvina 102
Thornton, Memorable 250
Thornton, Micajah 250
Thornton, Middleton 250
Thornton, Mildred 110
Thornton, P. L. 199
Thornton, Peter 158
Thornton, Polley 250
Thornton, Prior 250
Thornton, R. B. 199
Thornton, Reuben, Rev. 102
Thornton, Reuben, Sr. 200
Thornton, Rev. Mr. 229
Thornton, Salley 250
Thornton, Sarah 250
Thornton, Susannah 250
Thornton, Thomas 250
Thornton, Thomas H. 200
Thornton, Thomas, Rev. 102
Thornton, W. A. 199
Thorogood, John 134
Thorowgood, Margaret 134
Thorowgood, Robert 134
Thorowgood, Thomas Scarburgh 134
Throckmorton, Fanny 108
Thrurston, Mary 165,166
Thrustan, John 165,166
Thruston, Alfred 166
Thruston, Algernon Sidney 166
Thruston, Am 166
Thruston, Buckner 166
Thruston, C. M., Colonel 166
Thruston, Catherine 166
Thruston, Charles 166
Thruston, Charles M. 166
Thruston, Charles M., Colonel 166
Thruston, Charles Minn 166
Thruston, Charles Minn, Colonel 166
Thruston, Edmond 165
Thruston, Edward 166
Thruston, Edward, Jr. 165
Thruston, Eliza 166
Thruston, Elizabeth 166
Thruston, Elizabeth Taylor 166
Thruston, Eloise 166
Thruston, Fanny Badello 166
Thruston, Ferry 165
Thruston, Franc, Frane 165
Thruston, Frances 166
Thruston, Jemima 166

Thruston, John, Colonel 166
Thruston, Lucius Falkland 166
Thruston, Mary Buckner 166
Thruston, Mary Ruck 166
Thruston, Mildred 166
Thruston, Robert 166
Thruston, Sarah 166
Thruston, Susannah 165
Thruston, Thomas 165
Thruston, Thomas Whiting 166
Thurman, Caroline E. 287
Thurston, Ann 179
Thurston, Eliza 278
Thurston, Eliza T. 166
Thurston, Lucy May 179
Thurston, Susan 278
Tidball, Josiah 158
Tilley, Elizabeth 204
Tillman, Clarissa 155
Tinsley, Ann A. 194
Tinsley, Peter 286
Tittswortfi, Mary A. 116
Tittsworth, Elizabeth M. Seay 116
Tittsworth, Ferrell 116
Tittsworth, George F. 116
Tittsworth, James T. 116
Tldball, Frances Lee 158
Toler, Charles S. 242
Toler, David C. 242
Toler, Sarah 242
Toler, William H. 242
Tompkins, Bennett, Capt. 138
Tompkins, Elizabeth 138
Tompkins, Margaret J. 100
Tompkins, San 133
Trapper, Dr. 236
Travers, Eliza 158
Travis, Edward 207
Tribble, Andrew 267
Tribble, Andrew, Rev. 266
Tribble, Dudley 267
Tribble, Frances T. 266
Tribble, James P. 267
Tribble, Jchn, General 267
Tribble, Martha 267
Tribble, Mary 267
Tribble, Nanry 266
Tribble, Patsey 267
Tribble, Peter 266
Tribble, Robert 0. 267
Tribble, Sally B. 266
Tribble, Samuel 266
Tribble, Silas 266
Tribble, Thomas 266
Trueheart, Amanda 285,286
Trueheart, Elizabeth 285
Trueheart, William 285,286
Trweatt, William 95
Tucker, Alice 279
Tucker, Ann 279
Tucker, Carolina Henrietta 279
Tucker, Courtney 279
Tucker, Cynthia B. 277
Tucker, Cynthia Beverly 276
Tucker, Elizabeth 140,278
Tucker, Frances 278
Tucker, Gawin Corbin 279
Tucker, Joanna 278,279
Tucker, Joanna, Jr. 279
Tucker, John 278,279

Tucker, John Pulman 279
Tucker, Lucy J. 95
Tucker, Martha 278
Tucker, Mary 278
Tucker, Richard 279
Tucker, Robert 278
Tucker, Robert, Colonel 279
Tucker, Robert, Jr. 279
Tucker, Sarah 278,279
Tucker, William 141
Turnball, Charles 134
Turnball, Robert 135
Turnbull, Alexander 134
Turnbull, Andrew, Rev. 134
Turnbull, Anne 135
Turnbull, George, Rev. 134
Turnbull, Mary 135
Turnbull, Mary Cole 135
Turnbull, Rachel Robinson 134
Turnbull, Robert 135
Turnbull, Thomas Crawford 135
Turnbull, William 134
Turnbull, William Cole 135
Turner, Catherine 192
Turner, Elinor 252
Turner, Elizabeth 252
Turner, George 252
Turner, Nancy Jane 240
Tutt, John 214
Tyler, Betsy A. 267
Tyler, Elizabeth Arm1stead 268
Tyler, John, Judge 268
Tyler, Maria Henry 268
Tyler, Mary E. 113
Tyler, Watt H., Dr. 113
Tyree, Coca P. 146
Tyree, Cyrus 146
Tyree, Cyrus Hardy 146
Tyree, Emily M. 146
Tyree, F. D. 146
Tyree, Francis 0. 146
Tyree, James L. 146
Tyree, John P. 146
Tyree, Lemuel H. 146
Tyree, Martha Ann Virginia 146
Tyree, Mary W. 146
Tyree, Nancy C. 146
Tyree, Sarah Elizabeth 146
Tyree, Thomas J. 146
Umbarger, DelUah 232
Upshaw, Laurie 210
Upshaw, Sanders 210
Urick, Alan Dennis 241
Urick, Eleredith Sanders 240,241
Urick, Harriet 241
Urick, John William 241
Urick, Lcbs Cordelia 240,241
Urick, Lois Alarra 241
Urick, Meredith Sanders, Jr. 241
Vail, Amas L. 218
Van Clear, Mettle 99
Van DeGraple, Eliza Jane 181
Van Meter, Abraham 246
Van Meter, Ann 246
Van Meter, Anne 246
Van Meter, Benjamin Franklin 246
Van Meter, David 246
Van Meter, Garret 246
Van Meter, Hannah 246
Van Meter, Henry 246

Van Meter, Isaac 246
Van Meter, Jacob 246
Van Meter, Joseph Inskeep 246
Van Meter, Rebeckah 246
Van Meter, Sarah Inskeep 246
Van Meter, Solomon 246
Van Meter, Susannah 246
Van Meter, Tabitha 246
Vandevanter, Ann M. 239
Vandevanter, Blanche Lillian 239
Vandevanter, C. M. 239
Vandevanter, Cornelius M. 239
Vandevanter, HattLe May 239
Vandevanter, I. C. 239
Vandevanter, Isaac C. 239
Vandevanter, J. William 239
Vandevanter, James William 239
Vandevanter, Lucy Elizabeth 239
Vandevanter, Mary Eliza 239
Vandevanter, Maurice Grimsley 239
Vandevanter, Rodney Washington 239
Vandevanter, S. J. 239
Vandevanter, Sarah Jam 239
Vaughan, Lucy M. 111
Vaughan, Mildred A. 123
Vaughan, Rebecca E. M. 111
Vaughan, William 113
Vaughn, E1iza J. 184
Vaughn, Ralph C. 213
Visnoski, Deny Allen 249
Vivian, Virgil 173
Vivion, Betsey 173
Vivion, Jam 173
Vivion, John 173
Vivion, Mary 173
Vivion, Nancy 173
Vivion, Polly 173
Vivion, Sally 173
Vivion, Thacker 173
Waddel, James, Rev. 271
Waddel, Mary Smith 271
Waddel, Nathaniel 271
Waddy, Annie Catherine 185
Waddy, Anthony 262
Waddy, Garland Thompson 185
Waddy, Hannah 262
Wade, Ann 263
Wade, Elizabeth 264
Wade, Robert, Sr. 263
Wade, Sarah 263
Wagner, Barbara 98
Wainhause, Francis 134
Wainhouse, Dorothy 134
Wainhouse, Margrabe 134
Wainwright, Martha 95
Walker, Am 260
Walker, David 260
Walker, Deborah Anne 164
Walker, Elizabeth 164
Walker, Fanny Allen 164
Walker, George 163,164
Walker, George Michael 164
Walker, Hugh 166
Walker, I. F. 224
Walker, Isaac 224
Walker, J. 163
Walker, J. L. 164
Walker, James Robert 164
Walker, John 111,163,164,173
Walker, John L. 163

Walker, John Littlebury 164
Walker, John William 168
Walker, John, Dr. 111
Walker, Judith 164
Walker, Judith Bray Shields 164
Walker, Judy B. I. 164
Walker, Littleberry 163
Walker, Littleton Harwell 224
Walker, Lucy F. 224
Walker, Lucy Finey 225
Walker, Many 282
Walker, Margret 278
Walker, Martha E. F. 111
Walker, Mary 164
Walker, Mary Christian 163,164
Walker, Mary Susan 164
Walker, Mary U. P. 164
Walker, Mattie Bates 164
Walker, Nancy 163,164
Walker, R. 164
Walker, Rebeckah 164
Walker, Rebekah Allen 164
Walker, Richard 164
Walker, Richard Wilcox 164
Walker, S. I. 224
Walker, Sarah 111,260
Walker, Seaborn I. 224
Walker, Thomas 110,173
Walker, Thomas J. 164
Walker, Thomas Ledbetter 164
Walker, Virgil 173
Walker, Walker 276
Walker, William 163,173
Walker, William Edward 164
Walker, William P. 164
Walker, William Page 164
Walker, William, Jr. 164
Wall, Martha Elizabeth 218
Wallace, B. J., Rev. 99
Wallace, Elizabeth 266
Wallace, Kate 199
Wallace, Susan Frances 94
Wallace, W. P. 99
Waller Rose 186
Waller, Agnes 184
Waller, Agnes Carr 184,185
Waller, Alice C. 185
Waller, Ann 272
Waller, Anna 184
Waller, Anne 206
Waller, Annie Catherine 185
Waller, Archibald Pinckny 185
Waller, Benjamin Carter 207
Waller, Benjamin, Judge 206
Waller, Cardlisle Waddy 185
Waller, Caroline 185
Waller, Caroline Ann 185
Waller, Carr 184
Waller, Clara 207
Waller, Dabney Jordan 185
Waller, Dabney Jordan, Jr. 185
Waller, Dabney W. 185
Waller, Dabney Washington 184,185
Waller, Dahney 184
Waller, Dolly Ann 107
Waller, Dorothy 184
Waller, Dorothy Elizabeth 206
Waller, Dorothy Vivian King 185
Waller, Edward Pinckney 185
Waller, Elizabeth 107,184

Waller, Elizabeth Dabney 184
Waller, Elizabeth M. 184
Waller, Elizabeth Pleasants 185
Waller, Frames 207
Waller, George 'ISrler 185
Waller, Hampden Pleasants 185
Waller, John 184,206
Waller, John Mercer 185
Waller, John Thomas 185
Waller, Jordan 186
Waller, Judith Anna 185
Waller, Kate Clarice 185
Waller, Louisa 185
Waller, Martha 206,288
Waller, Mary 184,206
Waller, Mary Ann Dabney 184
Waller, Mary Elvira 185
Waller, Pomfrett 184
Waller, Raymond Minor 185
Waller, Robert 206
Waller, Robert Hall 207
Waller, Roberta Lee 185
Waller, Rose Garland 185
Waller, Sarah 184
Waller, Sophia Woodson 185
Waller, Thomas Carr 184
Waller, William 107,207
Waller, William Macon 107
Wallet, George Washington 185
Wallis, Colonel 102
Walton, Alfred 151,152
Walton, Allan 151,152
Walton, Charles Woodson 151,152
Walton, Cynthia Barron 152
Walton, Elizabeth Mary Ann 225
Walton, Elmer 151,152
Walton, Emily Caroline 152
Walton, Emma Bates 151,152
Walton, Everett 151
Walton, F. B. 151
Walton, Fred B. 151
Walton, Frederick B. 152
Walton, Frederick Bates 151,152,160
Walton, Grace 151
Walton, Guy 151,152
Walton, Howard 151,152
Walton, Isaac R., Major 224
Walton, Joseph Wilkerson, Captain 225
Walton, Louisa Conway 151,152,160
Walton, Lucius A. 152
Walton, Lucius Augustus 151,152
Walton, Madelon 151
Walton, Mary P. 152
Walton, Mary Peyton 151
Walton, Maude 151,152
Walton, Nancy Fleming 151,152
Walton, Raymond 151
Walton, Robert A. 152
Walton, Robert Alfred 152,152
Walton, Roger 151,152
Walton, Roy 151,152
Walton, Shirley 151,152
Walton, Thomas Woodville 151,152
Walton, Virginia 152
Walton, Virginia Feild 151
Wamsley, Daniel 237
Wamsley, Joseph 237
Ward, Anselm 236
Ward, Anselm Lynch 206
Ward, Charles Henry 206

Ward, Charles Lynch 206
Ward, Charles Terrell 206
Ward, Dorothea 206
Ward, Elizabeth 249
Ward, Floyd 206
Ward, Frances 156
Ward, James Dearing 206
Ward, Lucy 206
Ward, Lynch 206
Ward, Mallie 206
Ward, Martha Catherine 206
Ward, Mary 206
Ward, Mary Elizabeth 206
Ward, Petey Ocey 206
Ward, Robert Henry 206
Ward, Robert Palmers 206
Ward, Samuel 249
Ward, Susan 206
Ward, Susan Virginia 206
Ward, Virginia 206
Ward, William 249
Ward, William Patrick 206
Ward, William, Rev. 203
Ware, Lucy 282
Waren, Frank 250
Warfield, Harry H. 142
Warren, Eliz. B. 164
Warren, Elizabeth 164
Warren, Jean D. 167
Warren, Jean W. D. 168
Warren, Leon Albert 228
Warren, M. S., Dr. 163
Warren, Marie Daveiss 167
Warren, Michael S., Dr. 164
Warren, Rebecca Allen 163,164
Warren, William 167,168
Warren, William A. 163
Warterfield, Ann 151
Warterfield, Betsy W. 151
Warterfield, Cliff A. 151
Warterfield, Elizabeth W. 151
Warterfield, Harry T. 151
Warterfield, James G. 151
Warterfield, James, Sr. 151
Warterfield, Jessey M. 151
Warterfield, Mildred 151
Warterfield, Peter 152
Warterfield, Peter W. F. 151
Warterfield, Phillip J. 151
Warterfield, Ursela A. 151
Warterville, Orville P. 151
Warwick, William 111
Washington Richard 277
Washington, Arm Aylett 275
Washington, Augustine 275
Washington, Betty 276,277
Washington, Bushrod 275
Washington, Corbin Aylett 276
Washington, Cynthia 277
Washington, Edgar C. 277
Washington, Effie 277
Washington, Effy 277
Washington, Elizabeth 276,277
Washington, Ellen 277
Washington, George 276,277,278
Washington, George Corbin 276
Washington, George W. 277
Washington, Hannah Bushrod 275
Washington, Henrietta 277
Washington, Henry 277
Washington, Henry A. 276,278
Washington, Henry Augt. 277
Washington, Henry Augustine 276,277
Washington, Henry Augustine 277
Washington, Jane 275.276
Washington, John '1, 276,277,278
Washington, John 277
Washington, John Edward 168
Washington, Julia 277
Washington, Julia Augusta 275
Washington, Law. 278
Washington, Lawrence 276,277,278
Washington, Lawrence Augustine 277
Washington, Lawrence Gibson 277
Washington, Leasy 277
Washington, Lloyd 276,277
Washington, Lucy B. 277
Washington, Martha 275
Washington, Mary 277
Washington, Mary Amelia 168
Washington, Mary Ashton 277
Washington, Mary W. 276,277
Washington, Mary West 276
Washington, Needham L. 275
Washington, Orlando Fairfax 277
Washington, Orlando T. 277
Washington, Pilary A. 277
Washington, Richard 276,277,278
Washington, Richard Henry 277
Washington, Robert J. 277
Washington, Robert James 276
Washington, Sallie Tayloe 277
Washington, Sally 277
Washington, Sarah 275 ,276
Washington, Sarah Ashton 276,277
Washington, Sarah Augustine 277
Washington, Sarah T. 277
Washington, Sarah Tayloe 274,275,276,277,278
Washington, Selma 277
Washington, Virginia Elizabeth 168
Washington, Walker 277
Washington, William A. 276
Washington, William Aug. 275,276
Washington, William Augt., Colonel 276
Washington, William Augt., Jr. 276
Washington, William Augustine 275,276,278
Washington,, John Taylor 277
Washinton, Julie E. 275
Waterfield, Micajah G. 151
Watkins, Darian Smith 251
Watkins, Dawson Edward 142
Watkins, James A. 259
Watkins, Lavinia A. 93
Watkins, Leila Alice 251
Watkins, Martha 259
Watkins, Mary 259
Watkins, Ruth Josephine 242
Watkins, Samuel 259
Watkins, William 259
Watson, Ada 152
Watson, Anne 223
Watson, David 231
Watson, Francis 231
Watson, James A. 131
Watson, Mary 231
Watson, Mary Parker 231
Watson, Nancy 231
Watson, Prudence 231
Watson, William 231
Watts, Elizabeth C. 111

Watts, Ellza 139
Watts, Henry H. 139
Watts, Lucy 223
Waugh, Abner, Rev. 157
Waugh, Judith 124
Wayman, Charles 275
Wdltca, Ada 151
Weaver, Alexander Franklin 243
Weaver, David B. 243
Weaver, Jacob 243
Weaver, Jacob W. 243
Weaver, John C. 243
Weaver, Mary Elizabeth 243
Weaver, Rebecca 243
Weaver, Sarah S. 243
Webb, Jarth 122
Webb, John 122,213
Webster, Anthony 274
Webster, Elizabeth 274
Webster, Elizabeth 274
Weir, Hugh 171
Weir, Mary McKee 171
Weir, Samuel Tasker 184
Weiseger, Eliza Richison 181
Welborn, Virginia 257
Welch, B. J. 226
Welch, Bessie 226
Welch, Bettie Jackson 226
Welch, Daisy Barbour 226
Welch, Elizabeth J. 226
Welch, Frances Ann 228
Welch, Francis A. 228
Welch, Irene C. 225
Welch, John N. 228
Welch, Irem 226
Welch, Irene Westerman 226
Welch, Luther M. 228
Welch, Mary Egleston 225
Welch, Mary Elizabeth 226
Welch, Mildred Irene 226
Welch, S. B. 226
Welch, S. B., Sr. 226
Welch, S. M. 226
Welch, Sylvester 226
Welch, Sylvester Burditt, Jr. 225
Welch, Sylvester Morgan 226
Welch, Sylvlester Burnditt 226
Welcon, Alice Ashton 226
Well, William 231
Wellcome, Henry S. 248
Wellford, John Spotswood 109
Wellford, Kate Y. 109
Wellford, Preston 110
Wells, Martha 288
Werth, Mary M. 269
West, Matilda 281
West, Amanda Minerva 190
West, Catherine 281
West, Charity 234
West, Elis Jackson 190
West, Eliza 190
West, Elizabeth Ann 190
West, Ellis 234
West, Francis, Colonel 143
West, Harriet Hatley 190
West, Harriet Louisa 190
West, John, Lt. Col. 281
West, Joseph 190
West, Margaret Hall 190
West, Martin Valney 190

West, Mary Hall 190
West, Susanna 143
West, Thomas J. 234
West. Prudence Harris 190
Whatley, Betty 199
Wheeler, Elizabeth 171
Wheeler, John 171
Wheeler, Martha 171
Whitaker, Catherine M. 194
White, Ann 286
White, Ann B. 271
White, Arthur 140
White, Catherine C. 234
White, Claude Marshall 192
White, David H. 123
White, Elizabeth 104,286
White, George 104
White, Hannah 104
White, Helen 234
White, Hugh 271,272
White, Jacob 267
White, Jerusha 266
White, Jesse 234
White, Joseph 104
White, Lucinda 162
White, Lucy Elizabeth 239
White, Lucy K. 250
White, Martha 104,267
White, Mary 104~49
White, Mary Brown 104
White, Nancy 104
White, Rebecca 104
White, Rev. Mr. 111,119
White, Richard 104
White, Samuel 104
White, Sarah 104,286
White, Sarah C. 286
White, Thornas 286
White, V. N. 192
White, Volney Needham 192
Whitehead, Dempsey 160
Whitehead, Eliza Ann 160
Whitehead, Eva E. 160
Whitehead, Ida C. 160
Whitehead, Jatn M. 93
Whitehead, Jesse 160
Whitehead, Jesse T. 160
Whitehead, Julius I. 160
Whitehead, M. A. 93
Whitehead, Martha W. 92
Whitehead, Mary 91
Whitehead, Sarah 160
Whitehead, Sarah E. 160
Whitehead, Virginia T. 160
Whitehead, William J. 160
Whitehead, William J. 257
Whitfield, John 156
Whiting, Ann 109
Whiting, Eliza T. 166
Whiting, Elizabeth 140,266,283
Whiting, Elizabeth Thruston 166
Whiting, John 140
Whiting, Robert 140
Whiting, Thomas A., Colonel 166
Whiting, Thomas, Colonel 166
Whitlock, Mary 190
Whitmore, George 95
Whitmore, George A. 95
Whitney, Adelbert 0. 154,155
Whitney, Adelbert Oswell 154

Whitney, Arthur M. 154
Whitney, Clarence 155
Whitney, Maggie A. 154~55
Whitney, Maggie Oswell 154
Whitsitt, Seluda Harris 123
Wiatt, James C. 200
Wilburn, L. Oakey, Rev. 256
Wilkersan, Am Margaret 229
Wilkerson, Elizabeth 199
Wilkerson, John 199
Wilkerson, John Newman 229
Wilkerson, Maelcha 199
Wilkerson, Peggy 229
Wilkerson, W. S. 229
Wilkerson, William S. 229
Wilkins, John T. 177
Wilkins, R. A., Colonel 114
Wilkins, Richard A. 114
Wilkinson, James 132
Wilkinson, Julia Ann 132
Williams, Mary 195
Williams, Alice Kennon 117
Williams, Alice Rosely Kennon 117
Williams, Ann 265
Williams, Ann E. 100
Williams, Anna Roberta 1176
Williams, Carter N. 117
Williams, Carter Nelson 117
Williams, E. A. 117
Williams, E. K. 117
Williams, Edwin A. 117
Williams, Edwin A., Jr. 117
Williams, Edwin Anderson 117
Williams, Elizabeth 117
Williams, Elizabeth A., Mrs. 117
Williams, Frances 265
Williams, Henry Sinclair 117
Williams, I. H., Rev. 283
Williams, Isabel 256
Williams, John Garter 117
Williams, Lucy Williams Page 117
Williams, Margaret 220
Williams, Martha 265
Williams, Mollie 163
Williams, oracles E. 17
Williams, Rice 265
Williams, Roger 117
Williams, Roger Andrew 117
Williams, Rowena 258
Williams, Sallie 262
Williams, Sarah Ann 222
Williams, Thomas 117
Williams, W. 222
Williams, William James 117
Williams, William James 117
Williamson, Obedience G. 123
Williamson, Obedienoe Green Bailey 120
Williamson, Samuel, Rev. 186,187
Willianrs, Erasmus Kennan 117
Williarns, Anna Nelson 117
Williarns, Henry S. 117
Williarns, Hugh G. 257
Willis, Barbara 194
Willis, Edward Bennett 255
Willis, George Lewis 200
Willis, Laura 255
Willis, Laura Guthrie 255
Willis, Laura Isabel Guthrie 255
Willis, Lelia Goodson 255
Willis, Micajah 211
Willis, Mildred 157
Willis, Richard H. 265
Willis, William 255
Willis, William Henry 255
Wills, Ann 156
Wills, Elizabeth 216,217
Wills, Francis 226
Wills, Isabella 216
Wills, James 216
Wills, Mary 156
Wills, Mathew 216,217
Wills, Moses 156
Wills, Nancy 216
Wills, Patience 156]
Wills, Patsy 216
Willson, Aquilla 259
Willson, Hannah 259
Willson, Rebecca 259
Willson, Samuel 259
Willson, Sarah 259
Wilson, Betty 277
Wilson, Betty Washington 278
Wilson, Henrietta 277
Wilson, John E. 276,277
Wilson, John F. 277
Wilson, Lawrence W. 277
Wilson, Mary 237
Wilson, Miss 185
Wilson, Priscilla 223
Wilson, Sarah I. 277
Wilson, Susan 137,277
Wilson, Susan Chaplain 109
Wilson, William 277
Wiltby, William B. 236
Windham, Anna Lane 242
Windham, Charles L., Jr. 242
Windham, Taylor Charles 242
Winslow, Eliza Wyatt 105
Winston, Ailsey 194
Winston, Ann A. 194
Winston, Barbara 0. 194
Winston, Barbara 194
Winston, Betsey 194
Winston, Bickerton 194
Winston, Elizabeth H. 191
Winston, George 191
Winston, George 8. 194
Winston, George D. 206
Winston, George Hendree 194
Winston, James 194
Winston, John 194
Winston, John T. 194
Winston, John, Jr. 194
Winston, Jonn, Sr. 194
Winston, Joseph 194
Winston, Joseph B. 194
Winston, Maria T. 194
Winston, Martha C. 194
Winston, Mary I. 194
Winston, Nichalas I. 194
Winston, O. D. 194
Winston, Patsey 194
Winston, Reuben T. 194
Winston, Sarah A. E. 194
Winston, Thomas 194
Winston, Thomas I. 194
Winston, Thomas, Sr. 194
Winston, William 0. 194
Winston, William 194
Wirt, Bertie P. 277

Wirt, Dabney C. 275
Wise, Mary 281
Wise, Charles 281
Wise, Elizabeth 281
Wise, George 281
Wise, Henry 281
Wise, John 281
Wise, Margaret 281
Wise, Nancy 281
Wise, Nancy S. 281
Wise, Nancy Selman 281
Wise, Peggy 281
Wise, Polly 281
Wise, Solomon 281
Wise, Trefania 281
Wise, William 251
Withers, Sue Dabney 117
Withers, William 214
Witherspom, Jere, Dr. 272
Witherspoon, Edmonia 128
Witherspoon, Essra Offutt 128
Witherspoon, Ezra Offutt 128
Witherspoon, Jere, Rev. 109
Witherspoon, O. 8. 128
Witherspoon, O. H., Dr. 128
Witherspoon, Oran Haws, Dr. 128,129
Wolsey, Thomas 239
Womack, Martha 101
Wood, Abraham 224
Wood, Anne 224
Wood, Betsy 224
Wood, Gabriel 224
Wood, Jdn 224
Wood, Joseph 224
Wood, Judith 224
Wood, Levi 224
Wood, Martha 273
Wood, Mary 224
Wood, Nathaniel 224
Woodridge, John R. 274
Woods, Nancy 219
Woodson, Ann 140
Woodson, Benjamin 227
Woodson, Caroline Matilda 140
Woodson, George 140
Woodson, Jane Eliza 254
Woodson, John Royal 254
Woodson, Mary Degrafenriedt 262
Woodson, Mary J. 254
Woodson, Matthew 254
Woodson, Pauline 253,256
Woodson, Phillip Stephen 254
Woodson, Polleny E. 227
Woodson, Sarah 140
Woodson, Sarah Ann 253
Woodson, Susan 151
Woodson, Susannah 227
Woodson, Virginia 206
Woodville, Rev. Mr. 179
Wormley, Eleanor 275
Wormley, Mrs. 275
Wormley, Ralph 275
Woten, Anna 91
Woten, Bell 91
Woten, Elizabeth 91
Woten, Ellender 91
Woten, Hugh 91
Woten, Jade 91
Woten, Jam 91
Wright, Marian 115.116

Wyman, Ann 192
Yates, Susannah 280
Yerby, Gordon Girallaoe 186
Young, Daniel P., Rev. 128
Young, Jade 206
Young, Rebeceh 199
Zentmeyer, J. N. 188
Zentrneyer, M. A, Mrs. 189

Other books by Jeannette Holland Austin:

1860 Paulding County, Georgia Census

Alabama Bible Records

DeKalb County, Georgia Probate Records

*Fayette County, Georgia Probate Records: Volume II
Annual Returns, Inventories, Sales, Bonds, 1845-1897*

Georgia Bible Records, Supplement, 1772-1940

Georgia Obituaries, 1740-1935

Georgia Obituaries, 1905-1910

Jackson County, Georgia Tombstones
Jeannette Holland Austin and Dorothy Holland Herring

Masters of the Low Country: A History of the Georgia Colony

North Carolina–South Carolina Bible Records

The Georgians Database: Genealogical Notes

Virginia Bible Records

The Five Disciplines for Christians

Biblical Practices to Achieve Maturity

Elliott Cooke

WIPF & STOCK · Eugene, Oregon

THE FIVE DISCIPLINES FOR CHRISTIANS
Biblical Practices to Achieve Maturity

Copyright © 2022 Elliott Cooke. All rights reserved. Except for brief quotations in critical publications or reviews, no part of this book may be reproduced in any manner without prior written permission from the publisher. Write: Permissions, Wipf and Stock Publishers, 199 W. 8th Ave., Suite 3, Eugene, OR 97401.

Wipf & Stock
An Imprint of Wipf and Stock Publishers
199 W. 8th Ave., Suite 3
Eugene, OR 97401

www.wipfandstock.com

PAPERBACK ISBN: 978-1-6667-4839-0
HARDCOVER ISBN: 978-1-6667-4840-6
EBOOK ISBN: 978-1-6667-4841-3

10/05/22

Unless otherwise indicated, all Scripture quotations are taken from the Holy Bible, New International Version®, NIV®. Copyright © 1973, 1978, 1984, 2011 by Biblica, Inc.™ Used by permission of Zondervan. All rights reserved worldwide. www.zondervan.comThe "NIV" and "New International Version" are trademarks registered in the United States Patent and Trademark Office by Biblica, Inc.™

This work is dedicated to the glory of my awesome God, and with appreciation to my beloved wife Lynda, my family (I love you so much), the churches I have served, my schools, my professors, friends, and countless others who have impacted my life. This book would not exist if it weren't for these.

Contents

Introduction: An Overview of The Five Disciplines for Christians | ix

Section One: Fellowship
1. "It Is Not Good for Man to Be Alone" | 3
2. "You Are the Salt of the Earth" | 16
3. "Let the Children Come" | 25
4. Section Summary: Fellowship | 34

Section Two: Bible Study
5. "Study to Show Yourself Approved" | 47
6. "He Spoke as One with Authority" | 57
7. "Take the Helmet of Salvation and the Sword of the Spirit" | 65
8. Summary Section: Bible Study | 70

Section Three: Prayer
9. "Men Began to Call upon the Name of the Lord" | 79
10. A Personal Testimony to the Power of Prayer | 88
11. "Teach Us to Pray" | 97
12. Summary Section: Prayer | 104

Section Four: Ministry
13. "My Food Is to Do the Will of Him Who Sent Me" | 113
14. "My Father Is Working until Now, and I Myself Am Working" | 120
15. "God . . . Works in You" | 125
16. Summary Section: Ministry | 131

Section Five: Witnessing

17 "Always Be Prepared to Give an Answer to Everyone Who Asks" | 153
18 "If We Deny Him, He Also Will Deny Us" | 166
19 "Entrust to Reliable People Who Will Also Be Qualified to Teach Others" | 171
20 Follow-Up to Witnessing | 179

21 Closing Remarks | 191

Resources | 195
Bibliography | 199

Introduction

An Overview of The Five Disciplines for Christians

IN THIS AGE OF *easy believism* (a term used to describe the thought that there is no price to be paid to be a Christian—it is also called *cheap grace*)[1] it is time someone stood up and said, "Be careful people of faith, lest you fall!" Some religious people listen to a great preacher on the television or internet and call it "devotions" or their Church service for the week. They attend some mega-church because of the great service they have on Sunday morning and think they are in fellowship, but in truth it's little more than an hour or two to assuage their guilt. Some people of faith read a nice story followed by a Scripture verse and call it Bible study. They go shopping for their grandmother and call it their ministry. They recite the grace they learned as a child before a meal and call that praying. This is not being a mature Christian. A Christian doesn't become mute when someone asks about faith or Jesus. A Christian doesn't sit at home alone on Sundays, but they get themselves to a fellowship. Some people think they are mature in their faith, but in truth their faith is atrophying.

I am being led by the Holy Spirit to remind Christians that God calls us to maturity in Christ, especially in the Western Church, where we enjoy the greatest freedoms and prosperity unprecedented in the history of the world. How could we be so immature that we are still being spoon-fed a steady diet of strained beans and mashed bananas? We have Bibles galore

1. MacArthur, "What Is Grace."

in many different versions and formats. There are numerous churches in just about every community and in some places, they are literally on almost every street corner. These churches exist in many denominations to fit our personal theology more closely. We live in countries where many people call themselves Christian. We have resources aplenty, both physical and intangible, to aid and assist us in our spiritual growth, and yet most Christians share that they have never been discipled in the faith. They share that they don't know what to say when someone asks them what they believe about Jesus. Most Christians have not identified their spiritual gift. Many say that they don't understand what the big deal is about abortion, homosexuality, and fornication.

Not only are many Christians lacking a full measure of maturity, but they are also often lacking the desire to do anything about it. Many Christians say they can't follow too deep of a sermon. They say they don't like to read. They report they don't have time for Church or ministry, but they never miss an episode of their favorite television shows. Christians spend hours surfing the internet and yet don't have time to study the Bible. They memorize sports statistics, song lyrics, and recipes, but complain they can't memorize a Bible verse. Many adult Christians feel that they are too old to be expected to learn all that "Bible stuff," but they manage to do some pretty complex things like file taxes, invest in the stock market, install a new program on their computer, and operate their DVR.

I was an online missionary with Global Media Outreach,[2] and I received emails from new believers around the world who have shared that they did not have access to a Bible and that there was no Church near where they live. They told me stories of walking twenty miles to meet with other Christians or being disowned by their families because of their choice to follow Jesus. I've led missions trips to the Dominican Republic and Mexico where believers gather at the Church whenever possible and all day on Sunday. They don't have lyrics projected on screens, worship bands or any musical instrument, but you will not hear a more passionate song of praise sung anywhere in the world.

Thomas Bergler, in his book *The Juvenilization of American Christianity*, blamed this lack of spiritual maturity on the growing practice of putting off adulthood.[3] In psychology it is called the Peter Pan syndrome; this is where people want to remain young forever. As a result, we have a

---

2. Global Media Outreach, "Home."
3. Bergler, *Juvenilization of American Christianity*.

An Overview of The Five Disciplines for Christians xi

generation of people who have had a *failure to launch*. Older folks idolize young people by doing everything possible to appear and act younger. Young people do everything they can to keep from getting old. We now have a generation of adults addicted to video games. The reputation of men at any age is "a boy with his toys." We don't work hard at anything except play. We have postponed being responsible and prolonged the years of our reckless abandon. Our society has rejected the natural progression of humanness toward maturity and has embraced the fantasy of the inhuman as we glorify the vampire, alien, and Superman; as if maturity is something that is unattainable by mere human beings.[4]

Trevin Wax in his article *Why Millennials are Leaving the Church* said that the world is coddled by the Church instead of being convicted by it.[5] People tend to live up to expectations and if the Church lowers its expectations, you get a form of Christianity that is "Christian Lite." As Wax reminded his readers, "Christianity without a cost is Christianity without the cross. And Christianity without the cross isn't Christianity at all."[6] Western Christians need a challenge to reach out for more than an impotent faith and embrace our calling to be more. It's time to grow up and fulfill our destiny. It's time to leave the immature behind and strive toward a more mature faith.

Christianity is at a crossroads. Will we continue to be a leading force, raising up a generation of mature believers who inspire the world to follow Christ, or will we believe matters of faith are relegated to our private lives only? What will steer the course of the Church toward spiritual maturity is a revival of spiritual discipline. Christians around the world will need to get back to spiritual basics. Those people called by God's name need to turn, humble themselves, and pray. Unfortunately, Christians don't know what they are turning from or turning to. Today's believers will not submit to any authority including God. They just don't know how to pray anymore. Wake up Christians! We've gotten fat, lazy, and undisciplined.

We must relearn what it means to be spiritually disciplined and mature. In fact, most people, even the ones reading this and agreeing with what I am writing, don't even know what the Christian's disciplines are. They are recounted in both the Old and New Testaments repeatedly.

4. Bergler, *Juvenilization of American Christianity* (Speech at Regent University).
5. Wax, "Why Millennials are Leaving the Church," 3.
6. Wax, "Why Millennials are Leaving the Church," 3.

An honest search of the Bible will uncover these giant themes which the Bible teaches are imperative for spiritual growth. There are five of them, but without looking at the table of contents of this book (which you just read three minutes ago) can you name them? Are you guessing or do you know? Could you teach them to someone else? If you are a mature Christian, you know them because you use them many times each day and have done so for years. You have taught them to your family members, to Church groups, and to individuals you have mentored. Others have listed more than five spiritual disciplines. Some may use different terminology, but in essence, when all is boiled down it comes to these five disciplines: fellowship, Bible study, prayer, ministry, and witnessing.

Others might ask where are the disciplines of love, patience, kindness, and the like? Well, those are the fruit of the Spirit. They are something the Holy Spirit produces in the mature Christian. They are not something you can muster up by sheer will and practice. They are not ingrained by repetition; they are produced by God in the lives of those fully surrendered to him. So, if you want to have God's love, mercy, forgiveness, etc., grow to maturity through practicing these five disciplines. Others will ask, where are worship, discipleship, fasting, and such? Well, worship is encompassed in the five disciplines as it involves an attitude of prayer, often practiced in fellowship with others (at Church), and may even have elements of ministry (as in a spiritual service of worship). Discipling happens in the context of fellowship and Bible study. Fasting is a special form of prayer. So, as you will read, I have boiled down what others list as ten or twelve disciplines to the primary five disciplines.

These are the five linchpins of the mature Christian. When one comes to faith in Christ, God uses these five things to grow one to a certain level of maturity in Christ. Just as a plant needs sunlight, water, and nutrients or a gasoline engine needs spark, fuel, and oxygen, Christians have spiritual needs. That's right, I said needs. These five spiritual disciplines are not optional, they are necessities. Without them one will not grow, one will die (spiritually speaking). Without these disciplines there is no strength or drive in our spiritual life. You might think that because you attend a worship service on Sunday morning, say grace at mealtimes, and read a verse a day that you are a mature and growing Christian, but there is so much more. Have you ever wondered why there is no power in your prayer life? Ever wonder why your witness isn't more effective? Ever wonder why you have difficulty understanding the mysteries of the faith? There is a whole other level of maturity or understanding that you have not reached, and in truth, just when you think you have achieved a certain level of growth, the Lord will open your eyes to yet another level yet to be attained. It never ends, at least in this life.

Some of you might think that if you have some of these spiritual disciplines you will have at least some measure of growth or maturity, but the truth is it takes all five disciplines not just tons of one or even lots of two, three, or even four of these disciplines. You can give a plant water and fertilizer but without sunlight it will die. If it receives sunlight and water but not any nutrients it will eventually die. If you provide an engine with gas and spark but deny it oxygen it will not run. If you pump gas and oxygen into an engine, but there is no spark it will not turn over. Imagine an automobile with one, two or three of its wheels missing, you would not expect to go anywhere in such a vehicle. So, it is with the Christian. We need to have all five disciplines in our lives to function as we were designed.

Many people don't care to grow to Christian maturity. They think, "I'm a Christian. I'm going to heaven. I don't want to live God's way. I'm very satisfied living life my way." Such thoughts are not from God, but just might be from our spiritual enemies. People with such thoughts just might be enemies of God themselves, thinking they have true faith when they don't. A desire to grow into the image of Christ is proof of genuine faith. Growing in your faith benefits God's kingdom, your community, and your family. There's just too much at risk to have such a nonchalant attitude toward our spiritual maturity.

Each section of this book focuses on one of these disciplines. Since they are all necessary, I suggest you read them all, even the disciplines you think you have a handle on, because you may learn something crucial to your spiritual growth and maturity. I do not believe that they need to be read in a certain order, and perhaps it is best to start with the section that focuses on the discipline you struggle with the most and move on from there. Each section will have chapters devoted to different aspects of a discipline, which were inspired by certain verses or stories from the Bible. Those truths you understand already, read carefully to reinforce what you already know and those things which sound new, strange, or confusing read twice. Then attempt to put these truths into practice. The last chapter in each section is designed to help you do just that. It will contain practical insights into the discipline as you seek to implement them in your lives.

My prayer is that you will grow, mature, and share these truths with others and in so doing spark the last great revival before the coming of our precious Lord.

> "He is the one we proclaim, admonishing and teaching everyone with all wisdom, so that we may present everyone fully mature in Christ" (Col 1:28, NIV).

Section One

Fellowship

Chapter 1

"It Is Not Good for Man to Be Alone"
—GENESIS 2:18

WHEN ONE IS ALONE it is rarely good, but even when there are two together it isn't always healthy. Even when we have that special someone, we can still be lonely because we don't have that all-important number one relationship filled in our lives, and I'm not talking about a mate. I'm talking about your relationship with God.

God created man to love and serve Him. When we deny ourselves a relationship with Him, we walk around with a hole in our heart, and we truly are alone. How does one have a relationship with God? Believe that God sent His only Son, Jesus the Christ, to die on the cross to pay the penalty of your sin. Pray to Him and ask for forgiveness and that will initiate the beginning of a beautiful friendship that will bloom and blossom into something that will never wilt or die. Turning to God in this way is fulfilling your purpose. It satisfies that need to relate to our Creator.

God is supreme. There is no one like Him. He is the only wise and true God. God knew of the potential for loneliness humans would face, being the only one of their kind. God, the great cosmic ruler of the universe, created angels, the world, and mankind, as more than mere objects for play; He created them out of a desire for interaction. And God did not want robots that would have no choice but to obey Him, so He gave us free will. With that free will both the angels and humans stumbled in their relationship with God. A third of the angels rebelled from God and left their heavenly standing to become God's enemies, but two thirds of the heavenly host decided to stay in a right relationship with God.

Like the fallen angels, mankind also turned away from God and sinned against Him by willfully disobeying Him, but unlike those fallen angels, God would devise a plan that would offer humans the opportunity of a right relationship with God. The angels who did not fall would have a relationship with God, but only humans, who took advantage of this salvation, would have a special invested relationship with God. God gave His one and only Son to save humans, and any of them who would embrace the good news of the gospel would enjoy an undying gratitude and love for their Savior. This would make for the best kind of relationship, not one forged out of God's decree, but one that would be birthed of God's mercy, forgiveness, and love.

God understands what it is like to be alone. When Jesus was preparing for His anguishing crucifixion, He was alone in a garden (just like Adam). He didn't like being alone so He called Peter, James and John to draw a little closer so He wouldn't feel abandoned (but they all passed out and fell asleep leaving their Lord all alone again and again). When He was arrested all His disciples ran away to leave Jesus surrounded by His enemies. Even from the cross Jesus cries out, "My God, My God, why have you forsaken Me?" (Matt 27:46). So, God understands loneliness and had a plan to combat it.

When God created man He said, "It is not good for man to be alone" (Gen 2:18). But man was not alone, he had God. Adam had that all-important relationship with God. He had fellowship with God Himself. What Adam was missing was a relationship with someone like himself. So, God had all the animals come before the man but there was not a suitable helper found among them (Gen 2:20). He was the only one of his kind. Even the animals existed in pairs and groups which included male and female. Adam needed someone like he was. He was the pinnacle of creation. Adam walked around the garden and enjoyed rock star status. One might naturally ask, "Wasn't fellowship with God enough for Adam?" Though humans were made in God's likeness, God is wholly other. Man is not like God (as the devil suggested they would become). Adam was the only one of his kind and hence he was all alone. God alone does indeed satisfy all of our desires and needs, but God chooses to do this through others. It was all part of His larger plan for man.

Technically Adam was not alone, and neither was Jesus in the garden or on the cross, but such technicalities don't provide for God's perfect plan for man. Adam needed fellowship with God and others like him. His relationship with God would fulfill Him, but his fellowship with others would teach him very special lessons. God knew that because Adam was supreme amongst all of creation that he would think of himself as better than everything else. It's lonely at the top. God understands this all too well. God did not want Adam to be tempted to think that he was so perfect and special that he would consider himself God's equal. This was the temptation the fallen angels did not withstand, pride. God would not let this happen a second time.

To complete the task of raising up a people for Himself, God humbled Adam by giving him a wife (hey guys, no jokes here) and allowing them to sin. God would then set a plan in motion to bring humans back into a proper relationship with Himself. There would be a second Adam who would come from the offspring of man and woman, who would be God Himself, and He would lay down His life for all humanity. Those who believed and trusted in this Christ would be raised up out of their sinful ruined state to be, as it were, born again eventually achieving a state of perfection. Only through our being saved from our fallen broken sinful selves would we become truly perfect and ready to serve God for all eternity with a love and passion unknown by the angels.

When God made Adam, he intended to make an entire race of humans who would love and serve Him. For this to happen God had to make woman. God used a rib from Adam to form the woman. He did not use dust as He did with Adam. As Thomas Aquinas famously taught, God used the rib, not the foot or the head.[1] This was to signify that Eve would be a coequal with Adam, not someone in submission to be walked on by him or a tyrant to rule over him. She was taken from a rib close to his heart to show the affection they would share. Eve was taken from a rib under Adam's arm to symbolize the protective tendencies he would have toward her. She would walk alongside him, not under, over, behind, or ahead of him. They had more than a likeness with each other—there were important differences too. These differences would ensure a special interest and attraction toward each other. In addition, they would share a oneness and unity that would ensure the propagation of the species bringing great joy and happiness in their special relationship.

Adam could not produce progeny by himself. He needed a wife to procreate and propagate the species. Adam would be the first of many. It was not good that man be alone. According to God's plan, humans should exist within a multitude of mankind. This multitude of humanity would build community, society, culture and eventually civilization.

---

1. Aquinas, *Summa Theologica*, I.I:468.

Together we have a synergy which allows us to accomplish so much more than we could on our own. Adam could not do this alone, he needed others. God's plan was that Adam "be fruitful and increase in number" (Gen 1:28), filling the earth and subduing it. This was one command man was all too pleased to obey. As a result, nations were born so God might redeem a multitude for Himself from a diversity of people.

It is interesting to note that Adam was alone at one point, and it was declared not good. God made Eve and no one would ever be alone again. It was not Adam's singleness that God saw as "not good." God said it was not good for man to be *alone*, not *unmarried*. Marriage is not the solution for everyone's loneliness, it was the solution for Adam. It's okay to be an unmarried individual among the rest of humanity because a single human is not alone. Marriage is not for everyone. Jesus was single, but He lived in community with brothers and sisters, and He invited all people to follow after Him. This is God's plan that we live together in harmony and unity under God, loving and obeying Him. And the second part of His plan was that we love and forgive each other. This is the great commandment, to love God and others, and on this commandment all other laws and plans for man depend.

Adam and Eve were supposed to have a symbiotic relationship that was mutually edifying. Their purpose was to build each other up, but instead they fell from God's graces by falling for a delusion. Cain and Abel were supposed to help each other through thick and thin, but instead Cain in a fit of jealousy killed Abel. Jacob and Esau were supposed to work together to promote God's plan of blessing the earth through their family, yet they struggled over birthrights and subsequent blessings. Jealousy caused Joseph's brothers to sell him into slavery and they would have missed out on salvation if it were not for the forgiveness of Joseph. Saul and David were supposed to lead the nation of Israel in righteousness, but Saul saw his loyal servant David as a threat and strived to kill him.

You see, sin is in our spiritual DNA. We reject God's plans and laws for us. We were meant to live in fellowship with our brothers and sisters in Christ, but instead of being a family we bail out on them and shun the fellowship because of our thin skin and our lack of forgiveness. We refuse to live together in harmony. And now today there are a huge number of Christians sitting at home refusing to be part of God's plan for man, which is being part of the Church, God's holy bride. (Please note the capitalization of the word Church. This is an important distinction in understanding the rest of this chapter. Church with a capital C refers to all Christians everywhere while church with a small c refers to a local group of Christians.)

Why do we reject God's plan for help? We all need that support network around us to care and nurture us. We have doctors, teachers, lawyers, farmers, and family, but what about people who will meet our spiritual needs? Prayer and Scripture reading have been removed from the public arena. Where does the Christian turn to be spiritually encouraged? If Christians don't turn to other Christians for fellowship, instruction, and support they won't get it anywhere else. God's plan is for man to love and enjoy Him forever and He has given us other humans to remind us of this. We serve as reminders and examples for each other. Without each other we just may forget to turn to God and start trusting in ourselves.

God didn't just make a companion for Adam, someone just like Adam. God made him a woman. Men and women are not like each other, there are important differences. In many ways they were opposites, and these opposites attract each other and compliment each other. God didn't create us as sexual beings just for the pleasure of it; He gave us the ability to procreate. He wanted man to have many like him; He wanted man to live in community. God made sex pleasurable just to make sure mankind would give birth to others so they would not be alone. God made Eve for Adam not so he would simply have a companion, but because God wanted a nation of humans living together. Think about it, God could have made Steve instead of Eve. Then man wouldn't be alone, he would have a helpmate, but God didn't do that. He made a companion that could compliment the man, one that could help him procreate. God wanted man in fellowship with many not just a few. In numbers there is strength.

God blessed mankind with men and women. Adam would have both sexes involved in his life. He would have someone to hunt with and someone to dress his wounds (I know this might sound sexist, but I didn't assign either sex to either role, you just assumed I did). There would be a plethora of people to relate to and as iron sharpens iron so one person sharpens another (Prov 27:17). If you want a keen (sharp) edge you must have many irons sharpening you and you them. Each one having their own gifts and talents so they could rub off on each other and a synergy would result. How boring would it be if we were alike? Look at all the beautiful relationships God gave us, husband and wife, mother and son, father and daughter, sister and brother, boyfriend and girlfriend, best friends, teacher and pupil, and thousands more. Each of these relationships teaches us something about God. From the variety and diversity of these relationships comes the unity and harmony God designed as part of His plan for man.

No man is an island to himself. Life takes a team effort. You wouldn't even exist if it were not for your mother and father. Civilization takes people working together using their expertise and experience to benefit the whole of society, each one doing their part to contribute. For us to reach our highest potential we must live together with others. No creation or work of a single human is truly the work of themselves; it is the culmination of all the people involved in that one individual's life. We stand on the shoulders of those who have gone before us, and we can't truly accomplish anything by ourselves. When one is separated from the collective, one merely ekes out an existence. On our own we revert to a baser animalistic existence, but when we are in community, we have a greater chance to live life abundantly.

God created man for fellowship. Man was not a toy that God put on a shelf, nor did He leave man in his package. God unwrapped man and plays with him. We bring God great pleasure when we interact with Him. This relationship with God is the sole purpose of man. God wants us to love Him and enjoy Him forever. When a man rejects this truth, he rejects God. When man rejects God, he is not functioning as God desires. He is broken and can not live up to the potential God has for him. A train may think that jumping the tracks and taking off on its own is true freedom. It can reject the narrow course set out by the tracks as limiting its potential, but the moment it jumps from the tracks it becomes stuck and unable to move. Only by staying on the tracks is the train free to travel the entire country and truly be free. As it is with the train, so it is with man. Apart from God we can do nothing (John 15:5)!

At this point I would be remiss if I did not offer hope for those readers convicted of their need to make things right with God. If you have jumped the track of your relationship with God, you can get right back on course by asking Him to place you on the right track. Just as the train cannot lift (or even steer) itself back on the tracks, so you cannot get right with God by yourself. You must be lifted out of your situation. Each of us has turned to his own way. We all have sinned and fall short of God's design. Each of us find ourselves so easily entangled in disobedience and it is only God, because of His love for us, who can set our feet on the right path once again. God became a man in the person of Jesus to show us the way to live and then He gave His life to pay the penalty for our wrong doings. You see someone must pay for the train to be placed back on its tracks. Are you that train? Have you messed things up between you and God? Have you hurt others? God can make all things right again.

If you are convinced this is your need, pray to God right now. Say something like:

> God, I've gotten off track with You. I have rejected You and Your ways. I've made a mess of things and I need Your help. I am sorry. I need You to forgive me and make things right between us again. I want to accomplish Your plan for my life, but I'll need Your help. I believe Jesus paid the price for me to be picked up, cleaned off, and placed on the right track again. I can't do this by myself, please help me. I need You. I love You. In Jesus' name I pray, Amen.

Nothing pleases God more than when you pray such a prayer of sincere repentance. Know this, that God loves to forgive you and He will do His part to accomplish His plans for you. He will come by your side and help you time and time again. He desires a relationship with you, and He has placed others around you to help you too. Don't reject that help. Turn to other Christians. Find a fellowship of believers who will encourage your relationship with God.

Getting right with God and staying right with Him will help us fulfill God's purpose for us. He has chosen to use others to remind us of this. In fact, this link between our love for God and others is so important that Jesus taught that the great commandment, to love God, was linked to loving others. After all, mankind was made in God's image, so when we love others, in a sense, we love God. Loving those whose lives are in right relationship with God is especially pleasing to God. Ephesians 2:19 tells us that, "Consequently, you are no longer foreigners and aliens, but fellow citizens with God's people and members of God's household." This is why we are to do good, especially to those who belong to the family of believers (Gal 6:10).

God loved us so much that He sent His one and only Son, Jesus. I tell my congregation that God would rather die than live without us. God gave us this example; He came to us. He did not wait for us to come to Him. In fact, the Scriptures tell us that He came while we were still sinners, while we were still His enemies. If this is God's example, then we should do likewise. We should go to others and love them, even if they offend us or are our enemies. Man was created for fellowship and is desperately seeking somebody to love and someone who will love them unconditionally. If we want to be loved unconditionally then why do we place conditions on those we love? Why are we so quick to take offense and so unwilling to forgive? Why do we shun God's gift of fellowship with other Christians by rejecting God's Church? If we will embrace and love the fellowship of believers, then perhaps many of them will embrace and love us. If we reject them (who were made in God's image and who are closest to Him) what is to keep God from rejecting us? Jesus gave us the standard in the Lord's Prayer when He said, "forgive us our debts, as we also have forgiven our debtors" (Matt 6:12). Those are frightening words. How would you like to be judged by the same standard you judge others? When we choose to love others, especially those who might be hard to love, then we are being like our heavenly Father and pleasing Him. Against such behavior there is no judgment.

Most people are familiar with the story of Cain and Abel. They both made a sacrifice to God, but God esteemed Abel's sacrifice more than Cain's. Cain was so angry that he killed his brother. When God asked him where his brother was, he replied, "Am I my brother's keeper?" (Gen 4:9). Well, the long and short of it is that yes, we are our brother's keeper. Cain should have loved his brother and followed his example instead of becoming insanely jealous and killing him. In the New Testament Jesus taught us to love our neighbors. A man asked Him, "Who is my neighbor?" (Luke 10:29). Jesus responded by telling a story of a man who is attacked and an enemy of his came along and found him. Instead of passing him by, like others were doing, an enemy stopped and cared for the man. Who was being the good neighbor? The enemy Samaritan was being a good neighbor (hence the term Good Samaritan). Go and do likewise was the command. You see both the Old and New Testaments teach us to love each other and to be there for each other. It doesn't matter if the person is in your family or even if he's your enemy, you are to love each other.

There is a spiritual principle here. How you treat others is how you will be treated. Whatever a man sows that shall he also reap (Gal 6:7). What goes around comes around. If you care for others, then someone will be there to care for you. If you are part of someone's support network, then most likely they will be part of yours. We all need a support network of people in our lives to be examples to us, to tell us when we are wrong, to bandage our wounds when we've been attacked, and to help us in our time of need. It's therapeutic to have people we can trust to whom we can ask questions and vent our frustrations. We all need people, who will listen to us, put up with us, comfort and remind us that there is a God in Heaven who loves us and forgives sin. Likewise, we need to be those things for others. This is a mutual reciprocity. It is our duty, our responsibility, and God will hold us responsible. This is God's plan to keep us and preserve us. If you obey this spiritual principle (generally speaking) you will live long and prosper, if not then you can't expect God's blessing upon your life.

This is why being in fellowship with other Christians is a spiritual discipline. Without it we can't please God. Without it we shouldn't expect God's blessing. We will not grow as a Christian if we hate other Christians and ignore God's provision. So, brother (or sister), where art thou? Why are you not active in a local church? How is it that you think that watching a preacher on a screen is as good as (or better than) going to church? How can a Christian hate other Christians? How can you ignore God's commands? O, brother, how art thou? Are you feeling like your prayers bounce off the ceiling? Do you have questions for which you don't know the answers? Are you lonely, lost and confused? Then get yourself to church! What are you waiting for? It's like having a well-stocked kitchen but sitting at the table starving to death. Sure, sometimes when I open the refrigerator the cheese has gone moldy or the milk has spoiled, but I don't stop going there to get something to eat. That would be foolishness. In fact, the more I go to the refrigerator and eat of its contents then things inside don't perish because I make sure they don't by eating them before they spoil.

In every family there is bound to be jealousy, anger, and strife and this is true for the church family as well. The Church is made up of people. People are sinners. Therefore, the Church is made up of sinners. Whether or not you attend a church, both you and the people in it are still sinners. The only difference is that they have each other and you have only one or two people on whom you can count. In your home your family has squabbles, but you chose to stay and work things out. You forgive each other and continue living together. After all blood is thicker than water and you stick together. Well, if blood is thicker than water, then Jesus' blood should be like crazy glue. Nothing should be able to separate us from this love of God that is in Christ Jesus and in our fellow Christians. Jesus prayed for us Christians just before He left this world that we might be one, even as the Father and the Son are one (John 17:11). He taught that the whole world would know that we were Christians if we had love for each other. Well, no wonder why the Church is impotent and dying, Christians who could make a difference are sitting on the sidelines refusing to obey God. They reject each other and in doing so reject God

Himself. The body of Christ has lost its feet and hands because some will not go to church and play their part.

Earlier on I led you in a prayer of repentance, perhaps this is a good time to lead you who might be feeling convicted again in another prayer. The first step back to a vibrant spiritual life just might be confessing your lax ways toward fellowship and asking God to give you and your family a spiritual family and a spiritual home. Say something like,

> Dear God, I know I have been neglecting to feed my soul with fellowship. I ask You to help me. You know all my reasons for not going to church. You know all my excuses and you know all that I need. Please forgive me for my lack of faithfulness and restore me into fellowship. Lead me to the right church of Your choosing where You can minister to me, and I might be able to minister for You. In Jesus' name I pray, Amen.

I don't know where I would be if it were not for the Church. My job took me away from family and friends. Our support network instantly became my wife and me. Sure, we found a new doctor, had new coworkers, and made new friends, but we lost our entire extended family and many of our closest friends. At church we found people who loved us, and they became grandparents, aunts, and uncles to our children. These dear ones became my brothers, sisters, mother, and father. It reminds me of when Jesus said of his disciples gathered around Him, "Here are my mother and brothers" (Matt 12:49). I don't know how people make it through life without a good church. The church teaches us to care, share, and to fight fair. I love my church and will do whatever I can to promote and protect it.

One Old Testament story that has mass appeal is the story of Noah's ark. Proving that the remains of the ark are on Mount Ararat has occupied archaeologists for centuries. Historians cite the fact that many civilizations around the world have their own version of the famous biblical account. Theologians have told us that the ark is a "type" of Christ. They say it represents Jesus and that only in Christ there is salvation. I would rather liken the ark to the Church. I don't believe that attending a church saves anyone, but I do believe that it is God's appointed vehicle to save people. The ark didn't save Noah and his family, God did. God used the ark as His way of doing so. God saves us through the blood of Christ, but it is the Church (all Christians, the body of Christ-not a building or a denomination) that God uses to share the gospel with others so they can be saved from the consequences of their sins. Church doesn't save people. Church attendance will not gain anyone entrance into heaven, but it is a place where the nonbeliever will hear the good news of forgiveness of sins through faith in Jesus' shed blood. Hence church is a saving place, just like the ark (and your big box store).

We are told in Genesis 7:23 that they were all safe in the ark. If you were outside the ark, you were swept away in the flood, but in the ark, you were warm, safe and dry. God didn't have Noah build a fleet of ships for each of his family members. Noah was instructed to build one ark for all. If there were many ships the chance of survival would have been better. If there were more boats the chances that one of them would survive would go up. It was a huge gamble to only build one ship. It was placing all the proverbial eggs in one basket. One rock, one rogue wave, one mishap, and they were all lost. But that was God's plan, that they weather the storm *together*. The Church is the ark, and the fellowship is the family.

Someone will ask why there is not just one type of church like there was one ark? Since it is impossible for the Church to all meet in one place, the Church of God is split into many little fellowships and groups of churches called denominations. By meeting in various groups in a variety of locations everyone has the opportunity for fellowship. Each individual church is a microcosm of the Church universal. They are meant by God to be vehicles of salvation. Places one can go to have their questions answered and have the truth proclaimed. They are meant to be safe havens in the storm of life. They serve as hospitals of hope and healing. They are supposed to be beacons of absolute truth in a world of subjective opinions. Unfortunately, not all churches are these things. Some churches, and even entire denominations, have lost perspective. They have drifted into the storm of relativism and have forgotten the truth. Others are places of discord and strife. People have their experiences and most of us have heard horrible stories of dysfunctional churches, but just because problem churches exist, this does not exclude the fact that there are still some great churches out there. You wouldn't stop going to the doctor's just because you heard a story about a doctor who amputated the wrong leg. You might choose to not go to that doctor and find another, but you would still desire medical care. You wouldn't stop going out to eat just because one meal at one restaurant was not as you expected. There might be a church in town that no longer preaches the gospel or maybe there is one where you were hurt by an uncaring person, but those are not good reasons to abandon attending church. Church is God's ark for today. Don't try to tread water in the storms of life. You will go down into the depths like so many others. The church can be your life raft of safety.

Ecclesiastes tells us that when one is alone, he can be overpowered, but when two are together they can defend themselves. There is safety in numbers. The lone Christian is indeed vulnerable. We are like sheep in the midst of wolves in sheep's clothing. Christians are being scattered by the opposition. Once we are separated Satan hunts us down for the kill. Satan may not be able to take away our salvation, but he does the next best thing, he sidelines us. He isolates us and causes us to cower in our corner. Satan silences us from sharing the reason why we have this hope within us. When we are alone, we forget that we have a sure and certain hope, that we are children of the King, and that we shall reign with Christ for all eternity. When separated from the Church we are not being encouraged and reminded of the things of the faith. We become impotent and mute. Christians are neglecting the gathering of themselves together and this allows Satan to take so many good people down to hell with him.

Until the day of the flood, people thought Noah was crazy. There he was miles from any water and he's building an ocean liner. He built the ark for years. Imagine the ridicule he had to endure. Picture Noah's sons in the marketplace trying to purchase more gopher wood. In the same way the world looks at the Christian as crazy to go to church. Church, in their mindset, is a dead and archaic institution which has long outlived its usefulness. Church is a place where you sit on sixteenth-century furniture, sing seventeenth-century music, accompanied by an eighteenth-century instrument, and hang out with nineteenth-century-minded people. "Why would any intelligent person waste their time with such nonsense?" Even as you read this you might be tempted to hide the cover of this book lest anyone find you reading such "dribble." As it was for Noah before the flood, so it is for Christians today. But the floods are indeed coming. The waters will rise. Trouble will overtake those not spiritually prepared. Economic hardships will come, illnesses will take hold, and death will visit all of us, and what will those without a spiritual support network do? They will hope that there is a God. These will hope that they have lived good enough to merit His favor. They will pray that there is a heaven. Those without faith will die in fear and doubt. Not so the Christian steeped in fellowship. The Christian in fellowship will be strengthened and reminded of the promises of God. They will experience the peace of God which passes understanding and the joy of the Lord.

The Christian who is being encouraged in a fellowship will have a definite hope that their Father in heaven will deliver them.

You see, all who entered the ark were safe while all others perished (Gen 7:23). Even the dumb animals knew to gather at the appointed place at the appointed time. Sure, this made the ark a smelly zoo of a place, but I'd rather a year in a zoo than take my chances treading water. At church you might have to put up with some awfully strange people and maybe some of them smell pretty bad too, but I'd rather be safe than sorry. The nice thing about the church in most Western countries is that you don't have to hunt to find one. There is a good bible teaching church within a short drive from your house. I bet they meet on Sunday morning around ten or eleven o'clock in the morning. Going to church is like falling off a log, it's easy. I once had a guy who was new to our church come up to me and share that he started coming because we offered a new 9 a.m. service, which fit into his schedule. But now after attending church for six months he shared that church was the reason for the day and that he would come no matter what time it was offered. Even his recent illness could not keep him away. Our church had become his spiritual family. We had become an important part of his support network. He had a huge extended family that he looked forward to seeing each week. My prayer for him was that he would continue to grow in grace and find himself interacting with his new Christian brothers and sisters each week. After all, seven days without fellowship makes one weak (pun intended).

Chapter 2

"You Are the Salt of the Earth"
—MATTHEW 5:13

THERE IS A STRANGE story in Genesis 19 about Abraham bartering with God for the souls of others. God and Abraham were overlooking wicked Sodom and Gomorrah and God told him that He was going to destroy those cities and all who dwelt there. Abraham, perhaps fearing for his nephew Lot and other innocent people living there, negotiated a peace treaty. He asked if God would still destroy the cities if there were fifty righteous people living there. God conceded that for the sake of fifty He would spare the cities. Abraham then asked, what if there were only five less than fifty, would God destroy them all if there were only five less. God said for forty-five He would spare the cities. Abraham got God all the way down to ten righteous people and God agreed to spare them all if ten righteous people could be found. Too bad Abraham didn't go down to one. God showed mercy on Lot and his family, but He did destroy those two cities and all living there.

We are told by Jesus in Matthew 5:13 that we are the salt of the earth. Salt has several important properties. First, salt adds flavor to food. Second, as anyone living in a cold climate knows, it melts ice. And third it is used to cure and preserve things. Dear Christian, you and I are to add flavor to our communities. We are supposed to bring out the best in others and help them see God more clearly. God uses us to melt the cold hearts of many by warming them up to the gospel by winning them over with how we live our lives. God does not judge the world yet because we are still in it. The only reason God has not destroyed this world is because

He loves us. And so, the sun shines on both the just and the unjust. But with how few will God continue to show mercy to the masses? Will God spare your community if only fifty righteous can be found? What if less than ten are found? Do you really want to find out? Don't lose your saltiness and become useless. Be the salt your world desperately needs.

Your church is the community's saltshaker. Have you ever gone to salt your food and shook the shaker over your corn on the cob dripping with butter, but no salt came out? How disappointing that is. Your hands all messy with butter, you decide you can't fill the shaker, and you eat the corn unsalted. It doesn't taste as good, but you're not going to wash your hands, get the sea salt from the cupboard, fill the shaker, and then pour the salt on your now cold corn. For salt to be useful it must be ready and in its proper place, the saltshaker. Our communities need salt, but when they turn to the saltshakers, are they full and ready or are they near empty with all the salt clumped together? It's not the saltshaker's fault. As salt belongs in a shaker so Christians belong in a church.

A little salt goes a long way. Have you ever gone to use the saltshaker on your crispy French fries and the top came off the shaker pouring the entire contents on your meal? I was in youth ministry for over twenty years, so I've seen this too many times to recount. The meal is ruined. No matter how hard you try to scrape off the excess, it's just too salty. Some people only need a little bit of salt not the entire shaker full. How much salt people like or need is based on the individual. Some saltshakers are huge and have large hole to allow the salt to pour out freely with little effort while other shakers are small with tiny holes, and you have to shake violently for a minute just to get enough to taste it on your food. Each have their place and are used by different individuals at different times and for different reasons. So, it is with the Church today. Churches exist in various sizes and shapes. They have different doctrines and various degrees of liturgies. Some will say, "That's why I don't go to church, it's fractured and disjointed. It's not being what God intends, the unified body of Christ." To which I reply, no, it is exactly being the unified body of Christ. You see a body is not made up of all one part. Imagine if the whole body were made up of eyes or were one big eye. How would it get around without legs and feet? How would the body hear anything without ears or feed itself without a mouth? God has so apportioned the body, His Church, with great variety so together we might function in harmony while each one does their part receiving direction from the head, Christ Jesus.

There are so many different denominations and styles of worship out there; you're bound to find one that suits you. Some people like crowds, others hate them. Well, you've got mega churches and small churches. Bigger is not always better. Each has its advantages and disadvantages. It's a matter of personal preference. Some people like to hang out with people just like them and others like diversity. You can find these in churches too. Some people like a low liturgy and a contemporary feel to a church, while others do not. The point is there's a church out there for you.

If your church is not all it should be, see what God has called you to do about it. Don't just leave looking for the perfect church, it doesn't exist. Churches are made up of fallen people. The moment you join a perfect church it ceases to be perfect, but that doesn't mean we shouldn't strive to make it the best it can be. After you've given it your best (a fair shake if you will) and tried to work to make it better and you are still disappointed, then find another church. Don't just leave Church altogether. Don't let one bad apple of an experience spoil the whole bunch of opportunities facing you.

People like to play "if" games, especially when it comes to church. They say, if only the church would meet earlier or later in the day then I would go. If they didn't play that loud music . . . If they were closer to my house . . . If they were more friendly . . . If they were less judgmental . . . If they were less hypocritical . . . The game goes on and on. It's excuse after excuse. Of course, not everyone in the church is judgmental. One person one time offended them, and they hold it against everyone. I've heard loud music played with hymns as the organ blasted fillings loose and I've heard contemporary songs played so softly you could barely hear them. I've seen people commute an hour each way to their church of choice and they will tell you it is so worth it and I've seen people too lazy to walk next door. It all comes down to priorities and obedience. Will you make fellowship a priority?

My wife is fond of saying there are two different types of people who come to church. The first type is the "Here I am" person. This person comes and waits for people to come and greet them. They expect others to make them feel comfortable. They expect others to invite them to various programs and ministries. They believe church exists for them and that it is the church's job to meet their needs. Such people suck a church dry. They take and take and never seem to give back. People try to meet their needs, but in truth they can never meet all of them leaving both the "Here I am" person and the parishioner incredibly frustrated. The other type of person is the "There you are" person. This type of person walks through the doors of the church walks over to someone and says, "Hello, my name is . . ." They don't wait for others to make them feel welcome. They already feel welcome because this is their Father's house after all. God alone is asked to meet their needs and they look to be used of God to meet other people's needs. They are quickly assimilated and endear themselves to many in a relatively brief period. Which are you, a "Here I am" person or a "There you are" person? All it takes is for you to flip the switch in your head that takes yourself out of the center of the world and put Jesus there.

The influence a church can have on a life is amazing if one is open to it. When you see a bunch of "There you are" people it is exciting and contagious. I wish all churches were filled with such people, but sadly this is not the case. The Church does not exist for us, we are the Church, and we exist for God. God asks us to live a life poured out for others and not ourselves. Sure, there are times when we ask for help because we have needs, however, for some people this is their default mode. Only God can change such a life. When you see a Christian acting like a "Here I am" person, it is because they are immature in their walk with the Lord, and they need the five disciplines in their lives. If you're attending a church, but not growing, perhaps you need to evaluate the level of commitment you have to each of the five disciplines.

I have decided to start this book with this section on fellowship because it is the only spiritual discipline that can involved all five disciplines at the same time. You see when you attend a fellowship of Christians there's more than just coffee and refreshments. Most often, there is also prayer, Bible study, witnessing and ministry in addition to fellowship. So, you get five for one. What a deal! So why are you still sitting at home alone? Why aren't you sharing this book with everyone you know? We need revival and you are vital to that revival. If revival doesn't start inside the Church, then it won't happen outside the Church. We Christians will be held accountable to God for what we did and didn't do. What will you say to God when He asks for an explanation?

God told Pharaoh, "Let My people go!" (Exod 5:1). God told Pharaoh, through Moses, to let the Hebrews go into the wilderness so they might worship Him there. Pharaoh's heart was hardened, and he would not let them go till God wore him down with ten nasty plagues. Then finally Pharaoh let them go. God still cries out today, "Let My people go" except now He wants us to go to church where we can worship together!

Who or what is your Pharaoh holding you back from obeying God? What is hindering you? What is hindering others around you? Share this message with them and maybe they will make a commitment to fellowship in a good Bible teaching church. You just may spark a revival. Start a small group book study with Christians not involved in a church and use this book. You'll have some interesting discussions, and you just may help them grow to a whole new level of maturity. Maybe all they need is a little truth to encourage them.

What are some of the hindrances that keep people from attending church? I'm a pastor so I've heard most of them. "It's my only day to sleep in." "Sunday is the only time I have to get things done around the house." "I used to go to church, but it didn't work for me." "I'll never go back there, I've never been so hurt before, and these were supposed to be my brothers and sisters." "The kids have sports and I've got to take them." "I'm divorced and I don't feel welcomed there anymore." "My husband won't let me go, and he says church is a crutch for wimps." "I'm in a wheelchair and they don't have ramps." "I can't get my kids interested." "I lost my faith a long time ago and I don't care anymore." "God loves everyone, even if they don't go to church." "It's not like going to church will get me into Heaven." When they say these things, they're really saying they have been hurt or are too lethargic to make the effort.

Going to church doesn't keep you from sleeping in. I know of very few services starting at 8 a.m. In most cases people could sleep till 9 a.m. and still get to church. If someone took two hours on Sunday to go to church, they would still have the rest of the day to get things done. After all, how many hours a week do we watch television? If we need more time in our lives, why not start there instead of with church. If a church is not a good fit for you, find one that is. You can't judge all churches by the one you attended when you went once. Going to a good church may not gain you entrance into Heaven, but it will point you in the right direction and encourage your spiritual growth. If there are people at a church who turn you off, then go to another. Your spouse doesn't have to go with you (though it is preferred). If you look hard enough, you will find a church that even your spouse and children would like. It's true, there's not one church that will appeal to everyone. It all comes down to priorities. Will you make the effort to attend a place of fellowship on a regular basis or not? Becoming part of a fellowship takes commitment. Find a good church and give it three months, I believe your life will be transformed to where you will be closer to God than you've been in a long time.

God says, "If My people, who are called by My name, will humble themselves and pray and seek My face and turn from their wicked ways, then I will hear from heaven and forgive their sin and heal their land" (2 Chr 7:14). Who are God's people? Christians. And what other people group is called by the name of God (or His Christ) if it is not Christ-ians? I heard a disturbing fact that three of five people not in fellowship in a local church are Christians.[1] Stephen Mansfield in his book *Re-Church* said that of the millions of un-churched adults in America, 20 percent are born again Christians.[2] Shame on Christians! How can we expect people to embrace God if we can't embrace each other? A house divided against itself will fall. How can Christians hate fellow Christians? Real Christians have a love for each other. Can you imagine a body fighting against itself? We may not always agree about everything, but we should have each other's back.

Satan and his minions love to see Christians staying home. He laughs at Christians in isolation. He's got them just where he wants them, alone. Christians are much easier to deal with when they are by themselves feeling like they are a powerless minority, but when a Christian is committed to fellowship, that's a real threat to the devil. In fact, it is the church, not the individual Christian, which the gates of Hell shall not prevail against. Together we are strong. You just have to ask yourself, "Which side am I on?" A day may come when going to church could cost you your life? In fact, in many places around the globe that is the case and yet people take the risk. Such a love puts the Western Christian to shame. We sit in the lap of luxury, in the cradle of freedom and have little if any desire to find ourselves among God's people on His day. Seven days without God makes one weak (pun intended).

We are told in Joshua 3 that the children of Israel crossed over the Jordan *together*. They didn't cross one at a time. Can you imagine God having to separate the waters thousands of times to accommodate everyone's crossing schedules? No, God performed a miracle, separated the waters once and they all were there together waiting for the hand of God to make a way and when He did, they crossed at the same time in the same place. Could you imagine someone refusing to cross with the rest because he had other things to do or because they didn't get along with some people in the group? There were no other crossings. If someone

---

1. Barna Group, "Millions of Unchurched Adults are Christians."
2. Mansfield, *Re-Church: Healing your way back to the people of God.*

didn't cross with the rest, they were left out of the Promised Land. God is doing something great, but if someone refuses to go to the appointed place at the appointed time they will miss out. The one who rejects God's blessing shouldn't expect that He will deliver them a second time since they despised God's first rescue. Whatsoever a man sows that shall he also reap (Gal 6:7).

"No one told me this was my only chance." Really, what were you thinking when they were all on the other side, looked back at you, and pleaded with you to come before the river went back to normal? God is not a genie in a bottle, nor is He the great Santa Claus in the sky. God doesn't do what you want, He does whatever He pleases. His job is not to please you. He doesn't need you; you need Him. You exist to please Him. Don't say no to God. You will regret it someday. Those who were faithful to obey and cross over together shared an inheritance.

Elijah was a faithful prophet. He stood up to the prophets of Baal and to the wicked king. However, after a great victory when he was alone and isolated in a cave, we find him crying to God and complaining that "I have been very zealous for the Lord God Almighty. The Israelites have rejected Your covenant, broken down Your altars, and put Your prophets to death with the sword. I am the only one left, and they are trying to kill me too" (1 Kgs 19:14). But God reminds Elijah that he was not alone. Not only was God with him, but God had saved a whole group of other prophets and followers that Isaiah did not know about. There was Elijah alone and isolated in the cave and he lost perspective. He started to complain to God.

Something I can't understand is the Christian who thinks that when they move away from their church, they don't need to find another one right away. They tell themselves that they deserve a break, and they take a vacation from church. They tell their old friends that they just haven't found the right church, when the reality is they aren't really looking. A month turns into a year, which turns into a decade. They feel like there isn't a church as good as the one they left. They start to believe that no other church could ever possibly measure up to their last one, so they sit at home all alone and refuse to accept the truth that God always saves a remnant for Himself. They withhold their gifts and talents from a new group of believers. They tell themselves they've done their share and now they want to take it easy. They rationalize that it is time for others to take the lead, so they retire from fellowship and ministry. They just want a place where they can sit in the back row and let others do the work for a change.

I understand burn out. I understand the temptation to let others do what you are tired of doing. The best way to defeat this feeling is to do something else for the Lord for a period. If you've been a Sunday School teacher for ten years and you're feeling like you're the only one who is being faithful, and God forbid, you start to resent the students in your class, then it's time to do something different. Use other gifts and talents in other ways. Take up a new ministry, maybe visiting shut-ins or serve as a trustee for a while. Time away from your primary gift of teaching may be just what you need to rejuvenate your passion and desire to teach. You don't have to walk away from the church to take time off.

Maybe your spouse left you and you're going through a difficult divorce. You definitely need to take some time off from your ministry to heal. Burn out should be guarded against. As a pastor I don't want anyone to do anything begrudgingly. My goal is to have everyone doing what God has equipped them to do. When people are using their gifts and talents with joy and passion, there is a renewing of strength that comes from the Lord. It's a beautiful thing to witness. Don't let yourself think that you are the only one. When you find yourself saying this it should be a warning that you are losing focus and perhaps need a change.

God teaches us, "How pleasant when brothers live together in unity" (Ps 133:1). The opposite is just as true, how sad it is when brothers are isolated in disarray. Unity is pleasant. When people who are not family choose to live together as though they are, well, such love and commitment is impressive. That's what a church is, a group of people who are not related choosing to be a family of faith. That kind of love, commitment, and unity is impressive and even enviable. It is the best kind of witness. God loves this when it happens, and He blesses those who make it happen. Let's bring pleasure to our heavenly Father by being what He has asked us to be, His children, made in His image, acting just like Him. Please God by bearing with one another, overlooking each other's short comings and living harmoniously as His family.

Proverbs teaches us, "As iron sharpens iron so one person sharpens another" (Prov 27:17). As a young teen I had a rock polishing kit. You take a bunch of rocks, some powder, water, and put it all in a tumbler. Then let that tumbler turn on motorized rollers for months to get beautiful, polished stones fit for setting in jewelry. When you want to sharpen a sword, you take it to the blacksmith who puts it in the fire, places it on the anvil to bang out any nicks and dings in it. After he's got it flat and smooth, he then takes a file or a stone to it to ware the edges so fine that they become sharp. The Christian goes to church and rubs shoulders with other Christians and our rough edges rub against each other until they are smoothed out and we become bright and keen for Christ. We learn from each other. We see good and bad examples. We're reminded of the truth. Friction is inevitable. When it comes to fellowship, there's friction or it is fiction. Real relationships produce heat. Some go to church and play the game and pretend to love each other, but it's fake. It's not real because they don't work things out, they just pretend to have a unity and the result is a fiction not a real relationship forged by friction. These honest relationships hold us accountable.

The plea I make to you is not a new one. Isaiah wrote, "Come let us reason together" (Isa 1:18). God wanted His people to get together and think about the path back to God's blessing. They needed to do this together, not just individually. They needed to recount their history. They needed to repent of their sins both individually and corporately. They needed to consider God's plan for restoration. And they needed to commit themselves to following God's plan back into His good graces. By sharing together their limited understandings they would learn from each other and have a synergy of understanding and come to a clarion conclusion. They would stand on each other's shoulders and catch a glimpse of the big picture. Let the church bells ring, "Come let us reason together!" We can't do it alone.

The Church needs to be the salt of the earth. We need to use our influence to guide and direct our society. God always preserves a remnant for Himself. Jeremiah 23:3 says, "I Myself will gather a remnant." Churches today are the remnant in your community. Romans 8:29–30 says, "For those God foreknew He also predestined . . . And those He predestined, He also called; those He called, He also justified; those He justified, He also glorified." To these He gave abilities. Those abilities are not a gift for the individual who receives them, but for those with whom they are in fellowship. God will cause all things to work together for good. This is the work of every real Christian and for every true church.

Chapter 3

"Let the Children Come"
—MATTHEW 19:14

JESUS AND HIS DISCIPLES had been working hard. People were constantly pressing them for a meeting, a miracle, or a message. The disciples were bodyguards and bouncers. They would set a perimeter around Jesus and acted as gatekeepers. They would talk to people, find out what they wanted, and would decide if they should get an audience with Jesus. People were bringing children to Him for healing, which was fine. Healing children always played well with a crowd, but the town's parents were bringing their children to Jesus simply for a blessing. Jesus' schedule was too busy, so they started turning these pesky requests away, but Jesus rebuked His disciples and said, "Let the little children come to me, and do not hinder them, for the kingdom of heaven belongs to such as these" (Matt 19:14).

When I was young, on summer evenings the kids in the neighborhood would gather to play kick the can, hide and go seek, or capture the flag. Dusk would come upon us and that was the best time to lurk in and out of shadows and creep up on some unsuspecting prey. Sometimes people hid so well you couldn't find them no matter how many people looked for them. As night came on and it was time to go home, we would end the games by calling out, "Ollie, ollie, oxen free, all come home." Upon hearing this everyone would slink out from their hiding place knowing the game was over and it was safe to do so. Well, God is calling out to His children everywhere, "Ollie, ollie, oxen free, all come home." He wants us to come out of our hiding and come home to church and eventually to our heavenly home.

Jesus taught us to be like a child in our faith. Jesus loves His little children, and we are all His children, precious in His sight. For such is the kingdom of heaven. Who would dare to forbid His children to come home? Well, some parents have heard the call, "Ollie, ollie, oxen free, all come home" and they are ignoring the call. They are telling their children the game is not over and to just ignore the call. God will hold such parents responsible. A parent's job is to train up a child in the way they should go. That way is toward God and that way leads through your local church. Why not bless your children this week and bring them to church? Jesus is calling, "Come home." Come to Jesus.

Jesus also said, "I have longed to gather your children" (Matt 23:37). Perhaps He has been longing for your family to come to Him. God might tell you, parents, "I gave you your children, but please note that they are mine and I only loaned them to you." They are God's offspring not just yours. They might seem to be in your image, but in truth they were made in God's image first. God has wanted to gather your children together, but sometimes you don't cooperate. There are even those who would even want to scatter these young ones. Such people want to protect their children from God. What a silly thought. I have often marveled as our society seems to work so hard to limit children's exposure to God. They take away prayer, the Bible, and free speech about Jesus. What are they so afraid of? Are they thinking that children will read the Bible and become terrorists? Are they afraid that if students come to believe in Jesus, they would stop having promiscuous sex? Are they really afraid of the ethics, morals, and values their children will learn? It has never made sense to me. I just don't get it.

You've heard people call someone a mother hen. This usually means in today's vernacular that such a person is a helicopter parent. Another phrase used to describe someone who is upset is, "Mad as a wet hen." Well, God likens Himself to a hen wanting to gather her chicks under its wings. He also says, "But you would not have it." I pity the fool who tries to stand between a mother and her young. It doesn't matter what species. A mother will give her life for her young. God wants to nurture and protect His children, but we are like the foolish child running away from their parent toward the burning stove or busy street. Do you know what shepherds used to do with wondering sheep? They used to break their leg to keep them from wondering, getting lost, or worse yet, getting eaten by a wolf. The famous picture of Jesus with a lamb on His shoulders is just that. You see when a shepherd broke the leg of a lamb that lamb would then become totally dependant on the shepherd to carrying them when the flock would move on to greener pastures or to the watering hole. Often the shepherd and lamb developed a strong bond that continued even after the bone was healed. The lamb would stay by the side of the good shepherd and the shepherd would sleep next to his favorite lamb for warmth on the cold nights. There's safety in the chicken coop. There's safety in the flock. Jesus is our mother hen/good shepherd (I know this is mixing metaphors, deal with it). He longs for you, but will you have Him?

Jesus was about twelve years old, it is said, when Mary and Joseph brought Him in a caravan with other friends and family to Jerusalem. When it was time to leave for home Joseph and Mary thought he was in the caravan hanging out with the other boys his age, but later it was found out that Jesus was no where to be found. Was this a lapse in judgment on behalf of the parents? They should be applauded for taking Him to the temple, but they seemed to shirk their duties to watch over their son. Perhaps they were busy with their other younger children. Maybe they were distracted by conversations with other adults. Good for you if you've taken your children to church, just don't drop the ball when you take them home. You still have spiritual responsibilities to live a godly lifestyle and give your children a good example. You still have to teach your children about Jesus. It's not the Sunday School teacher's responsibility, it's yours. They are there to help you, not to take your place.

Joseph and Mary started their search for their lost son. They traced their steps all the way back to Jerusalem. There they searched the city, asking all sorts of questions. Finally, they found Jesus at the temple talking with the teachers of the law, who were very impressed with His understanding, but Jesus' parents were scared, upset, and relieved. They chided Jesus, perhaps wanting to shift the blame from them. I can hear them now, "Where have you been? How dare you worry us like this? Why couldn't you just follow the caravan?" Jesus' response was, "Why were you searching for me? . . . Didn't you know I had to be in my Father's house?" (Luke 2:49). This verse reminds me of the many children who come to church, but their parents won't. The kids beg their parents to take them to church, but it always seems like an inconvenience and a hassle. Their parents are glad to get rid of them for a while so they can go shopping or finally get some peace and quiet, but they really don't get it. Their children are saying, "Don't you understand? I have to go to church. I love youth group. It's the only place I feel accepted and loved. You have to take me. Please!" It is important for all of God's children, both young and old, to be in the house of the Lord. How about your family? Do you bring your kids to church and drop them off at the door, or do you take them inside and sit down next to them? There is great power in learning together.

One time when Jesus felt the power of God to preach "He called His disciples to Him" (Luke 6) to the side of a hill and gave the greatest sermon ever preached, the Sermon of the Mount. Jesus' followers could not hear Him unless they gathered together and came to where He was. If you are His disciple, He is calling you today. He's not just calling you; He's calling all His children to gather together so He can teach you all in the same place, at the same time, so we can achieve a unity and solidarity. While they were together on that mountain side Jesus selected some of His followers to be apostles. These were those who would be with Him everywhere He went. These were the one's He would send ahead of Him as His advance team to prepare the way for the Lord. Who knows what great plans the Lord may have for you? It is through the gathered that He confirms His call upon your life.

Jesus spoke of a man having a banquet in Luke 14:16–24. The invitations went out, but people started making excuses. I just bought a field said one, please consider me excused. Another said he just bought a pair of oxen and he had to try them out, so he could not come. Another had just gotten married so he would not be going either. Unlike this story, church is not just a rich man holding a banquet. It is God Himself calling to all people everywhere. And it is not just to a banquet He invited us; it is eternal glory in heaven. Who would say no to such an offer? Every time you refuse the invitation to gather with other Christians for the purpose of worship, prayer, and hearing from God you are rejecting His invitation. In the above story others took their place, the door was shut and those originally invited would not be let in because they turned down the invitation. Today may be the day of God's favor, but a night is coming when no person, no matter how much they wish they could, will be able to accept His gracious invitation.

After a particularly difficult sermon (found in John 6) many who gathered in the crowd decided to stop following Jesus. He turned to the twelve and asked them, "You do not want to leave too, do you?" (verse 67). I love Peter's response, "Lord, to whom shall we go? You have the words of eternal life. We believe and know that you are the Holy One of God" (verse 68). There is no where else the Christian can turn, but to Jesus, and He entrusts His word to the Church, to keep it, to teach it, and to proclaim it. Where else can you turn today to hear the truth found in God's Word? The wisdom of this world found in all the universities, books, and laboratories will never compare.

You may hear a great sermon on the television, but how does that person's life match up to what they preach? In truth you can never know. You don't know the person and you don't even know anyone who knows that person. You're taking it all by faith that they have your best interest in mind, but that may not be the kind of interest ($) they have in mind. You can't ask them your questions and get a response. You may think that reading a godly person's books is as good as going to church to hear some lame sermon from no one special, but once again you don't know that author, just their reputation. God's Word isn't just preached; it's lived out as an example for all to see. Jesus didn't just teach us how to live, He showed us. The reason Jesus is the most influential person in history is because He left us an example of how to love our enemies. He showed us how to serve, and He tells us to go and *do* likewise. Blessed is the person who not only hears the teachings but who also puts them into practice. That's what I love about small churches. It's easy to tell if someone is practicing what they preach. The teaching is so much more powerful when you respect the person speaking and you know they love you and your family.

Jesus gives the invitation for everyone to come and follow Him, and some followed for poor reasons. This is why Jesus at times taught difficult lessons, to weed out the wheat from the tares. When many stopped following Jesus because His teaching was too much for them to handle, this was a good thing. Some people are turned off by the gospel, church, or Christians, but such people are probably tares anyway. Some non-Christians will sneak through into fellowship at your local church. This even happened to Jesus. In the gospel of John chapter 6 verse 70 Jesus tells His disciples, "Did I not choose you and yet one of you is a devil?" He was speaking of Judas Iscariot who would betray Jesus for thirty pieces of silver. Don't assume that everyone inside a church is a Christian or even interested in following Jesus. There are all sorts of reasons to attend a church. Some people do it for economic reason. They might be in a certain type of sales and are looking to network and find more clients. Others come to church because the person they hope to marry attends there. Some people attend simply because of societal pressure to conform. There may be such a devil as a Judas in your church fellowship. Just as judging all the disciples as wicked because of Judas, it would be wrong to judge all Christians as hypocrites because of one bad apple. Realizing this before one even darkens the door of a church helps prepare one for disappointment and disillusionment. Even a genuine Christian will let you down, but you don't go to church because it's filled with perfect people. You go because God has given you a family, which in the long run will help you grow in your faith.

You more than likely have someone in your extended biological family who you would rather not hang out with, but they are and will always be part of your family. At family gatherings you just steer clear of that uncle, aunt, or cousin. You acknowledge them as part of the family, you are polite, but you don't go out of your way to pretend that they are your favorite. You love them from a distance, and you keep hoping things will change and the relationship could grow into something better. In God's family we are that less-lovable relative that the angels sit in wonder as to why the Father puts up with us and gave His only Son for us. People are fond of calling churchgoers judgmental yet in doing this they are in fact the ones who are being judgmental. I heard a story of one woman who was new to town and a local pastor invited her to his church. She told him that she would never go to church again because they're all filled with judgmental hypocrites. To which he answered, "Well then, you should feel right at home." Stop judging the Church of God, let Him judge His own Church.

Jesus taught that we Christians should love one another (John 13:34). We can't love people we refuse to gather with, that's not showing love. Likewise, saying we have love for someone but refusing to celebrate a relationship with them is not love at all. Having an emotional affection for someone at a distance might be one kind of love, but it's not very relevant. Love isn't just a feeling; it's an action and a commitment. By being part of a church family, we are committing to that family. We are saying that we accept them and love them enough to identify with them. We're throwing our lot in with them. By gathering together, we will have many opportunities to demonstrate our love to them and they in turn will be able to demonstrate their love for us.

The early Church was gathered together in obedience as Jesus had commanded and they were all in one place (Acts 2:1). What happened to them as they were gathered for one of the first church services, was something no one would want to miss. At least on this occasion the Holy Spirit came upon all who gathered, and they spoke in tongues. This was the official birthday of the Church. Before this day the Spirit of God would come and go upon believers, but after this day Scripture teaches that the Holy Spirit would come and stay upon true believers. Imagine if one of the disciples missed this day like Thomas had missed Christ's first appearing to the ten other disciples. God works in powerful ways when those with faith gather together in one place. Jesus performed miracles when people of faith gathered. Jesus told His disciples that whatever they agreed upon on earth would be bound in heaven. He also told His disciples that wherever two or three of them were gathered together that He would be there in their midst. What is God doing down the street at your local church? If you are not there, you'll never know, and I guarantee you are missing out.

In Acts chapter 2 in verses 42 through 47 we read that the early church regularly gathered together in the temple courts and shared everything in common. "Selling their possessions and goods, they gave to anyone as he had need" (verse 45). When one is part of a fellowship sharing and generosity is common. Hand-me-downs get passed around, people share rides, and invitations of various sorts abound. This can be crucial for the young family trying to make ends meet. This network of assistance is invaluable to the family who has moved away from their extended families. Why spend money putting a pool in your back yard when friends from church have given you an open door to enjoy theirs? When you need a job and you share that need with your church family, someone may know of a position that would be just right for you. Membership has its privileges and it is such a positive thing for your whole family. Are you denying your children and spouse much needed assistance? Are you willfully refusing the help of your local church because of pride or a previous experience? Why do we do this to our families?

As a result of the early Church's generosity, it grew, and many were coming to faith in Christ. This support and assistance the early Church offered was crucial at the time because Christians were undergoing persecution. It could be concluded that the greater the persecution upon individual Christians the more important the protection of a fellowship of believers will become to those being harassed. One could also surmise that as Western society moves increasingly toward a post Christian society, Christians will have increasing need for the support network the local church has to offer. Large groups of Christians will work together to defend their human rights. Someday soon the local church will be the only place one will be able to go to be encouraged in their faith in Christ. We might be spoiled now with the freedoms we enjoy, but those freedoms which have been challenged for decades, are eroding, and are in increasing jeopardy. Do not think that our children will enjoy the same society we did. The world is evolving and changing, often for the worst, because increasingly more people are hostile toward the Christian faith. If we don't encourage the faith of our children, they (and certainly our grandchildren) may even end up being the ones to persecute the future Church.

In Acts chapter 16 we read of how Paul was falsely arrested in Philippi. God freed him from his shackles and opened the doors of the prison during the night with a powerful earthquake. The jailer fearing for his life was about to kill himself, but Paul called to him and told him all the prisoners were still there. The jailer came running in, dropped to his knees before Paul and said, "What must I do to be saved?" (verse 30). Paul tells him that he must believe on the Lord Jesus Christ and that this was not just for him, but also for his entire family. How unfortunate would heaven be if you were saved, but those with whom you share life didn't make it? God doesn't only want you saved; He wants your whole household saved. Sure, the chains are gone, and you are free to go where you want, but staying in fellowship with your brothers and sisters in Christ will lead your whole family toward salvation.

In Hebrews 10:25 God tells us not to neglect the gathering of ourselves together. He does this for a reason. It is for our benefit. I liken it to a grandmother looking into her daughter's refrigerator and cupboards and telling them to go to the store to buy some fresh fruit, vegetables, milk, and meat. She's not doing this because she knows the grocer and wants to help him out financially. She's doing it because she knows their child needs a better diet to live a healthy life. Too many of us would rather live on Ramen Noodles, coffee, and Spaghetti O's, but if we continue to ignore God's wisdom, we will pay for it. Maybe not today or tomorrow, but someday, and we may pay for it dearly with our lives. Someone once said ignorance is bliss, but in truth it is tragic, especially when one is unaware about the only way to be saved or to save one's family. Why would someone want to neglect God's way toward Him, especially knowing how much God loves them and gave up for them? Stop neglecting the spiritual needs of your family.

"If we claim to have fellowship with him yet walk in the darkness, we lie and do not live by the truth. But if we walk in the light, as he is in the light, we have fellowship with one another, and the blood of Jesus, his Son, purifies us from all sin" (1 John 1:6–7). Are you walking in darkness or light? If you have fellowship with other Christians you're walking in the light, but if you call yourself a Christian and yet don't have fellowship with other Christians, you deceive yourself and the truth is not in you. Ephesians 2:8 says, "For by grace you have been saved through faith and this is *not of yourself*." The truth is, you are not saved by yourself, and you are not saved for yourself. You would not have come to faith if it were not for the Church. You may not have come to faith *at* a church, but you *were saved* when a Christian (all Christians make up the Church) shared the gospel with you! You were saved by Christ as He used the efforts of His faithful Church. Statistics tell us that many people were involved in your salvation; the person who brought you to church when you were young, the person who first shared the good news with you, the first Christian who's life impressed you, the person who prayed with you to become a Christian, and all the people who were involved in saving each one of those people, and so on, and so on, and so on.

Did you know that many of the *yous* in Scripture are plural—such as in Matthew 5:13 and 14? "You (plural: you all) are the salt of the earth . . . You (plural: you all) are the light of the world." The individual Christian is not the salt of the earth or the light of the world. *We* are the salt of the earth; *we* are the light of the world. Individually you are not a lighthouse; you may not even be a firefly. 1 Corinthians 12:27 tells us, "Now you (plural) are the *body* of Christ." *We* are the body of Christ. *You* are not the body of Christ! You are an atom in the fingernail of the body of Christ! *Alone* we are nothing—this is what makes the fact that Jesus died for you so amazing! *We* are the bride of Christ. In Ephesians 2:22 *we* are being built *together*. *Alone* we are a brick; *together* we are the New Jerusalem.

In John 17:11, 21–22 Jesus prayed that we Christians might be one. Christ wanted us to be together, not apart. Christians love being forgiven they just don't like to forgive. They are often thin skinned, take offense, and remove themselves from fellowship. They isolate themselves away from their brothers and sisters and then wonder why Christians aren't more caring. I think the world calls us Christians hypocrites because we call each other hypocrites. The Church is impotent because we are not together as God has designed. We are fractured and splintered and as a result the Church can not function as God wants. You could make a difference down at the local church of your choice, not to mention the difference you'd be making at home with your family.

Chapter 4

Section Summary: Fellowship

How to Find Fellowship

THERE ARE A FEW ways to find fellowship with other Christians, but first I must dismiss any argument that the type of fellowship I have espoused in the previous three chapters can happen at a meaningful level as a result of technologically assisted communication. This includes books, telephone, television, internet, tweeting, texting, Skyping, Zooming, and others. Sure, information can be transferred through these formats, but fellowship is so much more than an information exchange. To reject face to face direct contact with other Christians and believe that true deep relationships can develop without what I call *life exchange* is to delude oneself. I am more than what I say and so are you. I continue to exist even though the book is closed, or the electronic appliance is turned off and so do you. In truth the best form of fellowship would be to live together and limit the time spent apart. The best form of fellowship looks like family life or communal living.

We may be able to talk to each other and even see each other's faces, but it is a poor substitute for fellowship. Just ask any soldier separated by deployment. Phone calls, email, and video conferencing are not a substitute for being with your family and friends. Do these modes of communication benefit us? Of course, they do. Do they help to maintain relationships that are strained by distance? Yes, but they don't build the relationship. Ask someone who has a friend that has moved away if they are closer now than they used to be. Even if they call every day, email every night and tweeting continually throughout the day, the relationship now lacks many of the most common shared experiences. It is through sharing experiences that relationships are built. These modern electronic mediated forms of communication are poor at sharing experiences. If relationships or fellowship were to be placed on a continuum with zero being no relationship and ten being the highest and best, technologically assisted communication would rarely foster a relationship above the lower third.

I am not saying that technologically assisted communication doesn't have its place in relationships or ministry. I am not saying that they can't enhance relationships. I'm not saying that they haven't been a godsend to people and couples challenged by distance. Of course, such media have benefits, but they also have limitations. There are some of you that are downright angry at me right now for putting down your beloved lifestyle. I am not putting it down. I have a PhD in *communication*. I love technology. I am an adjunct professor who teaches *online* classes. I served as an *online* missionary with Global Media Outreach.[1] I love *Facebook* and I have over four-thousand Facebook friends. I check my *email* throughout the day. My *cell phone* battery only lasts half a day because of all its use. I pushed one of our churches to be the first church in our community to have a *website* and another to be among the first to *stream* its services. I believe Christians must take advantage of such technology, but I also believe that we must not be seduced by it. It's not that you can't develop intimacy through such mediums, you can, but there are limitations. God so loved the world that He sent His one and only Son, not an email. Jesus, in the great commission, tells us to go into all the world and make disciples. Yes, one way we can do that is through the internet, but He wants us personally involved, as personally as He was.

Technologically enhanced communication may provide a certain level of fellowship, but this level of relationship is not what God desires. Use such technologies to supplement and augment your communication, but do not deceive yourself into thinking that information equals relationship. If you are sitting at home engaging only in the electronic Church, you are missing out. Rejecting getting together with Christians and Christian fellowship are on opposite ends of a spectrum. Why aren't you involved in a local fellowship? Such a position is at odds with God's

---

1. Global Media Outreach, "Home."

will for you. Church, by definition, is not something done by or for oneself. The Church is the body of Christ; of which all believers are a part. Forgive those who have hurt you and get thyself to church! When you do this, you do two things to benefit yourself. Your sins will be forgiven (remember Jesus taught us to pray, and forgive us our debts as we forgive our debtors) and you will have all the benefits of fellowship.

So, if technology by itself doesn't provide fellowship the way God intended, how do we get it? We must seek out other Christians face to face and develop a relationship with them. "My neighbor is a Christian does that count?" That's a start. "I know a couple of Christians involved in my PTA." Great, but are you sharing spiritual life together? Are you in a committed relationship to each other with such strong bonds that they have become family to you? "Sure, we're best friends." Do you pray for each other? "I pray for them every day." Do you pray with them? Do you praise God together and worship together? Are you learning about God and His will for your life together? Do you study the Bible together? Do you share in ministry together? Fellowship is more than friendship. As the word fellowship implies, it is two people in the same boat (fellow and ship). It's "sink or swim *together*." It's a covenant relationship. If the ship goes down, you both drown, so you work like mad to bail out the water and keep the ship from sinking. Such fellowship is rarely accomplished in social interaction in your community.

The best way to foster fellowship is through attending and joining a local church and getting involved in a small group with some of those people. "Can't I just go to a Bible study? Why do I have to join a church?" Bible studies begin and end. People start attending and then stop. Some meet weekly and others meet monthly. Some are restricted to one gender or topic and do not offer a full range of relationships and experiences. Attending bible study is a good start, but just like the commitment of marriage binds people together in ways that living together just can't, nothing says I'm committed to another Christian like entering into a covenant relationship through church membership. "How about just attending regularly? Isn't that commitment?" Sure, attending a church on a regular basis is making some level of commitment, but the relationship is not cemented. I liken it to going steady verses being married. Staying at home watching a streamed part of a service is like staying at home Friday and Saturday night reading romance novels. Knowing a few Christians in your community is like having a few friends of the opposite sex. Going to a Bible study is like dating. Attending a church is like going steady. And becoming a member of a church is like getting married. With each step there is a deeper level of commitment and a more meaningful relationship. Here's another; staying at home reading your Bible all by yourself is like saying you're a sports fan. Having a few Christian friends is like watching a few games. Getting involved in a Bible Study is like going to a few games. Regularly going to the same church is like buying season tickets. And being a church member is like buying season tickets, buying jerseys, and wearing them all the time, traveling with the team to root for them when they are on the road and never missing a game.

"There's a difference between being a fan and being a fanatic, you know." There are some out there who think what I am purposing is fanaticism. They think I'm some sort of Jesus freak and I won't stop until everyone is just like me. First, it would be hell if everyone were just like me. Second, I am fanatical when it comes to Jesus. He died in my place. The most important question I have for you dear Christian is when did you stop being fanatical about Jesus? After all that He has done for us, how could anyone not do whatever He asks? All He asks us is to love our fellow believers. I'll do anything for my Jesus and if that means putting up with other sinful, fallen Christians, so be it. Jesus taught us how to love and enables us to truly love. If Christians can't love one another what hope is there that anyone can love?

How to Find a Good Church

"Fine, I'll trying going to church again. How do I find a good church?" I'll start by making sure you understand that there are no perfect churches. If you find one, the moment you attend it, it ceases being perfect. You also need to know that some people find different aspects of a church more appealing than other people. So, not every church is the best fit for everyone. I think that is why God has allowed His Church to splinter into so many different types of churches, so you could find a church where you would feel at home. Some people respond to formal traditions and liturgy, others enjoy a non-traditional church that is spontaneous. Others feel at home in a large church while still others desire a small fellowship. Such personal preferences are important and may be able to be accommodated by a good church within easy driving distance of your home, but such preferences are secondary to other considerations. After all, finding the right church is not as much about you as it is about the church you are considering.

A good church preaches and teaches from the *Bible*. If the Sunday School classes don't focus on God's Word more than the words of people, then that church is not a good Bible teaching church. If the pastor doesn't read a passage of Scripture and explain its application for life today, then that is not a Bible preaching church. Keep looking until you find one that does. Christians are supposed to be people of the book (the Bible). If you attend a church that does not give the Scriptures preeminence, then you will not grow in your understanding of the Word of God. If the preacher talks about the headlines more than God's truth as written in the good book, then he is not a faithful steward of his charge. While we're on the subject, if the preacher talks about money in every sermon and regularly speaks of giving money to receive a blessing from God, then find another church. That person is not thinking of the things of God. They are more interested in building an empire than the body of Christ. Any church, or preacher for that matter, should not be judged on one visit or one sermon. You are looking for the tendency of the church or pastor to teach from the Bible. You just might hit one service where the pastor is giving their quarterly stewardship sermon. Give it a month or so to make a proper evaluation.

A good church has *people coming to know Jesus*. There are plenty of Bible teaching churches who focus on teaching Christians only and there are some Bible teaching churches who focus on teaching the unsaved, but a good Bible teaching church focuses on both educating Christians and non-Christians about the Word of God. As a result, people will come to faith in Christ and Christians will grow in Christ. Some people think this means every service must end in an altar call. This is not necessarily a good indication that people's lives are being transformed. A truly evangelistic church will declare how to become a Christian at most every service and always encourage people to believe in Jesus' death on the cross. There should be some sort of call to commitment frequently. Visitors and guests will be commonplace. It may not be a large church because of turnover in the community, but a good church is going to reach people and help them grow in their relationship with God. You'll have to listen for testimonies.

A good church is going to value *prayer*. They don't have to have hundreds of people at a Wednesday night prayer service. That's not necessarily a good indication that a church values prayer. Maybe instead of counting numbers you should consider percentages. What percent of the church attends the various prayer opportunities? Which is evidence of a more dynamic commitment to prayer a church of five thousand with three hundred at a midweek prayer service or a church of one hundred with fifteen? The first is 6 percent of the congregation attending a prayer meeting and the second is more than double that, so it's not always how many attend. And it's not even the percentage of people who attend a meeting; it is also how much time they spend in prayer. Some churches' idea of an hour-long prayer service is to sing a song or two, preach a twenty–thirty-minute sermon, spend fifteen minutes sharing prayer requests and spending five minutes listening to someone pray.

My goal for a good prayer service is to have half the time spent in prayer and those prayers need to be brief and led by many people. Not everyone is expected to pray, but most people will. A praying church will offer more than just one opportunity to gather for prayer. They pray in short sentence prayers and their prayers are not always asking for things. Such a church will spend time giving thanks to God, glorifying Him for who He is, not just what He's done. People will pray for others and not just for themselves. They will have a prayer calling chain for emergencies. People will stop in the middle of conversations and say, "Let's pray about that" and then do it. Such a church will publish a prayer list and encourage people to pray. The leadership will be committed to prayer and will talk about answers to prayer, giving God the glory. Attending a prayer service will give you a deeper understanding of a church's spiritual maturity.

A good church is going to be *mission minded*. A good church is not just going to support missionaries, they are going to live like missionaries. They will work to use their gifts and talents for the furtherance of the gospel. Such a church is going to send at least 10 percent of their budget to missionaries and mission organizations, and they are also going to have outreach teams working to encourage the whole church to show the love of God and get the good news out locally. They are going to have children and youth ministries that not only teach the Bible, but also encourage involvement in living the Christian life in such a way that others are reached. A missional church will not depend on staff to do the work of the church. More than half the congregation will be involved in regular ministry.

A good church is going to be *relational*. The moment you walk into a relational church people will offer to help you or show you the way to the nursery or sanctuary. They will greet you and shake your hand, and I'm not talking about the greeters at the door (they're supposed to greet you).

You should get an invite to come back. Not all pastors have the luxury of greeting all visitors before the service, but the people sitting around you do. If you attend a church for a month and no one knows your name and you've never been personally invited to a church activity, event or to do something with someone, then keep looking for a friendlier fellowship. Some of you might not care about this and maybe you even want to sit in church and be anonymous, but I tell you that this lack of relational interaction is an indicator of spiritual maturity. It tells you if the church truly cares for others or if it's just a social club for members only. This is the natural outgrowth of a missions minded church.

These are the crucial characteristics of a good church: Bible believing/teaching, sound doctrine, praying, missional, and relational. All those other things like; do they have multiple services, are there thousands of people attending, is the quality of music good, do they use the King James Version of the Bible, is the building new construction, or is the preacher dynamic, are all points of personal preference. I always encourage people to major on the majors and minor on the minors. If there is a great new church being built and your friends go there and the music is great, but the preacher is always asking for money, other than your friends no one else knows you, the Bible is not held in high esteem, and there seems to be no interest in prayer, then it may not be a good church for someone wanting to grow as a Christian. You might finally stop by an old small unimpressive looking church building and find out that they are a great place to grow. Looks can be deceiving when it comes to looking for a church, especially when you know what you're looking for.

When looking for a good church, ask God to lead you. Talk to other Christian friends about their churches. Give churches a call and ask them questions about their bible study offerings, prayer ministries, and their missions' program. Check out their website. Ask people in the community what they know about the church. When you visit a church give it a fair try and attend for a few weeks in a row. Visit it with your family. Ask them what they liked and didn't like about the church. Try to figure out how good a fit that church might be for your family. If you are single, ask a friend to go along with you to get their input. Remember appearances can be deceiving and you're not looking for a perfect fit, you're looking for the best fit. There will always be flaws and areas we would want to change.

Some of you have fifty churches within an easy drive of your home so don't give up. Attend a church for at least four months before you start looking into membership. Don't leave a church too quickly. Take your time and don't be too quick to take offense. Attend any church (or club or any group) long enough and people will disappoint you and let you down. It won't be all roses all the time, nothing in life is. My wife expects her team to win every game. I want them to have a good season (win 60+ percent of their games or get in the playoffs). You don't want to join a church and then leave it. That hurts the church and you. This is why it is so important to do a good search before you settle on a church. One last consideration might be which church would be most blessed by your attending it. Remember, it's not about you and your needs and wants. It's about obeying God by being one with the body of Christ. Whatever you do, don't give up until you find a church family to call your spiritual home. You won't grow in your Christian life without good fellowship.

Tools for Church Hunting

Here are a couple of websites you could use to find churches in your area. You might find a few churches you didn't even know existed. If you're new to an area these sites could be invaluable to you. I encourage you to find a church close to where you live. How close is close? How far do you want to travel each way three times a week? A highway could make a church fifteen miles away within your search area. Traffic might make a church five miles away too far.

www.churchangel.com[2]
www.churchfinder.com[3]

When and How to Leave a Church

"I'm involved in a church, but after reading this description of a good church and evaluating my spiritual growth, I need to find another church. What should I do?" First, make sure your church is a place you need to leave. In a few years, I would imagine that every parishioner is tempted to leave their church at least once. This is often the result of a rash decision and the work of the evil one. Leaving a church is like going through a divorce. It is not to be considered lightly. Just because a new church starts up and is growing by leaps and bounds doesn't mean you should jump ship and join the new start up. Don't think the grass is greener somewhere

2. Church Angel, "Find a Church."
3. Church Finder, "Find Churches Near You."

else. It often does look greener, but that may be because of all the weeds (or manure). Take at least three weeks to leave a church. Know why you are leaving. If your church is not preaching and teaching the Bible then fine, leave, that is of major importance to your spiritual growth. If they are not missions minded, relational, or committed to prayer then fine, these are major considerations for a best church fit. Rarely is a church not meeting a certain criterion, it's more like a matter of degrees. Is my church missions minded enough? Are they Bible believing enough? Do they lack a passion for prayer? Is the church relationally adequate? Is there a better church fit for me? Would it be worth the turmoil and travail of ripping myself and my family out of this fellowship to gain only a slightly better fellowship? Is this God's will for me? These are all questions you need to ask yourself, God, and other Christians you respect.

After you've asked and answered the above questions then plan an exit strategy. First, pray and think about any parting blessings you can leave the fellowship. Maybe before you leave you would work to make something wonderful happen for the church to demonstrate your love for them. Then plan who you will tell about your decision to leave. Then plan where, when, and how you will tell them. Then you will need to explain why you are leaving. If you've ever broken off a dating relationship, you know how difficult this can be. If done properly and if it is part of God's will, it could end up blessing the church you leave. When they hear why you are leaving maybe they will work to improve that area of their ministry. Help them understand that it is for your spiritual growth that you need to follow God's leading and make this change. In truth you are not leaving the Church (there is only one Church), you are simply moving to a different corner of the vineyard, a corner better suited to your gifts, talents, and needs.

If you have a history of leaving churches, then leaving another church is not going to necessarily be the answer this time either. Such a person should think one hundred times before leaving again. Such a person develops a reputation and may be spiritually unstable. If you searched for the best fit church properly then you should rarely have to make a move unless there are major changes in your church or in the other churches in your area. Others of you have never even looked for a church. You're still in the church your parents took you to forty years ago. Some of you might be doing yourself a big favor by taking the time to evaluate whether the church you are in is a good church and a good fit for you. All sorts of emotional attachments will work against you to make

Section Summary: Fellowship

a move to benefit your spiritual growth. You'll be tempted to stay in a bad church because somehow you think it would be disrespectful to your parents. You'll be too afraid of hurting people's feelings to do what God is asking you to do. You need to find a new church as soon as you leave an old one. Don't think that you need a break from church. You need fellowship just like a fish needs water.

Section Two

Bible Study

Chapter 5

"Study to Show Yourself Approved"
—2 TIMOTHY 2:15

Did you know that it was through God's spoken words that all of creation came to be? For we read seven times in Genesis 1 "And God said, "Let there be..."" then shortly after such a statement we read, "And it was so." God's spoken words are powerful and His written Word, the Bible, is just as powerful. In Hebrews 4:12 we read, "For the Word (speaking of the written Word, the Bible) of God is living and active. Sharper than any double-edged sword, it penetrates even to dividing soul and spirit, joints and marrow; it judges the thoughts and attitudes of the heart." In the Old Testament we read, "The grass withers and the flowers fall, but the word of our God stands forever" (Isaiah 40:8). His Word is not only powerful, but it is enduring. His Word doesn't change, it doesn't loose its potency, and it will not go forth in vain. For we read in Isaiah 55:11, "My word that goes out from my mouth: It will not return to me empty but will accomplish what I desire and achieve the purpose for which I sent it." Nothing can thwart God's plans or His Word. He never takes His words back. He never changes His decrees. God is the same yesterday, today and forever (Heb 13:8). Numbers 23:19 says, "God is not a man, that he should lie, nor a son of man, that he should change his mind. Does he speak and then not act? Does he promise and not fulfill?" When God says something, He means it. He doesn't lie (Titus 1:2). If He promises something, He follows through on it. If He declares something, it is so. You can trust God's Word.

Right now, you are saying to yourself, "I can't read the Bible, it's too archaic. I can't understand it. I fall asleep when I read it." I'd like to point out to you that if you've been reading this book up to this point then you have read over forty Bible verses and passages. Most every paragraph focuses on a Bible verse. I've structured this whole book around God's Word. It's just one big, long Bible study. "But you make it make sense." That's the reason I started with fellowship, until you are more mature it can be difficult to motivate yourself to read the Bible daily. New readers often will start in Genesis and attempt to read straight through the Bible, but when they get to the "begats" a few chapters into it they give up. (This is why I encourage new Bible readers to start in the gospel of John.) When we were babies our parents, spoon fed us mashed carrots and bananas, but now that we are older, we feed ourselves steak and popcorn. The same thing happens with Bible reading. When we first start out, we must take in small amounts of easy verses and mature believers must help us understand what we've read, but soon we take our first steps and try reading on our own. Sure, we fall, but we get right back up and keep trying until we are running on our own.

If you are a Christian who is not steeped in the Word of God then you are easy prey for the evil one to distract, tempt, and cause to fall. Consider the serpent in the garden that confronted Eve and said, "Did God really say, 'You must not eat from any tree in the garden'?" (Gen 3:1). She wasn't sure, she had missed that lesson. If you don't know what God says about homosexuality, fornication, drinking, disobedience, lying, etc. then you will fall prey to the lies of this world as they try to squeeze you into their mold. Instead, be transformed by the renewing of your mind (Rom 12:2) through the Word of God.

This generation is facing great moral and ethical dilemmas because of their lack of understanding of basic biblical principles. Satan is whispering to this generation, "Did God really say having sex is a sin? How could it be if He created it? All the studies show that it is healthy for you. After all it's good preparation for marriage." And people today are buying into this lie hook, line, and sinker. As a result, we have unwed mothers, abortions, divorce, and general unhappiness in an area where God intended there to be one the greatest blessings. Outside the context of marriage, sex is selfishness run amuck. Satan tells us these lies time and time again concerning all of God's commands until we are all doing as we see fit in our own eyes and dismissing God's will entirely. The Bible is not just another book; it is the Book of books. It is God's Word.

"Study to Show Yourself Approved"

We need to be able to combat the temptation of the devil to question the truth of the Bible as Jesus did when He was tempted in the desert. What is it that Jesus did (in Luke 4) each time Satan tried to distort the Word of God or take it out of context? Jesus dug down into His wealth of scriptural knowledge and cited Scripture appropriately ("It is written . . ."). Jesus was able to refute Satan because of His wealth of knowledge of the Bible. We can do the same thing. In Luke as well as in the Matthew 4 account, a parallel passage, Jesus correctly uses Deuteronomy 8:3 to combat the twisted temptation of the Devil, "Man does not live on bread alone, but on every word that comes from the mouth of God." That's how important God's Word ought to be to us. It's like daily bread. I can only imagine that verse was the impetus of the title of one of the most widely used devotional guides *Our Daily Bread*.[1]

We need to feed on God's Word daily. We need to "Let the word of Christ richly dwell within you, with all wisdom teaching and admonishing one another with psalms and hymns and spiritual songs, singing with thankfulness in your hearts to God" (Col 3:16). Please note the connection between God's Word and fellowship. God's Word is something we study together, admonishing *one another*. The above passage is in the plural. Studying the Bible with other Christians is so much more effective than studying it alone. They don't necessarily tell you what to believe about a verse or passage, the Holy Spirit does that, but they do give you different perspectives that you can learn from. After all, "As iron sharpens iron, so one man sharpens another" (Prov 27:17). Hanging out with other Christians who share this passion for God's Word will be a great benefit to both your understanding and your implementation of God's Word.

The Bible is like no other book. It is the number one world's best seller of all time. In fact, the Bible is made up of sixty-six different books (or Scriptures). It was the first book ever printed. It has been translated into more languages than any other book. It can be read in the native language of 90 percent of the world's population. It was written by over forty different authors who represent many different backgrounds. When was the last time forty persons agreed on something so complex? Some were well educated, others were not. Some held positions of high esteem others did not. They were kings, warriors, judges, musicians, herdsmen, fishermen, a cup bearer, a physician, a tax collector, a rabbi, prophets, historians, and politicians among others. They wrote in different countries

---

1. Our Daily Bread Ministries, "Our Daily Bread."

(Egypt, Sinai, Israel, Babylon, Persia, Asia Minor, Greece, and Rome) and in three different languages (Hebrew, Aramaic, and Greek).

The Bible was written over a period of fifteen hundred years. There has been more written about the Bible than any other subject. It is unique in reputation, is cited by the greatest minds and has incredible influence in literature. Much of the world's greatest literature uses the Bible to connect with readers. You can't fully understand many of the greatest works of literature without an understanding of the Bible (and yet it is not allowed in some public schools). The Bible was written on stone, clay, papyrus, animal skins and metal. One would think that with all these variables that the Bible would be a hodgepodge of ideas and reflections, and some see it as such, but the truth is it is a unity of thought and material. It tells God's story of the redemption of humankind. Both Old and New Testaments tell of the Messiah coming to earth and dying for the sins of the world. When one uses proper exegesis, the Bible has no contradictions. The same cannot be said of the Koran or the writings of Confucius:

Book	Religion	Author	When Written	Time It Took
Koran	Muslim	Mohammed	AD 610–632	22 yrs
Five Classics	Confucianism	Confucius	500 BC–289 BC	211 yrs
Book of Mormon	Mormonism	Joseph Smith	AD 1823–30	7 yrs
The Bible	Christianity	40 Authors	1400 BC- AD 110	1500 yrs

No other book comes close to being as universal and timeless. And I haven't even touched on the countless testimonies to the transforming power of reading the Bible.

The Bible is the Word of God, the literal words of God, not just the words of humans. If it were the words of people, it would be impossible to have the agreement of thought and story, especially in its day. The writers of the Bible surely could have come up with a better story, truths, and Messiah than what the Bible presents. What person, much less alone people who in most cases didn't even know each other, would concoct the idea that God Himself would atone for mankind's sins by becoming a man and dying on a cross? The premise of the Bible seems like insanity. The fact that the Bible's teachings and stories seem so ludicrous combined with the fact that Jews (the very people God saved the world through) and intellectual elites, find its wisdom laughable causes one to ask; couldn't even a diluted person come up with something more believable? It's too preposterous to be anything but from God. This is God's own reasoning:

> For the message of the cross is foolishness to those who are perishing, but to us who are being saved it is the power of God. For it is written: "I will destroy the wisdom of the wise; the intelligence of the intelligent I will frustrate." Where is the wise man? Where is the scholar? Where is the philosopher of this age? Has not God made foolish the wisdom of the world? For since in the wisdom of God the world through its wisdom did not know him, God was pleased through the foolishness of what was preached to save those who believe. Jews demand miraculous signs and Greeks look for wisdom, but we preach Christ crucified: a stumbling block to Jews and foolishness to Gentiles, but to those whom God has called, both Jews and Greeks, Christ the power of God and the wisdom of God. For the foolishness of God is wiser than man's wisdom, and the weakness of God is stronger than man's strength. (1 Cor 1:18–25)

The argument I make in not simply that the Bible sounds like nonsense therefore it must be true. The Bible is not nonsense. It may seem ludicrous and foolish to some, but the foolishness of God is wiser than that of humans. It is a beautiful madness. God is so angry with sin and the fact that His children are separated from Him that He would rather die than live without them. The Bible is more than great literature; it is His story, the greatest love story, and God's Word. How else could this mere book be so preeminent?

The Bible may have been written by men, but these men wrote as inspired by God. God used them with their unique writing styles, idioms, and language to tell His story and share His truth. God inspired these men to write the very words He wanted them to write. In some cases, God even told them exactly what to write and they dictated it. Not only was God involved in the original authorship of the Bible, He also was involved in securing and guarding its purity. It was fashioned into scrolls, pages, and codices by scribes, who in some cases could not even read what they wrote to ensure exact duplication. We can have complete confidence that this book is still the very Word of God.

It is unique in its survival, concerning its number of manuscripts and in its integrity of copies. God protected the translation of His Word time and time again. Ptolemy II, king of Egypt around 250 BC, commissioned seventy-two Hebrew scribes to translate the Hebrew Old Testament into Greek. He locked them into seventy-two different rooms and seventy-two days later they all came out with identical translations. Such are the miraculous stories surrounding the copying and translation of the Bible. Peter penned these words about the Holy Scriptures, "Above all, you must understand that no prophecy of Scripture came about by the prophet's own interpretation. For prophecy never had its origins in the will of man, but men spoke from God as they were carried along by the Holy Spirit" (2 Pet 1:20–21).

Some still argue the authenticity of the Bible, especially the New Testament. They say others came along much later and rewrote the Bible to support the "cult of Christ." There is a tremendous weight of evidence that the Bible is what it says it is, a collection of eyewitness accounts and histories. I find it strange that no one doubts Homer's *Iliad* or Plato's *Republic*, but they doubt the authenticity of the Bible. Here's how the Bible stacks up against other accepted ancient writings.

Author	Book	Written	Earliest Copies	Gap	# Copies
Homer	Iliad	800 BC	c.400 BC	400yrs.	643
Herodotus	History	480 BC	c.AD 900	1,350yrs.	8
Thucydides	History	460 BC	c.AD 900	1,300 yrs.	8
Plato	Republic	400 BC	c.AD 900	1,300 yrs.	7
Demosthenes		300 BC	c.AD 1100	1,400 yrs.	200
Caesar	Gallic Wars	100 BC	c.AD 900	1,000 yrs.	10
Livy	History of Rome	59 BC	4th C/10th C	400–401,000 yrs.	1/19
Tacitus	Annals	AD 100	c.AD 1,100	1,000 yrs.	20
Pliny	Secundus History	AD 60	c. 850	750 yrs.	7

Author	Book	Written	Earliest Copies	Gap	# Copies
	New Testament	AD 50–100	c.AD 114 (fragments)	50 yrs.	
			c.AD 200 (books)	100 yrs.	
			c.AD 250 (most N.T.)	150 yrs.	
			c.AD 325 (complete)	225 yrs.	5,366 frags & books

(Taken from *The New Evidence that Demands a Verdict* by Josh McDowell Copyright © 1999 by Josh McDowell. Used by permission of HarperCollins Christian Publishing. www.harpercollinschristian.com)[2]

Add to this proximity in the age of the earliest manuscripts of the Bible, the fact that 5,366 manuscripts and fragments date to within 225 years of the original and compare this to the other works and you start to understand that the Bible is not like any other book. It is totally reliable, trustworthy, and authentic, and it is more so than any other book of ancient literature.

Some will argue, "How do we know we have the right writings? Others wrote gospels, how come they are not included?" Such questions are simply answered by a look at early Church fathers' quotations. Such an attack is based upon the misguided assumption that Emperor Constantine established the "cult" of Christ around AD 325. A careful look at the literary evidence will dispel such myths. The early church fathers and eyewitnesses of those who sat under the teaching of the apostles wrote about which writings were authoritative and which were not. A look at their writings where they quote verses and passages from accepted Scriptures, but not from the false writings of the Gnostics and others, authenticates the Bible we know today. The following is a report of some of the early church fathers' quotation of Scripture:

---

2. McDowell, *New Evidence that Demands a Verdict*, 38.

Section Two: Bible Study

Patriarch	Date	Gospels	Acts	Pauline	Other	Rev.	Totals
Justin Martyr	AD 133	268	10	43	6	3	330
Irenaeus	AD 202	1,038	194	499	23	65	1,819
Clement of Alexandra	AD 212	1,107	44	1,127	207	11	2,406
Tertullian	AD 220	3,822	502	2,609	120	205	7,258
Hippolytus	AD 235	734	42	387	27	188	1,378
Origen	AD 254	9,231	349	7,778	399	165	17,992
Eusebius	AD 339	3,258	211	1,592	88	27	5,176
Totals		19,368	1,352	14,035	840	664	36,289

(Taken from *The New Evidence that Demands a Verdict* by Josh McDowell Copyright © 1999 by Josh McDowell. Used by permission of HarperCollins Christian Publishing. www.harpercollinschristian.com)[3]

Additional citations by Clement of Rome (AD 95), Ignatius (AD 110), Polycarp (AD 156), Cyprian (AD 258) and others, along with the above prove that well before the Council of Nicea (AD 325) there was an established cannon of Scripture. The Bible as we know it is not a late invention of people wanting to create a new religion. It is the reliable, accurate, dependable, supernatural work of God.

There is little room for doubt. The Bible is a unique book. Its origins are from God Himself. Every bible should come with this warning in bold print across the front cover: "Warning-Reading this book will change your life! Read at your own risk." It has an effect like no other book. In Hebrews we read this verse, "For the Word of God is living and active. Sharper than any double-edged sword, it penetrates even to diving soul and spirit, joints and marrow; it judges the thoughts and attitudes of the heart" (Heb 4:12). You can't trust your senses. You can't trust your feelings. You can't trust the latest textbook, but you can trust the Bible.

3. McDowell, *New Evidence that Demands a Verdict*, 43.

It is the supreme authority given to us by God. Paul, in his letter to the Colossians, said, "Let the Word of God dwell in you richly" (3:16).

When one stops to wonder, why I should let this book have preeminence in my life, one is confronted with 2 Samuel 22:31 which claims, "The Word of the Lord is flawless." Psalm 33 verse 4 says, "The Word of the Lord is right and true." Psalm 119:89 states that, "Your Word, O Lord, is eternal." Isaiah 40 verse 8 says, "The grass withers and the flower fades but the Word of our God stands forever." Psalm 119 states, "Your Word is a lamp to my feet and a light to my path" (vs. 105), "I have hidden Your Word in my heart that I might not sin against You" (vs. 11), and "How can a young man keep his way pure? By living according to Your Word" (vs. 9). This is why we should, "Do your best to present yourself to God as one approved, a workman who does not need to be ashamed and who correctly handles the Word of truth" (2 Tim 2:15). The Bible is self authenticating. All you have to do is read it, study it, and let it prove itself to you. The Bible validates itself, Jesus attests to its authority, and God Himself validates them both through His seal of approval on them both with miracles that can not be explained away.

Psalm 1:1–6 tells the wise person,

> Blessed is the man who does not walk in the counsel of the wicked or stand in the way of sinners or sit in the seat of mockers. But his delight is in the law of the Lord, and on his law he meditates day and night. He is like a tree planted by streams of water, which yields its fruit in season and whose leaf does not wither. Whatever he does prospers. Not so the wicked! They are like chaff that the wind blows away. Therefore the wicked will not stand in the judgment, nor sinners in the assembly of the righteous. For the Lord watches over the way of the righteous, but the way of the wicked will perish.

Whose counsel are you seeking? Do you find yourself listening to the wicked, mocking sinners of this age or are you meditating on the Word of God? One way to tell might be to consider the outcome of your life's efforts. Are you prospering? Are you living a God blessed life? Do you want to? Stop listen to the voices of this age and immerse yourself in God's Word. You won't be doing it for just yourself either. Those around you will be impacted by your example. Deuteronomy 6: 1–9 commands us:

> These are the commands, decrees and laws the Lord your God directed me to teach you to observe in the land that you are crossing the Jordan to possess, so that you, your children and

their children after them may fear the Lord your God as long as you live by keeping all his decrees and commands that I give you, and so that you may enjoy long life. Hear, O Israel, and be careful to obey so that it may go well with you and that you may increase greatly in a land flowing with milk and honey, just as the Lord, the God of your fathers, promised you. Hear, O Israel: The Lord our God, the Lord is one. Love the Lord your God with all your heart and with all your soul and with all your strength. These commandments that I give you today are to be upon your hearts. Impress them on your children. Talk about them when you sit at home and when you walk along the road, when you lie down and when you get up. Tie them as symbols on your hands and bind them on your foreheads. Write them on the doorframes of your houses and on your gates.

Does the Word of the Lord consume you? Are you obsessed with it? Are you always thinking about it? There is great promise if you do, a long life and prosperity. Ignore the Bible at your own peril. Jesus stated, "He who rejects Me and does not receive My sayings, has one who judges him; the word I spoke is what will judge him at the last day" (John 12:48). The Word of God will judge you and sentence you to death or life. It seems to me you might want to study up for this test.

Jesus said, "The words I have spoken to you are spirit and they are life" (John 6:63). You cannot grow as a Christian and ignore His Word. It's the Christian's recipe for success. A story is told of a child who wanted to make his mother a birthday cake. She liked yellow cake. He knew he needed flour for the cake, and he wanted it to be yellow, so he went out and picked a bunch of dandelions (yellow flowers = yellow flour). For the icing he scraped the inside of the freezer. Obviously, the child did not end up with a cake. We might smile at such a story and think it quaint, but the truth is children can get away with it, but we are not children. We should know better, but we don't. We think we know God's will and His way, and we just head off in the direction we think is best, but we find ourselves in all sorts of trouble. Don't ignore God's recipe for success. Proverbs 14:12 says, "There is a way that seems right to a man, but in the end, it leads to death."

Chapter 6

"He Spoke as One with Authority"
—MATTHEW 7:29

IN MANY EDITIONS OF the Bible, Jesus' spoken words are written in red letters. This was to identify the very words of Jesus. Some people mistakenly believe that we can only trust the words in red. This is simply not true. The entire Bible is God's Word. Yes, the very words Jesus spoke are interesting because as the people in the crowds that followed Him said, "He speaks as one with authority." Peter himself when the Lord asked the disciples if they were going to stop following Him said, "Lord, to whom shall we go? You have words of eternal life" (John 6:68). Wherever Jesus spoke the people were amazed (Matt 22:22). They were awe-struck by Jesus' teachings, but Jesus Himself showed the greatest respect for God's Word (not just the words in red). Jesus spoke to God about God's Word and said, "Your Word is truth" (John 17:17). Jesus had authority when He spoke because He based His teaching on the Word of God. Anyone who speaks the truth from God's Word is going to be perceived as wise. But the one who mocks God and scoffs at God's Word will come to ruin. They do so because they have rejected God's truth and therefore lack understanding. After all, the Proverbs tells us, "A scoffer seeks wisdom and finds none, but knowledge is easy to one who has understanding" (Prov 14:6).

I have met many people who have rejected the Bible and dismissed God's Word. They often consider it little more than fairy tales and on par with Greek mythology. They declare knowledge and understanding superior to the Bible, but when things come apart, they ruminate that they just don't understand. If only they had some of that humility when they started, they might not have neglected God's wisdom. "There is a way that seems right to a man, but in the end, it leads to death" (Prov 14:12). I find that most people believe they are right. When confronted with someone else's opinion that's different from theirs they simply agree to disagree. It's hard to trust someone else, especially a God you can't see. Every time we drive down the street, we trust complete strangers to obey the rules of the road (an amazing act of faith). To trust others, one must have faith. The real reason some people just can't trust the Bible is that they lack faith.

To have faith in the Bible does not require one to blindly accept everything it says. Faith does choose to accept things it does not fully understand, but it is not blind, nor is it without reason. Christians somehow have gained the reputation of being mental midgets, but this is simply not the case. Many of the intellectual elite's schools of choice were founded by Christians. Harvard, Princeton, and others still have divinity schools. A lot of our civilization's greatest philosophical, scientific, and literary minds were and are Christians. Bacon, Copernicus, Dante, Kepler, Galileo, Descartes, Pascal, Newton, Pasteur, Kelvin, Aquinas, Milton, Chesterton, Eliot, Lewis, Augustine, Bach, and Handel, are among a long list of famous Christians and they were giants in their fields. It takes great intellect to understand the tenants of the Christian faith and yet it makes so much sense that children readily embrace faith in Christ. The Bible is a thinking person's book. It not only gets you thinking, but it also educates and imparts wisdom. It is one thing to have knowledge but quite another to make wise choices and this is what the Bible teaches.

One day rulers, the elders and the teachers of the law, met in Jerusalem to question Peter and John. These were the most educated of their society. Acts 4:13 tell us, "When they saw the courage of Peter and John and realized that they were unschooled, ordinary men, they were astonished, and they took note that these men had been with Jesus." These were no ordinary men because they had been schooled by Jesus. Have you been schooled by Jesus? If you are reading the Bible on a daily basis, you are. If you want to distinguish yourself from your peers, if you want to have an opinion that matters to others, school yourself in God's Word. Don't just read books about the Bible, read the Bible for yourself. God wants you to read the Bible so He can whisper into your mind. He will give you understanding and insight beyond yourself. This wisdom from above will be noted by others.

The Bible is the owner manual for the human soul. All we have to do is read it and follow it. When we disregard its wisdom, we get off track and loose our way. When we follow it, we build on a firm foundation. Don't think that you know better than God. Deuteronomy 4:2 warns us not to add to God's Word or to take away from it. God doesn't need an editor. An army can't choose to follow some of orders but disregard others. God has given us clear orders to follow; to pretend He hasn't is to our peril. We must resist the thought that we are our own god.

Jesus Himself tells us that God's Word is truth (John 17:17). It is wholly trustworthy (Pss 19:7, 111:7, and 119:86). Titus 1:9 reminds us, "hold firmly to the trustworthy message as it has been taught, so that (you) can encourage others by sound doctrine and refute those who oppose it." When someone hands you a treasure map you don't pretend North is South or say East is West. Not if you want to find the treasure. You follow it exactly, because the one who has hidden the treasure has been there and you must trust the map. Jesus has been there, and we must trust Him and His guidebook, the Bible. Think about it, God is omniscient, He knows everything. His knowledge transcends time. He knew what twenty-first century beings would need to hear way back when the Bible was written. You can't say that about science. What was "true" in Copernicus' day is no longer "true." Science continues to update human knowledge and understanding. It has to do this because human knowledge is limited, it develops and grows, but God's knowledge is so much superior to man's knowledge. God doesn't need to update His understand or His Word like science has to with their textbooks. You're the one who needs to update your understanding with the perfect wisdom revealed in the Bible.

When I was growing up television shows often focused on fathers. Since then, I have learned that indeed the Heavenly Father does know best and wise people will acknowledge it. Jesus' mother, Mary, was one who understood that God knew best. When she was told that she, a virgin, would become pregnant by the power of God and that she would give birth to the Savior of the world, she said, "May it be unto me as you have said" (Luke 1:38). Now that's faith. She accepted the fact that God knew best, and she was willing to go along for the ride. Many of us are control freaks. We like to be in the driver's seat, but that doesn't cut it when it comes to God. He demands that He sit there, and you move into the back seat. There used to be a bumper sticker which said, "God is my co-pilot," but that is not quite indicative of the Christian's relationship with God. God is the King of kings. He will not play second fiddle to anyone. If the president showed up, you would offer him the seat of honor. Place God on the thrown of your life and read His Word, the Bible, daily. He will get you to where you need to be, just trust Him, and read His wisdom daily.

If it's written in the good book, it will happen. You can trust it and take it to the bank. Jesus came to the temple one day and found the money changers in the temple courts selling animals for sacrifice. Jesus was enraged with this because He knew God's Word. He made a whip and drove the money changers out of the courts overturning their tables and yelling, "It is written! My house will be a house of prayer!" (Matt 21:13). Jesus let the Word consume Him. His anger was a righteous indignation. He knew the way God planned things to be and He was moved to make it so. God's plans and His will won't be thwarted. How will you know what God wants if you're not reading His Word? Let the Bible consume you. It is written, "For I know the plans I have for you," declares the Lord, "plans to prosper you, and not to harm you, plans to give you hope and a future." (Jer 29:11).

Without the Word you will fall into temptation. We stumble and fall even with the Word; how much more susceptible would we be without it? Without bible study we will not be able to distinguish between truth and a lie, we will not know what the right thing to do is. The Bible is our measuring stick. It's how we know right and wrong. We dare not trust ourselves; we can't trust our fellow man, but we can always trust God. God doesn't lie. He is a good God who desires to give good gifts to His children because He loves us. The Bible is one of God's greatest gifts to us. 2 Timothy 3:16–17 tells us that, "All Scripture is God-breathed and is useful for teaching, rebuking, correcting and training in righteousness." The education one receives from a lifetime of reading, is better than any PhD. We spend hundreds of thousands of dollars on a college education, but the Bible and its education, is free. All it takes is time, effort, and discipline to read it daily. The person whose life is trained by it is noteworthy.

So why is your Bible still on the shelf? Do me a favor, if you are reading this book right now and you haven't read your Bible today, go find it and read something from it right now. I'd rather you read God's Word than mine anyway. You can always come back to this book later.

It's really all about priorities. Give God's words first place over all your reading, television watching and internet browsing. We used to have a saying, "No Bible no breakfast." Reading your Bible daily is just that important for a Christian. Barna recently reported (2021) a survey stating that only 11 percent of the U.S. read their Bible daily and 29 percent don't ever read their Bibles.[1] And yet their surveys indicate that the number one predictor of spiritual maturity is daily Bible reading. No wonder the maturity level of Christians in the West is in decline, they are no longer people of the book. If God's faithful aren't reading the Bible, then the not so faithful surely will not and the world will have an easier time squeezing us into their mold and Satan will have an easier time tripping us up.

"All men are like grass, and all their glory is like the flowers of the field; the grass withers and the flowers fall, but the Word of the Lord stands forever" (1 Pet 1:24–25). Our ways, our plans, our accomplishments don't really amount to much. It's all a chasing after wind. But the Word of the Lord lasts. God will not contradict it. He will not go against it. Man can't stop its prophecies from coming true. When I think of the word *stand*, I think of a sentinel who stands guard. They are there keeping watch and they are on the ready. They don't sit, they stand. They don't sleep; they don't get distracted with television or music. They know that they serve an important function and that lives are on the line. If they fail their own life may be forfeited. I think of the great ancient city of Rhodes, which was a port, and at the entrance to the port was a huge statue standing guard over the port, with one foot on one side of the entrance and the other foot on the other side. He held a torch in one hand as he stood guiding friends to their safe haven of rest and yet stood guard against intruders. This is what I think of when I hear the words, "the Word of the Lord stands forever." And though this giant Colossus is no longer standing over the port of Rhodes, God's Word will always stand guiding all those seeking safe harbor in God's kingdom.

Deuteronomy 6:17–19 warns, "Be sure to keep the commands of the Lord your God and the stipulations and decrees he has given you. Do what is right and good in the Lord's sight, so that it may go well with you, and you may go in and take over the good land that the Lord promised on oath to your forefathers, thrusting out all your enemies before you, as the Lord said." Do you want it to go well with you? Christians who practice these five disciplines live a God blessed life. The very first Psalm makes this clear:

> Blessed is the man who does not walk in the counsel of the wicked or stand in the way of sinners or sit in the seat of mockers. But his delight is in the law of the Lord, and on his law, he meditates day and night. He is like a tree planted by streams of

---

1. Barna Group, "State of the Bible 2021: Five Key Findings."

water, which yields its fruit in season and whose leaf does not wither. Whatever he does prospers. Not so the wicked! They are like chaff that the wind blows away. Therefore, the wicked will not stand in the judgment, nor sinners in the assembly of the righteous. For the Lord watches over the way of the righteous, but the way of the wicked will perish. (Ps 1:1–6)

This psalm contrasts those who seek God's knowledge with those who don't. The word blessed means happy, so happy is the person who turns to God's Word and obeys it. They are like a well-watered fruit tree producing an abundant harvest. Whatever they do prospers. They have the Midas touch. It's not that way for those who disregard God's Word and disobey His commands. They become insignificant. They are objects of scorn and ridicule. Their lifestyle leads to death. The difference between these two groups is that one reads the Bible and strives to live by it and the other does not. People may think they know right from wrong; they may think they remember the values they were once taught when they were young, but they run the risk of doing as they see fit in their own eyes. They may be remembering wrong. They may have encountered some influences which have confused their understanding of God's way. In the Psalm it speaks of a tree that is planted. It is rooted and doesn't move. It stays right there by the stream, so it remains well watered. You don't water your house plants once and never water them again. You watch them and water them when they need it sometimes every day. You went to Sunday School when you were young. That's great. I'm sure it helped you when you were young and may still have some affect, but back then as you studied the Bible you were doing so with a limited mental capacity. Your ability to understand concepts have changed and grown. You can now understand subtle nuances. You can drink more deeply and comprehend more.

I enjoy watching children's films. A child understands the basic story, identifies with certain characters, and learns the morals taught, but the writers will often have all sorts of material clearly targeted for adults that the kids just don't get. The kids may even react at these adult targeted moments, but they don't understand it fully. It was purposefully placed there to entertain the adults who take the children to the film. It makes the film more than just a kid's film. It becomes a family film. The Bible was written so that it could be read on many different levels. It's so simple that a child can understand it and yet so deep that wise people will be amazed by it. It is timeless, ageless, and relevant to every generation. The same passage can speak powerfully to many different people undergoing many different experiences. One passage can be applied so many ways. It can have many different lessons. Why do you think the Bible is the world's number one best seller of all time? It is a blockbuster.

Not continuing to read the Bible because you already read it is like not eating because you did it once before. Think about that, your tastes have changed. Things you use to turn your nose up to when you were young are now your favorite foods. You have developed a distinguished pallet. You appreciate a meal that blends various flavors and textures together in just the right way to complement each other and enhance the subtle differences to tantalize the taste buds. Things you would never even think of trying have proved to be a delightful surprise. In the same way how, you read the Bible changes, grows, and matures. I continue to learn different lessons from passages I've read thousands of times. It's not just ink on a page. When you read it, the Holy Spirit becomes your guide. He gently leads and guides the reader in understanding the words they are reading, and He helps the individual apply what is read to their personal situation. Reading the Bible without seeking the help of the Holy Spirit is like a child trying to bake a wedding cake without a baker's help. This is why you should always start your Bible reading with a little prayer asking God for help.

I'd like to close this chapter out with an appropriate passage from Proverbs. This is what Proverbs 2:1–22 tells us:

> 1 My son, if you accept my words and store up my commands within you,
>
> 2 turning your ear to wisdom and applying your heart to understanding—
>
> 3 indeed, if you call out for insight and cry aloud for understanding,
>
> 4 and if you look for it as for silver and search for it as for hidden treasure,
>
> 5 then you will understand the fear of the LORD and find the knowledge of God.
>
> 6 For the LORD gives wisdom; from his mouth come knowledge and understanding.
>
> 7 He holds success in store for the upright, he is a shield to those whose walk is blameless,

⁸ for he guards the course of the just and protects the way of his faithful ones.

⁹ Then you will understand what is right and just and fair—every good path.

¹⁰ For wisdom will enter your heart, and knowledge will be pleasant to your soul.

¹¹ Discretion will protect you, and understanding will guard you.

¹² Wisdom will save you from the ways of wicked men, from men whose words are perverse,

¹³ who have left the straight paths to walk in dark ways,

¹⁴ who delight in doing wrong and rejoice in the perverseness of evil,

¹⁵ whose paths are crooked and who are devious in their ways.

¹⁶ Wisdom will save you also from the adulterous woman, from the wayward woman with her seductive words,

¹⁷ who has left the partner of her youth and ignored the covenant she made before God.

¹⁸ Surely her house leads down to death and her paths to the spirits of the dead.

¹⁹ None who go to her return or attain the paths of life.

²⁰ Thus you will walk in the ways of the good and keep to the paths of the righteous.

²¹ For the upright will live in the land, and the blameless will remain in it;

²² but the wicked will be cut off from the land, and the unfaithful will be torn from it.

There are two ways to approach life, with God's help or without. You can have the benefit of His divine wisdom or not. Daily reading your Bible will enable you to face whatever life throws at you. It doesn't take long, and it has a cumulative effect.

Chapter 7

"Take the Helmet of Salvation and the Sword of the Spirit"
—EPHESIANS 6:17

IN PAUL'S LETTER TO the Ephesians in chapter 6 he tells us to put on the whole armor of God. There's the belt of God's truth, the breastplate of righteousness, shoes that enable us to share the gospel, the shield of faith, the helmet of salvation, and the sword of the Spirit which is the Word of God. A lot has been said about this passage, such as the first five pieces of armor are defensive in nature. The belt of truth girds our loins (and holds up our pants), the breastplate protects our vital organs, the shoes give us a sure foundation, traction, and keep our feet from injury, the shield of faith deflects the arrows of our enemy, and the helmet protects our head or mind. The only offensive piece of armor we are to put on is the sword of the Spirit (notice that it's the Spirit's sword not ours). As a pastor I am holding back and fighting the urge to elaborate on the first five pieces of armor, that is for another day. In this chapter I'd like to discuss with you the way we use the Bible to benefit the kingdom of God.

First it should be noted how much the five defensive pieces of armor depend on the Word of God. We know truth (the belt) through the Bible. We can live rightly or are awarded Christ's righteousness (breastplate) because of our relationship with Jesus, something we never would have been able to do without the Word. We could not share the gospel (shoes) if we didn't read about it in the Bible. We would not have come to faith (the shield) without the good news found in God's Word. We would not have salvation (the helmet) had not someone led us to faith in Christ using the gospel message of the Bible.

The Bible teaches us about the five spiritual disciplines. We would not understand what fellowship is, were it not for the Word. We would not know where to go for fellowship if the Bible didn't point us in the direction of the Church. People wouldn't know how to pray without the Bible giving us examples and telling us how. The importance of prayer would not be understood without God telling us through His Word. We would not know what to say when we witness if it were not for the Bible telling us the good news of the gospel. The Christian wouldn't know of the importance of serving God and our fellow man through ministry, without the Word explaining it to us and commanding us to do it.

If you've been a Christian for a while, you must know by now that we are in a spiritual battle. We are not in a political struggle, nor are we fighting against other religions. We are not wrestling against other people. We battle against unseen evil forces of wickedness, against darkness in this world. We appear as lights in this darkness. The light of the gospel cuts through the darkness like a knife through butter. That knife is the sword of the Bible. The Word is a double-edged sword (Heb 4:12). It cuts both ways. With it we can distinguish the difference between the truth and a lie. It is a mirror with which we can see what we really look like to God, and it is measuring rod we can share with others so they can see if they measure up.

The Word of God works inwardly to benefit the Christian trying to live a life worthy of the calling with which we have been called and it works outwardly to help others refute crooked ways of thinking. It can be a broadsword, thick and heavy, able to deliver a powerful blow or it can be a scalpel, subtly dividing bone and marrow, to promote healing. It is an offensive weapon to defeat the enemy, the devil and it assists us in our war against the cancer of sin in our lives. By reading the Bible we know what is healthy and what is sinful, and we know who our friends are and who our enemy is.

In our spiritual battle the Bible can be wheeled by an uncoordinated novice or an experienced warrior. In the spiritual operating room, it can be used by a well-intentioned child or skilled doctor. Which are you? We know the Word of the Lord, the Bible, is always sharp. It's ready and powerful. It's not the sword that needs sharpening; it's the soldier using it. The problem is not with the Bible; it's with those who wheeled it. In basic training every soldier is issued the same type of rifle, but only a few become marksmen. Even though their life depends on it they don't always care for their gun as they should. With Christians our riffle sits on the shelf collecting dust and as any gun collector will tell you not keeping a gun clean can cause it to miss fire. Do you know where your Bible is? When was the last time you polished up on it? Do you know the books of the Bible in order? Can you find references quickly or does it take you quite a while to find verses? How many times have you read through the Bible? Reading though it once is like giving your rifle a good cleaning once. Some great Christian leaders made it their practice to read through the Bible every year.

I first read through the Bible when I was sixteen. I wasn't a good reader, and it took forever. I would get bogged down in the genealogies or in the laws for the Levitical priesthood. It took me a year and a half to complete the task. I found I understood the great literary works discussed in my English classes better after I read the Bible. Every few years I would undertake to read through the Bible again with the same result. I benefited greatly every time I read through it, but it would take a while. Then while on a mission's trip to the Dominican Republic I met Zeral Brown a missionary and founder of TIME Ministries. He shared with us his daily devotion reading plan, which I had not seen before then. He would read three chapters a day. On Monday he would read from the Pentateuch, on Tuesday he would read from the historical books, Wednesday he would read from the wisdom books, Thursday he would read from the major prophets, Friday he would read from the minor prophets, and Saturday he would read from the New Testament and on Sunday he would read whatever he liked or catch up if he missed a day. This system helps you stay motivated.

On Monday you might be trudging through the genealogies, but on Tuesday you would have a great story of the children of Israel. Wednesday was always a breeze for me in the wisdom literature. Thursdays might be interesting. Friday was the toughest for me, but Saturday was a delight. It wasn't like the whole week I was stuck in the same boring spot making my devotions a chore rather than a delight. Reading the Bible straight through from cover to cover is like bowling with mittens on. Why put yourself at a disadvantage? Reading the Bible should not be drudgery. It should be something you look forward to every day. It should be a joy. The Bible was not written in that order anyway. It is dear to me. It's like a family member.

You don't become an expert on Shakespeare by reading a sonnet. Memorize the books of the Bible in order. Memorize some of the more important verses of the Bible with citations. Using flash cards is very helpful. Memorize where to find important passages. This will help you know where to turn to find out about important subjects. There's nothing more frustrating than discussing basic principles of the faith with someone and not remembering where you read it. Having such knowledge readily at your disposal will help alleviate your apprehension about sharing your faith with others. Reading books about the Bible are good and helpful, but do not mistake reading this book, Bible handbooks, encyclopedias, theology books, commentaries, devotional books, or books written by your favorite Christian author, for bible reading. Nothing can replace your Bible.

The Bible will teach the art of submission as well as how to honor your parents and grandparents. People learn how to get along with siblings. They will be exposed to God's ideal for the family. Everything they read in the Bible will not be a good example. They will see plenty of poor examples as well. Young adults will be better prepared for marriage as they will learn the art of giving oneself wholly to their spouse to build them up and help make them the best they can be. Married people will have practical help in fighting the temptation to commit adultery. The Bible teaches parents how to raise their children. They will be given both positive and negative examples of childrearing and see their consequences. Older parents will be given the wisdom to handle turbulent times with teens, young adults, and grandchildren. In the Bible we learn God's plan for the family. You won't find that anywhere else. As the world increasingly desires to squeeze people into a new definition of family the Bible may soon be the only place to learn what a godly family is.

By your reading the Bible you will be a benefit to your community. People you work with, your neighbors, friends, and others you come in contact with will see the difference Christ has made in your life through the power of His Word. You will learn how to be a true neighbor. You will learn about the importance of friends and how to treat them. You will learn how to work together with team members and building others up. When your life is poured out like this you will have opportunities to share your faith. Your personal witness will be so much more effective as you will know how to share the gospel effectively. You will learn to pray for your government officials. You will know how to respect others and how to be a good citizen. In this age the Bible may be the only place where you really learn to serve your fellow man rather than self.

If you regularly read your Bible, you will be a benefit to your church. In Sunday School classes, Bible studies, and just in conversation you will have insights that come from God. People will listen to you because you will be speaking as one who has authority, not because you are haughty or you lord your Bible knowledge over anyone, but because you point others to God's wisdom, which is the only true authority. You will discover your spiritual gifts and use them effectively. You will learn to lead others in the ministry. You will be able to teach others because you yourself have been taught by God. You will have vision to encourage and motivate others because you will be tuned to the Holy Spirit. You will be able to listen critically and keep other leaders from stepping away from sound doctrine. Nowadays there are churches which have strayed from the authority of God's Word and their congregations are paying the price. You may even be in such a church, all the more reason to read your Bible and let your light shine so God's Word will once again have its place in the church.

Most of all, reading God's Word will make you a ready workman. He will be able to entrust you with greater responsibility because of your good foundation. God will not be ashamed of you because you are not ashamed of Him. He will take special pleasure in you, His obedient child. You will know God's marching orders and He will have greater confidence in you. You will be ready in season and out of season, thoroughly prepared for every good work. Some day may you hear God say, "Well done thou good and faithful servant."

Chapter 8

Summary Section: Bible Study

How Do I Get Into Reading My Bible?

For some of you, reading the Bible will be easy, like falling off a log, for others (especially non-readers) it will be a struggle. I don't ask that you take on more than for which you are ready. If you are new to reading the Bible, I suggest you start with the Gospel of John. Read a chapter a day or whatever feels right for you. Sometimes you read a single verse and you are so blown away, that you must think about it for the rest of the day. Other times you read the whole chapter. The important thing is that you make time every day. It's best to start your day reading the Bible because it gives you something to think about and use the rest of the day.

 Do you enjoy the outdoors? Then take your Bible for a walk. Do you like music? Then play some instrumental music while you read your Bible. Light some candles. Try listening to one of the many cds that have someone reading the Word on it. Get a box of Scripture verses and take one with you every day. Pull that card out a few times during the day and place it back in the box. The next day take a new one. Whenever you are waiting for a red light, an appointment, or for the copy machine pull that card out and read it. Do you like sports? Write your favorite passage or verse onto a baseball, football, or hockey puck. Do you spend hours and hours of your time at the computer? Then find a site where you can read the Bible (I suggest *Bible Gateway*)[1] or find a

---

1. BibleGateway, "Home."

screen saver with Bible verses scrolling on the screen. Many sites offer a verse of the day for your screen.

I think you might be getting it by now. What are you passionate about? Incorporate it into your Bible reading. If you like to paint, then paint what you read in the Bible. If you like to read murder mysteries, then use your memory verse card for the week as your bookmark. Have devotions every morning with your cup of coffee. I like to occasionally incorporate a hymn book. Set up a regular routine or change it up every day. On Mondays have devotions in the morning on the porch, on Tuesdays have it at your favorite lunch spot, Wednesday have it before bedtime, Thursdays you could do your Bible reading in the park, Friday listen to a reading or podcast on the way to work. Saturday you could share devotions with your spouse or person you are dating, and Sunday you could reread a verse you heard in church that was especially meaningful to you. Whatever works for you. Sometimes it is like the seasons, you need a regular routine for a while, and then you need variety, so you change things up for a while. Sometimes you need the gospels, at other times you crave the Old Testament. Try reading a chapter of Proverbs every day for a month. There are thirty-one of them, so it fits nicely in many months. Make a list of your top fifty Bible verses.

Journaling

Something you may find interesting, and something I recommend is journaling. Get a notebook, diary, or journaling book and write about your Bible reading. You place the date on the top of the page, the verse or passage you read, list insights you have learned from the passage you read, write questions you have about what you read, list any prayer requests (or things you have been dealing with lately), write out a sentence prayer for guidance, or write whatever you like. Keep a prayer request page noting when prayers were answered and how. Many people do a short version of journaling in their Bibles. It is not a sin to write things in your Bible. Use colored highlighters. Get a wide margin Bible so you have more room to write in. Start your own chain reference system linking verses and passages together that might be related or are about a similar topic.

The great thing about journaling is that you can go back over your week and see patterns and themes that the Lord is teaching you. You can be reminded about things you have questions about and reinforce important concepts. You can have a place to organize your prayer requests which can become a testimony page to remind you how faithful God is to answer your prayers. It is interesting to go back and read a journal after years have passed. You can see that you have grown and matured in your Christian walk. If you try journaling and it doesn't work for you, try doing it once a week or once a month. It may not be something that helps you in your Bible reading right now, but in the future it might click.

What Kind of Bible Should I Read?

There are so many kinds of Bibles. There are Bibles designed for teenagers, women, men, hunters, soldiers, fishermen, athletes, businesspeople, and probably anything else you can think of. There are picture Bibles, archeological Bibles, Bible magazines, devotional Bibles, family Bibles, comic book style Bibles, and dating Bibles. Some Bibles come on DVD, cd, and in electronic file format for your iPod, smart phone, and reader. There are Bibles in many different translations; there's the King James, Revised Standard, New American Standard, New International Version, The Message, and many more. Some Bibles are very precise in their language and literal translations of the original language. There are Bibles which interpret the original language into today's vernacular. There are study Bibles with lots of extra materials like maps, illustrations, charts, graphs, commentary notes, chain references, articles, profiles, overviews, and a condensed concordance. There are large print Bibles and pocket-sized Bibles. Some are expensive and others are cheap. Purchasing a personal Bible can be overwhelming.

There are a few questions which will help guide your selection of a Bible. Depending on what you use it for might steer you toward or away from one type or another. Will it be for personal study or reading? For ease of reading, you might choose a Bible with no notes or references, large print, in a readable version such as *The Message*. If you will be writing in your Bible, then you might want to note how much blank space is on a page to make your notes. Will this be a Bible that stays on the end table, or will you be carrying it everywhere? If you are taking it everywhere then you might want a durable leatherbound, small light weight Bible. If it will stay in one place you could consider a paper or cloth cover, large study Bible with all the bells and whistles. Are you new to reading the Bible? You might prefer a Bible with tabs for the different books of the

Bible. If you are only interested in the New Testament then you can save a lot on price, size, and weight by purchasing a New Testament.

Talk to friends about which Bible they prefer. Which version does your church or pastor use? Try the various versions out. Borrow a Bible and read it for a week. You can buy a Bible from Walmart, a local Christian bookstore, or online. Most Christians will end up with quite a variety of Bibles. I still have my first serious study Bible. It is the most precious book I own. If you are buying your first or only Bible, might I suggest a Study Bible, in a modern translation of your choice, and leather bound. It might be a little cumbersome taking it with you on vacation, to the office, or church, but if you are going to buy only one car, why get a used two-seater, with a broken radio and nonfunctioning wipers? Go top of the line. Spend the extra money, it will last longer and be of more use to you. Obviously, if you can't afford to buy a Bible, pick one up for free. Gideons give them away. You can find New Testaments or Gospel of John in paperback free for the taking in most churches.

I Don't Understand What I Read. Can Anything Help Me?

There are books called commentaries, which explain passages to you. You can read them in conjunction with your Bible reading. Some of these are for serious scholars and pastors and others are for laypeople. You can get a handbook which gives you an overview of every book of the Bible or a Bible commentary which has quick and simple summaries of every chapter of the Bible. You can buy a more in-depth commentary on a given book of the Bible. Ask questions of your church friends or pastor. Attend a Sunday School class and a Bible study where you can ask questions and listen to other people's questions. You will soon realize you are not alone in your quest to understand the Bible. There are also devotional books written by popular Christian authors on topics or books of the Bible which will explain passages in a relevant and practical way. Some of these authors are a delight to read as they use humor and narrative to help you see the application of a given passage, but once again do not mistake reading a commentary or devotional book for reading the Bible.

Make sure you start your reading with a simple prayer asking God to help you. The pages of your Bible are filled with ink on every page, but that's all it is, without the help of the Holy Spirit. Reading God's Word is not just a cerebral process. Reading your Bible is as much about your heart as it is about your mind. It's part of your ongoing conversation with God. In prayer we talk to Him and through His Word He talks to us. There are other ways God talks to us, such as through other people, circumstances, answers to prayers and the like, but only in the Bible do we have something that is tried, trusted and true. If you read something you don't understand, ask God what it means. He may be holding something back for which you are not ready. Remember God wrote this book for you. These are a collection of love letters from the one who loves you more than any other. Sometimes it's just a matter of putting your Bible down and meditating upon it for a while. When you come back to it, somehow it makes sense. God is like that, He does things in His time when we are ready, when the timing is just right.

What Is the Difference between Bible Reading, Bible Study, and Bible Memorization?

Reading the Bible is for getting the big picture. It helps us understand what God has done in general ways. Reading large portions of the Bible gives us an overview and helps us put the different pieces together. It's like viewing a completed puzzle, you can see how the pieces all fit together and you can get the idea of what the picture is all about. We use Bible reading for inspiration and general understand. Bible study, on the other hand, is taking smaller portions, or even verses, and doing a careful investigation. It's like taking the puzzle apart and taking each piece and categorizing them by color, shape, and size. We use Bible study when we don't understand something. It's slower and more gradual. It's asking questions about the details, which one reads, and it gives a different understand that reading does not always supply. One is impressionistic and the other is diagnostic. One is the work of the artist painting with broad strokes and the other is the work of the surgeon performing exploratory surgery.

Bible memorization is taking the ink on a page and hiding it in your heart. It allows you to have God's Word with you always. It's a practical application of the desire to let God's Word dwell in you richly. You commit to memory verses and even passages that have particular importance to your life or witness. We don't memorize the Bible to show off, nor do we try to impress people about ourselves. Memorizing Scripture is helpful for the individual because God will bring the verse to mind in various situations and circumstances to teach or remind us about something.

Some verses have the power to bring others to faith in Christ or to help heal a hurting soul.

Always memorize the citation along with the verse so you can find it. Some people take on a certain memory verse as a life verse. What's a life verse you ask? Well, it can be your purpose in life, what God keeps bring up to you, or the greatest thing you admire or respect. It can mean many different things to many different people, but when you come across yours it leaps off the page and you don't even have to memorize it. It is so profound, so wise, and so true that you can't help but remember it (like a first kiss). How do I find my life verse you ask? Read the Bible regularly. God will show you. Some people have many.

Joining for Devotions

Nothing beats personal private devotions for the individual, but children and families need help, direction, and an example to follow. Having devotions with your spouse, children, or your entire family has great benefits. For one thing you are all focused on the same thing at the same time. It gives you shared experiences, which bind you together. It impresses the importance of Bible reading upon all. Having joint devotions not only holds you accountable to have them, but also holds you accountable to live out what you read. It encourages others, especially children to go and do likewise. "But what do I do if my spouse doesn't want to do family devotions?" It is to their shame, and they will be held accountable someday, but so will you. Just because your spouse doesn't take out the garbage, doesn't exempt you from taking it out. Imagine how foul a house would smell if no one took the garbage out. If you take the initiative to have family devotions and do so humbly (giving opportunity for others to take the lead) you will be rewarded for your faithfulness. Who knows, others might surprise you and want to lead as they grow in their understanding of the Word.

Couples who are dating would be wise to set up a pattern in their relationship of spending time together in God's Word. Parents need to help their young children with their devotions. Activities, music, and games can be incorporated to make family devotions fun and exciting. Creativity is the key when working with children. If you struggle in this area, there are a plethora of devotional ideas for families found in books and on the internet. When having family devotions, you use the Bible appropriate for the youngest of the participants (even if it's a picture Bible). God's Word is so profound that no matter how simple the presentation He can speak powerfully to any open heart. "Isn't joining with others for devotions really group Bible study?" Yes and no. It is group Bible study but what makes it different from other group Bible studies are the relationships involved. The relationships are so close and intimate that joint devotions with others can be just as personal as private devotions, and sometimes it can be even more personal.

Children are great sponges and soak up God's Word easily. They are hearing the greatest story ever told for the first time. Don't be afraid to get your children memorizing verses either, they seem to have a knack for it. Put a verse on each plate before breakfast and ask each one to share their verse and what it means to them. Write a verse on the back of an appropriate jigsaw puzzle. When the family is putting it together, lead them in a predetermined discussion. Then when the puzzle is completed tell them there's a secret message from God for the family on the back of the puzzle. Use crayons, paints, and clay to help express what the verse being considered might mean. Keep a joint journal. There are plenty of creative things you can do for all ages. Children who are raised in such a way will have a better chance of incorporating Bible reading into their personal quiet times and to continue the tradition with your grandchildren someday.

Section Three

Prayer

Chapter 9

"Men Began to Call upon the Name of the Lord"
—GENESIS 4:26

AFTER ADAM AND EVE were kicked out of the garden, they still had contact with God. Cain and Abel worshipped God, sacrificed to Him, and spoke to Him. They began to procreate, and other men and women were born. These new people undoubtedly heard the story of the creation and fall of man. Perhaps people longed for the days of Adam and Eve when they could relate to God face to face. Whatever their motivation we read in Genesis 4:26 that they began to call upon the name of the Lord. I can hear them now, "Where are You God? I want to talk to You! How come You are hiding Yourself from us?" It was undoubtedly their sinfulness which kept God at a distance, but it was then that people learned to call out to God in prayer. Before that they spoke to Him face to face. It would be like your spouse being deployed to Afghanistan and only being able to email them from now on.

Prayer is talking to God. You can speak in an audible voice, or you can speak to Him in your mind. You can write your prayers in a journal. God is the Almighty God who can hear your prayer no matter where you are. He always has good reception (full bars). God is so great that He can listen to everyone praying at the same time. He is omnipresent, which means He can be with you listening to your prayers at the same time He is halfway around the world listening to a million other prayers. Talk about multitasking! There is no proper form for prayer and there are no right words you need to use. God knows and understands our hearts. He can read the mess of our minds and know what we mean. He is the awesome God of the universe, the all-powerful, and all knowing, only true God. He must be respected, reverenced, and feared. When one comes to Him in prayer, they might want to check their pride and arrogance at the door. God desires us to humble ourselves before Him, to ask for forgiveness. Beyond that, He is a loving heavenly Father, and we can climb up on His lap and call Him Daddy. We can't tell Him anything He doesn't already know. We can't shock Him with our honesty or bluntness. He understands that sometimes we get angry at Him. He is not threatened by our outburst (though He may sometimes be disappointed with our attitudes).

Prayer is crying out to God, "I'm here! Remember me?" It is an innate need to connect with God. This need is a response to fill what the seventeenth-century philosopher Blaise Pascal called "a God shaped vacuum in the heart of every man which cannot be filled with any created thing, but only by God."[1] Pascal called it an "infinite abyss." We can't help but cry out to God. God has left His fingerprint in our soul. We are His offspring; we are His children. We've run away from God, and we have this gnawing guilt. Part of us wants to run home and another part of us wants to continue in our defiance. Man's calling out to God is from the part of us that wants to be home with God once again.

Prayer, like Bible reading, should not be a chore. It should be as natural as breathing and as easy as talking to a friend. You don't have to be in church. You don't have to be in private. You can be at work, school, or at the mall when you pray. God is everywhere and He's always listening. In fact, He is waiting for you to talk to Him right now, so why not stop and talk to Him.

When we talk to God in prayer it is an exercise in faith. Praying pleases God. When we pour out our hearts to Him, we are acknowledging Him as God, sovereign over all. Prayer is also an act of love. When we pray, we are saying that we care. We don't just care for ourselves, but we desire to align ourselves with the Only One powerful enough to hear and answer our prayers. It's a swearing of allegiance. Prayer is the making of a covenant, "You be my God and I will be Yours." We pledge our devotion, and He is willing to serve as our benefactor. In prayer we praise God, thank Him, confess to Him, and ask Him for things. This is called the

---

1. Pascal, *Pensees*, 425.

A.C.T.S. of prayer; *a*doration, *c*onfession, *t*hanksgiving, and *s*upplication (supplication comes last because prayer is least about asking for things).

Listening is an important part of prayer too. Focus on God not yourself. Place yourself at the foot of His throne and wait for an audience with the King. Then when you get there wait till you are spoken to, then you may answer. Somehow, we have it all mixed up. We barge into His presence and start making demands of God then we rush out without ever listening to what He has to say. I tell people that the most neglected part of prayer happens after we say amen. We've let our requests be made known, but we don't listen for the answer. Then we wonder why what we have asked for hasn't come true yet, as if the great genie in the sky must grant our wishes.

God answers every prayer request with yes, no, or wait. "Would God really say no to His children" you ask? Don't you say no to yours? Can you imagine a world where every child's request is answered in the affirmative? What an awful world that would be. In the same way God says no to some of our requests because He sees the big picture. He knows better than we do what we need and when we need it. The Christian who has truly learned to pray has learned that prayer is all about respect, trust, and faith. Even Jesus when He was in the garden prayed, "Nevertheless, not My will but Yours be done" (Matt 26:39).

Prayer is the exercise of our faith and sometimes that exercise gets intense. Sometimes it's a request that we are passionate about, and God says no or wait. Maybe He waits to answer our prayer, so we double our efforts and our passion. Sometimes we argue and fight with God. I suppose it's sort of like a child throwing a temper tantrum. The child kicks and screams, but as a parent we understand it's time for their nap. In the same way God understands our weaknesses, questions, and anger. He loves us despite the hissy fits we throw. Sometimes our earnest and respectful prayers change God's plan. Jacob wrestled with the angel all night until he was blessed (Gen 32:24). Jesus told a story about the persistent neighbor who finally got what he needed from his friend because of his refusing to take no for an answer (Luke 11:5–8). On one occasion a Canaanite woman came to Jesus and asked for her daughter to be released from her demonic possession (Matt 15:21–28). Jesus at first ignores her, but because of the woman's persistence her request is finally granted. King Hezekiah was told by the prophet that God said he was about to die, but he earnestly pleaded with God for a longer life, and it was granted (2 Kgs 20:1–11). On another occasion God told Moses He was going to wipe out the children of Israel for their worshipping a golden calf, but Moses pleads with God on their behalf and God changes His mind (Exod 32:7–14). These stories and others remind us of the power of persistent prayer. There are some things that can only be accomplished through prayer, and I don't know about you, but those are the things I want to see done.

There are so many examples of prayer in Scripture. Jonah, the reluctant prophet, was one who was honest in his prayers. Not only do we have a great example of a prayer of repentance in Jonah chapter 2 when he was in the belly of the fish, but we also have him honestly pouring out his heart in disappointment after Nineveh repents and God relents. God is big enough to take your honesty. He's also discerning enough to judge the attitude of your prayers to see if they are righteous or not. God loves us so much that sometimes He takes our emotions into account. He understands us because He was a man once. He was tempted in every way just as we are but was triumphant in resisting against sin. Jesus himself prayed with great emotion as He sweat drops of blood and asked the Father, "May this cup be taken from Me" (Matt 26:39).

So, the next time you're thinking you disagree with God, let Him know what you're feeling, but do this with gentleness and respect. For Jesus also said right after the above prayer, "Yet not as I will but as You will" (Matt 26:39). Jonah in his prayer in 4:2–3 bitterly cried out to God, "Isn't this what I said, Lord, when I was still at home? That is what I tried to forestall by fleeing to Tarshish. I knew that you are a gracious and compassionate God, slow to anger and abounding in love, a God who relents from sending calamity. Now, Lord, take away my life, for it is better for me to die than to live." We might view Jonah's attitude as childish, but let's face it, we all get that way every now and then.

A few years back much was made of the prayer of Jabez.[2] In essence it is how to justify asking God for blessings. In 1 Chronicles 4:10 we read, "Oh, that you would bless me and enlarge my territory! Let your hand be with me and keep me from harm so that I will be free from pain." Wilkinson went into explaining how Jabez was really asking for blessings so that he might not cause pain or harm to others. When you think about it that way it sorts of sounds like extortion or blackmail, but God grants this man's request. Do not be afraid to ask God for blessings with right

---

2. Wilkinson, *Prayer of Jabez*.

motives. He is the good and perfect Father in heaven who enjoys giving good things to His children.

In James 4:2–3 we read, "You do not have because you do not ask God." James also goes on to say, "When you ask, you do not receive, because you ask with wrong motives, that you may spend what you get on your pleasures." The rightness or wrongness of our prayers has less to do with what we ask for and has more to do with why we ask for something. We cannot hide our motivations from God. He knows the thoughts, attitudes, and desires of our hearts and minds. So let your prayers be heard, but you might want to check yourself first. Make sure you don't have any un-confessed sin in your life. Be honest with yourself and ask why you want what for which you ask. Is it for yourself (the poorest of reasons), others (a better reason), or for the glory of God (the best reason)? Moses in Exodus 32 was able to convince God to change His mind by praying that God's reputation was at stake. Bridle your heart not your tongue when it comes to prayer.

We are told in Scripture that the Spirit makes intercession for us when we don't know what to pray (Rom 8:26). Hannah is a good example of this. In 1 Samuel 1:10–16 we read,

> In her deep anguish Hannah prayed to the Lord, weeping bitterly. And she made a vow, saying, "Lord Almighty, if you will only look on your servant's misery and remember me, and not forget your servant but give her a son, then I will give him to the Lord for all the days of his life, and no razor will ever be used on his head." As she kept on praying to the Lord, Eli observed her mouth. Hannah was praying in her heart, and her lips were moving but her voice was not heard. Eli thought she was drunk and said to her, "How long are you going to stay drunk? Put away your wine." "Not so, my lord," Hannah replied, "I am a woman who is deeply troubled. I have not been drinking wine or beer; I was pouring out my soul to the Lord. Do not take your servant for a wicked woman; I have been praying here out of my great anguish and grief."

The most important part of Hannah's prayer was her deep anguish and grief, and even when the words would not come out of her the Holy Spirit heard her heart and made intercession for her. Hannah's request was for her sake so she would save face with her family. She felt useless and shamed because she was barren. Being a mother was what she wanted all her life, but she was denied. God saw her plight (He needed a great deliverer and prophet anyway); He decided to use Hannah, answered her prayer, and through her raised up a great and godly spiritual leader for Israel, Samuel. God can sometimes work your wants, needs, and desires into His plan, but you've got to show Him how earnest you are and exercise your faith.

Solomon was a great example of prayer and right attitude. When he was dedicating the temple (2 Chr 1) he made an extravagant sacrifice in worship as an offering. God is so touched by his worship that He asks Solomon what he might want. Here we have God willing to give Solomon, riches, long life, and great glory, but Solomon asks for a wisdom and knowledge to be the best ruler he could be over God's people. God is so pleased with the request that He gives Solomon wisdom, knowledge, riches, glory, and long life, not because he asked for these things but because he asked for wisdom and knowledge for the sake of others and not for himself. O that our desires would so please the Lord that He would bless us in abundance.

Jesus was asked by His disciples to teach them how to pray and in Matthew 6:9-13 we have a sample prayer (called the Lord's Prayer). In this passage we are taught to worship God in our prayers and then to ask for the immediate necessities of the day. Asking for forgiveness is an important part of this sample prayer too, but the bulk of the prayer is worship and praise, not asking for things. Jesus' prayer is quite simple. It's not long and it is focused on God not us. It's focused on His will not ours. In that same chapter Jesus taught about how prayer is not an opportunity to look good in front of others. It is an intensely personal and private thing that we sometimes share with others. He reminds us that our loving heavenly Father knows what we need and that He will take care of us.

Christians often have a misguided ideal of what a prayer warrior is. They have in mind someone who prayers in the King James language and for hours on end. In the life of Jesus, we see someone who yes, got up early in the morning or stayed up some nights to pray, but he also had time to preach and travel about. He went to parties and spoke to individuals. My point is that He was not always on His knees. His life was lived as a prayer. He teaches us that our actions are often louder than our words and that a prayer devoid of a righteous life is powerless. When Paul admonishes us to pray without ceasing (1 Thess 5:17) he's encouraging us to not give up, not to keep praying every moment of every day. He wants us to live in an attitude of prayer. To let prayers flow through our everyday experiences naturally.

Some people ask for signs when they pray. They ask God to meet their pre-arranged criteria to confirm His will. Asking for a sign or *fleece* comes from Judges chapter 6 where Gideon asks God for confirmation of God's will by making a fleece of wool wet in the morning but the ground around dry. Gideon wakes up the next morning and the fleece is wet, and the ground is dry, but the morning dew might have simply evaporated leaving the dew in the fleece only. To make sure Gideon prays a second prayer asking that the fleece be dry and the ground around it to be wet on the next day. He wakes up and it is so. Asking for signs often will cause confusion. What we think is God's answer may be a natural occurrence or simply coincidence.

Asking for a sign is really asking God to confirm His will with some special occurrence of His power. Someone might say. "If this is the church You want me to attend then when I walk through the door have a motorcycle race out." Then they go to church and a kid with a motorcycle on his shirt runs past them on their way in the door. That's not exactly what they prayed for, but God has a wonderful sense of humor. Then they're left not knowing if that was God or just a coincidence. People usually ask for something impossible or farfetched. I think people just want to know for sure what God's will is. They don't trust their own judgment to discern God's will; they want God to tell them plainly. The only problem with asking for a sign is that God is not bound to your deal. Just because you ask for a sign doesn't mean He's going to give you one. If you ask for something to happen or not and God does not answer your request, whatever happens by chance is taken as God's will when He said nothing concerning your request. Often you end up even more confused than before.

Some people would tell you that asking for a sign is putting God to the test. After all Deuteronomy 6:16 commands "Do not tempt the Lord your God." Others will tell you that it is your faith that is tested. Very rarely does God tell us to put Him to the test. One such place where God tells us to test Him is in Malachi 3:10 where He tells us to test His faithfulness to provide for the tither (one who gives ten percent of their income to the Lord). The Israelites were constantly testing God in the wilderness, and He chided them for doing so. A good example of this is Exodus 17:1-7 where Israel was in open rebellion at Massah. Moses had to give them a sign (water from the rock) to confirm what they should have already known that God would always be with them and provide for them. If Jesus, when tempted by Satan in the wilderness (Matt 4:6-7), was not willing to put God to the test why are we so quick to do so? Gideon was afraid and full of doubt. Who could blame him for putting a fleece out? It was an exercise of Gideon's faith.

God understands our need for direction and assurance. He does not always demand blind faith, but I believe there is a difference between confirming God's will and asking for God's will. Confirming God's will indicates that you think you know God's will already, whereas asking for God's will means you don't have a clue. Using a fleece to confirm God's will is often a natural reaction to the realities of following God. However, it is risky to use a fleece to determine what God's will is. Either way when using this method you must bathe your request in prayer, fasting, and righteousness.

I would caution you if you want to pray for a sign. Be careful how you word your prayer and do this sparingly. When you pray for a fleece put some thought into it. Doesn't it take greater faith to believe that God will work all things together for good for those who are called according to His purpose? Asking for signs might betray a less mature walk with the Lord. It says that you're not sure about His promise and you want Him to back up what He has said with a miraculous demonstration. A mature person of faith trusts and believes God's Word.

I've often thought that prayer would be overwhelming to me if I were God. Imagine everyone praying different things all at the same time. Only the true God would be able to handle it. Think about it, people are praying all around the world twenty-four seven, three hundred and sixty-five days a year, in every imaginable language, year after year since shortly after the creation of the world. I get tired after five minutes when my grandson keeps asking "Why." Those whose prayers please God, whose lives are pleasing to Him. God calls saints. The real true Christian is supposed to be a saint. Saint is not a title awarded by humans; it is a title bestowed by God. In Romans 1:7 we learn that Roman Christians are called saints. Elsewhere Paul uses the terms believers and saints interchangeably. The Bible uses this term sixty-seven times and it is never used to identify a special class of Christian. All true believers seem to be given this title. I say all this to bring us to Revelation 5:8 which tell us that the prayers of the saints continually come up before the Father as a type of incense. They are like the aroma of freshly baked bread in the house of God. Your simple and humble prayers are pleasing to God. They are a joy to Him.

Your prayers make a difference. Not only are they heard by God, but He will act upon your request and take your needs and wants into consideration. He will even use His mighty powers for your good. There is no other act more powerful than the prayers of a righteous person. When a Christian is on their knees no government official has more authority. All the military might of the world pales in comparison to the force that is brought to bear when you pray. It is the most important thing you do, or don't do, every day. When you pray the devil shutters. When you pray Satan flees. Why would you not start every day in prayer? Why would you not start everything you do with prayer?

Chapter 10

A Personal Testimony to the Power of Prayer

THERE ARE MANY INSPIRING stories on the internet concerning prayer. No doubt you've read some. A missionary is about to be attacked, but halfway around the world some faithful group of twenty-six Christians burdened for him are in prayer and the attackers stop because they see twenty-six armed guards protecting the missionary. Such accounts are always astounding but often are met with skepticism. Rather than regale you with such stories I will tell you what has happened to me. It started in college when I used to joke with my friends about how I was going to start a book called *Godincidences,* where I would proclaim the mighty hand of God in my life. I now wish I wasn't kidding. I encourage you to start your own memoirs. You might be able to disclaim all other stories, but you will never take away the truth of these firsthand accounts of mine for me.

I was my senior year in high school. I had an old standard Chevy my stepmother had given me. The battery was dying so I always parked it on a hill so if it didn't start, I could jump start it by rolling it down the hill and popping the clutch. After work I picked up a friend and went to tell my mother I was going to Sears to buy a battery. I thought my mother was at an auction house in town, so I went there. The parking lot was sloped on a hill, so I parked up at the top. I shut off the car and we got out finding the place locked up with no one around. We went back to the car, and I tried to turn the engine over, but the battery was completely dead. I pushed in the clutch and let it roll backwards down the parking lot and popped the clutch. The car started and then stalled in the street at the bottom of the hill in a slump. My friend and I tried to push the car to get it going both forward and backward however, we could not get far because of the grade of the hill. We were stuck. This was in the day when people didn't have cell phones. There were no pay phones. In fact, we were out at the end of town in the middle of nowhere. There were no houses around and it was a couple of miles back to town.

What would I do? After sitting in the car for a while talking about our options my friend and I decided to pray and ask God for help. We prayed and got out of the car, leaned up against the car, and waited for a car to pass by so we could hitch a ride. Suddenly, a hitchhiker came upon us and said, "Let me help you push the car so you can get it going." I thought this was strange because we didn't have the hood up. We had no sign. We didn't have our thumbs out. How did he know we needed a push to get the car started? Had he seen us? No, he was nowhere when this whole thing started and only came walking up presently to the situation after we prayed. I didn't make much of it then, but it really made me wonder after. My friend and I tried, and we could not get the car up the hill for twenty minutes. This stranger comes along and tells us to get in the car and he would push us. We told him it would take all three of us to push the car and he told us he'd be fine and to get in the car. We did, he pushed the car, got it rolling, I popped the clutch and the engine started up.

He was hitchhiking so I offered him a ride. I told him I'd take him anywhere he wanted to go, after all, he just did me a huge favor, but he said, "No thank you. I'm going on much further." "Could I at least give you a ride to the interstate?" "No thanks, I'll be fine." "Well, let me at least give you some money for helping us." "No thanks, I've got all I need." "Okay, well, thanks for the push." And I drove off. The funny thing about this story is that as I pulled away, I saw him in the rearview mirror one minute and the next instant he had vanished. Where had he gone? It was a deserted area and no place for him to hide. At that moment I knew God had answered our prayers and sent an angel to help us. Who knows what dangers God saved us from on that day? Since then, I always pay attention to my battery and my prayer life.

The next year I was driving home from a discipleship meeting with a mentor in a Rambler I had picked up after the Chevy. It was late and drizzling. I was coming around a corner on a wooded stretch of road and there was a car heading straight for me on my side of the road. There was a telephone pole and woods to my right so I could only pull over so far. I tried to brake but was unable to stop. I prayed, "Oh God, help!" That was all I had time to pray. The oncoming car was on me. Their left headlight and my right headlight seemed to pass through each other as our cars passed by without hitting. I can relive that instant of my life and remember every detail. I have no explanation for how our cars did not hit in a head on collision. I know what I saw; two objects occupied the same space at the same time. I have no other way to share it. It is impossible I know. There is no other way to put it; it was a miracle.

Maybe these examples are too much for some of you. I can assure you that there were thousands of other prayers that were answered less dramatically. There were many times I prayed for the weather to change and low and behold it changed. The weather defied the forecast and everything that was happening in the towns around, but where we needed it, God poked a hole through the massive weather front and stopped the rain. There are thousands of little things I have prayed for, and He has been favorably disposed to grant most of my requests. If it was all chance, then how is it that 90 percent of the time what I asked for came true? If it was all chance, I should expect a 50 percent response.

There was one time my girlfriend (my now wife, Lynda) was about to break up with me for kissing another girl. She was extremely hurt. She stormed out of the house and went for a walk. I prayed that the Lord would change her heart and that she would forgive me. As she was walking, she asked that if God wanted us to continue dating that He would send her a sign and just then a shooting star raced across the sky. I guess you could say our love was like fireworks. She forgave me and forty-two years later; we're married with three children. I had prayed for a wife who would be able to withstand the rigors of ministry, support my ministry, and who would join me in service to our Lord. Enter Lynda.

When we were about to become first time parents the doctor came in, after twenty-seven hours of back labor, with the news that the baby was in a transverse position and the heart rate of the child indicated that the baby was in distress. He was concerned for the baby's life and told us to prepare for an emergency caesarian section. Lynda and I prayed for the baby's life, and I boldly asked that God allow things to change and for the baby to be delivered naturally and within a few minutes the doctor came in expecting to go to surgery and found that everything had changed, and Lynda delivered our firstborn, Hillaire, moments later. God has faithfully answered prayers for my family time and time again.

Speaking of my wife, Lynda was feeling especially poor one Sunday morning. It wasn't an illness, but more like a tiredness and spiritual struggle that she was dealing with. Before she left to teach Sunday School she prayed to God and said, "God, I know You are there, but I really need a hug from You this morning and I know you're probably giving me one, but I'm sorry I just can't feel it." She got to her classroom and her class was going up to the sanctuary for a program. The children were lined up to leave when suddenly a little boy came running toward her with his arms wide open yelling, "You know what Mrs. Cooke? I love you!" When he hugged her, she shared that instead of falling apart an incredible peace came over her. Lynda knew that was an answer to her prayer. God gave her the hug she needed, and that hug has gotten her through many hard times since. That little boy will never know just how much God had used him, but my wife does, and someday in glory they will sit down together, and she will share that story with him, and they will hug again. I want to be there for that one and to thank that young man for his ministry to my wife.

One time when I was out jogging my keys had fallen out of my pocket. I retraced my steps, a three-mile trek, twice and was unable to find them. I was tired and needed to get somewhere when finally, I stopped and prayed, "God, I can't find my keys. You know where they are, could You please help me find them. I have some important ministry with the youth group to get to. In Jesus' name I pray, amen." When I opened my eyes right there in front of me on the side of the road were my keys. What are the chances that they would be at that spot where I would choose to finally pray and ask God for help? Since then, I have realized that God cares even about lost things and is sometimes just waiting on us to ask Him for help. I know He was laughing at me as I ran around looking for my keys time and time again, just waiting for me to ask Him for His help. I know if I had asked Him sooner, I would have found those keys sooner. It was like God was trying to teach me something.

Another time I was working on the car, and I took a nut off and placed it on the engine and when the time came for me to put it back in place, I could not find it. It was not where I put it. I crawled under the car with a flashlight, searched the ground and the undercarriage for it, but I could not find it. I crawled up literally on top of the engine looking everywhere inside, and in every nook and cranny, but the nut was nowhere to be found. Once again, in frustration I cried out to God for His help. When I opened my eyes there it was right in front of me on top of the engine. That time I heard Him laugh. These last two happened to me as a young married man as God was teaching me to ask Him for help even with the small stuff. I've learned that if you don't want to lose things and if you want to have everything go well, start your project in prayer, no matter how mundane and unspiritual it is, and God will help make things go far better than when you try to function in your own strength and wisdom.

As a pastor I have learned to pray before every meeting at church and before every ministry in which I take part. I pray about all my preparation for ministry, and I pray for the results of the ministry in which I am involved. But it took me a while to learn to pray about non-ministry things. I had a dichotomy in my world, parts of it were spiritual and the other half was secular, but God showed me that there was no divide and that He wanted to be intimately involved in every part of my life. Occasionally, when I'm doing a project around the house, and something goes awry I inevitably stop to realize that I didn't start in prayer and start laughing at my foolishness and God and I have a chuckle as I ask for forgiveness and for His assistance yet again. It seems this was an important lesson that God does not want me to forget. Without Him I can do nothing!

Don't get me wrong, there have been a few times when I didn't get what I prayed for. I've asked for some pretty selfish things and God knew better than me and gave me what I needed, not what I wanted because it was in my own best interest. Some things I will have to ask Him about though. One time I was camping with my son, Kyle, with a good friend and his son. It was a wet week as we backpacked and canoed through the wilds of Algonquin Park in Canada. In the evening if the rain permitted, we would troll the lakes fishing. Two of us would paddle while the other two would fish. My friend and his son would catch these beautiful fish and my son's eyes would bug out of his head, but we weren't so lucky. I wanted my son to have a great experience, but it rained every day, and he wasn't catching any fish. I could see his frustration growing each day. The last time fishing I passed on my turn with the rod so Kyle would have twice the chance of catching a fish. With every paddle (all week long) I prayed, "Father, please let him catch a fish . . . Please let him enjoy this experience." But he never did catch a fish on that trip and the trip was remembered as something that he survived. As a father I was brokenhearted for him. I was so disappointed that God did not answer my prayer. I know it seems quite trivial and I would gladly trade those prayer requests in Algonquin for more important answers elsewhere, but it doesn't work that way.

It's not like we only have so many "wishes" that God grants. God's power is not limited. He could grant every prayer request all our lives long, but have you ever met someone who always gets what they want? Too often they end up thinking they are entitled to everything and are not grateful for anything. I will still ask God someday about my prayer for my son to catch a fish, but I already know the answer. "Elliott, you lived a full life and we've been through a lot together, and your greatest disappointment was that I didn't help your son catch a fish? There were lots of other prayer request I would have gladly answered for the real needs of others, but you never asked. Talk about being disappointed." (Ouch, maybe I won't ask Him after all.) You don't always get what you want from God. After all it's not about us, it's about Him. He is the Good Father in heaven who gives good gifts. He doesn't give us snakes when we ask for bread. As Christians, walking around with the power of prayer in our pockets, we start to feel like we live a charmed life, as if no harm will ever come to us, like God has to give us what we want. We run a danger of thinking that God owes us. This is not what prayer is.

Prayer is the exercising of our faith in a close, intimate conversation with God. I find that when my prayers are focused on others or on things that God would be interested in that He answers those prayers at a much greater rate. It reminds me of John 15:7 where Jesus says, "If you remain in Me and My words remain in you, ask whatever you wish, and it will be done for you." When we seek first His kingdom and His righteousness then our prayers are going to be things that God wants to do anyway. I'm not saying that God doesn't care about you the individual. I'm not saying that you shouldn't pray for little things and things for yourself. When we are young children, our parents take our immaturity into account when dealing with us. God is the same way. When I was a baby, I got away with slapping my dad's face, but when I got older, I never would have gotten away with that. When I was a baby, I got away with screaming for my bottle, but as a teen I never would have gotten away with screaming for my allowance. I believe that God deals with us differently during different stages of our lives. The more mature we are in Christ, the more He expects our prayer requests to be selfless and for His kingdom.

Vacation Bible School (VBS) was a big deal at one of our churches. It was one of our flagship ministries. We did it well and the community loved the opportunity to send their children. One year we worked hard to prepare for the program and prayed for the best VBS ever. The month of our VBS road work put up an inconvenient detour cutting off entire neighborhoods from easy access. It rained three of the five nights of our VBS, and our attendance was down a third. We were concerned and wondered why God did not answer our prayers for an abundance of children and many decisions for Christ. Wouldn't this please God? Weren't we praying for and seeking God's will? What we learned in our evaluation was the fact that 20 percent of the children who came to VBS made decisions to accept Christ as their Lord and Savior. 24 percent were new children representing new families reached. What we see as obstacles and failures is in fact God working His will behind the scenes. Without that rainy night a mother may never have said, "That's it, you've been in the house all day. You're going to VBS!" Without that detour a family who would have usually not driven past our church had to, saw our VBS, and sent their kids. You never know what is best to ask for when you pray, but you have to trust the one who is in control and knows best.

One Sunday morning I woke very disturbed by a detailed dream I had. I shared the dream with my wife, Lynda. It was about the Senior High Sunday School class I would be teaching in just a couple of hours. In my dream a couple of girls were very disrespectful, disruptive, and argumentative. I shared with my wife the very things that were said. She dismissed it as a bad dream. In my final preparations for class, I prayed that if the girls did act out like they had in my dream that God would give me the ability to change the way I handled the situation. In my dream, everything I said and did, seemed to incite the girls in their attack. I got to the classroom early and prayed once again. As my class got underway, I was dumbfounded as my dream started to be lived out just as I had shared with my wife. God helped me hold my tongue and gave me wisdom to handle the situation with grace. An adult helper in the class with me was not so fortunate. A lot of the attack that was against me in my dream was now refocused upon him. As it was going on I prayed that God would diffuse the situation. This was a spiritual battle like I had never known. After class I didn't have the chance to debrief with my helper because I had the service to prepare for. I knew I would have a chance to discuss things with him later. While I was off preparing with other leaders for the morning service, my wife was approached by my classroom helper who started to share that he just had the worst Sunday School class experience of his life. My wife asked him if there were two girls involved. He said yes. She told them who they were. He confirmed their identity. She told him the types of things they said. He said, "That's right. I guess you already heard." Lynda told him that she hadn't talked to me since early that morning and about the dream that I had shared with her before class. Both of them were dumbfounded. As horrible as that class was it could have gone even worse had not God told me about it ahead of time and if I had not been fully clothed in prayer to deal with the situation.

I tell people that prayer is having a conversation with God. Most people refer to prayer as talking to God, but I believe that God speaks to us in prayer too. While we pray, God brings to our minds certain Scriptures as answers to our prayers. He speaks to us in a still small voice in our minds and hearts. He speaks to us after we say "Amen." God speaks to us throughout our days, and we speak to Him. Life is an ongoing conversation with God. The only question is, are we listening? God desires to have a relationship with us. He wants to be our best friend. Without prayer this cannot happen. As I have said not many of my experiences with prayer are this dramatic and it is the countless common prayers that actually help me to believe in the power of prayer.

One time, a young man in my congregation asked me to help him promote his need for a car. He had three thousand dollars to spend on it. I prayed that someone would give him a car. I shared his need at prayer meeting later that night and the people prayed for him. He came up to me that Sunday to share that someone, not from our church, gave him a car. He was so excited to have his first car and was amazed that it was given to him. I was not so amazed. I just smiled. That's just like my God. God knows what we need before we ask. He loves us and wants to provide for us. This wonderful young man, a son of missionaries, was blessed and our prayers for him were answered.

This is the most common type of answer to prayer I have experienced. I still call them Godincidence because only God could work this way. You might be tempted to call them coincidences; I call them the mighty hand of God because of the vast number of coincidences. I suppose that one such happening could indeed be a coincidence, but when hundreds of such coincidences just happen, then they become proof of the power of prayer. It's the preponderance of evidence that proves to me the power of prayer. It's overwhelming and amazing. I pray you will see this same power of God manifest in your life as you take more seriously this whole idea of prayer to God.

Without devotion to prayer a Christian simply will not experience Godincidences. They will miss out on the blessings of experiencing this power of God in their lives. One's faith is proven by the evidence that comes from a life of prayer, without it one's faith is immature. You may not share this conviction about prayer, but I challenge you with this; give it a season. Go to prayer meetings. Pray regularly. Keep a prayer journal. Watch your faith grow as you see the hand of God like you have never seen before. Without the discipline of prayer, a Christian will simply not grow in the faith. It is a key and central discipline meant to grow a Christian to maturity in Christ. The only question is, will you use it, or will you simply let this opportunity pass you by?

Chapter 11

"Teach Us to Pray"
—LUKE 11:1

Jesus was once asked by His disciples, "Teach us to pray" (Luke 11:1). Jesus gave them the Lord's Prayer as an example. I've mentioned elements of this prayer already, but I would like to discuss with you how to pray. Many people find praying difficult. They feel like they don't know how to pray. I'm not sure if they just find talking and expressing themselves difficult or if they truly have trouble with prayer. Sometimes people just have a difficult time putting into words what they are thinking. They get tongue tied and feel it all comes out wrong. This discourages them from praying. This happens to people who pray out loud as well as people who pray quietly in their minds. If this is you, I can help. I'll start with what prayer is not.

Certainly, there are those who have a difficult time praying out loud. They worry over what other people will think of their efforts. They don't want to be embarrassed so they don't pray at all. They keep their prayers private; between themselves and God. Jesus said, "And when you pray, do not be like the hypocrites, for they love to pray standing in the synagogues and on the street corners to be seen by others. Truly I tell you, they have received their reward in full. But when you pray, go into your room, close the door, and pray to your Father, who is unseen. Then your Father, who sees what is done in secret, will reward you" (Matt 6:4–6). Praying out loud in church or in a group of people can be dangerous and lead you to sin. Jesus tells us that there are some people who love to be heard by other people. That's their motivation for praying. They want attention.

This is not what prayer is all about. People who are tempted to pray for attention ought to curb their praying in public and focus on praying in private. Jesus is not saying that all prayer should be done in private. Jesus Himself prayed in large and small groups. What Jesus was teaching was that prayer is not about proving to others that you are a good Christian.

Some people attend the midweek prayer service because "that's what good Christians do," and they want to be known as a good Christian. They pray long prayers with language which is not normal to their speech. The whole thing starts to take on heirs like a performance. Pride comes before a fall. I'm not busting people for using flowering speech or those who pray long prayers, but rather those who do such things to be seen by others. Somehow praying like this in front of others raises their self-esteem. We pray because our relationship with God needs it. In prayer we pour out our hearts to God, not to a group. Sometimes others might hear our prayers, but our prayers are not directed toward people, they are directed to God, and motivated by their love for Him and a desire to commune with Him.

There are many reasons to pray in public and doing so is not a sin. When we gather together for prayer or turn our attention to God in prayer in a group setting, we are agreeing with each other's prayers. We know that if two or three Christians agree on earth it will be bound in heaven (Matt 18:17–19). Sick people are encouraged to seek out their spiritual leaders to have them pray in a group over them (Jas 5:14–15). Many of the examples of people praying in Scripture are found in public settings. Many of the commands to pray are made in the plural ("you all" pray . . .). By joining together in prayer our faith and requests are strengthened exponentially. If your representative in congress hears from you on an issue, you get a form letter in return, and they do whatever they want. When they get thousands asking them for something they do it. Yes, sometimes the squeaky wheel will get the grease, but a broken-down machine gets the mechanic's full attention (or at least should). So, corporate prayer has its place in the life of every Christian, after all the early Church was continually gathering for prayer (Acts 1:14). What matters is who the prayer is directed toward, and if others are willing to agree with your prayer.

When praying in public, to keep from drawing attention to yourself, pray in short bursts and allow for a group conversation with God. Use sentence prayers. Don't dominate the prayer time. Take turns allowing others equal time. Listen to what others are praying. Agree with them in your heart or say amen. If they pray for it and you agree with them, then you don't have to pray for it again. Some might think that you didn't think they did a good enough job in their prayer, or it shows that you were not listening. Now if you pray for different aspects of the same thing that's fine. Allow silence to simmer. You don't have to fill up the silence with vocalized prayer. Such times are important to listen to what the Holy Spirit might be saying to you.

Not all prayers should be voiced. Even in a group setting there are certain things that would be inappropriate to pray out loud. Prayer can lead to gossip as we pray about things no one is supposed to know about. You can always share about an "unspoken" request. People can lift your need before God without knowing the specifics because God, who knows all secrets, will know what it is even if the group doesn't. General prayers of confession are wonderful, but airing your dirty laundry makes others feel uncomfortable. Use general language and speak the specifics to God quietly in your heart.

As I have emphasized previously, don't simply ask God for things. Praise Him. Thank Him. Group prayers should always include a general repentance and request of God to forgive His people from their sin. The Lord's Prayer is a group prayer because it is in the plural. Consider the fact that it is brief, reverent, and general. He includes a confession and a simple supplication. Your motivations for leading God's people in prayer are the spiritual needs of the people and your faith in God's ability to hear and answer your corporate requests

In prayer you do not address people or demons. There is only one God and Lord over all. Some people are in the habit of rebuking Satan in prayer. Engaging demons while you are praying to God is disrespectful to God and elevates the demon as if they are on the same level as God. Demons are not omnipresent. They can't hear your prayers unless they are present. Demons flee when Christians pray. How do you feel when someone is talking to you and then in the middle of your conversation, they turn their focus to someone else and ignores you for a while? You see their eyes focus off in the distance then they call to someone across the room. Sometimes they do this in mid-sentence. Such disrespect is not polite, but in prayer it is just downright rude. You wouldn't do this when addressing the President, why do you think you can do it with God?

The smaller the group praying with you the more intimate the setting is. Pray is sometimes shared with a single prayer partner. When you pray privately with just one other person you hear more of their true heart and attitude in prayer. Give me five minutes of praying with someone and I'll learn more about them than I could in working with them for months. Listening to someone in private prayer is like looking through a window into their soul. They are more honest. This is why opposite sex prayer partners is not always a good idea. When looking for a prayer partner find someone who is a Christian, you respect, and you can trust to keep your confidence. You might want to find someone around your age because they would better understand what you're going through. If you are married, you might want to find someone who is married. The next time you meet with them ask them how it's going with that prayer request they shared with you. Do this regularly and your souls will be knit together, and you will see the power of God unleashed in your lives. When praying with a prayer partner you need to establish an agreement of confidentiality at the beginning, otherwise it could lead to great hurt.

Prayer is not only to be done at church; it is to be done anywhere. It's not just performed at mealtimes; it's done whenever you have the urge or a need. I like to always have an empty chair around because it reminds me of the presence of God. The chair not only reminds me of the presence of God, but it also reminds me to talk to Him and include Him in my everyday life by praying to Him. Some people believe that there is a special prayer language. They think you must use certain words and phrases in a prescribed manner for your prayer to be heard. I suppose this is why written prayers abound and some people would rather read a prayer than to make one up on their own. Using someone else's written prayer would be like you sending your spouse a love letter I wrote intended for my wife. Now we will often cite poetry in our love letters, but what makes a love letter great is that it is the expression of one's own feelings. In the same way prayers composed by the individual praying them are more representative of our feelings. Prayer is simply talking to God. There are no right words as much as there is a right attitude. Prayer must be sincere and respectful. Some of the best prayers I ever heard were prayers uttered by children with poor language skills. It's their pure innocence that shines through the prayer and pleases God. We can do the same.

When you pray, stay within your natural vocabulary. Don't use words that you don't know. If the prayer has deep meaning for you then it will have deep meaning for God. If you try to represent yourself as something you're not, then God will see through your charade and such prayers are not very pleasing to God. Be brutally honest with yourself and with God. Be more real than you are with your best friend and God will draw near to you. He's not keyed in on certain words; He's keyed into your heart. People who are not Christians or who just became Christians aren't well versed in the highly technical religious jargon used by those in the church. That's okay with God. Non-Christians see our flowery language as evidence of our arrogance and hypocrisy. So, when praying out loud in public please use the k.i.s.s. principle; *keep it short and simple.*

Private prayer is a matter of personal preference. You can kneel, stand, sit, or prostrate yourself. You can have your eyes open, closed, or focus upon an object (as long as you're not praying to the object). You can pray out loud or in your mind. You can write your prayers and even burn them if you like. Some people like to pray clutching a cross. You can hold your hands palms up toward heaven, you can fold them in your lap, or you can raise them above your head. Whatever you think is respectful and appropriate is fine. Some of these things can make prayer more meaningful for you. God sees your heart and will hear the prayer offered in faith. The important thing is to direct your prayers to God.

Some people like to pray to Mary or some other saint. Some people like to pray to dead relatives. In the Old Testament Jewish believers are never seen praying to anyone other than God. Jesus never prayed to dead believers, nor does He ever encourage us to pray to saints. The New Testament never encourages us to pray to anyone other than God. The whole tradition of praying to dead believers, on one level, makes sense; after all they are in God's presence and have His ear. So, if God is not listening to you maybe if you talk to some other mediator God will listen to them. The only problem with this is that people, dead or alive, are not omnipresent nor are they omniscient. They can't hear your prayers and they can't mediate for you. Scripture tells us that there is only one mediator between God and man, Jesus (1 Tim 2:5).

Jesus tells of a story of Lazarus and a rich man (Luke 16), they both die, and Lazarus goes to heaven and the rich man goes to hell. There in hell the rich man is in torment by the fames and the rich man calls out to Abraham for relief, "Father Abraham, have pity on me and send Lazarus to dip the tip of his finger in water and cool my tongue, because I am in agony in this fire" (vs. 24). Abraham says there is nothing that can be done because a great chasm separates them that cannot be crossed. Lazarus is not allowed to go talk to the rich man's family. Lazarus is enjoying comfort and pleasures at God's side. Lazarus shows no care for this conversation. The rich man is told that his family have the scriptures and Jesus and that they should turn to them.

Surely Mary holds a special place in Jesus' heart as she served as His earthly mother. She is to be revered for her work and sacrifice. God highly esteemed her and so should we, but to pray to her does not make sense from Scripture. Jesus even asked His beloved disciple to care for Mary and treat her as his own mother because she would need his help (John 19:27). If she had power and could answer prayers, she would not need a guardian to watch over her. If she were so great, why were the apostles leading the church and not her? I have great respect for Mary as God's chosen vessel to give birth to our Lord, but to assume that she is given power to answer prayers is a stretch and may even be considered blasphemous. When I was in graduate school, we were told to cite primary sources, not secondary sources, because they held greater authority. Why would anyone go to a mediator in prayer when they can go directly to the Father themselves is beyond me.

I'm certain Mary has a special position in her relationship with Jesus. I'm certain she is revered in heaven by all the saints. When I get there, I will give her honor, but she is not God just because she gave birth to Jesus. She is called the mother of God, but we must remember that she was only the mother of Jesus. Jesus did not come into existence when He was conceived in Mary's womb. He is God, eternally existent. Mary has no power or authority over Jesus. Sure, Jesus submitted to her authority when he was on earth but that was His choice, it was not a result of her position. Jesus also submitted to Caesar and paid taxes to him, but this does not mean we should pray to Caesar. Focus your prayers on Jesus, the Father, or the Spirit (after all they are God).

Sometimes your grief may be so great that you don't know what to say. That's no reason to not come before God. He knows what you need before you ask (Matt 6:8). Even when you don't know what to say in prayer, the Spirit prays for you (Rom 8:26). This is a strange experience. You come before Him, beat your breast, and cry your tears and God knows what you need and what is on your mind. He knows what you would ask for if you could. I find this kind of time with God a very powerful form of prayer. Just because you don't know what to say is no reason to not spend time with Him. If you were sick but didn't know what was wrong, you'd still go to the doctor wouldn't you? Not knowing what was wrong is in fact the reason you would go to the doctor. Well, the same principle applies when you don't know what to pray. Even when I don't know what to pray, just coming into the presence of the Lord comforts me, and I leave with a peace that passes all understanding.

God is waiting and longing for us to turn to Him in prayer right now. He never tires of our time together. He wishes we would never leave. Someday we never will leave, but until then we have this special time with Him in prayer. It's the best way to start our day. It's the best way to end our day. Prayer is a great mini vacation from our humdrum life. It's where we need to go when we are facing problems. After all, "If any of you lacks wisdom, you should ask God, who gives generously to all without finding fault, and it will be given to you" (Jas 1:5). Christian companies should encourage its employees to pray. When we have a problem, it is the first place we should go. As Christians we are most powerful when we are on our knees. We are strong when we are weak. We need to humble ourselves before the Lord and He will lift us up, and who doesn't need that.

Chapter 12

Summary Section: Prayer

JUST LIKE WITH ANYTHING else, we learn by doing. Don't worry about saying prayers correctly or waiting till you can "do it right." If you were in a burning building, would you try to get out, or would you just sit down and wait to be rescued? There's no good reason to wait to pray. Maybe you say grace over your meal three times a day. That's great, but there's so much more that you're missing out on. When it comes to prayer, if you are respectful, humble, and directing your prayers to God, you can't go wrong. It's the most natural thing for the Christian to do. In this chapter I will address some of the questions you still might have, but even if you don't understand it all, take my advice, just start doing it.

What Is Fasting?

Jesus was once asked why His disciples didn't fast and His response is found in Matthew 9:15, "The time will come when the bridegroom will be taken from them; then they will fast." When the disciples had Jesus in a face-to-face relationship, He was easier to understand and talk to, but now that we no longer enjoy that type of relationship it is harder, and so we fast. Fasting is going without to focus on prayer. You can fast from food, television, music, or whatever you like. Giving something up for Lent is a form of fasting. It is showing God that you are sincere and determined. We take the time saved from our denying ourselves to pray. Fasting has most commonly come to mean going without food. We fast for medical testing, but that is not a religious fast. Spiritual fasting always involves prayer. God looks down from heaven, sees someone fasting, and says, "Now there's someone who really wants to be heard." It's a statement of sincere faith. It's prayer on steroids.

How Do I Fast?

Did you know that breakfast is named after the breaking of the fast? Usually fasts come due to an urgent need so people don't have time to plan a fast. They just don't feel like eating and spend the time in prayer instead. Now that I've described it that way, many of you are realizing that you have fasted. Sometimes this fast lasts a few meals. Sometimes you know ahead of time that you want to fast, and you can plan it. I'd like you to understand that it is not the length of your fast that is important. Some people think that by fasting for forty days, as Jesus did (Matt 4), that they will be heard because they have reached a certain number of days or time. There is no magic number of days or time for a fast. I've done some prolonged fasts and it gets easier to go without food the longer you go. When you're fasting and your stomach starts to growl, it is so cool because it is a reminder of your prayer need. It's like your stomach is praying without words.

When planning a fast, I like to start my day fasting. I wake up, get on my knees for a prolonged time of prayer, and skip breakfast. By ten or eleven o'clock my stomach reminds me I'm fasting and that I should be in prayer. Every time I think about food or eating or hear my stomach growl I pray. I try to not let anyone know I'm fasting. If I'm offered food I simply say, "No thank you." I might go to bed early and wake up at certain times throughout the night to pray and then break my fast in the morning with breakfast. Denying yourself food can be dangerous and some of you with compromised health should ask your doctor if you are healthy enough to fast for a full day. You must drink water when you fast. The body can go for a very long time without food, but you can become dehydrated in a short period of time without fluids. Some people will only drink water when they are fasting, others will drink any liquids they want and only deny themselves solid food. Juices will provide your body with calories to burn. Remember that coffee and tea are diuretics and dehydrate your body. When you drink juices, you still feel it because your stomach doesn't have much to do and will growl.

During a stricter fast (drinking water only) I find all my senses become heightened and I feel like I am closer to God. I feel like I can hear Him more clearly. I have His attention and He has mine. He speaks to me in ways I normally would miss out on. I hear and see Him in ways I would normally not be paying attention to. I find God speaks to me in many ways. A peace comes over me. I may not get the answer I am looking for, but God reassures me, and He usually opens my eyes to see the big picture. He shows me pieces of the puzzle I was missing and gives me understanding. The overall spiritual benefit from a fast is incredible. I will say that these benefits do grow the longer you fast. Fasting is not a magic pill or a silver bullet that makes everything alright. It is part of the discipline of prayer that is a lifestyle which will help lead one to Christian maturity.

Consider Biblical examples of people fasting. The people of Nineveh were able to convince God of their repentance by fasting (Jonah 3:7) and as a result were spared destruction. Paul, before he starts his career as a missionary, gathers the church and they fast for this launching of a new ministry (Acts 14:23). This is reminiscent of the way Jesus started His ministry except He went off by himself (Matt 4:1). The Israelites fasted when they were on the brink of annihilation (Esth 4:3), when they were in captivity (Dan 9:3), and when they wanted to rebuild the walls of Jerusalem and the temple (Neh 9:1). Also remember that King David fasted and prayed when he was receiving the consequences of his sin with Bathsheba and his son was dying (1 Sam 12:16). After seven days of fasting his son still dies. What parent wouldn't do whatever he could to spare their child? God used this time to prepare David and to speak to him. There are many reasons to fast; repentance, starting a new venture, needing insight or wisdom, health concerns, or some other request. Some people just incorporate fasting as a regular part of lives by fasting one meal a week, one day a month, or a week every year. They just regularly use this form of intense prayer because they know of its benefits. Remember, fasting without prayer is not very beneficial. It is prayer that is the spiritual discipline.

What Is a Prayer Vigil?

A prayer vigil is when a person or group of people spend the night or part of the night keeping watch in prayer. This time is usually spent in prayer and meditation. When a group of people do this, they can take shifts or different watches throughout the night, or they can join all together for an all-night session of prayer. It is usually done to prepare for a special event or for a specific purpose. I've been part of a vigil for New York City that was going on for years by area churches in the NYC region. People would sign up for an hour session and the sessions went on twenty-four hours a day, three hundred and sixty-five days a year. That vigil was never ceasing. Someone, probably many people, were always praying for the city on any given day and at any given time. A vigil can be called for by an individual church. People can pray at home or the church. When it is organized by a church, they often put together a sheet that directs the participants' mediations. There might be a Scripture verse or passage to read, some questions for reflection, a song to sing, and topics or specific items to cover in prayer.

Once when Peter was in jail and was supposed to be tried the next day (Acts 12:1–19), the early church called a prayer vigil for his deliverance. While the church spent the night in prayer the Lord sent an angel in answer to their prayers and rescued Peter by freeing him from his chains and opening the doors of the prison. Peter goes to the house where the church is praying and tells them of his deliverance. When Pearl Harbor was bombed, and the United States entered World War II there were many churches calling prayer vigils. The National Day of Prayer, the first Thursday of May, is a call for our nation to spend time in prayer for our country. Some people keep the Easter prayer vigil the night before Easter morning. Others keep vigil on Christmas or New Year's Eve. Some might do it before getting married, leaving on a tour of duty, going on the mission field, before getting ordained, or at the time of illness of a loved one. There are many reasons to keep vigil. It is not a magical practice; it is a demonstration of faith. It is similar to the idea of fasting.

Do I Have to Pray at Church?

Prayer is to be practiced by the Christian everywhere, not just at church. We are called to be people of prayer. Philippians 4:6 says, "Be anxious for nothing, but in everything by prayer and supplication with thanksgiving let your requests be made known to God." 1 Timothy 2:8 says, "Therefore I want the men *in every place* to pray, lifting up holy hands, without wrath and dissension." The call is to pray in every place not just at church, but church is meant to be a place of prayer. Jesus upon visiting the temple came upon people trying to make money. He railed against them and threw them out of the temple saying, "Is it not written: 'My house will be called a house of prayer for all nations? But you have made it a den of robbers'" (Mark 11:17). Though we no longer have a temple and meet in churches the principle remains the same. Church needs to be a house of prayer; a place where people can go to pray and hear from God. As people talk to one another and find out prayer needs from each other they should stop to pray. Prayer ought to permeate the place we call church, but church is not the only place to pray.

What Is Prayer Language?

Perhaps you've heard of a special prayer language that Christians use when they pray. This is not using King James language like "Thou" or "Art." The term prayer language refers to speaking in tongues. The ability to speak in tongues is a gift bestowed by the Holy Spirit. Unless He enables you to speak in tongues you can't do it. You can pretend to do it but doing so is an obvious cry for attention and an attempt to validate one's faith to others. Not every Christian speaks in tongues (1 Cor 12:30). It is often misunderstood to be proof that one has become a Christian. Some Christians believe unless you speak in tongues you are not a Christian. It is used by some as a sort of litmus test. This idea is not taught in Scripture but is a bastardization of passages such as Acts 10:45-47 and Acts 19:1-7. The gift of tongues is first seen in Acts 2 on the day of Pentecost when the disciples had the Holy Spirit come upon them and they spoke in foreign languages as a demonstration to those present that God was validating their message. Since that first day of the early Church the gift of speaking in tongues seems to have died out for the most part but some cling to an unintelligible personal and private prayer language (1 Cor 14:9) and call that speaking in tongues.

Paul teaches the Corinthian church about the use of tongues within the congregation during public worship in 1 Corinthians 14. In this chapter he teaches that the use of tongues is to speak to God not men (1 Cor 14:2). Paul further teaches that tongues do not edify the church body (1 Cor 14:17). He admonishes the church to speak plainly and not in tongues in public worship services (1 Cor 14:19). Tongues should be used in limited fashion in worship services (two or three at most-1Cor 14:27) and even then, it should only be allowed when someone is there able to interpret. This teaching relegates the use of tongues to a private prayer language for the most part.

Many have used this issue to divide the church. I beg of you reading this now to work to build up the body of Christ and not tear it down. Stop defrauding you brothers and sisters by saying that those who speak in tongues are being used of Satan (possible blasphemy), or that if someone does not speak in tongues, they are not a Christian or that they are not spiritually mature. These types of claims are not from God. They hurt many and lead people astray. Such behavior does not please our Lord. If you are so led of God to speak in tongues do so in private prayer and remember that speaking in tongues without demonstrating love makes you a noisy gong or clanging cymbal (1 Cor 13:1). If you do not have the gift of tongues, seek and use other gifts. It is time for the Church to major on the majors and to minor on the minors; the gift of tongues is minor among gifts and minor in church life. Let's not blow it out of proportion. We have greater work to do and more important things to focus on. God is the one who teaches and leads each one as He sees fit.

How Do I Keep a Prayer Journal?

In a prayer journal you write what you prayed and when. It is important to date your requests. Note when God answers the prayer and how. You then have a record you can look back over. God doesn't always answer our requests yes, remember sometimes God says no or wait. You should log these answers to your prayers on the same page with the date of when He answered the request. When you have done this for a year or more you can look back over your prayer requests and God's answers. This helps you understand where your heart's desires truly are, and it helps you learn how God tends to work in your life. You might gain insight into what God wants to teach you. You might learn how God speaks to you. Some people incorporate their devotions on the same page or notes from a sermon they heard at church. They use it as a spiritual diary. With this added information it becomes even clearer how God works and what He is trying to teach you.

A prayer journal is also a great way to remember prayer requests from other people. As a pastor I get lots of requests for prayer and if I didn't write them down, I would forget them. This is a one-page overview of say a month's requests. This makes for a quick and easy reference of prayer requests and a list of things to pray for. Your list of answered prayers can become a list of things to thank God for as well as a list for encouraging your heart when you are thinking that your prayers are bouncing off the ceiling. Years later you can read through your journal and see how you have grown.

Every Time I Pray, I Fall Asleep, What Can I Do?

I can't think of a better way to go to sleep. Who knows that your subconscious continues to pray in ways you don't know? The Lord ministers to us in our sleep. But if you want to make sure you don't fall asleep in prayer, try praying with your eyes open, pray kneeling, lift your hands, or pray shorter prayers. Don't pray when you are tired. Remember it is better to pray and fall asleep than to not pray at all. Give yourself a break. It's not a big deal. If anything, it shows a peace that passes understanding. It reminds me of Peter sleeping chained in prison on the night pending his possible execution. It may just be a symptom of a clear conscience. I wouldn't worry about it, unless it is happening in group prayer and you're a loud snorer.

Section Four

Ministry

Chapter 13

"My Food Is to Do the Will of Him Who Sent Me"
—JOHN 4:34

IN JOHN CHAPTER 4 we see Jesus entering a Samaritan village. He sends His disciples to find food for lunch while He stays by the well to refresh Himself. He has an encounter with a Samaritan woman and has an opportunity to witness to her. What I mean by witness is that He shared with her God's plan for forgiveness. He reveals Himself as the Messiah and she believes in Him, confesses her sin, and runs to tell everyone in the town about her experience. When Jesus' disciples come back, they are amazed that Jesus was talking to a Samaritan woman and tries to get Him to eat some lunch, but Jesus tells them, "My food is to do the will of Him who sent Me" (John 4:34). By saying this Jesus is declaring that there is something more important that eating. What could be so important? Doing *ministry*. When someone becomes a Christian, they don't go to heaven right away. You know God could have worked it out that way, but He didn't. He leaves us here to share the good news of God's forgiveness and His plan of salvation with others.

Eating is something we do three times a day (or more if you include snacks). We devote hours to it every day. We hunt, grow, or shop for food. We cut coupons, drive to three different stores, and pay large sums of money to buy food. We preserve, prepare, cook, and serve our food. We set tables, clean dishes, and put leftovers away. Then we start thinking about our next meal. Eating consumes us (pun intended). It devours all our time, energy, and resources. Too bad we Christians don't hunger and thirst for righteousness, fellowship, bible study, prayer, ministry, witnessing, and God like that. We spend maybe two to four hours a day on our appetite, but Christians only have five minutes to devote to God. Jesus said, "My Food is to do the will of Him who sent Me" (John 4:34). All too often we hurry through the time it takes to devote to these five disciplines. If we regularly eat our meals that way, we end up with heartburn. If we live our spiritual lives that way, we may end up without a heart burning for Jesus.

Why is it that God always gets our leftovers? We give Him what is left over after we pay the bills, we prepare for ministry according to how much time we have left over after a busy week, and our efforts are halfhearted because we are exhausted from our busyness. It's all about priorities and discipline. We fool ourselves into thinking that we can take short cuts when it comes to living the Christian life, but God will not accept a sacrifice that isn't first rate. The story of Cain and Abel taught us that. In Genesis 4 Cain brought some of the produce from his farm as an offering to God, while Abel brought the choice parts of an animal sacrifice. God accepts Abel's offering and does not accept Cain's. God is Holy and we must treat Him holy. This means respecting everything related to Him. It means doing our absolute best for Him. And it means doing everything else as if we were doing it for the Lord (Col 3:23).

We are Jesus' hands and feet. He went back into heaven and left us here with the task of representing Him. We are His ambassadors. God gives us spiritual gifts and talents to use for His glory. There are so many ways God can use you. Did you know that God gives every Christian at least one spiritual gift and that He expects you to use that gift to help build the kingdom? You've no doubt heard the expression "use it or lose it," well that applies to your spiritual gift too. Sampson (Judg 13–16) ignored his spiritual ministry to be a deliverer of God's people and instead got a little too friendly with the enemy. He did not treat the gift of God with respect when telling the secret of his strength to Delilah. She had his enemies shave his head and God removed his strength. Sampson didn't use his gift to glorify God. He misused it. He took it for granted. He didn't treat it as holy. In the end he was a pathetic figure chained between two pillars, blinded, and stripped of his strength and dignity. But the story doesn't end there. Like Jonah, Sampson comes to his senses and prays a prayer of repentance vowing to do the will of God. Well, God hears from heaven and restores Sampson's great strength and Sampson pulls the house down upon himself and the enemies of God. Sampson could have spared himself a lot of trouble by taking his charge seriously and staying true to his calling. Too bad he had to learn this lesson the hard way. How about you? Are you taking your ministry too lightly? Will you have to learn your lesson the hard way?

The story of Sampson reminds me of a young man in one of my churches. He was an athlete, bright, and a natural leader. He was good looking and popular with the girls and everyone else for that matter. He came to church and youth group regularly and came from a great Christian family. He knew the Bible and had faith in Christ. Some other kids in the church were considering starting a Bible Club on the local high school campus and they told me that they would do it in a heartbeat if they could get this young man to join them. After all, if he joined them, they would not be rejected as a bunch of Jesus freaks. That's how charismatic his personality was. I approached him with the idea of joining the others in starting the group and I will forever hear his chilling response in my mind, "I know I should, and I know that someday I will probably regret it, but I can't commit social suicide like that. I'm sorry, but I won't be joining them." I often wonder does he regret that choice? Did he start a pattern of rejecting God's ministry for chasing after wind (Eccl 1)? He could have done so much good for the kingdom of God. I wonder what he has accomplished for the kingdom since then. Has he squandered his spiritual blessings and missed out on what God wanted for him?

I knew of another Christian man that attended a church of mine. He was successful in business, had a beautiful wife, and wonderful children all following the Lord. He was highly respected, and his opinions were always highly regarded and sought after. He had wisdom and insights that were seemingly from God above. He had a great understanding of God's Word and applied it appropriately. Year after year he was asked if he would serve on this board or that committee and every year the answer was the same, "No." He never gave a reason he would just say no. He was not involved in any ministry. He did not serve on any team and only came to Sunday morning services. He never served in a short-term situation either, not when the church was looking for a new pastor, and not when the church had troubles. He was committed to his family (a noble priority) and his career. He had a summer home and would be gone for many weeks especially in the summer. Hey, he worked hard and I'm sure he earned the break. I never begrudged him that. He was blessed of the Lord and who am I to argue with God? But the church needed him several times. They would have greatly benefited from his wisdom and may have been diverted from many poor choices, but his voice was not heeded because it was never heard.

On the other hand, I believe people can get so involved in church and ministry that they lose sight of their relationship with God. They lose their families as their marriages crumble and their children resent God for taking them away. Sometimes people can get so heavenly minded that they are no earthly good. They are so busy serving at church that their neighbor's needs are going on unmet. They are like the scribe who passed by on the other side when he saw the injured traveler on the side of the road cut and bleeding (Luke 10:25-37). I'm sure that scribe rationalized to himself that he had an important meeting to get to at the synagogue. I'm sure he didn't want to contaminate himself with the bloody mess and make himself unclean because he had important ministry to do. So, we too often get so involved in church work that we forget the needs of our fellow human beings and leave the work of compassion and kindness to the Samaritans of this world.

Many people confuse loving God with working in church. I understand the dangers of placing church above God and family. Having said all this, there is a danger in neglecting your spiritual gift, not developing it, and not using it. It's a balancing act that requires discipline and right priorities. You must know the season and when it is right to serve and when it is right to not serve. You might have to say no so you don't become over committed and end up giving God less than your wholehearted effort. If serving in a ministry is never happening in your life, you will never grow as a Christian. You will never receive the blessings God has for you. Ministry is exercise for your faith and provides many valuable opportunities to grow. People think that ministry is about serving others, and though that is true, it is more about God and your being obedient to do what He asks of you. You might be the only Jesus someone will ever see, but if you're not ministering to others, they may never see Jesus at all.

Every Christian is given at least one spiritual gift, an ability that comes from Him for the purpose of building up of the body of Christ (the Church). Ephesians 4:8 teaches, "When He (Jesus) ascended on high, He took many captives and gave to His people." There are many gifts, but one God who coordinates these gifts so that a local group of Christians is fully equipped for the work God wants them to do, fully equipped until someone refuses to use their gift. Then the church is not functioning as it should. Others without the right gift try to do someone else's job, something they're not gifted in. They are distracted from their primary area of service covering for someone else. When this happens still others are stretched trying to fill holes and gaps left by the ones covering for someone else. As you can see, even one person not doing what God intends for them to do can have a cascading affect upon all ministries. Sure, God can raise up someone else and give them the gift to fill the void but woe to the one who balks at God's will.

We don't all have the same gift. As Romans 12:6 explains, "We have different gifts, according to the grace given to each of us." We are the body of Christ. All are not hands. All are not feet. All are not tongues. 1 Corinthians 7:7 says, "But each of you has your own gift from God; one has this gift, another has that." God gives a few of each gift as befitting the needs of that particular body (or church) according to the purpose for which He designed it. 1 Corinthians 1:7 teaches that churches have everything they need, "Therefore you (plural) do not lack any spiritual gift as you eagerly wait for our Lord Jesus Christ to be revealed." As Christians we all want to hear our Lord someday say, "Well done thou good and faithful servant, enter into your rest." Unfortunately, some might hear, "Well, looks like you made it by the skin of your teeth." It's too bad so many opt out of God's blessing for them. If you want a promotion in business you've got to prove your worth by taking care of business and be a company person. If you want to be a good soldier, you follow orders. If you want to please God, you trust and obey.

According to Romans 11:29 we are told that God's gifts as well as His call are irrevocable. He doesn't take them back, but you can let them atrophy. What is your calling? What is it that you are supposed to be doing for Him? Someone else is depending on you to be F.A.T. (an acronym for *F*aithful, *A*vailable, and *T*eachable). You are needed at your local church so get involved in a balanced way. Use your gifts and talents to bless others. You are part of God's plan for that church. Without you they lose their power and effectiveness. Hebrews 2:4 says about the message of salvation that, "God also testified to it by signs, wonders and various miracles, and by *gifts* of the Holy Spirit distributed according to his will." Your gifts are an important validation of the gospel. People seeing you exercising your gifts and talents in a body of believers will speak powerfully to them about the truth of the gospel. You are an important cog in the machine of God's mercy. The rockets which nations launch into space involve some of the newest cutting-edge technology. Yet one little seemingly insignificant malfunctioning part can turn the entire ship into a very costly piece of space junk. You count and others are counting on you.

Jesus also spoke of the importance of doing God's will. In Matthew 6:20 Jesus commands us to store up treasure in heaven. He wants us to use our spiritual gifts and talents to make a heavenly investment. Here on earth, we spend a lifetime saving for retirement and then, just as we are about to retire, all those savings can evaporate in an instant as the stock market crashes. We invest in friendships and marriages for years and then they move away, or a spouse divorces you. Even successful investments in this life will only produce value in this life. Jesus wants us to realize a greater rate of return. The people that come to God because He uses us will live forever. We will never be separated from God or our brothers and sisters. Why spend your life on things that will not last? Why not work for a reward that will last forever?

When you get involved and use your gifts and talents it sets an example for others in the church and for your children. When your fellow parishioners see you working for the kingdom of God, they are encouraged to use their gifts and talents. Then the whole church starts to function as it should and God's purposes for your church start to be realized. When your children see you are using your gifts and talents, they learn that serving others is more important than only focusing on yourself. They realize that everyone has at least one spiritual gift and they start to investigate what theirs is. Even young people need to use their gifts. The earlier they identify their spiritual gift and start using it the stronger it will become. You as a parent may only have forty to sixty years to store up treasure in heaven but your children may have sixty to eighty years. Young people are not just the church of the future; they are an important part of the Church today.

Youth can go where you cannot. They can do what you are unable. Encourage your children to identify their spiritual gift and to start using it. Encourage the young people in your church to use their gifts and talents. Let them be part of the Church today. After all it is going to be theirs one day anyway. You want your church strong and functioning when your generation is too old to keep up. Young people may not do things the way you would, but your generation didn't always do things the way your parents preferred either. Learn to start sharing control and authority now or there will be problems later. Always be working with someone younger to take over for you. If the whole Church does this, then we will not experience a power outage in the future and the mighty Church of God will continue to experience uninterrupted leadership and witness.

If you are not using your gifts in a local church, then you are discouraging the 20 percent of the people who do 80 percent of the work. You're setting an example for others in the church that they can just attend on Sunday morning, put twenty dollars in the plate, and feel like they are part of the body of Christ. Well, you may be a part of the body of Christ, but you may be a useless appendage that the body might be better without. You are setting an example of selfishness for your children and dooming them to a treasureless heaven (if they make it all). Ephesians 2:10 says that we are saved to perform good works which God prepared for us to do. James teaches that faith without works is dead. You prove that your faith is real by your good works. Don't get me wrong, we are not saved by the exercising of our gifts (or good works). We are saved by faith alone. Don't disappoint our Lord who gave His life for you. Get involved in a ministry and use your gifts and talents.

Chapter 14

"My Father Is Working until Now, and I Myself Am Working"
—JOHN 5:17

GOD WORKED SIX DAYS and rested on the seventh. God has seemingly entered a Sabbath rest from His work of creating, but Jesus indicates that the Father is still at work. God is still holding all things together, answering prayers, watching over His creation, and working all things together for the good of them that love Him. He does not slumber, nor does He sleep. God is the Great Judge. Nothing escapes His gaze. Talk about a good work ethic, God's not lazy. He's on top of His game doing what needs to be done. He will one day create a new heaven and a new earth. And His Son is no different.

Jesus was one who worked. After a long hard day of traveling, preaching, and healing, when the whole world was seemingly pressing around Him just to touch the hem of His garment, when His disciples were exhausted and falling asleep, what would Jesus be doing? Climbing a mountainside and spending the night in prayer. Before the sun would rise Jesus would be up preparing for the day in prayer and meditation. Jesus did the hardest work of all time. He paid for the sins of the world and works as our advocate and mediator. He went to heaven to help prepare a place for us. He's hustling on your behalf. He's pouring out His life for you. He's a worker and He's given us the greatest example of serving our fellow human. If this is how the God of Heaven works and if this is how the Savior of the World works, then we had better be working too.

I understand that we are not God. We don't have endless strength. We are not all powerful. We grow tired and we get weary. We can't do what God can do, but we can do what the He has given us to do and has prepared us to do. Jesus said, "We must work the works of Him who sent Me, as long as it is day; night is coming, when no man can work" (John 9:4). Jesus also said, "The harvest is plentiful, but the workers are few. Ask the Lord of the harvest, therefore, to send out workers into his harvest field" (Matt 9:37–38). Everyone wants to enjoy the harvest, but few want to help make it happen. It sort of reminds me of the children's story of the little red hen. No one would help the hen with the work of planting, picking, grinding, and baking, but everyone was eager to help with the eating. The hen says, no way. Why should you get the blessings but leave all the work for me? Maybe you'll remember this next time I ask you to help me. Everyone wants to go to heaven, but few are willing to do what the Father asks.

Jesus taught that, "Anyone wanting to be first must become the slave of all" (Mark 10:44). Jesus was the perfect example of a servant. He even said that "the Son of Man did not come to be served, but to serve, and to give His life as a ransom for many" (Matt 20:28). This attitude of service is the mark of a true Christian. We should have this same attitude that Christ had, who although He existed in the form of God did not regard equality with God something to be grasped but humbled Himself and took on the form of a servant (Phil 2:5–11). The King and Lord of the Universe stripped, wrapped a towel around Himself, and washed the disciples' feet. If He was willing to humble Himself and serve, we should be willing to do the same.

God made us to serve. Even from the beginning there was work to be done. Among mankind's first jobs we were to rule over creation (Gen 2:26), be fruitful, multiply (Gen 2:28), to work the garden, and care for it (Gen 3:15). He gave us the job of naming all the animals (Gen 2:19). Unfortunately, God increased the difficulty of our work because of our disobedience (Gen 3:17). Paul taught that if someone didn't work then he shouldn't eat (2 Thess 3:1). Those not doing what God has asked of them often find themselves in trouble. Take King David as an example (2 Sam 11). At the time when kings went out to war David stayed behind and did not lead the army. He delegated the work to subordinates and he stayed home. From his roof top he saw Bathsheba, the wife of Uriah, one of his most loyal officers, bathing. This was the wife of a close friend, someone who had served with David from the beginning. David lusted in his heart and invited Bathsheba to his bed. Then to cover up her pregnancy he had her husband Uriah, his friend, killed. All this happened because David would not do what God expected of him.

There are plenty of examples in Scripture and in modern life of people who neglected the work to which God had called them. Barak (Judg 4) was a great military commander of the Israelite army. God asked him to attack but he was not so keen on the idea. He would not go to war unless Deborah went with him. He hid behind the skirt of a woman and balked at God's will for his life. Well, at least he did go to war, but he was not known as a man of courage. He did win the battle, but the victory was Deborah's not his. He had the opportunity to obey God's will and be highly esteemed by the people, but he initially shirked his responsibilities.

Jesus told a parable of a man giving a great banquet in Luke 14:15–23. He had his servants make all the preparations and then he sent his servants to everyone on the guest list to announce the start of the banquet. The guests all started making excuses. The man told his servants to fill up his house with strangers and unfortunate people. He told the servants that not one of those who had said no to his invitation was allowed to change their mind and try to come. Well, they ended up missing the party of a lifetime. It's downright dangerous to say no to God or to balk at His will.

Have you ever seen a work crew on the side of the road? Often you see one man, in a hole, working like crazy while four others stand around watching. Passers by say, "Look at those men, being paid to do nothing." How do you feel when you are working, a bunch of people come by, and watch you work? They start talking, distracting you, and they don't lift a finger to help you. You try to be polite but deep inside you're wishing they would either help or leave. Well, God is working, and many Christians are just standing around watching, doing nothing to help out. At churches all around the world there are Christians laboring to keep the church going and to get the message out but for everyone working there are four others standing around doing nothing to help. If you are one of those on the sidelines, I implore you to get involved.

Could you imagine a football team trying to win a game but only two people take the field? Can you imagine the rest of the team just standing on the sidelines hooting, hollering, and telling the two on the field to run faster and try harder? How do you think that team is going to do? How do you think those two players are going to look at the end of the game? Do you think they would show up for the next game? How would the fans feel about that team? What would the other team think

"My Father Is Working until Now, and I Myself Am Working" 123

of their opponent? It's rather comical to consider except you know where I'm going with this. Your church is that team. We need to run in such a way to win the prize, not standing around watching the few.

Are you wondering why your church isn't growing? Are you wondering why your church isn't firing on all cylinders? Well, are you doing your part? Are you supporting the church with your tithe? Are you involved in a ministry team? Are you using your gifts and talents? Are you encouraging others to use their gifts? We are supposed to spur one another on to love and good deeds (Heb 10:24). Imagine how your church would be if everyone pulled their weight and encouraged each other? You need to set the example in your church. You need to start the next great revival before the Lord comes again. Be a servant.

Do you remember the parable of the three servants entrusted with the bags of gold (Matt 25:14–30)? One was given five bags of gold. He invested it and it made five more. Another servant was given two bags of gold. He invested it and it made two more. The last servant was given one bag of gold, but he did not invest it. He dug a whole and buried it. When the master returned and settled the accounts, he was pleased with the first two servants and he gave them more responsibilities, but with the last servant he was not pleased. He became enraged at the "wicked and lazy" fellow and had him thrown into the darkness where there was weeping and gnashing of teeth. The lesson of this parable could not be any clearer. God gives us gifts and talents and He expects us to invest them. He wants us to put them to work for the Kingdom of God. Those who do will be blessed and those who don't will regret it.

Each Christian has been given a very special charge. Paul teaches in 2 Corinthians 5:18, "Now all these things are from God, who reconciled us to Himself through Christ, and gave to us the ministry of reconciliation." These gifts and talents we have been entrusted with are to be used so people may be reconciled to God. If you don't get involved in a ministry, people will be lost. We are at war with the forces of darkness. Their goal is to drag as many people down to hell with them as they can, but God does not want any to perish. He sent His only Son to pay the penalty of their sins by dying on the cross, and He's given us this message of reconciliation, which we must share, so people can embrace God's gift of forgiveness through faith. Your obedience or disobedience has tremendous ramifications. People you know and love are hanging in the balance.

God has equipped us for this work by giving us gifts and talents, but He's also given us each other and the gift of His perfect Word, the

Bible. We are not alone in this ministry; we have the body of Christ, His mighty Church. We need to work together as a team. We are not alone. God Himself is with us too, never leaving us, never forsaking us. And He's given us the power of His Word. Paul taught that, "All Scripture is inspired by God and profitable for teaching, for reproof, for correction, for training in righteousness: that the man of God may be adequately, equipped for every good work" (2 Tim 3:16–17). God's Word is wisdom that guides and directs us in this work. It speaks to all believes, coordinating our efforts. God's Spirit also works from within all believers to lead us in the direction we should go, and He tells us what we should say.

Make no mistake, all people will be judged, even Christians. Paul teaches that Christians will be judged at the Bema Seat of Christ when each person's works will be tested (1 Cor 3:13–15). This judgment is not to determine if we go to heaven or hell, if we are trusting in Christ, that's already settled. This judgment is to determine the quality of our lives and the rewards we will get in heaven. If the work we did was for God it will last, but if it was not, it will be burned up. The work we do for the Father is worth doing because it lasts and has eternal rewards. The reward, as far as I'm concerned, is not literal jewels in a crown, but people who will be there in heaven because of our work. They will seek us out and say, "Thank you for giving to the Lord." Every time we see them walking down the streets of gold, we will have the satisfaction of knowing that we were used by God to make an eternal difference. When a contractor builds a house, he can look at it and say, "I built that." Unfortunately, that house will fall down or burn up someday. The work we do for God will never be destroyed.

So, as we have seen in this chapter, God has equipped His people for works of service, so that the body of Christ may be built up (Eph 4:12). If we are obedient and use our gifts, we please our God. If we don't use our gifts, we disappoint our Lord and run the risk of missing out on God's blessing. God could always raise up someone else to do what He's asked you to do. God's plan will not be thwarted, but if He does then you will miss out on being used of God. The harvest is plentiful, but the workers are indeed few. I'm praying that you would be convicted to do the work that God has for you joyfully and wholeheartedly. If Christians reading this would pledge to not shirk their responsibilities and get involved in ministry then revival would come to His church, people would be won to the Lord, and God would be well pleased.

Chapter 15

"God . . . Works in You"
—PHILIPPIANS 2:13

AFTER THE LAST COUPLE of chapters I believe a word of warning and further explanation needs to be made. God is the one who works through us. I know the previous chapters made it sound like I was asking you to get involved and to use your gifts and talents in ministry, but the truth is, I'm only asking you to open yourself up to God's working through you. As a Christian God dwells inside believers through the indwelling of the Holy Spirit, who never leaves us or forsakes us. It is the Holy Spirit that produces fruit in us (Gal 5:22). He also gives us the words to say when we don't know what to say (Mark 13:11; Luke 21:15; Matt 10:19). It's almost like we are God's puppets. He uses us as He sees fit and does with us as He pleases. He leads us and guides us to accomplish His good pleasure. We are His hands and feet.

We can get in the way of the Holy Spirit working through us by taking over and doing as we see fit in our own eyes. When we take matters into our own hands and we operate, not in the Spirit, but in our own strength and abilities. There is a qualitative difference between our own understanding, talents, and abilities and the understanding and gifts the Holy Spirit gives us. We can get understanding from our own experience or from others, like through books or in classrooms. We should seek this kind of knowledge. It has its place and is helpful. But the knowledge that comes from above comes from God and is not based on theories of mankind. God's understanding of things is perfect and true. It doesn't need to be updated. It never changes. God's truth and ways are perfect.

Textbooks must be updated. Theories are proven wrong. New insights are gained, and teachers must change what they teach. God's understand doesn't need to be updated and is not susceptible to new discoveries.

God's wisdom comes to us through reading His Word, the Bible. It comes to us as the Holy Spirit whispers into our minds insights from above. It comes to us as other Christians share God's truth with us. It comes to us as God leads us through circumstances. Who wouldn't want perfect knowledge and understanding? James teaches that, "the wisdom that comes from heaven is first of all pure; then peace-loving, considerate, submissive, full of mercy and good fruit, impartial and sincere" (3:17). If your understanding does not have these qualities, then it is not from God. When we operate in this less than perfect knowledge then we are in danger of leaving God's truth and plan in favor of functioning in our own strength and insight. Our insights are faulty and do not accomplish the plans of our Lord.

In a similar way God's power and strength are available to the Christian as we yield to the Holy Spirit. We don't do what we want, but rather we do what God tells us to do. When we are obedient God adds to our actions His power and His authority and accomplishes so much more than we ever could on our own. God working through us is effective, while our operating on our own is ineffective. We have a choice; we can take matters into our own hands, spin our wheels, and end up with nothing for all our efforts or we can yield to God's ways, let His power flow through us, and accomplish God's will. Unfortunately, Christians and even entire churches sometimes are tempted to function in their own strength and power. They forget to ask God what His will is and they just do what has been done in the past or they do what looks good to them. Then they sit back and wonder why their efforts aren't being blessed.

In the same manner we can use our abilities and talents instead of functioning with our God given gifts. For instance, people who are career teachers are often asked to teach in the Sunday Schools and youth programs. Maybe they are teachers because God has given them the spiritual gift of teaching, but that is not always the case. Someone who teaches may only have human training and understanding of education. Sure, this can be used to the glory of God, but what if God has given them the gift of hospitality and He wants them to serve in that ministry? They end up spending all their time and energy preparing lessons instead of hosting and making people feel welcome. Another person with the spiritual gift of teaching is denied the opportunity to fill that spot on the Sunday

School staff and no one is filling the void of helping people become assimilated into the body of Christ. The person with the spiritual gift of teaching whose spot is filled by the career teacher ends up serving in another ministry such as on an evangelism team but is ineffective because they are functioning outside their area of giftedness. The professional teacher is getting burned out teaching all the time and is quietly building up resentment. Their ministry is hampered because they are not doing what God wants them to do.

Occasionally a church leader makes a decision and asks someone to serve without first asking God who He wants to serve. These unsuspecting dear saints think such a leader must have God's leading; they even think that it's a confirmation of God's will for them. Pastors and other leaders should be leery of pressing people to serve when they are hesitant. If it's God's will then He will work in the person's heart to lead them to want to do it. The best way is to start with God. Ask Him what He wants. He'll let you know.

The Spirit filled life involves surrendering to God and yielding to Him fully. It's a matter of getting yourself out of His way. Often God wants to work in tremendous ways, but we hinder the work. We mess it all up. Just because you are a Christian does not mean you are living a Spirit filled life. The Spirit filled life is not how much of the Spirit we have, it's how much of us the Spirit has. It takes a conscience daily effort to place the Spirit in the driver's seat of your life. It takes starting each day in prayer asking for God's will for your life to be done. It takes starting each project and making each decision in prayer. The more we surrender to the Spirit the more God can use us and work through us. Just pray a prayer something like:

> "Heavenly Father, I want your will to be done in my life. I want Your power to flow through me. I want to be used of You to accomplish Your will. Forgive me of my sins and for all the times I head off on my own and leave You behind. I surrender to You fully and ask that You take control of my life. Take all of me and do with me as You wish. In Jesus' name I pray, Amen!"

If you pray that prayer, be prepared for God to answer and when He does you will be sorely tempted to take matters into your own hands. Fight that urge and continue to let God have His way.

Paul in his letter to the Ephesians blessed them saying, "Now to Him who is able to do exceeding abundantly beyond all that we ask or think, according to the power that works within us" (3:20). This verse represents my blessing on those of you who have struggled in this spiritual discipline of ministry and have just now decided to surrender to God's will for your life by letting God use you and the gifts He has given you to minister to others. You have just become a servant of the Most High and His power and authority will flow through you. Just remember you serve Him; He doesn't serve you. After all it is a terrifying thing to fall into the hands of the living God (Heb 10:31). Let Him have His way and don't get in His way. Be a ready and fit vessel, ready for the Master's use.

After all, Christians are God's children. Scripture plainly teaches this. John 1:12–13 states, "Yet to all who did receive Him, to those who believed in His name, He gave the right to become children of God—children born not of natural descent, nor of human decision or a husband's will, but born of God." So, if we are God's children we should take after Him. If God is working until now, so should we. If we are part of the family, we have a responsibility to our Father to do our chores and participate in the upkeep of the home. We have obligations to our brothers and sisters. We should not bring disgrace to our family. We should obey the family rules. If we don't, we run the risk of being the black sheep of the family and receiving a limited inheritance. Perhaps such a person is not a family member at all. I know when I was growing up, I spent a lot of time at a neighbor's house. Just because I was there all the time did not make me part of their family. Just because they accepted me, loved me, included me, and treated me like I was a part of the family didn't mean I was. I had no chores or responsibilities.

At this point I would like to point out that you might think you are part of God's family because you hang out with Christians. You might think you are a Christian because your parents are. You might wish and hope for forgiveness and eternal life in heaven, but you may not have these things because you never trusted in Christ's death on the cross, asked God for forgiveness, or let Him into your life. If you call yourself a Christian but can't stand Christians, you may not be a Christian. If you think you are going to heaven but have no evidence of your faith through your good works, you may not be a Christian. People who religiously go to church on Sundays but will have nothing to do with the ministry may not be Christians. Christianity is not a religion. It is a relationship. This relationship with God through Jesus Christ, is a loving and caring relationship that works both ways. Christians love their Lord so much that they feel the need to use their gifts and talents for the cause of Christ.

As Christians we are supposed to produce fruit. In Matthew 3:8 Jesus warned people who would claim to have faith to, "Produce fruit in keeping with repentance." Remember we may not be saved by our works, but we are saved to produce them.

Some people will say that they can produce their good works outside the local Church. They say they can't stand the Church because it is filled with hypocrites. No one likes hypocrisy but being saved by Christ constrains us to live for Him; it also gives us a love for one another. How can you claim family membership without ever spending time with that family? Imagine a son who never comes home for dinner, never sleeps in his own bed, and never even talks to other family members. When his little sister is sick in the hospital, he won't even visit her, call her, or send her a card. Wouldn't you say that such a fellow has grown apart from his family? Wouldn't you say that such a person has denied his family? Now imagine such a person getting sick and calling his siblings names for not visiting him in the hospital. Imagine the nerve of such a person showing up after fifty years of such behavior to collect his inheritance. Let not that man think that he will receive a dime.

The truth is the world is full of people claiming one thing but doing another. The Church did not corner the market on hypocrisy. If you pressed a person who believes the Church is full of hypocrites, they would probably only be able to name a few people at church who disappointed them in one way or another. I'm sorry, but that's what happens in families. In our families we love each other deeply. We want to spend all our time together. We do everything together. All that time together is bound to produce a few moments of friction. The great love families have for each other causes them to forgive. An even greater love binds the whole Church together and we bear with one another. We overlook our differences and bear with one another. It's a choice, a commitment that we make, and like marriage that commitment, makes us stronger. Sure, there are weaker brothers, but in the church, we work to help them grow because we love them and are committed to them. Stop blaming the Church so you can get out of your responsibilities. Wasn't it a Christian who shared the gospel with you that got you saved? Wasn't it the Church that played an important role in your salvation? Don't cut them off and stop neglecting your role in the family of God.

Did you know that our most important ministry is not to others anyway? It's not saving the lost, it's worshipping God. Look at Revelation 7, 19, and 22 (and many other places in the Bible). Man was made to worship. It's our destiny. Try doing that outside the Church. Sure, it can be done but not regularly or effectively. Going to a worship service in a church greatly enhances the probability that you will fulfill your destiny to worship God. There is no other public place to turn where our spiritual relationship will be encouraged, and worship is permitted. The Church is God's ordained vehicle to bring His grace to the world. There are three institutions ordained of God: the family, the government, and the Church. The Church is the only one of the three that will last for eternity. Using your gifts and talents in a church amplifies your effectiveness. When your gifts are used as part of a coordinated effort of the church, the gates of hell will not prevail against us. The Church is struggling, and they need your help.

Chapter 16

Summary Section: Ministry

What Is a Spiritual Gift?

A SPIRITUAL GIFT IS something that God gives to His children at the moment of their conversion to faith in Christ. It's sort of a reverse housewarming gift. Usually, the friends and new neighbors drop by to bring a gift for the new home. It's their way of blessing the move and saying good luck. Well, when the Holy Spirit moves into your life to take up residence, He brings a special gift for the owner of His new home. It's not obvious at first. In fact, since you just started your life in Christ the gift is small and not very impressive. It's like a starter set of china or seeds for your garden. You politely say thank You, put them down, and go on with enjoying your new relationship with Jesus. Many Christians don't even know about this gift or paid it any attention.

The Scripture has lists of spiritual gifts and books have been written on the subject. The first and seminal work on the subject was written by a friend of mine, Leslie Flynn. I read his *19 Gifts of the Spirit* when I was a young man seeking to discover my spiritual gifts.[1] When I was older, I worked at Les' church, and he was still there as the pastor emeritus. There are other books you can use to help you identify what the gifts of the spirit are and how they are given. There may be nineteen as Les described or perhaps the lists in the Bible are not meant to be exhaustive. The gifts of the spirit are broken down into categories; speaking gifts, serving gifts,

1. Flynn, *19 Gifts of the Holy Spirit*.

and signifying gifts. The speaking gifts are gifts of prophecy, evangelism, shepherding, teaching, exhortation, knowledge, and wisdom. The serving gifts are helps, hospitality, giving, government, mercy, faith, and discernment. The signifying gifts are miracles, healing, tongues, and interpretation.

You will note that these are not to be confused with the fruit of the Spirit (Gal 5:22), love, joy, peace, patience, kindness, goodness, faithfulness, gentleness, and self-control. The fruit of the spirit are character distinctives (something you are) while the gifts of the Spirit are meant to bless others (something you do). Perhaps it may seem like a subtle distinction but it's really an important one. The fruit of the Spirit are produced in all obedient Christians, while the gifts of the Spirit are given individually to different people. It is possible to have more than one spiritual gift, but I've never met someone with more than eight or nine of them. Every Christian has at least one and the fewer that are found in a person the more powerful they tend to be.

Think about it, if you have a number of gifts your time and energies are divided. When you have only one gift you can focus on using that gift exclusively. God gives the gifts very judiciously. He gives them to each one just as He sees fit. As Christians, each already possessing our own spiritual gift, we cannot envy or covet others with different gifts. We need to be glad for the gifts that God has given to others and focus on our using our gifts as God desires. When each Christian is focused on their own gift(s) and using it to the glory of God then the body of Christ is fully functioning.

Spiritual gifts are different from natural talents that people learn (or have been born with). Talents can of course be used to the glory of God, but they should not be confused with gifts given by the Spirit. Talents have a human origin, while spiritual gifts come from God. Both gifts and talents can be developed and grow but the real distinctive is that talents can be learned, the gifts cannot. With the gifts God has either given it (or them) to you or not. What He has given you may be a starter kit that you build into a more mature gift, but it starts with God not yourself.

How Do I Discover My Spiritual Gifts?

There are websites you can use to help you identify your spiritual gift(s). They will take you through a questionnaire, when if answered truthfully, will point you in the right direction. I simple search engine query into spiritual gifts test will yield several of them. My favorite site is found at www.kodachrome.org/spiritgift.[2] The test is just a start. It is possible to get a false positive when taking such a spiritual gift test and then you could waste years of time in frustration trying to use a gift you don't have. Therefore, it is important that after you take a spiritual gift survey you share the results with godly Christians who know you well. They can confirm if the test is pointing you in the right direction or not. The last step of confirming your gift is to do ministry with it. If your experiences are positive, and once again confirmed by others, then you have found your area of giftedness. If people don't confirm what the test indicates, you might want to retake the test. Perhaps you could ask some of those you trust, and who know you well, to take the test as if they were you. You then could compare their answers and your answers. Where there is agreement there is a higher likelihood of something being your spiritual gift. It really does take all three, the test, validation of others, and confirmation of experience. Once you have all three in agreement, congratulations, you have found your spiritual gift(s).

How Can I Do Ministry More Effectively?

Perhaps you have identified God's spiritual gift for you, and you are using it effectively, but you desire to use it more effectively. You will want to ask the Lord what you should do. You might want to ask Him if He wants you to use your gift in concert with other Christians. Perhaps He will lead you to work with others with the same gift or perhaps He will direct you to work with people with complementary gifts to supplement what you may be lacking. Effectiveness is greatly enhanced by the team of people you place yourself within. Sometimes you can become more effective by not working with a certain person.

Who's to say that someone gifted with evangelism who chooses to work with an evangelist and is used by God to bring thousands to Christ is greater than the brother or sister with the same gift who chooses to work in a small local church and is used to lead only a few hundred to Christ. You might be tempted to say the one who saves thousands is more effective than the one who saves hundreds, but what if the one saving hundreds leads the next Billy Graham to Christ and that person goes on

2. Ellis, "Online Spiritual Gifts Test."

to save millions? Which of the two is more effective now? God knows what He is doing. You've heard the saying, "There are no small parts, only small actors." Well, there are no less significant roles to be played in the body of Christ. Each one must do their part as God leads.

You must always keep in mind that God may not be calling you to be tremendously successful in the world's eyes. Perhaps He's just calling you to be faithful, plant seeds, and let someone else come after you to get the credit. If you are doing ministry to be praised by people, then you are not doing God's will. After all, when it comes to using your spiritual gift, how do you gauge effectiveness? How do you know if God is pleased? I believe if you are at peace, can sleep at night, are in a right relationship with God and others, and have asked God what you should do, then He's led you to what you are doing, He's producing fruit through you, and you are where you need to be. We've all seen highly successful ministries that were rotten at the core. Success in ministry is not measured the same way as it is in secular society. God doesn't call us to be successful; He calls us to be obedient. Don't you want to hear, "Well done thou good and faithful servant"? Effectiveness is a worthwhile consideration, but it does not trump God's direction.

What Is a Ministry Team?

A ministry team is a group of people working in ministry together. It could be a committee or people working alongside each other in ministry at a church or para-church ministry (a Christian organization that is not a church), or it could be a group of friends working together outside any organized ministry. Sometimes they find themselves working together because they share a passion and at other times, they just all volunteered at the same time. They could have been thrown together by a leader or they could have chosen to serve together. Sometimes they share the same gift and often they complement each other's giftedness. The important thing is that they work together as a team, each of them doing whatever needs to be done for the success of the ministry. Hopefully that means functioning in their area of giftedness, however it could also mean being willing to do whatever needs to be done. The individual gets lost in the team effort when everyone strives to accomplish the goal. Each team member has their area of specialization, but they also learn each other's roles because they never know when they may be called upon to perform someone else's function.

Teams usually benefit from knowing each other well and there are ways for people to get to know each other better. Team building and trust exercises could help your team function more effectively. In a team approach to ministry the individual is willing to sacrifice all for the sake of the ministry. The team learns to work together flawlessly. They become a well-oiled machine and here's the best part, they produce in abundance. There is a synergy which happens with good teamwork, and when God adds His blessing to a ministry accomplished by a true team, it soars. Though I call these groups of people ministry teams, they are not in competition with other ministry teams. Often ministry teams will work with other ministry teams. Before joining any ministry team, you will want to devote time in prayer about your decision, ask the Lord if it is a good fit for you, and if it is where He wants you.

What Do I Do If No One Will Do Ministry with Me?

There are a few examples of people doing solo ministry. Jesus was by Himself when He ministered to the woman at the well (John 4) and Philip was alone when he witnessed to the Ethiopian eunuch (Acts 8:26) so we should not shrink back from opportunities to minister to others or share the gospel individually. When God places a single opportunity for you to meet someone's need (spiritual or otherwise) do not hesitate, but when you are looking to regular ministry you should not go it alone. Jesus had His disciples, whom He sent out in pairs. There is a principle here; I call it the Timothy principle. If you take someone else along with you on your ministry journey then you have a prayer partner, helper, and someone to take your place someday. You can provide valuable training or be trained by your partner in ministry.

There's a second issue here also. You should always perform regular ministry under authority. Jesus was under the authority of God the Father (John 17:2), the disciples were under Jesus' authority (Matt 10:1), and Paul and Silas were sent out under the authority of the church at Antioch (Acts 15:40). You must have an authority over you and your ministry to safeguard it from abuse and possible heresy. You want to have such a seal of approval upon your ministry to lend credibility to your cause and instruction. You need to have someone holding you accountable and aiding you with helpful evaluation so you can do your ministry even better.

If you can't get approved to do the ministry you desire by a church or organization, or if no one will join you in ministry, you must ask yourself, why is that? It could be that people don't believe you should do it. They may see things that you don't. This confirmation of the body of Christ is an important step in determining your call (whether God wants you to do it or not). Perhaps God has given you an idea that someone else is supposed to flesh out. Perhaps God is saying not now. Perhaps you don't have the gifts and talents necessary for the task. Take time to pray about this. Don't just charge off on your own and make it happen. Christians are supposed to be the body of Christ not a bunch of Lone Rangers (even the Lone Ranger had Tonto).

Perhaps people don't understand your ministry. Maybe your plans need more organization and polishing. Maybe they have questions and concerns that you have failed to address. Do your homework; pray, evaluate, pray, plan, pray, pursue, and pray again. There are many different ministries, organizations, and individuals to work alongside. Don't get discouraged when a ministry door is closed to you. It usually means God has something else for you to do. Be gracious and kind. Keep your judgment and disappointment in check. Sometimes God doesn't want us to do, He wants us to listen.

How Often Do I Need to Be Involved?

I understand that you must provide for your family. I understand that you have doctor appointments, soccer games, school meetings, homework, and family obligations. It doesn't take long to use your gift. You don't have to use it in church. I'm not telling you that God has a 24/7/365 ministry for you. Some are called to a great time-consuming ministry and others are not, but all are called. You probably don't have to serve eight hours a day, six days a week unless you are in full time paid ministry. Sunday School teachers teach for an hour on Sundays and spend five hours or more preparing to teach that one hour. That's only six hours per week out of one hundred and sixty-eight or 3.5% of your time. That's not even a tithe of your time. And that's one of the more involved ways to minister. Some ministries are far less time consuming. Visiting a nursing home once a week for an hour is a great ministry. Walking across the street to shovel your neighbor's driveway is another great ministry and witness. If you want your gift to grow, use it regularly.

It's funny, when I go away on vacation and don't preach for a few weeks I feel it. If you don't go to the gym for a month, you feel it. It's amazing how fast we start to atrophy. The same holds true for our ministry. We can lose our edge quickly. If you don't use it, you lose it. Abraham Lincoln was once asked, "How long do a man's legs have to be?" And his response was, "Long enough to reach the ground."[3] How often do you have to serve in a ministry? As long as it takes. God doesn't have us punch a time clock. If God has a job for us to do, we should do it no matter how long it takes. If He's given us a consistent ministry, we should be faithful and take the time to give God our best effort. He doesn't deserve our leftovers. I would recommend getting involved in a weekly ministry. I'm not talking about going to church or attending Sunday School. I'm talking about serving others and using your gifts and talents. Attending is not ministering.

Pastors can spend twenty hours preparing a single sermon. Vacation Bible School directors spend months preparing for a weeklong ministry. Writers can spend years writing a single book. Musicians practice a lifetime to perform their opus magnus. Some ministry is done daily, some is done weekly, and still others are performed monthly. Certain ministries are once in a lifetime and others are annual. The above question has the wrong focus. It's asked by a person who is looking to do the bear minimum just to get by. In everything you do you should want to do all things to the glory of God (1 Pet 4:11, 1 Cor 10:31). You should work until the ministry is accomplished well and to the glory of God.

If you find yourself doing ministry begrudgingly then you had better stop and pray for direction. Some of the greatest advice I ever received was that when one is choosing a career "do what you're passionate about." This advice is true for ministry as well. God has perfectly prepared you for the task He wants you to perform. If you are regularly functioning out of your area of giftedness, then you might want to rethink and pray about what you are doing. God has given the local church body everything it needs to do what He wants them to do.

When you find your niche, the ministry God has called you to, it is a pleasure to serve and the time it takes to perform is a joy to give. You find yourself going over and above what others might think is required. You go the extra mile because it is your baby. If this used to be the case,

---

3. Quotefancy, "Abraham Lincoln Quote."

but no longer is, perhaps you need a break. Sometimes you've been doing the same thing so long that you need a sabbatical to recharge your batteries. Perhaps you've become burned out, don't even know it, and can't recognize it. The expectations and pressure to perform and continue the ministry have robbed you of the joy you once had. Nobody should want ministry to be done for the sake of having a ministry. Ministries exist to meet the needs of people. If there are no people with that need then the ministry is not necessary and keeping up with appearances becomes a drain on valuable resources, time, and energies. Something churches often overlook is that there are seasons in ministry. There is a time to do ministry and there is a season to rest from ministry. Here's a shocker, ministries die. Sometimes it is best to let a ministry die so the needs might be met in a new or different way. Occasionally you need to step away from a ministry to follow God's leading. If you are involved in a regular ministry, make sure you're taking time to recharge your batteries (reading books on the subject, going to conferences and seminars, taking time off, etc.).

What Are Some Tools to Help Me Minister?

It depends on the ministry. I can't imagine a teaching ministry that doesn't use the Bible. Almost anything you own or possess can be used to the glory of God. There was a family in our church who had a swimming pool, and they would open it up for fellowship. Their pool was one of the tools they used to exercise their gifts of hospitality. Cooking (a talent) could be used as a tool in your ministry of helps as you prepare a meal for someone who just came home from the hospital. Your baseball card collection could be used for a special evangelistic meeting featuring athlete's testimonies or a baseball speaker. Just look around. What do you have that you could use in your ministry? Think creatively. Often you have a hobby or activity that you enjoy, well guess what, you can use that in your ministry. You enjoy golf and you have the gift of evangelism share the gospel with those you golf with. You're trying to lose weight, start a weight loss group at your church and use your gift of administration. Your ministry shouldn't be work. It should be fun and something you're passionate about. Computers, cars, paint brushes, tents, you name it; they can all be used in ministry. Your skills in writing, listening, budgeting, and singing can all be used alongside your gift to serve others and glorify

God. God loves to take what is lying around or what is at hand and do the miraculous with it.

Your two best tools in ministry are prayer and the Bible (I bet you're not surprised by that). Pray through each phase of evaluation, preparation, and execution. Base your ministry on biblical principles; not on fads that come and go. Thirdly, you want to have helpmates that are suitable for you; coworkers who enable you, not detract from the ministry. It is possible that an assistant is doing an adequate job but may not be right for the situation. Don't settle for adequate. Surround yourself with people who are passionate about doing the work. You want burdened people who are gifted with you so a synergy will happen in your ministry. You can then feed off each other's energy and enthusiasm. If you're not feeling it one day, they can bolster your spirit and vice a versa, and when you're both on, watch out.

Beyond spiritual qualities there are no silver bullets that will make your ministry the best. Sure, there are books, curriculum, and magazines you should study. Yes, there are seminars and conferences of which you should take advantage. There may be equipment and technology you will want to use, and by all means use them, but these are not the ministry, nor will they do the ministry for you. God needs a clean heart devoted to the work. He wants us to be passionate about what we do. He wants us to do our ministries to His honor and glory. He commands us to love those to whom we minister.

There are sound ministry principles of which you will want to take advantage. Evaluation is something you need to do before preparing for any ministry and something you need to do after every ministry opportunity. Let those you are ministering to have input as part of the evaluation. Don't just evaluate your part in the ministry; evaluate the need for the ministry. Evaluate the people receiving the ministry. Evaluate the outside community. Evaluate the setting and climate. Keep records and document things for easy reference. Stay organized; I know this takes time, but it will save you so much more time in the long run and will be invaluable to others who come after you to know what was going on and how to continue.

Preparing properly will put you in good stead as well. You should have more than you need so you can receive the added blessing God will send your way. If you think you need so many of something, you get more, so when more show up than expected you can accommodate them. You need to have more activities prepared than you will need. Always have a contingency plan (be flexible as needed). Set up well ahead of time. Show up early and stay late (taking advantage of those teachable moments that happen with the first few who show up and the last few who leave). Preview all visuals and audios which are going to be used. Have policies, procedures, expectations, and codes of conduct so everyone knows what to expect and what to do in various situations. Rehearse and try out all gear, equipment, and activities. In other words, don't just show up and fly by the seat of your pants. As you can see the best tools for ministry are not usually external things you might use in ministry but are inward qualities and characteristics the minister has for ministry.

How Do I Make Time for Ministry?

How do you not? There are two different philosophies of ministry; if it's worth doing it's worth doing poorly, verses, if it isn't done with excellence then it's not worthy of God. God deserves our best and He demands it. Sometimes our best might only be five loaves of bread and two fish (Matt 14) in the presences of unrealistic expectations. God can use our inadequate best to meet the needs of others by performing a miracle (I feel this way almost every time I preach). So don't use your inadequacies as an excuse to not do what God wants you to do. Having said that, God is deserving of the very best (first fruits), not leftovers and hand me downs. Don't withhold your best from God and don't be afraid to surrender your worst.

You make time for ministry the same way you make time for anything else that is important in your life. Often the priorities of a person direct how they spend their time. As a Christian desiring to grow to maturity you must realize that ministry is vital. Once you realize this and understand that it is more important than other things you spend time on, then you can reapportion your time commitments. I would encourage you to start with a list of things that are important to you, and then prioritize that list. Placing things in order of importance is a great exercise and probably should be done every few years just to make sure something isn't slipping up the ranks. After you have a prioritized list of things in your life, make another list of how you spend your time. Compare and contrast those lists. If you are spending time on things which are not a priority for you then you need to reconsider if you need to be involved in that activity. Every choice you make affects everything on your list. Don't let the little things in your life squeeze out the important things.

Tell others who can help you and hold you accountable to reprioritize your life. Ask them to pray for you as you commit to a new way of life.

For instance, you might have God, spouse, children, work, church, extended family, exercise, ministry, etc. as priorities. You'll notice I didn't just write family; I broke that category down into three different parts: spouse, children and extended family. I do this to prioritize my spouse over my children. Children can consume our time and can threaten the priority of continuing to work on our relationship with our spouse. I also have three different categories that many people would lump together: God, church, and ministry. My relationship with God is not the same thing as church, which is not the same thing as ministry. My relationship with God includes my time spent studying the Bible, praying, and meditating. These can be done at church, home, or anywhere, but they are done every day. Church includes going to Sunday service, Sunday School, Bible Study, Wednesday Prayer Meeting, etc. Ministry is time spent using my gifts which may be at church or elsewhere. A person might spend fifty hours a week on work while spending only six hours on their relationship with God and yet they might list God above work in their list of priorities. It is often the case that the time allotment will not match a prioritized list. The important thing is that they are on both lists. Often, we can make time for ministry by cutting back on frivolous involvements.

What Do I Do When I Feel God Asking Me to Do Something, but I Don't Feel Adequate to Do It?

First, you work to confirm that God is asking you to do something. Pray about it. You can ask other Christians who know you well what they think about you doing that ministry. You test the waters by watching others do that ministry. You volunteer to get involved with no commitment. If God shows you some inadequacies, then look for training and pray for God to gift you in that area. Find others who have what you are lacking and learn from them or delegate certain aspects of that ministry to them. If God truly calls you to do something He will provide the resources to get it done. Stop walking by sight, walk by faith. Trust in God, not in your own abilities. Remember, God didn't ask you to do it, He asked you to let Him do it through you, so get out of His way and obey.

If God is asking you to do something, then He will make you able to do it. God doesn't call the qualified, He qualifies the called. Remember you are not alone; God is with you. You have all the power and authority of the universe on your side helping you. Some people think God has called them to do something, but they are misreading the intention. For instance, a person might feel God is calling them to be a full-time missionary to a foreign land, while God has called them to walk across the street and witness to a neighbor. God's call needs to be confirmed. It's not just a feeling. God will often give you a desire but not always (take Jonah or Moses for instance).

If your spiritual leaders are not in agreement with what you think is God's will and it goes against your abilities, then no, God has not asked you to do that. If you think God is calling you to start a new ministry at your church, but you don't have time for it and you don't want to do it, but others are believing God wants you to do it, then it might be God's will. Perhaps He just wants you to start it, train someone else to run it, and then withdraw. Perhaps God will change your heart and give you the passion you're missing after you show your willingness to be obedient to His call. Perhaps God is about to give you a new spiritual gift. Perhaps God knows you better than you know yourself (there's no doubt about this). You don't want to fight God. It's a losing battle. Remember the lesson Jonah had to learn the hard way.

Will I Still Go to Heaven If I Don't Do Ministry?

I just may surprise a few people here by saying no to this question. Do you find this shocking? You will want to remind me that we are saved by faith not works. I will remind you that we are saved by faith (not works) to do good works (Eph 2:8–10). I will remind you that faith without works is dead (Jas 2:26). Your works, or your ministry, is proof of your faith. If you don't love God enough to want to serve Him, why would you want to live with Him forever? Now sure there are some people who will come to faith in Christ on their deathbed who will not have a chance to get involved in ministry. They will go to heaven without works, but that is not what you asked. You asked if you, with full understanding, complete intent, and many opportunities, can disobey God and still go to heaven. I'm speaking of an entire life lived without any ministry whatsoever. Balking at God's will at a single point in time may be dangerous, but doing so, by itself, will not keep you from entering glory.

Jonah was asked of God to go to his enemies and preach the gospel to them, but he refused and tried to run from God. God turned Jonah around and got him to where he was supposed to be, and Jonah did share about God with the people of Nineveh. When Jonah was running, he was miserable, and it could have ended in his death, but he repented of his disobedience and acquiesced. He was not happy about it, but God used him to bring salvation to an entire city.

You do not have permission to disobey God. He will deal with you severely if you disobey Him. I know you're afraid and don't want to do what He is asking you but look at the alternative; severing your relationship with God, being cut off from the power of God, and the guilt and sadness of an un-repented sin. You need to confess your disobedience, ask for His help, and make restitution. Who are you going to fear more, God or your fear of what might happen (Matt 10:28)? The fear of the Lord is the beginning of wisdom (Ps 111:10), and wisdom is knowing the right thing to do and having the ability to do it (Jas 3:13-18). If you lack wisdom (and bravery) then ask God who gives to all His children generously and without scolding (Jas 1:5).

In heaven each believer will be given a crown (1 Cor 9:25; 1 Pet 5:4) and there will be jewels in that crown; a jewel for each great work we accomplished for the glory of God. A friend of mine is fond of saying to herself, and sometimes others within earshot, "Plink, plink," meaning that jewels from her crown have just fallen out because of her actions or thoughts. When you get to heaven do you want to just barely make it, crawling before Jesus and saying, "I made it," or do you want to come and say, "Here my Lord," and show Him all the gifts and deeds you did for Him? Don't come before Him empty handed. Bring an offering. Do what He asks you to do.

How Can I Do Ministry from Home?

You can do ministry in your home with your family and to your family. You could perform ministry in your home to others if you invited them into your home and say, cook them a meal or babysit their children. You can be part of a prayer chain from home. You can do ministry from your home to others around the world. With the advent of the internet, you can reach out and minister to people anywhere in the world. I was a cyber-missionary for two years with www.GlobalMediaOutreach.com.[4] I led people to Christ and discipled people from all over the globe. I was also involved in a financial ministry found at www.Kiva.org[5] where I gave interest free micro business loans in Jesus' name (literally, I use Jesus' name).

You could write a regular "verse of the day" post on your Facebook page. You could write emails to others to encourage them or pray for them. Of course, you can still use a telephone and even regular mail. You can do your ministry anonymously if you like. Your home is a great place for ministry. You can write letters to a Christian brother or sister imprisoned for their faith in some closed country. You can write world leaders on behalf of a Christian concern. You can join a correspondence ministry. You don't have to leave your door to make a spiritual impact on the world. All it takes is a stamp or an internet connection. Become your churches webmaster or join the Online ministry team. There's so much you can do with a computer. Help a church ministry by doing weekly reminder calls for them from your home. Call the elderly and have a phone visit. You could start a hotline ministry. Enlist others to join you. Use a pass around cell phone that people take with them for their shift. Design a book of counseling helps and referrals. Have people come to your home for weekly training and sharing. Start a story line, where kids can call each week for a story with a spiritual lesson about God's love or a gospel invitation.

You can use your possessions in ministry. Open your pool up to the women and children of your church every Friday for Pool Day. Host a missionary (and their family) to stay with you. Open your spare room to someone in need like a woman in a crisis pregnancy. Be a foster parent. Host a Super Bowl party with sports celebrity testimony. Host a weekly Bible study for your neighbors. Babysit for the families in your church. Invite newcomers to your church and another individual/family from your church to dinner and help them get to know each other. Start an informal counseling ministry. Invite people over for coffee and listen to them. Host a desert at your home for your Sunday School class. Invite the youth group to have a meeting in your home or yard. Offer a class in your home (maybe how to use the computer or how to decorate a cake). Host an Easter egg hunt for your neighborhood children with gospel

---

4. Global Media Outreach, "Home."
5. Kiva, "Home."

presentation. Start a weekly prayer meeting. Pray about it and try to think outside the box.

I Used to Have a Gift, but I Don't Anymore, What Do I Do Now?

People often feel like they have lost their gift or that God has taken it away. They feel like God has punished them like He punished Samson (Judg 13–16) by taking away his strength. In truth Samson literally gave his strength away when he betrayed his people and God by treating his gift with contempt. He told Delilah the secret of his Nazarite vow knowing that she would betray him to his enemies. The point of Samson's story is that we can grieve the Spirit and his power won't flow through us when we become disobedient or backslidden. The gift of God is still there for the true believer, it's just hindered by our sin. If you are thinking that your gift is gone you might want to do some soul searching and pray through Psalm 139. Repent and make restitution for your unfaithfulness. Ask for your gift to be restored for God's glory. When He restores it be careful not to fall into temptation again.

Often our gifts atrophy from lack of use and we think it has gone away when it is still there. If the gifts and calling of God are irrevocable then we never really lose our gifts. If you want your gift back, then you will need to get right with God. Confess your sin, make amends to those you've wronged, and ask God to restore your gift. Perhaps your circumstances have changed so that you can no longer use your spiritual gift in the same way, you just need to figure out how to use your gift in a different way. Once again you can ask God to show you how you can use your gift in your new situation. You may have become shut in, moved to a new community, or have suffered some sort of malady that makes continuing to use your gift in the same way impossible, but all you have to do is think creatively about new ways to use your gift.

Perhaps your gift was not a spiritual gift at all. Perhaps it was a talent. Talents are not spiritual gifts, and though the Holy Spirit can help you develop your talent and use it for God's glory, there is no expectation that it will always be there. Sometimes the opportunities to use your gift are no longer present. A retired pastor will not have as many opportunities to use his gift of preaching (although anyone can preach anywhere at any time). Sometimes you just need to understand how to use your gift in the new context in which you find yourself. Older saints often feel like their time for doing ministry has passed and that it is time for younger people to step up and take over; while I understand the grain of truth in what they are saying, there is no retirement from ministry in the Bible. We must serve God all our days. I've seen people who had the gift of hospitality when they were younger continue that same ministry in their nursing home as nurses, workers, and other residents were attracted to their room because of their kind ways and words.

You've probably not lost your spiritual gift; you just need to understand how to use it in a new context. For instance, if you have the gift of preaching, but have lost your voice, ask God to open a different avenue for you to preach through writing (whether publishing or through social media). Maybe you need to take some time off or to take a bit of a Sabbatical from ministry before you engage in it again. Pray about it and talk to some trusted Christian friends. Don't give up on your gift. If you take care of it, and your relationship with God, the Holy Spirit will continue to use you all the days of your life.

If People Aren't Blessed by My Ministry, What Do I Do?

Perhaps you need to retest and make sure you have the gift you think you have. Perhaps you still have that gift but are using it wrongly. Maybe God is trying to redirect your efforts (ask Him if you need to make changes). Maybe there is a sin in your life impeding your effectiveness (ask for forgiveness). Perhaps you are undergoing a time of testing or persecution from demons (ask for God's protection). Satan hates it when God is winning a battle. He will do what he can to disrupt successful ministry. A former church of ours had a very successful Vacation Bible School each July, and like clockwork Satan would try to distract and thwart the workers and their efforts. Each year we persevered and overcame the various obstacles set before us and with God's help and blessing, the ministry continued to produce results for the kingdom of God. You might want to ask a few Christian leaders you respect what they think about your ministry. You may want to ask the people you are ministering to what they think. Most importantly you need to talk to God about it. If it is true that your ministry is no longer effective, it may be time for a change. Pray about it. God will lead and guide you.

If people aren't blessed by your ministry, you had better give that careful consideration as to whether to continue or not. If Christians aren't blessed by your ministry, then that is most likely confirmation that you should not be doing it. This does not mean that you shouldn't do ministry, it just means you shouldn't do that ministry. It is not necessarily a lack of confirmation of giftedness. Sometimes you must try a few ministries before you find the one that is right for you. Why would you want to continue to do something if you are ineffective at it?

When Should I Stop Doing a Ministry?

When you lose your passion for the ministry or get burned out. If the seasons have changed and the ministry is no longer relevant, or meeting a need, then step out and try something different. If God is calling you to something else, then don't be afraid to stop doing one thing and start doing something else. Often people have a hard time letting go and they hang on too long. If you are thinking it may be time to stop doing a certain ministry then pray to God about it and He will answer, guide, and direct you. List the things that should not keep you from doing a ministry. If you are doing something worthwhile for God, you will face opposition. Opposition is Satan's way of hindering God's work. He will use circumstances, people (even fellow Christians), and all sorts of fiery darts to attack your ministry. When under attack consider the source, in many cases it is a backhanded compliment. If your ministry has recently had a failure or setback, it is not necessarily a time for quitting. It's a time for evaluation and learning. It's a time for making sure it doesn't happen again. Let's face it, God is the one who does the work anyway, we just give Him the space to operate.

It is a sad situation when God has stopped doing a work, but people are continuing to go through the motions. It's such a waste of time, energy, and resources. Churches are notorious for this. A certain ministry is thought to be the litmus test for a true church or true faith, so they prop up an old, outdated ministry that is no longer meeting any needs and the church ends up working for the ministry rather than the ministry working for God. In some instances, well-meaning workers in a ministry can actually work against God. There's an old saying, "Let go and let God." Where He's working is where you want to be.

When Can I Retire from Having to Use My Gifts and Talents in Ministry?

Do you really have to ask? Never! There are no excuses. God has left us here for a reason. Sometimes those reasons change as the seasons change, but He always has work for us to do. Think how old and tired Caleb was when God asked him to conquer the Promised Land and carve out his inheritance. Elderly people are some of the greatest assets a church has, and they often are underutilized. I have to say, shame on the church that pushes out the older saints who are participating in ministry and shame on older saints who decide to stop serving their Lord in the cause of Christ. Even when you are shut in your home and can't do what you used to do, you can always pray. Prayer is one of the most underappreciated ministries and yet it is the most effective. There is never a reason to give up praying.

Some people have worked in the church all their life and can't wait to sit back and let others do the work for a change but the problem with that kind of thinking is that there is no mention of retirement in Scripture. In fact, Scripture teaches that the gifts and call of God are irrevocable (Rom 11:29). Taking a back seat in our old age only leads to a burden being placed on others to do your work, your gifts and talents will start to atrophy, and your spiritual growth will be hindered. I always say, "stay active or rust." I'm not saying that God wants you to do more and more until the day you die. It is quite possible that God indeed wants you to slow down or let others take up the leadership of certain things, but that does not mean that He doesn't have something He wants you to do.

We had a retired organist in our church and when our organist left, I asked her if she would take over. At first, she said she couldn't, that it had been too long, and that she was too old (she was ninety). I asked her to try anyway, and she reluctantly tried. After a few weeks she got her chops back and was flying over the keyboards. I loved seeing Ethel play in our blended services. What an example she set for the congregation. Even the young people marveled at her abilities. Much younger people would often say, "Well, if Ethel can still be serving the Lord, I guess I shouldn't say no." Ethel served as our organist for nine additional years until she passed. It kept her young and gave her something to look forward to doing. She had a sense of worth to the work of the Lord. She had something to live for. She didn't just sit at home wishing the Lord would take her.

Think of the great people of faith that God used in their old age: Abraham (one-hundred years old), Sarah (ninety), Moses (eighty to one hundred and twenty), Aaron (eighty-three to one hundred and twenty-three), Noah (five to six hundred), Joshua (eighty-five), Eli (ninety-eight), Zacharias, Simeon, Anna, Daniel, and the aged apostle John. Each of these were over eighty years of age and used of God in very important ways. What would have happened to the faith if they had said that they were too old to be of service to God? I often tell shut-ins that they still have an important ministry. I remind them that they at least have the responsibility to pray for the ministry of the church. I update them regularly on the prayer requests and they take this ministry seriously. I remind them of the witness they still have and the example they still set for others (especially their families). If God has you here, He has you here for a reason. No one who puts their hand to the plow and then stops is worthy of the kingdom of God (Luke 9:62).

Section Five

Witnessing

Chapter 17

"Always Be Prepared to Give an Answer to Everyone Who Asks"
—1 PETER 3:15

WHY DOES THE LORD admonish us through His servant Peter "to always be prepared to give an answer to everyone who asks you to give the reason for the hope that you have" (1 Pet 3:15)? That's a good question. Could it be that without saving faith people will spend eternity separated from God and their loved ones in a place where there will be weeping and gnashing of teeth (Matt 8:12, 13:42, 13:50, 22:13, 24:51, 25:30 and Luke 13:28)? Yes, and this is an important point; there is a hell (Matt 5:22, 5:29-30, 10:28, 18:9, 23:15, 23:33; Mark 9:43-47; Luke 12:5; Jas 3:6, 2 Pet 2:4; Rev 20:14-15). This may not be a popular view to espouse nowadays. People don't like to think of God as a judge separating loved ones for all eternity (Matt 25:31-33). They would rather think of Him as a kind and loving old man who accepts everyone. There's only one problem with this idea, that is not how God has revealed Himself in the Bible. When we think that way, we are remaking God in the image of what we think He ought to be, and we delude ourselves.

Do I have to remind you, God is who He is (Exod 3:14)? You might be sincere in your belief that there is no hell and that if there were, God would only send the worst of the worst there, but you are sincerely wrong. Jesus states, "I am the way and the truth and the life. No one comes to the Father except through Me" (John 14:6). God wants us to be prepared to share the gospel (the good news of forgiveness of sins and eternal life) because it is only through believing this wonderful truth that we are forgiven. We are not saved because we are good or good enough. "For all have sinned and fall short of the glory of God" (Rom 3:23). "Each of us has turned to our own way" (Isa 53:6). "There is no one who seeks God" (Rom 3:11). None of us is good enough because "all our righteous acts are like filthy rags" (Isa 64:6). It's not like there is a giant balancing scale in heaven and all your bad deeds are on one side and all your good deeds are on the other, and which way the scales tip determines where you go. If that were the case, could you imagine God sending the person who only had one more bad deed than good to hell and the one who had only one more good deed to heaven? Talk about arbitrary and capricious.

God has a perfect standard to which none of us measure up, but He also has a perfect plan through which all of us can be saved, faith in Christ. When you think about it, it is not God who determines who goes to heaven and who goes to hell, it's the people themselves. Each one can embrace faith or reject it. This is what seals their fate. All are without excuse because God has made Himself known to them (Rom 1:20). God asks us to make it as clear as possible to them and to remind them of the importance of making the decision to trust in Jesus. You might be the one to explain it to them in such a way that they finally understand.

God wants all people to be saved (Isa 45:22 and 1 Tim 2:4). The mean one is the Christian who refuses to share the good news they enjoy. Maybe they share it with their children but are afraid to share it with others out of fear of rejection, so they let people march off to a Christ-less eternity. How much do you have to hate your fellow man to refuse them the antidote for the disease they have? Can you really say you are doing right if you see a person drowning in a pool and do nothing to save them? You have the serum in your hand. You have the life preserver at your side. Throw them the lifeline; share the gospel with all who will listen (I know mixing metaphors . . . indulge me my mind is racing one hundred miles an hour).

Jesus commands us to, "Go and make disciples of all nations" (Matt 28:20). This is The Great Commandment, not the great suggestion. In the Greek this command is in the plural and continual sense. He wasn't just asking the apostles to do it. He wasn't asking the collective Church to do it. He was asking each one of us to do it and to keep on doing it until He returns. God asked us to do it; that should be enough to motivate us to do it. We don't have to understand everything. We don't have to know why He commanded it. The soldier's job is to obey orders. God is the perfect commander who never makes a mistake. We can trust His orders are always true and right.

When we obey this command to share the reason why we have this hope within us, it pleases God. He takes great delight in His children who love Him and obey Him. Whatever pleases God ought to please the Christian as well. I'm not saying that there is never any anxiety over witnessing, only that we should still want to do it. At the end of my first date with my wife, Lynda, I was apprehensive about kissing her goodnight, but I still had an intense desire to plant one on her. It was my goal. It was one neither of us will ever forget. It was worth going through all the butterflies and worry. If I totally wimped out and didn't kiss her, we may never have ended up husband and wife. In the same way you should want to share the gospel with others even though you are apprehensive. If you do, you may be used of God to lead someone to faith in Christ. They will be in heaven because of what Christ had done and what He did through you. There is no greater feeling than being used of God to lead someone to the Lord. Once you do it you want to do it again and again. It is why we are left here on this earth.

It is easier to believe when we hear the testimony of others. This is why testimonials are so often used and effective in advertising. It's easier to understand when someone explains it to us and answers our questions. Romans 10:14–15 says:

> How, then, can they call on the one they have not believed in? And how can they believe in the one of whom they have not heard? And how can they hear without someone preaching to them? And how can anyone preach unless they are sent? As it is written: "How beautiful are the feet of those who bring good news!"

Church, we need a pedicure. We need to beautify our feet by preparing to be a witness in season and out of season because God is depending on us and because others' eternal lives are hanging in the balance.

If people don't hear the gospel from Christians, then they will hear a different gospel from the world. They will be left as sheep without the shepherd. They will become prey for Satan who will continue to tell them that they are not so bad and that they are good enough. They may believe the lie and never make it to heaven. Your family, friends, neighbors, and co-workers need you to be bold and courageous. This world needs Christians to stop being afraid to share the gospel; "For the Spirit God gave us does not make us timid, but gives us power, love and self-discipline" (2

Tim 1:7). These are the power of the gospel, the love for our fellow man, and the self-discipline to be prepared to share.

We must be prepared. The doctor who studies up and prepares for surgery is going to be more successful than the one who doesn't. Have you ever heard a sermon that was not prepared? It's often not very pleasant to hear. How would you like your contractor to come to your house unprepared without the right materials and equipment? It would be like taking a cross country road trip in your seven-year-old sedan without checking the oil, transmission fluid, brake fluid, spare tire, tire pressure, and wiper fluid. It's just plain foolish. The lumber jack who is prepared with a sharp ax is going to do five times the logging in half the time and half the effort of the one who is not prepared. Stop working so hard at what you think God wants you to do and prepare for what God has called you to do. He's called us all to share the gospel. He even tells us how to do it; love one another and proclaim that Jesus died on the cross for sin.

The best way to prepare to witness is to start praying. Stop reading this and pray about your witness. To whom does God want you to share your testimony? Ask God. What does he want you to say? Ask God. Should you use a tract? Ask God. Should you take someone with you? God knows so ask Him. Where should this encounter take place? Pray about all these things and more, but don't forget to listen for God's answers. God answers through His Word (the Bible), His leading (a quiet inaudible voice or feeling), circumstances, and other godly people. Ask others to pray for and with you. Maybe you already have someone on your heart or mind, and you want to witness to them. Maybe you have no idea who you should witness to, and you need to ask Him to point someone out. Witnessing starts and ends with prayer. You start by asking for direction (not His blessings on your plans) and you end with praying with the individual to make Christ their leader and forgiver or you pray that God will use someone else to bring them in.

After you've prayed about witnessing, make a plan. Do you know what you are going to say? Do you have some basic salvation Scriptures memorized or have them marked in a Bible? Have you practiced and rehearsed? Do you have contingency plans (what if they say this or that and what to do if someone else joins in)? Have you earned the right to witness to this person if this is friendship evangelism? How well do you know this person? What are their likes and dislikes? What approach would work best with them? Do you have a brief two-minute story about how you became a Christian? Do you know how to share the gospel in two minutes or less? I know this list of questions seems intimidating but it's not. In fact, you don't have to have any of this preparation done. God may give you an opportunity that catches you completely off guard and unprepared. You should still share the gospel, remembering that some plant, others water, but God causes the growth.

You will not harvest the souls of everyone to whom you witness. Often it is a team effort. Sometimes you will never know until glory that the questions you planted in their mind were instrumental to their pursuing Christ. My wife had a friend who told her this story of coming home from a Navigator's meeting in Maine. He picked up a hitchhiker and started to witness to him. The hitchhiker didn't pray the sinner's prayer but later another Navigator picked up that same hitchhiker and shared the gospel with him. The guy was like, "You're the second one today to tell me this." To which his friend said, "I think God is trying to get your attention. Maybe you should listen more closely." God orchestrates all His various efforts in ways we will never know.

It is always best to be as prepared as possible even for the unexpected. Carry tracts in your bible and in your car. Practice by rehearsing with friends as you take turns role playing. Practice drawing the bridge illustration. Rehearse using the wordless book or bracelet. Memorize the Roman Road. Reading books on evangelism is a great way to keep the fire burning. Read through the Four Spiritual Laws until you can read it upside down (because you will be facing the person you are witnessing to and directing them page by page through it). Form a prayer support team who will be praying for you. Attend witnessing courses. There are many different types of witnessing. You can go door to door and witness to people you don't even know. Walk up to a stranger in the mall or on the street. Witnessing to strangers is preferable to some people because they don't know them and may never have to see them again. The fear of rejection is far less. Others would much rather witness to people they know because strangers frighten them and it's much easier to share with someone they have a relationship with. Maybe you don't know which you would like. Try them both, even if you're scared to death of the one. You might surprise yourself and find it exciting and easy.

Keep your presentation brief. You don't want to over share because that could turn them off. Your personal testimony should come in two versions the full long version (five minutes) and your Reader's Digest version (two minutes or less). When witnessing use the shorter version. Practice it and time yourself. It should have three parts; your life before

Christ, how you came to Christ (including the gospel), and lastly your life since becoming a Christian. You should also be able to share the gospel in around a minute (this is often part of your testimony). The gospel should go something like this, "God loves you so much that He sent His only Son, Jesus, to die on the cross for you, to pay the penalty for your sin. If you trust in Him, and what He has done for you, you have God's forgiveness and eternal life. This is faith. It is a gift that you can't earn and like any gift you have to accept it." All are sinners (I am a sinner), God loves us and has a plan to save us, Jesus died for sin, each one must accept this free gift of forgiveness by believing these premises. Ask the person you are witnessing to if they want to trust God and pray now. Pray for them, give them material, offer help (discipleship).

You'll have to learn how to read people (if they are antsy or put off) and learn what kind of questions to ask. Here's a sample list of possible questions you might ask during a witnessing encounter:

Would you like to know for sure you are going to go to heaven? (1 John 5:13)

Do you have a few minutes for me to share with you about how you can restore your relationship with God?

Do you know how to get to heaven?

Do you know what Jesus says about how to get to heaven?

What makes a person a Christian?

Do you have a few minutes to help me with a survey? (Using a survey is a good tactic when approaching complete strangers.)

What would be the worst thing that could happen to you after you die?

Do you know the gospel? May I share it with you?

Would you mind if I read through this little booklet called The Four Spiritual Laws with you? It will only take a few minutes.

Do you know what is going to happen to you after you die?

How prepared are you to meet God?

Do you like free gifts?

Did you know that you can know for sure that you will inherit eternal life? (1 John 5:13)

If you were to die right now, where would you spend eternity?

If you died, met Jesus at the pearly gates, and He were to ask you, "Why should I let you into My heaven?" what would you say?

Here are a few extremely important types of questions you should ask at the end of your explanation:

> Do you now believe for the first time what I just shared with you?
> What keeps you from trusting in Jesus?
> Would you like to pray with me?

Of course, these questions aren't all discussion starters. You should have an introduction planned out. This list is just an example of the different type of questions you should be thinking about as you have opportunity to share with someone and as you discern what direction you should take in your conversation.

You should never be rude, judgmental, pushy, or unkind. You are representing Christ and every other Christian that person will ever meet. You will be shaping their impressions and feelings toward the Church. You could turn someone off to the gospel by your actions and your words so be very careful. Be respectful. Don't answer your cell phone in the middle of an encounter (turn it off before). Don't tell them they are wrong; simply tell them what the bible says. Say something like, "That's an interesting viewpoint. Thank you for sharing it. The Bible says that . . ." Witnessing is an awesome responsibility; this is another reason we should be prepared. We will sound more convincing if we give a more confident, well thought out, and reasoned answers. You will want to anticipate their questions but never cease to truly listen to them. You will want to have direct eye contact the whole time yet read their body language.

When witnessing to a stranger, say in a mall, you should look for a person who seems to have the time and not someone in a rush. You might stay away from someone engaged in certain activities like eating or reading. You might also avoid people who are with friends. You might want to find someone that is most like you, the same age, gender, and dress. Always ask the person for permission to share with them. Say something like, "Excuse me, but do you have a few minutes for me to share some good news? My name is . . ." When you are witnessing to strangers, door to door, you don't have the luxury of carefully selecting to whom you might witness. They could open the door and it becomes obvious that now is not the right time; maybe the Super Bowl is on, maybe they have guests, or perhaps they have a dripping paint brush in their hand. In such an instance you should be prepared to quickly introduce yourself, explain what you are doing at their door, leave a tract or an invitation, and promise to stop by another time. If they are not busy and they invite you inside you should not enter, especially if the person is of the opposite sex. If you have someone with you perhaps you might consider entering a home but use caution when doing this.

When witnessing to friends and acquaintances remember you want to earn the right to share. That means putting in the time to listen to them share about what they are passionate about. All your listening will pay off tremendous benefits as you get to know their likes and dislikes. Then you will know what the best approach to might be. For instance, if your girlfriend was abused by her father, you might not want to talk about how God the Father loves us and has a wonderful plan for her life. If they have recently had a traumatic event such as a surgery, you may be able to use that as an example by saying something like, "Just like you went to see the doctor when you suspected something was wrong with your body, we need to turn to Jesus when we suspect something is wrong with our spirit . . ." or "I'm so glad you overcame cancer. You know sin is a cancer which needs to be dealt with and cut out before it has a chance to spread. Luckily, we have Jesus, the Great Physician, who has never lost a patient . . ." You can work into the conversation hobbies, interests, activities, objects in their home, and tons of other things you become aware of because you are listening and observant. The person will sense your interest in them and appreciate you for it. Ideally you are tailoring your presentation to them not reciting a script from memory.

When doing friendship evangelism, you will want to spend time with them. If they are going shopping, and invite you to go with them, go. When they come home from the hospital after surgery make them a meal for them and visit them. Invite them out for coffee frequently, then when you invite them out for coffee and plan to share the gospel it won't come out of the blue. You will be able to share as a trusted friend in the natural course of events and it won't seem so contrived or like an intervention. You should raise the flag of Christ frequently in conversation. This is not witnessing; this is simply talking about your involvement in the faith so you can demonstrate how natural it is to have a vibrant everyday faith. Occasionally, say something like, "I'll pray about that." Things like, "Church was great today" might lead to more or it might not, but you keep your faith in your relationship (which is what I call raising the flag of Christ) so that when you do share the gospel with them it doesn't come out of left field.

Whoever you share the gospel with you will probably want to do it in private or semi-private. Choose a setting where they would feel safe. You can do it in a public setting if you can have a private conversation. I've shared Christ with many people at McDonalds, Starbucks, and parks. Anywhere can be the right place. When God says, "Now's the time" then share wherever you are. When they start asking spiritual questions try turning the conversation toward the gospel. Practice doing this. They felt comfortable enough to bring up the subject and if there is no resistance to your leading them to talk about the gospel then go for it. In such cases it doesn't matter where you are. I've shared Christ with people in bathrooms, on roller coasters, and in the middle of large rock concerts. You must be listening to them and the Lord. You must be reading the signs and taking advantage of opportunities to share. Again, not in a pushing way; not *constantly* raising the flag, not trying to turn *every* conversation to the gospel, just trying it occasionally, as it feels right. It should be natural. It should flow out of the situation and the relationship.

When you have a strong urge to share the gospel with someone it's probably the Lord leading you. When you can't get it out of your mind, or when the person keeps giving you openings to share the gospel, this is of and from the Lord. You must be faithful to take advantage of the opportunity and share. If you've been praying and preparing, then you have nothing to fear. God is with you, and He will give you the words to say. You don't have to answer every one of their questions. You shouldn't argue them into heaven (like that ever works anyway). You simply share what you know. Share Christ's story, your story, and then ask them about their story. Tell them that the Bible says Jesus, God's Son, died on the cross to rescue us from all our mistakes. Tell them how you came to believe in Jesus. Then ask them what they believe about Jesus. If they don't give a Christian response, then state the plan of salvation and ask them if they want to receive the gift of God's forgiveness.

Don't get sidetracked from the gospel. Don't let questions about creation, the trinity, or the little pygmy in Africa get you off talking about Jesus and how he died on the cross for sin. If you are talking about Jesus and turning the conversation toward Him, and away from issues and controversies (like homosexuality, religious wars, schisms, etc.), then you are heading in the right direction. It is a ploy of Satan to sidetrack us when we are sharing. Some people use questions about these side issues as a defense mechanism. They don't want to be confronted with their sin, so they try to make it about something else. Say things like, "I wasn't there when God created the world, but I do know that He created us to have a relationship with Him and that we messed that up through sin. That's why He sent Jesus to die on the cross for us; to save us . . ." or "Homosexuality? It's not my job to judge. The Holy Spirit is the one who convicts the world of right and wrong. I was convicted of my sin, and I came to believe that Jesus died on the cross to take my place." Use whatever they bring up as a springboard to the gospel, but be sensitive, respectful, and gentle. If it starts becoming argumentative then cool your jets and stop. Pray in your mind for them and ask God if you should move on. Maybe you were only supposed to bring them so far and someone else is supposed to finish the job. The Spirit moves in mysterious ways.

Be sensitive to how they are receiving your presentation. Do you sense they are coming to Christ out of fear? Fire insurance is a good thing to buy but illegal if you are planning on burning down your house. They can't accept Christ's forgiveness if they simply want a license to sin. You also want to carefully discern if they are coming to Christ because others want them to become Christian. Such commitments often are not genuine. Many accept Christ to get their boyfriend or girlfriend to say yes to a proposal of marriage. They play the game for a while but soon fall away proving their so-called faith was a rouse. As a pastor I won't consider marrying a couple if they don't share the same faith. When I share this often someone is ready to accept Christ. People will do anything given the proper motivation, but we are not trying to manipulate people into becoming Christians.

We don't want the people to whom we are witnessing to become Christian out of fear, guilt, a desire to please others, or as a response to an emotional appeal. We want them to accept the claims of Christ because they see their personal need for a Savior. We want to introduce them to their new first love. We're not trying to fill a quota. The goal is not to make converts; the goal is to make disciples. Disciples grow after they accept Christ. Disciples mature to the point that they go out and make disciples. After you pray with a person to accept Christ hopefully your relationship to that person has only just begun. In some cultures, if you save someone's life you are responsible for them for the rest of their life. Even if the person you lead to the Lord is a stranger, you should share some contact information with them or have some program of follow-up that you can suggest to them. This should be part of your preparation.

Give them the name and address of three good churches in the area. Offer them a bible or promise to send them a bible. Have follow-up material on hand to give to them. Give them a bible reading plan. There are many resources like this for you to use. They are inexpensive to purchase and even new testaments are relatively cheap so have a bunch on hand. If you are not prepared to disciple them in the faith, then have the name and contact information of someone who is able to do that for them and tell them to expect a call from that person.

Encourage them to share about their decision to accept Christ with others as soon as possible. This will help them cement their new faith. Introduce them to others who might be a resource to them, people like your pastor, a Sunday School teacher, a deacon from your church, etc. Share some helpful Christian websites. Introduce them to your Christian friends. Explain to them the importance of fellowship with other Christians to encourage their new faith. Give them a copy of this book. You are like their spiritual father or mother, and they are a little newborn. Get their contact information and call them, write them, text them. Find out how they are doing. Answer their questions. Let them know you are there for them. Ask them how you can pray for them. Bring them to a worship service, bible study, and prayer meeting.

Keep a journal of your witnessing activity. You can use it for prayer purposes or just to make you aware of opportunities. See how many times a month you share your faith. Set goals to better your best week. Write down your plans to witness to specific people. Take notes after friendship encounters with pre-believers (that's what I like to call non-Christians God has burdened me with). List reminders and insights about how to do evangelism better. Write down verses you want to memorize. Have a page of resources or where you can find such and such. Keep a record of every person you prayed with to accept Jesus Christ as their Lord and Savior.

Some of you have the gift of evangelism and will have the opportunity to share your testimony in front of groups. You may have the opportunity to preach. Don't be afraid to stick to the simple gospel truth and give an invitation. You know you have the gift of evangelism when you see God using you to win people to Himself. Don't neglect that gift. Practice it and use it. Use it with individuals and in groups. Encourage others to witness. Teach, train, and help others to do evangelism. Some of you will want to test the waters with a short term missions trip.

One of the biggest parts of the Great Commission is to "Go." You don't have to go very far to find someone who doesn't know Jesus Christ as their Savior. You can do missions right in your own neighborhood. In certain metropolitan areas you can even do cross-cultural missions work within a mile of your home. The word "Go" in the Great Commission is not used to necessarily tell us all to go to far-away lands in order to witness; it means go across the town, across the street, and sometimes across the room. As Christians we can't sit there and wait for the world to come to us. We can't put up our church sign and wait for them to come; we must go to them. We must take initiative. Jesus didn't save us from His throne in Heaven; He came down (incarnational theology) and lived among us. In the same way, Christians must go to the lost.

Churches have become too laid back. We think the programs will entice them to come, where they will hear the gospel, and get saved. When they come, we talk about the weather and other trivial topics and leave the heavy work of evangelism to the professional paid staff of the church to do. Few people in the church do follow-up anymore. They don't invite them to dinner or a bible study; they don't call them after their visit to church with an invitation to something. They don't go and visit the family to explain what the church is all about and to welcome them. They certainly don't talk about matters of faith with them. A person or family that comes to church is saying that they are interested in spiritual guidance or that they have a spiritual need. If we can't approach this group with the gospel, we'll never reach those outside the church. If showing up is 80 percent of the job, then all we have to do is go to the pre-believers within our sphere of influence prepared to share the gospel and take advantage of the opportunities God brings our way. Many Christians are praying for revival and God wants to pour out His Spirit on all people but He's waiting for us to go to them. Be the answer to your prayer and go witness.

People often think that witnessing is best done by developing relationships with people and winning them over with their lifestyle, waiting for them to be ready, and then simply answering their questions. I say they are half right. There are many people who will never ask why you have this hope. Friendship evangelism is a great tool, but in Acts 8 Philip went to the Ethiopian (as he was led by the Spirit). He created the opportunity by running alongside the chariot. Philip spoke to him first and asked him if he understood what he was reading. What would have happened if Philip didn't obey the Spirit and come alongside the chariot? He'd probably still be wandering around in the desert. Do you ever wonder why you feel like you're in a spiritual desert? Maybe you've been neglecting this spiritual discipline long enough. It's time dear Christian; take the next step in your spiritual maturity and be obedient to witness.

I'm reminded of Moses who in his encounter with God at the burning bush (Exod 3 and 4), was asked to go to Egypt and tell Pharaoh to set God's people free. He was scared to death. Moses came up with all these excuses; he didn't have the authority to do it, he didn't know what to say, he wasn't a good speaker, what if people didn't believe him . . . Sound familiar? God says to Moses, "Who gave human beings their mouths?" God would go with him and give him the words to say, but Moses still didn't want to obey God. He liked his new life in Midian and did not want to go back to his old stomping grounds to mix it up with a dangerous crowd. Moses asks God, "Please send another." God became furious with Moses. Have you been asking God to send someone else in your stead? You wonder why it seems like your prayers are bouncing off the ceiling and why you don't see the power of God demonstrated in your life; well, this could be the problem. Is it possible you are not being obedient to God in this matter of witnessing?

God doesn't ask you to win the world or to be successful every time; He asks you to be faithful. Will you be faithful? The results are God's work not yours. Perhaps this is the last step God is waiting for you to take before He pours out His blessing on your life, your family, your church, or your world. God has sent me into your life through this book to encourage you in this matter. Fear keeps good people from doing the right thing, but God does not give us a Spirit of fear. Fear paralyzes the prey of the roaring lion of this world. It's like I'm watching the National Geographic Channel and I see the gazelle in the sights of the hunting lion. I'm screaming at the flat screen for the poor animal to get up and go, but it doesn't until it's too late. Don't put it off any longer. Start your prayers and preparations; for this day we go to battle to snatch the souls of friends, family, and complete strangers from the fires of hell.

Chapter 18

"If We Deny Him, He Also Will Deny Us"
—2 TIMOTHY 2:12

THE DEMONS BELIEVE IN God and want forgiveness, but they don't have it. Everyone wants to go to heaven, but not all will. Salvation takes true repentance, not just being sorry about our sin. It takes a turning from our way to God's way. It takes a surrendering to His will and not ours. To be saved you must embrace this attitude unequivocally. You have to let Him reign and rule in your life. You have to at least want to have God's will being lived out in your life. No one is perfect. We stumble and fall. We take back control of our lives from Christ from time to time as we seek our will and not His, but He brings us back to our senses and we confess our folly and give Him back the control of our lives.

If a Christian says no to God's command to witness continually, willfully, and with full awareness, then their faith may not be true faith at all. Their actions (or in this case, their lack of being willing to witness) speak to the quality of their faith. They're not surrendered. In the long run you can't hold back from God and call yourself a mature Christian (well, you can, but you're lying). Up till now most were happy with my treatise because it was easy. They believe in Jesus. They enjoy fellowship. They read the bible. They pray. They enjoy doing ministry. They agree with everything that has been said here until they came to that last chapter and now, they're ready to throw this book out the window. They're writing an email right now to give me a piece of their mind. They're going to set me straight. They're sick of being told they must witness. They don't want to do it, and no one is going to make them. Until you are obedient to witness you are suck in your spiritual growth.

I get it. Such a Christian wants God's salvation on their terms. They want forgiveness without compliance. They want easy grace. The only problem is that's not what God has offered. God's grace is costly. Unless we are willing to give up everything to follow Christ, we are not worthy to be called His disciple (Matt 10:37–38; 13:34 and 44). God wants us to trust and obey, not trust and shrink away. Anyone who puts his hand to the plow and then stops is not fit for service in the kingdom of God (Luke 9:62). We were all fine with following Christ until He asked us to witness and now some just want to pretend that He didn't ask.

When I asked Lynda to marry me, I was in youth ministry. She knew I had the call of God upon my life. She was on board with everything that came with it, except if I went into the senior pastorate. After serving the Lord in youth ministry for twenty-two years, at the ripe old age of forty, God asked me to be a senior pastor. That was some conversation with Lynda, but God had worked in her heart to prepare her for the switch, and she was willing to support me (for which I will always be grateful). The point of this story is that God understands where we are at and what type of commitment, we are willing to make when we first turn to Him. He knows that in truth few of us are fully surrendered when we first come to Christ. We are as surrendered as we can be at that time, but God loves us too much to leave us there. He grows us, opens our eyes, and helps us to see other areas of our lives needing to be surrendered.

When I first accepted Christ, I was twelve years old. I didn't have a job. I wasn't married. I didn't have children. I surrendered all that a twelve-year-old could, but since then God has called me to make fuller and more meaningful commitments to Him. I have had to continue to surrender to Christ; things I may have said no to as a preteen. If I knew that I would have to clean up after my sick dog and hold him in my arms as he was put to sleep, I don't think I would have gotten him, but somehow my commitment grew as did my love and I wanted to do those unpleasant things. In the same way a growing Christian can't continue to deny Jesus any corner of their lives. The true Christian will eventually succumb to His will. God tells us in his Word, "Therefore let us move beyond the elementary teachings about Christ and be taken forward to maturity, not laying again the foundation of repentance from acts that lead to death" (Heb 6:1, try reading the next few verses).

1 John 2:23 says, "No one who denies the Son has the Father. He who confesses the Son has the Father also." A Christian can't deny Jesus before others. They can't deny Jesus' will to be done in their life. We were all taught to pray, "Your will be done, on earth as it is in heaven" (Matt 6:10). Even Jesus, when He didn't want to do what God was asking of Him, prayed, "My Father, if it is not possible for this cup to be taken away unless I drink it, may your will be done" (Matt 26:42). Someone may say, "Well, even Peter denied the Lord three times." Yes, he did but he didn't continue to deny Him. Jesus confronted Peter in a tearful encounter of restoration and after that he would never deny the Lord again. I must say it again, "whoever denies Me (Jesus) before men, I also will deny before my Father who is in heaven" (Matt 10:33). Someone may say, "But refusing to witness is not the same thing as denying the Lord. I'm not recanting my faith." It may not be recanting your faith, but it is a sin of omission.

Rather than denying God's will for your life wouldn't you rather hear from God, "Well done thou good and faithful servant"? Wouldn't you rather hear, "I know your works. Behold, I have set before you an open door, which no one is able to shut; I know that you have but little power, and yet you have kept my word and have not denied my name" (Rev 3:8). You say, "Well, sure I'd rather hear those things, but I can't witness. You don't understand, you're a pastor, it's easy for you. It's impossible for me." But nothing is impossible with God. "I wish I could." If you want to do it, but feel you can't, then God can work with that. If there is a part of you who wishes you could obey God in this area, but fear has its grip on you then you are in good company. Adam hid from God out of fear because of his disobedience. Moses balked at God's plan out of fear. Jonah didn't want to go to Nineveh because he was afraid that his enemies would be saved. Peter denied our Lord three times out of fear that he would be killed. And yet, in each case God was able to work in and through each one of these reluctant believers.

They had to come to the end of themselves. They had to confess that they couldn't do it and that God would have to do it. Then they had to surrender themselves and let God do it through them. You say, "I freeze up and can't do it." That's my point, you can't do it, but you can let Christ do it. Ask God to do this work of witnessing through you. Ask Him to prepare you. Ask Him to fill you. Ask Him for such great love for Him and your fellow human that you'd be willing to let Him witness through you. He will take you step by step through the necessary preparation. Slowly your heart will change as you envision yourself surrendered to the

Lord and Him speaking through you. He will place a support network around you to help you with each and every step He is going to take through you. Your part in all this is to get out of His way. So, when He is trying to say something, you've practiced and rehearsed, don't change the direction of the conversation.

Perhaps you are ready to pray this prayer:

> God, I have been holding back from You. I want to fully surrender to Your will in my life. I want to stop doing it my way. I need You in control of my life. I have been pretending to have my act together, but I am a mess. Clean me up. Forgive me of my disobedience. Cast my fears aside and replace them with such love for You that I will become an effective witness. Let Your power flow through me, a clean and fit vessel. Prepare me for all You have in store for me. I surrender all. In Jesus' name I pray, Amen!

It's that simple and that hard, but you'll never regret it. If you just prayed this prayer you need to tell someone about your commitment to witness. Tell another Christian, tell your pastor, tell your spouse, tell someone. Think of it as practicing witnessing to non-believers. Other Christians will be thrilled about your commitment to fully surrender and engage in evangelism. They will support you and encourage you. Some of you might be on the church board, Sunday School teachers or even pastors. Don't be embarrassed to share. There's a great old hymn, *I Love to Tell the Story*.[1] In it, it says, "I love to tell the story for those who know it best seem hungering and thirsting to hear it like the rest." Feed the Christians around you with your story. Others may take the bold step you just took. Maybe revival will break out in your church.

Increasingly there is a whole world of people who have never heard the good news of the gospel. There is a whole generation of young people whose parents are not taking them to church or leading their children to Christ. Schools are not allowing Christ or the Bible in School anymore. Public displays of faith are disappearing because it is perceived as illegal. You can't witness at work. The town can't put up the nativity. Today's children are growing up knowing very little about the historical Jesus, much less about the Biblical Jesus.

I had a girl in one of my youth groups who came to one of our meetings because a friend invited her. She heard us talking about the Bible and Jesus and she said, "I really don't understand what you're talking about.

---

1. Hankey, *"I Love to Tell the Story."*

My parents never brought me to church or taught me anything about Jesus or the Bible. They were brought up Christian, but they don't talk about Him. I know Jesus was a man who started a religion, and His birthday is Christmas, but that's all." After I picked my jaw up off the floor, I shared some of the basics of the gospel. She was wide-eyed and was asking all sorts of questions. Over the next few weeks, she gave her heart to Christ. Your world is full of people who have never heard, and they need you to share the reason why you have the hope that you have. No wonder many countries are becoming post Christian societies; Christians are refusing to share the gospel (even with their own children).

Chapter 19

"Entrust to Reliable People Who Will Also Be Qualified to Teach Others"
—2 TIMOTHY 2:2

CAN YOU IMAGINE IF whoever shared the gospel with you never did? You are a Christian because of them, and you might not have become one without them. Jesus shared the good news with Peter, Peter shared it with Joseph, Joseph shared it with Simon, Simon shared it with Priscilla, Priscilla shared it with her daughter Mary, Mary shared it with her fiancé who would become her husband Marcus, Marcus shared it with the commander of the guard Maximilian, Maximilian shared it with Constantine, Constantine shared it with . . . and on and on it goes down through the ages until it came to you. These people shared with some who embraced the faith, but for everyone who accepted the faith there were seven who didn't. Actually, it was more like Jesus shared the good news with ten thousand and five hundred came to faith; they shared it with one hundred thousand and five thousand came to faith who shared it with a million . . . who shared it with ten million . . . and so on, and so on.

The world population is over eight billion, of which about 30 percent claim to be Christian, which is about 2.4 billion. Unfortunately, anywhere from 32–40 percent of the world has never heard the gospel which amounts to 3.2 billion (more than the number of Christians).[1,2] If those 2.4 billion Christians would be obedient to share the gospel with everyone, they have the opportunity, the whole world would hear of the

1. Joshua Project, "Global Statistics."
2. One World Missions, "Missions Education."

gospel of Christ in less than two years. You start with 2.4 billion Christians sharing their faith and at the end of the first year you would have 2.4 billion people would hear the gospel, and by the end of the second year the whole world would have heard the gospel. Of course, not everyone who claims to be a Christian is a Christian and there are geographic and ideological challenges. Even if only 10 percent of purported Christians were faithful to share the gospel you would start with two hundred and forty million and in just over five years everyone in the world would have heard the gospel of Christ. If only one Christian in one-hundred would be faithful to follow this plan of witnessing the world would be reached in just over eleven years. Don't you think we should be able to get one in one-hundred Christians motivated to share the gospel? Unfortunately, since the world has not yet heard the good news about Jesus, we can assume that not even one in one-hundred is faithful to share the good news (not even 1 percent).

Each one of us has people depending on us to be part of this gospel chain, this legacy of faith. What legacy are you leaving? Will people remember you as the person who played an important part in their coming to know Christ or will you not be given a second thought when you move out of town? Earn a reputation of loving your Lord so much that your faithfulness drew others into a closer relationship with Jesus. Be an example to other Christians and encourage them to go and do likewise. Just as every person born has two biological parents, every Christian born again has a spiritual parent; someone who shared with them so they could embrace the faith. Granted it could have been a printer/publisher, an author, or a Christian teacher with a internet show. The Christian often remembers the one who helped them come to know the Lord.

I was twelve years old when I attended Camp Pine Ridge for Boys in Rumney, New Hampshire (now known as Rumney Bible Conference). It was 1971 and I have no idea who the counselor was who shared the gospel with a small group of boys gathered for devotions that day, but two of us responded and prayed to accept Jesus Christ as our Lord and Savior. His name may not have been remembered by a twelve-year-old boy, but now that I am older my appreciation for that young man is never lacking. If he had not been faithful to share the gospel with us that day, hundreds of people who I have led to the Lord may never have come to know Christ, and who knows about the other twelve-year-old who accepted Christ that day. Some of those I have led to the Lord are pastors, missionaries, and churchmen and women, and God knows how many they have reached with the gospel. Even if that young man at Pine Ridge had only won two boys to the Lord, he still may have been partially responsible for a thousand or more people coming to Christ in his lifetime and perhaps millions in future generations. Don't break the chain of faith extending down through the generations.

Are the Christians in your local fellowship impassioned to witness? If not, fan into flame their faith; encourage them to share. If they don't care to share their faith, find a group of Christians who are being faithful to witness. Don't let a dead church (no matter how many activities they have) hold you back. It's hard enough to witness without a wet blanket smothering the embers of your faith. When Christians don't witness, they discourage the others around them like a wet blanket. Such churches may look like the real thing, but they are a sham. They are little more than a country club meeting to satisfy their own needs. They are religious, but do not share how to have a relationship with Jesus. Is your church in danger of losing its lampstand?

Sharing the gospel is not just part of a witnessing chain; your witnessing is part of a spiritual chainmail armor of the Church. The breastplate which was commonly used in Christ's time by armies to protect their soldiers eventually gave way to something lighter and more flexible, the chainmail. It is a garment weaved of metal. The strength of the mail was from its tight weave. Nothing could get through because trauma to one link in the mail was spread out to the other links in the area; and so, the attacking force of a blow, from say a sword, was mitigated. The Church is like a chainmail garment. We are not Christians in isolation. We exist as a body made up of many parts. We depend on each other. We work in the ministry alongside one another. We all work together for there is only one cause, the cause of Christ. Chainmail is often thought of as defensive, but it is because of this strong defense that a warrior has the confidence to rush ahead offensively.

In the same way because Christians who are united and intent on the same purpose (to share the good news) have courage to charge forth against the gates of hell which shall not prevail against us. Interestingly, when one piece of the mail was broken the wire could become a dangerous metal spike which could cause small little cuts and punctures in the warrior's flesh, which often would become infected and end in death. The very thing that was to protect a soldier could cause their death. Don't be the chink in the armor of Christians in your area. Don't be a weak spot for the enemy to exploit. Don't hurt the work of the body of Christ. Repair the chainmail of your church because, whether you realize it or not, we are at war against the army of darkness (Paul tells us in Ephesians 6 to be clothed in the full armor of God because we wrestle against principalities and powers).

As important as witnessing is, the Great Commission is to make *disciples*, not to witness. Witnessing is the important first step in the "making disciples" process. The difference between witnessing and discipling is the same as the difference between helping someone become a believer in Christ and helping someone grow in their new faith in Him. When you witness to someone, and they accept Christ you become spiritually responsible for them. You become their spiritual parent in the faith. They are looking to you to help them understand what they just did. They are a spiritual newborn. We don't just discharge newborn babies out of the hospital on their own; we entrust them to loving parents who take them home and raise them.

In the same way when you birth someone into the kingdom of God you must continue to care for them. You must invest your life in them. You must make the time to meet with them on a regular basis (say once or twice a week for at least twelve weeks). When you get together with them you pray with them, study the Bible together, answer their questions, introduce them to other Christians (and the church), and you teach them how to, in turn, share their faith. There are materials and books you could work through together, but the most important part of the discipling process is for you to impart yourself to your disciplee. This takes time and a caring relationship, but the result is that they become like you ("It is enough for students to be like their teachers" Matt 10:25). They have seen Christ in you and have followed you as you have followed the Lord until they can follow the Lord by themselves.

Some might think that making disciples is a spiritual discipline (and it is) deserving of its own section (and it is), but I have chosen to combine making disciples with witnessing because you can't make disciples without making converts. Witnessing is the beginning of the Great Commission and disciples are the result of the Great Commission. They are not the same thing, but they are closely related and bound together in the same spiritual discipline. It is possible to spend your life winning people to the faith and moving on to the next convert all your life long, but that is not what is supposed to happen. Even the world's greatest evangelists have carefully planned a follow-up program because they understand their responsibility to those who come to faith through their ministry.

"Entrust to Reliable People Who Will Also Be Qualified to Teach Others"   175

Because there are so many who come to faith through their ministry, they must delegate this responsibility.

I think it's kind of sad that they miss out on building a relationship with their spiritual offspring. There's nothing more satisfying or rewarding than to be use of God to lead someone to faith in Christ and then to develop a lifelong relationship where you can see them grow in their faith. There are others who feel called to disciple new Christians that have just come to faith through the ministry of others. Both (evangelists and disciplers) are needed, but I find both sort of sad. The evangelist who never disciples is like being a surrogate mother who never raises a child and the one who disciples only is like a foster parent who has no children of their own.

I know there are many ways to have and be a family (the analogy of course breaks down and I am not passing judgment on different ways of being a family) but desiring a family, planning for one, giving birth and raising your child (bone of your bone and flesh of your flesh so to speak) has been one of the most rewarding accomplishments of my life that I wouldn't trade for anything. In the same way the mature Christian was made to reproduce; not just to witness and birth others into faith in Christ, but to also disciple them and help them grow in the faith. You're not a parent just because you give birth. You're a parent because you raise a child to maturity. There are some that you will never see again and must trust them to the Lord for discipling. He will raise someone up to do the work that you can't, but when you are able you must step up to complete the task by discipling them to maturity in Christ.

There is a thought that until a church founds a daughter church that it is not a mature church. In the same way, Christians who have not led a person to faith in Christ and discipled them to maturity are not mature themselves. After all God doesn't call us to be successful, He calls us to share. The results are up to Him. Those who witness a little have a little Christian maturity; those who witness much have a greater maturity. If you want to develop your ability to witness hang out with Christians who do it and those who God has used to draw people to Himself. Watch such people and learn from them. Go with them. Emulate them.

Prayer is said to be the life blood of the church, the blood of martyrs is the seed of the church, but the future and health of the church hangs on evangelism and discipling. If your local fellowship is not growing numerically, eight times out of ten it is because Christians aren't witnessing and discipling. I believe most Christians think salvation is for them. It is something they need to receive; it is not something they need to share. They leave the work of evangelism to the professionals; the paid clergy or those with the gift of evangelism. This type of thinking is what we would now call an *entitlement* mindset rather than a servant's attitude, and yet God commands us in His Word to have the same servant mindset that Christ had (Phil 2:5–8). We are not to think of ourselves only, but we are to think of others as more important than ourselves (Phil 2:3–4). When we consider the needs of the unsaved around us, we must understand that their needs are greater than our own.

If you're a Christian and you're resting on your laurels because you have previously done great ministry or because you have been used of God to win others to Christ in the past, then you are missing out. In Matthew 25 the people who are sent to hell argue, "But why? Didn't we do wonderful deeds in Your name?" Jesus, when he was confronted by the religious rulers about His saying they were not saved, chided them for doing the works of Satan (John 8:41). Satan, as we know, masquerades as an angel of light (2 Cor 11:14). He doesn't say, "Here I am, the prince of darkness! Follow me and do as I do." No, he looks good, sounds right, and does what looks like noble deeds. All of the apostles evangelized until their death. Jesus says, "No one who puts a hand to the plow and looks back is fit for service in the kingdom of God" (Luke 9:62). Paul speaks of finishing the race when he said, "However, I consider my life worth nothing to me; my only aim is to finish the race and complete the task the Lord Jesus has given me—the task of testifying to the good news of God's grace" (Acts 20:24). There is no retirement from the Great Commission. Evangelism is the passion of the true believer their whole life long.

The one who evangelizes will face rejection, ridicule, and reprimand, and it's not always from a human source. Satan gets mad when someone threatens his territory, and his territory is the souls of those who do not believe the gospel. A Christian witnessing is a direct threat to him. When you are involved in evangelism there are far more troubles, problems, and conflict. We must pray that the works of the evil one would be thwarted. We must be reminded of the spiritual warfare we are entering. Many know firsthand how upset the demons get and what they are capable of to try to distract us from sharing the gospel with the lost. The hearts and minds of young people are especially desirable territory in this war.

Think about it; a twelve-year-old has sixty-ninety years to serve our Lord and be a witness for Him. If Satan can keep these children from even hearing about Jesus, his job of deceiving and leading people down the wrong path is much easier. Young people haven't developed habits or patterns for their life yet. If God gets a hold of them, they will be hard for Satan to sidetrack. If Satan can mess up a young person's life (turn them on to drugs, get them pregnant, have them thrown in prison, etc.) then, even if they come to Christ later in life, they will have baggage to deal with which may keep them from being effective. They will have an Achilles heel where Satan could plant doubts or feelings of inadequacies. Satan can't keep Christians from going to heaven and get them to join him in hell, but he can work to minimize their witness and effectiveness for the cause of Christ. He tries to silence Christians through intimidation and fear. The world is heading toward hell already and if he can keep Christians in check then he can take many with him into a Christ-less eternity.

Interestingly, young people are the most open to the gospel as well as being more susceptible to being led astray than older people. Most people who come to know Christ do so before their fifteenth birthday (different surveys range from 82–85 percent). Only 5 percent of Christians come to the Lord after the age of thirty. When you think about it, it makes sense. Children don't have as much to surrender and give up when becoming a Christian. Adults have families, careers, reputations, etc. to cause them to shrink away from a gospel invitation. Satan knows all this, and he works to keep the Church from reaching all people with the gospel, but he especially works to keep young people in the dark. He only has to do it for ten to twenty years and he's pretty much ensured that they will never become Christians. It is easier for Satan to work to keep a person from hearing the gospel for ten-twenty years than to deal with a Christian for sixty years or more. If you've ever had insects in your home, you know you don't just kill the adults; you have to get the eggs in the nest, otherwise they will keep hatching and producing. Satan is trying his hardest to keep as many people as possible from following God, so he takes an active role in youth ministry. I can personally attest to this as I was in youth ministry for twenty-two years.

If Satan has a strategy to keep people lost, the Church better strategize to win the lost. The Master has a plan for evangelism that works (or else Christians wouldn't exist). We had better get on board with it and encourage other Christians to get to work. Sure, we should especially look to share the gospel with youth, but we also need to wake up the sleeping giant. That sleeping giant is the many Christians who are not fully engaged in witnessing. If we can get others to take a more active role in sharing their faith, then we can target an untapped resource to grow the Church. The Western church is lagging behind other nations' church movements because many Western Christians are too frightened to share the gospel. When will we get it? Faith is on the decline in the Western world because we are not doing our job.

This book may not be a fascinating work, nor entertaining. It's not a very good self-help book and there aren't enough stories. It's just not what people are looking for. That's why I wrote it. It is not what others are writing about. It is not what people are seeking, but they should be! Everyone wants to feel good about themselves instead of taking a good long look in the mirror. It may not be what people are looking for but since when do people do what's best for them. I believe God inspired me more than a few times when I was writing this book and I know it is exactly what many Western Christians need to hear. I ask my readers to listen to the Spirit's instruction. To them who have ears to hear let them hear what the Spirit says to the churches.

When I was writing this it was the opening night of VBS and as I was writing, thunderbolts were crashing down all around our little country church. Some might think God must be angry, but as I have shared with you, satan gets angry and he was trying to discourage attendance. I stopped writing, prayed and the skies parted. God is good and we shared the good news with those who came. Don't let the storms of life dissuade you from the work still to be done.

Chapter 20

Follow-Up to Witnessing

What Is the Gift of Evangelism?

NOT ALL CHRISTIANS HAVE the spiritual gift of evangelism. Evangelism is sharing the gospel to non-Christians. Notice I didn't say anything about success rates. They say Billy Graham, arguably the greatest evangelist the world has ever know, has won more people to Christ than anyone in history, but he has also shared Christ with more people who didn't become Christians than anyone else in history (like Babe Ruth and his homeruns and strikeouts). The work of bringing someone to faith is not ours; it is the work of God. Success has little to do with the gift of evangelism. God just tags certain people with a special ability. They are just better at it than the rest of us. That doesn't mean the rest of us shouldn't bother. People with the gift of evangelism will not be able to reach all the pre-believers out there.

Saying that because you don't have the gift of evangelism, you don't have to witness, is like being a professional baseball player who doesn't bother to show up for a game because there are three all-stars on the team. "They're future Hall of Famers," you say, "and they have skills and abilities that are far beyond mine, so they don't need me. They can win the game all by themselves." Such a scenario would be ridiculous. In the same way the Church is a team with many players with different abilities and gifts. Some play first base and others are in the outfield. They each have roles to fill, and no matter how gifted the star players are, if the team hopes to win the game it is going to take everyone doing their part. Each one contributes something in the course of a game in order to compete, but when everyone understands their role, and does it to the best of their abilities, there is a synergy that happens, and the team becomes greater than the sum of its parts. Everyone plays like a superstar and superstars play like men amongst children.

God has fitted and gifted His Church in such a way that we can accomplish great things if we all do our part. Yes, to some He gave the gift of evangelism but that doesn't mean that He doesn't want all Christians to witness.

What is the Roman Road?

The Roman Road is not some ancient cobble stone street in Italy; it is a specific course of Scriptures found in Paul's letter to the Romans. They are usually shared in order. Memorizing these Scriptures and practicing using them will put you in good standing when witnessing to someone needing to hear the gospel from God's Word. Here are the verses:

Romans 3:10 (All Have Sinned) "As it is written: There is no one righteous, not even one"

Romans 3:23 (All Have Sinned) "for all have sinned and fall short of the glory of God"

Romans 5:12 (Sin's Penalty) "Therefore, just as sin entered the world through one man, and death through sin, and in this way, death came to all men, because all sinned."

Romans 6:23 (Sin's Penalty) "For the wages of sin is death, but the gift of God is eternal life in Christ Jesus our Lord."

Romans 5:8 (Christ Paid the Penalty) "But God demonstrates his own love for us in this: While we were still sinners, Christ died for us."

Romans 10:9 (Salvation through Faith) "That if you confess with your mouth, "Jesus is Lord," and believe in your heart that God raised him from the dead, you will be saved."

Romans 10:10 (Salvation through Faith) "For it is with your heart that you believe and are justified, and it is with your mouth that you confess and are saved."

Romans 10:13 (Salvation through Faith) "Everyone who calls on the name of the Lord will be saved."

You can highlight these in your Bible and have the person read them, then you can explain it to them and answer their questions. There are also tracts that use the Roman Road, and you could use one of them. They are not the only salvation verses you could use (there are many), but this Roman Road is a favorite of many. Here's a partial list of some of the other ones I like to use:

John 1:12 "Yet to all who did receive Him, to those who believed in His name, He gave the right to become children of God."

John 3:16 "For God so loved the world, that He gave His only begotten Son, that whoever believes in Him should not perish, but have everlasting life."

John 3:36 "Whoever believes in the Son has eternal life; whoever does not obey the Son shall not see life, but the wrath of God remains on him."

John 14:6 "Jesus said to him, I am the way, the truth, and the life: no man comes to the Father, but by Me."

Acts 4:12 "Salvation is found in no one else, for there is no other name under heaven given to men by which we must be saved."

2 Corinthians 5:17 "Therefore if any man be in Christ, he is a new creature: old things are passed away; behold, all things are become new."

Ephesians 2:8–9 "For it is by grace you have been saved, through faith—and this is not from yourselves, it is the gift of God—not by works, so that no one can boast."

Hebrews 9:27–28 "Just as man is destined to die once, and after that to face judgment, so Christ was sacrificed once to take away the sins of many people; and he will appear a second time, not to bear sin, but to bring salvation to those who are waiting for him."

1 John 5:11–12 "And this is the testimony: God has given us eternal life, and this life is in his Son. Whoever has the Son has life; whoever does not have the Son of God does not have life."

Revelation 3:20 "Behold I stand at the door and knock, if anyone hears my voice and opens the door, I will come in to him and dine with him and he with me."

Use some of these or find your own favorite verses to share. There are many more. The important thing is that you prepare to give an answer to anyone who asks you why you have this hope within you.

What Do You Do If They Don't Want to Hear the Gospel?

If people say I don't want to hear all that "garbage," then stop talking. Instead of using words focus on actions and behaviors which will point people to Christ, sometimes more effectively anyway. Just because someone doesn't want to hear the gospel now doesn't mean they will never be open to hearing again. You always want to be gentle and respectful. Just because they might be rude doesn't give you the right to tarnish the cause of Christ. Remember you want to earn the right to be heard and you want to leave them wishing they had listened to you. If you do it right, they will at least always know who they can turn to.

What Do You Do If They Don't Want to Accept Christ after Hearing the Gospel?

Some people need time to digest all they they've heard. You don't want to pressure them into making a decision and you don't want a decision based on fear or guilt. You want them to come to Christ for the right reasons. Make sure their questions are answered to the best of your abilities. Let them know you are there for them if they have any more questions or to pray with them when they are ready. It is not uncommon that the seed of the gospel must be planted before it can germinate and take root. You have done your part; you've been faithful. Perhaps someone else will take them the rest of the way. Sometimes it's sort of like tag team evangelism. You can't make someone a Christian no matter how hard you try and coercing them into praying a prayer does not mean that they became a genuine Christian either. Trust that God is in control. Pray for and with them. Don't forget to continue to pray for them and to follow up later if you have the opportunity.

Why Did God Leave It up to Us to Share the Gospel?

That's a very good question. Surely, He could do a better job at it than we could. It must be for our benefit. I tell people who come to faith that the more they tell others about their decision to trust in Christ, the more they cement their faith (or secure a real and genuine faith). By telling others they are exercising their new faith and the muscle of faith starts to grow and get stronger. It's sort of like learning a new word; if you use it ten times as soon as you learn it, you own it and will never forget it. By sharing you are proving that your faith is real and genuine. Of course, there are many other acts (or fruit) that the new Christian will start to produce which prove the validity of one's faith, but one of the very first is to be quick to share one's faith story with others. Witnessing is not just for the older Christian or the most mature, it's just as important to the new Christian. If God did not give us the charge to witness and make disciples our faith would be a selfish, ingrown, and immature. God doesn't need us to witness, we need to witness to grow in our faith. God understands this and that is why He commands us to witness and make disciples.

How Do You Know If Someone Is a Christian Already?

To find out if someone is a Christian or not you have to watch their life. "By their fruit you will recognize them" (Matt 7:16). Jesus told those who claimed to have true faith that they had better do works in keeping with their faith (Matt 3:8 and Luke 3:8). This could be misleading as you can find some non-Christians who have plenty of good works, so it is not just how they live their life, it is also why they live their life. It's a matter of faith. So, you ask them what they believe about Jesus. You ask them their faith story. You don't just ask them if they are a Christian because many people falsely believe that because their parents are Christians or because they go to church or because they are not Jewish or Muslim, they must be Christians. You're not a hamburger because you go to McDonalds; you're not a Christian because you go to church. To truly determine if someone is a Christian takes time, objectivity, and exposure.

How Do You Witness to Someone You've Already Witnessed To?

Just because you witnessed to someone once doesn't mean you should check them off your list. People often have to hear the gospel multiple times before they trust in Christ. How many times did you have to hear before you accepted Christ? Could you imagine a teacher saying something once to their class and expecting them to know it? Once you've already shared the gospel with someone you have already broached the subject with them, and it should be easier to bring it up again. You should not assume they remember everything you told them previously. You basically share the same simple gospel message over again using different language, Scriptures, or illustrations. Perhaps the first time the language didn't connect with them. Ask them what questions they have. Make sure you listen. Write down notes after witnessing so you can know how to pray and so you can prepare to share again later. You always want to approach others with the gospel with gentleness and respect, whether it is for the first time or the 101st time.

How Do You Witness to Someone You've Known for a Long Time?

When you've known someone for a long time but have neglected to bring matters of faith into the relationship it can be very difficult and intimidating to witness to them. Usually there is fear that your relationship will change or that they will reject what you're sharing and reject you too. The truth is that your relationship with them is going to change sooner or later. It will either change when you witness to them (by them becoming Christian or rejecting Christ) or it will change when they are separated from you for all eternity because they never came to know Christ as their Lord and Savior. Do you really want to see them walking off to hell and turn back toward you and say, "Why didn't you tell me? I thought we were close!" If they were close before sharing with them, you will continue to be close after. Look at it as a way to strengthen your relationship.

It doesn't have to be awkward. At least it shouldn't be. You should have a testimony before them. They should know of your faith. They should know that you're involved in your church and that you are a person who likes to pray about things. It always starts there; let them see your spiritual side so when you do finally share with them it doesn't come as a surprise or out of left field. You could start by telling them your faith story (your life before Jesus, how you came to trust in Jesus, and your life since). Just because you've gone years without discussing such things doesn't mean you can't. Bite the bullet, pray about it, be courageous and just do it!

Do You Have to Have All the Answers to Be Effective?

You do not have to have all the answers to witness to someone. They may not even have any questions. The gospel is simple enough. All have sinned. There is a penalty to pay for sin (death). Jesus died to make the payment for us. We must each accept this free gift. Children can follow the logic. It is a logical premise and conclusion. It is a valid and reasonable belief. Sure, people have questions about evolution, angels, and pigmies in Africa, but what does all that have to do with the gospel and their decision? Often questions end up sidetracking the response to the gospel. You can often tell if a question is genuine or if it is a ruse. Answers to certain questions can cloud the issue at hand. You're asking them if they believe one plus one equals two and they want to know if the quadratic formula can be used to prove the existence of God. It may be an interesting question and you could discuss it later, but it is not what you are talking about right now. As quickly as possible bring them back to the gospel and their response to it.

There are certain people who must have the entire system understood before they buy into it and I suppose I understand that, but I like to remind them that I may not fully understand how a television works, but I still own one and enjoy it. You can't fully understand God. He is not a system to be proven; He just is. You can always tell them that you don't know the answer and that you will investigate it and get back to them. This gives you the opportunity to develop a relationship. You can regroup, pray, find the answer, and think through a better plan to share with this person. One of the worse things you can do is to answer a question to which you don't have the answer. Also, if you are going to answer a question, answer their question, not the one they are not asking. Keep your answers succinct. Don't bring up more questions with your answer. Use the k.i.s.s. principle, "*keep it simple saint!*"

What Do I Do If They Want to Become a Christian but Don't Want to Pray?

People may believe but just don't know what to say. They've never prayed before and are intimidated by the question, "Would you like to pray now to receive God's forgiveness?" You should offer to pray for them. Ask them to repeat your prayer phrase by phrase. Make sure you break your prayer down into short phrases and pause after you say each one allowing them to repeat what you just said before you say the next phrase. Maybe they can't even repeat a prayer because they are feeling so overwhelmed. Invite them to say the prayer you are going to pray out loud quietly in their heart (or unspoken in their mind-to think it) and remind them that God will hear their prayer. It is always more desirable to get them to pray using their own words or to at least get them to say the words out loud. Somehow it is more sincere and memorable (this too will help them cement their faith), but don't make them do something they don't want to do. Coming to Christ is an act of volition (the will) not a verbal contact. It must be a sincere belief. The sinner's prayer is not a magical incantation that removes sin.

What Words Need to Be Prayed to Become a Christian?

There are not exact prayers or words that must be said to become a Christian. I knew a teenager who became a Christian by sitting on a park bench all by himself watching a beggar on the street. He had just heard the gospel and in his heart, he reasoned that he was no better than a worthless beggar in the eyes of God, so he said he decided to believe. When I asked him what he prayed he said, "Well, it wasn't really a prayer, it was more like a decision. In that moment I could feel my heart being changed and God coming upon me." His life was indeed changed (love ya Goose). The words are not as important as the attitude of the heart. I've heard people mumble some pretty incoherent stuff over the years and they ended up with the most amazing faith I've ever seen. I ask people to pray something like, "I'm sorry God for all the bad things I've done. I believe that Jesus died to pay the penalty for my sin. Forgive me and make me your child. Lead me and take control of my life. In Jesus' name I pray, Amen!" There are a few elements represented in this type of prayer: confession of sin, belief in Jesus' sacrifice for them, asking for forgiveness, and handing over lordship of one's life to Christ. Prayers can be long or short.

What Is the Wordless Book?

The wordless book is a book without words. The covers and each page are a different color which reminds us of a different aspect of the gospel. Charles Spurgeon seems to be the first to use this concept in 1866. Spurgeon's color scheme only had three colors; black (representing our sin), red (representing death-the consequences of sin and Christ's death for us), and white (representing how our sins are washed away and how Christ makes us pure again).[1] Since those days, green (representing our growing in Christ after we choose to trust in Christ), and gold (representing the golden streets in heaven where we will end up living with God for eternity) have been added. You can use Scripture verses in your presentation as you like. You can buy these books and use them in your presentation of the gospel. These books are often used with children who can't read lengthy explanations anyway. It also comes in a second form, the wordless bracelet (also available for sale). The same five colors are seen in the five beads representing the same five principles. (You could even get creative and use a box of crayons.) After a presentation the book or the bracelet can be given to the child to help them remember what the gospel is.

What Is the Bridge Illustration?

The bridge illustration is a simple diagram of a great chasm with God and heaven on one side and all humanity on the other side. The fires of hell are often added in the midst of the chasm. This illustration can be drawn on a napkin at a restaurant or on the back of a paper placemat. All you need is a piece of paper and a writing utensil (you can even use a crayon). You explain how the chasm is impossible to cross on our own (it's like the Grand Canyon). You can draw a few people trying to jump the gorge (representing trying to get to heaven by doing good works) but no matter how hard we try we always fall short (for God is holy and we are not-we must be sinless to get to heaven). You then draw a bridge and write Jesus on it and explain how God provided a way for us to cross over into heaven by having Jesus die on the cross for our sin. All we have to do is believe in Jesus and what He did for us to cross over and have forgiveness of sin and the hope of eternal life. You can use appropriate Scripture verses. You can embellish upon this illustration, and you don't have to be particularly artistic to use this. With just a little bit of practice you'll be ready to use it in a moment's notice.

---

1. Blue Letter Bible, "Spurgeon's Wordless Book."

What Questions Should I Put On My Evangelizing Survey?

If you chose to canvas a neighborhood, parking lot, or mall with a survey, it's easy enough to design your own. You just ask questions about sin, Jesus, and forgiveness. Don't ask too many questions so you can say something like, "Excuse me, do you have time to help me with a survey? There are only five questions, and it takes less than a minute." You should have a clipboard with the survey on it as you read from it. For instance, you could ask something like the following questions in your survey:

1. Do you believe that all people have done wrong things?
2. Did you know that the Bible says that anyone who does wrong things will not go to heaven?
3. Did you know that the Bible says that Jesus was sent by God to die on the cross for the wrong things we've done?
4. Did you know that the Bible says we must each choose to trust this good news to be forgiven of our wrong doings?
5. Would you like to know how you can know for sure you are going to heaven?

If they say yes to the last question you can go into a gospel presentation. Make sure they understand that the survey is over but that you would be happy to share what the Bible says about knowing for sure that they are going to heaven (1 John 5:13). Using the bridge illustration, you could go on to explain the gospel and ask them if they would like to pray to God to ask for forgiveness and receive this free gift. The survey alone could take about a minute (depending on the type and how many questions you use) and the gospel presentation should be brief as well and should take no more than an additional five minutes (including prayer). The whole thing could take five to six minutes. Whether you get to share the gospel or not make sure you thank them for their participation. Also, make sure you at least have copies of *The Four Spiritual Laws*[2] (or some other tract). If they pray to accept Christ, you can ask them if they would like to have future contact with someone who could help them understand the decision they just made and get their phone number or email address for follow-up.

---

2. Bright, *Four Spiritual Laws*.

What Is Team Evangelism?

Team evangelism is when more than one person is involved in the process of sharing the gospel with someone. It could be people praying for you as you share the gospel. It could be someone who goes with you to share the gospel. It could be that you share with a person once and then tell someone else about the conversation and then they would follow-up with another conversation later. There are many ways to use the team approach. You can practice with a team; rehearsing and role playing to prepare to share the gospel. You can debrief after an opportunity to evaluate how to do a better job next time. You could use a tag team approach where you share something this week, someone else shares something next week and someone else gives that same person an invitation to a church activity. Witnessing does not have to be a solitary venture. There are many ways to have the support and assistance of others, all it takes is cooperation, creativity, and communication. Ask others to join with you today.

What Does a New Christian Need to Do?

The first thing you want to encourage a new Christian to do is to tell others what they just did. After they say amen look around to see if there is someone with which they could share their decision. Make it a safe person (in some cases that might be a family member, in other cases it would not be a family member-it depends on the person). Ask them if they mind if you ask so and so to join you so they can share what they just did. Then call them over and ask them to share. You should try to pick a Christian who can positively reinforce their decision to follow Christ. You should encourage them to share with as many people as possible. You should also be prepared to offer some form of follow-up/discipleship before they leave.

You will want to encourage them to connect with a church (by attending regularly), bible study or other group of Christians. They will need the encouragement and support of Christians as Satan will try to discourage their newfound faith. If they don't have a Bible, it would be nice to offer them at least a New Testament, but they should be encouraged to read the Bible every day. You might even offer them some form of suggested readings. You should also encourage them to pray at various times throughout their day about everything. Something else new Christians should be encouraged to do is to be baptized. This may not come up until the discipleship phase of your relationship but when Philip won the Ethiopian to Christ, he baptized him immediately (at the Ethiopian's request, Acts 8:36–38).

What Do I Do If Someone Doesn't Want to Be Discipled?

If someone has just prayed asking God to forgive them of their sin because of what Jesus did for them but they do not want to meet with someone regularly for discipleship, maybe they don't understand what you are asking them to do. Perhaps they think you are trying to get them to commit to a program. Make sure they understand that it's just having someone in their life they can meet with for encouragement and support as they start this new life in Christ. Explain to them that they may have questions about the passages they start reading or need help finding or fitting into a good church. This discipleship relationship should be with someone of the same gender and similar age. In a church setting at an alter call it is best to have trained people to call on and match up with the convert right there on the spot.

After all your explanation if they still are not interested in being discipled then all you can do is to pray for them and trust God to bring someone into their life. You could take it a step further and share with someone who might know them that they refused discipleship and maybe they could offer or share with them how they were discipled and what a difference it made for them. Ultimately it is the Holy Spirit who teaches us anyway so trusting them to the Lord (and continuing to pray for them) is not a bad thing at all.

Chapter 21

Closing Remarks

THESE SPIRITUAL DISCIPLINES ARE designed by God for Christians. I suppose Jews, Muslims and others might be tempted to use these disciplines in their faith traditions. I have no idea how that would work or what it would look like. I am inclined to think that it would not work because most other faith traditions are not evangelistic, nor do they have a holy book quite like the Bible. Secularists might attempt to modify the ideas in this book to encourage a sense of harmony but that would be like cutting the legs off a horse and then entering him in a race and expecting him to win (rather absurd I know).

 Thank you for taking the time to read this book. I know it couldn't have been easy and represents a substantial time investment. I do believe it to be of tremendous value to people who do not know Christ but especially to young Christians and Christians who have not seen the power of God demonstrated in their lives in a while. These five disciplines are scriptural and imperative to attain maturity in Christ. It is impossible to get there without all five being exercised in healthy doses by the Christian. I encourage you to share this book with others who could benefit from it. Pass it around to your friends. Start a bible study with this book as your text. Use it one on one with a new Christian as you seek to disciple them in the faith. My hope is that this will become a work that will be of use to Christians for decades to come.

 In this book I have laid out God's plan for growth; the five disciplines of fellowship, bible study, prayer, ministry, and witnessing. Look, if you have a problem with the five spiritual disciplines you do not have a problem with me but with God. These five truths are taught from one end of the Bible to the other (as I have attempted to demonstrate). In my opinion of the five disciplines the one which is most needed in communities today is fellowship. People would rather watch a church service on television or an internet stream, listen to a sermon on YouTube, and read books like this. So many Christians today are angry, disappointed, or disillusioned with the church and yet *we* (Christians) are the Church. We've got to stop expecting Christians to be perfect. Real Christians (you and me) are a messy lot. Anyone can sound good on television, radio, or in a book, but we all have warts. Grace sees the warts and chooses to love anyway; just like God did when He sent His son.

Jesus said, "Upon this rock I will build my church." Paul spoke of bearing with one another. Hebrews 10:25 speaks on not giving up on the assembling of yourselves together. Ecclesiastes 4:12 speaks to the safety of fellowship. People in churches receive the encouragement and support to live out their Christian life. It's a place to use your gifts in ministry, a place where you can join with others to accomplish more than you can by yourself. Church for the Christian is like water for the fish. It's our natural environment. Take us out of it and we start to die, not all at once like our friend the fish, but slowly over time. Something special happens when Christians gather together (where two or three are gathered there I am in their midst, if you agree on earth, it will be bound in heaven, God inhabits the praise of His people . . .) and some have been missing out for quite a while. I'm trying to be a good friend and speaking the truth in love. I care too much to let some continue to think that they don't need church.

I make myself available to anyone to help them understand the concepts in this book. I welcome your questions, corrections, and challenges. I'm sure this work could be improved and if it is needed, I would welcome the input. May God bless you in your spiritual pilgrimage and quest for Christian maturity. I leave you with this prayer:

> Holy Father, You are the God of second chances. You proved that by sending Your one and only Son, Jesus, to give us a second chance. We are blowing it and continue to need your forgiveness. Forgive us and help us please You. Thank You that Jesus died for sins past, present, and future. Thank You that His death still atones for us. Thank You for loving us too much to let us remain as we are. Thank You for being a perfectionist and for having high expectations for us. I pray that the person holding

Closing Remarks

this book and reading these words will bring You great joy as they practice Your five disciples for Christians. I pray that they will triumphantly implement them with ease in their lives. I pray that Your mighty Church will be revived by turning to Your simple ways. I ask all this in Jesus' name, Amen!

Resources

For speaking engagements, email: elliottc2@verizon.net.
The thoughts I have expressed in this book are not just my own. There is significant scholarly research coming out to support these truths which I have gleaned from the scriptures. I have included a valuable short list of some of those studies below. This is to show the science supporting the authority of the Bible.

Acevedo, Gabriel, Christopher G. Ellison, Xiaohe Xu. "Is it really religion? Comparing the main and stress-buffering effects of Religious and secular civic engagement on psychological distress." *Society of Mental Health* 4, 2 (2014) 111-128.

Bradshaw, M., and C. G. Ellison. "Financial Hardship and Psychological Distress: Exploring the Buffering Effect of Religion." *Social Science and Medicine* 71 (2010) 196–204.

Burdette, A. M., C. G. Ellison, T. D. Hill, and N. D. Glenn. "'Hooking Up' on Campus: Does Religion Make a Difference?" *Journal for the Scientific Study of Religion* 48 (2009) 535–51.

Ellison, C. G., and J. S. Levin. (1998). "The Religion-Health Connection: Evidence, Theory, and Future Directions." *Health Education and Behavior* 25 (1998) 700–20.

Ellison, C. G., and K. L. Anderson. "Religious Involvement and Domestic Violence among U.S. Couples." *Journal for the Scientific Study of Religion* 40 (2001) 269–87.

Ellison, C. G., J. B. Barrett, and B. E. Moulton. "Gender, Marital Status, and Alcohol Behavior: The Neglected Role of Religion." *Journal for the Scientific Study of Religion* 47 (2008) 660–77.

Ellison, C. G., J. D. Boardman, D. R. Williams, and J. S. Jackson. (2001). "Religious Involvement, Stress, and Mental Health: Findings from the 1995 Detroit Area Study." *Social Forces* 80 (2001) 215–49.

Ellison, Christopher G., Matt Bradshaw, Kevin Flannelly, & Kathleen Galek. "Prayer, Attachment to God, and Symptoms of Anxiety-Related Disorders Among U.S. Adults." *Society of Religion* 75 (2014) 208-233.

Ellison, C. G., M. Bradshaw, S. Rote, J. Storch, and M. Trevino. "Religion and Alcohol Use Among College Students: Exploring the Role of Domain-Specific Religious Salience." *Journal of Drug Issues* 38 (2008) 821–46.

Ellison, C. G., A. M. Burdette, T. D. and T. D. Hill. "Blessed Assurance: Religion, Anxiety, and Tranquility Among US Adults." *Social Science Research* 38 (2009) 656-67.

Ellison, C. G., A. M. Burdette, and W. B. Wilcox. "'The Couple That Prays Together': Race, Ethnicity, Couples' Religious Involvement, and Relationship Quality among Working-Age Adults." *Journal of Marriage and Family* 72 (2010) 963–75.

Ellison, Christopher G., Reed T. Deangelis, Terrence D. Hill & Paul Froese. "Sleep Quality and the Stress-Buffering Role of Religious Involvement: A mediated moderation analysis." Journal for the Scientific *Study of Religion* 58, 1 (2019) 251-268.

Ellison, C. G., and D. Fan. "Daily Spiritual Experiences and Psychological Well-Being Among U.S. Adults." *Social Indicators Research* 88 (2008) 247–71.

Ellison, C. G., B. K. Finch, D. N. Ryan, and J. J. Salinas. "Religious Involvement and Depressive Symptoms among Mexican-Origin Adults in California." *Journal of Community Psychology* 37 (2009) 171–93.

Ellison, C. G., and R. A. Hummer, (eds.). *Religion, Families, and Health: Population Based Research in the United States*. New Brunswick, NJ: Rutgers University Press, 2010.

Ellison, C. G., M. L. Vaaler, K. J. Flannelly, and A. J. Weaver. "The Clergy as a Source of Mental Health Assistance: What Americans Believe." *Review of Religious Research* 48 (2006) 190–211.

Gassaway, J. M., T. Reischl, and S. Witcher. "The Relationship between Church Attendance, Family Distress, Difficult Life Circumstances, and Children's Academic Achievement." *NHSA Research Quarterly* 1 (1997) 44–45. doi: 10.1207/s19309325nhsa0102_6

George, L. K., C. G. Ellison, and D. B. Larson. "Explaining the Relationships between Religious Involvement and Health." *Psychological Inquiry* 13 (2002) 190–200.

Glanville, J. L., D. Sikkink, and E. I. Hernandez. "Religious Involvement and Educational Outcomes: The role of social capital and extracurricular participation." *The Sociological Quarterly* 49 (2008) 105–37. DOI: 10.1111/j.1533-8525.2007.00108.x

Henderson, Andrea, K. and Christopher G. Ellison. "My Body Is a Temple: Eating Disturbances, Religious Involvement, and Mental Health Among Young Adult Women." *Journal of Religion and Health* 54 (2014) 954-976.

Hill, T., A. M. Burdette, C. G. Ellison, and M. A. Musick. "Religious Attendance and the Health Behaviors of Texas Adults." *Preventive Medicine* 42 (2006) 309–12.

Hill, T. D., C. G. Ellison, A. M. Burdette, and M. A. Musick. "Religious Involvement and Healthy Lifestyles: Evidence from the Survey of Texas Adults." *Annals of Behavioral Medicine* 34 (2007) 217–22.

Hummer, R. A., C. G. Ellison, R. G. Rogers, B. E. Moulton, and R. R. Romero. "Religious Involvement and Adult Mortality in the United States: Review and Perspective." *Southern Medical Journal* 97 (2004) 1223–30.

Hummer, R. A., R. G. Rogers, C. B. Nam, and C. G. Ellison. "Religious Involvement and US Adult Mortality." *Demography* 36 (1999) 273–85.

Johnson, B. R. "A Tale of Two Religious Effects: Evidence for the protective and prosocial impact of organic religion." In *Authoritative Communities: The Scientific Case for Nurturing the Whole Child*, edited by Kline, K. K., 187–225. New York: Springer, 2008.

Jung, Jong Hyun and Christopher G. Ellison. "Discovering Grace at the Table: Prayers at mealtime, marital status, and life satisfaction in later life." *Research on Aging* 44 (2021).

Krause, N. M., and C. G. Ellison. "Forgiveness by God, Forgiveness of Others, and Psychological Well-Being in Late Life." *Journal for the Scientific Study of Religion* 42 (2003) 77–93.

Krause, N. M., C. G. Ellison, and K. M. Wulff. "Church-based Emotional Support, Negative Interaction, and Psychological Well-Being: Findings from a National Sample of Presbyterians." *Journal for the Scientific Study of Religion* 37 (1998) 725–41.

Krause, Neal, Peter C. Hill, & Robert Emmons. "Assessing the Relationship Between Religious Involvement and Health Behaviors." *Health Education & Behavior* 44, 2 (2017) 278–284.

MacQueen N. "The Benefits of Regular Church Attendance." *Sunday Software*. https://sundaysoftware.com/the-life-benefits-of-church-membership/

Muller, C. L., and C. G. Ellison. "Religious Involvement, Social Capital, and Adolescents' Academic Progress: Evidence from the National Educational Longitudinal Study of 1988." *Sociological Focus* 34 (2001) 155–83.

Powers, D. A. and C. G. Ellison. "Conservative Protestantism and Church Attendance Effects on Teen Pregnancy and Pregnancy Outcomes." Presented at the annual meeting of the Population Association of America, Philadelphia, PA, 2005.

Szaflarski, M., P. N. Ritchey, A. C. Leonard, J. M. Mrus, A. H. Peterman, C. G. Ellison, M.E. McCullough, and J. Tsevat. "Modeling the Effects of Spirituality/Religion on Patients' Perceptions of Living with HIV/AIDS." *Journal of General Internal Medicine* 21.5 (2006) S28-S38.

Vaaler, M. L., C. G. Ellison, and D. A. Powers. "Religious Influences on the Risk of Marital Dissolution." *Journal of Marriage and Family* 71 (2009) 917–34.

Webb, A. P., C. G. Ellison, M. J. McFarland, K. Morton, J. Lee, and J. Walters. "Divorce, Religious Coping, and Depressive Symptoms in a Conservative Protestant Religious Group." *Family Relations* 59 9 (2010) 544–57.

Wolfinger, N. H. and W. B. Wilcox. "Happily Ever After?: Religion, Marital Status, Gender and Relationship Quality in Urban Families." *Social Forces* 86 (2008) 1311–1337.

Bibliography

Aquinas, Thomas. *Summa Theologica*. Translated by the Fathers of the English Dominican Province. Allen, TX: Christian Classics, 1981.
Barna Group. "Millions of Unchurched Adults are Christians." https://www.barna.org/barna-update/article/12-faithspirituality/362-millions-of-unchurched-adults-are-christians-hurt-by-churches-but-can-be-healed-of-the-pain#.UhL4Cz_lfms.
———. "State of the Bible 2021: Five Key Findings." https://www.barna.com/research/sotb-2021/.
Bergler, Thomas E. *The Juvenilization of American Christianity*. Grand Rapids: Eerdmans, 2012.
———. "The Juvenilization of American Christianity." Speech at Regent University Faculty Retreat, Virginia Beach, VA, August, 2013.
BibleGateway. https://www.biblegateway.com/.
Blue Letter Bible. "Spurgeon's Wordless Book." https://www.blueletterbible.org/Comm/spurgeon_charles/sermons/3278.cfm.
Bright, Bill. *The Four Spiritual Laws*. Tract. Campus Crusade for Christ.
Church Angel. "Find a Church." www.churchangel.com.
Church Finder. "Find Churches Near You." https://www.churchfinder.com/.
Ellis, Ken. "Online Spiritual Gifts Test." www.kodachrome.org/spiritgift.
Flynn, Les. *19 Gifts of the Holy Spirit*. Wheaton: Victor, 1974.
Global Media Outreach. https://globalmediaoutreach.com/.
Joshua Project. "Global Statistics." http://joshuaproject.net/great-commission-statistics.php.
Kiva. "Home." www.Kiva.com.
MacArthur, John. "What Is Grace?" https://www.oneplace.com/ministries/grace-to-you/read/articles/what-is-grace-10339.html.
MacQueen, Neil. "The Benefits of Regular Church Attendance." https://sundaysoftware.com/the-life-benefits-of-church-membership/.
Mansfield, Stephen. *Re-Church: Healing your way back to the people of God*. Austin, TX: Barna, 2010.

McDowell, Josh. *The New Evidence that Demands a Verdict*. Nashville: Thomas Nelson, 1999.

One World Missions. "Missions Education." http://oneworldmissions.com/site.cfm?PageID=5521.

Our Daily Bread. "Devotions." https://odb.org/tag/devotions/.

Pascal, Blaise. *Pensees*. Translated by A. J. Krailsheimer. London: Penguin Classics, 1995.

Wax, Trevin. "Why Millennials are Leaving the Church." http://www.churchleaders.com/pastors/pastor-articles/169302-why-millennials-are-leaving-the-church-a-response-to-rachel-held-evans.html#.Uf2J-u2QIFE.email.

Wilkinson, Bruce. *The Prayer of Jabez*. Sisters, OR: Multnomah, 2000.

www.ingramcontent.com/pod-product-compliance
Lightning Source LLC
Chambersburg PA
CBHW060607230426
43670CB00011B/2012